Differing Visions

Differing Visions

Dissenters in Mormon History

Edited by
Roger D. Launius and Linda Thatcher

Foreword by
Leonard J. Arrington

UNIVERSITY OF ILLINOIS PRESS

Urbana and Chicago

This book is printed on acid-free paper.

Library of Congress Cataloging-in-Publication Data

Differing visions : dissenters in Mormon history / edited by Roger D.
Launius and Linda Thatcher.
    p.   cm.
    Includes bibliographical references (p. xxx–xxx) and index.
    ISBN 0-252-02069-3 (alk. paper)
    1. Dissenters, Religious—United States. 2. Mormons—United
States. 3. Church of Jesus Christ of Latter-Day Saints—
Controversial literature—History and criticism. 4. Mormon Church—
Controversial literature—History and criticism. I. Launius,
Roger D. II. Thatcher, Linda.
BX8645.5.D54   1994
289.3'09—dc20   93-5463
                                                          CIP

For the memory
of
Oliver Cowdery,
David Whitmer,
and
Martin Harris,
faithful believers
who dissented.

Contents

Foreword
Leonard J. Arrington   ix

Acknowledgments   xiii

Introduction: Mormonism and the Dynamics of Dissent
Roger D. Launius and Linda Thatcher   1

1. David Whitmer: Faithful Dissenter, Witness Apart
   Ronald E. Romig   23

2. "Such Republicanism as This": John Corrill's Rejection
   of Prophetic Rule
   Kenneth H. Winn   45

3. William E. McLellin: "Mormonism's Stormy Petrel"
   Richard P. Howard   76

4. The Fruit of the Branch: Francis Gladden Bishop and
   His Culture of Dissent
   Richard L. Saunders   102

5. James Colin Brewster: The Boy Prophet Who Challenged
   Mormon Authority
   Dan Vogel   120

6. William B. Smith: "A Wart on the Ecclesiastical Tree"
   Paul M. Edwards   140

7. The Old Fox: Alpheus Cutler
   Danny L. Jorgensen   158

8. Stephen Post: From Believer to Dissenter to Heretic
   M. Guy Bishop   180

9. The Flight of the Doves from Utah Mormonism to California
   Morrisitism: The Saga of James and George Dove
   Richard Neitzel Holzapfel   196

10. Henry W. Lawrence: A Life in Dissent
    John S. McCormick and John R. Sillito   220

11. Frank J. Cannon: Declension in the Mormon Kingdom
    Kenneth M. Godfrey   241

12. Joseph W. Musser: Dissenter or Fearless Crusader for Truth?
    Martha Sonntag Bradley   262

13. Fawn McKay Brodie: Dissident Historian and Quintessential
    Critic of Mormondom
    Newell G. Bringhurst   279

14. Maurine Whipple: The Quiet Dissenter
    Jessie L. Embry   301

15. Richard Price: Leading Publicist of the Reorganized Church's
    Schismatics
    William D. Russell   319

16. Apostate Believers: Jerald and Sandra Tanner's Encounter
    with Mormon History
    Lawrence Foster   343

17. Sonia Johnson: Mormonism's Feminist Heretic
    Alice Allred Pottmyer   366

Contributors   391

Index   395

Foreword

Leonard J. Arrington

Religion has been both a unifying and divisive force at every level of human society throughout its existence. In the United States, however, an astonishing number of burgeoning religious organizations have flourished, each with divergent ideas and each sparking castoffs who have set out on their own spiritual journeys when they could no longer accept the authority of the institution of which they had once been a part. Perhaps the unique nature of the American experience, the fact that there is a clear separation of church and state, has fostered this proliferation. Whatever the reason, many have joined differing groups in search of fresh teachings, new leadership, or unique interpretations. In some instances, seekers have become so discouraged in this quest for truth that they abandoned organized religion.

This spiritual quest has been just as much, perhaps more so, the case with those embracing Mormonism in all its varieties as with the larger American Christian tradition. Unfortunately, dissension within the Latter-day Saint tradition has been a neglected phase of the church's history, one perceived as less than "faith promoting" and somehow suspect. Accordingly, little study has been given to either dissenters or to the variety of factors motivating people to forsake the faith of Mormonism. *Differing Visions: Dissenters in Mormon History* attempts to make accessible some of the elusive figures in this history, people whose names, for decades, have produced raised eyebrows.

The nineteen persons analyzed in this book represent a broad spectrum of one-time Saints. The profiles have little in common. The dissenters are both male and female, and they cover all periods and ages. They have few distinguishing attributes in terms of education, social position, economic standing, or cultural ideas. Their unification, however, lies in their single-minded purpose to strike out on their own and reinterpret the Mormon experience from their own individual perspectives. Many started their own religious organizations, but few claimed that they were new. Virtually all maintained that they were continuing what they perceived as the truths of Mormonism. Some left quietly, and others, although never joining another group, continued as opponents of the church they once warmly espoused.

The diversity and richness of the individual biographies contained in *Differing Visions,* however, belies the common themes that run through the lives of each dissenter. Several general conclusions have emerged from this cooperative historical exploration. First, the essays provide a useful recovery of little-known information about the lives of the people profiled. As only one example, John Corrill, so important to the early development of the institution and one of its dominant figures in Missouri in the 1830s, has been a shadowy figure without real form to most students of Mormon history. The essay here presents far more information about him than was known before and serves as a corrective to past neglect. Even David Whitmer, who has been discussed in numerous historical publications, has been cast in a new light with the emphasis on his developing conflict with Joseph Smith and his dissent from what he believed were incorrect policies by the church in the latter 1830s. In such instances, the contributors to this volume have come to grips with several ignored facets of Mormon history. The essays also correct the lack of attention of the role of dissent and the role of dissenters in the development of the religion. This creates, in addition, a more rounded portrait of Mormon religious history than previously expressed.

Second, one of the points that has come out of these essays is that there have always been numerous ways in which the life and work of Joseph Smith, Jr., could be interpreted. At least some of these ways can be arguably viewed as legitimate and internally consistent although perhaps radically different from the mainstream of Mormon thought. The realization that the vision of the kingdom of God could be different to different people, and, more important, that there might be more than one path to reach it, can be a useful perception for those who confidently assert that they possess the "truth."

Third, the dissenters profiled in these essays were motivated to take their courses away from orthodox acceptance of the religious institution for reasons that were not generally self-serving. They were principally moved by conscience and questions of right and wrong to take the action to reject the formal Mormon institution and strike out on their own. For example, Henry W. Lawrence left the movement because he became convinced that the organization had departed from the principles of Christianity. He had forthrightly sought to point out errors, anxiously seeking to show others the errors he perceived. His arguments were not mere rhetoric; there is no evidence to indicate that he was motivated to protest the church's actions by anything other than conscience. In the end, he took his efforts elsewhere and worked for the goals he considered part and parcel of the Mormon faith broadly considered. The same could be said of many other dissenters profiled in this collection.

Finally, these essays reveal that none of the dissenters could ever fully reject the movement once having been associated with it. This was partly a matter of the subjects chosen, but evidence thus far indicates that in many cases remnants of the religion remained embedded in dissenters regardless of how intensely they disliked the institution, the doctrine, the leadership, or whatever. They were rarely able to just walk away and not have the movement affect them.

All of the essays in this volume are useful additions to the historical literature of the Latter-day Saint tradition. Not everyone will agree with the conclusions expressed by the individual authors, nor will they find some of the biographical figures particularly sympathetic. Frankly, neither do I. Each chapter, however, presents a balanced portrait and an intimate analysis of those who have helped to shape the Mormon experience. This collection should be the beginning, rather than the end, of a discussion of diversity within Mormonism.

Acknowledgments

As in any book, numerous debts were incurred over the course of its production. We acknowledge the support and encouragement of a large number of people associated with the study of Mormon history and want to thank many individuals who materially contributed to the completion of this project. Of course, Richard L. Wentworth and Elizabeth G. Dulany of the University of Illinois Press provided encouragement and ideas for proceeding with the work. Mary Giles, our copy editor, brought order to the various formats of the chapters and materially improved this publication with her questions.

In addition to the individual essay authors, who deserve much credit for whatever success this book might have, several individuals read all or part of this manuscript or otherwise offered suggestions that helped us more than they will ever know: James B. Allen, Lavina Fielding Anderson, Valeen Tippets Avery, Milton V. Backman, Jr., Davis Bitton, Alma R. Blair, Peter Blodgett, Robert B. Flanders, John E. Hallwas, Marvin S. Hill, Jeffery O. Johnson, F. Mark McKiernan, Linda King Newell, Max H. Parkin, Lee Penent, D. Michael Quinn, Michael S. Riggs, Donald R. Shaffer, Steven L. Shields, A. J. Simmonds, E. Gary Smith, W. B. Spillman, Grant Underwood, Clare D. Vlahos, Edward A. Warner, and David J. Whittaker. Our thanks are also gratefully given to the staffs of the Reorganized Church of Jesus Christ of Latter Day Saints Library-Archives, the Historical Department of the Church of Jesus Christ of Latter-day Saints, the Utah State Historical Society, the Missouri Historical Society, the Huntington Library, the Brigham Young University Library, and the Illinois State Historical Society. Without their assistance this book could not have been completed.

Introduction:
Mormonism and
the Dynamics of Dissent

Roger D. Launius and Linda Thatcher

On a cloudy autumn day in September 1634, two hundred passengers disembarked from a ship onto a cluttered wharf in Boston, Massachusetts Bay Colony. They were pleased to be in Boston, in spite of the squalor of that outpost of civilization established only four years earlier, for they considered it a holy land consecrated for a great experiment in Christian living. The "errand into the wilderness," as it was sometimes called, excited the early Puritans for they believed they would finally be able to worship God as they thought He intended, without bishops or kings or meaningless ritual. Among the immigrants were Anne Hutchinson and her husband, both enamored with the possibilities of living a saintly life in a new world free from the sins of the old. She did not realize that within a short period she would become embroiled in a theological controversy like had never before been seen in Massachusetts and that would make her one of Puritanism's most famous religious dissenters.

John Winthrop, the colony's governor and eventually one of Anne Hutchinson's chief protagonists, described her as "a woman of haughty and fierce carriage, of a nimble wit and active spirit, and a very voluble tongue."[1] She was a match for any thinker in the new colony, as well as probably in England. Anne Hutchinson was a Puritan zealot convinced that the Anglican church, with its emphasis on salvation by works, bred hypocrisy and was a cancer on Christendom. The Hutchinsons' Boston home soon became the location of weekly meetings, where she led members of the local Puritan congregation in discussions of the minister's sermons. Starting as a small group, the circle gradually expanded to more than eighty people. Hutchinson's keen and imaginative mind soon moved beyond the accepted doctrines of Puritanism, becoming less orthodox as time passed. Her supporters also became more radical, and the discussion group began to take on the character of a dissenting religious movement.[2]

Anne Hutchinson's theological ideas started from the Puritan principle that God granted salvation without regard to the human condition; grace was a free gift to some, but no one could earn it. From that point she departed from Puritan theology, denying that good conduct could ever be a sign of salvation and affirming that the Holy Spirit resting in the hearts of the Elect, as those blessed with salvation were called, relieved them of the necessity of obeying earthly laws. By emphasizing piety, she argued, Puritan ministers were deluding their congregations into the false assumption that good works were a result of God's grace. That was, she believed, precisely the fallacy taught by the Anglican and Catholic churches. Moreover, personal revelation could supplant the authority of the ministers, and each individual had a duty to obey God's voice rather than the commands of either church or state. The complete decoupling of salvation from good works—antinomianism—was a dangerous idea, for it justified a total disregard for the rules of society by those so graced by God. Anne Hutchinson's espousal of antinomianism challenged the authority of the ministers and even the secular government to use the covenant of grace as a means of enforcing orthodoxy.

The force of her intellect and the fervor of her convictions helped sway numerous Puritans, and by 1637 the community was divided. The New England divines tried unsuccessfully to contain the antinomian controversy, but by midsummer it was clear that official action would be required. In November 1637, Anne Hutchinson was brought before the authorities on the charge of heresy. The trial was lively as both sides jousted verbally. Hutchinson was flawless in her defense until she admitted in a closing statement that she had personal revelations, and then she prophesied that "if you go on in this course you will bring a curse upon you and your posterity, and the mouth of the Lord hath spoken it."[3] The court found her guilty of heresy and banished her from the colony.

She then journeyed to Rhode Island. In banning her from their midst, the guardians of Puritanism rid their movement of a serious challenge to accepted theological teachings and religious authority. In the same process they excised some of the strength of their religious movement—the dynamic thrust of people of good character who challenged accepted notions—as well as forces that reinvigorated and reshaped their institution. They were forced to choose between the Scylla of priestly function that pointed toward maintenance of a status quo of both religious power and theology and a Charybdis of prophetic insight that might allow greater innovation from its members but could potentially destabilize the institution. They chose in favor of preserving the priestly order.

The antinomian controversy has been played out in a variety of forms throughout American religious history. Anne Hutchinson's case was not the first, and far from the last, expression of American religious dissent. Both institutions and dissenters have been fundamentally affected by these events. This has perhaps been more true of Mormonism than in other religious traditions. To analyze this phenomenon requires a preliminary consideration of the identification and expression of dissent in the Mormon context. Such dissent can arise from any one of these or a combination of factors: intellectual disagreements; sociocultural differences; demographic characteristics; a lack of integration, influence, power, or participation; or a misunderstanding over individuals' intentions.[4] Religious dissent extends from its purest form—individual disobedience motivated by a belief that both the integrity of the Gospel as personally understood and the honor of self are at stake—all the way to such less lofty goals as desires for personal power and wealth. Charisma, of course, due to its volatile nature, has always been a potent source of dissent and schism. Regardless of the motivating forces in time, dissent naturally leads to a dialectical struggle over power, influence, and authority within an institution.[5]

The Mormon movement itself arose in the midst of a crisis of authority and sought to identify, support, and establish a new authority to resolve both the unanswered and unsatisfactorily answered religious questions of the early nineteenth century. In heralding the coming of a new foundation for Christian faith, the beginning of Mormonism was a decisive and ringing dissent from all existing churches and theologies.[6] In the most famous of all accounts of the First Vision, a religious experience that happened around 1820 and in which Joseph Smith, Jr., was reportedly told that he would become a prophet and "that all religious denominations were believing in incorrect doctrines, and that none of them was acknowledged of God as His church and kingdom. And I was expressly commanded to 'go not after them,' at the same time receiving a promise that the fullness of the gospel should at some future time be made known to me."[7] In a more candid moment Smith even suggested that all other religious groups were an "abomination in his [God's] sight, that those professors were all corrupt, that 'they draw near me with their lips but their hearts are far from me, They teach for doctrines the commandments of men, having a form of Godliness but they deny the power thereof'."[8]

Smith's willingness to dissent from the established authority of his era and locale and to strike out on his own religious journey set him in bold contrast to most other Americans. Although the early nineteenth century was an era of spiritual quickening, most religious enthusiasm was coopted into the institutional structure of mainline denominations.[9]

Religious dissenters were committed to ideas and a philosophy, or a theology, that motivated their lives. For these people, ideas had consequences. Even the most Machiavellian person would be forced to admit that ideas of political loyalty, ethical responsibility, doctrinal superiority, genetic or some other type of determinism, or historical inevitability have wrought consequences of great proportion in the development of humanity. It is a measure of the importance of these religious ideas that people holding them, such as Joseph Smith, Jr., and other dissenters, affirmed in their lives, and often in their deaths, that their ideas did matter.

Joseph Smith, Jr., was a radical who challenged accepted religious and social notions on virtually every front. Smith and others like him, according to the historian Edwin Scott Gaustad, were "1) tough on bishops, and all other entrenched exercisers of ecclesiastical authority; 2) hard on creeds and all other dogmatically defined or uncritically assumed, proposition-packaged truth; and, 3) in constant tension with mainstream U.S.A., sometimes trying to alter the direction of the majority, other times asking only that society leave it alone."[10] Society has often dealt harshly with dissenters. Sometimes, like Anne Hutchinson, they were exiled; sometimes, like Joseph Smith, they were killed. They were rarely ignored, although when they were that was the religious dissenter's harshest punishment. Dissenters who survived, however, often claimed at least a small following and established a new ecclesiastical institution. This is what happened with the early Latter Day Saint movement, and it became the most successful of all American-born churches.[11] Smith created his own organization interested in preserving its own institutional power. While Smith and his followers were bound to torment society, dissenters within his own circle soon began tormenting him. The irony of the tormenter becoming the tormented, within Mormonism, is too rich to be ignored.

Joseph Smith erected his own brand of religious authority in early Mormonism. In the Restoration scheme of things, if one accepted Smith's religious authority, one also accepted a social, political, economic, and cultural system. Early Mormonism rejected the central features of the emerging *Weltanschauung* now called modernity—a pluralistic, scientific, secular approach toward life.[12] Smith's organization sustained earlier Medieval conceptions of human existence, the creation of a utopian theocracy, and themselves as the covenant people of God above all others. It embraced an absolutist image of right and wrong, with Smith and his faithful always right, and was therefore intensely skeptical of American pluralism if for no other reason than it recognized many perspectives. Mormonism was exceptionally critical of Jacksonian America's unbridled, self-interested individualism, and increasingly it viewed the United States as a society that was highly secular and profane. Mormonism was, therefore, intensely sectarian, even creating the sense of a religious movement that was something separate and distinct from Christianity.[13]

Marvin S. Hill emphasized these conceptions by arguing persuasively that the early Mormon attempt to develop a communal utopia under theocratic control during the 1830s and 1840s was partially a reaction against the increasing importance of democratic, competitive, secular tendencies and the overall decline of religion in America. The Mormon church, therefore, "sought to revitalize this magical world view [like had been present in medieval society], combine it with elements of more traditional Christianity, and establish a theocratic society where the unconverted, the poor, and the socially and religiously alienated could gather and find a refuge from the competing sects and the uncertainties they engendered. His efforts to do so would bring him into conflict with leaders and others of the established order who were otherwise-minded."[14]

The emerging emphasis on personal freedom in America was an unnerving ingredient in the general sense of alienation felt by converts to Mormonism toward those around them.[15] A reactionary approach toward America was institutionalized in the 1830s as Mormonism shifted from charismatic or spiritual power to hierarchical priesthood authority.[16]

The shift to hierarchical religious authority in early Mormonism was a natural and perhaps necessary ingredient in response to the pluralism surrounding the institution, and this in itself fostered dissent. The Latter Day Saints early established an ecclesiastical structure in which authority flowed from Smith at the top to subordinates in the organization. At the same time, there was room for a more democratic approach that located religious authority in the lower levels of the organization. It found support in the Mormon scriptural record authorizing the elders to "conduct the meetings as they are led by the Holy Ghost."[17]

In a movement that also valued spiritual experiences as evidence of God's covenant with them, as Larry W. Conrad has noted, it was not an unnatural step from thinking in response to spiritual awakening that "one is *an* authority to thinking that one is *the* authority." The two constructs for religious authority made Mormonism especially conducive to internal dissent, and Smith was forever trying to minimize schism that might result from it. Especially critical to the issue of religious authority was who had the right to define theological and political positions. Founded on the concept that the ancient priesthood had been restored to Mormonism after having been lost in a great apostasy, Joseph Smith claimed that he and his supporters alone possessed the authority and truth necessary for salvation. Dissenters from Mormonism, in effect, concluded that exclusive claims to authority and theological truth were conferred on them rather than residing in the ecclesiastical machinery.[18]

Mormonism's position on religious authority has fostered a series of internecine struggles for power and influence, as more than a hundred schismatic movements have emerged from it since 1830.[19] Periodically, individuals with different perspectives on issues ranging from fundamental doctrinal questions to bureaucratic tiffs have challenged the movement's leadership. Joseph Smith, Jr., had to deal almost from the beginning of the formal establishment of the Mormon movement with unruly coreligionists who had emerged from essentially the same background as he. Struck by the sense of religious authority imbued in Mormonism, by the promise of spiritual awakening, and by the possibility, even probability, of personal revelation, they argued for an understanding of truth as a dynamic. They asserted that it was not unchangeable; that its ultimate focus was in the individual, not in the state or the church.[20] These beliefs were manifested in a series of challenges to Smith's suzerainty over the direction of policy, organizational trajectory, and doctrinal conceptions. These dissenters reinterpreted the ideas of Smith's "restoration" in a variety of ways. All worked along a continuum, however, between the established tradition of Mormonism and the cosmic ideals of Protestantism and American civil religion.

In response to these challenges, Smith sought to establish ever-tighter control over the movement, ironically moving from the position of dissenter to ecclesiastical authority. He erected a strong organization with authority to make pronouncements for the membership. Consolidation of authority, therefore, was an early and persistent goal of the Mormon leadership. Perhaps the best examples of this were Smith's statements in the *Doctrine and Covenants* giving himself the final authority on ecclesiastical questions. For example, when Hiram Page challenged, apparently with some success, Smith's right to receive revelations binding on the whole church in September 1830, Smith dictated an emphatic revelation that ended Page's career as a prophet: "But, behold, verily, verily I say unto thee, No one shall be appointed to receive commandments and revelations in this church excepting my servant Joseph Smith, Jr., for he receiveth them even as Moses; and thou shalt be obedient unto the things which I shall give unto him, even as Aaron, to declare faithfully the commandments and revelations, with power and authority unto the church."[21]

Another member, known to history only as Mrs. Hubble, challenged Smith's authority to receive revelations a few months later, and his response was an even stronger revelation. "But verily, verily I say unto you, that none else shall be appointed unto this gift [of revelation] except it be through him," the document stated, making it impossible for another person to assert authority as a prophet in the church.[22] These were essentially ecclesiastical actions to proscribe the influence of dissenters on the members of the institution.

They were not fully successful. Some early Latter Day Saints, less alienated from American society, emphasized the positive aspects of pluralism and decried what they perceived as an omnipresent pressure to conform to unique characteristics. Over a period of years, repeated differences of opinion surfaced over the policies, doctrines, and direction of the church. At times these differing elements contended one with another to the extent that a dissenting element was identifiable. Many of those dissenters had positions worth considering, in some instances they were probably right, usually they were honest in their dissent. Yet those interested in the Mormon experience have tended to dismiss these people as apostates, charlatans, or even psychopaths. Some probably fell into any one of these or other categories of a more subtle nature. Many, however, were honest searchers for religious truth. They believed sincerely that they possessed religious truth, or at least a greater portion of it than the institutional church, and worked to persuade others to their positions. In some instances they were probably not so sure that they had the answers as they were that the answers did not reside within the halls of the institution. These searchers had a profound influence on the history of Mormonism; they helped shape perspectives for the larger body of Saints and offered alternative ideas, some of which eventually prevailed within the movement.

The experiences of Oliver Cowdery, Martin Harris, and David Whitmer are a case in point. They had been some of the earliest and most stalwart of Mormonism's converts. They had testified to the divinity of the Book of Mormon and had persevered persecution and hardship for the sake of Mormonism. They were also among some of the prophet's closest friends and supporters and had been a critical component of early Mormonism's organizational machinery. Yet they found themselves outside the movement in 1838. As a result, they were vilified as traitors who had rejected the gospel, with a special place in hell reserved for them. Historians have seen fit to record the lives of these three men selectively, applauding their early support for the church, decrying or ignoring their dissent, and ultimately celebrating their repentance and return to the movement or their continuing testimony to the truthfulness of the Book of Mormon.[23] At no time, however, has their dissent been analyzed seriously. There were reasons for what they did, as they most likely did not suddenly take leave of their senses and at the same time take leave of the church. This raises the question of what prompted them to pursue a different religious course.

This dissenting role has been played out in Mormonism over and over again. For instance, following the disastrous Zion's Camp expedition to Missouri in 1834, several church officials in Kirtland, Ohio, challenged Smith's role.[24] They charged him with a number of crimes ranging from discrepancies in policy and doctrine to differences of opinion on insignificant issues. The dissent culminated in a serious rift in the church in 1837 and 1838. Many church members left or were excommunicated at that time, including the three witnesses, more than half of the Quorum of Twelve Apostles, and Bishop Edward Partridge as well as a number of members of lesser stature. The dissent was devastating to both the church and the disillusioned members who had believed in the "fullness of the gospel."[25]

What prompted this rift in the organization? The answers advanced have ranged from purely economic interpretations to explanations that create simple cause-effect dichotomies about the nature of apostasy and rebellion.[26] The issue, however, was much more complex than the specific complaints. Marvin S. Hill has offered a compelling analysis of the dissent that was demonstrated in Kirtland. Hill found that the Saints' complaints were only symptoms of a larger discontent over the fundamental nature of the church:

> In the upheaval at Kirtland, which carried over into Far West, Missouri, the degree of control to be possessed by the church and its leaders, the degree of consolidation in the kingdom was at stake. Dissenters like the Cowderys, the Whitmers, Burnet, McLellin and Brewster, wanted a more open society, closer to the values and traditions of evangelical Protestantism, while those who supported Smith tolerated a more closed society based on higher law, where the Saints were of one mind an[d] one heart, ready to do battle against the ungodly.[27]

The real issue was concerned with the shape of the future church and whether or not it would be part of mainstream American religion.

Many of these dissenters' criticisms were directed toward working out a position on the church's relationship to society. Much of the concern revolved around the nature of church government and its role somewhere between authoritarianism and complete freedom for the membership. Many dissenters expressed concern over what they thought was the development of a tyranny in the church. Warren Cowdery, the brother of Oliver and the editor of the *Messenger and Advocate,* warned against authoritarianism:

> If we gave all our privileges to one man, we virtually give him our money and our liberties, and make him our monarch, absolute and despotic, and ourselves abject slaves or fawning sycophants. If we grant privileges and monopolies to a few, they always continue to undermine the fundamental principles of freedom, and, sooner or later, convert the purest and most liberal form of Government into the rankest of aristocracy. . . . Whenever a people have unlimited confidence in a civil or ecclesiastical ruler or rulers, who are but men like themselves, and begin to think they can do no wrong, they increase their tyranny and oppression and establish a principle that man, poor frail lump of mortality like themselves, is infallible.[28]

One dissenter, Benjamin Winchester, said that Joseph Smith, Jr., while preaching in the Kirtland Temple, claimed that he "was authorized by God almighty to establish his kingdom—that he was God's prophet and God's agent and that he could do whatever he should choose to do, therefore the Church had NO RIGHT TO CALL INTO QUESTION anything he did, or to censure him for the reason that he was responsible to God Almighty only."[29] Winchester suggested that such an attitude demonstrated the fundamentally authoritarian direction toward which the church was moving.

The dissenting attitude in Kirtland continued in western Missouri during 1837 and 1838 as well and led to the development of such organizations as the Danites. This organization, led by Sampson Avard, began with the intention of enforcing orthodoxy among the Mormon membership and evolved into a vigilante movement, with all the abuses that have characterized those movements through the years. More important, however, was the appearance that a significant minority of church members were unwilling to acquiesce in the direction in which the institutional church was heading.[30] Of course, the greater the authoritarian nature of the institution, the less room there was for nonorthodoxy and the greater probability there would be for dissent.[31] All the factors came together for widespread dissention within Mormonism in the latter 1830s.

The undercurrent of concern over the direction of the movement was not washed away with a purging of dissenters from Mormonism during 1837–38. It arose again in Nauvoo in the mid 1840s. Many influential Latter Day Saints, led by William Law, a counselor to Joseph

Smith in the First Presidency in the early 1840s, and other prominent Mormons who had much to lose and little to gain by dissent left the movement because they were convinced that the organization had departed from the true principles of the gospel. This alternative position, therefore, was not merely started to gain something. Some of the most solid and respected individuals of the community were involved. Perhaps their secular stature contributed to their dissent; having a larger stake in mainstream American society than most of their Mormon brethren, they may have been less willing to overturn social, political, and economic institutions.[32]

These dissidents worked to expose what they considered the evils of the leadership in a newspaper called the *Nauvoo Expositor*. On June 7, 1844, they issued the paper's only number. This newspaper has been remembered largely for its affidavits about the practice of plural marriage by church officials and condemned as the catalyst for Smith's death. Digging below the surface of this controversial issue, the dissidents were protesting what they viewed as an erosion of the rights of the Saints to direct the church. The editors affirmed that they "know of a surety, that the religion of the Latter Day Saints as originally taught by Joseph Smith, which is contained in the Old and New Testament, Book of Covenants, and Book of Mormon, is true; and that the pure principles set forth in those books, are the immutable and eternal principles of Heaven, and speaks a language which, when spoken in truth and virtue, sinks deep into the heart of every honest man." Although accepting the purity of the movement at the beginning, these Saints asked Smith to function more democratically within the institution. They claimed that he had become a tyrant who did as he pleased without the regard for others that a man of God should have. They added that he was mixing religion and politics, even to the extent of declaring himself a candidate for the presidency of the United States in 1844. Furthermore, they complained that Smith had started teaching other doctrines, besides plural marriage, that were contrary to the gospel they had embraced. Those who opposed Smith's actions, they said, were dealt with harshly by ecclesiastical authorities.[33]

The publication of the *Expositor* raised a furor in the community, and Smith, acting as mayor of Nauvoo, and the city council agreed that the press had to be silenced by the police force. William Law immediately swore out a complaint against Smith for inciting a riot and unlawfully destroying property. Smith was arrested on this charge, as well as some others drummed up later, and while he was incarcerated in the Hancock County jail, a mob shot him and his brother, Hyrum, on June 27, 1844. In an irony of the foremost magnitude, whether one believes all the charges levied by William Law against Smith matters not; the prophet was vulnerable to the mob because he had been arrested for exercising injudiciously the very power Law had accused him of exercising injudiciously.[34]

Perhaps the greatest of all dissenting episodes took place following the death of Joseph Smith, Jr., when church members could not agree on either a leader or a theological direction. Out of that experience no fewer than fifteen important groups emerged. The largest, of course, was led by Brigham Young, and it was successful in capturing the organizational machinery virtually intact. Because of differing ideas about the manner of presidential succession and religious authority, it was unable to secure the whole membership, however. This divergence of ideas among the members cast doubt on the legitimacy of any one method of succession over another as the appropriate means of determining the "truth" of a given faction. The issue was most assuredly unclear and—based upon prophetic declaration, organizational evolution, priesthood authority, and scriptural precedents—there were several ways in which an individual within Mormonism could legitimately claim succession to the presidency. D. Michael Quinn, who delineated eight legitimate methods of Mormon presidential succession, concluded that "by the summer of 1844 [at the death of Joseph Smith, Jr.] there was no explicit outline of presidential succession in print."[35]

From the confusion on the issue, it would be easy to see how so many different individuals and, eventually, Mormon churches, each with legitimate claims, could assert that they were the continuation of the early Latter Day Saint church, each labeling the others as dissenting and heretical organizations. Those factions of Mormonism went on to develop their own institutions, from which later members dissented in turn. The result has been a propagation of Mormon groups during the more than 160 years since the chartering of the original Latter Day Saint church. In 1986 approximately fifty organized groups still functioned under the umbrella of Mormondom.

Clearly, dissent has been a significant force in the church and a dynamic that has continued throughout the movement's history. Most explanations of religious dissent have emphasized a particular explanation based on sociocultural differences between the institution and the dissenters: lack of participation, power, or influence within the institution, which results in status anxiety; misunderstandings over intentions; or unorthodox beliefs and practices. Research on Mormonism, including the essays contained in this volume, suggest that Mormon dissent has been largely motivated by a complex social interaction process within specific sociocultural and historical contexts. The

actions of dissenters were motivated by meaningful interpretations of
their Mormon conceptions, by specific existential conditions, by conflicts between leaders over critical issues, and by desires for institutional
power and authority. Most people did not deliberately set out to dissent, and their actions were not the result of deliberate, rational actions. They were generally less motivated by personal gain than by com-
mitments to principles as they defined them.

In spite of the plethora of religious dissent that has been present in
Mormon history, and its generally idealistic expression, internal disagreements have not been seen in any corner of Mormondom as legitimate. "By its own nature," wrote Paul M. Edwards, "dissent weak-
ens the power the church was constitutionally designed to strengthen."
Without at least some of this power the institution could not meet the
majority of its members' needs. If the church's power were effectively
challenged, the argument suggests, the movement would fall of its own
weight. "There can be no real dissent within the group because the
leadership reflects—and the consent of the people authorizes—the 'General Will' of the body."[36] This basic approach makes clear how the institutional church acknowledges truth in a legalistic manner. On this
score, the view expressed in the Book of Mormon has generally been
acknowledged as authoritative: "it is not common that the voice of the
people desireth anything of the contrary to that which is right; but it
is common for the lesser part of the people to desire that which is not
right."[37]

For more than a century and a half, writes Paul Edwards, Mormonism has asserted that the essence of the General Will is mediated by a
member's "passionate *concern* for and involvement with another (even
an institution) and the *duty* espoused by this concern." The chief point
of this has been a generally accepted belief that, to a large measure, members in good standing believe love for the institution requires an obedience that acknowledges contractual love as ownership. In the Mormon
tradition, then, one cannot really dissent if one truly loves the gospel.
"The arguments against dissent have tended to revolve around the assumption that personal feelings must bow below that of the church, that
no disagreement be allowed to harm the church." Dissent, therefore, has
not been an acceptable form of action in Mormonism.[38]

There has traditionally been another way in which dissent has been
placed outside the legal assumptions of Mormonism. The members have
been taught to expect answers not only to their theological, but also
to their social and political questions. Accordingly, church officials have
been expected to respond to every question with an answer rather than
acknowledging the complexity of the questions. Dissenters have a pro-

pensity for framing questions without clear-cut answers, and the move-ment's leadership has often viewed these as threats to harmony. The leaders become, almost by default, defenders of an institution created by humanity rather than prophets calling members to righteousness. In addition, Mormon dissent has been limited by the members' ten-dencies to confuse power and authority. "Power is the ability to take control and to obligate others to you," wrote Edwards, "authority is the right to do so. Power begins at the top with the authority being delegated, thus people tend to assume that power is authority and thus consent to power. Finally, tolerance for dissent implies a pluralism that Mormonism never accepted and was brought into being to stamp out."

Those who have not accepted these assumptions quite so readily have been the most consistent dissenters throughout the history of Mormon-ism. People in that category have usually tasted both power and influ-ence—as well as professional acceptance and understanding—outside the church and have been relatively comfortable in other circles. They have become "increasingly aware of their own authority by virtue of knowl-edge and ability, while at the same time more aware of their lack of pow-er within the institution. This group includes the intellectuals (and clos-et skeptics), as well as those faithful to the tradition but not necessarily the doctrine. It also includes persons who have come to believe that their opinions reflect an honest minority." These individuals have often con-sidered themselves challenged—and usually blocked—by those who con-trolled the institution. They have felt "excluded from power because they have been neither rich enough (in terms of holding authority) nor poor enough (willing to trade obedience for protection)." It is probably no anomaly that many of the dissenting movements arising out of Mormon-ism have been led either by secularly successful individuals or by intel-lectuals of one stripe or another.[39]

Dissent in the Mormon tradition has developed overwhelmingly neg-ative connotations. This is true in large measure because the institu-tion's antipluralistic and exclusivistic claims have prompted Mormon leaders of every faction to perceive dissent as, for the most part, dis-loyalty. Mormonism could not let its defectors go unchallenged; their comments always signified unrest and probable difficulties for the church. Without rebuttal, dissenting positions took on greater sub-stance. Always dissenters, such as William E. McLellin or Frank J. Cannon, were characterized as misbegotten, woeful malcontents whose arguments were without foundation. The problem was with the dis-senters' characters, not with the church or its leadership. Often the personal sins of the dissenters were trotted out for public display. If none were immediately at hand, they might be made up as in the case with David Whitmer. Crimes real and imagined were described in a depth not seen except in the most vicious political campaigns. Dissent was often explained as the result of personal fault.[40]

The dissenters, because of flaws in their characters, were threats to the integrity of the gospel and deserving of expulsion. The institution was always judged to be sound, the dissenters themselves were defective. One historian concluded:

> Defectors became a kind of bogey to haunt all inhabitants of the Mormon kingdom. Without vigilance and strength of character they [other members], like the defectors, could become overwhelmed by the baseness of their character and, thus, open to Satan's enticements. In this way blame was shifted from the kingdom to the individual defector. More importantly, dissent was portrayed as the outward sign of personal weakness and sin. Dissent, therefore, could no more be tolerated than sin itself. This attitude within the kingdom militated against any legitimate expression of doubt. There was no loyal opposition within the kingdom of God. As no dissent from orthodox opinion was allowed either the inhabitant accepted it or he was compelled to withdraw.[41]

This process has always served as a defense mechanism for the various institutions of Mormondom. Mormon groups have used it to protect themselves from extra-hierarchical pushes for change from within.

The emphasis on the negative aspects of dissent has prohibited Mormonism from recognizing the positive consequences of social conflict. The delineation of orthodoxy and dissent from it have four central repercussions. First, it helps to define the normative or ideological boundaries of Mormonism, thereby clarifying the sometime fine line between what are and what are not legitimate positions. While the dissenters themselves might be lost in this process, those who remain recognize a demarcation of orthodoxy that is relatively strong. For example, Joseph Musser's twentieth-century polygamy, although rooted in the tradition of nineteenth-century Utah Mormonism and therefore consistent with his conceptions of what Mormonism should be, was determined to be heretical. Although Musser and his supporters were lost in the struggle over this issue, it set a standard for orthodoxy that was not lost on other members. Second, the struggle over issues within Mormonism has typically generated solidarity among the membership as they rally together to either punish the deviants or to save them from unorthodoxy. The opposition to a Henry Lawrence, a Fawn M. Brodie, or a Richard Price galvanized the institution more than had no threat been perceived. Third, it can relieve stress and tension within the group as members "blow off steam" in the process of working through the issues sparking dissent. Finally, dissent serves the positive function of providing a warning sign to church leaders that real concerns need to be reconciled if the group is not to schism.[42]

Dissent, as with power and authority, is really a neutral term. It is a positive term for those supporting the dissenting position, as with Martin Luther and others who dissented against the Catholic church, or as with Joseph Smith, Jr., and the Latter Day Saints who dissented against American Protestantism and society. Catholic leaders, of course, did not support Luther's dissent and took action to silence him before he did much damage to the ecclesiastical order. Likewise, religious groups in Jacksonian America thought Joseph Smith in error and took action to quell his influence. The perspective on the issue, it seems, has always been conditioned largely by the side of the fence on which the individual participant stands. Unity of purpose instead of uniformity of belief has been an often-stated, admirable goal. However, in a religion based on revelation, people have often honestly believed that God is on their side—or they are on God's side—and therefore operate under the perceived divine imperative to demand capitulation rather than compromise.[43]

These issues are the concern of this collection of biographical essays drawn from more than 160 years of Mormon history. Founded on the principle of personal revelation and disgust for other established Christian churches, Mormonism has been a dynamically evolving institution since its creation. The movement has attracted, and thrown off, a wide divergence of people, each with remarkably differing interpretations of the "truths" of Mormonism. These "centrifugal tendencies" in Mormonism have been largely ignored by historians, and dissenters have usually been simply written off as apostates.[44] These essays seek to describe the vision of Mormonism that captured converts, to understand the particulars of the lives of certain dissenters and what prompted them to take the courses they took, to assess the factors intrinsic to the movement that prompted dissent, and to analyze the development of a major American religion from the perspective of a dissenting tradition.

This collection represents an attempt to offer an honest assessment from the standpoint of selected individuals about the dissenting tendency in Mormonism and how it affected the movement. To achieve this purpose the authors analyzed the careers of their subjects with a view to illuminating what attracted them to the Latter Day Saint movement, compelled their activity, and ultimately prompted them to dissent in either a public or private manner from the religious institution.

Equally important, the individual authors have examined the continued influence of Mormonism on their subjects, which seems to have
been more lasting than the dissenters would admit. To reorient a cli-
ché, you can take the people out of the church but you cannot take
the church, or more precisely its social and behavior system, out of
the people.

Our curiosity for this subject was piqued by the insights offered in
The Gnostic Gospels by Elaine Pagels,[45] Pagels used the Gnostic documents discovered since World War II to show that an entirely different
interpretation of Jesus existed from that of orthodox Christians and to
show that there was a conflict in the ancient world over how the mission of Jesus would be taught. Either side could have won, but what
was remarkable was that the Gnostics used the same information to arrive at entirely different perspectives on Christianity than did the orthodox. For a time it appears that either the Gnostics or the Pauline Christians might be successful in capturing the institutional Christian church.
Over the years, however, the position currently accepted as orthodox
Christianity gained credence, and the Gnostic approach was gradually
exterminated. In the same way, Brigham Young interpreted the Nauvoo
experience as the best and most advanced manifestation of Mormonism
and worked to ensure its preeminence, whereas William Smith or any
number of other later nineteenth-century dissenters thought it represented
much that was wrong with the church and strove to assert their own
positions. In contrast, the early twentieth-century Mormon dissenter
Joseph Musser believed that Mormonism's rejection of plural marriage,
which the church officially practiced until 1890, was a sign of apostasy
and required his opposition. Much the same could be said for Richard
Price, the Reorganized Church's present-day dissenter who has led a rebellion predicated on a supposed return to the "pure truths" of the organization taught earlier in its existence. Only by investigating these differing perspectives can one appreciate the divergent churches and peoples
claiming the heritage of Mormonism.

Any collection of historically oriented essays, especially those biographical in character, raises an immediate criticism: Why were some
subjects included while others of seemingly equal importance were
omitted? There can never be a satisfactory answer to this question. Our
criteria for choosing particular subjects and omitting others rested on
three interrelated factors. First, the subjects had to be of interest and
importance to Mormon history in and of themselves. There also had
to have been a reasonable chance of furthering the study of dissent in
the institution through profiling each subject. This omitted such people as Mrs. Hubble, the 1830 prophetess who challenged Joseph Smith's

authority and is at best a footnote in Mormonism's history.[46] Second, although there has not been much work on the subject of dissent, there seemed no reason to duplicate serious recent scholarship concerning some notable dissenters within Mormonism. For this reason, such people as William Law, who withdrew from the church in 1844 and began his own protest movement, have not been included. Third, of course subjective factors were involved in the selection of topics, for example, whether or not a scholar was willing to take on a particular essay. In some instances individuals were asked to write essays but were forced to decline for a variety of issues.

The list of dissenters included in this book is, nonetheless, a useful cross-section of people from a variety of periods, theological perspectives, and geographical locations. From David Whitmer to Sonia Johnson, all the essays capture something of the vitality of Mormonism and bespeak the contrasting perspectives of the institution. They are offered as the first, rather than the definitive, effort to understand the diversity of the Saints. Each was written by a scholar well versed in the subject, someone who in many instances has spent years studying the person or related events. The authors include members of the Utah Mormon movement, the Reorganized Church, a variety of other Christian denominations, and the religiously unaffiliated. Some derive their livelihood from one of Mormondom's institutions, whereas others work outside that community. Although each writes from a personal perspective and with their own voice, all are united in a commitment to historical inquiry and understanding. All of the essays in this book are printed here for the first time, although in some instances the authors might have written on the same or a related subject in years past.

NOTES

1. John Winthrop, "A Short History of the Rise, Reign, and Ruin of Antinomians, Familists and Libertines, that Infected the Churches of New England," London, 1644, in *Antinomianism in the Colony of Massachusetts Bay, 1636–1638*, ed. Charles Francis Adams (Boston: Publications of the Prince Society, 1894), 138.

2. See Perry Miller, *Orthodoxy in Massachusetts, 1630–1650* (Cambridge: Harvard University Press, 1933); Emery Battis, *Saints and Sectaries: Anne Hutchinson and the Antinomian Controversy in the Massachusetts Bay Colony* (Chapel Hill: University of North Carolina Press, 1962); Kai T. Erickson, *Wayward Puritans: A Study in the Sociology of Deviance* (New York: John Wiley and Sons, 1966); Edmund S. Morgan, *The Puritan Dilemma: The Story of John Winthrop* (Boston: Little, Brown and Co., 1958).

3. Quoted in Erikson, *Wayward Puritans,* 98.

4. These reasons have been advanced by numerous students of sociology. See Gus Tuberville, "Religious Schism in the Methodist Church: A Sociological Analysis of the Pine Grove Case," *Rural Sociology* 14 (1949): 29–39; Christopher Dawson, "What About Heretics: An Analysis of the Causes of Schism," *Commonweal* 36 (1942): 513–17; Anthony Oberschall, *Social Conflicts and Social Movements* (Englewood Cliffs: Prentice-Hall, 1973); and H. Richard Neibuhr, *The Social Sources of Denominationalism* (New York: Meridian Books, 1929). James S. Coleman, "Social Cleavage and Religious Conflict," *Journal of Social Issues* 12 (1956): 44–56; William Gamson, *Power and Discontent* (Homewood: Dorsey Press, 1968); and Rodney Stark and William S. Bainbridge, *A Theory of Religion* (New York: Peter Lang, 1987) stress a lack of participation, power, or influence as determinative of dissent. The primacy of intellectual or ideological reasons for dissent have been accentuated by Edwin Scott Gaustad, *Dissent in American Religion* (Chicago: University of Chicago Press, 1973); John Wilson, "The Sociology of Schism," *A Sociological Yearbook of Religion in Britain* (London, England: SCM Press, 1971), 4:1–21; and Mary Lou Steed, "Church Schism and Secession: A Necessary Sequence?" *Review of Religious Research* 27 (1986): 344–55.

5. See S. N. Eisenstadt, ed., *Max Weber on Charisma and Institution Building: Selected Papers* (Chicago: University of Chicago Press, 1968), and Eric Hoffer, *The True Believer: Thoughts on the Nature of Mass Movements* (New York: Harper and Row, 1980).

6. This issue is too well accepted to be debated. For analyses see Marvin S. Hill, *Quest for Refuge: The Mormon Flight from American Pluralism* (Salt Lake City: Signature Books, 1989); Dan Vogel, *Religious Seekers and the Advent of Mormonism* (Salt Lake City: Signature Books, 1989); Richard L. Bushman, *Joseph Smith and the Beginnings of Mormonism* (Urbana: University of Illinois Press, 1984); Klaus J. Hansen, *Mormonism and American Culture* (Chicago: University of Chicago Press, 1981); Mario S. DePillis, "The Quest for Religious Authority and the Rise of Mormonism," *Dialogue: A Journal of Mormon Thought* 1 (Autumn 1966): 68–88.

7. Joseph Smith, Jr., "Historical Sketch, March 1, 1842," in *The Personal Writings of Joseph Smith,* ed. Dean C. Jessee (Salt Lake City: Deseret Book Co., 1984), 213.

8. Joseph Smith, Jr., "History, 1838," in *The Personal Writings of Joseph Smith,* ed. Jessee, 200.

9. The importance of the Second Great Awakening of the first three decades of the nineteenth century in the United States has been studied ad nauseam. See John B. Boles, *The Great Revival, 1787–1815* (Lexington: University Press of Kentucky, 1972); Nathan O. Hatch, *The Democratization of American Christianity* (New Haven: Yale University Press, 1989); George M. Thomas, *Revivalism and Cultural Change: Christianity, Nation-Building, and the Market in the Nineteenth Century United States* (Chicago: University of Chicago Press, 1990); Mark Noll, ed., *Religion and American Politics: From*

the Colonial Period to the 1980s (New York: Oxford University Press, 1990); R. Laurence Moore, *Religious Outsiders and the Making of Americans* (New York: Oxford University Press, 1986).

10. Gaustad, *Dissent in American Religion,* p. 142.

11. The two major groups of Mormonism spell the last part of their names separately. The Church of Jesus Christ of Latter-day Saints uses a hyphen and small *d* in the last part of its name. The Reorganized Church of Jesus Christ of Latter Day Saints omits the hyphen and capitalizes the *D.* In the first generation of the church evidence suggests that the official name was Church of Jesus Christ of Latter Day Saints, and it will be referred to in that manner in this introduction. Individual essays in this book will apply the accepted usage of the time and Mormon group.

12. For concise discussions of modernity see Anthony Gibbons, *The Consequences of Modernity* (Stanford: Stanford University Press, 1990); Jurgen Habermas, *The Philosophical Discourse of Modernity* (Cambridge: Polity Press, 1987); Jean-Francois Lyotard, *The Post-Modern Condition* (Minneapolis: University of Minnesota Press, 1985).

13. On sectarianism see Bryan R. Wilson, *Sects and Society* (London, England: Heinermann, 1961); Roy Wallis, *Sectarianism* (New York: John Wiley, 1975); and Roy Wallis, *The Road to Total Freedom: A Sociological Analysis of Scientology* (New York: Columbia University Press, 1977). The "peopleness" of Mormonism has been brilliantly analyzed in Jan Shipps, *Mormonism: The Story of New Religious Tradition* (Urbana: University of Illinois Press, 1985).

14. Hill, *Quest for Refuge,* 17.

15. On these arguments see Peter L. Berger, *The Sacred Canopy* (New York: Doubleday Anchor, 1969), 111–12; and Kenneth H. Winn, *Exiles in a Land of Liberty: Mormons in American 1830–1846* (Chapel Hill: University of North Carolina Press, 1989), 6–17.

16. A. Bruce Lindgren has noted that early Mormon religious authority was patterned on the Book of Mormon model of charismatic power, not on priesthood ordination. The shift to priestly authority came later. See A. Bruce Lindgren, "The Development of the Latter Day Saint Doctrine of the Priesthood, 1829–1835," *Courage: A Journal of History, Thought, and Action* 2 (Spring 1972): 439–43. Dan Vogel suggested that the emergence of assertions of angelic ordination as described in the early 1830s represented an attempt to strengthen the authority claims of Joseph Smith and to consolidate control by meeting literalistic seeker's expectations of both spiritual endowment and angelic ministry. See Dan Vogel, *Religious Seekers and the Advent of Mormonism* (Salt Lake City: Signature Books, 1988), 120.

17. *Book of Doctrine and Covenants* (Independence: Herald Publishing House, 1970), sec. 17:9; *Doctrine and Covenants of the Church of Jesus Christ of Latter-day Saints* (Salt Lake City: Deseret Book Co., 1981), sec. 20:45.

18. Larry W. Conrad, "Dissent among Dissenters: Theological Dimensions of Dissent in the Reorganized Church," in *Let Contention Cease: The Dynamics*

of Dissent in the Reorganized Church of Jesus Christ of Latter Day Saints, ed. Roger D. Launius and W. B. Spillman (Independence: Graceland/Park Press, 1991), 203–9, quotations from 206, 207.

19. On the factions of Mormonism see the catalog, Steven L. Shields, *Divergent Paths of the Restoration* (Bountiful: Restoration Research, 1986); Steven L. Shields, *The Latter Day Saint Churches: An Annotated Bibliography* (New York: Garland Press, 1987).

20. See the argument in Mark P. Leone, *Roots of Modern Mormonism* (Cambridge: Harvard University Press, 1979), 221.

21. *Book of Doctrine and Covenants,* sec. 27:2; *Doctrine and Covenants of the Latter-day Saints,* sec. 28:2–3.

22. *Book of Doctrine and Covenants,* sec. 43:1b–2a; *Doctrine and Covenants of the Latter-day Saints,* sec. 43:4.

23. The best work on the three witnesses is Richard Lloyd Anderson, *Investigating the Book of Mormon Witnesses* (Salt Lake City: Deseret Book Co., 1981), but it fails to deal with the issue of dissent.

24. For a fuller description of this event see Roger D. Launius, *Zion's Camp: Expedition to Missouri, 1834* (Independence: Herald Publishing House, 1984), 159–65.

25. The dissenting movement in Kirtland is described in Milton V. Backman, Jr., *The Heavens Resound: A History of the Latter-day Saints in Ohio, 1830–1838* (Salt Lake City: Deseret Book Co., 1983), 310–41; Hill, *Quest for Refuge,* 55–80; Winn, *Exiles in a Land of Liberty,* 106–28.

26. The economic interpretation of Kirtland dissent is usually tied to the failure of the church-sponsored Kirtland Safety Society Anti-Banking Company. For this view see Scott H. Partridge, "The Failure of the Kirtland Safety Society," *Brigham Young University Studies* 12 (Summer 1972): 437–54; Dean A. Dudley, "Bank Born of Revelation: The Kirtland Safety Society Anti-Banking Company," *Journal of Economic History* 30 (December 1970): 848–53; Robert Kent Fielding, "The Mormon Economy in Kirtland, Ohio," *Utah Historical Quarterly* 27 (October 1959): 331–58; and James B. Allen and Glen M. Leonard, *The Story of the Latter-day Saints* (Salt Lake City: Deseret Book Co., 1976), 113–14.

27. Marvin S. Hill, "Cultural Crisis in the Mormon Kingdom: A Reconsideration of the Causes of Kirtland Dissent," *Church History* 49 (September 1980): 286–97, quote on 296.

28. *Latter Day Saint Messenger and Advocate* 3 (July 1837): 538.

29. Quoted in Charles L. Woodward, "The First Half Century of Mormonism," 195, New York Public Library.

30. Without going into a long recitation of this crisis in the church and the Danite operation in Missouri, we would recommend Stephen C. LeSeuer's, *The 1838 Mormon War of Missouri* (Columbia: University of Missouri Press, 1987). For a short general study of the crisis in Far West see F. Mark McKiernan's dated essay "Mormonism on the Defensive: Far West," in *The Restoration Movement: Essays in Mormon History,* ed. F. Mark McKiernan,

Alma R. Blair, and Paul M. Edwards (Lawrence: Coronado Press, 1973), 121–40. A recent publication emphasizing his dissenting nature is Philip R. Legg, *Oliver Cowdery: The Elusive Second Elder of the Restoration* (Independence: Herald Publishing House, 1989).

31. Ideas on freedom and authoritarianism have been developed in Wallis, *Road to Total Freedom.*

32. On these leaders see, Lyndon W. Cook, "William Law, Nauvoo Dissenter," *Brigham Young University Studies* 22 (Winter 1982): 47–62; Robert Bruce Flanders, *Nauvoo: Kingdom on the Mississippi* (Urbana: University of Illinois Press, 1965), 305–10; John Frederick Glaser, "The Disaffection of William Law," in *Restoration Studies III,* ed. Maurice L. Draper and Debra Combs (Independence: Herald Publishing House, 1986), 163–75. In *Quest for Refuge* (chapter 2), Hill describes the early Saints as generally destitute and the social and economic policies of the church they embraced as radical, in part because there was little for the Saints to lose in a complete restructuring of society.

33. *Nauvoo* [Ill.] *Expositor,* June 7, 1844.

34. Dallin H. Oaks, "The Suppression of the *Nauvoo Expositor,*" *Utah Law Review* 9 (Winter 1966): 862–903; Dean C. Jessee, "Return to Carthage: Writing the History of Joseph Smith's Martyrdom," *Journal of Mormon History* 8 (1981): 3–21.

35. D. Michael Quinn, "The Mormon Succession Crisis of 1844," *Brigham Young University Studies* 16 (Winter 1976): 187–233, quote from 187.

36. Paul M. Edwards, "Ethics and Dissent in Mormonism: A Personal Essay," in *Let Contention Cease,* ed. Launius and Spillman, 246–47.

37. Mosiah 13:35, in Book of Mormon (Independence: Herald Publishing House, 1966).

38. Edwards, "Ethics and Dissent in Mormonism," 248.

39. Ibid., 249–50.

40. This is documented repeatedly in the essays that follow. See especially those on William E. McLellin, David Whitmer, Francis Gladden Bishop, Henry Lawrence, and Frank J. Cannon.

41. Gordon D. Pollock, "In Search for Security: The Mormons and the Kingdom of God on Earth, 1830–1844," Ph.D. diss., Queen's University, 1977, 292–93.

42. See Lewis Coser, *The Functions of Social Conflict* (Chicago: The Free Press of Glencoe, 1956); Ralf Dahrendorf, *Class and Class Conflict in Industrial America* (New York: Oxford University Press, 1959).

43. Some of these ideas are developed in Donald J. Breckon, "The Politics of Dissent and the Reorganized Church," in *Let Contention Cease,* ed. Launius and Spillman, 157–61.

44. On "centrifugal tendencies" see Leonard J. Arrington, "Centrifugal Tendencies in Mormon History," in *To the Glory of God: Mormon Essays on Great Issues,* ed. Truman G. Madsen (Salt Lake City: Deseret Book Co., 1972), 163–77.

45. Elaine Pagels, *The Gnostic Gospels* (New York: Harper and Row, 1979).

46. We do not even know her first name, from where she came, or where she went. See Backman, Jr., *The Heavens Resound,* p. 60.

1

David Whitmer:
Faithful Dissenter, Witness Apart

Ronald E. Romig

David Whitmer was one of the most significant figures in early Mormonism. Whitmer's prominent role as a key early supporter of Joseph Smith, Jr., and his witness to the divinity of the Book of Mormon has ensured that his career as a Latter Day Saint became well known. Yet, most investigation has focused exclusively on his role as one of the three Book of Mormon witnesses. Whitmer's dissent from the church in the mid 1830s, culminating in his withdrawal in 1838, makes him an especially significant subject for consideration in the first generation of the church. In spite of his exile from the church, throughout the remainder of his long life Whitmer's feelings, beliefs, and perceptions about his experiences demonstrated his faithful dissent. This essay will describe Whitmer's attraction to, envelopment in, and withdrawal from Mormonism.

David Whitmer was the fourth child of Peter Whitmer, Sr., and Mary Musselman Whitmer, born near Harrisburg, Pennsylvania, on January 7, 1805.[1] Not long thereafter, the family removed to the state of New York, "at a point midway between the northern extremities of Lakes Cayuga and Seneca, two miles from Waterloo, seven miles from Geneva, and twenty-seven miles from Palmyra."[2] In this community Peter Whitmer, Sr., was known as "a hard working, God-fearing man, was a strict Presbyterian and brought his children up with rigid sectarian discipline."[3] The family, in spite of apparent industriousness, was poor. David Whitmer, it seems, received only a limited education.[4]

Whitmer first came into contact with Joseph Smith, Jr., and the message of the Restoration through Oliver Cowdery, his brother-in-law. Whitmer recalled that he first became interested in Smith's work during a business trip to Palmyra in 1828: "A great many people in the neighborhood were talking about the finding of certain golden plates by one Joseph Smith, Jr., a young man of that neighborhood. Cowdery and I, as well as others, talked about the matter, but at that time I paid but little attention to it, supposing it to be only the idle gossip of the neighborhood. Cowdery said he was acquainted with the Smith family, and he believed there must be some truth in the story of the plates, and that he intended to investigate the matter."[5] Not long after his initial meeting with Smith, Cowdery became convinced of his religious mission and worked to interest David Whitmer in Joseph Smith's activities.

Whitmer recalled that he eventually went with Cowdery to meet Smith and was impressed by the young seer's sincerity and commitment. He wanted to help Smith with the Book of Mormon and soon moved him into his parents' house to free him to work on the translation full time. The men became close friends during this time and spent hours discussing religious ideals and precepts. Later in his life, Whitmer left this description of the young prophet: "Joseph Smith was a man of great magnetism, made friends easily, was liberal and noble in his impulses, tall, finely formed and full of animal life, but sprung from the most humble of circumstances. The first good suit of clothes he had ever worn was presented to him by (my brother) Christian Whitmer."[6]

David Whitmer was wholly taken with Smith. For Whitmer, Smith's demeanor seemed to stimulate singular experiences, elevating perceptions far above everyday farm activities. Despite obvious incongruities, the teachings and actions of Joseph Smith fostered a creative expectation within. In that sense, Smith was more the visionary artist than purveyor of institutional religion. His representations appealed not so much to reason but influenced some universal subjective truth within. His visions opened a window between the spiritual and natural world for David Whitmer that he had never perceived before. In such an animated atmosphere, Whitmer said that he experienced something that increased his spiritual intimacy with the Divine.

David Whitmer's role in the developing church provided him with what everyone desires, extreme personal satisfaction. The depth of his family's involvement reinforced this feeling. In a clannish family such as Whitmer's, there is a great need, even urgency, for each family member to be part of, support, and advance family beliefs. With his family so intimately engrossed in the Restoration movement, David Whitmer was impelled to join and thereafter remain part of the "in" group. The attraction of the Restoration's religious knowledge combined with strong familial incentives proved especially powerful.

He firmly believed that he was a participant in a string of divinely initiated experiences occurring in relation to the translation of the gold plates of Mormon. All of Whitmer's recorded actions for the rest of his long life confirmed that he perceived the coming forth of the Book of Mormon and the organization of the Latter Day Saint church as a genuine representation of divine interaction with humanity. Numerous instances demonstrated this basic belief throughout Whitmer's lifetime. He accepted these unique religious experiences, even though by their very nature they could only remain subjective to others not having first-hand knowledge of them.[7]

Ironically, the opening Restoration events took place as forces of democratization and industrialization promoted an increase of individualism and religious liberalism. At this time many were reacting to perceived limitations of religious control over the common man. The era invited intellectual individuality with new emphasis on opportunities afforded by education. Yet, to others such an awakening suggested a man-centered rather than a God-centered future. Accordingly, these liberalizing tendencies were opposed by those who sought to conserve social traditions and the historic role of religion. Joseph Smith, as has been suggested by several recent scholars, distrusted the pluralism developing in American society. His thinking reflected a reaction against the divisions of society being created from the effects of the Reformation, capitalism, and nationalism. Smith conceived that man could only be secure when theocratic order from a Kingdom of God held dominion.[8] Whitmer's philosophy on this issue is less clear, but he appears to have been more accepting of American pluralism than Smith. This fundamental difference of worldviews fostered a growing tension between the two men. Eventually, Whitmer came to contest the prophet's envisioned rules of an earthly Kingdom. Over the next few years, he was to find that keeping peace with Joseph Smith would increasingly demand his conformity to a developing unique worldview.

In June 1829, Smith invited Whitmer's deeper involvement in the Restoration work by calling him through revelation to additional responsibilities. Smith told him, "you are called even with the same calling with which he [Paul] was called."[9] Later that same month, Smith baptized Whitmer in nearby Seneca Lake. Immediately thereafter he was ordained an elder.[10] Soon, he became one of the witnesses to the Book of Mormon. He remembered that he accompanied Smith, Martin Harris, and Oliver Cowdery into the woods, where they began to pray. In a short time "a light appeared and it grew brighter until an angel stood before us."[11] Whitmer added: "In the midst of this light, but a few feet from us, appeared a table upon which were many golden plates, also the sword of Laban and the Directors. I saw them as plain as I see you now, and distinctly heard the voice of the Lord declaiming that the records of the plates of the Book of Mormon were translated by the gift and the power of God."[12] This encounter became the core religious experience of David Whitmer's life. It served as a benchmark for what had preceded and all that followed. The fact that he affirmed this experience throughout his life illustrates how deeply he had internalized it.

Joseph Campbell has observed much about the value of myth in adding purpose to human lives.[13] Without myth, divine heroes, and mentors to guide, where can meaning in life be found? Who can say at what point the excesses of credulity are harmonized by the benefits that result to the individual from the power of the myth? In much the same way, Whitmer's witness of the divinity of the Book of Mormon was the cusp at which the divine met the mortal.

At this early date, Joseph Smith launched into a pattern of behavior that he would emulate throughout his life. This, too, would set him and Whitmer at odds. Smith regularly envisioned new and larger dimensions to church scope and interest. Intrigued by reflections of a heavenly order in the scriptures, he aspired to turn this symbolism into literal reality. An essential element of his undertaking was the authoritative organization of the church. Although preaching and missionary efforts represented a preliminary church structure, Joseph Smith longed for the literal restoration of Christ's church, which he perceived as having been long since withdrawn from the face of the earth. The release of the Book of Mormon to the public on March 26, 1830, seemed to signal the beginning of this new phase of church design. Just days after the Book of Mormon was off the press, Smith called the faithful to a April 6 meeting at Peter Whitmer, Sr.'s log house to organize the church in accordance with New York state law.[14]

David later interpreted this action as a negative development in the Restoration's history. He reflected:

> I consider on that day the first error was introduced into the Church of Christ, and that error was Brother Joseph being ordained as "Prophet Seer and Revelator" to the church. . . . None of us detected it [the error] then. We had all confidence in Brother Joseph, thinking that as God had given him so great a gift as to translate the Book of Mormon, that everything he would do must be right. That is what I thought about it. It grieves me much to think that I was not more careful, and did not rely upon the teachings of Christ in the written word.[15]

After formal chartering, under Smith's leadership, church organization would continually evolve and grow, just as the church's name itself would take a variety of forms through succeeding years. Participants would find that the ultimate church organization and its priesthood structure was far from fully envisioned or wholly in place on the day the church was organized. Additions and adjustments that were soon to add to the "principles" of the gospel held in 1830 presented considerable difficulty for David Whitmer and other members inclined to take church claims and organizational structure more in line with the views held in larger American society.

Shortly after the organization of the church, Smith returned to Harmony, Pennsylvania, to arrange and copy the prophet's revelations. During this time, Oliver Cowdery, who was living with the Whitmers, sent a letter to Smith that revealed serious disagreement among early members, including David Whitmer, the first such instance recorded in church history. There was an error in one of the commandments, Cowdery informed Smith, who quoted the letter in his history:

> "And truly manifested by their works that they have received of the Spirit of Christ unto the remission of their sins." The above quotation, he [Cowdery] said, was erroneous, and added, I command you in the name of God to erase these words, that no priestcraft be among us. . . . In a few days afterward, I visited him and Mr. Whitmer's family, where I found the family, in general, of his opinion. . . . It was not without both labor and perseverance that I could prevail with any of them to reason calmly on the subject.

Finally, with Christian Whitmer's assistance, Joseph Smith "succeeded in bringing, not only the Whitmer family, but also Oliver Cowdery, to acknowledge they had been in error."[16]

David Whitmer and others of his family were inclined to render their own interpretations of what was appropriate doctrine in a manner reminiscent of the strongly congregational attitude of most American Protestants. Smith's strong feelings about the source of religious authority, however, always mitigated against this pluralistic tradition. The power of his winning ways and arguments induced them all to accept his rendition. The pattern established by this early encounter was often repeated and amplified. In a number of successive instances David Whitmer found that he was not in initial agreement with Smith's opinion about church doctrine or procedure, but in most cases he eventually submitted to Smith's view, at least publicly.

Although Whitmer later minimized his recollection of early disagreements, it prompted internal questions of Smith's tight control over the direction of the church through his presidential office. Smith probably perceived this tension as well, for he soon gave Whitmer revelatory advise on the subject: "David, you have feared man and have not relied on me for strength. . . . You have not given heed unto my Spirit, and to those who were set over you, but have been persuaded by those whom I have not commanded; wherefore, you are left to inquire for yourself, at my hand, and ponder upon the things which you have received."[17]

Whitmer accepted this statement as prophetic counsel at the time, but the tension between his view of religious ideals and those of Smith continued. It was something of a push-pull relationship. Whitmer was struck by the deeply moving religious experiences that he had felt at the founding of the church, and he sought to remain true to them.

At this early stage of church development, Whitmer wanted desperately to make a place for himself among the Latter Day Saints and used his relationship with Joseph Smith to influence the direction of unfolding events. Up to this point, he and other members had felt free to exercise their equal participation in the development of the church. During the very early period, Smith may have felt some hesitancy and even entertained some little fear that his longstanding supporters might desert him, for he was dependent upon them for both physical and social support. However, Joseph Smith came to feel a growing assurance in his position. It seems that members increasingly accepted his authority in community and social, as well as doctrinal and procedural, matters. Although some may perceive this as the emergence of an expression of Smith's assurance of divine sanction and a reflection of the courage of his convictions, his success, from Whitmer's perspective, established an evolving pattern of domination that ultimately harmed many in the movement as it escalated.

Such matters seemed of small consequence at the time. Whitmer's concern was surmounted by Smith's charisma and by the depth of their personal relationship. Although these frictions were patched up, Whitmer's later recollections show that they did not leave him unaffected. He suggested that Smith's mistakes were related to his overarching confidence in the prophetic position and his merging of sacred and secular issues that should be left separate. Although he acquiesced outwardly, Whitmer took a course of supportive dissent and quietly determined to work from within for what he perceived to be correct principles. In every visible sense, however, he acted the part of the true believer and no doubt hoped and believed his efforts would, in the end, assist in the inauguration of God's Kingdom as he envisioned it. Aflame with the hope of assisting in the accomplishment of something perceived of such worth, Whitmer remained circumspect in his actions for several years.

At the same time in the early 1830s that Whitmer was beginning to question some of the actions Smith took in directing the church, the prophet perceived the need for a more effective church structure. Following the Mormon missionary detour to Kirtland, Ohio, in the fall of 1830, a large number of new converts, most of them members of a church pastored by Sidney Rigdon, had entered Mormonism.[18] The incorporation of Rigdon and his followers into the church seemed especially to stimulate the need for a greater organizational adjustment and change. Rigdon soon came to supplant Oliver Cowdery and Whitmer as Smith's most intimate advisor in the church affairs. Whitmer wrote somewhat bitterly:

> Rigdon . . . worked himself deep into Brother Joseph's affections, and had more influence over him than any other man living. He was Brother Joseph's private counsellor, and his most intimate friend and brother for some time after they met. Brother Joseph rejoiced, believing that the Lord had sent to him this great and mighty man Sydney Rigdon, to help him in the work. Poor Brother Joseph! He was mistaken about this, and likewise all of the brethren were mistaken, for we thought at the time just as Brother Joseph did about it.[19]

Rigdon's importance in the church was graphically stated to Whitmer in 1832 when Rigdon was called as the prophet's first counselor in the newly created First Presidency of the Church. In this emerging organizational structure David Whitmer and several other early members of the church held no official position.[20]

With the conversion of a large number of people in northern Ohio, Smith elected to relocate church headquarters to the area. Accordingly, stalwart members began gathering to Ohio in the spring of 1831.[21] David Whitmer did so for a short time, but in the summer of 1831 he followed Smith's prompting and moved again to Jackson County in western Missouri. It was during this period that he began to express in more public ways his disagreements with Smith. As Smith increasingly looked to Sidney Rigdon for advice, he became less bound to his traditional supporters. Indeed, Rigdon also came to have a profound influence on the direction and organization of the movement.

The early shift from New York state to Ohio provided Joseph Smith an enormous opportunity. During these adjustments, he seemed to sense that change was a important ally; from the very beginning he counted upon it to accomplish his ends. He noted that such startling alterations allowed him to forward his religious goals. People and resources were easily diverted toward church purposes as change interrupted normal routines. Indeed, had things remained static he would have had very little opportunity to guide the growth of the church. The institution could not have developed so rapidly had not change been so frequent nor used as effectively. This course created a ready source of energy and enthusiasm that propelled the church forward and allowed Smith to experiment with his inspiration and ideas. He had a knack of mounting and maintaining ever-new challenges to keep members interested and involved. He also seemed to have an intuitive understanding of this dynamic and became a master of innovation. As new members were drawn into the group, he found places for them and created new and ever-expanding organizational structures to embrace them,[22]

Whitmer's later reflections on this aspect of Mormonism suggest, even though he still identified with the ideals of the original organization, that he questioned much of the church's direction from an early point. For instance, when Smith wanted to print the revelations he had received, Whitmer objected because of his understanding that the revelations were directed to individuals and believed that they were not intended as doctrine for the whole church. Whitmer described the meeting in which Smith proposed this project: "A few of the brethren— including myself—objected to it seriously. . . . and withstood Brothers Joseph and Sydney to the face. . . . that it was not the will of the Lord that the revelations should be published."[23] Whitmer's heavy investment into the movement and peer group pressures made him unwilling to sacrifice his membership in the group over such disagreements, however. He continued as a member in good standing, harboring ill feelings about it, something of which Joseph Smith was well aware and sought to defuse.[24]

By this time the colonization effort in Jackson County was well underway. Smith's initiation of a parallel church organization in Jackson County to administer the affairs of Zion inadvertently presented Whitmer an even greater opportunity to nurture his growing dissent. Promoting a separation of Kirtland and Jackson County created a situation in which the independent-minded, such as David Whitmer, found themselves freer to develop a shared perspective at variance with Joseph Smith's. Free from Smith's immediate influence, Whitmer found a new level of individuality deep within and sought to manifest it in directing the local church along lines more palatable to his personal conceptions.

He developed, for example, a position on the Law of Consecration different from that of Smith's. The Hiram, Ohio, branch's departure for Missouri in the spring of 1832, coincided with David Whitmer's. Members from the Hiram branch, arriving in Jackson County in June 1832, settled around what became the Whitmer settlement in Jackson County.[25] This relationship suggests a close connection that may also reflect a common philosophical and theological perspective. Before the

Hiram branch's departure, Harvey Redfield was hurriedly dispatched from Kirtland in an effort to persuade the members of the branch to obey the revelations requiring consecration, but they refused to consecrate their financial resources before departing.

In response to such circumstances, *The Evening and the Morning Star* printed the following remarks: "One very important requisition for the saints that come up to the land of Zion, is, that, before they start, they procure a certificate from three elders of the church, or from the bishop in Ohio, according to the commandments; and when they arrive to present it to the bishop in Zion, otherwise they are not considered wise stewards, and cannot be received into fellowship with the church, till they prove themselves by their own goodness."[26] The Hiram branch's refusal to consecrate before starting represented a growing discontent with the operation of the Law of Consecration.

The Whitmer family, which had moved to Jackson County as a group, worked closely with the members of the Hiram branch to clear land and develop a neighborhood of log houses that was sometimes called Fayette, reminiscent of the area of New York from which the Whitmers had come. It was also known as Timber Branch and the Whitmer settlement. Whitmer's appointment as presiding elder provided ecclesiastical leadership within the community.

Gathering church members produced a grand transformation of the wild lands upon which they settled. Despite internal and external difficulties, church members were soon established on the land and began to reap the benefits of their hard work. They began to sense a growing discontent among their nonmember Jackson County neighbors, however. Several hostile incidents were directed at the church during the summer of 1832. Although church members were occasionally threatened and some of their homes were pelted with stones and brickbats at night, no great damage was done until 1833.[27]

Although violence had erupted earlier between the Mormons and the Missourians in Independence and surrounding settlements, serious trouble for church members living in the Whitmer settlement did not begin until October 31, 1833. As part of the larger conflict, about forty non-Mormons, many armed with guns, moved against the settlement. Ten or twelve houses belonging to church members were unroofed and partly demolished. The Missourians also took two men and whipped and pounded them with stones and clubs, leaving barely a breath of life in them. One of the men beaten was Hiram Page, David Whitmer's brother-in-law.[28] News of the attack rapidly spread to the other church settlements. The day following the raid, Whitmer unsuccessfully led an effort to secure a peace warrant against leaders of the mob. He advised branches of the church to gather into bodies as best they could for their own preservation.

After church members at Independence and other settlements suffered similar attacks, the affair finally came to a head at the Whitmer settlement. On Monday, November 4, 1833, a large party of Missourians gathered above the church's Big Blue settlement and attacked a ferry operated by church member Orrin Porter Rockwell. After minor destruction the mob left. However, the Latter Day Saints, hearing of the attack, started out to offer assistance. In the process a group of nineteen members, including David Whitmer, ran into the Missourians more or less by accident.[29]

The Mormons were pursued into the Whitmer settlement, where a pitched battle ensued. Whitmer, who participated in the action, later related: "The mob destroyed a number of our dwellings and fired upon the little party of Mormons, killing one young man and wounding several others. The Mormons returned the fire, killing the leader of the mob, a Campbellite preacher, named Lovett."[30]

The unhappy escalation of hostilities that this action signaled resulted in the forced expulsion of the Mormons from Jackson County. In the process, members lost their homes and possessions. They scattered throughout the region, with most fleeing north across the Missouri River into Clay County. Reflecting upon the expulsion, Whitmer expressed second thoughts about the Jackson County gathering: "I regard it as an error, one that brought evil upon the church. I believe that God will finally gather his people, but not in the sense and way as taught by Joseph. . . . All attempts at Gathering will prove futile until the Day of the Lord comes."[31] All efforts by Joseph Smith and the church leaders to resolve the Jackson County difficulties, including a relief project called Zion's Camp, proved unsuccessful.[32]

In an effort to ensure the leadership of the scattered Missouri church, and perhaps to placate Whitmer, Smith ordained Whitmer president of a newly organized Missouri High Council on July 8, 1834.[33] It is clear that many Latter Day Saints believed this ordination designated Whitmer to be Smith's successor. Indeed, Joseph Smith admitted in a High Council meeting on March 15, 1838, that "the ordination of David Whitmer, which took place in July 1834, [was] to be a leader, or a prophet to this Church, which (ordination) was on conditions that he [Joseph Smith, Jr.] did not live to God himself."[34] Much later, John C. Whitmer wrote to John Snyder: "Brethren, we have told you before about the prophecy which Bro. Joseph Smith gave in 1834 to Bro. David. We have the old yellow time worn paper, among the sacred papers of our dear brother. This prophecy has been fulfilled. It says of

Bro. David that 'he shall be a ruler in Zion when he is old and well stricken in years.' *He* shall say to the faithful, 'Go forth, and build up the waste places of Zion.'"[35]

Whitmer seemed to keep his belief about this in a proper perspective. He told Zenos H. Gurley, Jr., in 1885: "I regard my authority as an elder for Christ given me of God before that time as superior to any honor which Joseph could bestow upon me by any such ordination."[36] In later life Whitmer even argued that the presidency was contrary to the laws of Christ and that Smith was in apostasy for creating it.[37]

With the situation in Missouri in disarray, Joseph Smith recalled some of the key church leaders to Ohio in 1834–35 to participate in church educational and organizational activities. One major aspect of the activity during this period involved the completion of the Kirtland Temple. David Whitmer went to Kirtland as requested, but he continued to function as the president of the Missouri church. Although extremely uncomfortable about the disaster that had occurred in Missouri, at Kirtland he participated in the heady atmosphere of a growing and developing church. The anticipated realization of spiritual endowment in the temple counterbalanced for Whitmer, as it did for the majority of the Saints, the debacle in Missouri.[38]

An instance that clearly demonstrates Whitmer's willingness to participate as a full partner in church activities but that also shows something of the strain between he and Smith, occurred during the selection of the Twelve. On February 14, 1835, Joseph Smith called a meeting of those who had made the journey with Zion's Camp to Missouri. He described the need to establish a Quorum of Twelve Apostles and asked the three witnesses to the Book of Mormon to serve as a committee to make the selections. Whitmer was pleased to assist, and Whitmer met with Oliver Cowdery and Martin Harris to choose the Twelve. Smith was not happy with the witnesses' selection of Phineas Young to the quorum, however, and imposed his wish that William Smith, his younger brother, be ordained instead. Oliver Cowdery wrote, "Brother David and myself yielded to his wish, and consented for William to be selected."[39]

Despite David Whitmer's attempts to remain positive about the church, he struggled to suppress growing apprehensions about Smith's leadership. Whitmer's brother, John, wrote that beginning not long after the July 1834 ordination Smith began to denigrate David Whitmer "and abuse him as his natural custom was to do with those whom he feared, lest they should become great in the sight of God or man, therefore, he harangued the conference and sought to destroy the confidence of the people present in D. Whitmer."[40] Despite this, Smith involved Whitmer in important events and decisions, including numerous worship and educational activities in Kirtland. For instance, at a crucial meeting with the prophet in the temple on January 21, 1836, Whitmer participated in a ritual washing and anointing. Oliver Cowdery, another participant, recorded that those gathered "washed our bodies with pure water before the Lord, preparatory to the anointing with the holy oil." He added, "After we were washed, our bodies were perfumed with a sweet smelling oderous wash."[41] This was prelude to a unique spiritual experience that lasted the night.[42] Whitmer was also an honored participant in the dedication of the Kirtland Temple on March 27, 1836, testifying that he saw angels in the building during the service.[43]

If these spiritual events buttressed Whitmer's faith on the Restoration gospel, his faith in Smith as a prophet continued to flag. Most of his concerns stemmed from the increasing secular power and influence he saw the prophet wielding. From Whitmer's perspective, Smith's and the institutional church's incursion into nontraditional arenas of his life was inappropriate. More comfortable with the pluralism of Jacksonian America, Whitmer did not fully support Smith's broad interest in using the church's political and economic influence to achieve favorable outcomes of issues.

While Smith tried to blend governmental and ecclesiastical power, Whitmer remained strongly in favor of the separation of church and state affairs. He was not alone in this belief. Oliver Cowdery, for example, wrote a letter to his brother Lyman in 1834, revealing a conviction that he feared the church's potential to ascend the role of government and thereby foster a spirit of intolerance that might transcend the justice and equality of individual liberty.[44] These political activities clearly highlighted a growing concern over what some intimated to be Smith's assumption of "monarchial powers."[45] Whitmer later expressed his dismay at the church hierarchy's meddling in secular concerns. He recalled: "Poor Joseph! He was blinded and became ensnared by proud, ambitious men. I labored hard with him to get him to see it—from 1835—and God alone knows the grief and sorrow I have had over it. . . . The majority of the members—poor weak souls—thought that anything Bro Joseph would do must be all right."[46]

These issues came to a boil among the Mormons of Kirtland during the summer of 1837, when the church-sponsored wildcat bank failed, generating a great deal of mistrust between Smith and several leading members.[47] Some Saints, unable to rationalize the heady expectations for the future just a few years earlier with the economic and political disaster of the present, called him a "fallen Prophet" and urged his overthrow. Brigham Young charged David Whitmer with taking a leading role in organizing opposition against Smith's leadership: "On a certain occasion several of the Twelve, the witnesses to the Book of Mormon, and others of the authorities of the Church, held a council in the upper room of the temple. The question before them was to ascertain how the Prophet Joseph could be deposed and David Whitmer appointed the President of the Church."[48]

Despite such accounts, Whitmer firmly denied being involved in any such activity. Smith responded like a treed bear and informed the church that, according to Donna Hill, "Oliver Cowdery, David Whitmer, John Whitmer, William W. Phelps and others were in transgression, and would lose their standing unless they humbled themselves and made satisfaction."[49]

These events, and Joseph Smith's response, certainly dampened Whitmer's enthusiasm for the church organization, if not the gospel as he understood it. The prophet's friendship, his commitment to the founding experiences of the church, or the group dynamics that had tempered his dissent thus far could offset the developing pattern of separation growing between the two. Whitmer and other dissenters soon returned to Missouri. On September 4, 1837, Smith wrote to John Corrill, a member of the Missouri High Council, to suggest perceived transgressions of Whitmer, Oliver Cowdery, and others. It was apparent to Smith that a tide of change was rising against him, and he believed that Whitmer and Cowdery were leading it.[50]

By early 1838 it had become clear to Whitmer, and to other dissenters, that they must break with Joseph Smith. After that time Whitmer began, in good conscience, to examine alternatives to activity in the church. Oliver Cowdery wrote to his brothers Lyman and Warren in February 1838 about the dissenters' activities:

> At a meeting of the following members of the Church of Latter Day Saints, viz, F. G. Williams, D. Whitmer, W. W. Phelps, J. Whitmer, Jacob Whitmer, Lyman E. Johnson, and Oliver Cowdery . . . to take into consideration the state of said church and the manner in which some of the authorities of the same have for a time past, and are still endeavoring to unite ecclesiastical and civil authority and force men under a pretence of incurring the displeasure of heaven to use their earthly substance contrary to their own interest and privilege, and also how said authorities are endeavoring to make it a rule of faith for said church to uphold a certain man or men *right* or wrong. . . . David Whitmer, Oliver Cowdery, F. G. Williams were appointed a committee to draft a declaration and resolutions. . . . W. W. Phelps, John Whit-

mer and Luke E. Johnson were appointed a committee to look
for a place for the above named individuals in which to settle
where they may live in peace.[51]

David Whitmer's participation in these activities indicate that he understood the full extent of the rift between himself and organized Mormonism. In essence, Whitmer had grown increasingly disgruntled over
a period of years with the church's policies in Kirtland and had declared doctrinal and economic independence.

In February 1838 Joseph Smith arrived in Far West, Missouri, and
immediately took action to isolate and silence the objections of Whitmer and other dissenters to his perceived abuses. At Smith's instiga-
tion, on April 13, 1838, the Far West High Council preferred charges
against Whitmer:

> Charge First. For not observing the word of wisdom, for un-
> christian-like conduct in neglecting to attend to meetings, in unit-
> ing with, and possessing the same spirit with the Dissenters, in
> writing letters to the Dissenters in Kirtland unfavorable to the
> cause and to Br Joseph Smith jr.
> 3rd For neglecting the duties of his calling.
> 4th. For seperating himself from the cause and the Church
> while he has a name among us.
> 5 For signing himself President of the Church of Christ in an
> insulting letter to the High Council.[52]

Whitmer sent a statement to this body that made it clear he no longer
considered himself a member of the church:

> You sir with a majority of this Church have decided that cer-
> tain Councils were legal by which it is said I have been deprived
> of my office as one of the Presidents of this Church I have thought
> and still think they were not agreeable to the revelations of
> God, ...
> Believing as I verily do, that you and the leaders of the coun-
> cils have a determination to pursue your unlawful course at all
> hazards, and bring others to your standard in violation of the
> revelations, to spare you any further trouble I hereby withdraw
> from your fellowship and communion—choosing to seek a place
> among the meek and the humble, where the revelations of Heav-
> en will be observed and the rights of men regarded.[53]

The High Council chose not to take further action against him but
"decided that David Whitmer be no longer considered a member of
the Church of Christ of Latter day Saints."[54]

David Whitmer and others of like mind thought they could remain in their homes near Far West, the Mormon stronghold in Caldwell County, Missouri, following these events, but stalwart supporters of Smith would not allow it. Their actions raised sufficient excitement among the members that the Whitmers and Cowderys felt compelled to leave the area. Whitmer claimed divine intervention in his June 1838 decision to leave Caldwell County and resettle in Richmond, Missouri. He commented that God "told me to 'separate myself from among the Latter-day Saints, for as they sought to undo me, so should it be done unto them'."[55] Whitmer's level of understanding of his own dissent is revealed in a later observation: "If the heads of the church had not gone into error I would not have been called out from among them, but would have been commanded to continue to work with them."[56] Under different conditions, he may have never removed himself from the church or separated from Joseph Smith.

In the end, circumstances terminated the relationship. Whitmer was forced into a perspective from which he had to acknowledge his internal feelings and growing dissent. But even in this, his dissent was not directed primarily against the church, but rather against Smith's seemingly ever-enlarging power to lead the organization in directions that ran counter to Whitmer's understanding of what religion should do. He wrote to Joseph Smith III: "I loved your father; I upheld him as far as he taught the doctrine of Christ; yea I loved him so much and had so much confidence in him, that I followed him into many errors before I was aware that I was trusting too much in 'an arm of flesh,' instead of trusting in God only, and relying upon 'that which is written.' . . . Your father was once a humble man; but he became ensnared by Sidney Rigdon, David Patten, Brigham Young and others."[57]

For David Whitmer, the story of Mormonism in the mid 1830s had become a horrific episode in which those things that he held dear were sacrificed as the church moved into more secular activities and replaced the pluralism of the nation with a monolithic worldview aimed at theocracy.

Whitmer's unique contribution to dissent came in the nature of his separation. Unlike many other dissenters, upon his defection he did not move in the extreme. Although he may have sometimes appeared weak in Joseph Smith's presence, his individuality and commitment to an ideal led to a relatively quiet dissent for most of his career in the church. Following his separation, Whitmer manifested remarkable characteristics of personal strength and determination that put his beliefs and church experiences in a larger perspective. Contrary to human nature, which often compels one, especially in need, to seek the support and justification of a group of peers, he remained apart. Although Whitmer departed the "in" group, he did not cultivate the affection of the outside world.[58]

About ten years later, after the death of Joseph Smith, Jr., at Carthage, Illinois, Whitmer briefly associated with some church members as a result of the efforts of William E. McLellin, a former apostle who had been cut off from the church in 1838. McLellin visited Whitmer in September 1847 and persuaded him to serve as the leader of the new church organization from his home in Richmond. McLellin wrote, "I then led those four men [Hiram Page, David, John, and Jacob Whitmer] into the water and administered to them in the name of the Lord Jesus. . . . And we all partook of the bread and wine in remembrance of the Lord Jesus. I then confirmed those who were now new born into the Church of Christ. . . . We all stepped forward and laid hands upon David and reordained him to all the gifts and callings to which he had been appointed through Joseph Smith."[59]

Whitmer was only partially convinced of his role as president of the new church. His brother-in-law Hiram Page wrote, "We had not as yet come to an understanding, but consented to the organization after three days of successive entreaties. Now we acknowledge that the organization was not in accordance with the order of the gospel church."[60]

After his brief 1847 encounter with McLellin, Whitmer reinvested his energy into his Richmond livery stable business, David Whitmer & Sons. In addition to stabling and renting horses, Whitmer & Sons provided chauffeuring services. In this way Whitmer established a solid reputation as a businessman and outstanding citizen, gaining great respect among his western Missouri neighbors, serving as mayor of Richmond in the 1860s.

Several years passed during which David Whitmer lived in the obscurity of his work. However, in his later years, as other early members of the church died, he was frequently interviewed about his early experiences. These interviews pointed up the persistence of Whitmer's fundamental commitment to the latter-day gospel as he understood it. On the whole, they serve as a splendid reflection of the growth of dissent in the early years of the Restoration movement.[61]

It is not possible to close an examination of the life and dissent of David Whitmer without noting his one last attempt at effecting a church organization during his last years of life. Even after Joseph Smith III took his place as head of the Reorganized Church and gathered many midwesterners from various factions dating from the early organization around him, a few continued to look to David Whitmer as a legitimate successor to Joseph Smith, Jr.[62] He finally accepted this calling. In 1876 he set about establishing what he called the Church of

Christ and claimed his right as president by virtue of his 1834 ordina-tion.[63] This church movement was envisioned as the reestablishment of the early church in an authoritative condition. It never attracted more than a small group of Whitmer's associates in Richmond, Missouri, and a few believers from the Kirtland area. His 1887 pamphlet "An Ad-dress to All Believers in Christ" was written in an attempt to promul-gate the Church of Christ. A short time later, on January 25, 1888, Whitmer died, and his movement soon faded.[64]

A summation of David Whitmer's life appeared in *The Return*, a Whitmerite newspaper, and reveals much of his character and strength of conviction:

> There were many opportunities for him to adopt the Phariseeism position, both with the believer and unbelievers in the Book of Mormon, but he preferred to be one of the people in very fact, isolated yet among all classes, a fellow mortal burdened with the guardianship of the sacred manuscript of the Record of the Ne-phites, a servant of God as an Elder in the Church of Christ, and the witnessship to the voice of god and the vision of a just man made perfect before the shekina of the Holy Presence of the Lord God Almighty. . . . A prominent journalist once said to him, "Dav-id Whitmer, would to God I had your knowledge of my maker." He remarked that she and all had the same knowledge or path to it without the burden it imposed. That there was not anything in this world that caused him so much temporal vexation as his position, but it was a life work and he had put his shoulder to the plow and would never turn back for he knew that his Re-deemer liveth, and that his burden was for the relief of the na-tions and the glory of America.[65]

Whitmer was perceived throughout his life as a believable witness. His personal conduct during his disciplined separation earned him much admiration and respect as a steadfast witness of the literal ori-gins of the church. His experiences sustained a lifelong witness of the Book of Mormon. His faithful dissent ultimately focused on adminis-trative abuses perpetrated by the church leadership rather than foun-dational assumptions. By maintaining a firm witness of the Book of Mormon and the Restoration, his continued expression of dissent as-sumed an authoritative bearing. His impact upon the larger movement continued until his death; it was almost as though he never really left. Whitmer characterized his position when he wrote, "I stand to-day just where I and the others stood in the early days of the church when the Bible and the Book of Mormon were the rule and guide to our faith."[66]

Phillip R. Legg has theorized that Oliver Cowdery served as the conscience of the church until his expulsion.[67] David Whitmer's presence may have significantly promoted Cowdery's limited accomplishments along these lines, and during his later years Whitmer seemed to assume that role symbolically. In 1888 the Reorganized Church's newspaper commented that "almost from his first acquaintance with Joseph Smith, David Whitmer held dissimilar views from him in respect to doctrinal matters and methods of church government, which gradually increased up to 1836–8."[68] At the same time, Whitmer's willingness to stand up and be counted when he perceived improprieties in the direction in which the church hierarchy was taking the movement was a measure of the man. In such a climate, David Whitmer should be remembered as one whose vision of the role and path of the gospel in the lives of the Saints differed. It was not necessarily a more or less appropriate vision, but a different one. In that process, the Saints have been enriched.

NOTES

1. Mary Cleora Dear, *Two Hundred Thirty-Eight Years of the Whitmer Family, 1737–1976* (Richmond: Beck Printing Co., 1976), 41; Andrew Jenson, *Latter Day Saint Biographical Encyclopedia* (Salt Lake City: Andrew Jenson Historical Company, 1901), 1:263. See also Ebbie L. V. Richardson, "David Whitmer," M.A. thesis, Brigham Young University, 1952.

2. "Mormonism," *Kansas City* [Mo.] *Journal,* June 5, 1881. See also Diedrich Willers, *Centennial Historical Sketch of the Town of Fayette* (Geneva: Press of W. F. Humphrey, 1900); *Salt Lake Herald,* August 7, 1875.

3. "David Whitmer on His Death-Bed," *Chicago Tribune,* December 15, 1885, interview reprinted in *Saints' Herald,* January 2, 1886, 12–14.

4. *History of Ray County, Missouri* (St. Louis: Missouri Historical Co., 1881), 529; John J. Snyder to Paul M. Hanson, January 31, 1923, Hanson Collection, Reorganized Church of Jesus Christ of Latter Day Saints Library-Archives, Independence, Mo.

5. *Kansas City Journal,* June 5, 1881.

6. "David Whitmer Interviewed," *Saints' Herald,* November 15, 1881, 347.

7. Whitmer's commitment to these ideals has been shown authoritatively in Richard Lloyd Anderson, *Investigating the Book of Mormon Witnesses* (Salt Lake City: Deseret Book Co., 1981), and Richard L. Anderson, "David Whitmer: Unique Missouri Mormon," in *Missouri Folk Heroes of the Nineteenth Century,* ed. F. Mark McKiernan and Roger D. Launius (Independence: Independence Press, 1989), 45–59.

8. This case is ably argued in Marvin S. Hill, *Quest for Refuge: The Mormon Flight from American Pluralism* (Salt Lake City: Signature Books, 1989). Similarly, Kenneth H. Winn, *Exiles in a Land of Liberty: Mormons in America, 1830–1846* (Chapel Hill: University of North Carolina Press, 1989), provides a rationale of divisive tensions as a result of disparate views of republi-

canism among members. Dan Vogel, *Religious Seekers and the Advent of Mormonism* (Salt Lake City: Signature Books, 1988), assesses the impact upon the movement of competing assumptions regarding religious Christian primitivism and universalism, highlighting such underlying issues as charismatic witness of authority versus legalistic justification.

9. *Book of Doctrine and Covenants* (Independence: Herald Publishing House, 1970), sec. 16:3b; *The Doctrine and Covenants of the Church of Jesus Christ of Latter-day Saints* (Salt Lake City: Deseret Book Co., 1982), sec. 18:9.

10. H. H. Smith, "Biography of David Whitmer," *Journal of History* 3 (July 1910): 301; Joseph Smith, Jr., *History of the Church of Jesus Christ of Latter-day Saints*, ed. B. H. Roberts (Salt Lake City: Deseret Book Company, 1978), 1:51; David Whitmer, *An Address to All Believers in Christ* (Richmond: N.p., 1887), 32.

11. Edward Stevenson, "Interview with David Whitmer," December 22, 1877, Church of Jesus Christ of Latter-day Saints Historical Department, Salt Lake City.

12. *Kansas City Journal,* June 5, 1881; Joseph Smith III and Heman C. Smith, *History of the Reorganized Church of Jesus Christ of Latter Day Saints* (Independence: Herald Publishing House, 1967), 1:46. See also *Deseret News* [Salt Lake City], December 24, 1885; *Chicago Tribune,* December 15, 1885.

13. Joseph Campbell with Bill Moyers, *The Power of Myth* (Garden City: Doubleday and Co., 1988).

14. Smith and Smith, *History of the Reorganized Church,* 1:67–68.

15. Whitmer, *Address to All Believers in Christ,* 33–34.

16. Smith and Smith, *History of the Reorganized Church,* 1:113–14.

17. *Book of Doctrine and Covenants,* sec. 29:1a–c; *Doctrine and Covenants of the Church of Jesus Christ of Latter-day Saints,* sec. 30:1–3.

18. F. Mark McKiernan, *The Voice of One Crying in the Wilderness: Sidney Rigdon, Religious Reformer 1793–1876* (Lawrence: Coronado Press, 1971), 36.

19. Whitmer, *Address to All Believers in Christ,* 35.

20. On the church's organizational development see, D. Michael Quinn, "The Evolution of the Presiding Quorums of the LDS Church," *Journal of Mormon History* 1 (1974): 21–38.

21. Lyndon W. Cook, *The Revelations of the Prophet Joseph Smith* (Provo: Seventy's Mission Bookstore, 1981), 24–25. Whitmer participated in the June 3, 1831, conference at Kirtland, in which the first high priests were ordained. See Donald Q. Cannon and Lyndon W. Cook, eds., *Far West Record: Minutes of the Church of Jesus Christ of Latter-day Saints, 1830–1844* (Salt Lake City: Deseret Book Co., 1983), 6.

22. An analogy for this was offered in the development of American Puritanism. See the path-breaking study by Kai T. Erickson: *Wayward Puritans: A Study in the Sociology of Religion* (New York: John Wiley and Sons, 1966). It has also been demonstrated in other studies: Peter L. Berger, *The Heretical Imperative: Contemporary Possibilities of Religious Affirmation* (Garden City: Doubleday, 1979); Edwin Scott Gaustad, *Dissent in American Religion* (Chicago: University of Chicago Press, 1973); J. Milton Yinger, *Religion in the*

Struggle for Power: A Study in the Sociology of Religion (Durham: Duke University Press, 1946).

23. Whitmer, *Address to All Believers in Christ,* 54–55.

24. Smith and Smith, *History of the Reorganized Church,* 1:223.

25. John Poorman, a New York convert, was at Hiram at the time of the mobbing of Joseph Smith and Sidney Rigdon in February 1832. Poorman eventually lived in the Whitmer settlement in Jackson County. Levi Jackman and John Follett were also from the Hiram area and constructed homes near the Whitmers in Jackson County. "List of Members in Jackson County, Missouri," N.d., LDS Historical Department.

26. "The Elders Stationed in Zion to the Churches Abroad," *The Evening and the Morning Star* [Independence, Mo.] 2 (July 1833): 111.

27. The best work on the overall Mormon experience in Jackson County, Missouri, remains Warren A. Jennings, "Zion Is Fled: The Expulsion of the Mormons from Jackson County, Missouri," Ph.D. diss., University of Florida, 1962.

28. Brigham H. Roberts, *The Missouri Persecutions* (Salt Lake City: George Q. Cannon and Sons Publishing, 1900), 96. See also John Corrill, "From Missouri," *The Morning and the Evening Star* 2 (January 1834): 124; Philo Dibble, *Early Scenes in Church History,* Faith Promoting Series, no. 8 (Salt Lake City: Juvenile Instructors Office, 1882), 82–83.

29. Corrill, "From Missouri," 125; Alexander Majors, *Seventy Years on the Frontier* (Chicago: Rand, McNally and Company, 1893), 46–47; Henry Alanson Cleveland quoted in "Journal History of the Church of Jesus Christ of Latter-day Saints," November 4, 1833, LDS Historical Department.

30. *Kansas City Journal,* June 5, 1881.

31. Zenos H. Gurley, Jr., "Interview with David Whitmer," January 14, 1885, typescript in Reorganized Church Library-Archives. See also Zenos H. Gurley, Jr., "The Book of Mormon," *Autumn Leaves* 5 (1892): 451–54.

32. On this paramilitary relief column see Roger D. Launius, *Zion's Camp: Expedition to Missouri, 1834* (Independence: Herald Publishing House, 1984).

33. Whitmer was ordained president of the church in Missouri. See Cook, *Revelations of the Prophet Joseph Smith,* 25; D. Michael Quinn, "The Mormon Succession Crisis of 1844," *Brigham Young University Studies* 16 (Winter 1976): 194.

34. Cannon and Cook, eds., *Far West Record,* 151.

35. John C. Whitmer to John J. Snyder, February 3, 1888, Whitmer Family Papers, Reorganized Church Library-Archives.

36. Gurley, "Interview with David Whitmer."

37. Whitmer, *Address to All Believers in Christ,* 28, 33–34, 42, 45–48.

38. The anticipated spiritual endowment has been discussed in Lauritz Petersen, "The Kirtland Temple," *Brigham Young University Studies* 12 (Summer 1972): 400–409; and Roger D. Launius, *The Kirtland Temple: A Historical Narrative* (Independence: Herald Publishing House, 1986), 58–74. The results of this expectation are analyzed in Marvin S. Hill, "Cultural Crisis in the Mormon Kingdom: A Reconsideration of the Causes of Kirtland Dissent," *Church History* 49 (September 1980): 286–97.

39. "Journal History of the Church," February 27, 1848, LDS Historical Department; Gurley, "Interview with David Whitmer."

40. F. Mark McKiernan and Roger D. Launius, eds., *An Early Latter Day Saint History: The Book of John Whitmer* (Independence: Herald Publishing House, 1980), 176.

41. Leonard J. Arrington, ed., "Oliver Cowdery's Kirtland, Ohio, 'Sketchbook'," *Brigham Young University Studies* 12 (Summer 1972): 416.

42. Joseph Smith, Jr., Diary, January 21, 1836, in *The Personal Writings of Joseph Smith*, ed. Dean C. Jessee (Salt Lake City: Deseret Book Co., 1984), 145–48.

43. Smith, Diary, March 27, 1836, ibid., 180.

44. Oliver Cowdery to Lyman Cowdery, January 13, 1834, Oliver Cowdery Papers, Huntington Library, San Marino, Calif.

45. *Latter Day Saint Messenger and Advocate* 3 (July 1837): 538; Joseph Smith, Jr., *The History of the Church of Jesus Christ of Latter-day Saints*, ed. B. H. Roberts (Salt Lake City: Deseret Book Co., 1976), 1:273; Charles L. Woodward, "The First Half Century of Mormonism," 195, New York Public Library.

46. "Letters of David and John C. Whitmer," *Saints' Herald,* February 5, 1887, 92–93.

47. On the Kirtland bank see Marvin S. Hill, C. Keith Rooker, and Larry T. Wimmer, "The Kirtland Economy Revisited: A Market Critique of Sectarian Economics," *Brigham Young University Studies* 17 (Summer 1977): 389–475.

48. "History of Brigham Young," *Deseret News,* February 10, 1858.

49. Donna Hill, *Joseph Smith: The First Mormon* (Garden City: Doubleday and Co., 1977), 214.

50. Joseph Smith to John Corrill and the Church in Zion, September 4, 1837, in *Personal Writings of Joseph Smith*, ed. Jessee, 352.

51. Oliver Cowdery to Lyman and Warren Cowdery, January 30, 1838, Cowdery Papers, Huntington Library.

52. Cannon and Cook, eds., *Far West Record,* 177.

53. Ibid.

54. Ibid., 178.

55. Whitmer, *Address to All Believers in Christ,* 27.

56. David Whitmer, *Address to Believers in the Book of Mormon* (Richmond: APMLI, 1887).

57. "Letters of David and John C. Whitmer," 89.

58. Whitmer was among the militia during the siege of Far West and declined an opportunity for retribution.

59. Smith and Smith, *History of the Reorganized Church,* 3:89.

60. *The Olive Branch; or, Herald of Peace and Truth to all Saints* [Kirtland, Ohio], August 1849, 27–28.

61. These interviews have been analyzed in Anderson, *Investigating the Book of Mormon Witnesses,* 79–92.

62. William E. McLellin, letter fragment (bottom of page 2 missing) to My

Dear Friends, February 1870, Miscellaneous Letters and Papers, Reorganized Church Library-Archives.

63. *Latter-day Saints Millennial Star,* December 16, 1878, 785–87; Joseph Fielding Smith, *Life of Joseph F. Smith* (Salt Lake City: Deseret Book Co., 1938), 239; James R. B. Vancleave to Joseph Smith III, September 29, 1878, Joseph Smith III Papers, Reorganized Church Library-Archives.

64. See the following articles from the *Saints' Herald,* February 11, 1888, published at the time of his death: "David Whitmer's Special Work" (81–83); John A. Robinson's description of Whitmer's funeral (89); and reprints from *Richmond Democrat,* January 26, 1888, and *Chicago Times,* January 26, 1888 (93–95).

65. *The Return* [Davis City, Iowa], 3 (December 1892): 4–5.

66. "Letters of David and John C. Whitmer," 93.

67. Phillip R. Legg, *Oliver Cowdery: The Elusive Second Elder of the Restoration* (Independence: Herald Publishing House, 1989).

68. "David Whitmer Dead," *Saints' Herald,* February 4, 1888, 67.

2

"Such Republicanism as This": John Corrill's Rejection of Prophetic Rule

Kenneth H. Winn

On August 31, 1838, Joseph Smith, Jr., threatened to walk on John Corrill's neck.[1] By that time Corrill's growing disaffection from Mormonism both angered and frightened Smith. One of the earliest converts to the church from a remarkable harvest reaped by missionaries in Ohio during the fall and winter of 1830–31, Corrill had risen to prominence in the church and played a key role in its eight-year sojourn on the Missouri frontier. Widely popular among the Latter Day Saints and respected by nonchurch members as well, his opposition to the prophet threatened to spread a rebellious spirit through the church and abet the charges of critics who were not Mormons. When, in fact, two months after Smith's confrontation with Corrill, the church lay prostrate before its enemies and the prophet languished in jail, Smith blamed the disaster on Corrill and a handful of other dissenters, whom he described as "illbred and ignorant" men "whose eyes are full of adultery and [who] cannot cease from sin."[2]

Today nearly all historians turn aside Joseph Smith's fury at Corrill and acknowledge Corrill's integrity, decency, and ability to hold fast to principle when the passion around him ran high.[3] Rooted in strong beliefs arising from his Christian primitivism and his dedication to republican liberty, these qualities were manifest not only in Corrill's actions, but also in his *Brief History of the Church of Christ of Latter Day Saints,* which offers an insightful account of life in the church as he knew it and is, perhaps, the single most important source of information for events surrounding the Mormon War in Missouri.[4]

John Corrill would have been wholly obscure without his eight years in the church. We know almost nothing about his life before his conversion and only slightly more about it after he left Mormonism.[5] Like other early Mormons he was of New England ancestry, born on September 17, 1794, near Barre in Worcester County, Massachusetts. He later married a woman named Margaret with whom he had at least five children.[6] By trade an architect, he has also been listed as a carriage builder and a surveyor; it is likely he worked as all three. Although his educational background is unknown, his relative skills as a writer and his small library evince some formal schooling.

By the fall of 1830 Corrill was living at Harpersville, Ohio, when four Mormon missionaries passed through the area on their way west.[7] They caused quite a sensation. Claiming to preach the pure uncorrupted gospel of the apostles as derived from an ancient religious book discovered in upstate New York, they found many eager listeners. John Corrill, however, was not one of them. Several days after the missionaries departed, he idly thumbed through the Book of Mormon and dismissed it as a fraud designed to make money.

What changed his mind was the conversion of Sidney Rigdon, a former Campbellite minister who was leading a restorationist group in Kirtland, Ohio.[8] When Corrill first learned of the missionaries' intention to see the minister, he fully expected Rigdon to expose them as impostors. Corrill was dumbfounded to learn that both Rigdon and most of his followers had converted to the new faith. He was convinced that Rigdon, whom he admired deeply, had made a horrible mistake and set out accordingly for Kirtland to correct Rigdon's wayward course. Upon his arrival, Corrill was disgusted. Religious enthusiasm convulsed the village. Rigdon, when he found him, refused to argue, saying that "he was beyond the land of contention, and had got into a land of peace."[9] When Corrill asked him if the scriptures were not sufficient for salvation, Rigdon responded that the Bible warned of great peril and judgment in the last days and God now sent messengers to announce that those days were at hand.

Corrill departed from Rigdon in a reflective mood. Perhaps, he decided, he had been too hasty in his judgment. Rather than risk fighting against God he decided to investigate seriously the Book of Mormon and to compare it closely with the Bible. After several weeks of study Corrill returned to Kirtland to rescrutinize the Mormon community with the intent of catching the church's leaders in fraud. Corrill was deeply skeptical and used the Bible to review the claims of Mormonism.

Within six weeks, however, he had formulated a number of arguments on behalf of Mormonism.[10] First, he reasoned that God had once sent prophets and new revelation to the world, so why not now? Even if Joseph Smith had been a bad man before his call to prophethood, as some claimed, had not Moses murdered a man and then been called by God while fleeing justice? He also found he could not automatically dismiss the genuineness of the Book of Mormon. He recognized that the Bible revealed references to scripture it did not contain, as well as stories and predictions of both hidden and future revelation. Could the Book of Mormon be the other scripture mentioned in the Bible?

Significantly, Corrill found that Ezekiel 37:15–21 had declared that there would be two religious records, one for the house of Judah (the Bible) and one for the house of Joseph, both of which would be joined in the gathering of the tribes of Israel. To Corrill, the Book of Mormon looked like the record of Joseph, containing many things the prophets had spoken of as necessary for the arrival of the Millennium. Corrill also found perfect harmony in the ethical codes espoused in both the Book of Mormon and the Bible, both promoting the principles of morality, piety, honesty, and godliness. In the end, this line of reasoning convinced him that Mormonism was "much nearer the religion of the Bible than any other [he] could find." Even so, he pronounced himself "not fully satisfied" and declared that he would leave the church should he ever discover it practicing deception.[11]

The story of Corrill's conversion points up both his dedication to private judgment and his biblicism. Both of these placed him within the fold of what is known as Christian primitivism. Led by people like Alexander Campbell, Barton Stone, and Elias Smith, the primitivist movement was a potent religious force in the early nineteenth century. Primitivists believed that innovations down through the ages had corrupted the original purity of Jesus' teaching and called for a return to the ways of the apostolic church. They, accordingly, demanded the abolition of all tradition, hierarchy, and theology that had accreted to Christianity over the centuries. Deeply influenced by the radical republicanism of the American Revolution, they were especially angered by the priestcraft they believed ministers of the traditional Protestant churches practiced. Exalting the Christian's independent judgment over that of a church elite, they urged that all faith be grounded exclusively on their common-sense reading of the Bible. Dedicated rationalists, the primitivists had little use for emotional or mystical religion. For them the Bible was somewhat like the constitution from which Christians reasoned. One convinced sinners to embrace the truth by the strength of one's argument.[12]

Like Corrill, most Mormons were, at least initially, Christian primitivists, but they differed from other restorationists in a number of ways. They tended to emphasize the Old Testament in a way that was unique among primitivists. More important, the Mormons had a greater need for certainty. Confused and repulsed by the rivalries among Protestant denominations fired by the Second Great Awakening, most found little religious solace in the many ambiguities and vagaries of the Bible.

The Book of Mormon, in good measure, represented an attempt to bring order to what the Saints perceived as religious chaos. Still, even that was not enough. Absolute certainty necessitated that they turn to a prophet who could speak for God. This spiritual yearning left converts thirsting after communion with the Holy Spirit and the angels of Heaven, leaving Alexander Campbell's dry rationalism far behind.[13]

Thus, the seed of John Corrill's dissent was present even before his conversion. He never strayed sufficiently far from his primitivist roots to remain for long a faithful follower of Joseph Smith. Corrill would never surrender his private judgment to the authority of prophetic rule. And not only did he extol reason and individual judgment, but he also had a natural distaste for intense emotional display in religion. In contrast to most other Mormons, Corrill joined the church not because it gave him greater religious security but because the church's precepts accorded with his reason—a position with fateful consequences.

On January 10, 1831 John Corrill finally joined the church, and a few days thereafter he was ordained an elder. At the same time Kirtland underwent a good deal of change. Three weeks after Corrill's baptism, Joseph Smith arrived, bringing the New York Saints with him. On February 9 Smith received a revelation, "the Law of Consecration," putting the church on a communitarian footing and at the same time sending the elders out on a preaching mission in pairs. Corrill, for his part, was happily yoked with Solomon Hancock. Together they went to New London, Ohio, where they built a new church of thirty-six members.[14]

Corrill's and Hancock's success was not atypical. The church grew very quickly during this period, and in ways not always to Corrill's liking. His revulsion for strongly emotive religion was tested early. From its start, he complained, too many visionary spirits had joined the church, sorely trying "the feelings of the more sound minded." Most of these enthusiasts were young, and Corrill, thirty-seven and older than most Mormon converts, had little sympathy for their youthful excess. As he described them, these enraptured converts "saw wonderful lights in the air and on the ground, and would relate many great and marvellous things which they saw in their visions. They conducted themselves in a strange manner, sometimes imitating Indians in their manoeuvres, sometimes running out into the fields, getting on stumps of trees and there preaching as if surrounded by a congregation;—all the while so completely absorbed in visions as to be apparently insensible to all that was passing around them."[15]

Fortunately, only a small minority engaged in such behavior. "The more substantial minded" among the Saints, Corrill noted, "looked upon it with astonishment" and believed it "from an evil source." Periodic outbreaks of religious frenzy nevertheless continued for another six months until Smith, under pressure from a number of elders (clearly including Corrill), received a revelation condemning these outbursts, which finally brought them under control. Corrill pronounced the revelation "very gratifying."[16]

Even as Joseph Smith sought to contain antinomianism among the Mormons, he began to give the church greater organizational structure. On February 4, 1831, the prophet received a revelation calling Edward Partridge to serve as a bishop to the church. This revelation took Corrill, who initially had a primitivist's suspicion of church offices, by surprise. He later observed that "this was the first time that I knew or even thought there was to be a Bishop in the Church but on reflection I knew that there were bishops in old times, and I said nothing against it."[17] That he had undoubtedly known and liked Partridge, who had been one of Rigdon's prominent parishioners, probably influenced him as well. The two, in fact, had a close relationship during the next few years. On June 3, 1831, Smith "restored" the Melchizedek priesthood and chose Corrill as one of the first high priests. He then named Isaac Morley and Corrill as Partridge's first and second counselors.

The following day Smith received another revelation calling Corrill to travel to "Zion." The Mormon missionaries, who had sparked the mass conversions in the Kirtland area, had chosen a site for the gathering of the Saints on the western edge of Missouri at Independence. The Saints' belief that the advent of the Millennium depended upon reconverting the Indians living nearby to their ancient religion had dictated the site's selection. Preaching as they went, about thirty elders left Kirtland for Missouri on June 19, 1831. Shortly after their arrival in Jackson County, Missouri, God confirmed Zion's location and, on August 3, the Saints dedicated a temple site. Smith then appointed a number of elders to remain while he, Rigdon, and some others returned to Kirtland. One of those asked to remain was John Corrill.

Corrill played a central role in establishing the church in Missouri. He served as a superintendent of schools, kept the official record of the Saints in the region, and helped administer the affairs of the church. Corrill's wife and children came to Independence in the fall of 1831, among the first of a steady stream of immigrants. By July 1832 the growth of the church necessitated the Mormon settlement's division into branches, one of which Corrill headed.[18]

Although pledged in revelation as a "land of peace," Missouri brought trouble to the Saints from the start. With the arrival of the first Mormons in Missouri a rift began to be apparent in the church between the group in Missouri and the larger body in Ohio.[19] Missouri bishop Edward Partridge repeatedly clashed with Joseph Smith and Sidney Rigdon over church policy. Partridge apparently held a highly decentralized view of church authority, giving the Missouri church virtually complete authority over its own affairs. Smith and Rigdon, by contrast, were in the process of assuming greater authority and creating a more centralized hierarchy. While Smith thought Partridge disrespectful of his prophetic authority, Partridge was concerned about creeping authoritarianism. In response to this challenge the prophet received a revelation warning Partridge to end his disobedience and another revelation clarifying the lines of authority between his role as president of the High Priesthood and that of the office of bishop.[20]

This did not end the tension. In 1832, at the behest of Missouri church leaders, John Corrill wrote to Smith about the problem, accusing him of grasping after monarchical power. The prophet, in turn, responded informally in a letter to Missouri leader W. W. Phelps on July 31, 1832, that he had "learned by Broth[er] John's letter that the devel had set to work" stirring up the Missouri Saints' hearts. He said he would "not fellowship the letter" nor "plead guilty to the charges made against me."[21] More formally, on January 14, 1833, Orson Hyde and Hyrum Smith on behalf of the Kirtland church responded to Corrill's letter, claiming that rather than "seeking after monarchical power and authority" Smith had sought merely to "magnify the high office and calling whereunto he has been called and by the command of God, and the united voice of this church. It might not be amiss," Hyde and Smith cautioned the Missouri leadership, "for you to call up the circumstances of the Nephites [in the Book of Mormon], and the children of Israel rising up against their prophets, and accusing them of seeking after kingly power, and see what befell them, and take warning before it is too late."[22]

Although Hyde and Smith noted that the prophet's authority rested on both God's call and the voice of the church, the theocratic and democratic values contained within Mormonism would inevitably clash. John Corrill's commitment to republican liberty was closely tied to his Christian primitivism—and was deeply ingrained in his nature—making him Partridge's natural ally. The skirmishes over power between the two regional churches would soon disappear in reconciliations and later events, but this argument prefigures the larger and more vicious quarrels in which Corrill would become entangled and would eventually lead to his withdrawal from the movement.

The unregulated immigration of eastern Saints to western Missouri caused friction between the two churches; more importantly, it turned the non-Mormon, or "old citizens," of Jackson County against the Saints. In part this resulted from the coming of the church's zealous poor to Missouri. Enthused with millennial expectancy and having few belongings to hold them to Kirtland, these converts immigrated to Zion in the belief that the bishop would provide for them through the Law of Consecration. As John Corrill remembered with disgust, church members

> had been commanded not to go up in haste, not by flight, but to have all things prepared for them. Money was to be sent up to the bishop, and as fast as lands were purchased, and preparations made, the bishop was to let it be known, that the church might be gathered in. But this regulation was not attended to, for the church got crazy to go up to Zion. . . . The rich were afraid to send up their money, and the poor crowded up in numbers, without any places provided, contrary to the advice of the bishop and others, until the old citizens began to be highly displeased.[23]

By May 1832 about three hundred Mormons had settled in the Independence area. A little more than a year later, the number had reached 1,200, and the speed of immigration was increasing. Corrill observed that the old settlers "saw their country filling up with emigrants, principally the poor" and "if left alone, [the Mormons] would in a short time become a majority, and, of course, rule the county." Many of the old citizens tried to escape the situation by offering to sell out to the Mormons, but church members had no money with which to pay for their land.[24]

Discontent with the church among non-Mormons first surfaced in the spring of 1832, and by July 1833 had become so dominant that extralegal action resulted. It was not simply the Saints' poverty that bothered them, but their clannish self-righteousness, their too often articulated boast that Jackson County belonged to them by revelation, their belief that in the event of hostilities the Indians would rise up and help slay unrepentant non-Mormons, and, not least of all, their fear that those Yankees would provoke a slave uprising by encouraging the immigration of free blacks to Missouri. This led to violence on July 20 when, after a breakdown in negotiations between the two groups, a mob of 150 men marched into the Mormon community, destroyed the Mormon press, razed the newspaper office, and tarred and feathered Edward Partridge and another church member.

With still no satisfactory resolution, the mob returned three days later and forced John Corrill and other church officials from their homes and into the public square. They were threatened with death and assured of the complete destruction of the church unless the Saints agreed to leave the county. Corrill and some of the other brethren offered their lives to the mob in exchange for the safety of the church, but they were met with rebuff. Under these circumstances the Mormon leaders felt they had no choice except to agree to the old citizens' demands. The church officials themselves were given until January 1, 1834, to leave; the rest of their brethren were to be gone by April 1. For unspecified reasons, the mob chose John Corrill and A. S. Gilbert as the two Mormon officials allowed to remain and wrap up the church's official business. This act began a pattern. Corrill seems to have been the Mormon whom non-Mormons could tolerate best. During the next five years he would help negotiate the Saints out of three Missouri counties and into one of them.[25]

Yet for all of the Mormons' apparent obnoxiousness, the old settlers had never charged any Saint with an illegal act. Corrill, who could view his church with a dry eye, remarked that "up to this time the Mormons had not so much as lifted a finger, even in their own defence, so tenacious were they for the precepts of the gospel,—'turn the other cheek'."[26] The Saints consequently saw no reason to live up to an unjust agreement made under duress. The salvation of the church, the salvation of their souls, depended upon following God's command to build up Zion. They accordingly appealed to the Missouri governor, who urged them to seek legal counsel. Although the Saints doubted the law's efficacy in Jackson County, they hired lawyers on October 30, 1833.

News that they had done so set off five days of violence beginning on October 31. In a campaign of terror, the old citizens whipped men and pulled down houses. In one famous incident, Corrill and a number of the brethren came upon some men sacking A. S. Gilbert's store. The group fled, but the Mormons did catch a man named Richard McCarty, whom they took before a justice of the peace. The justice, however, refused to issue an arrest warrant, and the Mormons let McCarty go. Ironically, the next day, Corrill, Gilbert, and some others, were arrested for assault and battery and false imprisonment upon McCarty's complaint. As Corrill remarked: "Although we could not obtain a warrant against him for breaking open the store, yet he had gotten one for us, for catching him at it."[27]

In the face of these events, the Saints found themselves perplexed about how to respond to aggression, wondering what their religion demanded of them. According to Corrill, the Mormons finally decided that each man had the right to defend himself, his family, and his home, but, because a single person would be inconsequential in face of a mob, church members might justifiably band together.[28] The result was a pitched battle between the Mormons and Missourians that left two old settlers and one church member dead and others wounded.

Word of the battle came while Corrill and the others stood before a judge for "assaulting" Richard McCarty. At the same time a mob formed at the courthouse with the intent of lynching the brethren. Fortunately, in Corrill's words, "the court esteeming it too dishonorable to have us killed while in their hands, on our request shut us up in the jail to save our lives."[29] Finally convinced that only the Mormons' departure from the county could prevent massive bloodshed, Corrill, Gilbert, and Isaac Morley soon left the jail to persuade the Saints that the church must leave.

As violence escalated in November 1833, the Saints flew out of Jackson County in all directions. While some found hostility elsewhere, those who made it to neighboring Clay County received sympathy and material aid. Like other Mormons, the expulsion left John Corrill and his family scrambling for shelter. Eventually he and Edward Partridge located an abandoned log shanty, most recently used as a stable. As Partridge's daughter, Emily, recalled, the two men cleaned the shanty as

> best they could and moved their families in. There was one large room, and a leanto, but that was not of much use, as the floor was nearly all torn up, and the rats and rattlesnakes were too thick for comfort. There was a large fireplace in the one habitable room, and blankets were hung up a few feet back from the fire and the two families, fifteen or sixteen in number, were gathered inside of those blankets to keep from freezing, for the weather was extremely cold, so cold that the ink would freeze in the pen as father sat writing close to the fire.[30]

Corrill divided the next nine months between providing for his family's basic needs and protesting the injustice done to the Saints. Letters of petitions and appeal bearing his name with others flowed to Fifth Circuit Court judge John F. Ryland, Missouri governor Daniel Dunklin, militia colonel Samuel Lucas, and President Andrew Jackson, and when these all failed, a generalized appeal to the American people, their leaders, and "the ends of the earth." On February 23, 1834, Corrill and a number of elders returned to Jackson County under the protection of fifty members of the Clay County militia, which was led by one of their former lawyers, David Rice Atchison, to testify to their ill-treatment before a court of inquiry. The hearing came to an end, however, when the court dismissed the militia, sending the Saints marching double time back to Clay to the strains of "Yankee Doodle."

Public sentiment clearly would not sustain an investigation in Jackson County.[31]

For his part, Governor Dunklin expressed sympathy for the Saints and encouraged the legal investigation in Jackson County. Later he indicated that he would support the use of troops to return the Mormons to their land, but he warned that the troops would withdraw after the Mormons were resettled. Accordingly, Joseph Smith, after receiving a revelation, recruited about two hundred armed men from Kirtland and elsewhere and on May 5, 1834, set out to hold Zion once the Saints were reestablished. Although the Mormons attempted to keep the purpose of "Zion's Camp," a Mormon army from Ohio, secret, all of Missouri soon learned of its coming. Rumors flew fast and furious about the approach of fanatical zealots who in unreasoning revenge would cut the throats of women and children in their beds. Writing to the Ohio brethren shortly before the camp's arrival Corrill scoffed at such rumors, suggesting that the Missourians seemed to think that the Saints were morally no better than their persecutors. We have "no thoughts," he wrote, "of ever returning in the night time, or in the *mob like* manner which they represent to the people: for as we design to be governed in all cases by the laws of the land, we shall therefore return under the protection of the Governor, as he has promised us." The Saints, he said, had no need to surprise, "for we mean to act only on the principles of self defense in all cases."[32]

With the approach of Zion's Camp, moderate politicians scrambled to head off the looming conflict. On June 10, 1834, Judge Ryland wrote to Mormon leaders to request permission to organize a meeting in Liberty between Mormon and Jackson County representatives. Corrill, acting on behalf of a church committee, wrote back to Ryland and warmly agreed to a meeting. But, he warned the judge, they would never sell their land. Allowing the old settlers to purchase the land that the Saints held sacred, he added in a note to their lawyers Alexander Doniphan and David Atchison, "would be like selling our children into slavery." The ensuing meeting on June 16 predictably failed. The Jackson Countians offered to either buy out or sell out to the Mormons: one choice religiously unfeasible, the other economically so.[33] When the Saints and the old citizens seemed again on a violent course, Governor Dunklin abruptly withdrew his offer to help the Mormons reclaim their property. Without his aid Zion's Camp collapsed, and Joseph Smith reluctantly but realistically abandoned plans to march into Jackson County.

The expulsion from their divinely appointed settlement and the subsequent failure of Zion's Camp left the Missouri church disoriented.

Moreover, Zion's Camp struck many Missourians more like an invasion than a rescue mission, and it cost the church the goodwill of many Missourians who had previously been sympathetic to the Saints. To reduce tension between the Mormons and their neighbors, on July 31, 1834, at a meeting of local church High Council in Clay County, its president David Whitmer counseled the Saints to forego voting in the upcoming elections. He also appointed John Corrill and three other leaders to hold a series of meetings throughout the county to tone down recent spiritual excesses by teaching proper doctrine and to instruct the Mormons on how to avoid further inflaming Gentile opinion against them.[34]

Earlier, on June 23, Joseph Smith had called Corrill and the other leading elders in Missouri to return to Kirtland to receive their "endowments" and help build up the kingdom. Corrill left for Kirtland sometime in the fall of 1834. From that time until the following summer his activities are almost entirely unknown. Because many of the returning elders went out on preaching missions, perhaps Corrill did as well.[35] On April 8, 1835, he received a patriarchal blessing in Kirtland that declared that none "would surpass him in understanding pertaining to architecture," and which prophesied that he would "build the house of the Lord in Zion." Perhaps he worked on the Kirtland Temple at this time, but this seems unlikely.[36] Corrill's name finally begins appearing again regularly in the historical record on August 17, 1835, when, as the acting bishop of Missouri, he ceremonially accepted as "true" the compilation of revelations and teachings known as the *Doctrine and Covenants* at the General Assembly of the church.[37]

This also began the period in which he seemed happiest in the church and during which he spent a good deal of time with Joseph Smith. Most of this association was friendly and routine. The prophet, for instance, recalled a pleasant day of travel and discussion with Corrill on October 4 en route to a meeting in Perry, Ohio. When the misarranged meeting fell through, they went on to visit non-Mormon relatives of Corrill's in the neighborhood and passed the time agreeably. On November 1 Smith noted in his diary a "fine discourse" by Corrill at meeting. Five days later, he recorded his chastisement of both his wife, Emma, and Corrill for leaving the meeting before the sacrament. On December 9 the prophet listed Corrill as giving (or repaying) him $5 during a period of need. Three days later, Smith and Corrill went together to pray for a sick sister.[38] And during the winter of 1836, Corrill apparently joined the prophet and other leading elders in the study of Hebrew under Joshua Sexias.[39]

At the same time, Corrill had far more serious dealings with the prophet as well. On September 24, 1835 a small group of church leaders met to discuss the means of retaking Zion. Spirits ran high. They agreed they would petition Missouri governor Dunklin again for help, but, in Joseph Smith's words, they determined to "go next season, to live or die on our own lands" and covenanted to struggle with their enemies to the death if need be.[40] According to John Whitmer, the meeting produced more than covenants. By revelation the prophet created a "war department" with the prophet at its head and David Whitmer as "captain of the Lord's Host." Officers were Frederick G. Williams, Sidney Rigdon, W. W. Phelps, John Whitmer, John Corrill, Hyrum Smith, and Oliver Cowdery.[41] Curiously, while this event has the flavor of a turn toward the militarism that overtook the Saints a few years later, it is worth noting that six of the men listed became dissenters against the later militaristic policies.

Perhaps the most important sign of the esteem in which the prophet held Corrill during this period came with his appointment on January 15, 1836, to supervise the completion of the Kirtland Temple. At the command of revelation, the Saints had strived mightily to complete the temple for more than two years, and Smith had laid great emphasis on the work, promising that great spiritual gifts would be conferred on the Saints at the building's completion. Corrill, for his part, found the work quite gratifying and described the finished interior of the temple with pride in his *Brief History of the Church*.[42]

The day after Corrill received his appointment to oversee the completion of the temple, the prophet invited Corrill, Oliver Cowdery, and Martin Harris to participate in a purifying ritual in anticipation of the temple experience. As Cowdery described the ritual in his sketchbook, it began with the preparation of pure water. They then "called upon the Lord and proceeded to wash each others bodies; and bathe the same with whiskey, perfumed with cinnamon. This we did that we might be clear before the Lord for the Sabbath, confessing our sins and covenanting to be faithful to God. While performing this washing unto the Lord with solemnity, our minds were filled with many reflections upon the propriety of the same, and how the priests anciently used to wash always before ministering before the Lord."[43]

Corrill noted after one of the subsequent purifying ceremonies that they took the sacrament "in which they partook of the bread and wine freely, and a report went abroad that some got drunk," but as to that Corrill commented that "a similar report, the reader will recollect, went out concerning the disciples, at Jerusalem, on the day of Pentecost."[44]

When, at last, on March 27, 1836, the Saints dedicated the temple, spiritual enthusiasm reached unprecedented proportions and continued for some days. Many considered it the most moving experience of their lives. Corrill, who generally disapproved of such things, this time refrained from criticism, observing somewhat laconically in his *Brief History of the Church* "that from the external appearance, one would have supposed the last days had truly come."[45]

As the temple neared completion, Corrill and other Missouri elders began planning their return to Clay County and the families they had left behind. On March 11, 1836, a church council formally appointed Bishop Edward Partridge, John Corrill, Isaac Morley, and W. W. Phelps as the "wise men of Missouri" and gave them money to help buy land to provide for immigrating Saints. A month later, accompanied a short distance by the prophet and other friends, the wise men finally began their journey back home.

What they found upon their return was a good deal of trouble. As Mormon numbers in Clay County grew, the old citizens grew restive and then finally lost sympathy for the Saints. Their complaints about the church soon echoed those of Jackson Countians. Because of the steady influx of immigrants, the Mormons, they said, were about to overrun the county. Church members had not only bought up most of the good land, they continued, but they had also informed the old settlers that the whole region really belonged to Mormons by revelation. Moreover, they foolishly or maliciously tampered with the Indians, opposed slavery, and possessed eastern habits and opinion that mixed poorly with those of the other residents. Fortunately, the two sides, balanced precariously on the precipice of bloodshed, pulled back as moderates on both sides sought a peaceful solution. On June 29, 1836, a group of Clay Countians formally asked the Mormons to leave the area, and, although protesting that "the Mormons had committed no crime," the Saints agreed to go.[46]

To help find a new home for the Saints, Corrill again stepped to the fore. He took the lead in negotiating for a gathering spot in nearby Ray County throughout the summer. In these meetings Corrill was circumspect, asking for a "resting place" from persecution and pledging that should the day come when "Ray County requires the 'Mormons' to leave it entirely, we [would] feel disposed to do so on our part and urge and advise our brethren to do the same."[47] Such behavior paid off, and with the help of their former lawyers and Clay Countians Alexander Doniphan, David Atchison, and Amos Rees they were allowed to settle without opposition on unincorporated land attached to Ray County north of where most of the old citizens were located.[48] The Mormons purchased property upon which they built their main settlement, the town of Far West, on August 8, 1836. Corrill took a particularly active role in resettling the Saints, purchasing 1,600 acres of land on the church's behalf. At the same time that church members began moving into the area, Clay County's state representative Alexander Doniphan negotiated a bill through the legislature on December 29, 1836, incorporating the territory north of Ray County as Caldwell County.[49]

The Missouri church spent the next year in almost completely unaccustomed harmony. As Corrill pointed out, the Mormons successfully demonstrated to their neighbors that although "they laboured under many disadvantages, on account of their poverty and former difficulties" they were industrious, and many in the non-Mormon community responded with employment and with loans to buy land. "Friendship" at last, said Corrill, "began to be restored between [the Saints] and their neighbors, the old prejudices were fast dying away."[50]

Corrill divided the year between helping the church reorganize its life and reorganizing his own. In April 1837 he helped price and sell lots in Far West. In May the Missouri High Council selected him as the church's agent and as the "Keeper of the Lord's Storehouse." In June he received the High Council's approval to engage in the mercantile business. In August the High Council relieved him of some of the press of duty by appointing Titus Billings in his stead as counselor to Bishop Partridge. In November, along with several other church leaders, he scouted out sites for new settlements for in-coming Mormon immigrants. And in December he helped design a voluntary "tithing" plan (those of means would pay 2 percent of their net worth annually) to meet church expenses.[51]

As the relative peace of 1837 drifted into 1838, submerged tension appeared within the Missouri church. They were immeasurably exacerbated when Joseph Smith, in flight from angry apostates and creditors, arrived in the spring. Amid great chaos, the Kirtland settlement had broken up in the wake of economic collapse, most symbolically represented by the failure of an unchartered Mormon bank, whose success, dissenters charged, had been guaranteed by revelation. At the same time, a small but influential group, of whom David Whitmer was the most prominent, had fallen into disaffection over changes in the church. Most appalling in their view was the proliferation of church offices, which they believed took the church away from its primitivist origins.

Corrill had left Kirtland before the crisis erupted. And although he shared none of its bitterness, he looked upon the whole affair with revulsion. The Kirtland church, he thought, had shamefully lost its moral bearings in its euphoria over newfound wealth. Buoyed by a sea of credit, they had "suffered pride," he said, "to arise in their hearts and became desirous of fine houses, and fine clothes, and indulged too much in these things, supposing for a few months that they were very rich." Even later, writing from the perspective of a dissenter himself, Corrill remained remarkably even-handed in his disapproval, finding both sides lacking in charity. The dissenters, he said, accused the church leadership of "tyranising over the people, and striving constantly after power and property." Church leadership countercharged the dissenters with "want of faith" and with being "guilty of crimes, such as stealing, lying, [and] encouraging the making of counterfeit money." The result was catastrophic: "instead of pulling together as brethern, they tried every way in their power, seemingly, to destroy each other." The church's enemies, he continued, successfully exploited these divisions until the community's existence was brought to an end.[52]

Corrill's response to the burgeoning ecclesiastical hierarchy also set him off from such dissenters as David Whitmer who offered a more orthodox primitivist critique. The reason lies in Corrill's overriding commitment to republicanism. Although he had a primitivist's suspicion of church offices, he examined the Bible and either found support for their creation or, when scripture proved silent, believed that Christians were free to judge for themselves. What ultimately reassured him about these innovations, however, was their apparent guarantee of republican liberty. The church offices were organized into various independent administrative or missionary bodies, which protected liberty through checks and balances and ultimately reserved sovereignty to the people. In Corrill's understanding, all of these branches were

equal in power, that is to say, each had a right to discipline their own members, and transact other business of the church within their calling, and a decision of either one of these bodies, when in regular session, could not be appealed from to any other, for one had no right or power to reverse or overthrow the judgement or decision of the other, but they could all be called together and form a conference, consisting of all authorities, to which an appeal could be taken from either one and the decision reversed ... but besides this, Smith and Rigdon taught the church that these authorities, in ruling or watching over the church, were nothing more than the servants to the church, and that the church as a body, had the power in themselves to do any thing that either or all of these authorities could do, and that if either or all of these authorities became deranged or broken down, or did not perform their duty to the satisfaction of the church, the church had a right to rise up in a body and put them out of office, make another selection and re-organize them and thus keep in order, for the power was in the people not in the servants.

Consequently, where Whitmer saw personal ambition leading to the introduction of priestcraft into the church, Corrill saw the development of the same sorts of checks and balances that the founders had written into the American Constitution. More important, these arrangements rested upon the consent of the laity, and in the end he "concluded there was no danger where full power and authority was reserved to the people."[53] For all of its plausibility, however, Corrill's analysis was fatally flawed, grossly underestimating the effect of prophetic power on classical republican arrangements.

When Joseph Smith arrived in Far West on March 14, 1838, the Missouri Saints were overjoyed to see him. John Corrill formed part of a welcoming party that escorted Smith to the new settlement. Relieved to have arrived among friends, the prophet nonetheless remained deeply embittered over Kirtland's turmoil.[54] Although in firm control of the Missouri church, Smith soon grew determined to put down the dissent that had arisen in Kirtland and spilled over into Missouri.

A number of church leaders who had grown disaffected with the prophet's leadership, David and John Whitmer, Oliver Cowdery, and W. W. Phelps, among others, already lived in Missouri. The previous fall, Smith had visited Far West in an effort to end differences between him and the two Whitmers and Phelps, whom together formed the Missouri church's presidency. But tension persisted. With obvious disrespect for the prophet's leadership, the dissenters, in turn, sparked an uprising against their own authority when, in defiance of church policy, John Whitmer, Phelps, and Cowdery sold their land in Jackson County, an action tantamount to denying the faith. Accordingly, on February 5, 1838, the Missouri High Council put Whitmer and Phelps on trial, as they did David Whitmer, whom they accused of violating the "Word of Wisdom" and for engaging in "un-Christionlike conduct."

Although the Missouri Saints overwhelmingly favored Phelps and the Whitmers' dismissal from office, John Corrill "labored hard" on the presidents' behalf. According to the minutes of the High Council, Corrill claimed that, although he did not uphold iniquity, he thought that authority over the accused lay with the bishop and his twelve councilors rather than the church's High Council—a view also held by Bishop Partridge and Corrill's friend Solomon Hancock.[55] Corrill's concern for proper procedure probably emanated from his belief that liberty within the church was predicated on proper institutional arrangements. This line of thinking, however, may have appealed to him for other reasons as well. Although he did not approve of the presidency's actions, time would soon reveal his increasing dislike of the church's heavy-handed control over the Saints' temporal affairs. Moreover, a trial before the Bishop's Council would probably have the accused before more friendly—or at least less hostile—judges. Corrill's effort, however, was for naught. All three men lost their offices.

This action confirmed the dissenters' beliefs about Smith and authoritarianism in the church, and they began organizing resistance to the ecclesiastical tyranny they perceived. Upon his arrival, the prophet approved the High Council's actions, and Corrill "confessed" the error of "his former conduct." When the High Council deemed his confession inadequate, he "made perfect satisfaction." During the next few weeks the High Council excommunicated the leading dissenters from the church. This time the High Council's action met with Corrill's approval. He disapproved of the malicious behavior of the dissenters, especially that of Oliver Cowdery, whom he thought had sought to harass the prophet and other church leaders with lawsuits.[56]

In the wake of their expulsion from the church, the dissenters did not repudiate their faith but remained loyal to a different understanding of Mormonism. Rather than quietly melt away, they hoped to awaken others to perceived corruptions in the church. This determination enraged Smith and Sidney Rigdon, who responded by launching a purity crusade, reminding the Saints that their salvation in the last days depended upon their perfect union. In response, zealots began holding meetings to decide how best to silence the dissenters. In one such meeting in early June 1838 a variety of methods were discussed, with some participants even calling for the dissenters' murders. Corrill was appalled and vociferously opposed such measures, much to the irritation of Sidney Rigdon, who warned Corrill that his attempt to interfere with actions directed at the dissenters put his own well-being at risk. Much chastened, Corrill soon learned that these meetings continued although he no longer received an invitation to attend them.[57]

The new militancy directed at the dissenters surfaced publicly on June 17, 1838, when Rigdon preached what has been popularly called the "Salt Sermon" because of its text from Matthew 5:13: "Ye are the salt of the earth: but if the salt have lost his savor, wherewith it be salted? It is thenceforth good for nothing, but to be cast out, and to be trodden under the foot of men." Rigdon argued that the dissenters had lost their savor by abandoning their faith and deserved ill-treatment. The Salt Sermon had the desired effect. During the next few days, a frenzy of anger welled up against the dissenters. Corrill secretly warned the dissenters of just how much danger they were in. Shortly thereafter, eighty-three of the prophet's loyalists signed a "Note of Warning," giving the dissenters three days to leave Caldwell County or face forcible expulsion. When the dissenters left the county in search of legal aid, zealots turned their wives and children out of their homes, and Mormon-controlled courts ordered their property confiscated for debt.[58]

As hostility toward those who would criticize the church leadership reached a fever pitch, it found institutional expression in the creation of a secret paramilitary force called the Sons of Dan, or Danites. Led by Dr. Sampson Avard, whom Corrill described "as grand a villain as his wit and ability would admit," the Danites bound themselves together through covenants that sanctioned serious crimes if undertaken in the service of the church presidency.[59]

The expulsion of the dissenters and the rise of the Danites finally pushed John Corrill into dissent. He "looked upon with horror the treatment of the other dissenters and their families, and considered it as proceeding from the mob spirit."[60] His dissent, however, was a silent one. By invitation he had attended two Danite meetings, and what he saw scared him: "The teachings of that society led them to prohibit the talkings of any persons against the presidency; so much so, that it was dangerous for any man to set up opposition to any thing that might set on foot, and I became afraid to speak my own." Although publicly silent, Corrill privately began working against the militant drift of the church, quietly exposing the Danites to others when he could.[61]

The crisis that began in Kirtland and eventually swept Corrill up in Missouri marked a major turning point in early Mormon history, pitting the theocratically minded devotees of the prophet, who regarded opposition to the church leadership as opposition to God, against more libertarian minded dissenters, who rejected the First Presidency's claim over their temporal affairs and the authoritarian demand for blind obedience. To Corrill and other likeminded Saints, the Danites represented an ugly betrayal of the early church, working in direct contradiction to both the Book of Mormon and previous revelation. The Danites' willingness, in Corrill's words, "to use any measures whatever, whether lawful or unlawful, to accomplish their purpose, and put down those that opposed them [both within and outside the church] perverted the former belief and notions of the church; for the church always believed that judgments, pestilence, disease, famine, great troubles and vexations, were sooner or later to be poured out upon all the wicked, and cut them off in the course of time, and this . . . would be done by God himself."

The whole point of the gathering of the Saints, Corrill continued, was to purify oneself in a place of refuge from the judgments upon the wicked that were to come. The Danites had now usurped the role of God in the work of retribution. Unfortunately, said Corrill, the approval Smith and Rigdon gave the Danites, even though they did not know the details about their actions, made it "clearly evident to me that the leaders of this faction intended to set up a monarchical government, in which the presidency should tyrannize and rule over all things."[62]

The church leadership understood that Corrill and others disapproved of the measures taken against the dissenters, but they put this down to unmanly squeamishness and a failure to appreciate the severity of the crisis. Sidney Rigdon derisively dismissed charges of antirepublicanism in these measures, snorting that when people do not wish for certain individuals to live among them, "it is the principle of republicanism itself that gives that community a right to expel them forcibly and no law will prevent it."[63] In late July, Rigdon said he "strongly suspected" John Corrill was "using [his] influence against the presidency of the church" and declared that Corrill and others like him would have to be put down. Neither Rigdon nor Joseph Smith, however, took any action against him at the time.

On August 6, 1838, the citizens of Caldwell County elected John Corrill as their representative to the Missouri legislature. In many ways this was quite natural. He was very popular among the Missouri Saints and had repeatedly demonstrated his ability to negotiate with non-Mormons. Moreover, unlike many other prominent church members, he could meet both the state and local residency requirements for election.[64] Perhaps equally important, although the presidency had its suspicions about Corrill's orthodoxy, it did not understand the depth of his hostility to recent church developments. The best irony of his election, however, was that it came with the strong-arm support of the Danites. Unsurprisingly, Corrill does not point this out in his *Brief History of the Church*. What he does note, however, is that, shortly before the election, Danite officers met with the First Presidency, selected a slate of candidates, and then passed out tickets with their approved choices printed on them throughout the county. Most Mormons concluded that the ticket represented God's will and went along with it. God, happily, like most Mormons, favored Democratic candidates.[65]

Within weeks of his Danite-approved election, Corrill had become all but irretrievably alienated from the church. The origins of the open breach between Corrill and Joseph Smith came over a revelation reinstating comunitarianism, which the church had abandoned in the wake of the expulsion from Jackson County. In May 1838, Smith and Rig-

don, both of whom had suffered severe economic losses in the service
of the church, requested from the High Council $1,100 and a land
grant in compensation for work performed other than preaching. Although the High Council approved the request, it threw church members generally into an uproar and was quickly rescinded.

On July 8 the prophet received a revelation putting the church back
on a communal basis, which, among other features, gave financial support to the church's leadership and consequently invited skepticism over
the motive for the revelation.[66] Although participation in the new economic arrangement was supposedly voluntary, those who proved slow
to join were subjected to pressure. In a public address Sidney Rigdon
warned that church members who failed to cooperate would "be delivered over to the brother of Gideon and be sent bounding over the
Prairies as the dissenters were." With a good deal of bluster, Sampson
Avard did attempt to frighten those people whom he suspected of less
than full cooperation, pointedly hinting to Corrill and Reed Peck that
death awaited those who did not comply with the revelation.[67]

Avard was right to suspect Corrill, for he did not accept the revelation, suggesting that the reintroduction of communitarianism created
economic divisiveness among the Saints. His dim view of the presidency's economic leadership in Kirtland may have also influenced his view,
or, like others, he perhaps thought an economic revelation benefiting
Smith and Rigdon smacked of priestcraft—a view consistent with his
Christian primitivism. So, too, the efforts to make compliance compulsory may have bothered Corrill, a position consistent with his lib-
ertarianism and in marked contrast to the strictly voluntary economic
plan he had devised earlier with Bishop Partridge. Finally, of course,
he could have had a self-interested motive. He later claimed he had in
excess of $2,000 worth of property in Missouri, making him well-off
by church standards. This, however, seems unlikely given the voluntary liquidation of his property a few months later to help the needy
Saints. In any event, Corrill deeply disapproved of the revelation and
readily shared his opinion with others.[68]

By August's end the church leadership had had enough. As Smith's
scribe George Robinson wrote at the time, "Br[other] Corril[l]'s conduct for some time past has been very unbecoming indeed, especially
a man in whom so much confidence has been placed."[69] When on August 31 Smith and Rigdon learned that Corrill had told some recently
arrived converts "that he had no confidence in the revelation" on communitarianism, they were livid and sought him out publicly. The prophet, beating his fists together, angrily told Corrill, "if you tell about the
streets again that you do not believe this or that revelation[,] I will

walk on your neck Sir." Smith warned Corrill that Peter himself had told him that he had hung Judas for betraying Christ, implying the same sort of fate might await Corrill. Corrill's behavior, he continued, endangered the dissenter's salvation. If he did not change his ways, the prophet declared, he would keep him out of Heaven, even if doing so meant Smith meeting Corrill at its entrance with his fists.[70]

Corrill responded to this attack with warmth of his own and, quite bravely, under the circumstances, told Smith he might reach Heaven's gate first, suggesting that it might be he who kept the prophet out. According to George Robinson, Corrill proceeded to tell Smith that he would "not yeald his Judgement to any thing proposed by the church, or any individuals of the church, or even the voice of the great I Am given through the appointed organ as revelation, but will always act upon his Judgement. Let him believe in whatever religion he may. He says he will always say what he pleases. For he says he is a Republican and as such, he will do, say, act, and believe what he pleases." Robinson, for his part, was astounded by Corrill's effrontery. "Mark such Republicanism as this," he wrote, "that a man should . . . [pit] his own Judgement . . . [against] the Judgement of God."[71]

It was in this moment of drama that the inherent structure of John Corrill's conflict with his church, a conflict whose origins were present from the time of his conversion, most clearly manifested itself. For most Saints, sovereignty over their lives lay with the man who spoke for God. Together, with one heart and mind, they would build God's Kingdom. Yet because the Lord had warned them, "be ye one or be ye not mine," dissenters imperiled the Saints' salvation and were in rebellion against God.[72] Corrill, by contrast, joined the church because as a Christian primitivist he thought its precepts accorded with his reason. An unfettered right to reason and believe as he wished, principles he associated with republican liberty, remained at the base of his faith. When these principles clashed with the reality of prophetic rule, Corrill's allegiance to the church was shaken.

Although it by no means abated, the quarrel between Corrill and Joseph Smith soon disappeared in the swirl of larger and more important events. Although the Mormons had been at peace with their neighbors since their first settlement of Caldwell County in 1836, the apocalyptic fervor that had swept the church in the late spring of 1838 not only led to the suppression of the dissenters but also caused the Saints to adopt a militant stance against potential foes outside the movement. This new belligerence rekindled the flames of anti-Mormonism. On August 6 an election riot between Mormon and non-Mormon voters in Gallatin in Daviess County triggered rapidly escalating hostilities that soon inflamed all of northwestern Missouri. Appeals to Governor Lilburn Boggs and other politicians proved fruitless. With no aid forthcoming from the government and inspired with a millenarian enthusiasm, the Mormons took to the offensive.

Corrill regarded the decision for Mormon military operations as the height of folly that would only bring destruction upon the church. Initially, he attempted to challenge the church's course, telling Smith "that they would have the whole state upon them." The prophet retorted that once the mob discovered the Saints were willing to fight, all combativeness would be knocked out of its members. Thus rebuffed, Corrill shrank from any further attempt to halt battle preparations. "I knew they were jealous of me as a dissenter," he wrote, "and that it was of no use for me to say any thing more; in fact, I felt it was necessary for me to look out for my own safety."[73]

As well he might. On October 15, Joseph Smith proposed sending Mormon troops into Daviess County. He asked and received approval from the citizens of Far West that any church member who refused to participate in these operations have their property confiscated for the use of those who did.[74] Even more ominous were the so-called bayonet resolutions whereby dissenters could be forced at bayonet point to lead the Saints into battle. Reed Peck wryly noted that Corrill, W. W. Phelps, John Cleminson, and several others, "had the honor of being enrolled in one of these [military] companies and under the bayonet resolutions and marched into Daviess County."[75] These resolutions notwithstanding, Corrill did not lead anyone into battle. On October 18, Mormon troops plundered and burned parts of Gallatin, Millport, and a number of other nonchurch settlements. Laid up in camp with a bad leg (or so he claimed), Corrill watched with horror as triumphant Mormon soldiers spoke of vanquishing mob after mob until they reached St. Louis. "Many," he lamented, "had the weakness to believe that God would enable them to do it."[76]

Instead, the so-called Mormon War was almost at an end. On October 25, 1838, in an attempt to rescue two of their spies, forces clashed with what they thought was part of the anti-Mormon mob. What they had done instead was attack a duly authorized state militia. Although the militiamen were anti-Mormon in sentiment, the battle changed the whole nature of the conflict. Acting on orders from the governor, troops from all over northwestern Missouri poured into Caldwell County and after the massacre at Haun's Mill forced most Mormons to retreat to Far West. Joseph Smith had realized by this time that the Saints could not win and asked Corrill and a handful of well-known dissenters with contacts among the non-Mormons to help arrange for a surrender. He told Corrill and Reed Peck "to beg like a dog for peace."[77]

Initially, the prospect for securing acceptable terms of surrender seemed promising at first, but the anti-Mormon militia General Samuel D. Lucas took a hard line. John Corrill, as one of the Mormon negotiators, was especially concerned about how Lucas would react to Governor Boggs's so-called Extermination Order, giving the militia carte blanche to kill the Saints. "This order," Corrill wrote, "greatly agitated my mind. I expected that we should be exterminated without fail." So also feared the prophet, who upon being told of the order declared "he would rather go to state-prison for twenty years, or . . . die than have the people exterminated." This concern was not realized. Instead Lucas specified that church leaders give themselves up for punishment; that the Saints surrender all arms; that all Mormons who had participated in the hostilities deed their property to the state for indemnification of the old settlers who had lost theirs; and that all Mormons not being held for trial leave Missouri. Church officials agreed to the terms, and Corrill, with other go-betweens, turned Smith and selected other Mormon leaders over to the militia.[78]

In November, Corrill testified at a court of inquiry concerning Danite activities, and church military raids into Daviess County. If Corrill, however, had abandoned his belief in Mormonism, he did not abandon the Mormon people. Although he could have easily left church members to their fate, Corrill not only spoke on their behalf to the authorities but also gave his money to the church's poor—all he had. By selling his property he was able to distribute about $2,100 to nearly 160 needy families.[79] Corrill typically gave each recipient about $3 dollars, although there was a wide difference in contributions based on need. For instance, he gave 18 cents to Sherman Brown but $44.60 to Titus Billings. Although some of the money ended up in the hands of old friends like Edward Partridge ($15.04), the jailed Alexander McRae, a fanatical Danite of whom Corrill disapproved, received $2.88, which Corrill undoubtedly gave to McRae's wife. Two of Joseph Smith's brothers benefited from Corrill's largesse as well: Samuel ($9.62) and William (75 cents).

On December 19, 1838, Corrill proved his fidelity to the Saints again, when one month after he assumed his seat in state legislature as Caldwell County's representative, he introduced two memorials on behalf of the Mormons. The first was from church members in Daviess County, who prayed for release from the "treaty" signed at Far West compelling them to leave the state. The second memorial from the church detailed the mistreatment of the Saints from arrival in Jackson County to the Mormon War and asked that all property taken from them during this period be restored and, as in the first petition, requested that their forced emigration be halted.[80]

In presenting these petitions Corrill began a bit diffidently, yet as reported by the *Missouri Republican,* he said that the Mormon "people, despised and persecuted as they were, were still his constituents, & he was therefore bound to speak on a subject in which they were so deeply interested." In his *Brief History of the Church,* Corrill rather laconically noted that his presentation of the Saints' petitions "produced some excitement in the House." The petitions, in fact, caused an uproar, as one representative after another from the western part of the state rose to vilify the Mormons as the most base and degraded wretches ever to blight their portion of the state. Declaring themselves unwilling to hear such disgraceful slander, they claimed their constituents to be the finest people on earth and perfectly incapable of committing the atrocities of which the Mormons accused them. By focusing on the improbable parts of the church's charges (the rape of Mormon women by militiamen, for example) they managed to dodge the church's more substantial charges and ignored the question of the forcible expulsion of innocent men, women, and children from the state. By the time they had finished their attack, Corrill had fallen into complete retreat and volunteered to withdraw the memorials, only to see them tabled instead.[81]

John Corrill wrote his *Brief History of the Church of Christ of Latter Day Saints* sometime in the winter of 1839, concluding his narrative with his service in the legislature. The book, however, ends with a number of reflections. In one sense he still acknowledged the appeal of the church and attributed the Saints' success in winning converts to their skill in theological argument. If Smith and Rigdon had "manifested a truly Christian spirit," he wrote, "it would have been very difficult to put them down. But their impudence and miscalculations, and manifest desire for power and property, have opened the eyes of many, and did more to destroy them than could have possibly been done otherwise." Hostility from outside, he believed, was the only thing holding the church together. Without it "they would have divided and subdivided so as to have completely destroyed themselves and their power, as a people, in a short time."[82]

As those remarks had been directed to those outside the church, his last thoughts were addressed directly to his former coreligionists:

> I have left you, not because I disbelieve the Bible, for I believe in God, the Savior, and religion same as ever; but when I retrace our track, and view the doings of the church for six years past, I can see nothing that convinces me that God has been our leader; calculation after calculation has failed, and plan after plan has been

overthrown, and our prophet seemed not to know the event until too late . . . and still we were commanded in the most rigid manner, to follow him, which the church did, until many were led into the commission of crime; have been apprehended and broken down by their opponnents, and many have been obliged to abandon their country, their families, and all they possessed, and great affliction has been brought upon the whole church. . . . But where now may you look for deliverance? You may say, in God; but I say, in the exercise of common sense and that sound reason with which God has endowed you; and my advice is to follow that, in preference to those pretended revelations which have served no better purpose than to increase your trouble, and which would bind you, soul and body, under the most intolerable yoke.[83]

Thus ends the published version of Corrill's book with the same strong affirmation of the Christian primitivist's faith in independent reason that brought him into the church and the same commitment to republican liberty that caused him trouble after his conversion—a commitment underscored by the crossed out last line of the manuscript version of the book: "For my own part, I had rather enjoy liberty in Hell than suffer bondage in Heaven."[84]

When the Missouri legislature ended its session in mid February 1839, Corrill left his seat, never to return. His constituents had left the state, and there was no longer any reason for him to be there. Despised and officially considered a traitor to the Saints, Corrill was formally excommunicated by the church on March 17, 1839. When on April 21 he wrote Thomas Watson & Sons, whom he had engaged to print his *Brief History of the Church*, he was living in Springfield, Illinois, where he said he intended to remain for the season.[85] Sometime before January 1840 he moved to Quincy, Illinois, where many of the Saints who had fled Missouri had originally found shelter and safety, and some remained. Despite his departure from the fold, he stayed sympathetic to the Mormon people and joined the Saints in petitioning the federal government for redress of the injuries suffered by church members in Missouri.[86]

John Corrill died in early 1843, his reputation and finances in tatters. He owned no real property, and his personal effects were valued at $265.86, including, as was the custom of the time, the clothes of his wife and children. His book had met with an indifferent reception. The three hundred copies he had left at the time of his death were valued at $4. His integrity and basic decency were overshadowed by charges that he had betrayed the prophet and the church.[87]

NOTES

I would like to thank my research assistant, Lisa Hefferman Weil, for her help in preparing this essay.

1. Reed Peck, *The Reed Peck Manuscript* (Salt Lake City: Modern Microfilm, n.d.), 13, 34.

2. Scott H. Faulring, ed., *An American Prophet's Record: The Diaries and Journals of Joseph Smith* (Salt Lake City: Signature Books in association with Smith Research Associates, 1987), 222–23.

3. For a sampling of views by divergent historians, see Richard Lloyd Anderson, "Atchison's Letters and the Causes of Mormon Expulsion from Missouri," *Brigham Young University Studies* 26 (1986): 11; F. Mark McKiernan, "Mormonism on the Defensive: Far West, 1838-1839," in *The Restoration Movement: Essays in Mormon History,* ed. F. Mark McKiernan, Alma R. Blair, and Paul M. Edwards (Lawrence: Coronado Press, 1973), 138–39n2; Marvin S. Hill, *Quest for Refuge: The Mormon Flight from American Pluralism* (Salt Lake City: Signature Books, 1989), 225n65; Stephen C. LeSeuer, *The 1838 Mormon War in Missouri* (Columbia: University of Missouri Press, 1987), 40.

4. John Corrill, *A Brief History of the Church of Christ of Latter Day Saints . . . With Reasons of the Author for Leaving the Church* (St. Louis: n.p., 1839).

5. Short biographical sketches containing some information on Corrill's early life are found in Andrew Jenson, *Latter-day Saint Biographical Encyclopedia* (Salt Lake City: Andrew Jenson History Co., 1901), 1:241–42; Dean C. Jessee, ed., *The Papers of Joseph Smith* (Salt Lake City: Deseret Book Co., 1989), 1:480–81; Lyndon W. Cook, *The Revelations of the Prophet Joseph Smith* (Salt Lake City: Deseret Book Co., 1981), 58–59.

6. The children were named Betsy, Nancy, Whitney, Foster, and Mary. There was possibly a sixth child. A John W. Corrill, of uncertain relation, served as the administrator of his estate. John Correll Estate Box 287, Adams County Court House. These papers are missing. In 1975, however, the Genealogical Society of Utah microfilmed them, and they are presently available on film roll 933951.

7. This account of his conversion is based on Corrill, *Brief History of the Church,* 7–9.

8. On the life and career of Sidney Rigdon, see F. Mark McKiernan, *The Voice of One Crying in the Wilderness: The Life of Sidney Rigdon, Religious Reformer* (Lawrence: Coronado Press, 1971).

9. Corrill, *Brief History of the Church,* 8.

10. Ibid., 10–16.

11. Ibid., 16. Corrill may have punched up his initial skepticism in light of later events, but it is nevertheless consistent with his behavior over the course of his career in the church.

12. Richard T. Hughes and C. Leonard Allen, *Illusions of Innocence: Protestant Primitivism in America, 1630-1875* (Chicago: University of Chicago

Press, 1988), 102–33; Nathan Hatch, *The Democratization of American Christianity* (New Haven: Yale University Press, 1989), 67–81; Kenneth H. Winn, *Exiles in a Land of Liberty: Mormons in America, 1830–1846* (Chapel Hill: University of North Carolina Press, 1989), 9–10, 48.

13. Hughes and Allen, *Illusions of Innocence*, 33–52; Dan Vogel, *Religious Seekers and the Advent of Mormonism* (Salt Lake City: Signature Books, 1988), 36–41.

14. Corrill, *Brief History of the Church*, 17.

15. Ibid., 16.

16. Ibid., 16–17.

17. Ibid.

18. Donald Q. Cannon and Lyndon W. Cook, eds., *Far West Record: Minutes of the Church of Jesus Christ of Latter-day Saints, 1830–1844* (Salt Lake City: Deseret Book Co., 1983), 52, 58, 65, 234, and passim.

19. *A Book of Commandments for the Government of the Church of Christ* (Zion: W. W. Phelps and Co., 1833), 48, 59–64. For a discussion of the problems with the Missouri site, see Robert Kent Fielding, "The Growth of the Mormon Church in Kirtland, Ohio," Ph.D. diss., Indiana University, 1957, 48–55.

20. Vogel, *Religious Seekers and the Advent of Mormonism*, 112–14; *Doctrine and Covenants of the Church of Latter-Day Saints, containing Revelations Given to Joseph Smith, the Prophet* (Kirtland: F. G. Williams and Co., 1835), secs. 64:17 and 107:59, 65–69.

21. Dean C. Jessee, ed., *The Personal Writings of Joseph Smith* (Salt Lake City: Deseret Book Co., 1984), 245–46.

22. Joseph Smith, Jr., *History of the Church of Jesus Christ of Latter-day Saints*, ed. B. H. Roberts (Salt Lake City: Deseret Book Co., 1978 ed,), 1:318–19.

23. Corrill, *Brief History of the Church*, 18–19.

24. Ibid., 19.

25. On the Jackson County conflict, see Ronald E. Romig and John H. Seibert, "First Impressions: The Independence, Missouri, Printing Operation, 1832–1833," *John Whitmer Historical Association Journal* 10 (1990): 51–66; Winn, *Exiles in a Land of Liberty*, 87–100.

26. Corrill, *Brief History of the Church*, 19.

27. *Evening and Morning Star* [Kirtland, Ohio], January 1834. See also Oliver Cowdery's remarks in the March 1834 issue.

28. Ibid., July 1834.

29. Ibid., January 1834.

30. As quoted in Max H. Parkin, "A History of the Latter-day Saints in Clay County, Missouri, from 1833 to 1837," Ph.D. diss., Brigham Young University, 1976, 188–89; for a similar account by Emily's sister, Eliza, see 50.

31. F. Mark McKiernan and Roger D. Launius, eds., *An Early Latter Day Saint History: The Book of John Whitmer* (Independence: Herald Publishing House, 1980), 97–98; Smith, *History of the Church*, 1:451–52, 479, 483–85, 487, 488–90, 492, 2:75–76, 89; *Evening and Morning Star*, March 1834, August 1834.

32. *Evening and Morning Star,* June 1834. On this expedition, see Roger D. Launius, *Zion's Camp: Expedition to Missouri, 1834* (Independence: Herald Publishing House, 1984).

33. Smith, *History of the Church,* 2:89–92, 96–99, 107, 113–14, 135–36. Corrill attempted to spark new negotiations for another month until it was clear that further effort was useless.

34. See, for example, the problems of the Hulet branch, ibid., 1:137–41. See also Cannon and Cook, eds., *Far West Record,* 78; *Evening and Morning Star,* September 1834; Parkin, "Latter-day Saints in Clay County," 234–35. Corrill's disapproval of unbridled religion had made his appointment a natural one, but it assured he would come into conflict with Lyman Wight. Wight and Corrill's careers in the church had been quite close. Wight had ordained Corrill a high priest, as second counselor to Bishop Partridge, and had served as his traveling companion to Missouri during the summer of 1831. Yet the two men could not have been more different. On August 21, 1834, Corrill brought Wight up on charges before the church High Council for advocating the false doctrine that "all disease in this church is of the Devil and that medicine administered to the sick is of the Devil, for the sick in the church ought to live by faith." Wight, for his part, acknowledged that he believed this to be true, and this, in turn, led to a debate that ended with President David Whitmer ruling that God had made medicine to help people and that it need not be neglected. See Cannon and Cook, eds., *Far West Record,* 96–97.

35. Smith, *History of the Church,* 2:112–13; Corrill, *Brief History of the Church,* 22; Jessee, ed., *Papers of Joseph Smith,* 481; Milton V. Backman, Jr., et al., comps., *A Profile of Latter-day Saints of Kirtland, Ohio, and Members of Zion's Camp, 1830–39: Vital Statistics and Sources* (Provo: Brigham Young University, 1983), 104.

36. His name does not appear on Backman's list of "Latter-day Saints who received a special blessing in Kirtland for working on the construction of the Kirtland Temple, March 7–8, 1835." See Backman, *A Profile of Latter-day Saints,* 99.

37. *Evening and Morning Star,* August 1835.

38. Faulring, ed., *An American Prophet's Record,* 36, 46, 50, 72, 75.

39. This is a conjecture based upon a favorable remark he made about Sexias in his *Brief History of the Church,* 22–23, and the books in Hebrew listed in the inventory of his estate. See Estate Box 287, Adams County Court House.

40. Smith, *History of the Church,* 2:281–82.

41. McKiernan and Launius, eds., *An Early Latter Day Saint History,* 151.

42. Faulring, ed., *An American Prophet's Record,* 109; Hill, *Quest for Refuge,* 51–52; Corrill, *Brief History of the Church,* 21–22.

43. Leonard J. Arrington, ed., "Oliver Cowdery's Kirtland, Ohio, 'Sketch Book'," *Brigham Young University Studies* 12 (Summer 1972): 410–26.

44. Corrill, *Brief History of the Church,* 23.

45. Ibid.

46. McKiernan and Launius, eds., *An Early Latter Day Saint History,* 154;

Smith, *History of the Church,* 2:436, 449–52; Winn, *Exiles in a Land of Liberty,* 102–4; Corrill, *Brief History of the Church,* 26.

47. As quoted in Anderson, "Atchison's Letters," 12–13. See also Parkin, "Latter-Day Saints in Clay County," 269.

48. The Saints agreed that they would buy out any settlers who did not wish to live near them and foreswore settling on a northern strip of land claimed by Ray County. Peck, *Reed Peck Manuscript,* 3; Parkin, "Latter-Day Saints in Clay County," 270; Anderson, "Atchison's Letters," 12–13.

49. Cannon and Cook, eds., *Far West Record,* 105–6; Parkin, "Latter-day Saints in Clay County," 267.

50. Corrill, *Brief History of the Church,* 26; see also Peck, *Reed Peck Manuscript,* 4.

51. Cannon and Cook, eds., *Far West Record,* 103, 113, 114, 117, 124, 127, 129–33; *Elder's Journal,* November 1837; Lyndon W. Cook, *Joseph Smith and the Law of Consecration* (Provo: Grandin Book Co., 1985), 75–77. The High Council also granted Corrill a daily payment of $1.50, along with other officials, when serving as the church's agent.

52. Corrill, *Brief History of the Church,* 27. On the Kirtland situation see Winn, *Exiles in a Land of Liberty,* 109–21.

53. Corrill, *Brief History of the Church,* 24–25.

54. Jessee, ed., *Personal Writings of Joseph Smith,* 355. This was, in part, reflected in the so-called political motto of the church, which Smith wrote several days after his arrival in Far West. In the motto, the prophet extolled the Constitution and the Founding Fathers, virtue and truth, aristarchy and democracy, and other positive ideas, but he gave equal space to disapproval of such evil as tyrants, mobs, aristocrats, and the practitioners of priestcraft and gave special attention to "those who invent or seek out unrighteous and vexatious lawsuits." At Smith's behest, Corrill and seven other church leaders signed the motto.

55. Cannon and Cook, eds, *Far West Record,* 137–41.

56. Ibid., 151–52, 166.

57. Peck, *Reed Peck Manuscript,* 6; Corrill, *Brief History of the Church,* 30; John Corrill in Missouri General Assembly, *Document Containing the Correspondence, Orders, &c., in Relation to the Disturbance with the Mormons.* . . . (Fayette: Missouri State Legislature, 1841), 110.

58. Corrill in *Document Containing the Correspondence,* 110.

59. Corrill, *Brief History of the Church,* 31; LeSueur, *1838 Mormon War in Missouri,* 40–43; Winn, *Exiles in a Land of Liberty,* 123–24, 130–31.

60. Corrill, *Brief History of the Church,* 30.

61. Corrill, in *Document Containing the Correspondence,* 111; Phelps, *Document Containing the Correspondence,* 121–22.

62. Corrill, *Brief History of the Church,* 31–32.

63. Peck, *Reed Peck Manuscript,* 8.

64. The Missouri constitution required that representatives be residents of the state for at least two years and residents of their county for one year before election. Caldwell County had been legally incorporated on December 29, 1836.

65. Corrill, *Brief History of the Church,* 33.

66. *The Return* [Davis City, Iowa], October 1889; Smith, *History of the Church,* 3:32; Cook, *Joseph Smith and the Law of Consecration,* 77–81.

67. Peck, *Reed Peck Manuscript,* 8–9, 12.

68. Corrill, *Brief History of the Church,* 26–27, 45–46. See also John Corrill's petition, "To the Honorable the Senate and House of Representatives of the United States in Congress Assembled," MSS 942, fd 7, Archives and Records, Harold B. Lee Library, Brigham Young University (original in the National Archives and Records Administration, Washington). My thanks to David J. Whittaker for securing a copy of Corrill's petition for me.

69. Faulring, ed., *An American Prophet's Record,* 209.

70. Peck, *Reed Peck Manuscript,* 13, 34.

71. Faulring, ed., *An American Prophet's Record,* 209–10.

72. *Book of Commandments,* 40:22.

73. Corrill, *Brief History of the Church,* 36–37.

74. Corrill longed to gather his family and flee, but punishment awaited those caught leaving, and he never found a good opportunity. Ibid., 37.

75. Ibid.; Corrill, in *Document Containing the Correspondence,* 112–13; Peck in ibid., 117; Phelps in ibid., 122–23; Peck, *Reed Peck Manuscript,* 19–20.

76. Corrill, *Brief History of the Church,* 38.

77. Ibid., 41; Peck, *Reed Peck Manuscript,* 24.

78. Corrill, *Brief History of the Church,* 41. Lucas's notion of trying the church leaders for their alleged crimes consisted of no more than a quick court martial, after which he ordered their execution. Fortunately, Alexander Doniphan, whom Lucas ordered to execute the men, refused and promised to have Lucas tried for murder if the death sentence were carried out. This brought the quasi-legal lynching to an end.

79. Oliver Cowdery and Burr Riggs also sold their property to aid the poor. Ibid., 110–13; LeSueur, *1838 Mormon War in Missouri,* 222; John Correll Estate Box 287.

80. *Missouri Republican* [St. Louis], December 24, 1838. The second memorial is found in Smith, *History of the Church,* 3:217–24.

81. Corrill, *Brief History of the Church,* 44; *Missouri Republican,* December 24, 1838.

82. Corrill, *Brief History of the Church,* 45.

83. Ibid., 48.

84. The original of Corrill's manuscript is in the Missouri Historical Society Archives, St. Louis; pp. 1, 19, and 24 are missing from this document. The quotation is from 90. Corrill appended to his *Brief History of the Church* a passage from Joseph Smith's unpublished inspired translation of the Bible. The verses he selected are millenarian in content and run from the last sentence of Matthew 23 through Matthew 24. Writing to Thomas Watson & Sons, the publishers of the *Missouri Argus,* who were printing the book for him, he said that he included these lines "not out of disrespect for Smith or his followers[,] but merely to indulge the reader with a small specimen or sample of the new

translation." A little more candidly, at the end of the letter he added that he thought inclusion of the passage would "make the book more saleable[,] especially among the Mormons for many are hungry after that chapter." Corrill to Thomas Watson & Sons, April 21, 1839. Missouri Historical Society Archives.

85. Corrill to Thomas Watson & Sons, April 21, 1839.

86. "To the Honorable," MSS 942, fd 7.

87. Corrill's personal property was inventoried on March 9, 1843. His effects included furniture; items related to his work as an architect (books, carpentry tools, drawing instruments); and a fair number of books including four copies of the Book of Mormon, three copies of the *Doctrine and Covenants*, eight books in Hebrew (probably testifying to his attendance at Joshua Sexias's class), and Greek and Latin grammars.

3

William E. McLellin:
"Mormonism's Stormy Petrel"

Richard P. Howard

Dale L. Morgan, preparing his bibliographies of the churches of the Mormon dispersion, dubbed William E. McLellin (1806–83) "Mormonism's stormy petrel."[1] Morgan's image of McLellin suggests the use of such modifiers as *emotional, impulsive, opinionated, irritable,* and *controlling* in describing McLellin's nature. Considerable evidence supports this description, making McLellin a lively study in dissent. During a long life, McLellin flitted from one Mormon faction to another, searching for what he perceived as the absolute truth of the gospel. His was a desperate and seemingly fruitless search for God.

Born on January 18, 1806, in Smith County, Tennessee, McLellin's search shows up in one of his earliest known letters. Writing on August 4, 1832, about his conversion to the Latter Day Saints, McLellin described how two separate teams of Mormon elders visited him in his home at Paris, Illinois, in July 1831. Both groups were en route to Jackson County, Missouri, in preparation for the establishment of a zionic community there. The preaching of David Whitmer, one of the three witnesses to the divinity of the Book of Mormon and a member of the second team to visit Paris, so deeply impressed the gospel message on McLellin that he immediately left his settled life to follow Mormonism:[2] "My curiosity was roused up and my anxiety also to know the truth. And though I had between 30 & 40 students and the people generally satisfied with me as Teacher—yet I closed my school on the 29th July and on the 30th I mounted Tom and left for Indepen[dence]."[3]

McLellin arrived in Independence, Missouri, on August 18, 1831, only to find that Joseph Smith, Jr., the Mormon prophet, and many of the elders who had come to Missouri had already left to return to Ohio. But he acquainted himself with the Saints there and was baptized two days later. On August 24 he was ordained an elder, and the next day he headed eastward with Hyrum Smith. On this trip he preached his first missionary sermon (one and one-half hours in length) on August

28, 1831, during which he perceived his hearers as being touched by God's spirit. Encouraged by this, McLellin later preached to a packed court house at Jacksonville, Illinois: "the house though large was full of Judges, Lawyers, Doctors, Priests and People I think about 500. I spoke 3 hours and when done I cannot describe the joy of some, the consternation of others, and the anger of others."[4]

On their way to Kirtland, Ohio, the Mormon stronghold, McLellin and Hyrum Smith veered to Paris, where McLellin finished some personal business, bought Smith a horse, and preached to some of his friends and relatives. They eventually arrived in Kirtland on October 18, 1831. A week later, at a church conference at nearby Orange, McLellin first met Joseph Smith, Jr. McLellin's account of this meeting demonstrated something of his fundamental commitment to Smith and the Latter Day Saints: "On the 25th Oct. I attended a conference. General peace and harmony pervaded the conference and much instruction to me. From thence I went home with Jos. and lived with him about three weeks; and from my acquaintance then and until now I can truely say I believe him to be a man of God. A Prophet, a Seer and Revelator to the church of christ."[5] At this meeting McLellin asked Smith to inquire of God's will for his life, and Smith responded through revelation in rather minute detail.[6] McLellin was ordained at the conference to the office of high priest.[7]

McLellin's faculty for misjudging his social environment, which he demonstrated repeatedly in following years, came out during a church conference at Hiram, Ohio, in early November 1831. Church leaders were considering the publication of revelatory documents by Joseph Smith. McLellin saw himself as superior in literary attainment and ability to most of those around him, including Smith, and apparently boasted that he could write a revelation surpassing the ones available to the church through its prophet. Smith gave him a chance to try his hand. Predictably, McLellin's effort not only failed of its immediate objective, but the elders also rallied around Smith and bore witness to his revelatory prowess. Years later, after McLellin was out of the church, Smith wrote of the event:

William E. M'Lellin, as the wisest man, in his own estimation, having more learning than sense, endeavored to write a commandment like unto one of the least of the Lord's, but failed, it was an awful responsibility to write in the name of the Lord. The elders and all present, that witnessed this vain attempt of a man to imitate the language of Jesus Christ, renewed their faith in the fullness of the Gospel, and in the truth of the commandments and revelations which the Lord had given to the church through my instrumentality; and the elders signified a willingness to bear testimony of their truth to all the world.[8]

Thereafter Smith sent McLellin on a mission, perhaps to get him out of Kirtland.[9] McLellin left for his mission to the eastern states, but within a few weeks his complaints about being sent away had reached Smith, who admonished him through revelation at the January 1832 conference at Amherst, Ohio, and sent him with Luke Johnson on a mission to the southern states.[10] This time McLellin remained on a mission at Middlebury, Ohio, but then he suddenly returned to Kirtland and married Emeline Miller on April 26, 1832.[11] His record of unwillingness to carry out the wishes of Joseph Smith probably accounted for McLellin's December 3, 1832, excommunication, although he was apparently soon thereafter reinstated.[12] Perhaps fittingly, the last time McLellin's name appeared in Smith's revelatory instructions it was a rebuke. A document of March 8, 1833 read: "I [God] am not well pleased with my servant William E. M'Lellin." The document further admonished McLellin, who had by that time settled in Independence, to repent of his many failings.[13] In sum, the initial interactions between McLellin and Joseph Smith revealed a distance portending McLellin's eventual separation from the church.

Early on McLellin had moved to Independence and lived there until late 1833, when mob action forced him, with some 1,200 other church members, to flee to Clay County. There he remained for nearly a year. On July 3, 1834, he became a member of the Missouri High Council under the presidency of David Whitmer, further cementing the close relationship these two men had enjoyed since McLellin first learned of Mormonism from Whitmer. On July 9 he started for Kirtland with Joseph Smith and several other men; although he became ill and they had to leave him until he got well, McLellin settled in Kirtland in the fall of 1834.

Perhaps another instance of his relationship with Whitmer came on February 14, 1835, when McLellin began his brief tenure as a member of the Quorum of Twelve Apostles. The members of this quorum were chosen by the three witnesses to the Book of Mormon, one of whom was David Whitmer. The prayer of blessing given McLellin at the time may have influenced his self-perception:

Wisdom and intelligence shall be poured out upon him, to enable him to perform the great work that is incumbent upon him; that he may be spared until the Saints are gathered; that he may stand before kings and rulers to bear testimony, and be upheld by holy angels; and the nations of the earth shall acknowledge that God has sent him; he shall have power to overcome his enemies; and his life shall be spared in the midst of pestilence and destruction, and in the midst of his enemies. He shall be a prince and savior to God's people. The tempter shall not overcome him, nor his enemies prevail against him; the heavens shall be opened unto him, as unto men in days of old. He shall be mighty in the hands of God, and shall convince thousands that God has sent him; and his days may be prolonged until the coming of the Son of Man. He shall be wafted as on eagles' wings, from country to country, and from people to people; and be able to do wonders in the midst of this generation. Even so. Amen.[14]

Almost at the same time that he was called to be an apostle, McLellin's almost constant troubles with the church leadership became public. In the summer of 1835 he was disfellowshipped but restored on September 25, 1835, without a clear reconciliation. From this point on he seems to have lost confidence in some leaders in the church, although the attraction of Mormonism held sway. He could not leave the church, although he definitely considered doing so. That push-pull relationship with the church would become a part of McLellin's life ever after.[15]

Public disputes between McLellin and the hierarchy arose with the Kirtland church's disintegration and the flight of its leaders to Far West, Missouri, in the winter of 1837–38. Progress toward church stability did not materialize as he had hoped, and the failures of the organization to meet serious challenges of an economic and political, as well as a spiritual, nature created a serious crisis of conscience for McLellin. It seems from the scant records available for this period that he lost faith in the church leadership and was having second thoughts about continuing as a Latter Day Saint. This was a not uncommon development at the time. The most serious dissent of the church up to that point took place in 1837–38, and it prompted the withdrawal or excommunication of numerous church members. Among them were several high officials, one of whom was McLellin's mentor, David Whitmer.[16]

As church leaders relocated from Kirtland to Far West during the first part of 1838, McLellin became increasingly disenchanted with the organization. His dissent was well known to the senior leadership. The apostle David W. Patten took the opportunity at the April 7, 1838, conference to speak against him and four other apostles.[17] Finally, on May 11, 1838, a bishop's court tried McLellin for transgression. Joseph Smith, who was in attendance, related nothing of the outcome, only that he spoke with McLellin at the trial. In editing Joseph Smith's account for publication years later, B. H. Roberts inserted a footnote on this subject. He commented:

> the text is silent in relation to what action was taken respecting William E. McLellin, and the Far West Record is silent upon the subject also. In fact the minutes of the trial before the Bishop are not written in that record at all. It is known, however, from other sources that William E. McLellin was finally excommunicated from the church at Far West. Thence forward he took an active part in the persecution of the Saints in Missouri, being remembered by some as desiring to do violence to the person of Joseph Smith, while the latter was confined in Liberty prison.[18]

McLellin became a diligent opponent of the Mormon leaders but not necessarily of the Saints during the period that followed. He charged that Smith and his lieutenants had lost the vision of the early church and had been seduced by power and affluence. There is some evidence that while Joseph Smith and other church leaders were in jail in November 1838, McLellin led a search party through Smith's home "to confiscate books and papers that might prove damaging to the Mormons. The Danite constitution was reportedly found in a trunk filled with the Prophet's personal papers."[19] Smith wrote in an epistle from Liberty jail, in Clay County, Missouri, in December 1839 that turncoats William "McLellin, John Whitmer, D. Whitmer, O. Cowdery, Martin Harris, who are too mean to mention and we had liked to have forgotten them."[20]

From 1838 through 1843 McLellin essentially retreated from the Mormon scene. When the church was forced out of Missouri at the end of 1838, he moved to Hampton, Illinois, near Rock Island, began practice as a physician, and remained aloof from Mormonism until the autumn of 1843. He then began several intensive years of affiliation with a quick succession of dissenting factions. These affiliations culminated in his forming a group of his own at Kirtland from 1847 to 1849. Nearly twenty years after that group fell apart, McLellin spent several months affiliated with the faction led by Granville Hedrick at Independence.

The first of the factions to attract McLellin was that of George M. Hinkle, located at Buffalo, Iowa Territory, across the Mississippi River from McLellin's home. Hinkle, another Mormon dissident from the 1838 period, had gathered a group of about a hundred members there in 1840 and struggled for existence for several years. McLellin appeared at a conference of Hinkle's group on September 16, 1843, and accepted ordination to "be united with elder Hinkle in bearing the glad tidings of salvation to the world." McLellin apparently "straightway preached this to be the true, the only true church of God now on the earth."[21]

By mid 1844, both Hinkle and McLellin were active as apostles for the church and jointly launched a church periodical, the *Ensign*, with McLellin as editor. It gave him a forum for presenting his views about Mormonism. For instance, he had an intense disgust for the activities of Brigham Young and the apostles who were in control of the institutional machinery. When the editor of the nearby *Davenport Gazette* mistakenly suggested that Hinkle's group was "Mormon," McLellin offered the first of many published attacks on what he would later refer to as "Twelveitism": "One thing we have to say, and we want it distinctly understood—we have no bond of union or fellowship existing between us and the Mormons (so called.) Yet we do not feel disposed to persecute or injure them, or needlessly make any thrusts at them. We are for the Latter Day Saints to have and enjoy their rights as other churches; and when they trample upon the laws, and disregard other men's rights, then we are for their punishment."[22] In this mild put-down of Mormons, McLellin followed the lead of Hinkle, who was careful to convey his conviction of the wickedness of Nauvoo Mormonism while appearing if not conciliatory then at least adopting a live-and-let-live attitude.[23]

McLellin did not remain a part of Hinkle's group long. By October 1844 he was gone, and had he not voluntarily departed Hinkle would have forced him out on charges of apostasy in church court. Hinkle strongly criticized McLellin for reneging on the church and the gospel:

> It is awful to reflect upon the many thrilling discourses, positive declarations, and pointed testimonies borne from the public stand by this individual . . . since last April . . . no man of this age has made a louder pretence to the miraculous gifts of the gospel than Dr. McLellin. . . . He was, Paul-like, in his zeal against [those] . . . who apostatized or departed from the Church . . . he remarked, that when any one left this Church they were bound to lie; for, said he, the Devil will lead them to it. . . . He then determined to leave the church; and from thence forward sought to do all the mischief in his power.

Hinkle was convinced that McLellin had fallen into the same trap. "I am now convinced that he intends to destroy the faith of all those who he can have influence over," he added, "I deem it my duty to thus put you on your guard."[24]

From there, for a brief season in late 1844 and early 1845, McLellin affiliated with William Law's dissident group situated in the Hampton, Illinois, area. Law had been a member of the First Presidency, but with his family and a few friends bolted from the church in the spring of 1844 over doctrinal differences with Joseph Smith. McLellin cast his lot with people whom he called the "faithful" members of the First Presidency. He tried to bring Sidney Rigdon into this reform group on December 23, 1844, suggesting that the scattered Saints could unite under Rigdon and Law—the only surviving members of the First Presidency as the proper successors to the slain Joseph Smith: "the Lord has shown to me that by a union of President Law and yourself, together with each [of] your friends, that all the honest in heart among the Latter Day Saints and throughout the world will UNITE also, and form that company who will follow the saviour robed in white linen 'clean and white.'"

Even as he was making this proposal, McLellin also raised the possibility of his visiting Pittsburgh and joining Rigdon's movement. He wrote:

> You used to tell me that "I was a man after your own heart." One thing I know that on my first visit to Ohio, from no man did I receive so much intelligence concerning the divine volume as from yourself. But you could seldom act yourself in consequence of the abominable jealousy of him [Joseph Smith] with whom you were connected. And I am told by the brethren here that for the last five years you have been rather a spectator than an *active adviser* in those measures at Nauvoo, which have brought death upon the prophet and lasting disgrace upon the church. This gives me more confidence in you, and I am determined from this time forward to "be a man *after God's* own heart."[25]

In a postscript McLellin referred to thrice-weekly meetings he was attending at William Law's home, in which they enjoyed the spirit of God in prophecy. He seemed clearly a part of Law's tiny following at that point, but he was leaning plaintively toward Rigdon by the start of 1845.

An especially attractive feature for William McLellin was the strong statements in Rigdon's periodical blistering the Nauvoo Quorum of Twelve. Leaving Law's group, by March 1845 McLellin was in Pittsburgh and had his anti-Twelve views published in Rigdon's periodical. He condemned the Twelve as fallen beyond redemption. He affirmed that the church's proper leaders were comprised of a presidency of three, headed by Rigdon. McLellin's praise of Rigdon at that point was nothing short of pure eulogy. He urged this pattern of presidency on the church and closed his writing with a hint that he himself should like to stand with Rigdon in that inspired leadership: "I feel my interest identified with his, and I feel also to stand by him in all righteousness before God, while he stands as a man of God to plead with the world."[26]

Predictably, McLellin played an active role in the April 1845 Conference of Rigdon's Church of Christ.[27] Rigdon proposed a committee of Samuel Bennett, Jeremiah Hatch, Jr., McLellin, Joseph M. Cole, and George W. Robinson to draft a preamble and resolutions for the church on the Mormon Nauvoo problem. The goal was twofold: to take a definite stand against the perceived Nauvoo apostasy, and to inform the world of the chasm between the "true faith" of the Church of Christ. The committee met and delivered to the conference a document entitled "Preamble and Resolutions of the Church of Christ." The preamble began by noting the necessity of publicizing the differences between themselves and the Latter Day Saints at Nauvoo. It then lamented the way in which Nauvoo Mormonism had perverted the gospel and defied the laws of God and of the nation. The committee then framed these resolutions:

Resolved, That we hold no fellowship with the people calling themselves the church of Jesus Christ of Latter Day Saints, and can have no communion with them, unless they repent and obey the principles of righteousness and truth.

Resolved, That we maintain the truth and the truth only, at all hazards; renouncing at once, and for ever, the unsanctifying dogma, that it is sometimes lawful to lie.

Resolved, That our subjection to the law of God impels us to yield implicit obedience to the law of the land.

Resolved, That we maintain and do earnestly contend for the faith which was once, and is again, delivered to the saints, contained in the Bible, Book of Mormon and Book of Covenants.

Resolved, That we feel it a solemn and imperative obligation, we owe to God and our fellow men, to disseminate to the extent of our ability, correct information regarding certain pernicious doctrines and practices which are secretly taught by the leaders and many of the members, of the society called the church of Jesus Christ of Latter Day Saints; verily believing them

demoralizing and destructive, combining all the worst features
of barbarism, and containing all the elements of the wildest an-
archy, and would if unchecked by the power of truth, ultimately extinguish the species.[28]

McLellin's signature to these resolutions showed that at this stage he
was focusing his dissent on Mormonism as it then existed at Nauvoo.

Other indications of McLellin's swift rise in Rigdon's group included his selection as a member of Quorum of Seventy-three (along with
his old comrade, George M. Hinkle) and his designation as a member
of the Quorum of Twelve.[29] McLellin, a clerk of the conference, also
played a central role in discussions of other important issues. He spoke
several times at key points in the conference. Early in the week, just
after Rigdon had been unanimously sustained as prophet, seer, revelator, and translator to the Church of Christ, McLellin stood, took Rigdon's hand, and pledged "to stand by him and his family in all righteousness before God until the time of the end."[30] Two days later (April
9) McLellin confirmed a vision and revelation proclaimed by Sidney
Rigdon.[31] Later in the conference he reported his own revelation and
covenant. In it he had been commissioned to be a steward over the
bones of Joseph M. Cole, a fellow apostle and member of the Quorum of Seventy-three—also present at the conference, but who—according to McLellin's revelation—would be slain before Christ's Second
Coming.[32]

The conference on the last day unanimously endorsed the 1835
Doctrine and Covenants as the revelation of God and law of the
church. Later McLellin would reject the *Doctrine and Covenants,* but
at this point in the development of his Latter Day Saint antipathy
McLellin's endorsement of the 1835 *Doctrine and Covenants* was tantamount to rejecting the Nauvoo editions of 1844, 1845, and 1846.
McLellin's full break from all the major features of Latter Day Saintism
(except the Book of Mormon) would await the formation of his own
schismatic group in 1847.

Reports of the Rigdon conference of April 1845 soon reached Nauvoo. One elder, David Pettegrew, back in Nauvoo from a mission to
the eastern states, had contact with some of the Rigdon branches since
January 1845. He had read the Rigdon conference minutes and reacted strongly:

I left Nauvoo the 28th of last January, in company with Elder
Willard Snow, for the southeast part of Indiana. When we arrived
we found great trouble in the branches which we had built up
three years before. There were men among them of another spir-

it—the doctrine of Rigdon, and it was marvelous to witness the "wicked spirit" of those who had turned away from the faith. I never realized before the abomination and wickedness of dissenters. They drew after them a multitude of the baser sort, who stood and delighted to hear them ridicule and slander the prophet and people of God; by which *"the way of truth was evil spoken of."*

Warming to a denunciation of McLellin, Pettigrew recalled an event corroborated in no other source that I have so far found:

> It brings to mind what I witnessed in Jackson county, in 1833, a few months before we were driven from that place. The power of God was manifest on that land in our meetings, held by the elders. I remember in one of those meetings it was made known by prophecy and revelation, through T. B. Marsh, as the spirit gave utterance, "that McLellin would carry the things the Lord was revealing to his people, to the world, and would use his influence against the church to destroy it."
>
> McLellin wondered why T. B. Marsh uttered words against him:—Then another arose and bore testimony to what Marsh had foretold, by the same spirit; and a third arose and testified also, and we marveled! we sorrowed! we wondered! I shall never forget that scene. It was true, and when I read the Pittsburgh papers, and saw McLellin in with Rigdon, it brought the prophetic language of 1833, to my mind, and confirmed it. *McLellin goes against the church to destroy it!*[33]

Such characterizations did not bother McLellin, even if he knew about them. On May 28, 1845, he sent a letter to "Presidents Rigdon and Robinson" that reflected great optimism in the eventual triumph of their cause against the Twelve. He told of his revelation to go to Tennessee to visit his father, whom he would baptize, and who in turn would give him a father's blessing. All of this had come to pass, he wrote. Even more, he had prophesied the future in response to a question from his congregation, "Are you a prophet of God?" He commented: "The future was opened up before me and I rolled it off with a voice that started some of them from their seats. And I must say that I even felt some astonished myself at what I *saw and declared* the meeting closed, the people dispersed." While receiving his father's blessing McLellin's soul caught fire, and the future world opened to him, revealing "important events and scenes through which you and I will have to pass shoulder to shoulder, hand to hand, and heart to heart, before we shall see this world redeemed, sin destroyed, Satan bound, and the saints rise, and all the righteous enter into the rest of God, and dwell on the face of this earth in peace."[34]

From late May through August 1845, McLellin traveled and preached widely for Rigdon's Church of Christ. From Hampton, Illinois, to Philadelphia he labored tirelessly, preaching, baptizing, and helping local people resolve their conflicts. J. H. Newton, a member in Philadelphia, wrote feelingly of McLellin's "olive branch" qualities of ministry and paid tribute to him for the way in which he had quickened the believers there in their faith and commitment.[35]

From the sketchy evidence extant, McLellin by early 1846 had become convinced that the faithful of the church ought to gather at Kirtland. It also appears that by that time McLellin was no longer firmly a part of Rigdon's organization. In trying to influence others to this position, McLellin wrote to Leonard Soby in Philadelphia about the gathering and direction of the Rigdonites. Soby promptly wrote to Rigdon on February 2, 1846, questioning McLellin's course: "Why does he write to me to destroy my confidence in those I love? Oh I see the spirit of the Devil in this."[36] Rigdon responded by explaining that McLellin and some others had "apostatized from the church and kingdom of the living God, and are lifting their puny arms against the work of the Almighty." He then printed extracts of two McLellin letters in the *Messenger and Advocate,* and noted that McLellin had left Rigdonism altogether. His heart was at Kirtland—stronghold for the kingdom of God, in which place he soon would try to find the "rest of God."[37]

In April 1846 McLellin moved to Shalersville, Ohio, where he practiced medicine until moving to Kirtland the following October. During that time he apparently flirted for a few months with the movement of James J. Strang. In a letter to David Whitmer on December 2, 1846 McLellin stated that Strang had made overtures to him and even listed him as a member of his Quorum of Twelve. McLellin, however, disavowed any official affiliation with Strang's group, later attacking Strang's leadership in the columns of his *Ensign of Liberty.* In May 1848 he accused Strang of instituting strange oaths, covenants, bizarre ceremonies, and blood rituals and labeled him a "third-rate infidel," a "false prophet, and a base hearted man, whose great aim is to destroy others in order to build himself up."[38]

Seven months earlier, however, McLellin had passed through Voree, Wisconsin, the site of Strang's headquarters, to visit him and his followers. In October 1847 he engaged in a debate with James J. Strang. The two men had a heated exchange on the issue of McLellin's affiliation with Strang's group and whether McLellin had ever been on friendly terms with one of Strang's colleagues, John C. Bennett. McLellin hotly denied both points, and Strang responded by reading three letters from McLellin (two to Bennett, the other to Strang himself) into the record of the debate. He challenged McLellin to deny that he had written the letters. McLellin remained silent in the face of that challenge. The three letters, together with Strang's comments about them, ended the debate quickly, and McLellin never mentioned these matters again, even in his own publications. Summarized, the letters established the following points of reality about McLellin's membership in James J. Strang's group and his previous friendship with John C. Bennett:

1. McLellin's friendship with Bennett dated from 1831, and they had lived and practiced medicine in the same town in 1844 (presumably, Hampton, Illinois). On the basis of that friendship McLellin asked Bennett to write him a recommendation as a physician and a gentleman. McLellin also proposed entering a medical partnership with Bennett, indicating a willingness to spend the winter in Voree trying to work it out.

2. McLellin and Strang happened to be in Kirtland at the same time and had several long conversations about the church. McLellin found Strang to be very intelligent and gentlemanly and respected his claims as president of the Latter Day Saints.[39]

3. McLellin longed to be "with his Brethren" in Voree for the October 6, 1846 conference, but his workload was too heavy. He expected to visit Voree in "only a few months" but rejoiced in the close friendship he had with Bennett.

4. McLellin praised Strang and enclosed a separate message intended for Bennett to give him with the statement: "The nearer the relation and the more the intimacy between J.J.S. and myself the better for the *cause.*"

5. McLellin pressed Bennett to be his advocate for a responsible station in Strang's organization: "You may promise in my name all that you may think I am (by indefatigable perseverance) capable of performing. . . . Some things in this [letter] you will show to none save my friend Pres. J. J. Strang. In him I have all confidence."[40]

6. In a letter to Strang, McLellin strongly affirmed his gratitude to Strang for their lengthy August 1846 visit at Kirtland. He pledged his active participation in church work, describing his determination in this regard to be "almost unbounded." His "soul pants to dwell among the Brethren." He also urged Strang to

postpone the next conference until June 6, 1847, and to defer appointment of all important leadership posts until then [when McLellin would be able to attend]."[41]

7. McLellin stated his unchanging position regarding his "taking the oversight and management of some important business on my arrival" [at Voree] and hoped that Strang had not changed in his support. He was willing to help with the printing press for the church next spring but awaited Strang's advice.[42]

In their debate Strang exploited the content of those letters to demonstrate that McLellin's verbal and other published statements were at total variance with the reality suggested in the letters. It is probable that, because he was disappointed that Strang did not choose him for a top leadership role, McLellin distanced himself from Strang as soon as he could. Near the end of October 1846 McLellin, wounded by Strang's neglect of him, moved his family to Kirtland and began preparing for the launching of his own "Church of Christ." On December 2 he sat down to write a long and critically important epistle to old friend David Whitmer.

McLellin's object in writing to Whitmer at Richmond, Missouri, was to urge him to accept a calling as prophet, seer, and revelator to the church. That calling, McLellin argued, had been imposed on Whitmer on July 8, 1834 in Clay County, Missouri, by Joseph Smith, Jr. After the Zion's Camp debacle, just before returning to Kirtland, Smith had organized the Missouri High Council and appointed leaders for the Missouri church. He had set Whitmer apart to be president of the church in Missouri. McLellin, now writing in retrospect, reinterpreted that ordination in a wholly different light. What had not apparently occurred to McLellin before, he now wrote in the most definite and persuasive language he could summon:

> You will remember, [Joseph Smith] appointed a special conference at L. Wight's, on the 8th of July, 1834. Benj. Winchester and Leonard Rich have both told me that he laid his hands on you, in that conference, and appointed and ordained you to be the Lord's Seer, "in his stead," provided anything should befall himself, so as to remove him from time. I was at that conference part of the day, and well remember that I saw you ordained. Should Joseph transgress, he should not have power except to appoint another. Now all acquainted with his history, from that day to the day of his death, know perfectly well that he never had power with God to accomplish any one great or good object that he ever commenced. Every thing seemed to be marred in his hands, until finally he died "as a fool dieth," at the hands of his enemies.

Now brother David, inasmuch as the Lord has appointed you, you cannot shrink from your duty, and then have any hope of eternal life. You must obey, or sink in utter darkness forever. . . . But my dear brother, the church is bleeding at every pore, for the want of faithful Shepherds to take the oversight of the flock. . . . The church now calls upon you to come and take your place, and make the seat of the FIRST LEADERS in the church here in Kirtland. For this was the first Stake of Zion ever pointed out, in this generation. We have the promise that in this place, we shall have an endowment from on high. Then the Elders, thus prepared, shall go to Gentile and then to the Jew, in all the world, in power.[43]

To this point in the letter McLellin had denounced Joseph Smith, claiming that David's ordination on July 8, 1834, to the presidency of the Missouri church was directly consequent to Smith's transgression. This assertion rested on McLellin's interpretation of *Doctrine and Covenants,* section 43:2. By this theory, Smith had no further prophetic authority from then on; he was a fallen prophet during the last decade of his life. McLellin then projected his anger at the Nauvoo Twelve, as well as at other factional groups: "The apostate Twelve have fled to the wilderness, with a large body of followers, to endure the severity of the judgments of God, in their destruction, which is certain. Rigdon lives near Chambersburg, Pa., surrounded by only a *few* followers; but few as they are, their hearts are full of desires for blood and war. Strang pitched his head quarters in Voree, Wisconsin, and has made the *notorious* Dr. J. C. Bennett his chief counsellor and *Pontiff. Big title truly.*"[44]

McLellin then pled at length to Whitmer to make this a matter of prayer and to come and take his place. For whatever reasons David Whitmer chose not to respond to McLellin's letter. When he published it in the *Ensign of Liberty* in April 1847 McLellin noted that Whitmer had given him no answer.

McLellin's patience at Whitmer's long silence had already worn thin by mid January 1847. He, Martin Harris, and several other elders met on January 23 in Kirtland to name their organization officially "The Church of Christ." Two weeks later the first conference of the new group convened at Kirtland. One of the first actions of that conference was to hear and approve a committee report—written by McLellin, Leonard Rich, Jacob Bump, and three others—on the reasons for the emergence of the Church of Christ. Now, and in much more detail than McLellin had written to Whitmer, the "fallen prophet" theory began to take on a life of its own. They faulted Joseph Smith and other top leaders for a broad range of offenses:

1. Renaming the church in May 1834 as the "Church of the Latter Day Saints" when the original name had been designated by revelation.

2. Leading the militaristic Zion's Camp against the peace enjoined by the gospel. The camp had ended in disaster, an evidence of the Lord's displeasure.

3. Presuming to lead the church after July 8, 1834 when Joseph Smith appointed his successor, David Whitmer.

4. Making Sylvester Smith a scapegoat for Joseph Smith's sins committed during the military expedition of Zion's Camp.

5. Engineering the "endowment" at Kirtland Temple in March and April 1836, which failed of its expectation because the Lord would not endow with His spirit those who had so far drifted from divine purpose.

6. Establishing a mercantile business at Kirtland stocked with goods bought on credit when the Lord had commanded "to owe no man."

7. Founding a bank without a charter from the state legislature in clear violation of Ohio laws.

8. Engaging in land speculations with the city plat at Kirtland.

It was a set of indictments very close to those offered by other dissenters from the 1837–38 period, aiming mostly at the church's involvement in secular affairs.

This did not end the assessment, however. The committee also denounced the excesses of Nauvoo, seeing them as the logical outcome of the earlier transgressions summarized above. Because of these sins:

> Finally, the protecting, or rather the preventing power of God is withdrawn. "The wolves are on the scent," the Prophet and Patriarch of the Latter Day Saints are again taken prisoners, and soon the massive doors of the Carthage prison grate upon their hinges, as they are closed for the *last time* upon these strange, singular, and unfortunate men. Soon a lawless banditti of mobocrats rush forward and surround the walls of their prison. Infuriate madness, with the blackness of darkness of the infernal regions, sits on their brows. Willful murder is in their hearts. Another moment, and the—Hark! What do we hear? O! 'Tis the death groans of Joseph and Hyrum Smith. Ah!! see them fall!!! The fatal lead has pierced their vital parts. Their life's blood has crimsoned the jail of Hancock County. O! ye unfortunate men, we feel to bewail the manner of your end. O! that you had kept

the strict commandments of your God, and then lived in righteousness, and led the people of the Church of Christ onward to that "rest which remaineth to the people of God."[45]

Having demolished Joseph Smith's prophetic authority in this report, McLellin also sought to destroy the credibility of other factional leaders. For example, the April 1847 issue of the *Ensign of Liberty* contained a long, stinging rebuke of James J. Strang's claims to prophetic leadership.[46] He also undertook lengthy missionary tours, both East and West, to capture followers from Strang, Brigham Young, and Rigdon. He met, for example, with the Strangites in Pittsburgh led by J. M. Grieg, who later wrote to Strang of McLellin's visit:

I thought it important that you should know that "Scrutator's Angel" [McLellin] has recently favored this region of country with a visit, professedly to confirm the appointment of one David Whitmer to the successorship of Joseph Smith in the Seer's office; but really to boost himself into notoriety, and get subscribers to the Ensign of Liberty. I will give you some specimens of his statements here and in Brighton, that you may judge of his work and its probable influence upon the minds of the saints here—premising that in Brighton as well as in this place he had the privilege of saying all that he would to the saints. We gave up our meeting to him in both places, that he might deliver his message. I have not room to give but a few of [McLellin's] many queer and contradictory statements[:] "I cannot be mistaken (said he) about the history of the church, for I have a *good memory.*" But when asked how he came to join G. M. Hinkle, and afterwards, by special revelation, go 500 miles to join S. Rigdon, if he witnessed the appointment and ordination of David Whitmer to the Seer's office? his answer was—

"I forgot it."

"Joseph Smith had no power or authority to lead the church after 1834."

"No man can understand the Book of Doctrine and Covenants unless familiar with all the circumstances under which it was written."

The above are fair samples of his teaching. The effect of such teaching with the brethren of this place has been only to strengthen and confirm them in the truth. There is an old saying that, "Give the Devil rope enough and he will hang himself." We gave McLellin all the rope he asked for, and he has snarled himself up so badly that Oliver's revelations about Voree will never be able to straighten him up. I would advise the saints, whenever Mc. or any of the "immortal trio" at Kirtland [McLellin, Martin Harris, and Leonard Rich] visit them, to keep them talking. Only encourage them to talk and they will talk the "truth all to pieces."[47]

Grieg's letter was probably indicative of general response to McLellin's traveling ministry, given the early demise of McLellin's Church of Christ in late 1849.

On a western tour McLellin spent nearly a week with the Whitmers in Richmond, probably to press David Whitmer into action as church prophet. In publishing his record of the visit, however, McLellin told nothing of his main purpose in going there. At most, he was able to say of the visit: "Union of feeling, and harmony of action, governed our every movement. Brethren and friends, let me say to you, 'All is right, all is well,' with those witnesses."[48]

James J. Strang lost no time in chiding McLellin for being so evasive about his critical contacts with the Whitmers. He caustically honed in on McLellin's vexing leadership problem:

> off posts Wm. E. on a journey of four months to visit Whitmer and converse face to face, and returns without one scrap from him, and not even the assurance that he will accept the station of prophet. We have for a long time suspected that Whitmer and Cowdery[49] did not lend themselves to Mc.'s humbug, and now we are more assured of it than ever. If all was union and harmony, *what* was done so harmoniously? . . . If Wm. E. McLellin could have got ONE SINGLE WORD from David Whitmer or Oliver Cowdery, wherewith to prop up his cause, he would have made speed to give it the greatest possible publicity.[50]

Allowing for Strang's antipathy toward McLellin, one must still wonder just what transpired between McLellin and the Missouri recipients of his September 1847 visit. Not until August 1849—the last issue of the *Ensign of Liberty*—did McLellin report anything of substance regarding his encounter with the Whitmers. And what McLellin wrote confirms why he had said so little about the events before; his Missouri venture had failed:

> 1. The meeting members were McLellin, David Whitmer, John Whitmer, Jacob Whitmer, and Hiram Page. Four of them administered to David Whitmer for "strength to do his duty."
>
> 2. They approved the revelation given McLellin on February 10, 1847 at Kirtland, which provided for rebaptisms, reconfirmations, and reordinations to all who wished to unite with the Church of Christ.

3. Four revelations through David Whitmer were received, mostly directing McLellin to continue his work back at Kirtland, which included writing to expose the errors of apostasy in the various schismatic groups. The Whitmers and Page were enjoined to stay in Missouri against the day when they should reclaim their inheritances in Zion.

4. David Whitmer saw a vision in which McLellin was to possess a beautiful chest filled with precious things: wisdom and knowledge from God. This confirmed to McLellin a similar vision he had in April 1844 concerning these gifts to himself.

5. Acting on the pattern noted in paragraph 2 they rebaptized, reconfirmed, and reordained each other, including David Whitmer "to all the gifts and callings to which he had been appointed through Joseph Smith, in the general assembly of the inhabitants of Zion in July 1834" but *not* to be prophet and president of McLellin's Church of Christ.[51]

From this event the irrepressible McLellin could see the grave implications of that September meeting for his future. No wonder he had not cared to publish this record before. The closer he studied what had happened, the longer it took him to deal with the reality of his ultimate rebuff. The Whitmers had treated him with civility, even hospitality. But there was no mistaking their intent. They would not yield to McLellin's ingratiating presence and pressure among them. If it took four revelations and a vision to send McLellin away reasonably happy, then so be it. Back to Kirtland he had gone in 1847, hoping to keep alive his tiny, struggling band of dissenters.

McLellin's flagging hope for David Whitmer's seership vanished as he read, published in the August issue of the *Olive Branch*—the periodical of the James C. Brewster-Hazen Aldrich Church of Christ also at Kirtland—Hiram Page's letter of June 24, 1849. Page, speaking for himself and his Whitmer relatives in Richmond, renounced whatever of value to McLellin that might have transpired in the "conference" of September 1847. Page acknowledged McLellin's honorable motives in trying to affirm the Whitmers as good and honest people. The Whitmers, however, took exception to McLellin's claim of direction by the Holy Spirit in coming there and insisting that they organize in some church capacity. Page saw through to the center of McLellin's objective: "but it must come through him, which would give a sanction to all that he had done, which would give a more speedy rise to the cause than anything else could; and by our holding him up, he could build up the church according to its true order, which would be a source of consolation to us. But we had not as yet come to an understanding, but consented to the organization after *three days successive entreaties*. Now we acknowledge that the organization *was not in accordance* with the order of the Gospel Church."[52]

McLellin's Missouri heroes had resolutely distanced themselves from him, to the point that his claims to credibility were severely impaired. He could not make a career out of condemning Latter Day Saint apostates, so his wisest course would be to shift the focus of his life. In 1849 he retreated from the scene of religious debate and apology, moved to Linden, Michigan, and pursued his medical profession.

Mormonism was at the center of McLellin's being, however, and seemed to signal him now and then to reenter the fray whenever events caught his attention. Such an event was the coming of Joseph Smith III to the prophetic office of the Reorganized Church of Jesus Christ of Latter Day Saints in April 1860. In his inaugural address on April 6 young Smith had affirmed some things about his father and about early Mormon history. Smith's statements differed radically from what McLellin remembered and had written so vehemently back in the 1840s.

McLellin read the address as well as many other writings of Reorganization leaders. He thought about what to do and finally, on January 10, 1861, he wrote to Smith with the aim of educating the young prophet. The long letter's primary teaching points were:

1. The church should never have had two priesthoods, as the levitical priesthood was strictly Old Testament.

2. Christ was the last and great high priest; there was no need for any later high priests at any time. High priests in the Restoration were added later, not meant to be a part of the original church structure.

3. Joseph Smith, Jr., taught and practiced polygamy. All young Smith needed to do on this point was ask his mother, who had told McLellin during his trip to Nauvoo in 1847 that this was so.

4. Joseph Smith, Jr., was not as good a man as his son had proclaimed him to be on April 6, 1860.

5. Joseph Smith, Jr. died indebted ($200,000) from ruinous financial speculations.

6. The church under Joseph Smith, Jr., strayed from the original pure teachings. The Twelve in Utah represented today what was taught in the last years of his life.

7. The *Doctrine and Covenants* was an inferior work to the *Book of Commandments*.

8. Proper church leadership should be clothed with apostolic power. Joseph Smith III had no credentials along that line.

9. So many factions had risen and fallen, McLellin asked, what is it about the Reorganization that would equip it to survive?[53]

There is no evidence that Joseph Smith III answered McLellin's letter. How seriously he took McLellin's instruction can be guessed from the fact that, by his own admission, he never spoke with his mother on the polygamy question until February 1879. This was in spite of a second letter from McLellin received in 1872 that urged him, among other things, to ask Emma Smith about the matter.

Another evidence of McLellin's continuing interest in Mormonism was his letter to the editor of the *Truth Teller,* a periodical of Granville Hedrick's group in Independence. Writing in 1864 from his Michigan home, McLellin advanced the idea that the singular hallmark of ordained ministry in every age was the process of direct revelation between God and the minister.[54] McLellin did not argue with anything said in the periodical; he simply shared his insights. The editor printed his letter without comment.

The next evidence of McLellin's reviving interest in Mormonism was his announcement that he had united with Granville Hedrick's small group in Independence. Writing from Brownsville, Missouri, on July 12, 1869, McLellin told a friend why he had become a "Hedrickite":

In the first place he delivered a number of prophecies which have already come to pass. So his friends who heard him declare. I could tell you what they were—but no matter now. . . . They go back on the original principles as taught at first in 1830 and up to 1834 when they declare that Jos. fell. Dont you know that I published in the "Ensign" in 1847 that Jos. fell in 1834. . . . We set aside all extras as doctrine or principle which cannot be sustained by the New Testament, and that *inestimable inspired* book of Mormon. I went up to Independence to attend their conference which was to have been the 28 of May, but was put off until the 4th of June. They had meetings every day between the 28 and the 4th. So I had a good opportunity to investigate. And I set and said nothing during the meeting & conference, but on the 5th I stated to them precisely my position, that I was willing to believe Hedrick was a Prophet, and the church had chosen him to preside over the whole church, and I was willing to take him to preside. I heard, after he got there on the 1st, a great deal of his teaching, and of his decisions, I was willing to admit I could see wisdom in them. Hence I united with them.[55]

McLellin also preached his first sermon in nearly twenty years at He-drick's conference on June 6, 1869. Hedrick was more than pleased. While at the conference McLellin decided to move to Independence. Although he referred to his wife as "not very pious, or spiritual mind-ed," she "is willing to go with me to Zion." He bought a frame home near the Independence square for $1,500 and moved into it a few weeks later.[56]

McLellin's union with Hedrick's group lasted only a few months. He left the group on November 3, 1869. Near the same time his wife joined the Reorganized Church. In February 1870 he wrote about his feelings for Hedrick's group: "There are some fifteen or twenty of us here who cannot go with the Hedrick party. They are in reality noth-ing but Latter Day Saints. True they dont hold to polygamy, but they hold to many wild notions of that *infamous ism.*" He seemed to lean once again toward David Whitmer's presidency, having recently writ-ten and read to Whitmer his considered view on that matter. McLellin wanted to publish strong claims to prophethood for Whitmer, but Whitmer was not sanguine. He told him to do it only if McLellin "would publish it under [his] own signature."[57] An echo of the sum-mer of 1847, to be sure.

McLellin's dissent in his final years was primarily in the form of written letters, both private and public, against the claims of the Re-organized Church. There was an apparent anomaly, for both Reorga-nization missionaries and McLellin were constantly jousting with Utah Mormons. Common ground? No. McLellin fought them because he believed that their doctrines, stemming mostly from Joseph Smith, Jr., were false. Reorganized Church missionaries also fought them not only because they believed that their doctrines were false, but also as much because they said those doctrines were never taught or practiced by Joseph Smith, Jr.. So McLellin read Reorganized Church periodicals and tracts and went into his warring mode because Joseph Smith III and his followers simply did not know their history. Or even worse, if they did, they lied about it.

McLellin's approach would be to use his old ideas from the *Ensign of Liberty* magazines and rewrite them to meet the new challenges. The basic points of argument did not change greatly. He proceeded from a clear and deeply felt bias, expressed succinctly in a letter he wrote in October 1870:

I have been reading and writing most of the summer and fall so far I have quite a book of manuscript, expect to publish it some day but shall not until I get spiritual minded brethren around me to read and scan each treatise. I want it to contain pure truth and nothing else. I have five foolscap pages, reviewing [Davis H.] Bays and [Isaac] Sheen. And I have not spared! I perfectly dispise their miserable misrepresentations. I cant believe them honest, or that they want to know the truth. I tell you I *know* Josephism is built on a flimsy, sandy foundation, and God's truth will wash all the sand from under it! All Latter Day-ism is nothing on earth but sectarianism!![58]

McLellin also expressed a growing closeness to David Whitmer, spending time with the little Whitmer fellowship, where he felt the word of God to his soul. He rejoiced in not having contention with any sect or party, but simply basking in the presence of God. In this sense McLellin did not view his running letters of debate with Reorganization representatives as contention. Rather, he was simply enlightening those who walked in darkness. It was not his mission to convert and baptize "Josephites." He was only intent on setting the record straight and, having done that, waiting for more questions to explore from differing perspectives.

In this context, McLellin wrote letters to various inquirers, or to writers whose published views were offensive to the truth as McLellin saw it. Upward of a dozen of such letters are either on file in Reorganized Church Library-Archives or were published in the *Saints' Herald* during the 1870s. Most deal with the same issues, hobbies McLellin had been riding for much of his adult life. By the 1870s his dissenting voice, although strident and at times boringly repetitious, had lost whatever appeal it might have had to open-minded investigators. He had become a crank. When he died at his Independence home on April 24, 1883, few mourned his passing. McLellin was indeed Mormonism's stormy petrel: moody, blustery, self-absorbed beyond words to tell, yet an indefatigable crusader for the relative truths he knew as absolute truth.

NOTES

1. Dale L. Morgan, "A Bibliography of the Churches of the Dispersion," *Western Humanities Review* 7 (Summer 1953): 116.

2. McLellin was at that time a school teacher in Paris; a wife, Cynthia Anne, whom he had married on July 30, 1829, had recently died. Lyndon W. Cook, *The Revelations of the Prophet Joseph Smith* (Provo: Seventy's Mission Bookstore, 1981), 106–7.

3. William E. and Emiline McLelin to Beloved Relatives [Samuel McLel-

lin], August 4, 1832, Reorganized Church of Jesus Christ of Latter Day Saints
Library-Archives, Independence, Mo. This is a rare instance in which McLellin spells his last name as *McLelin*.

4. William E. and Emiline McLelin to Beloved Relatives.

5. Ibid.

6. *Book of Doctrine and Covenants* (Independence: Herald Publishing House, 1970), sec. 66; *Doctrine and Covenants of the Church of Jesus Christ of Latter-day Saints* (Salt Lake City: Deseret Book Co., 1968), sec. 66, commended McLellin for his repentance and reception of the gospel but urged him to continue the repenting process. Specifically, he was to shun his established temptation to commit adultery. He was also sent on a missionary tour eastward from Kirtland in the company of Samuel H. Smith, brother of Joseph Smith. His reward: "Continue in these things, even unto the end, and you shall have a crown of eternal life at the right hand of my Father, who is full of grace and truth" (sec. 66:12 [LDS]; 66:5g [RLDS]).

7. Donald Q. Cannon and Lyndon W. Cook, eds., *Far West Record: Minutes of the Church of Jesus Christ of Latter-day Saints, 1830–1844* (Salt Lake City: Deseret Book Co., 1983), 14.

8. "History of Joseph Smith," *Times and Seasons* [Nauvoo, Ill.], April 15, 1844, 496. Present at this special conference, according to the minutes in *Far West Record*, ed. Cannon and Cook, were "Joseph Smith, Jun., Oliver Cowdery, David Whitmer, John Whitmer, Peter Whitmer, Jun., Sidney Rigdon, William E. M'Lellin, Orson Hyde, Luke Johnson, Lyman E. Johnson" (15).

9. *Book of Doctrine and Covenants*, sec. 68:1; *Doctrine and Covenants of the Church of Jesus Christ of Latter-day Saints*, sec. 68:1–12.

10. *Book of Doctrine and Covenants*, sec. 75:2; *Doctrine and Covenants of the Church of Jesus Christ of Latter-day Saints*, sec. 75:6–11.

11. Emeline Miller was born on September 4, 1819, in Vermont. She and McLellin were married for many years and had three known children: Helen, William Clark, and Marcus W. Of this event, Joseph Smith, Jr., wrote to his wife, Emma Smith, on June 6, 1832: "I am not pleased to hear that William McLelin has come back and disobeyed the voice of him who is altogether Lovely for a woman[.] I am astonished at Sister Emaline yet I cannot belive she is not a worthy sister[.] I hope She will find him true and kind to her but have no reason to expect it[,] his Conduct merits the disapprobation of every true believer of Christ." Letter in Mormon Collection, Chicago Historical Society, and also published in LaMar C. Berrett, "An Impressive Letter from the Pen of Joseph Smith," *Brigham Young University Studies* 11 (Summer 1971): 517–23.

12. Joseph Smith, Jr., "History, 1832," December 3, 1832, in *The Personal Writings of Joseph Smith*, ed. Dean C. Jessee (Salt Lake City: Deseret Book Co., 1984), 17.

13. *Book of Doctrine and Covenants*, sec. 87:8c; *Doctrine and Covenants of the Church of Jesus Christ of Latter-day Saints*, sec. 90:35. McLellin had settled in Independence on June 16, 1832.

14. Joseph Smith, *The History of the Church of Jesus Christ of Latter-day Saints*, ed. B. H. Roberts (Salt Lake City: Deseret Book Co., 1965), 2:190–91.

15. Cook, *Revelations of the Prophet Joseph Smith,* 107.

16. On this important topic see Marvin S. Hill, "Cultural Crisis in the Mormon Kingdom: A Reconsideration of the Causes of Kirtland Dissent," *Church History* 49 (September 1980): 286–97.

17. Cannon and Cook, eds., *Far West Record,* 160. All of the apostles except William Smith, the prophet's brother, were later cut off from the church.

18. Ibid., 3:31–32n.

19. *Missouri Republican,* November 10, 1838, quoted in Stephen C. LeSueur, *The 1838 Mormon War in Missouri* (Columbia: University of Missouri Press, 1987), 180.

20. Joseph Smith, Jr., to the Church in Caldwell County, December 16, 1838, in *Times and Seasons* [Nauvoo, Ill.] 1 (April 1840): 82–86.

21. "Conference Minutes," *Ensign* [Buffalo, Iowa] 1 (October 1844): 62.

22. "Our Politics," *Ensign* 1 (August 1844): 30.

23. *Ensign* 1 (August 1844): 31–32.

24. George Hinkle, *Ensign* 1 (October 1844): 57–59.

25. William E. McLellin to President S. Rigdon, December 23, 1844, in *Latter Day Saints' Messenger and Advocate* [Pittsburgh], January 15, 1845, 91–92.

26. William E. McLellin to Brother [Samuel] Bennett, March 15, 1845, *Latter Day Saints' Messenger and Advocate,* March 15, 1845, 149–51.

27. By this time McLellin favored the name "Church of Christ" as the only acceptable title for followers of Christ. As he moved into Rigdonism, his influence on this matter seems apparent. Rigdon's periodical henceforth became *Messenger and Advocate of the Church of Christ.*

28. "Conference Minutes," *Messenger and Advocate of the Church of Christ,* April 15, 1845, 169, 176.

29. Hinkle, writing in April 1845, told his followers in Buffalo, Iowa, of what was in effect a merger between his group and Rigdon's Church of Christ. He also stated that all differences that had arisen between himself and McLellin no longer existed and that full confidence between them had been restored. *Ensign* 1 (April 1845): 156–57.

30. "Conference Minutes," April 7, 1845, in *Messenger and Advocate of the Church of Christ,* April 15, 1845, 169. Rigdon followed this demonstration immediately by nominating Samuel James and Ebenezer Robinson as his counselors in the First Presidency. The conference accepted both unanimously. Had McLellin intended his effusive vow of fealty to Rigdon to make him part of Rigdon's presidency, he must have been disappointed at the result.

31. *Messenger and Advocate of the Church of Christ,* May 1, 1845, 185–86.

32. "Conference Minutes," *Messenger and Advocate of the Church of Christ,* April 15, 1845, 168, 17, and May 1, 1845, 189.

33. David Pettegrew letter to *Times and Seasons,* May 1, 1845, 892–93.

34. William E. McLellin letter, *Messenger and Advocate of the Church of Christ,* July 1, 1845, 253.

35. Two McLellin letters telling of his labors that summer appear in the

Messenger and Advocate of the Church of Christ, July 15, 1845, 267–68, and August 15, 1845, 302–3 (see 315–16 for Newton's letter).

36. *Messenger and Advocate of the Church of Christ,* 1 (May 1846): 463.

37. Ibid., 463–64.

38. *Ensign of Liberty, of the Church of Christ* [Kirtland, Ohio, cited hereafter as *Ensign of Liberty*] 1 (May 1848): 90–91.

39. William E. McLellin to My Old and much Respected Friend [Dr. J. C. Bennett], August 14–18, 1846, in *Gospel Herald* [Voree, Wis.], December 2, 1847, 161.

40. William E. McLellin to Dear Doctor [Dr. J. C. Bennett], September 30, 1846, in *Gospel Herald,* December 2, 1847, 165.

41. William E. McLellin to Pres. J. J. Strang, September 27, 1846, in *Gospel Herald,* December 2, 1847, 165.

42. William E. McLellin to Pres. J. J. Strang, 166.

43. William E. McLellin to My old, well tried, and beloved friend, David Whitmer, December 2, 1846. McLellin, not hearing from Whitmer for many weeks, published the letter in *Ensign of Liberty* 1 (April 1847): 18–19.

44. William E. McLellin to David Whitmer, 19–20, emphasis in the original.

45. William E. McLellin, report of his committee to a conference of the Church of Christ at Kirtland, Ohio, February 6, 1847, in *Ensign of Liberty* 1 (March 1847): 2–13, summary and excerpts; emphasis in the original.

46. *Ensign of Liberty* 1 (April 1847): 29–32. The attack discredited the "letter of appointment" by Joseph Smith of June 18, 1844, Strang's angelic ordination, and his claims to having produced translations of ancient sacred writings.

47. "Extracts of Letters," *Gospel Herald,* October 7, 1847, 118–19.

48. William E. McLellin, "Our Apology—And Our Tours," *Ensign of Liberty* 1 (December 1847): 34–35.

49. McLellin had seen Oliver Cowdery at the latter's home near Voree the previous July, not in Richmond in September.

50. "David Whitmer, Ensign of Liberty, and McLellinism," *Gospel Herald,* January 13, 1848, 197. Strang challenged Whitmer to stop playing this waiting game, to publicize his position openly. "If he thinks he is a prophet, let him say it, and we will publish it. . . . If ye be honest men, speak."

51. William E. McLellin, "Our Tour West in 1847," *Ensign of Liberty* 1 (August 1849): 99–105.

52. Hiram Page to Alfred Bonny, Isaac N. Aldrich, M. C. Ishem, June 24, 1849, in *Olive Branch* 2 (August 1849): 27–29 (editor's commentary on 30). In more specific terms Page rejected, among other things, (1) the office of high priest; (2) the office of seer, stating the endowment is the work of the Holy Spirit to all who join the Church of Christ; and (3) the idea of the gathering of saints to a single center. In commenting on the letter, the editor notes that Page's stated position should thoroughly discredit McLellin, whom he described as "our most violent opposer" since the Brewster-Aldrich Church of Christ began in Kirtland in June 1848.

53. William E. McLellin to Joseph Smith, January 10, 1861, Reorganized Church Library-Archives.

54. He now spelled his name *McLellan* and did so consistently the rest of his life. Much earlier he had occasionally spelled it *McLelin.* Some early church records show his name as *M'Lellin.*

55. William E. McLellan to Our Very Dear Friends, July 12, 1869, Reorganized Church Library-Archives.

56. Ibid.

57. William E. McLellan, letter fragment (bottom of page 2 missing) to My Dear Friends, February 1870, Miscellaneous Letters and Papers, Reorganized Church Library-Archives.

58. William E. McLellan to My dear old friends, October 21 and 25, 1870, Reorganized Church Library-Archives.

4

The Fruit of the Branch: Francis Gladden Bishop and His Culture of Dissent

Richard L. Saunders

From its inception, the revelatory tradition in Mormonism engendered strife. The doctrine of modern, continuing revelation, begun by Joseph Smith and accepted by most groups claiming descent, leaves social order open to counterclaims that strike at the heart of ecclesiastical order. If one person may speak for God, why may not another? By claiming an ongoing dialogue with divinity, Joseph Smith opened the door to a social force he could barely control and eroded his religious authority.

The history of Mormonism is full of individuals who followed the prophetic tradition began by Joseph Smith. One individual who received little attention, even from his peers, was Francis Gladden Bishop. The progress of his life is a good illustration of personal religious opinions being given precedence over the doctrines and practices of the larger religious culture. Bishop's history also stands as an example of the tensions bred in Mormonism as the latter sought to establish cultural and ecclesiastical order—imposing a control structure upon the acceptable dynamics of revelation.[1]

Bishop was born the third son of Isaac Gates and Mary Hyde Bishop January 19, 1809, in Livonia, New York, about a hundred miles west and south of Palmyra. His parents were Methodists, a pietistic and evangelical sect, and raised their family with the strictures expected of believing parentage. Family Bible reading steeped Bishop in the prophecy and narrative of the book and initiated a life-long affinity for Holy Scripture.[2] So great was the impact of the Holy Writ upon young Bishop that in later life contemporary events became meaningful only if they could be interpreted to match some scriptural passage. It was also early in life that Francis Bishop assumed an interpretive structure of scriptural literalism. This literalist view later expanded to apply not just to scripture, but to virtually all that Bishop experienced, dictating his view of events and assigning meaning to the world's complexities. The Bible—more importantly, his interpretation of it—became the foundation of his worldview. He accepted the volume as absolutely authoritative and as literal truth divinely manifest.

Bishop was a product of the recurring sweep of religious revivals that characterized the Burned-Over District. By 1825 the cycle of revivalism begun by the evangelist Charles G. Finney had blazed near the Bishop home in Greece, just west of Rochester, New York. Caught in the spirit of the time, sixteen-year-old Francis made a public profession of Christian faith, and in 1826, four months after his seventeenth birthday, he received the first of several important visions to which he would refer in later life.

Relating the experience three decades later, of being "engaged in solemn prayer to God," he became insensible to his surroundings. Before him appeared a wall with an open doorway, allowing through it a brilliant light. Through this opening three persons passed into view. The trio looked on the boy and smiled, then ascended to the aperture and passed from view. Immediately, a different personage appeared. This individual, said Bishop, came "as a man." He, too, smiled on the boy. The vision closed; released back into consciousness, Francis Bishop contemplated the meaning and significance of what he had just experienced.[3]

Rather than having a clear understanding of what had happened, he was left to interpret value and significance from not much more than memory and his belief in the vision's actuality. It was not until after an indeterminate "later" that the vision's significance was comprehended. Francis finally concluded that the first three figures had been angels, while "by an impulse of the same character, I saw [the fourth to be] the Ancient of Days, of whom I had read in the Prophecy of Daniel."[4] This character, the "Ancient of Days," would become central to Bishop's religious interpretations and later views of contemporary events.

Unfortunately, he never recorded clearly his reasons for assigning this particular identity to the apparition. The impression is given that he had seen a vision but gained nothing more than the experience itself. By so identifying his visitor, the young Francis Bishop demonstrated a detailed knowledge of the Bible sufficient to isolate a distinct prophecy from the middle of the Old Testament that seemed to provide an identification for his visitant. Conversely, he may have matched the figure with an identity only after a period of purposeful study of days, weeks, perhaps even as long a year or two. In either situation, his application of exact scriptural statement is the earliest disclosure of the literalist intellectual process that shaped his later life.

Shortly after this vision, Francis Bishop joined "a society of people, who I believed were Christians."[5] His association was shortlived, however. The Bishop family moved from Greece, south to Allegheny County, after losing their home in 1829, and after another vision Bishop there became a preacher for the Freewill Baptists.

Three years later he converted to the infant "Church of Christ" and was baptized in July 1832.[6] His religious allegiance changed—at least overtly—as he picked up the Mormon banner, and so did the vehicle of his zeal and the social context of his expression. Yet as events would soon prove, his allegiance to the Restored Gospel was crowded aside by the importance of his personal experiences with divinity. In later years, as Bishop reflected upon his early visionary experiences, they gained significance and fostered a self-conviction that he was destined to play an important role in the unfolding latter-day work of God.

Within a few weeks of his baptism and ordination as an elder, a man by the name of Walton presented himself to the branch of the church to which Bishop belonged in Olean Point, New York.[7] Walton claimed he had been sent by Joseph Smith to preside over local congregations with credentials consisting of an ordination as a "High Priest after the order of Melchesedec."[8]

Bishop apparently occupied some position of authority in Olean Point, and the appearance of a rival challenged his influence. In the situation, however, he perceived an opportunity and decided to seek an ordination to the office of high priest himself. This would place him on an authoritative par with Walton and perhaps provide the chance for securing local leadership permanently. In the fall of 1832 Bishop traveled to Kirtland and laid his petition for ordination before a council there. The petition was denied. It was the opinion of the council that "he wanted a high station without meriting it, or without being called by the Spirit of God to that work."[9] Francis Bishop retained the priesthood office to which he had been ordained, that of elder, and returned to the Olean Point area seeking to prove himself as able as he was willing to carry the office and calling of high priest.[10]

Throughout his life Bishop considered himself "an inspired man of God" and his prayers to be of great faith, so there yet remained to his mind a way through the apparent impasse. He addressed his concerns— or made his claim—regarding the priesthood and the church to "the throne of grace." He asked for divine inspiration concerning two issues: a sign concerning the truth of his newly found faith (which, he said, he had begun to doubt), and, more important, he asked for understanding concerning the office of high priest, which Walton boasted and Bishop himself so desired.[11]

Before addressing the results of this query it is important to put Bishop's questions in context. They reveal his mental position and personal ideas as related to the Restoration gospel. The stated intent of his queries and the underlying motivations are, in fact, contradictory. Taken together the questions suggest that Bishop had mentally created a complex disguise for what he was actually concerned about. The first point, that concerning the truth of his new faith, the veracity of the Mormon claim, could have stood independently.[12] If Bishop became satisfied that the Mormons had no authority and were not what they claimed to be, then the second question, concerning "the character of the High Priesthood," was moot. Posing the second question implies that, even before he asked, Bishop had become satisfied with the validity of the Mormon claim. In fact, he wrote of himself in third person as "a man of great faith before God, [therefore] he could not believe himself deceived in this late faith."[13] Bishop had apparently become a believer in Mormonism; his first query may have been a disguise that concealed the motivation of the second.

The way in which his questions were expressed reflected Bishop's interest and attention in position by virtue of ordination as high priest. He had been refused by the church and thus, unable to secure an ordination to the office, he turned to the Lord. Bishop did not seem as concerned about his new-chosen faith as he was about the "nature of the High Priesthood," how the office was given—or gained—and what one could do with it. Asking for a demonstration of the validity of the Mormon cause was a guise to soften asking God outright to provide an ordination that could not be had otherwise. The undercurrent of what Bishop seemed to be asking was that he saw in the office of high priest an opportunity for the advancement of personal status and for movement toward assuming the significant position signified by his visionary "callings." Because ordination had been refused, how might the ecclesiastical order be circumvented? His questions implied that Bishop sought only a specific answer, one that would raise his social status and fit a preconceived idea of his cosmic importance. The response he received to his two questions satisfied the most personally important matter and served as the foundation of his later career as a schismatic leader in Mormon history.

While he was praying one night soon after, a messenger appeared at Bishop's bedside. Without introduction the being approached Bishop, placed his hands on the supplicant's head, and said solemnly, "I ordain you a High Priest." Having thus spoken, the visitant disappeared, and Bishop was caught away in a vision. He found himself seated on a throne with a crown on his head and a sword in his right hand. The visitor informed him that "this"—meaning the throne, crown, and sword—"is the power of the High Priesthood!" This action, Bishop later explained, was to teach him the character of the ordination that he had just received and which he examined exhaustively in his writings. At the same time, he was also told that Joseph Smith had fallen as a prophet and was rejected and that he, Bishop, would soon lead the church.[14]

Bishop wrote years later of being innocently unaware of the visit's grand significance. Actually, his writings suggest that in 1832 he had little or no idea of the meaning behind what had transpired. To fill the void Bishop again turned to his understandings and interpretations of the scriptures for an inspirational catalyst: searching the prophetic passages of the Old Testament, filtering his experience through scriptural prophecy, and fitting them to himself and his experiences. By virtue of his study, "the prophecies," he later wrote, "regarding the man, called the Branch, and also Elijah the prophet to come, and restore all things, were unfolded to me by *Divine* revelation."[15] For the first time, Bishop claimed to be "the Branch" spoken of in the Old Testament book of Zechariah. Drawing his ordination into line with the self-appointed significance of previous visions, he appears to have begun constructing a *Weltanschauung* in which he was not only a part but also moving rapidly toward the center.

As Bishop noised about his new authority, he was shortly summoned again to Kirtland to explain this ordination and "calling."[16] Thus confronted, he confessed his error but also used the occasion to relate a vision of 1826. He was told that "it was a matter of importance, and . . . I should yet understand it, as it regarded myself," but no interpretation was officially offered.[17] None was needed. Although to the council the young man's experience was one of many dreams and visions, for Francis Bishop the vision was a sacred appointment that set him apart from his peers. Regardless of the official position of church leaders, he had settled on his own interpretation and had already preached of his divine calling. Only months into his decade-long career in the Mormon church, the path into the future was marked for the young elder. He would wait for the Lord's call to further action, but Francis Bishop's mindset had become fixed and would change little in the next decade. Although he continued to partake in the Mormon cultural experience, his mental priorities and doctrinal values appeared little influenced by official teachings. Although it provided an environment, Mormonism did not really become a part of him. Rather, he assimilated its values and ideals as selectively as he had his previous experiences.

In the spring of 1833 Bishop was dispatched as a missionary. Over the next decade he served almost constantly in that capacity, traveling from Maine to North Carolina and from the East Coast to Tennessee. During this time Bishop remained virtually unsupervised and, although he was a missionary of the Restoration, Bishops's interpretations of scripture and Mormon doctrines often testified as much of his own calling as of the church's. He was first a missionary of his own call. His propensity to preach his own doctrine and scriptural interpretations were the source of constant irritation.

In early April of 1835, the leadership in Kirtland received a letter from one Gibson Smith, complaining about Bishop's religious teachings. The accusatory information in the letter prompted Kirtland High Council clerks Orson Hyde and William McLellin to post a suspension notice in the April 15 issue of the *Messenger and Advocate*. Smith's letter does not survive, but the charges he proffered against Bishop, surmised from existing records, concerned Bishop's doctrinal speculations and scriptural interpretations. Bishop yet harbored the love of concentrating on the "mysteries of the Kingdom" and a very literal interpretation of scripture. The published suspension notice specifically mentioned Bishop's stated view on one of his favorite subjects, his identity as one of the "two witnesses" in chapter 11 of the Revelation of St. John. Bishop was tried before the Quorum of Twelve Apostles and before the Kirtland High Council, again confessed his error, and was restored to active membership.

Despite his acknowledgment of error, Francis Bishop continued to indulge his personal beliefs about his early visions, which strongly influenced his interpretations of Mormon doctrine. From his visions he was committed to the idea that he fit high into the divine plan—somehow. But by 1835 his visionary "calling" had not yet coalesced into a clear destiny. Bishop was thus caught trying on prophetic stations (the "two witnesses"), seeking by trial and error the one into which he was destined to fit. Throughout his life, he clung steadfastly to his mental vision-sanctioned realities and used them like a sculptor uses an armature—as a foundation, a primary point of reference and direction—in determining his interpretation of scriptural "reality." These he fleshed out with the clay of Restoration doctrines, but the design was his own. What he taught as a missionary was Mormonism on the surface, but under that veneer lay the core of Bishop's own values. Between 1833 and the 1835 trials Francis Bishop had begun to test his call, feeling about for the niche that he believed the Lord had prepared for him.

In 1836, Bishop returned to Kirtland to receive the initial rites of the endowment at the Solemn Assembly following the dedication of the temple. Soon after, he departed for a flurry of brief missions and in the next three years preached in Washington, D.C., Pennsylvania, and Maryland. He continued his cycle of preaching interspersed with return trips to Kirtland until the summer of 1838, when he was laboring in Patrick County, Virginia, along the North Carolina border.

Early in 1839, as the Mormons were being driven from Missouri, persecution began in North Carolina. To give some positive attention to the Saints, Bishop wrote a manuscript that touched lightly on the rise of the church and tried to address the particular persecutions in Missouri from the Mormon perspective. The bulk of the work, a broad defense of the principles of American religious liberty, was more suited to his talents at emotive writing than at history. The draft was set in type and published under the title of "A Brief History of the Church of the Jesus Christ of Latter Day Saints," one of the first published nondoctrinal defenses of the young church and probably the first nonperiodical published history.[18]

Bishop concluded his missionizing and moved to Nauvoo some time before 1841 to occupy a home and lot directly north of the temple lot. Near the beginning of March 1842, Reynolds Cahoon, a member of the temple committee, happened to be at the temple site. While there he called at the Bishop home and chanced upon Bishop reading to his neighbors "something which he himself had written, illustrative of his Patriarchal blessing, and his Divine calling as the Branch, as sustained by the [scriptures]."[19] Cahoon lodged a charge against Bishop before the High Council. Although there is no record of the specific content of Bishop's text, Cahoon's charges and the trial record suggested that he was representing his work as revelation or doctrine and had placed it on an authoritative par with the pronouncements of Joseph Smith, acting as the prophet of the Lord and president of the church.

The charge centered on Bishop having publicized revelations and doctrines at variance with official teachings of the church.[20] To Francis, his work represented a harmless personal attempt to comprehend a patriarchal blessing he had received in Kirtland. To an outside observer, however, it appears that Bishop was trying to square his interpretation of Holy Writ to his perceived call and divine appointment. His action demonstrates that Bishop had not, even after a decade in the church, surrendered his belief in the authority of his early visions and regarded them as superior to the prophetic declarations of the prophet he claimed to follow. Although they had been labeled as false by that prophet, to Bishop they were still valid and yet marked a call to greatness. When previously confronted about these odd beliefs, Bishop himself had admitted a number of times, vocally at least, that he had been in error. Evidently, such acknowledgments were short-lived, a more certain assurance of truth being given to Bishop by the memory of his own experiences.

Once again, before a church council, at its insistence and understandably with some trepidation, Bishop produced and read parts of his revelations and written reflections on his call as "the Branch." From these pages he read "that he [Bishop] should yet lead the church; and that whosoever opposed him in his divine calling, would be Anathema, Maranatha." He must have been highly offended at the council's response: "the whole mass . . . appeared to be the extreme of folly, nonsense, absurdity, falsehood and bombastic egotism—so much so as to keep the Saints laughing, when not overcome by sorrow and shame."[21] It was Brigham Young's opinion that the reasoning was nonsense.[22] Even before Francis Bishop finished, it was clear that the elder who had once been rebuked before the School of the Prophets for so eagerly seeking a high priest's office had not since aligned his personal beliefs with accepted doctrines. His writings were testimony of that fact.

Ridiculous and incriminating as Bishop's scriptural interpretations seemed to the other council members, his friend and Nauvoo Stake president, William Marks, moved that the charges be dropped. With this motion on the table Joseph Smith addressed the council and illustrated the potential problems associated with heresy. After others had added their views, the High Council voted unanimously that the heretic be removed from membership in the Church of Jesus Christ of Latter-day Saints. The symbols of Bishop's offense, his writings, were committed to the coals of the fireplace; the gathered faces reflected a momentary brightening of flame, and the leaves were consumed.[23]

Two months after his excommunication, Francis Bishop placed an advertisement in the local paper, the *Wasp,* giving notice of his intent to leave Nauvoo and his desire to sell his two lots and houses.[24] After the sale advertisement appeared, William Marks and Hyrum Smith privately counselled Bishop to remain in the city, expressing confidence that the affair would blow over and that he could rejoin the church.[25] Had he accepted their advice, he may have rejoined and so remained more anonymous to history. While Bishop was waiting to close out his business in Nauvoo, revelations began again. This was the call to action for which he had waited so long.

In the spring or early summer of 1842 he was informed by "a promise of the Lord" to expect another visit from one of the three individuals who had visited him years before. Shortly after, while Bishop "was in the Spirit," an odd visitor who had recently requested to board a few days with the Bishops returned, stripped of mortal disguise, bringing instructions and information. Bishop's visitor gave his name as Nephi and claimed to be the same angel who had delivered to Joseph Smith the gold Book of Mormon plates. Bishop was informed that Christ's twelve apostles were elders, not high priests; that "Nephi" and his two companions had appeared in 1829 to Joseph and Oliver Cowdery as Peter, James, and John to appoint them apostles; and that those three, with John the Revelator, were the four angels of Revelation 7:1. John and the other two of the quartet soon appeared. After being instructed by them about the Book of Mormon and Bishop's impending responsibility in bringing forth the "work of the Father," Nephi returned with an admonition to fast and prepare to receive "seven sacred things."[26]

The next afternoon, Bishop retired alone for prayer and solemnly awaited the promised vision. He was not disappointed. Soon Nephi returned to present before him the gold plates from which Joseph Smith had translated the Book of Mormon and, curiously, the initial 116 pages of the Book of Mormon manuscript that the scribe Martin Harris had lost. Also exhibited was a sword taken from a Book of Mormon character named Laban, which represented the justice and wrath of God; the Urim and Thummim, or interpreters (a pair of seer stones) that Joseph Smith used to translate the Book of Mormon; a breastplate belonging to Moroni (the last Book of Mormon prophet and custodian of the plates); a ball-like brass compass, the Liahona or Directors, that had guided Lehi's party through the Arabian desert in the Book of Mormon; and a pair of interlocking crowns Bishop identified as the Crown of Israel and the Crown of Glory.

Through the next week Nephi returned repeatedly to display the sacred items. At the end of the appointed week Bishop was transported in vision to the throne of the Ancient of Days and there crowned.[27] He had now received the call to the greater work that for a decade he had been awaiting. These Nauvoo visions also provided or clarified the identity that he had sought in his claim as one of the "two witnesses." The balance of his life was dedicated to the attempt at realizing the greatness of his call.

The construction of Mormon Nauvoo and doctrinal developments in the church progressed oblivious to Bishop and his new-found authority. Finding himself ignored, he proceeded to do what other prophets had done when disregarded—he preached. He preached publicly but not widely in the city, foretelling the destruction of the temple and the driving of the saints into the wilderness. He was also given a chance to preach formally to the church, but without much success. It was around this time, probably privately, that he for the first time gathered a few believers around him and organized the "Kingdom of God."[28]

Francis Bishop and wife Irena left Nauvoo to settle temporarily in Augusta, still in the county, late in 1842. A year later he wrote to Joseph Smith, asking if he might be readmitted to church membership. His attitude was "I have been a good member of the Church," yet he understood that the motivation for the separation lay in his personal ideas. He did not apologize for or compromise his beliefs. Bishop maintained that his doctrines were his own and of no threat to the church he had served; he believed what he taught but supposed that neither his doctrine nor personal beliefs made any difference to the Saints. What Bishop ignored was that his was a theology intended to supplant, not supplement. He acknowledged that his "greater things" superseded those revealed through Joseph Smith. In Augusta, "exiled from Zion," he asked to be reinstated as a member of the church in good standing; if he could not, then Bishop asked that "no one called a Saint oppose me."[29]

For the next few years Francis Bishop remains untraceable. Then, some time during 1847, he received the divine commission to commence his work anew. One of the few clues Bishop offers relating to his activities was a cryptic remark that he had been instrumental in seven different movements in as many years. This action, he explained in retrospect, represented the seven dispensations of the earth's existence.[30] Less coincidentally, it was the number of failed followings Bishop began between 1847 and 1854. Unfortunately, he himself left little record of them. Details of three of the seven leadership attempts are known at least in part: one begun and abandoned in Voree, Wisconsin; another in Kirtland, Ohio; and his most successful one was in Council Bluffs, Iowa. The others remain as yet unknown to history.

Francis arrived in Voree, the home of James J. Strang's following, in response to a sarcastic challenge by the Wisconsin prophet in the spring of 1848.[31] He set about preaching of his divine call but attracted few to his claims. Bishop's doctrine had taken a step beyond his earlier supposition that he might be one of the "two witnesses." His preaching centered on the positions of the two witnesses spoken of in Revelation 11:3 and the olive trees of Zechariah 4:11. These, he claimed, were one and the same, the prophets who would come before the return of Jesus Christ at the opening of the Millennium. He identified the witnesses as Oliver Cowdery (who was living and practicing law close by but had been excommunicated a decade previous) and Joseph Smith, whom James Strang had been appointed to replace since his death.[32] The witnesses held only the Lesser or Aaronic priesthood and served as forerunners to himself, to "make his path straight" as John the Baptist had prepared the way for Christ. Bishop's 1832 ordination by the Ancient of Days and his Nauvoo visitations expanded his personal role as he claimed for himself the custodial care of the

High Priesthood and head of the new dispensation. He also claimed a dual identity as the incarnation of the Holy Spirit and as the "Branch of David."[33] As it happened, neither "witness" was interested in the role.

Faced with impending failure, Bishop staged a melodramatic opening of the Millennium atop the Hill of Promise. He ordained convert Sally Shumway a high priest (his was probably the first Mormon group to ordain women); blew the resurrection trump ("a tin horn blown long and loud," wrote Strang); raised an ensign to the nations; and called for the gathering of the Lost Tribes of Israel. Nothing happened. Strang and his followers remained amused but uninterested, and Bishop vacated Voree.

By the late fall of 1850 Bishop had relocated and settled into the society of his former home of Kirtland, Ohio.[34] Irena had died or divorced Bishop before this time, and it was to Kirtland that he brought his second wife, Phebe. In Kirtland Bishop began, as he had among the Strangites in Wisconsin and earlier, to preach of his divine calling as the Branch and as the rightful leader of the faithful. As evidence of his divine calling, he claimed to have the seven sacred things he had been shown in Nauvoo in 1842. In Bishop's new gospel dispensation, these seven items, he explained, were to be used collectively in bestowing the "ordinance of the Kingdom."[35] He also staged a performance that again was intended to establish the Kingdom of God. Bishop, his wife, and his brother Henry baptized themselves face down in the river that ran through Kirtland. Having performed this ordinance, Bishop "called himself the father and his Br[other] the son and his wife the holy ghost."[36] With their performance complete, Bishop and brother Henry rode off some time later to the small group of Latter-day Saint members in Cleveland. There Bishop preached his Ordinance of the Kingdom, speaking of how those who were faithful (to him, of course) would become kings and priests. His doctrines gained some believers; however, his success was short-lived. James Bay, a missionary from Utah on his way to England, was able to regain most of Bishop's Cleveland converts.

During his stay in Kirtland, Bishop had printed two doctrinal treatises. "A Proclamation From the Lord to His People, Scattered Throughout All the Earth" was an 8.5 x 21-inch, double-sided sheet intended to fulfill Zechariah's prophecy of a "flying roll" to go out over the earth, an act that was to herald the gathering of Israel.[37] In the summer of 1851, Bishop published a pamphlet, again from Kirtland, "An Address to the Sons and Daughters of Zion, Scattered Abroad, Through All the Earth."[38] The "Address" was intended to explain and expound the broadsheet revelation, the "Proclamation" as a commentary of sorts. It also called Bishop's faithful to gather to a Zion in the Great Salt Lake Valley.

Under the leadership of a contingent of apostles, the largest body of Mormons had fled the United States in 1846 and moved deeper into the continent. Settling a year later in a desert valley on the rim of the Great Basin, they established a city, free to practice their religion and prepare for the second coming of the Son of God. By 1851 the followers of Brigham Young and apostolic leadership enjoyed virtual political autonomy, ensconced firmly in the Salt Lake Valley. At no other time in history would the Mormon church maintain such control over an entire populace, Mormon and Gentile. The Gladdenites made an appearance in Utah as early as 1851, but because they found the social climate uninviting they left by mid 1854. To Francis Bishop goes the questionable credit for the rise of the first schismatic sect within the Saints' mountain retreat.

Bishop was unable to complete the trip to Utah. Instead, he remained in Kanesville, Iowa, while his following stirred in Utah. From Kanesville he supervised what remained of his followers, published three more pamphlets, and eventually organized "The Church of Jesus Christ of the New Jerusalem" in August 1854.[39] Bishop also became a property-owning charter member of the city of Council Bluffs when Kanesville incorporated that year.[40] In August, when Bishop's Utah converts arrived from Great Salt Lake City, they expected to find their leader, but Bishop had sold his property interests, gathered letters of recommendation from the local citizenry, and embarked inexplicably for the East. With their leader gone, the New Church, as they called themselves, quickly crumbled, and with it Bishop's most secure following. Francis Gladden Bishop had passed the pinnacle of his success.

The rest of Francis Bishop's life was spent in preaching of his divine call in a fruitless effort to again collect a church. In his final decade he is barely given passing mention in the letters and journals of those who encountered him. Leaving Council Bluffs, Bishop collected a small, short-lived following in Cincinnati before moving on to Washington, D.C., and New York City. After three years in the New York area Bishop moved westward again. He made a failed attempt to gather the scattered followers of Charles B. Thompson in 1860, settled and abandoned a community in Nebraska on the Platte River Road, and eventually made his way to Colorado.[41]

From Denver in early 1864, the would-be prophet wrote a series of long letters to Brigham Young, asking to be welcomed in to bestow the seven sacred things to the Utah Saints. In his years of trial and anonymity Bishop had not abandoned his doctrines. On the contrary, his doctrine constantly evolved to explain the repeated setbacks and disappointments Bishop encountered. His witnesses had unwittingly done their duty in years past and were now unneeded despite the fact that they had abandoned the cause. Bishop's role was personally to prepare the way for the Ancient of Days. Bishop himself was coming to Salt Lake to represent the Ancient of Days as this figure returned "to sit."[42]

Fifty-five-year-old Francis Gladden Bishop climbed down anonymously out of a stage or wagon onto the dusty summer streets of Salt Lake City in June or July 1864. What Bishop did while he was in Salt Lake remains a mystery. He certainly walked about the city and the temple grounds at its heart. He may have quietly visited former acquaintances from the past years of Kirtland and Nauvoo. It is also possible that he called on Brigham Young, although he is not mentioned in the office journals. It is fairly certain that he was not able to or did not fulfill his hopes to return representationally as the Ancient of Days. He remained quietly in the city through the fall. During a scarlet fever outbreak in November, the aging prophet took to his bed. On the last day of November 1864, Francis Gladden Bishop, who had recently returned to—but in his own mind had never left—the Mormon church, died in the Salt Lake Third Ward.[43]

He was a complicated man, and there is more to his story than odd personal beliefs. Those personal beliefs were the product of a significant religious past, beliefs that instead of being abandoned or exchanged or replaced or updated when their owner joined a new church were packed along with him. Thus Bishop's doctrines are a conglomerate of different religious influences, experiences, and practices.[44] From his earliest childhood came the love and knowledge of the Bible and its importance as a guide to past, present, and future reality. From Methodism under his parents, later as a Baptist circuit-rider, and as a Mormon missionary he gained opportunities for study and expression and was granted a de facto theological independence that allowed his self-importance to develop. While filling these several responsibilities there was no routine supervisory force keeping Bishop's doctrines in line with institutional doctrine. He was free to express opinion along with doctrine and, as his trials attest, did so. To this variety of influences is added Bishop's inner world of reality, his absolute conviction that he had seen visions and enjoyed divine aegis and responsibility. In actuality, these visions were the catalysts around which Bishop used his admixture of experience and interpretation to form doctrines. The human capacity for thought creates a world in which mental reality does not have to submit to narrow tests of actuality. Bishop's visions are representational of his ultimate—his personal—reality.

For a decade Bishop participated "faithfully" in the Mormon milieu, keeping and developing his beliefs silently without effective interference from ecclesiastical authority. Regardless of the state or direction of his personal beliefs, as long as the line between heterodoxy and orthodoxy was not breached publicly he remained a "faithful" church member. He had gotten into trouble only when he attempted to present his own opinions as doctrinally authoritative, when he had taught of them to others. It was by stepping beyond this ill-defined limit of appropriate behavior that Bishop invited censure. The ideas of individual members existed collectively as a force outside the church structure, a force that Joseph Smith in his official position and his successors might help guide but could never wholly control.

Properly identified, Bishop was a heretic, not an apostate. Heretics reinterpret, restructure, or reorder the social and emotional values of the parent group to coincide with personal beliefs and priorities. Often a single point of disagreement is isolated and serves as a catalyst that may assist in breaking other ties to orthodoxy and around which like-minded individuals may be gathered. Bishop's catalyst was the question of authority of his visions. For a true apostate the break may be made similarly but leads to a rejection of the group's values. The appellation *apostate* has been broadly and incorrectly used in all branches of Mormonism to tar unregenerate dissenters with the onus of their rebellion.

Writing of heretics and apostates in first-century Christianity, the Apostle John stated, "They went out from us, but they were not of us; for if they had been of us, they would no doubt have continued with us: but they went out, that they might be made manifest that they were not all of us" (1 John 2:19). Bishop's break in Nauvoo and shift from faithful church member to dogmatic heretic appears to be sharp, but his arraignments before church councils reveal that Bishop, like those of whom John spoke, had never been truly a part of the core of Latter-day Saint faithful. His personal beliefs, ideas, and interpretations formed the heart of his doctrine and understanding, doctrine that did not come from the pronouncements of the prophet he claimed to follow.[45] He and his ideas were immersed in Mormonism, not rooted in it. His beliefs drew strength from and were magnified and interpreted through the filter of Mormonism, but Bishop's personal beliefs—about himself, his world, and his experiences—in fact remained central to Bishop's identity as a Mormon. He actually had made his break with the Mormon church in 1832 when he silently refused to regard his visions and opinions as doctrinally invalid or as satanically motivated. He remained in the church for a decade after 1832 because he appeared to be orthodox. If Bishop appears nontypical of dissenters, it is because he serves only as a caricature of dissent. For Francis Gladden Bishop, as with any dissenter, disagreement in the form of personal doctrinal interpretations was at the root of dissent.

On a rise in the pioneer section of the Salt Lake City Cemetery is Bishop's sister's family plot, where he was supposed to have been buried. The stones marking the family graves—if there were any—have disappeared over time. In their place collectively stands a single granite monument to the family dead, placed there in the 1920s by Bishop's nephew. On the reverse is a list of the names of those in the plot. Near the bottom is the name of Francis G. Bishop. Unfortunately, Bishop does not lie near the marker that now bears his name. After a life full of missed opportunities and contradictions, he suffered a final injustice in death. On the cold December day that he was buried, he was not placed in the Brim plot but interred instead at the head of a draw among other "singles" from the city.[46] He is buried in the wrong grave—a final act of being in the wrong place at the right time.

NOTES

1. For more information on Bishop and the character of Gladdenism, see the larger work from which this chapter is summarized: Richard L. Saunders, "Francis Gladden Bishop and Gladdenism: A Study in the Culture of a Mormon Dissenter and His Movement," M.S. thesis, Utah State University, 1989.

2. Francis Gladden Bishop, *Zion's Messenger* (Council Bluffs: N.p., 1854); Anna Maria Bishop Brim, "Journal of Anna Maria Bishop Brim," microfilm of typescript, Utah State Historical Society, Salt Lake City.

3. Francis Gladden Bishop, "An Address to the Sons and Daughters of Zion, Scattered Abroad, Through All the Earth" (Kirtland, Ohio: N.p., 1851), 24.

4. Bishop, "Address to the Sons and Daughters of Zion," 26; Daniel 7:9.

5. Bishop, "Address to the Sons and Daughters of Zion," 24; Bishop, *Zion's Messenger*, 32.

6. Bishop, *Zion's Messenger*, 9, 31; Letter of Francis Gladden Bishop, February 4, 1840, in *Times and Seasons* [Nauvoo, Ill.] 1 (March 1840): 77.

7. An extensive examination of early church documents and collected genealogical materials has failed to identify Walton. It is possible that Bishop misspelled Micah B. Welton's name, although it is not certain if he held the office of high priest. See for the year 1832, Andrew Jensen, "A Chronological List of Missionaries from the Church of Jesus Christ of Latter-day Saints, 1830–1930," microfilm, Church of Jesus Christ of Latter-day Saints Family History Library, Salt Lake City.

8. Bishop, *Zion's Messenger*, 9. The office of high priest was first distinctly bestowed on June 7, 1831, and in the earliest days of the church was often referred to as the High Priesthood. See *Book of Doctrine and Covenants* (Independence: Herald Publishing House, 1970), sec. 52:introduction; *Doctrine*

and Covenants of the Church of Jesus Christ of Latter-day Saints (Salt Lake City: Deseret Book Co., 1982), sec. 52:introduction.

9. *Millennial Star,* November 20, 1846, 138.

10. Bishop made no mention of this failed attempt at securing ordination. He stated that he was sent to preach the gospel yet does not appear on the 1832 list of missionaries that LDS church historian Andrew Jensen assembled from church records. Compare Bishop, *Zion's Messenger,* 31, and Jensen, "A Chronological List of Missionaries."

11. Bishop, *Zion's Messenger,* 9–10.

12. Bishop, *Zion's Messenger,* 9; Bishop "Address to the Sons and Daughters of Zion," 29–30. In the earlier of the two versions, the "Address," he does not mention concern over the truth of the church's claims.

13. Bishop, *Zion's Messenger,* 9.

14. Bishop, *Zion's Messenger,* 9–10; Bishop, "Address to the Sons and Daughters of Zion," 29–30.

15. Bishop, "Address to the Sons and Daughters of Zion," 11.

16. *Millennial Star,* November 20, 1846, 139–40.

17. Bishop, "Address to the Sons and Daughters of Zion," 26.

18. F. G. Bishop, "A Brief History of the Church of the Jesus Christ of Latter Day Saints, from Their Rise Until the Present Time, Containing an Account of, and Showing the Cause of, Their Sufferings in the State of Missouri in the Years 1833–1838. And Likewise a Summary View of Their Faith" (Salem, N.C.: Blum and Son, 1839). The only known copy is today at the Library of Congress. The historian Dale L. Morgan incorrectly identified this pamphlet as published in Salem, Massachusetts. This is unlikely because Bishop was laboring in Virginia and North Carolina. See Dale Morgan, "A Bibliography of the Churches of the Dispersion," [Salt Lake City] *Western Humanities Review* (1953): 158.

Most works on the history of the Mormons had been written by non-Mormons and were less than favorable. Oliver Cowdery's famous letters were not published separately until 1844, and then in England. Two other Latter Day Saint pamphlets closely contemporary to Bishop's were John Taylor's "A short account of the murders, roberies, burnings, thefts and other outrages committed by the mob & militia of the State of Missouri, upon the Latter Day Saints" (Springfield: N.p., 1839); and Parley Pratt's "History of the late persecutions inflicted by the State of Missouri upon the Mormons" (Detroit: Dawson and Bates, Printers, 1839).

19. Bishop, *Zion's Messenger,* pp. 34–35.

20. The charges as recorded in the High Council minutes were typically general: of "setting himself up as a prophet and a revelator to the Church. Second for an improper course of conduct in meetings." See "Minutes of the High Council of the Church of Jesus Christ of Nauvoo, Illinois," March 11, 1842, Church of Jesus Christ of Latter-day Saints Historical Department, Salt Lake City, typescript at Utah State University Special Collections, Logan. Years later, when the official church history was being edited for publication in the *Deseret News,* extracted more from Smith's journal than from the official min-

utes, the second charge was ignored. In relation to this issue no additional information is extant.

21. "Minutes of the High Council," March 11, 1842.

22. Brigham Young, *Manuscript History of Brigham Young 1801–1844,* ed. Eldon J. Watson (Salt Lake City: Smith Secretarial Service, 1968), 115.

23. Bishop, *Zion's Messenger,* 34–36; "Journal History of the Church of Jesus Christ of Latter-day Saints," LDS Historical Department, March 11, 1842; Wilford Woodruff, *Journals of Wilford Woodruff,* ed. Scott G. Kenney (Midvale: Signature Books, 1984), 2:157–158; Young, *Manuscript History,* 115.

24. *The Wasp* [Nauvoo, Ill.], May 14, 1842, 3; Bishop, *Zion's Messenger,* 36.

25. Bishop, *Zion's Messenger,* 35–36; Francis Gladden Bishop to Joseph Smith, Jr., September 26, 1843, Joseph Smith, Jr., Papers, LDS Historical Department. Hyrum Smith's intervention here was not a unique case. At his trial for apostasy after the martyrdom, High Council member Leonard Soby testified that Hyrum Smith also sought to repair or downplay a breach between Soby and Joseph Smith. See "Minutes of the High Council," unbound, September 7, 1844, LDS Historical Department. Wilford Woodruff noted that Sidney Rigdon's excommunication had also been sidetracked by Hyrum's petitions to Joseph; see *Millennial Star* 5 (December 1844): 109.

26. Joseph Smith said that he received the plates from Moroni, the last Nephite prophet and last custodian of the plates. The Three Witnesses to the Book of Mormon were shown the plates by "an angel" but left no record of his identity. Presumably it was Moroni. The testimony concerning these men's vision of the plates is printed at the front of any copy of the Book of Mormon. See Joseph Smith, Jr., *History of the Church of Jesus Christ of Latter-day Saints,* ed. B. H. Roberts (Salt Lake City: Deseret Book Co., 1976), 1:33; Bishop, "Address to the Sons and Daughters of Zion," 27–28.

27. Bishop, "Address to the Sons and Daughters of Zion," 27, 29.

28. Bishop, *Zion's Messenger,* 36. In retrospect, this prophecy may have been written in a little-known Reorganized Church periodical that was published in Salt Lake City. See *The Messenger* 3 (January 1877): 1.

29. Francis Gladden Bishop to Joseph Smith, Jr., September 26, 1843, Joseph Smith, Jr., Papers, LDS Historical Department.

30. Bishop, *Zion's Messenger,* 11–12, 36. Bishop relied on a complex interrelation of Old Testament and Apocalyptic scripture to arrive at this conclusion. It centered on numerical correlation of the "seven Spirits of God" in Revelation and the stone with seven eyes of Zechariah. To Bishop, these eyes and spirits were symbolic of the earth's gospel dispensations, which were also represented by his seven movements.

31. *Gospel Herald* [Voree, Wis.], January 13, 1848, 203.

32. *Ensign of Liberty* [Kirtland, Ohio] 1 (March 1848). A letter from Oliver Cowdery to William E. McLellin cited there was dated July 28, 1847, from Elkhorn, in Walworth County, Wisconsin. See also Francis Gladden Bishop, "A Voice of Warning and Proclamation to All" [Voree, Wis.: N.p., 1848], 1–3.

33. Sarah Hall Scott to sister, March 31, 1848, Inez Smith Davis Papers

and Notes, Reorganized Church of Jesus Christ of Latter Day Saints Library-Archives, Independence, Mo.; *Gospel Herald,* April 20, 1848, 18; Isaiah 11:1; Jeremiah 23:5.

34. Bureau of the Census, Seventh U.S. Population Census (1850), Ohio, Lake County, 223.

35. Bishop, "Address to the Sons and Daughters of Zion," 11–13.

36. James W. Bay to Brigham Young, August 7, 1851, Missionary Reports, Brigham Young Papers, LDS Historical Department.

37. Bishop, "Proclamation"; Zechariah, 5:1–3. In his "Bibliography of the Churches of the Dispersion" Morgan incorrectly states that the text had been lost. A copy was located at the LDS Historical Department and was cited in his larger bibliography. Chad J. Flake, ed., *A Mormon Bibliography, 1830–1930* (Salt Lake City: University of Utah Press, 1978), 43.

38. Pages 46–47 of the fifty-page work bear a revelation dated June 15, 1851. A letter written to Brigham Young on July 30, 1850, refers to a copy of the "Address to the Sons and Daughters of Zion" sent under the same mailing, suggesting that its publication took place between the two dates. See Brigham Young Papers, Incoming Correspondence, LDS Historical Department.

39. Francis Gladden Bishop, "The Ensign. Light of Zion. Shepherd of Israel! and 'Book of Remembrance.'" [first division] (Kanesville, Iowa: N.p., 1852).

40. Iowa, Pottawattamie County, Deed Records, Book A, 348, Pottawattamie County Recorder's Office, Council Bluffs, Iowa. The lot descriptions are recorded in Plat Book K, 18–19.

41. *True Latter Day Saints Herald* 1 (August 1860): 185; Ezra Strong to Solomon Strong, February 7, 1856, Washington State University Special Collections, Pullman, typescript at Utah State University Special Collections; *Saints' Herald,* May 6, 1903, 411–12; Francis Gladden Bishop to Joseph Smith III, September 28, 1862, Joseph Smith III Papers, Reorganized Church Library-Archives; Francis Gladden Bishop to Brigham Young, March 20, 1864, 12, Brigham Young Papers, Incoming Correspondence, LDS Historical Department.

42. Francis Gladden Bishop to Brigham Young, March 20, 1864, April 3, 1864, and April 29, 1864, Brigham Young Papers.

43. Salt Lake County, Utah, Death Records, microfilm, LDS Family History Library, consecutive death no. 2269.

44. Bishop clearly does not fit into the pattern that Jan Shipps has identified as a standard Mormon cultural break with the past and reordering of historical value. See Jan Shipps, *Mormonism: The Story of a New Religious Tradition* (Urbana: University of Illinois Press, 1984), 51–65.

45. Joseph Smith was constantly faced with the problem of discouraging competing pronouncements while encouraging the seeking of inspiration. *Doctrine and Covenants of the Church of Jesus Christ of Latter-day Saints,* sec. 28; *Book of Doctrine and Covenants,* sec. 27; *Times and Seasons,* December 1, 1842, 32.

46. Sexton's Record Books, Salt Lake City Cemetery, vol. 2.

5

James Colin Brewster: The Boy Prophet Who Challenged Mormon Authority

Dan Vogel

Of all the would-be prophets to leave the Mormon fold during Joseph Smith, Jr.'s, lifetime, James Colin Brewster was perhaps the most prolific. Brewster was only ten when he reported receiving visions and recited chapters from purported lost books of ancient scripture. By his twenty-fifth birthday, Brewster had published several books of prophecy, edited a periodical, become one of the chief officers of a newly organized church, and founded a short-lived colony in New Mexico.

Young Brewster's prophetic model was Joseph Smith, Jr., and in most important ways he attempted to emulate the Mormon leader's career. But Brewster wished to succeed where he believed the Mormon prophet had failed, in the establishment of a utopian society. Unlike Joseph Smith, however, Brewster's following did not survive his prophetic failure. His life provides a fascinating study in the role of ambition, spirituality, and individualism in the development of the early Mormon church.

Brewster was born in Black Rock, Erie County, New York, on October 20, 1826. His parents, Zephaniah and Jane, joined the Mormon church in Westfield, Chautaugua County, New York, in the early 1830s and soon after removed to Kirtland, Ohio, with their two sons, James and Amsbury.[1] In 1832 Jane gave birth to a son, Hamlet, and in 1834 to a daughter, Letitia.[2] During their first years in the Mormon capital, the activities of the Brewster family were not unusual for recent converts. Zephaniah occasionally donated his carpentry skills to building the temple, for which he along with others received a blessing in March 1835.[3]

Following completion of the temple in 1836, the Kirtland community entered a period of spiritual and economic crisis. Although dissention was growing rapidly before the failure of the church-sponsored bank, the Kirtland Safety Society Anti-Banking Company, in May 1837, the failure was followed by a general conflict in which many members, including some in high ecclesiastical positions, rejected Smith's leadership, declaring that he was a fallen prophet.[4]

Perhaps spurred by the Kirtland conflict, a ten-year-old James Brewster received his inaugural spiritual manifestation. According to Brewster's recollection, he saw in vision an angel who showed him a large round table supporting "a vast quantity" of books. Addressing Brewster, the angel said: "The round table denotes equality, and the writings are ancient records that are to be written."[5]

In his autobiographical sketch, written in 1848, Brewster gave neither the angel's name nor the contents of the books he was shown. But church records indicate that on October 30, 1837, "Brothers Norris, Brewster, and others, presented to the High Council a plan for the better organization of the Church in temporal affairs, stating that Moroni had appeared to Collins Brewster." The council, however, decided that it was "a trick of the devil" and elected not to adopt any of his proposals.[6]

In response to this decision, the Kirtland High Council met on November 20, 1837, under the direction of John Smith, the prophet's uncle, to consider the recent conduct of James Brewster, his parents, and nine others. Charges had been brought against the group, according to church records, "for giving heed to revelations said to be translated from the Book of Moroni by Collins Brewster, and for entering into a written covenant different from the articles and covenants of the Church of Latter-day Saints, and following a vain and delusive spirit."[7] Brewster never mentioned any written revelations for this period, but the minutes of the meeting indicate that the clerk read them to the council.

Perhaps the most damaging evidence against the group, as far as church authorities were concerned, was their declarations of independence from institutional imperatives. One witness, for example, testified that "he had visited the accused and labored with them according to the law of the Church; that the accused justified themselves, seeing the Church had not lived according to the former revelations, and they considered the High Council and others were in transgression; and that most of the accused appeared to be determined to pursue their own way, whether right or wrong."

Another witness said that "the accused appeared to manifest a hard spirit against the Presidents of the Church and the High Council," while others testified that "they heard them speak against the heads of the Church and that Brother Joseph [Smith] had many things to repent of, and one of them said he thought some put too much stress on the

Priesthood." It was even rumored that Moses R. Norris had ordained James Brewster to be a "prophet."[8] Predictably the High Council decided to disfellowship Brewster and any of his followers who would not denounce him. Brewster, however, was not removed from the church at that time, according to one account, because he had promised to discontinue his activities.[9]

Fleeing from creditors, civil authorities, and dissenters, Joseph Smith left Kirtland for Far West, Missouri, on the night of January 12, 1838. The following July, a pioneer party known as Kirtland Camp left the Mormon stronghold to join Smith in Missouri. The Brewster family traveled with the party as far as Dayton, Ohio, where the Brewsters and the Higbys withdrew "for the want of a team to carry them with their families."[10] According to Brewster, it was in August 1838 near Dayton that he experienced another vision in which he saw the "lost books of Esdras," the writings of an ancient Israelite prophet. At that time, however, he was not permitted to read them. In September 1838, Brewster moved with his father to Springfield, Illinois, and in December he received another vision in which an angel declared to him that "it is the will of the Lord that you should commence and write those books of Esdras."[11]

On December 27, 1838, Brewster began work on what would become his first published work, an "abridgement" of the first, second, third, fourth, sixth, seventh, and eighth books of Esdras. But Brewster confessed that he could "not write so as to render it intelligible to any but myself so poor a writer was I at that period." By employing a number of scribes, among them his father, Brewster managed to finish the book, which was published in June 1842.[12]

Brewster's Prophet Esdras foresaw the events of the last days, including the upbuilding of Zion, the destruction of the wicked, and the return of Jesus. Esdras warned his latter-day readers that the time would soon come when God will "destroy the wicked and ungodly from off the face of the earth, that it shall not be polluted by the sons of unrighteousness for the earth shall be purified, and all those that dwell upon it must be righteous."[13] Esdras even gave a timetable for this destruction, stating that "forty, and eight days [years] shall pass away from the time in which the Kingdom of God is set up on earth [1830] until the earth is purified by fire, but the day in which the Son of Man cometh no man knoweth."[14] Predicting that the world would end in 1878 conveniently placed the return of Jesus at a comfortable distance and provided Brewster with sufficient time to develop his perceived prophetic mission to prepare the world for Christ's return.

Esdras warned that the wicked among the Saints could not escape the destroying fire. Esdras was particularly critical of church leaders: "Wo to the shepherds that will not feed the flock, that say the burden of the Lord is too great, and we cannot serve the Lord."[15] Possibly alluding to the church's financial difficulties in Kirtland, Esdras predicted: "And now I say unto you that the enemy of all righteousness has laid snares to destroy the saints of the most high, and he hath led away many unto darkness. And he hath made the gold and silver which he has created for them an abomination. . . . The saints that forsake the ways of the Lord shall not be prospered."[16]

Esdras also predicted the Brewsterite reorganization of the church. "When the kingdom of God is set upon the earth, they shall prosper for a time when many of the saints shall fall into darkness and half a them shall pass away when the kingdom of God shall be established anew upon the same foundation." He even predicted the general time when the reorganization would occur: "And now I say unto you, that when this book shall come forth ye may know that the time for to bring the House of God into order has arrived, that is the church."[17] Brewster, however, later admitted that at the time he believed Esdras' prediction pertained only to a reorganization of the existing church, not to the establishment of a new church. In fact, Brewster said, "when Joseph Smith and others went forward in Nauvoo, and was re-baptized and renewed their covenants, we hoped that this was the event spoken of, but in a short time we saw that this was not the fact, the organization was not upon the first foundation."[18] The Nauvoo rededication to which Brewster alluded began in 1842, but Brewster would later learn that this was also the year that Smith had secretly introduced the endowment ceremony, something that he subsequently became convinced had sent the church into apostasy.[19]

Apparently Brewster was also critical about Mormon actions during the Missouri persecutions of 1838. A few months following the massacre of Mormons at Haun's Mill, Brewster dictated Esdras' prediction: "How much evil wicked men have done on the face of the earth, they have slain many of the saints, they have burnt their cities, they have laid waste the land which was not theirs, and have slain the inhabitants with the sword, and this because of the evil which is in their hearts."[20]

Concerning Mormon retaliation on the Missourians, Esdras stated: "The saints shall not slay their enemies, . . . neither do they rob them, neither do they shed blood, the saints are not of the world. . . . Such as fear persecution fear not God."[21] Esdras further stated: "If there be not peace in Zion how shall it be built up, it must be built up, and if there be war it cannot be done, peace must be where the saints dwell,

God is a God of peace, and not of war, therefore his saints must dwell in peace, they shall not war with the nations round about, neither among themselves, for if they do either they shall fall."[22] Esdras provided a very effective voice for Brewster to criticize the Mormon hierarchy and wrap himself in the garments of ancient prophecy.

In response to persecution, according to Esdras, the true Saints "shall prophecy and speak with many tongues, and upon many the Lord will pour out his spirit. . . . They shall escape over the mountains like a fox, and they shall escape the power of their enemies, and no one shall find them."[23] This passage was the first allusion that Brewster was planning a migratory escape over the Rocky Mountains, although the location was not disclosed at that time. It was not until November 1840 that Brewster received a revelation that mentioned the gathering of the Saints "upon the river Bashan, beyond the wilderness of Deluen," and in April 1841 announced that the river of Bashan was the Rio Colorado.[24] When Joseph Smith, Jr., heard in 1842 about Brewster's plans to migrate with his small body of believers to California, he commented: "Brewster may set out for California but he will not get there unless some body shall pick him up by the way [and] feed him &c."[25] When considered in the context of Esdras' predictions and Brewster's full intentions, Smith's prediction proved truer than most thought at the time.

The ability of the teenaged Brewster to dictate the Books of Esdras sentence by sentence to scribes was seen by many of his followers as a demonstration of the young man's "supernatural power."[26] Despite his son's unusual talent, however, Zephaniah Brewster initially expressed doubt about the source of the revelations. His doubts eventually led him to take the first portion of the manuscript-in-progress to Joseph Smith in Nauvoo for his opinion, but the Mormon leader did not have time to read it.[27] Hyrum Smith, who was shown the Esdras manuscript during a visit to Springfield, advised Zephaniah Brewster to renew his efforts with Joseph Smith.

In June 1841, therefore, Zephaniah returned to Nauvoo and handed over the manuscript to Smith, who kept it six days.[28] He later recalled: "Brewster showed me the Manuscripts. I enquired of the Lord and the Lord told me the book was not true. It was not of him. If God ever cal[l]ed me, or spoke by my mouth, or gave me a revelation, he never gave revelations to that Brewster Boy or any of the Brewster race."[29] Brewster disputed Smith's version of the incident, arguing, "At that time, he [Smith] stated that he enquired of the Lord concerning it and could not obtain an answer. Since then, he told certain individuals that he did receive an answer that it was not of God."[30]

On March 29, 1842, Brewster announced that he had received a direct commandment to publish his translation of the Books of Esdras, which was issued as a pamphlet later that same year under the title "The Words of Righteousness to All Men." When Brewster's revelations came to the attention of church authorities in Springfield, Brewster and his father were "dealt with," a possible reference to their excommunication.[31] By December 1842, James Colin Brewster was no longer a member of Smith's organization. He admitted the church's action but said that "the only thing found against us was that we had not joined that branch of the church [at Springfield], and supposed we had not acted wisely in all things."[32]

On December 1, 1842, the Nauvoo periodical *Times and Seasons* noted that Brewster's Book of Esdras was "assiduously circulated, in several branches of the church" and denounced it as "a perfect humbug." The editor, the apostle John Taylor, concluded by affirming institutional imperatives, quoting the revelation that Joseph Smith had produced in September 1830 to discredit revelations Hiram Page had received through a stone: "No one shall be appointed to receive commandments and revelations in this church excepting my servant Joseph Smith, Jun."[33]

Taylor informed his readers that young Brewster was not a person to be listened to within Mormonism. According to the editorial, he "has professed for several years to have the gift of seeing and looking through or into a stone; and has thought that he has discovered money hid in the ground in Kirtland, Ohio. His father and some of our weak brethren, who perhaps have had some confidence in the ridiculous stories that are propagated concerning Joseph Smith, about money digging, have assisted him in his foolish plans, for which they were dealt with by the church." Taylor claimed that the Kirtland money diggers were "suspended" from the church but repented of their "ridiculous and pernicious ways."[34]

In March 1843, Brewster published a pamphlet addressed "To the Mormon Money Diggers," which responded to the charges made in the *Times and Seasons* editorial. Brewster denied the claim that he had used a seer stone as a "perfect falsehood," stating that "Joseph Smith and many of the first presidents of the church know it to be false, and at the same time knowing that they could not bring anything against our moral character have endeavored to injure us by publishing these falsehoods."[35] Brewster always maintained that his information came by open vision, but treasure-seeking was usually accomplished through the use of a seer stone or mineral rod.

Against the charge that Brewster, his father, and others in Kirtland sought buried treasure because they gave credence to anti-Mormon stories about Joseph Smith's treasure-seeking activities in New York, Brewster responded by stating that such stories were confirmed by Joseph Smith, Sr., whom he said had openly stated before a church council: "I know more about money digging, than any man in this generation, for I have been in the business more than thirty years." Brewster also said that the elder Smith had related in private conversation "many particulars, which happened in N.Y. where the money digging business was carried on to a great extent by the Smith family."[36] In fact, according to Brewster, it was the senior Smith who recruited his father and him to assist with the treasure-seeking. Brewster's father, however, "ever regarded money diggers with the utmost contempt," but, believing in Mormonism, he was persuaded by Joseph Smith, Sr., and others of "high standing in the church"—John Smith (assistant counselor in the First Presidency) and Alva Beman (president of the Kirtland elder's quorum) among others—to participate in treasure-seeking in Kirtland.[37]

Brewster's claim that he and his father had been recruited by the others seems to be supported by the fact that both Smith and Beman had an established history of treasure-seeking in New York.[38] The historical setting for these activities also seems consistent with Brewster's account. According to Zephaniah Brewster, it was during Kirtland's financial crisis in May or June 1837 that Joseph Smith, Sr., and the others engaged in their treasure-seeking activities.[39] A number of independent sources implicate Joseph Smith and other church leaders in a treasure-seeking excursion to Salem, Massachusetts, in August 1836, presumably also to resolve some of the economic pressure on the church.[40]

Despite such correlation, certain aspects of Brewster's denials are difficult to accept. Brewster's attempt to minimize he and his father's participation in treasure-seeking, for example, is unconvincing. Although Brewster indicated that his father was skeptical about treasure-seeking, he said nothing about his own attitude. His silence is likely because he played a central role in the activities. In fact, as Austin Cowles later reported, Brewster, who was then ten, had come to the attention of the Kirtland treasure-seekers because "he had the gift of seeing in vision distant objects not seen by the natural eye."[41] According to Brewster himself, he and his father were called to a private meeting in the temple, where Joseph Smith, Sr., Alva Beman, and Joshua Holeman laid hands on him and blessed him to be "a Prophet, a Seer, a Revealer, and Translator, and that I should have power given me of God to discover and obtain the treasures which are hid in the earth."[42]

However, Brewster confessed, "the men . . . went with me and my father several times in pursuit of money, but it was not obtained."[43]

While the editorial reported that Brewster was "suspended" from the church for his treasure-seeking activities in Kirtland, the record of Brewster's case is silent regarding the specific matter, mentioning only his written revelations and defiance of church discipline. Brewster, however, confirmed the treasure-seeking context of the church's action against him, stating that the "Brewsterites, as we were called by the Church, were all condemned, although many of the Counsellors, by whose vote we were condemned, had been engaged with us in the money digging business."[44] Brewster's admission would seem to indicate that his revelations were an outgrowth of his treasure-seeking activities. Evidently, he carried his charismatic treasure-seeking role much further than his mentors had anticipated.

Taylor also reported that Zephaniah Brewster "very frequently applied for an ordination, but has been as frequently denied the privilege, as not being considered a proper person to hold the priesthood."[45] Brewster countered by stating that his father was "ordained by the order of JOSEPH SMITH, without his requesting it, under the hands of J[ames]. Adams, High Priest and Patriarch, Elder [Edwin P.] Mariam, President—both of the Springfield church."[46] Brewster was likely correct, because Adams was still living in the area in March 1843 when he made this statement and could have easily disputed the claim.[47] Zephaniah Brewster did petition the Kirtland Elders' Quorum for ordination on January 4, 1837, but the ordinance could not have taken place until after September 1838, when the Brewsters moved to Springfield. Merriam was ordained in Kirtland in September 1837, but Adams, a resident of Springfield, was apparently not converted until after meeting Joseph Smith in November 1839. It also seems likely that Zephaniah Brewster's ordination would have taken place before the organization of the Springfield stake on November 5, 1840, because Brewster said that they had been censured for not participating in the stake.[48]

In the fall of 1841, Brewster began work on his abridgement of the ninth book of Esdras, which he completed in the winter of 1842. When it was published in July 1845 under the title "A Warning to the Latter Day Saints, Generally Called Mormons," it contained a prediction by Esdras about the fall of Nauvoo. "Wo unto the Idle city [Nauvoo] for their transgressions are many and the righteous among them are very few, and because of these they are spared, and when these turn to wickedness they shall be destroyed." Because the Mormons in Nauvoo "have been a wicked and rebellious people, . . . they shall be driven out of the land of their inheritance. As Israel was driven forth by Nebuchanezzer, king of Babylon; even so shall the ungodly perish and be visited with utter destruction in the last days."[49]

Brewster claimed in 1843 to have finished ten books of Esdras but complained that the lack of funds prevented their publication in their entirety. He later stated that in the years before its publication he had read the prediction of Esdras to "every member of the church that visited us," but "the belief that Nauvoo could not be overthrown was so firmly established in the minds of nearly every member of the church that the warning was received and its truths were rejected as a thing of nought."[50]

Even at the time Brewster's prediction appeared in print, few Mormons were aware that church leaders were privately making plans for a western migration of the church. Public announcement of the removal surprised many Mormons, who wondered how church leaders could abandon the nearly completed temple and the apparently prosperous city. By September 1846, Nauvoo's population of more than twelve thousand had been reduced to about five hundred. A traveler who visited the city soon after the exodus described its empty "gloomy streets," broken fences, weed-grown gardens, and vandalized houses as a "melancholy disappointment."[51]

The Mormon flight from Nauvoo greatly increased Brewster's prophetic prestige, causing some excitement among the Mormons at Springfield. In an 1848 editorial, Brewster took advantage of the situation, reminding his readers of the Prophet Jeremiah's words that a true prediction was a clear indication that God had sent him (Jeremiah 28:9).[52]

In his ninth book, Esdras had warned the Latter Day Saints in Nauvoo to "abhor all works of darkness and secret combinations; for these are from Satan and multiply evil upon the sons of men."[53] In subsequent publications, Brewster expanded on the theme of "secret combinations," explaining in 1849 that the church had departed from the faith by "imperceptible degrees" until 1842, when "the fatal step was taken by the introduction of a secret order in direct violation of almost every command in the gospel of Christ."[54] Brewster evidently had reference to Joseph Smith's introduction of the endowment ceremony in 1842. "The priesthood does not consist in high sounding titles, in secret combinations, in key words and mysteries," Brewster declared.[55]

The ninth book of Esdras also included the first clear reference to the need to establish a utopian colony in California (Bashan). Esdras predicted: "They who fear God shall escape through the wilderness, and go beyond the river Amli (Rio del Norte [Rio Grande]) unto the land of their inheritance, a land of hills, of vallies, of plains and pleasant places, which brings forth in abundance, that they who go there shall prosper. The land of Bashan shall be given to the saints." Esdras also predicted that they that go there "shall build cities."[56]

In the same book, Brewster also published an extract of the "Prophecy of Enoch," in which Enoch predicted that the government of the United States (Bethsula) would begin to fall in the seventieth year of the nation (1846) and that "in the same year that this nation, (the United States) shall begin to fall, shall the kingdom of righteousness arise."[57] Brewster commented in January 1850 that the prediction had been fulfilled in the Mexican War of 1846–48, which resulted in U.S. acquisition of New Mexico. "This territory, is," he wrote, "the cause of a dispute, which, even now, threatens the destruction of the Union." He added: "This is plainly foretold in those writings [of Esdras], and will surely come to pass."[58]

In March 1848, Brewster published "An Address to the Church of Christ, and Latter Day Saints," which also included the eleventh book of Esdras. In his address, Brewster argued that Joseph Smith was called only to organize the church, thus explaining Smith's failure to establish Zion and the political kingdom of God.[59] In another place, Brewster declared that the temporal kingdom of God had authoritatively commenced on July 3, 1846, when he received a revelation commanding him to "arise and do the work unto which thou art appointed. For unto you this day is given the power and the authority to establish and build up the kingdom of righteousness."[60]

Brewster's address also discussed the subject of migration to the West. He wrote: "the country designated for the commencement of this great work, is Eastern California, or the valley of the Colorado and Gila rivers, where the Saints are to gather from all the countries of the earth, and establish and build up the Kingdom of Righteousness, which shall never be left to other people, but shall stand forever."[61]

Brewster evidently had great plans for his colony. The eleventh book of Esdras included a prediction that Brewster's settlement in California would be sought by the most powerful nations of the earth, and "after ten years from the time they establish the kingdom, they shall be considered one of the nations of the earth."[62]

Dictated after the events had occurred, Brewster's Esdras predicted the murder of Joseph Smith and the Brewsterite restoration that would follow: "I saw that in the third year after the time (or year) that their first leader was slain, that a few gathered themselves together and established the kingdom anew upon the same foundation."[63] A footnote indicated that the church would be reestablished "within three years after the year commencing June 27th, 1844 [the date of Joseph Smith's death]," that is, three years after June 27, 1845. On June 26, 1848, at the last possible moment, the Church of Christ was organized with nine members, who appointed Hazen Aldrich president.[64] Aldrich had been a prominent member during Joseph Smith's lifetime, having served on the Missouri High Council and as one of seven presidents of the First Quorum of Seventy.[65]

As early as March 1846, Brewster wrote to James J. Strang, another would-be prophet, to inquire about his claim to be Smith's legal successor. "I have known ever since the death of Joseph," he wrote, "that the twelve were not in their place and that they had no right to the office of the first presidency. I also knew that some one (I knew not who) would arise and establish the church."[66] Brewster eventually rejected Strang's claims, concluding that Joseph Smith had left no "legal" successor and that the church had been "completely disorganized" at his death. Despite this disorganization, Brewster believed that "those who were legally ordained in the first organization, did not lose their priesthood by the disorganization of the church; for it is only by their own transgression, that those who have been legally ordained, can lose their authority."[67] The authority by which the Brewster-Aldrich organization was founded was the prediction in Esdras that the church would be reestablished.

Further organization of the church would not take place for more than a year. On September 29, 1849, at a church conference held at Springfield, Aldrich nominated James Brewster and Jackson Goodale as his counselors in the First Presidency. Although provision was also made for twelve apostles, elders, priests, teachers, and deacons, it is not known who, if any, were appointed apostles.[68]

At the time of the first church conference there was but two organized branches, one in Kirtland and the other in Springfield. By the second annual conference, Brewster reported, there were "several" organized branches in Ohio, Illinois, and Iowa, mostly consisting of former Strangites. By February 1850, Brewster was estimating church membership in the "hundreds."[69]

The first number of the new organization's periodical, the *Olive Branch,* was issued from Kirtland in August 1848, edited by Austin Cowles and published by Hazen Aldrich. It optimistically claimed that: "this herald or messenger to the saints and to the nations is designed to be a standard of truth for the benefit of the church and the world, from this its commencement henceforth, till the righteousness of Zion and Jerusalem go forth as brightness, and their salvation as a lamp that burneth, or in other words, till the law goes forth from Zion, and the word of the Lord from Jerusalem."[70]

In July 1849 the place of publication was changed to Springfield and Brewster was named editor. But in August 1850 the publication was returned to Kirtland, Brewster having departed for California to fulfill his dream of building a utopian society there. After the January 1852 issue, the *Olive Branch* was discontinued due to financial difficulties.

During its nearly four and a half year run, the *Olive Branch* published articles on doctrine, conference minutes, correspondence, and excerpts from Brewster's translations of Esdras and other ancient writings. Like Joseph Smith, Brewster eventually moved from the restoration of lost books seen only in vision to translations of existing ancient documents written in unknown languages. Brewster gave English translations of Mayan hieroglyphics that appeared on the plates in John L. Stephens's book *Incidents of Travel in Central America, Chiapas, and Yucatan,* a two-volume work that first appeared in 1841. In April 1851, the *Olive Branch* published Brewster's translations of Indian pictographs he found on rocks as he passed through New Mexico.[71]

In April and May 1850, the *Olive Branch* published Brewster's translation of six bell-shaped brass plates that supposedly had been discovered in an Indian burial mound near Kinderhook, in Pike County, Illinois, in 1843.[72] His translation of the strange characters covering the small plates differed from that of Joseph Smith's, who had also attempted a translation before his death. According to Brewster's translation, the plates contained the "History of the Altewanians," an account written by "Varamenta, the last of the Altewanians," whose people were destroyed in war with another nation about 400 A.D. However, subsequent testimony and recent scientific investigation indicates that the plates were forged by some residents of Pike County in an attempt to entrap Joseph Smith. Brewster and his followers accepted the translation as divinely inspired.[73]

In preparation for the move west, the Brewsterites were commanded through Esdras to gather (except those living nearer California) at Kirtland. In June 1849, a church conference was held in the Kirtland Temple, with Hazen Aldrich presiding. There, Austin Cowles and others refused to accept two of Brewster's revelations and were excommunicated during the following September.[74]

It was decided that the first company would leave from Independence, Missouri. Following Esdras' prediction, the company was to leave Independence after June 27, 1850, and to "arrive at the place appointed before the close of the year 1851."[75] Brewster planned to leave about July 1, 1850, but no later than August 1. He explained the importance of leaving on time: "The distance from Independence, Mo., to the mouth of the Colorado, is 1,800 miles; it will therefore require a little more than four months to travel that distance. Consequently, if we leave the frontier on the first of July, we will reach our place of destination in November. If we were a few weeks later, it will prevent any crops being raised until the next year."[76]

The first company of Brewster's group was organized at Independence on July 15, 1850, with Jackson Goodale as captain. Among the ninety-member company was twenty-four-year-old Brewster, his five brothers and sisters, and his parents. The company got a late start, departing with its twenty-seven wagons and two hundred head of cattle on August 5, 1850.[77]

Brewster had planned to pass through New Mexico in October. However, it was at this time that the company began to experience difficulties among its members. About October 9, they reached Las Vegas, New Mexico, where part of the company under the leadership of George Mateer separated and continued its journey toward California.[78] On October 19, 1850, Jackson Goodale was relieved of his command but continued to travel with Brewster's company. Brewster later explained that, "Jackson Goodale, the leader of the first company, was guilty of transgression of the law of God; consequently his authority to lead the company was on that day forfeited and lost."[79] Dissention in Brewster's company was perhaps the result of his decision not to continue the trip to the predicted location within the predicted time limit. According to his previous calculations, the company had another 749 miles to go. One source indicated that the teams were "considerably jaded" and that supplies were becoming scarce.[80]

On November 23, 1850, Brewster wrote from Albuquerque. By December 31, he was in Socorro, about seventy-five miles south of Albuquerque, where he, his family, and several members of the company were enumerated in the 1850 federal census.[81] In this source, Brewster's occupational designation was "Mormon Prophet," indicative of his perceptions of his own place in the world. On January 16, 1851, Brewster wrote from Socorro, relating that on December 4, 1850, he and a part of the company "crossed the Amli [Rio Grande] and entered into the land of our inheritance. . . . We have purchased a large tract of land, and that the settlement has *already been commenced.*"[82] The colony was situated not very far from Socorro in the valley of the Rio Grande. The new settlement was named Colonia, a name taken from the writings of Esdras. By February 16, 1851, Brewster was sending letters to the *Olive Branch* from Colonia, New Mexico.[83]

Meanwhile, Hazen Aldrich and others who remained at Kirtland began to express dissatisfaction with Brewster. In August 1851, Aldrich wrote in the *Olive Branch:* "We believe J. C. Brewster has misconstrued the Writings of Esdras to his own liking."[84] Brewster did not let that charge go unanswered. He reported a revelation concerning Aldrich that stated: "the advice that thou hast given to the first elder of the church, concerning the council of the Presidency of my church, is right, and in rejecting it he has rejected that which is good, and caused confusion and disorder by acting contrary to the order of the church, in taking upon himself the duties and privileges that belong to the council of three. Let him take heed lest he be found preventing the prosperity of the church."[85]

Mateer's company eventually reached Tucson, where they remained about a year. But the Oatman and Wilder families, together with John and Robert Kelly, decided to continue on down the Santa Cruz to the Gila River, where they encamped near the Pima Indian villages. Royce Oatman, however, decided to press on with his family to Fort Yuma. On March 19, 1851, while encamped on the Gila, Oatman was attacked by Indians who murdered him, his wife, and four children and took two female children captive. Oatman's eldest son, Lorenzo, escaped and rejoined the Wilders and Kellys near Tucson, from thence to Fort Yuma and eventually San Diego. Lorenzo proceeded on to San Francisco, where he was eventually reunited with one of his sisters and migrated to New York. Willard Wilder, son-in-law to Aldrich, and his family settled in Los Angeles, where Aldrich later joined them.[86]

Mateer's company also eventually reached California; the San Francisco *Daily Herald* of July 30, 1852, reported the arrival in California from the Gila of "some five or six emigrant families. They belong to the Brewster division of Mormons, who left Missouri some two years since, for the 'land of promise,' said by one of their heads to be located on the Gila, according to a special revelation from Heaven, made to the Head of their Church. . . . The few families that have succeeded in reaching this place . . .state that they have been deceived and betrayed, by their own folly—renounce Mormonism, and are to return to the old folds."[87]

Nothing is known about the success of the Brewsterite colony in New Mexico, but it soon began to break up. As late as September 20, 1851, Brewster was still at Colonia, but one report has him residing in Socorro, New Mexico, by July 1852.[88] Soon after Brewster apparently returned to the United States, having never reached California. In January 1853, Aldrich told a friend: "J. C. Brewster has returned to the States & says he is going to remain until that meeting is held in the Temple. . . . I have sent him the names of the subscribers to the Olive Branch & as soon as he can he will issue it again. He is now a going to take charge of the affairs of the church for I now expect to go to the Land of Peace [California] in the spring."[89]

Federal census records for 1860 indicate that at least some former members of Brewster's settlement had returned to Illinois, including Zephaniah and Jane Brewster.[90] James Brewster does not appear with his parents in the 1860 enumeration, and his location during the census year is unknown. Later in the decade Brewster was evidently living in Peoria County, Illinois, when Stephen Post baptized him and his wife into the group of Mormonism headed by Sidney Rigdon. On July 17, 1867, Post recorded in his journal: "Today I went down to Kickapoo creek near br Wilders where I baptized James Brewster & Elizabeth his wife. Confirmed them at their house."[91]

The Reorganized Church's official history states that Brewster was last heard of "lecturing in California in advocacy of the system known as spiritualism."[92] But there is no collaborative evidence regarding this matter. It is unknown how Brewster spent the remainder of his days, although it was certainly in relative obscurity. Brewster's prophetic showdown with Joseph Smith ended in failure. But his initial success was the result of Smith's ultimate failure to satisfy the yearnings of some of the early Mormon converts for adequate millenarian leadership. Although Smith may have correctly predicted the failure of his challenger—prophetic foresight is never more dependable than when one millenarian oracle predicts the failure of another—Smith had also failed to establish a zionic community of refuge and the political kingdom of God on earth. But Joseph Smith's institution adjusted to prophetic failure, whereas Brewster and his followers faded into obscurity. Despite comparable prophetic shortcomings, Brewster lacked the organizational skills and the charismatic leadership necessary to prevent his slipping into oblivion.

NOTES

1. The date of conversion for Brewster's parents is unknown, but it was before the birth of their third son, Hamlet, in Ohio in 1832. See Federal Census of New Mexico, Socorro, Valencia County, 1850, 320. James Colin Brewster would not have qualified for baptism until October 20, 1834. The 1830 census indicates that the family was located in Westfield, Chautauqua County, New York. After the departure of the Brewsters, Zephaniah Brewster's father-in-law, James Higby, was excommunicated from the Mormon church in Westfield in June 1833 "for circulating false and slanderous reports." Joseph Smith, Jr., *The History of the Church of Jesus Christ of Latter-day Saints,* ed. B. H. Roberts (Salt Lake City: Deseret Book Co., 1976), 1:355–56, 3:132; Kirtland Council Minute Book, June 24, 1833, Church of Jesus Christ of Latterday Saints Historical Department, Salt Lake City; Eber D. Howe, *Mormonism Unvailed; or, A Faithful Account of That Singular Imposition and Delusion, from Its Rise to the Present Time* (Painesville: E. D. Howe, 1834), 133–35.

2. Federal Census of New Mexico, Socorro, Valencia County, 1850, 320.

3. Smith, *History of the Church*, 2:206–7. The 1850 New Mexico census listed Zephaniah Brewster as a carpenter.

4. The failure of the Kirtland Safety Society and the ensuing conflict are discussed in Max H. Parkin, "Conflict at Kirtland: A Study of the Nature and Causes of External and Internal Conflict of the Mormons in Ohio Between 1830 and 1838," M.A. thesis, Brigham Young University, 1966, 178–225, 279–325; Milton V. Backman, Jr., *The Heavens Resound: A History of the Latter-day Saints in Ohio, 1830–1838* (Salt Lake City: Deseret Book Co., 1983), 310–41.

5. *Olive Branch* [Kirtland, Ohio] 1 (October 1848): 33.

6. Smith, *History of the Church*, 2:525.

7. Ibid.

8. Ibid. 2:526.

9. *Times and Seasons* [Nauvoo, Ill.], December 1, 1842, 32.

10. Backman, *Heavens Resound*, 342–67, 385; Smith, *History of the Church*, 3:129, 132.

11. *Olive Branch* 1 (October 1848): 33–34.

12. Ibid., 34–35.

13. James Colin Brewster, "The Words of Righteousness to All Men, Written from One of the Books of Esaras [Esdras], Which was Written by the Five Ready Writers, In Forty Days, Which was Spoken of by Esaras [Esdras], in His Second Book, Fourteenth Chapter of the Apocrypha, Being One of the Books Which Was Lost and Has Now come Forth, by the Gift of God, In the Last Days" (Springfield, Ill.: Ballard and Roberts, 1842), 14. See 2 Esdras 14:44–48.

14. Brewster, "Words of Righteousness to All Men," 21.

15. Ibid., 30.

16. Ibid., 13, 29.

17. Ibid., 33.

18. *Olive Branch* 1 (March 1849): 145.

19. See D. Michael Quinn, "The Practice of Rebaptism at Nauvoo," *Brigham Young University Studies* 18 (Winter 1978): 228–29.

20. Brewster, "Words of Righteousness to All Men," 10–11. On the Mormon-Missouri confrontation, see Stephen C. LeSueur, *The 1838 Mormon War in Missouri* (Columbia: University of Missouri Press, 1987).

21. Brewster, "Words of Righteousness to All Men," 32.

22. Ibid., 34.

23. Ibid., 11.

24. *Olive Branch* 1 (October 1848): 35, 1 (December 1848): 90.

25. Scott H. Faulring, ed., *An American Prophet's Record: The Diaries and Journals of Joseph Smith* (Salt Lake City: Signature Books, 1987), 265.

26. *Olive Branch* 1 (August 1848): 19.

27. Ibid. 1 (October 1848): 35.

28. James Colin Brewster, "Very Important! To the Mormon Money Diggers. Why do the Mormons Rage, and the People Imagine a Vain Thing?" (Springfield, Ill.: N.p., March 20, 1843), 2.

29. Faulring, ed., *An American Prophet's Record,* 265.

30. Brewster, "Very Important," 2; see also *Olive Branch* 1 (October 1848): 35.

31. *Times and Seasons,* December 1, 1842, 32. A stake had been organized in Springfield in November 1840, with Edwin P. Merriam as president (Smith, *History of the Church,* 4:236).

32. Brewster, "Very Important," 4.

33. *Doctrine and Covenants of the Church of Jesus Christ of Latter-day Saints* (Salt Lake City; Deseret Book Co., 1968), sec. 28:2; *Book of Doctrine and Covenants* (Independence: Herald Publishing House, 1970), sec. 27:2a

34. *Times and Seasons,* December 1, 1842, 32.

35. Brewster, "Very Important," 2.

36. Ibid., 4. On the Smiths' treasure-seeking activities in New York, see D. Michael Quinn, *Early Mormonism and the Magic World View* (Salt Lake City: Signature Books, 1987), 27–111; Roger I. Anderson, *Joseph Smith's New York Reputation Reexamined* (Salt Lake City: Signature Books, 1990).

37. Brewster, "Very Important," 2.

38. Concerning Joseph Smith, Sr.'s, treasure-seeking, see Quinn, *Early Mormonism and the Magic World View,* 28–32, 36, 56–58; for that of Alva Beman, see 35–36.

39. Brewster, "Very Important," 5.

40. Ibid., 4; *The Return* [Davis City, Iowa] 1:105–6; Joseph Smith to Emma Smith, August 19, 1836, in *Saints' Herald,* December 1, 1879, 357. See also David R. Proper, "Joseph Smith and Salem," *Essex Institute Historical Collections* 100 (April 1964): 93–97.

41. *Olive Branch* 1 (December 1848): 93.

42. Brewster, "Very Important," 3.

43. *Olive Branch* 1 (December 1848): 93.

44. Brewster, "Very Important," 3–4.

45. *Times and Seasons,* December 1, 1842, 32.

46. Brewster, "Very Important," 4.

47. James Adams died on 11 August 1843. See *Times and Seasons,* August 1, 1843, 287; Smith, *History of the Church,* 5:527–28; *History of Sangamon County, Illinois* (Chicago: Interstate Publishing Co., 1881), 77. Edwin P. Merriam died on September 14, 1842. See Milton V. Backman, Jr., comp., *A Profile of Latter-Day Saints of Kirtland, Ohio, and Members of Zion's Camp, 1830–1839: Vital Statistics and Sources* (Provo: Brigham Young University, 1983), 47.

48. Lyndon W. Cook and Milton V. Backman, Jr., eds., *Kirtland Elders' Quorum Record, 1836–1841* (Provo: Grandin Book Co., 1985), 22, 31; Smith, *History of the Church,* 4:20, 271, 236; Brewster, "Very Important," 4.

49. James Colin Brewster, "A Warning to the Latter Day Saints, Generally Called Mormons. An Abridgment of the Ninth Book of Esdras" (Springfield, Ill.: N.p., 1845), 1–2, 5, 8; *Olive Branch* 1 (December 1848): 89.

50. Ibid. 1 (December 1848): 89; Brewster, "Very Important," 6.

51. Charles Lanman, *A Summer in the Wilderness* (New York: D. Apple-

ton and Co., 1847), 30–33. On the fall of Nauvoo, see Robert Bruce Flanders, *Nauvoo: Kingdom on the Mississippi* (Urbana: University of Illinois Press, 1965), 306–41.

52. *History of Sangamon County*, 535; James Colin Brewster, "An Address to the Church of Christ and Latter Day Saints" (Springfield, Ill.: N.p., 1848), 5.

53. Brewster, "Warning to the Latter Day Saints," 4.

54. *Olive Branch* 2 (December 1849): 90. For Brewster's rejection of two orders of priesthood, see 89–94. Concerning Joseph Smith's development of two orders of priesthood, see Dan Vogel, *Religious Seekers and the Advent of Mormonism* (Salt Lake City: Signature Books, 1988), 112–21.

55. *Olive Branch* 2 (December 1849): 93. See also 1 (March 1849): 146, 1 (November 1849): 72, and 2 (February 1850): 122–27. On the introduction of the Mormon endowment, see David John Buerger, "The Development of the Mormon Temple Endowment Ceremony," *Dialogue: A Journal of Mormon Thought* 20 (Winter 1987): 36–46.

56. Brewster, "Warning to the Latter Day Saints," 5.

57. Ibid., 10.

58. *Olive Branch* 2 (January 1850): 99.

59. Brewster, "Address to the Church of Christ," 2.

60. *Olive Branch* 1 (December 1848): 91.

61. Brewster, "Address to the Church of Christ," 6–7.

62. Ibid., 11.

63. Ibid., 8.

64. *Olive Branch* 1 (November 1848): 82–83.

65. See Smith, *History of the Church*, 2:164, 203; *Olive Branch* 1 (December 1848): 94–95.

66. Quoted in Dale L. Morgan, *A Bibliography of the Churches of the Dispersion* (Salt Lake City: Western Humanities Review, N.d.), 113.

67. *Olive Branch* 2 (January 1850): 103–4.

68. Ibid. 2 (October 1849): 50, 2 (November 1849): 78, 79.

69. Ibid. 2 (February 1850): 127; Morgan, *Bibliography of the Churches of the Dispersion*, 113.

70. *Olive Branch* 1 (August 1848): 14.

71. Ibid., 16, 1 (January 1849): 109–11, 3 (April 1851): 133, 141–42. Brewster, for example, translated hieroglyphics above the heads of bas-relief figures on two sanctuary panels at Palenque's temple of the cross: "The King Ostima, who erected this temple, in honor of the God of walls and towers. . . . The nation of Paansa were governed for thirty years by the most Gracious King. . . . He ruled over all the country of the Ottomacoes, His dominion extended from the sea to the mountains; and all the tribes of Votan were tributary unto Him, His laws were just, and all the nations of Talpahan were under them." Although even now scholars do not understand Mayan hieroglyphics completely, what is known does not correspond with Brewster's translations.

72. *Olive Branch* 2 (April 1850): 158–60, 2 (May 1850): 161–65, 1 (August 1848): 16; 1 (December 1848): 93.

73. See Stanley B. Kimball, "Kinderhook Plates Brought to Joseph Smith Appear to be a Nineteenth-Century Hoax," *Ensign,* August 1981, 66–74.

74. Brewster, "Address to the Church of Christ," 16, 17, 23; *Olive Branch* 1 (November 1848): 82–83, 2 (July 1849): 2–11, 2 (October 1849): 50.

75. Ibid. 1 (January 1849): 103.

76. Ibid. 1 (December 1849): 95, 1 (January 1850): 98.

77. Ibid. 3 (October 1850): 37. Brewster enumerated the company, listing the names of heads of families and number in family as follows: Jackson Goodale (seven), 7 H Brewster (ten), John Prior (two), Ira Thompson (six), John W. Crandall (nine), A. W. Lane (five), Wm. J. Conner (three), Royce Oatman (ten), John Richardson (four), W. O. Wilder (four), George Meeter (Mateer) (ten), Wm. W. Lane (three), J. B. Wheeling (seven), A. Patching (seven), O. F. Beckwith (one), Robert Kelly (one), and John Kelly (one).

78. Ibid. 2 (October 1850): 37, 3 (April 1851): 142. Mateer's company apparently included the Oatman, Wilder, and Kelly families. Robert and John Kelly appear in Santa Fe in the 1850 New Mexico census (355, 358).

79. *Olive Branch* 3 (May 1851): 147.

80. Ibid. 2 (June 1850): 182; R. B. Stratton, *Captivity of the Oatman Girls* (New York: N.p., 1858), 51.

81. *Olive Branch,* 3 (April 1851): 142; Federal Census of New Mexico, Socorro, Valencia, 1850, 640. The Brewster family is enumerated as follows: Zephaniah (53), Jane (40), J. Colin (24), Amsbury (21), Hamlet (18), Letitia (16), Amaretta (11), and Alwilda (6). Other members of the company enumerated are Jackson Goodale and family, William J. Conner and family, John Prior and wife, and John Richardson and family (640).

82. Ibid. 3 (May 1851): 147.

83. Ibid. 3 (June 1851): 161; *New York Tribune,* May 28, 1851.

84. Ibid. 4 (August 1851): 13.

85. Ibid. 4 (November 1851): 65.

86. H. H. Bancroft, *The History of Arizona and New Mexico* (San Francisco: The History Co., 1889), 484–86; Edwin Corle, *The Gila: River of the Southwest* (New York: Farrar and Rinehart, 1951), 155–75; Stratton, *Captivity of the Oatman Girls;* Hazen Aldrich to Brother Alston, Willoughby, Lake County, Ohio, January 25, 1853, Reorganized Church of Jesus Christ of Latter Day Saints Library-Archives, Independence, Missouri. I am indebted to D. Michael Quinn for bringing this source to my attention. Aldrich died in 1873 in El Monte, Los Angeles County, California.

87. *San Francisco Daily Herald,* July 30, 1852, 2. The item from the *Herald* is a letter, dated July 17, 1852, from a correspondent in San Diego. Partly quoted in Morgan, *Bibliography of the Churches of the Dispersion,* 114.

88. Joseph Smith III and Heman C. Smith, *History of the Reorganized Church of Jesus Christ of Latter Day Saints* (Independence: Herald Publishing House, 1967), 3:71; *San Francisco Daily Herald,* July 30, 1852, 2; Morgan, *Bibliography of the Churches of the Dispersion,* 114.

89. Hazen Aldrich to Brother Alston, January 25, 1853.

90. Zephaniah Brewster is enumerated in the Federal Census of Illinois for

Litchfield in Montgomery County, 1860, 141 and 1870, 179. For Jackson Goodale, see Federal Census of Illinois, Pike County, Barry Township, 1860, 784.

91. Stephen Post Diary, July 17, 1867, Latter-day Saint Historical Department. My appreciation to D. Michael Quinn for this source.

92. Smith and Smith, *History of the Reorganized Church,* 3:73.

6

William B. Smith:
"A Wart on the Ecclesiastical Tree"

Paul M. Edwards

The identification of dissent is not always clear. For William Smith, it began with the realization that he was caught between his moral and legal (in keeping with God's plan) right to office, which was supported by illegal authorities, and legal authorities who failed to support him in his birthright. His dissent was against the violation of his perceived rights; it was against the denial of his office and calling; and, eventually, it was against changes in the true church created by both Brigham Young and Joseph Smith III.

The nature of his dissent was relative and subtle. It is often difficult for the orthodox to identify just what makes a dissenter out of a man with such a strong sense of loyalty to the Restoration. Orthodoxy in a living institution moves against the shore of tradition like the evening tide against the rocks, changing so gradually that only one measuring it against a stable point can tell that, in fact, the sea and the land are both different.

For most people, dissent is best explained as confrontation against existing authority, and certainly William Smith fits this description. Always vocal, sometimes belligerent, he never hesitated to make his own views known. But confrontation is such a small part of the total picture that it can, if one is not careful, cause one to completely misread the motives of the dissenter.

The life of William B. Smith is a case history of a man for whom the "original" understanding changed very little.[1] He was a man who found himself in the strange position of becoming a dissenter as events moved the mainstream away from him. These events seemed out of his control and beyond his ability to adjust. Smith discovered that he was in dissent when the church his family had formed, and in which he had served, was jolted by a series of blows. Major change occurred. In a very real sense the church had betrayed him, for it betrayed the "constitution" of the movement and thus violated the contract he felt he had made.

Smith was also a man who tried very hard to adjust to the "expectations of loyalty" as he watched those things he cherished most move in counterpoint with those things expected of him. If he was to remain in good faith with those he loved, and with the promise to which he was committed, he had to change.

Some would say that he was an opportunist, that he changed loyalties too quickly, and that he wore the livery of the house in which he wished to live. There are reasons to see this as true—in part. But equally true is the realization that William found legitimacy under the guidance of Joseph Smith, his brother and his prophet. He learned to accept the laws, and he was loyal to the doctrine and the traditions Joseph Smith established at Kirtland and Nauvoo. And when disaster challenged the security provided by that comfortable relationship, William Smith sought a secure place wherever he thought he might find it. He sought an alliance that would allow him to continue his relationship with the church. But each new pretender failed to provide what he needed, and finally he decided to try and establish it himself. But he failed. In the end, William Smith joined the Reorganization, with "Little Joseph," and attempted his last real chance to belong.

William Smith had been an acceptable sibling in the Smith family: a trusted and responsible member of the religious organization and a fairly careful exponent of the early doctrine. He was not without his disagreements even in the preassassination church. There is no doubt that he considered the Smith family as the royalty of the Restoration and, consequently, saw himself just a little above most persons. He assumed that his position and opinions would carry considerable weight. He was used to the fact that they did. Nothing in his personality or experience equipped him for exile—not exile demanded by the increasingly nationalistic postcrisis churches, nor a self-imposed exile. His heritage was one of disagreement and confrontation. When he died on November 13, 1893, he understood that he had failed to accomplish what had seemed so significant.

William B. Smith was born in Royalton, Vermont, on March 13, 1811, the sixth son born to Lucy Mack and Joseph Smith. He was five years younger than Joseph, Jr., but participated from the beginning as a member of the "founding family" and as an active part of the leadership. He served first as a teacher, elder, and then as a high priest. In 1835, while only twenty-three, he was called to serve in the Quorum of Twelve Apostles. He acted as the outspoken and committed "defender of the faith" while editor of the *Nauvoo Wasp* (1842–43). He was still a member of the Twelve when the mob in Carthage assassinated Joseph and Hyrum Smith in 1844.

Although he certainly caused his brother Joseph difficulty, both as a brother and as a member of the Quorum of Twelve, he remained in good standing. On one occasion Joseph rose to his defense after William had been chastised by the Twelve for arguing with Joseph: "as for my Servant William, let the Eleven humble themselves in prayer and in faith, and wait on me in patience, and my servant William shall return. I will yet make him a polished shaft in my quiver, in bringing down the wickedness and abominations of men and there shall be none mightier than he in his day and generation."[2]

Smith did return, and he served in the church's hierarchy for many more years. At the time of the assassination, William Smith was in the East on a mission as a member of the Twelve and, due to his wife's illness and a somewhat shadowy warning by the church clerk about his safety, he did not return to Nauvoo until May 4, 1845.

There is little evidence about how he responded to the deaths of his elder brothers on June 27, 1844, and the resulting death of Samuel on July 30, just a month later. He seemed greatly burdened with the fact that he was the only remaining adult Smith male. Although he was not to know the full implications it would hold for him, he must have been aware that he was in both a significant and a dangerous position. Certainly, the fact of his survival would alter his relationship with the leadership and put him in a situation in which his contribution would be changed considerably. Quite possibly there would be an effort to oust the Smith family altogether.

In the remaining years William Smith was to serve briefly as patriarch and, under Joseph III, as a missionary. He would hold a variety of offices in connection with separatists' groups, but always briefly and unsuccessfully. He would never again be at ease with his relationship to the hierarchy of the church.

There must have been serious questions in Smith's mind about whether he was, in fact, a dissenter. More, I would think, that he held tight to his understanding of the gospel made available by his brother the martyr. And, despite his efforts at adjustment, he was never again to serve as he felt called within any system.

There can be little doubt that William Smith saw himself as the rightful heir of the patriarchal authority held by his father, Joseph, Sr., and by his brother Hyrum. This was a heritage traced through the lineage of thousands of years. The Book of Mormon linked Lehi, and his son Joseph, to the ancient patriarch Joseph of Egypt by means of direct lineage. This was how Joseph Smith the martyr provided literal linkage from Adam to the modern period. Patriarchal lineage moved forward as well, wrapping the early church in "an almost ecstatic sense of destiny."[3] For Joseph of old was linked with a new prophet, to be called Joseph after his father, who would lead his people as did Moses.[4]

Joseph Smith, Sr., was ordained on December 18, 1833, by his son (a loop in the authority linkage) bestowing on the senior Smith the power of patriarchal ministries, primarily the blessing of the faithful. Later, as he lay dying on September 14, 1840, the elder Smith "sealed" these patriarchal powers upon his son, Hyrum.[5] Joseph Smith, Jr., confirmed this in revelation four months later when he acknowledged Hyrum was to take the

> office of priesthood and patriarch, which was appointed unto him by his father, by blessing and also by right, that from henceforth he shall hold the keys of the patriarchal blessings upon the heads of all my people, that whoever he blesses shall be blessed, and whoever he curseth shall be cursed; that whatsoever he shall bind on earth shall be bound in heaven; and whatsoever he shall loose on earth shall be loosed in heaven; and from this time forth, I appoint unto him that he may be a prophet, and a seer, and a revelator unto my church, as well as my servant Joseph, that he may act in concert also with my servant Joseph.[6]

William Smith held the position that he had inherited rights to the sealing power that Hyrum held. As the sole remaining adult member of the Smith family, he was, by every right of lineage and of blessing, the holder of the keys of the gospel passed from Adam through the Old Testament prophets to the new generation of patriarchs—Joseph, Sr., Hyrum, and now himself. Assuming that William held, at least at the beginning, ideas of primogeniture, Joseph Smith III would hold the keys in potential and the expression awaited only his maturity. Thus the stage was set for William to act, "to hold the sealing blessings of my church, even the Holy Spirit of promise, whereby ye are sealed up unto the day of redemption."[7]

The subtleties by which the role seemed so legal by means of lineal descent, but through which descent he did not claim Joseph's role, appear to be far more pragmatic than ecclesiastical at this point. As time went by, the line between the two became increasingly hazy. As early as August 8, 1844, Brigham Young addressed William Smith's role as patriarch in a lecture to Sidney Rigdon on the contrasting roles of presidency and patriarchy. Young received the support of the conference to wait and let the Twelve decide about the matter of the patriarch.[8]

Smith pushed his claim almost immediately. Writing while still in the East, he affirmed the role of Brigham Young as head of the Twelve who must govern, but pushed for a decision on the identification of the Patriarch of the Church. He wrote to ask that "the Brethren remember me and my claims in the Smith family" not for Joseph's role but for Hyrum's. The office, serving as father to the church "must continue in the Smith family while they live and are in the faith."[9]

By late September 1844, Brigham Young responded that "the right [of the patriarch's office] rests upon your head there is no doubt" and suggested that if William Smith did not prefer to vacate in favor of his Uncle John or Uncle Asael, he should present himself for ordination.[10]

In *Times and Seasons* the editors reported receiving a letter from William Smith stating he would soon arrive in the city: "It will be his privilege when he arrives, to be ordained to the office of patriarch to the church, and to occupy the place that his brother Hyrum did, when living; and he will stand in the same relationship to the Twelve, as his brother Hyrum did to the First Presidency, after he was ordained patriarch."[11] According to the official record of these events, Brigham Young affirmed the legality of this action by right of descent.[12] *Times and Seasons* further editorialized that "William is the last of the family, and truly inherits the blood and the spirit of his father's house, as well as the priesthood and patriarchal office from his father and brother, legally, and by hereditary descent."[13]

Uncle John, Joseph Smith Sr.'s brother who had been ordained by the prophet on January 10, 1844, as a patriarch, would have been a far easier choice.[14] But Brigham Young, acting on what he must have felt was divine consideration, ordained William Smith as "Patriarch to the whole church" on May 24, 1845. The Twelve had some difficulty with this but gave their approval.

The anticipated trouble was not long in materializing. Writing after his ordination, Smith addressed the readers of *Times and Seasons,* indicating his need for support as the last of the long-suffering Smiths; his recognition of the authority of the Twelve (equally and as a body); and he implied—at least it seems to have been inferred—that he would follow Christ rather than the Twelve. It is just possible, as Gary Smith has interpreted, that as patriarch William Smith might see himself also as "associate president" as was Hyrum Smith.[15]

In the same issue of *Times and Seasons* an article by junior editor W. W. Phelps appears to have been written to add fuel to the fire. Phelps identified Smith as "Patriarch over the whole church" and claimed for him that this was a right which he had inherited, as had Joseph, Sr., and Hyrum. Phelps held up the Smith family before the church and identified William as the representative of the family to the church.[16] Again, the subtle realization was that Smith's claim to the patriarch's office could also support a claim to be Joseph Smith's successor.[17]

The response to this was quick and powerful. John Taylor, the formal *Times and Seasons* editor and a member of the Twelve, followed up with an answer in the June 1, 1845, issue. Correcting the language Brigham Young used (which identified William Smith as patriarch for the whole church), Taylor pointed out that William had been *ordained* as patriarch to the whole church. This was, in fact, a change from previous understandings of the role. Smith, Taylor suggested, may well act as the senior patriarch holding presidential authority over other patriarchs, but not over the whole church.

Taylor must have known what he was doing, for previous understandings of the office had emphasized that both Joseph and Hyrum Smith were patriarchs *of* the whole church and were to hold the keys for *all* the people.[18] Taylor was nevertheless very straightforward in his interpretation. Did his role place William Smith over the whole church as president, he asked rhetorically? He then answered "no." The calling to Hyrum Smith, he interpreted, made him senior but not the general authority, for Joseph Smith was called to be "a presiding elder over all my church." Taylor wrote, "And from this it is evident that the president of the church, not the patriarch, is appointed by God to preside. But does not the Patriarch stand in the same relationship ·to the church, as Adam did to his family, and as Abraham and Jacob did to theirs? No."[19]

Rather, Taylor pointed out, the patriarch's office must fall under the direction of the Twelve because the Twelve are those who are authorized to ordain patriarchs. Taylor obviously chose to ignore the fact that neither Joseph, Sr., nor Hyrum Smith, as patriarchs, were subject to the direction of the Twelve.

One of the few concessions Taylor seemed to be willing to make was to admit that William Smith, as patriarch, held the sealing powers. Certainly Hyrum had this authority even though it was exercised under the permission of Joseph Smith, Jr. But when Smith attempted to exercise this, he provoked Brigham Young's displeasure. By August of 1845, only a couple of months after his ordination, he felt the need to write to Young and ask him what he was supposed to do about sealings. Young replied with a brilliant legalistic reading of the tradition. Certainly, Hyrum Smith had the power of sealings, he pointed out. He was the legitimate patriarch and counselor, as was his brother William. But the power of the sealing was not part of the power of lineal authority. The sealing power was not in Hyrum's lineage, rather it was in his ordination and calling. Even then he only acted on Joseph Smith's authority. Anyone sealed without this authority would go to hell. Besides, sealing had to be done in the temple and thus had to wait.

Following this, the relationships between Smith and the apostles steadily deteriorated to the extent that he was rejected as apostle and patriarch at a General Conference on October 6, 1845. Within the next two weeks, he was excommunicated from the Latter-day Saint movement, primarily for insubordination. He had been patriarch less than six months. With his dismissal the conflict raised by his lineage and authority was held in check. Because of the need to control William Smith's power, as well as his ambition, the sealing powers of the office were removed and the authority and influence of the "presiding" patriarch greatly diminished. Eventually, the office would be withdrawn from the hierarchy of contemporary Mormonism.[20]

Did William Smith receive the same office through lineage and ordination as his brother Hyrum? No. William felt that the role of patriarch could continue even though the role of the president had obviously changed. He seemed to feel that it was possible for there to be two persons who were, in effect, over the whole church: he as patriarch and father and Brigham Young as president of the Twelve and of the First Presidency. He believed he could function as spiritual head of the movement while Young served as leader of the priesthood and overall manager of the church. This, Smith concluded, was his right and was the intention of God in whose wisdom lineage served to pass office from father to son, from brother to brother.

Why was William Smith excommunicated? Several reasons seem apparent. He was certainly a difficult man who believed he was right and that his legal authority was being diluted. He had seriously questioned the legal rights of the emerging presidency. He had written to a Brother Little in August 1845 to express concern over efforts to restrict the Smith family and acknowledged "Little Joseph" as the true successor, "although some people would fain make us believe that the Twelve are to be perpetual heads of the Church to the exclusion of the Smith family."[21]

Smith was less than optimistically loyal. Parley P. Pratt suggested that he should not remain in the Twelve until he "thinks different," asserting that he had proof positive that Smith was an "aspiring man; that he aspires to uproot and undermine the legal Presidency of the Church, that he may occupy the place himself."[22] William Clayton was concerned with Smith's support for those who favored young Joseph Smith III for president and thought "there is more danger from William than from any other source, and I fear his course will bring us much trouble."[23]

By late 1845 William Smith was vocally in opposition to Brigham Young and the church and openly sought dissenters who, it must be as-

sumed, would support his view of his own responsibility. He apparently tried to hold up Joseph III before the remnant, asserting his right to
be president and, consequently, himself and Emma Smith as guardians
until young Joseph's maturity. Emma never gave such an idea public support but may well have supported it in principle. William Smith's efforts
at this point came to very little, and his support of George J. Adams—
who organized a church in Augusta in the Iowa Territory with Joseph
Smith III as president and William as patriarch—further pushed him into
difficulties with the Twelve. However, as Roger Launius suggests in his
biography of Joseph III, "his [William's] activities in Nauvoo in 1845
apparently did establish very firmly in the minds of the Smith family the
concept of lineal priesthood, the passing on from father to son the rights
and duties of the religion."[24] Certainly, the publication in 1845 of "A
Proclamation: And Faithful Warning to all the Saints scattered around
in Boston, Philadelphia, New York, Salem, New Bedford, Lowell, Pe-
terborough, Gilson, Saint Louis, Nauvoo and elsewhere in the United
States; Also, to those residing in the different parts of Europe and in
the Islands of the Seas" was an example of his opposition.

In a letter written November 22, 1845, in the *Millennial Star,* James
Kay makes reference to a pamphlet published by William Smith that
denounces the Twelve who, according to Smith, "are not, nor ever were,
ordained to be head of the church; that Joseph's priesthood was to be
conferred on his posterity to all future generations, and that young
Joseph is the only legal successor to the presidency of this church."[25]

The charges concerning Smith's immoral behavior seem questionable, not his behavior so much as the charges. In an excellent article,
Irene M. Bates makes a real case for saying that his reputation as violent, obscene, and licentious was greatly exaggerated.[26] Smith was a
man of his times, and both his appeal to his fists and his sloppiness
about marital formalities not only reflected his times but also the behavior that many members of the leadership of the church exhibited
in the 1840s. It is important to note, as Bates pointed out, that despite the charges—and such supportive events as Smith's resignation
of his apostolic office over difficulties with his brother in October of
1836—no action was taken against him, even at a time when others
were being prosecuted for the same sort of crimes. Regardless of the
seriousness of the charges, or the facts upon which they were based,
many of these complaints came before and during the Twelve's consideration of Smith's ordination and certainly were not new charges
on which to initiate action.

Following his excommunication, Smith made several attempts to
regain his position through a reconciliation with Brigham Young and

the Twelve, or in association with one of the splinter groups. Just what Smith had in mind at this point requires serious consideration; he seemed to be playing the various groups against each other. In March 1846 he sent separate petitions to the Twelve and to Strang. To James Jesse Strang he offered the support of "the whole Smith family," support he could not provide, and to the Twelve he made threats and demanded action.[27] He demanded of the Twelve a public recognition of his right as a Smith and of his office, an honorable share of the kingdom, and that the Twelve repent of their wrongdoings.

When Brigham Young and the other apostles reorganized the church at Winter Quarters, near present-day Omaha, in December of 1847, "according to the original pattern with a First Presidency and a Patriarch," Uncle John Smith was named presiding patriarch.[28] He was sustained in October 1848 "over the whole church" and on January 1, 1849, as "Presiding Officer over the Patriarchal Priesthood." Certainly John Smith, through assuming a more gentle relationship with the president, maintained the role of the Smiths in that office. In 1855 Hyrum Smith's son, John, was called to serve in the position of presiding patriarch.

During the winter of 1845 and 1846 William Smith served as pastor for a Baptist church in the East but left quickly because his Mormon views were considered heresy. In 1846 he joined the movement of James J. Strang, very likely because it offered a potentially legitimate alternative to Young's group. Sixteen years to the day after Joseph Smith organized the church in New York, William Smith accepted his perceived rightful role under Strang. He was invited by the General Conference at Voree, Wisconsin, April 6, 1846, to take his place as a member of the Twelve and as patriarch.

Once again unable to conform to the "illegal" system, Smith was expelled from membership in 1847. Launius makes the point that "Old Mormons drifted from one group to another searching for what they considered the 'true faith' of the original church. Had these factions not existed, the old church members might well have left Mormonism altogether. As it was, however, many of them remained loosely affiliated with Mormonism and receptive to the message of the movement that became the Reorganized Church during the 1850s."[29]

When his association with Strang failed, Smith accepted the need to identify his own movement and acknowledged the necessity of accepting the role as the logical (legal) heir to the presidency, at least for awhile. He claimed to have had a revelation in 1847 that certainly supported the view that he had in mind a presiding role. Published as a part of an appeal "To the Scattered Saints" in November 1848, he recounted the words of the revelation:

I have appointed thee, my servant William Smith, to take the place of my servant Hirum Smith, thy brother, as Patriarch unto the whole church, and to preside over my people, saith the Lord your God, and no power shall remove thee therefrom; and thou shalt be the prophet, seer, revelator, and translator unto my church during the minority of him whom I have appointed from the loins of Joseph thy brother; go on, therefore, and organize and set in order all the branches, for I have given thee full power and authority.[30]

Smith took his appeal to the public in a series of long and often-provocative broadsides that asserted his own point of view and, consequently, put down other contenders. He did attract a small group of followers but was not very successful in establishing the church.[31]

His idea was attractive, however, to many who had been waiting for a leader. One of these was Isaac Sheen, who sided with Smith and who was responsible for the publication of the *Melchizedek and Aaronic Herald*. In the nine issues published between 1849 and 1850 the publication presented Smith as the most logical successor to the presidency.

In the spring of 1850, William Smith met with the Saints in Covington, Kentucky. He had visited many of the scattered Saints, teaching them the doctrine of limited priesthood as it applied to the presidency of the church. He argued against the legitimacy of all others who claimed succession. It was his right, he taught, as uncle, natural guardian, and only surviving brother of the former president, to be president pro tem during the interim.[32]

William Smith wrote to David Powell on Christmas Day 1851 to explain that he held lineage back through Joseph Smith, Jr., who had the right to give it to his sons. "Since all were dead it followed he could give office to whom he pleased, but if we would ever have a son the Presidency would be his by right of inheritance," Smith commented. "If he had no son he could bestow it upon another, with 'Young Joseph' having first chance."[33]

In 1852 the Saints gathered at the Newark Branch in Beloit, Wisconsin, rebuked William Smith because he believed that he should serve as the leader of any considered reorganization, and that he would do so in his own right rather than as guardian for young Smith.[34] The claim was considered pretentious, and the Saints "discontinued all connections and fellowship."[35]

But to a large degree it was this division of understanding between Smith's followers and those who accepted his concept of lineage but not the affirmations of his own responsibilities that provided the environment from which the Reorganization would emerge. Smith's case for lineage was strengthened, and his case for guardianship weakened, by the simple passage of time. As Joseph Smith III grew to manhood and showed himself to be a man of maturity and concern—even if not yet dedicated to the church—the promise of a Smith to lead the Saints encouraged those who had been waiting, sometimes patiently and sometimes in connection with a temporary leader, for the time when this was possible.

It was perhaps Jason W. Briggs's contact with William Smith that brought the whole issue to a head. Briggs, after a brief association with Smith's followers at Covington, became more and more assured of the truth of the lineal doctrine that Smith proclaimed. He affirmed that the concept was scripturally sound and traditionally valid in Mormonism. He acknowledged that many had forgotten the doctrine and had suffered because of doing so. Although Briggs could go along with William Smith's lineage, he could not accept the fact that Smith acknowledged polygamy to his followers and had participated in overlapping marriages, if not in polygamy. Disappointed and disillusioned, Briggs sought guidance which, in time, led to the formation of the Reorganization.

A significant part of the message Briggs recorded affirmed the law of lineage by which the priesthood was transmitted through generations. But it warned that "wolves" had been preying on the church members and that William Smith had been allowed to serve as a representative of the rightful heir because of the prayers of Joseph and Hyrum Smith in order to respect the "law of lineage, by which the holy priesthood is transmitted," but "as Esau despised his birthright, so has William Smith despised my law, and forfeited that which pertained to him as an apostle and high priest." Smith and his spokesperson Joseph Wood, it stressed, "shall be degraded in their lives, and shall die without regard."[36]

William Smith still had some hope he could work this out with those who had migrated to Utah. On August 8, 1853, he wrote to Brigham Young to assert once again his right to remain in the Twelve. He appealed in the name of the Christ he served, the Smith family he now represented, and as an apostle and patriarch of the Church of Jesus Christ of Latter-day Saints. He was still acknowledging Brigham Young's authority in 1854 and again in 1855; making claims for his apostolic role and affirming his position.[37] At one time he even considered a trip to Utah to test the waters.[38] There appeared to be no interest on Young's part.

By the late 1860s, William Smith apparently identified the Reorganization as the only place in which he might find opportunity to serve in his rightful capacity. But the Reorganization did not respond to his appeals in the manner he anticipated. His nephew, Joseph Smith III, was not open to much consideration. He provided Smith with the opportunity to join with the Reorganization, indicating a willingness to recognize his Melchizedek priesthood, but warned him against pushing his claims for apostolic or patriarchal office.

William did not respond immediately and over the next few years continued to press his demands: that he be accepted on the basis of his former membership and that he retain his standing as an active member of the Quorum of Twelve. But after several years completely cut off, he lessened his demands so that by 1879 it was possible for the Reorganization to accept him as a member. They also acknowledged him as a member of the Quorum of High Priests.

For some in the Reorganization this was more than they wanted to give. Jason Briggs, expounding on his 1851 revelation, remembered that Smith (and Joseph Wood) had "wholly forsaken my law, and given themselves to all manner of uncleanness, and prostituted my law and the keys of power intrusted to them, to the lusts of the flesh, and have run greedily in the way of adultery."[39]

In September of 1880, William Smith wrote yet another appeal to the readers of the *Saints' Herald*, the Reorganized Church's official newspaper, trying to convince them that the church needed a patriarch and that he was without doubt the proper person to be set aside to that office.[40] But although the explanation caused some comment, there was not much discussion either way. Apparently there was little doubt either officially or in the minds of the general members that the role of patriarch was a valid position in the church. The office was firmly established in tradition and in scripture by Joseph Smith, Jr.

On March 6, 1881, William Smith pushed his position again: "when will this Church of Christ be clothed upon as a bride adorned for her husband. Not until she is organized in her perfection, with all the gifts and officers made complete in the Church. . . . It is the duty of the First Presidency to select and ordain the Patriarch, that is to fill the place left vacant by the death of Hyrum Smith."[41]

Jason W. Briggs, who had once followed William Smith and traced his belief in lineal priesthood to Smith's concepts along that line, was, nevertheless, very much against Smith on this. Writing on the same day that Smith's letter appeared, Briggs told his friend William Kelley that he had tried earlier to abolish the office of patriarch, a "wart on the ecclesiastical tree, unknown in the Bible or Book of Mormon."[42]

Perhaps this attitude explained why the Reorganization, seeking all the legitimacy it could find, would not have accepted William B. Smith as an apostle based on his original ordination—and why, under the circumstances of William's heritage, lineage, and presence in the Reorganization, he was not named patriarch. It is certainly understandable why Joseph Smith III would be reluctant to accept his uncle's ordination by Brigham Young. But once they had accepted him on his own baptism and his high priesthood, why did either not accede to the role of apostle, for which he had a calling, or to patriarch for which he had lineage?

There is certainly indication that Joseph Smith III deliberately put off naming a successor to his Uncle Hyrum until William Smith no longer contended for the position. Such a method of dealing with controversy was not uncharacteristic for the young Smith. Just a few months after William Smith's death, he provided further outlines on the nature of the patriarch's role. He made many inquiries and, on one occasion, voiced his opinion rather forcefully. "Grandfather Smith was the first; Uncle Hyrum the second patriarch. But the Reorganization has never had one; as it was grossly abused in the Utah Church, and we had *no revelation* restoring the practice."[43]

Three years later, in April 1897, Alexander H. Smith, his next-younger brother, was called to be the Reorganization's first patriarch. The Patriarchal Quorum gathered for the first time in April of 1903. Then, in 1910, Joseph Smith III gave further direction to the patriarchal minister, including the often-quoted "he is not to meddle with branch affairs or district affairs." This, of course, was interpreted as no meddling at all.[44]

In April 1913, Frederick A. Smith, the son of Alexander H. Smith, was ordained presiding patriarch and served until his cousin, Elbert A. Smith, was ordained. Elbert Smith served just short of twenty-five years. It was at the World Conference in October 1958 that Roy A. Cheville, long a professor of religion at Graceland College and a man with a "pastoral reputation," became presiding patriarch in a radical break with the lineal tradition.

For William B. Smith, Cheville's appointment would have been the ultimate failure. Whatever the reasons or validity behind these decisions, the phasing out of the role of the presiding patriarch in both the Latter-day Saint Church and in the Reorganization the ordination of a patriarch who was not a member of the Smith family—a point emphasized by the fact the Elbert Smith's son, Lynn, was at the time a member of the quorum—sealed the fate of William Smith's affirmations concerning the family rights to the office of patriarch.

The other aspect of William Smith's belief, that of lineal authority, remained strong in the Reorganization. When Joseph Smith III approached the end of his life and began to consider who would lead the church in the years ahead, he was convinced of the legitimacy of the doctrine of lineal succession as it applied to the presidency. This concept, strongly if often unwisely endorsed by William Smith, was certainly behind the calling of Joseph Smith III as president of the Reorganization, even though he himself always downplayed this aspect of his calling.

Joseph Smith III clearly felt that a direct descendent of Joseph Smith, Jr., should by birthright become president of the church. Such a calling needed to be the product of heritage, which was evident in the lineage of his son, Frederick Madison Smith, and divine appointment, which Joseph Smith III identified in his letter of instruction. William Smith had such a heritage but had only briefly enjoyed the calling.

As William Smith discovered, there can really be no effective dissent within the church. This is true because the leadership reflects—and the consent of the people authorizes—the general will of the body. These Rousseauian and Burkian assumptions explain how the institutional church identifies truth and acknowledges the primary principle of the Mormon General Will as prescriptive. As the church legalistically ascribes to Mosiah 13:35, "it is not common that the voice of the people desireth anything contrary to that which is right; but it is common for the lesser part of the people to desire that which is not right."[45] The contrariness of the dissenter makes that person of "the lesser part."

It is difficult indeed to evaluate William Smith's role in the development of the office of patriarch. There is little doubt that he made an impact on both the Latter-day Saint and Reorganized Church communities. His stubborn assumptions about the prerogatives of the Smith family may well have weakened any acknowledgment of those rights and yet perhaps saved them from oblivion for at least a while. One must seriously question whether the overall effect was to save or destroy what he had in mind. His passionate insistence on the rights to the office of patriarch may well have driven Brigham Young to give in to Smith's demands at first, then to counter his claims with expulsion, which weakened the power of lineage through charges of insubordination and misconduct.

Certainly the nature of Smith's claims, both during his discussions with Joseph Smith III and as recorded in those years while the Reorganization was struggling to be born, can be interpreted as preventing him being named to the office of patriarch. In so doing, he slowed the resurgence of the office until after his death. In both cases the efforts to control Smith and the power of his claims may well have led to the declining authority and effectiveness of that office.

On the other hand, William Smith's support of the right of lineage had to have been difficult for Brigham Young to understand when, as president of the Twelve and not as a member of the Smith family, he assumed leadership and later when the Reorganization made so much of the lineal authority of Joseph Smith III. In the Reorganization it was William Smith's insistence that urged Jason Briggs to further action and during the 1850s caused the new organization to push for young Smith to join them.

William Smith was convinced of his role as a member of the founding family, and he believed he was called of God to restore the power and authority of the priesthood in the latter days. He saw that obligation, and right, in terms of lineage and blessing. At no time did he withdraw from his belief that his position was correct, that it was the law of the church, and that it was in keeping with God's commandments.

That he was unwise in his presentation, and in many of his actions, does not discredit his beliefs. He understood that the church—under Brigham Young as the "new authority" and under Joseph Smith III as the "inactive authority"—had moved from its original position and thus was wrong. Because the church was wrong, he had no other role but to dissent. He tried to fight it, he tried to live with it, he tried to adjust to it pragmatically, but in the end all he could do was to dissent.

Why, one must wonder, did William Smith simply not leave as so many others had done? Why did he not avoid the pain and discomfort caused by so many years of frustration and rejection? His place among the family gave him special reasons that account for his behavior. In consideration of such a plight, I wrote in 1977 that "the family was, and is, under the greatest pressure to be a royal family. The family must account for, and maintain, the sacred mantle; to wear the royal robes. But the robes of prophetic vision are not the common garment, even of prophets; and men and women have carried those garments with them through six generations because they were not called to wear them and they had no place to lay them."[46]

NOTES

1. Several biographical articles have been published on William Smith: E. Gary Smith, "The Patriarchal Crisis of 1845," *Dialogue: A Journal of Mormon Thought* 16 (Summer 1983): 24–35; Irene M. Bates, "William Smith, 1811–93: Problematic Patriarch," *Dialogue: A Journal of Mormon Thought* 16 (Summer 1983): 11–23; Paul M. Edwards, "William B. Smith: The Persistent 'Pretender,'" *Dialogue: A Journal of Mormon Thought* 18 (Summer 1985): 128–39. William Smith adopted the middle initial *B* when he became a Union army volunteer in 1864 and retained it thereafter.

2. Joseph's Smith Journal, October 30, 1835, in *An American Prophet's*

Record: The Diaries and Journals of Joseph Smith, ed. Scott H. Faulring (Salt Lake City: Signature Books 1989), 47.

3. Richard P. Howard, "A Brief History of Patriarchal Ministry," in *The Patriarchs,* ed. Reed M. Holmes (Independence: Herald Publishing House, 1978), 21.

4. *Book of Mormon* (Independence: Herald Publishing House, 1966), II Nephi 2:10–35.

5. Lucy Mack Smith, *Biographical Sketches of Joseph Smith and His Progenitors for Many Generations* (Lamoni, Iowa: Herald Publishing House, 1912), 337–38.

6. *Book of Doctrine and Covenants* (Independence: Herald Publishing House, 1970), sec. 107:29a–d; *The Doctrine and Covenants of the Church of Jesus Christ of Latter-day Saints* (Salt Lake City: Deseret Book Co., 1982), sec. 124:91–96.

7. *Book of Doctrine and Covenants,* sec. 107:38; *Doctrine and Covenants of the Church of Jesus Christ of Latter-day Saints,* sec. 124:124.

8. Joseph Smith, Jr., *History of the Church of Jesus Christ of Latter-day Saints,* ed. B. H. Roberts (Salt Lake City: Deseret Book Co., 1978), 7:232.

9. William Smith to Brigham Young, August 24, 1844, Brigham Young Collection, Church of Jesus Christ of Latter-day Saints Historical Department, Salt Lake City. In this and subsequent quotations from the period, spelling and capitalization have been modernized.

10. Brigham Young to William Smith, September 28, 1844, in *The Prophet,* November 9, 1844, as quoted in Smith, "Patriarchal Crisis of 1845," 27.

11. *Times and Seasons* [Nauvoo, Ill.], December 1, 1844, 727.

12. Smith, *History of the Church,* 7:301.

13. *Times and Seasons,* May 15, 1845, 905.

14. Smith, *History of the Church,* 7:234, 241.

15. William Smith, "Patriarchal," *Times and Seasons,* May 15, 1845, 904–5. Despite the fact of this issue's date—before the date of William's ordination—it was actually printed some two weeks later, after the ordination (Smith "Patriarchal Crisis of 1845," 29).

16. *Times and Seasons,* May 15, 1845, 905–6.

17. See Robert Glen Mouritsen, "The Office of Associate President of the Church of Jesus Christ of Latter-day Saints," M.A. thesis, Brigham Young University, 1972.

18. Smith, *History of the Church,* 4:189: Smith "Patriarchal Crisis of 1845," 30.

19. "Patriarchal," *Times and Seasons,* June 1, 1845, 921.

20. See Smith, "Patriarchal Crisis of 1845." One hundred and thirty-four years later, on October 6, 1979, Eldred G. Smith became patriarch emeritus, and the office he held in the Latter-day Saint movement was discontinued.

21. William Smith to Brother Little, August 20, 1845, LDS Historical Department.

22. Joseph Smith III and Heman C. Smith, *History of the Reorganized Church of Jesus Christ of Latter Day Saints* (Independence: Herald Publishing House, 1968), 3:32.

23. William Clayton, Journal, May 23, 1845, as quoted in James B. Allen, *Trials of Discipleship: The Story of William Clayton, a Mormon* (Urbana: University of Illinois Press, 1987), 164.

24. Cited in Roger D. Launius, *Joseph Smith III: Pragmatic Prophet* (Urbana: University of Illinois Press, 1988), 42.

25. *Millennial Star* [Liverpool, England], May 1, 1846, 134; Smith and Smith, *History of Reorganized Church,* 3:30.

26. Bates, "William Smith, 1811–93," 11–23.

27. See Linda Newell's response to Paul M. Edwards, "William B. Smith and the Ordination Question," paper presented at the annual meeting of the Mormon History Association, May 7, 1983, Omaha; copy in my possession.

28. "General Epistle from the Twelve," *Millennial Star,* March 15, 1848, 86, as quoted in Irene M. Bates, "Uncle John Smith, 1781–1854: Patriarchal Bridge," *Dialogue: A Journal of Mormon Thought* 20 (Fall 1987): 84.

29. Launius, *Joseph Smith III,* 81.

30. Quoted in *Saints' Herald,* July 28, 1909, 701.

31. William Smith's broadsides are: "William Smith, patriarch and prophet of the most high God. Latter Day Saints, Beware of imposition." (Ottawa, Ill.: N.p., 1847); "A revelation given to William Smith in 1847, on the apostasy of the Church and the pruning of the vineyard of the Lord" (Philadelphia: N.p., 1848); and "Zion's Standard, a voice from the Smith Family" (Princeton, Ill.: N.p., 1848).

32. William B. Smith, *Defense of Elder William Smith. . . .* (Philadelphia: Brown, Bicking and Guilbert, Printers, 1851).

33. *The Messenger* [Salt Lake City], November 10, 1875, 5–6.

34. Edmund Briggs, deposition in *Abstract of Evidence No. 1720, Temple Lot Case,* U.S. Circuit Court, Kansas City, Mo. (Lamoni: Herald Publishing House, 1893), 208.

35. Smith and Smith, *History of Reorganized Church,* 3:209.

36. Ibid., 3:200; *The Messenger,* November 10, 1875, 1.

37. William Smith to Brigham Young, August 8, 1854, May 7, 1855, and February 13, 1859, all in LDS Historical Department.

38. Brigham Young, Office Journal, May 14, 1860, LDS Historical Department.

39. Smith and Smith, *History of Reorganized Church,* 3:201; *The Messenger,* November 1, 1875, 1.

40. *Saints' Herald,* September 15, 1880, 289–90.

41. Ibid., March 15, 1881, 86–87.

42. Jason W. Briggs to William H. Kelley, March 6, 1881, William H. Kelley Collection, Reorganized Church of Jesus Christ of Latter Day Saints Library-Archives, Independence.

43. *Book of Doctrine and Covenants,* sec. 104:17; Joseph Smith III, Letter Book no. 5, 140, Reorganized Church Library-Archives.

44. *Book of Doctrine and Covenants,* sec. 125:4c.

45. Paul M. Edwards, "Ethics and Dissent in Mormonism," 7, paper presented at the Sunstone Theological Symposium, August 1986, Salt Lake City.

46. Paul M. Edwards, "The Secular Smiths," *Journal of Mormon History* 4 (1977): 4. This was the Mormon History Association's Presidential Address, delivered April 23, 1977, at Kirtland, Ohio.

7

The Old Fox:
Alpheus Cutler

Danny L. Jorgensen

Alpheus Cutler, the "Old Fox," died in southwestern Iowa on August 10, 1864, at eighty years of age.[1] A New Englander, Cutler was an early convert to the new American religion established on the sixth of April 1830 by Joseph Smith, Jr. He participated in the growth of early Mormonism and gatherings of the Saints on the American frontier. A high priest, Cutler rose to considerable prominence in the Nauvoo Mormon church. He became a member of the elite inner circle around the charismatic Mormon prophet and an initiate of the novel, secretive Nauvoo Temple theology. After Joseph Smith's martyrdom in 1844, Cutler accepted the leadership of the Mormon apostles, followed Brigham Young across Iowa, and anticipated moving west with this largest single remnant of Nauvoo Mormonism.

During the late 1840s a Mormon branch at Silver Creek, under Cutler's leadership, became embroiled in a prolonged dispute with Council of Twelve president Orson Hyde and the High Council at Kanesville. Some of Cutler's associates eventually were disfellowshipped, and in 1851 he was excommunicated. Left with few alternatives, Cutler, who was called "Father" by about two hundred followers, founded the Church of Jesus Christ (Cutlerite) in 1853 as the successor to and a reorganization of Joseph Smith's religion.

Cutler and his followers were not attempting to reform Mormonism or establish a schismatic movement. They had been devout Saints, well versed in Nauvoo Mormonism, initiates to the temple rites, and even participants in celestial marriage, that is, marriage for eternity. They were unlike many of the Saints, especially the members of branches outside Nauvoo, who remained uninformed about temple Mormonism. They had not been among the dissidents within the Nauvoo church. Unlike Sidney Rigdon, James Strang, William Smith, and other rivals of Brigham Young and the Mormon apostles, Cutler did not aspire to be Joseph Smith's successor. He and his followers were not part of the original movement that later formed the Reorganized Church of Jesus Christ of Latter Day Saints.

Based on his membership in the Nauvoo Council of Fifty and ordination by Joseph Smith to Lamanite (Indian) ministries, Alpheus Cutler—much like the apostle Lyman Wight and Bishop George Miller, who also founded schismatic movements—expected to play a leading but specialized role within the Church of Jesus Christ of Latter-day Saints. Although Cutler and his followers subsequently rejected the practice of plural marriage, they were fully committed to Nauvoo Mormonism as mediated through Cutler's Council of Fifty membership, and they aimed to preserve and enact it while awaiting the building of Zion, the Kingdom of God on earth, the Second Coming, and the Millennium.

Alpheus Cutler was born February 29, 1784, in Plainfield, Sullivan County, New Hampshire. He was the second of ten children (the family was comprised of eight daughters and two sons) and the eldest son of Knight and Betsy Boyd Cutler. His ancestors, James and Anna Busby Cutler, were English immigrants who in 1635 resided in Watertown, Massachusetts. His father, Knight, was a Rhode Islander by birth and a veteran of the Revolutionary War. Alpheus Cutler achieved basic literacy, farmed with his father, and learned the trade of stone masonry. He was over six feet tall, heavy-set, and powerfully built. His disposition and manner were forceful, outspoken, and at times fiery. He was critical, possessed a sarcastic style, and frequently expressed himself in an extremely candid, sharp, and brusque manner.[2]

In 1808 Cutler married twenty-year-old Lois Lathrop, the daughter of Captain Samuel and Lois Huntington Lathrop, a prominent Lebanon, New Hampshire, family. Shortly thereafter the Cutlers moved to Upper Lisle, Broome County, New York, where three of their eleven children—Thaddeus (1809), Lois Huntington (1811), and Libbeus (1814), who died in infancy—were born. Cutler served in the military during the War of 1812, and his experience as a soldier was invoked frequently in subsequent years as a source of his leadership ability. Shortly after the war the Cutlers relocated to Chautaugua County in western New York near Lake Erie, where most of their other children— Louisa Elizabeth (1816), Sally (Sara) Ann (1818), William (1821), Benjamin Franklin (1823), Clarissa (1824), Emily (1827 or 1828), Edwin H. (1829), Betsy A. (1832), and Phineas (unknown)—were born. About 1830, the Cutlers' eldest son, Thaddeus, married Lemira Scott and moved to nearby Forestville.

It is not known whether the Cutlers were particularly religious before their conversion to Mormonism.[3] They may have been Congregationalists. The Cutlers resided within a forty-mile radius of the various locations of Joseph Smith's family and the family of Emma Hale before 1830. The Hale and Lathrop families probably knew one another. It seems likely that the Cutlers had some familiarity with Mor-

monism before 1832. Alpheus Cutler, like Joseph Smith, was steeped
in the magical worldview that pervaded the American culture of the
period.[4]

David W. Patten, a Mormon missionary, met the Cutlers around
1832 while preaching near his former home at Orleans. Following a
meeting in the Cutler home, Lois, the Cutlers' critically ill daughter,
requested a healing administration. Immediately thereafter she reportedly arose from bed, dressed, walked around the room, and declared
that she had been "healed by the power of God." Patten's preaching
and this apparent miracle resulted in the conversion and baptism of
eighteen people and the establishment of a Mormon branch at Silver
Creek, New York.[5] Alpheus Cutler was baptized on January 20, 1833,
and shortly thereafter ordained an elder.

About this time the Cutlers left New York and joined the Mormon
gathering at Kirtland, Ohio. They established farms, and Cutler used
his skill as a stone mason to help build the Kirtland Temple. He attended the School of the Prophets (a priesthood study group organized
by Joseph Smith) and was appointed to a committee responsible for
compiling the *Doctrine and Covenants of the Church of the Latter Day
Saints,* published in 1835. Having memorized the prophet's lectures on
faith and much of the *Doctrine and Covenants,* Alpheus Cutler possessed prodigious recall. He was notorious for his ability to call up
scriptural support for a particular point of argument.

Cutler actively supported Joseph Smith in the conflicts that splin-
tered the Ohio church. Present on March 27, 1836, for the temple's
dedication, Cutler, like many of the Saints, experienced ecstatic manifestations of the spirit accompanying this event. He "saw in a vision a
gold chain, suspended or draped, across the room and saw the Lord
descending on a long strip, which resembled a carpet. This Being
seemed to move toward him and spoke to him."[6] Belief in and use of
gifts of the spirit (speaking in tongues, healing, prophecy, the discern-
ing of spirits, and miracles) was prevalent among the Mormons, and
they were emphasized later by the followers of Cutler.

Lois H. Cutler married Almon W. Sherman at Kirtland in 1835. The
Shermans were early Mormon converts. Almon's brother, Lyman R.
Sherman, was called to the Council of Twelve Apostles, but died before ordination. Through the Shermans, the Cutlers were linked by kinship to several other eventual Cutlerite families. Another daughter,
Louisa Elizabeth, married Tunis Rappleye in 1836. The Rappleyes, like
members of other Cutlerite kinship groups, were among the Mormons
who eventually went to Utah.

In late 1836 or early 1837 the Cutlers and Shermans moved to northern Ray County to be near Saints gathered in Missouri, where they farmed along the Crooked River. Cutler may have constructed a bridge and mill on the Grand River around Richmond.[7] "When the cornerstones were laid for the [Far West] Temple on that Fourth of July, 1838, Alpheus Cutler was ordained by President Smith to be the 'chief architect and master workman of all God's holy houses'."[8] As a result of violence against the Mormons on October 27, 1838, the Cutlers lost their farms and crops in Missouri.[9] They moved to Commerce, Illinois (later renamed Nauvoo), selected homesites, and established farms in 1839. In April Cutler and the Mormon leadership slipped back to Missouri, when he laid the foundation for a temple at Far West, an event that marked Cutler's rise to prominence.

At the Semiannual Conference of the Church in October 1839, Alpheus Cutler entered the Nauvoo High Council and later the Nauvoo Temple's building committee. His drawings were selected by Smith to guide temple construction.[10] Cutler worked in the tithing office, and became a familiar figure among Nauvooans as the ringer of the bell calling temple laborers to and from work. A group of Mormons, under the leadership of Peter Haws and Alpheus Cutler, left Nauvoo in September 1841 to obtain timber in the pine country of Wisconsin along the Black River (on Indian land) for temple construction. A large raft of boards and timbers was shipped down the Mississippi River and arrived in Nauvoo in October 1842. Cutler regularly reported to the church regarding progress on the temple.[11] About 1842 or 1843 he testified before the governor in Springfield on behalf of Joseph Smith, and otherwise supported the prophet against detractors inside and outside the Church.

Cutler's most significant role in Nauvoo Mormonism came with his selection to the secretive Council of Fifty, a parapolitical body established by Joseph Smith for the purpose of achieving the Kingdom of God on earth. He was one of the first few men chosen for the council, and eventually he was ordained by special divine revelation through Smith to head a committee (that included Oneida Indian, Lewis Denna, a later follower) responsible for Lamanite ministries. Cutler's participation in the Council of Fifty symbolized and defined his membership in the elite, inner circle around the charismatic Smith.

As a member of the Fifty, Cutler received special instructions from the Mormon prophet regarding the Kingdom of God, as well as privileged information regarding the emergent temple theology, including celestial and plural marriage. Most of the apostles, who also belonged to the Council of Fifty, were away from Nauvoo for extended periods of time conducting missionary work and later campaigning for Smith's election to the U.S. presidency. Cutler remained in Nauvoo most of the time and therefore was a more continuous participant in the Council of Fifty's discussions. Alpheus and Lois Cutler were among the earliest, secret initiates to temple Mormonism. Like the wives of other eminent Mormons, Lois participated in the Nauvoo Relief Society presided over by Emma Smith, the prophet's wife.

By the time of Smith's death in 1844, the Council of Twelve and many of the Council of Fifty were practicing celestial and plural marriage, the most distinctive feature of temple Mormonism. Cutler was no exception. On January 14, 1846, he (at sixty-two) and Lois (fifty-eight) were sealed together for time and eternity. With Lois's consent and participation Alpheus also married Luana Hart Beebe for eternity this same day. On February 3, 1846, he took five more wives in temple ceremonies: Margaret Carr and her sister Abigail, Sally Cox, Daisey Caroline McCall, and Henrietta Clarinda Miller.

Very little is known about most of these women, and there is no record that any of them, except Luana, produced children by Cutler.[12] Luana Hart Beebe was born October 13, 1814—making her thirty-two when she married—in Lebanon, New Hampshire, the birthplace of Lois Cutler. The Beebes were early Mormon converts, and Luana's father (Isaac, Sr.) and several brothers (particularly Calvin) became prominent priesthood members and later Cutlerites. They were among some of the first Mormons to populate Jackson County, Missouri, where in 1832 Luana, who was sixteen, married a seventeen-year-old second cousin of Joseph Smith's, Orrin Porter Rockwell. By 1844, the union had produced five or six children (Emily, Caroline, Orrin Dewitt, Sarah, and one or two Josephs), five of whom (all excepting the Josephs) survived infancy. The Rockwells divorced about 1845.[13]

After Luana's marriage to Cutler, the Rockwell children, who remained with their mother, were sealed to him in the Nauvoo Temple. Luana's marriage to Cutler produced three children: Jacob Lorenzo (born February 18, 1846), Olive Luana (March 8, 1850), and Lydia Ann, whose birthdate is unknown. Lydia died in infancy, but Jacob and Olive survived. The paternity of these children was kept secret, however, even from them. Jacob used the surname of Boyd (Cutler's mother's maiden name) and was told that his father was a deceased scout for the Mormon Pioneer Company. Olive alternatively used the surnames Baldwin and Perry, reflecting Luana's subsequent marriages to Wheeler Baldwin and Isaac Perry.

Other members of the Cutler family, like other eventual Cutlerite families, also participated in plural marriage.[14] Clarissa Cutler, Alpheus Cutler's twenty-one-year-old daughter, married the apostle Heber C.

Kimball on December 29, 1845 in the temple. About this time, her sister Emily, sixteen, also married Kimball. A son, Abraham, was born to Clarissa and Heber, and a son, Isaac, was born to Emily and Heber. Clarissa and Emily did not go west with their husband. Both women subsequently repudiated their marriages to Kimball and then married Cutlerite men. Abraham and Isaac Kimball grew up among the Cutlerites, residing in Cutler's home and later in that of their Uncle Thaddeus's. They rejoined their father's family in Utah, however, during their early teens.

At the time of the Smiths' murders in June 1844 Cutler served as captain of the prophet's bodyguards. He helped bury the fallen leaders at Nauvoo in unmarked graves, so as to prevent them from being desecrated by mobbers. He also served briefly as an unofficial leader of the church. With the return of the Twelve to Nauvoo, Cutler acknowledged their leadership. Much of his time was spent supervising the completion of the temple, but he also was involved in councils of the Twelve and the Fifty. Unlike Brigham Young and some of the Twelve whom Emma Smith distrusted, the prophet's widow relied on Cutler. He served as an arbitrator between the Twelve and her over the next several years. With the decision to speed the Saints' removal from Nauvoo, Cutler was selected to captain a company. He joined Brigham Young and the Twelve as part of the Camp of Israel, which began crossing the Mississippi River to Iowa Territory in February 1846.

Alpheus Cutler arrived at the Missouri River on June 12, 1846. He wrote for the counsel of Young and the Twelve before crossing the river.[15] On the other side, he founded one of the first Mormon encampments, designated by Brigham Young as "Cutler's Park" in his honor.[16] During the summer of 1846 Father Cutler, as he was respectfully known, helped select the site of winter quarters. He was sustained as president of the Municipal High Council at Winter Quarters on August 6, 1846, making him one of the most important leaders of the exodus.

Over the summer and fall of 1846, some eventual Cutler followers crossed the Missouri. Other founding Cutlerites, like the Latter-day Saints generally, were scattered over Iowa. Some of them remained for an extended period at Mt. Pisgah, others created what they thought would be a temporary encampment at Silver Creek, while other eventual Cutlerites gathered at Farm Creek.[17]

In anticipation of an early spring departure from Winter Quarters, Cutler was selected as president of Heber C. Kimball's company on January 27, 1846. Why these plans changed is not clear.[18] At the Missouri (on Pottawattamie or Omaha land), Cutler met some Indians with whom he had been acquainted in New York, observing that they served in the army with him, ate and slept at his house, and "some of them are New York Gentlemen."[19] This meeting stimulated Cutler's interest in pursuing Lamanite ministries. He approached the Mormon leadership for permission to undertake an exploratory mission. Eye-witnesses later testified that Brigham Young blessed Cutler for his Lamanite calling before a collection of policemen at Winter Quarters.[20]

Cutler proceeded with this missionary effort. He hoped to secure government contracts to build mills and schools, operate them, and provide other forms of assistance, as well as to preach and to seek converts. He also discussed with Young the possibility of organizing the Indians for armed resistance to defend the Mormons should the army or militia be sent against them. Young expressed interest in the economic advantages of Cutler's undertaking and reminded him that Joseph Smith had committed to him and none other "the keys to open the Gospel to every Lamanite nation," but rejected organizing Indian resistance.

When Winter Quarters was abandoned in 1848, the governing high council and Cutler's position on it were dissolved. He relocated to Silver Creek, rejoined family and friends, and became president of the Silver Creek (Big Grove) Branch. If Cutler felt displaced when Apostle Orson Hyde became president of the reconstituted High Council at Kanesville (later Council Bluffs), there is no record of it. Whatever his feelings, he had made provisions for another challenging undertaking—his Lamanite ministry.

Brigham Young wrote Cutler on April 21, 1848, to encourage him to continue west. Cutler replied on April 23 that he would start as soon as "circumstance will permit," offered his best wishes and blessings, and signed the letter "your brother in the new and everlasting covenant," signifying his plural marriage participation.[21] Between 1848 and about 1853, Cutler and his associates conducted Lamanite ministries. The Cutlerites, as they had come to be known, established an encampment, which may have moved several times, among the Indians. They traveled between Silver Creek and the mission; some of the Cutlerites remained in Kansas continuously, while others—like Cutler and Bishop Luman H. Calkins—moved back and forth, stopping over at St. Joseph, Missouri, as well as visiting Mormon families and encampments along the river.

A majority of Cutler's followers were early Mormon converts, predominately former Protestants and New Englanders.[22] They embodied such basic values of this regional, early-nineteenth-century American culture as a commitment to republican ideology, and they resided around well-established villages in New England and later, as Mormons, on the American frontier.[23] Sometimes before, and certainly after, joining the Latter Day Saints they were geographically mobile. A majority of them had "common school" educations, some had learned trades, and a few had advanced schooling and—infrequently—some college. They farmed as a full or part-time occupation, some worked at more or less skilled trades, and a few were successful businessmen and merchants. They were not members of the upper classes, but neither were they impoverished.[24] A high proportion of eventual Cutlerites, in comparison with the general Mormon population, received temple endowments before leaving Nauvoo. Most of the eventual Cutlerite men had been ordained to the Mormon priesthood.[25]

On April 22, 1848, Orson Hyde wrote Brigham Young that there was "a good deal of disaffection" among the branches in Iowa.[26] Persistent rumors about Cutler's mission and teachings disturbed the Kanesville High Council. "Lamanism," as Cutler's teachings were referred to by the council, eventually was interpreted as heresy. Except for Cutler's later claim to exclusively hold the keys to the priesthood and authority for the Kingdom, however, there was nothing inherently heretical about Lamanism. It derived from the Book of Mormon's account of New World peoples, including a belief that the curse of dark skins placed on them by God for their earlier sins would be lifted in the latter days. Through their ministry, the early Mormons believed, the Lamanites would be redeemed and take their place in Zion.

Brigham Young subsequently would establish the priority of the apostles as having authority for the continuity of the Restoration, but Cutler was not alone in thinking that the Council of Fifty—from which his claims to Lamanite ministries derived—had an authority equal to or even greater than the Twelve. Apostle Lyman Wight's claims to authority also derived from this principle, and Peter Haws challenged the authority of Orson Hyde, as president of the Twelve, on these same grounds. Because the Council of Fifty operated secretly at Nauvoo and its existence was almost completely unknown outside Nauvoo, it is not surprising that Cutler's assertions were perplexing to many movement participants.

In September 1848, representatives of the Kanesville Council visited Cutler's Camp at the Big Grove on Silver Creek, and a meeting with Cutler and Calkins was arranged.[27] Summarizing this meeting, the High Council wrote to the First Presidency in the Great Salt Lake Valley: "We considered your pledge to the Old Fox a sacred one. . . . Our spirit seemed a little troubled, but we could see nothing wrong that we could get hold of, and thought it was quite probable that our feelings might be effected by the old gentleman's natural parabolical, allegorical, symbolical, mysterious, secretive way of telling things."[28] This description of Cutler is revealing and consistent with subsequent events and other indicators of his conduct.

The High Council gathered further information and made plans to visit Silver Creek. In the meantime (November 1848), Hyde wrote them a letter stating that "Father Cutler and Bishop Calkins were taking to themselves strength, and laying a plan that was calculated to destroy the life blood and best interest of the Church. The Brethren were counseled not to follow them any farther until the Books were balanced before the High Council, as the Big Head is a dreadful and contaminating disease."[29] Elder Stoddard was sent to the Big Grove Branch to read the letter to them, "and in the case the infection was likely to be spreading, to read it to the other Branches." The letter "stirred up a Hornet's nest," and a remark by Stoddard provoked a "severe lecture from Cutler" as well as a "flood of anathemas" from other members of the branch.[30]

The High Council received a response from the Silver Creek Saints defending their actions, disapproving of the actions of the council, and charging them with interfering with Cutler's mission. They responded, noting to Brigham Young that "if our first letter was rather high seasoned, and was calculated to produce excitement, our second one was decidedly of a mild and pacific character." Getting no response, George Smith was sent to Silver Creek, where he discovered that Cutler had "stuck a broad axe in his shinbone" and that he would come before the Council as soon as it healed.[31]

On December 15, 1848, Cutler, along with other Silver Creek Saints, arrived at Kanesville. They objected to an investigation of Lamanism before the council on the grounds that it involved Council of Fifty business, and consequently a more informal meeting was arranged. A lively argument ensued, during which Calkins disputed the council's understanding of Cutler's ministry. Eventually, the conflicting parties reached a compromise. The High Council agreed to sanction Cutler's mission so long as it did not harm the church. Cutler and his associates were to exhibit respect for the council's authority, and offer certain retractions.

A month later, however, Calkins wrote a letter disputing the minutes of the December 15 meeting. The High Council complained to authorities in Utah: "Because we would not hold still and suffer ourselves to be jumpt on rough shod, and rode down out of sight, we have been called usurpers, tyrants, and religious despots."[32] Hyde indirectly accused the Cutlerites of minting counterfeit money, organizing the

Indians for armed rebellion, attempting to reestablish the church in Jackson County, Missouri, and exhibiting an unwarranted piety.[33] From the standpoint of the Cutlerites' powerful New England republicanism, Hyde's actions no doubt were seen as tyrannical.

The case against Cutler, Calkins, and the Silver Creek Branch was taken up at the April 6, 1849, conference of the church in Iowa. Hyde summarized the problems, admitted to being a "little warm or heated at times," but noted that he was fortunate to have two "cool, deliberate and calculating" counsellors. He claimed that the Silver Creek Saints had seldom, if ever, come before the High Council cheerfully and were "very technical, and metaphysical." Objecting to a Cutlerite contention that the work of God would be "speedily consummated," he argued that "No enthusiastic flirts—no vain or wild chimera—no mysterious humbug is going to accomplish the great purposes of our Heavenly Father in these days." According to Hyde, "Father Cutler lies a little back in the shade, behind the curtain while Bishop Calkins is his organ and mouth-piece and the 'Magnus Apollo' to carry out his measures." Asserting the authority of the High Council, he observed, "If the Silver Creek Branch were as frank and honest as they pretend, they would say . . . that they regard Father Cutler as the highest authority on earth."[34]

Hyde's comments obviously reflect a conflict over authority, but they also reveal tensions between worldviews. As a college-educated man, Hyde was committed to Enlightenment rationalism, whereas Cutler and many of his followers exhibited a more esoteric, other-worldly, mystical, magical worldview. Both worldviews coexisted in early Mormonism but, with the death of Joseph Smith, a magic worldview gradually was displaced by one that was more pragmatic, rationalistic, and conventionally religious. Of the Cutlerites, Hyde—with characteristic rhetorical vigor—commented: "The wicked subterfuge is resorted to, in order to beguile the unwary, that the ancients have visited them, tongues and prophecyings are dealt out so profusely that the market is glutted. We are weak mortals; but when the Holy Spirit comes upon us, and we take an action upon those who have questioned our power, our right, and our jurisdiction, in order to get a lengthened term to do wrong, they will find, sooner or later, that what we bind on earth is bound in Heaven."[35] Under the leadership of such men as Young and Hyde, the charisma of Joseph Smith would become routinized, and a more priestly form of authority would replace prophetic authority.[36]

In defense of the Cutlerites, William Redfield of Silver Creek argued that Cutler "always sustained the heads of the Church," and he would "make full return to the authorities here" as soon as he got back. He further maintained that "if Bishop Calkins taught wrong things it was private, and not in public." Finally, he challenged, "let those who have said anything against the Branch prove it."[37]

The conference had heard enough, however, and upon the recommendation of President Hyde, Bishop Calkins was "dis-fellowshipped until he makes satisfactory retractions." Alexander Stanley's motion that Cutler's mission be suspended "until an investigation is entered into, and an understanding is given before the Authorities of the Church, and it is approved by them; and until he knows us and knows himself" was "[c]arried unanimously."

Hyde exhibited less and less patience for Cutler's cause, yet conference actions aimed to gain compliance. Cutler's mission had been suspended, but he was not disfellowshipped. Bishop Calkins had been disfellowshipped, but this action, rather than cutting him off from the church through excommunication, implied that membership might be restored. In spite of Hyde's speculations about Cutler, he had not openly defied the authorities.

On October 21, 1849, Brigham Young wrote to Cutler from Great Salt Lake City. Aware of Cutler's problems with the High Council, he offered assistance to the Iowa Saints in moving west and described in glowing terms the construction of the city, its comfortable homes and splendid farms. He counseled Alpheus to come west with his family by the next season, offered him a house, and indicated that his old friends would welcome him in a spirit of peace and fellowship.[38] For his part, then, Young hoped to keep the Old Fox and his followers in the movement. Their continued participation, however, was contingent on signs of westward progress.

The Iowa trek sapped the strength, resources, and resolve of Young's followers and resulted in considerable suffering, death, and apostasy. In spite of efforts by Iowa authorities to assist the westward migration, many of those who lingered declined help, and by 1849 they had begun to question earlier plans to continue to the Great Salt Lake Valley. A variety of factors mitigated against relocation: age (some were too old or too young), poor health and physical handicaps, insufficient commitment to Mormonism, lack of economic resources, and having established successful farms and businesses in Iowa.[39] It is not surprising that these conditions would contribute to personal differences, disagreements, conflicts, and bad feelings. Nor is it surprising that there would be conflicts over authority, or that rival leaders, such as Bishop Miller, Apostle Wight, and Cutler, would emerge and attract followings.[40]

Hyde perceived this situation, probably correctly, as threatening the success of the Utah Mormon movement. At the April 6, 1850, conference held at Kanesville, Cutler's case again was considered. It was resolved that if Cutler did not appear before the High Council and demonstrate a willingness to go to the valley, he would be disfellowshipped.[41]

Cutler responded on June 13 from his camp near the (Kansas) Caw River to Brigham Young's letter of the previous year. Referring to the work Young appointed him to do, Cutler said he needed another year or two so as to complete mills under contract. He defined this as a matter of honor to himself and the church. Once his work was complete, Cutler maintained, he would come to the valley or anywhere else that Young directed. Because it was Young whom appointed him, Cutler noted, he was appealing his disfellowship (a result of the conference resolution) directly to him.[42]

A High Council committee was appointed to investigate the Silver Creek brethren. Quite a number of Saints—Calvin Beebe, Jacob Myres, Michael Jacobs, Dana Jacobs, Sandford Jacobs, Ruben P. Hartwell, Herman Abels, Lewis S. Dalrimple, and Jehial Hildreth—were found to be "disaffected," and they were disfellowshipped.[43] The Saints were warned further that if they associated with these people, they too would be "cut off."

In 1851 Cutler and some of his followers remained in the Kansas Indian Territory with their mission to the Delawares. They had not completely renounced moving to the Great Salt Lake Valley, but they demonstrated no inclination to do so in the near future. They remained unrepentant and even defiant. Hyde had forsaken gaining the compliance of the Cutlerites. Responding to a letter asking about Cutlerism, he defined it in the *Frontier Guardian* as: "'The big Head,' swelling into sore accusation,—breaking out and freely discharging the corruption of Apostasy."[44] On April 20, 1851, Cutler was excommunicated from the Church of Jesus Christ of Latter-day Saints.

He and many of his followers sustained relations with family members and friends in the valley, but his excommunication effectively severed formal relations with Young and his organization. Some of them pondered the possibility of moving west from time to time, and a few families eventually went to the valley and rejoined this organization.

In 1851, under pressure from civil authorities in Iowa, Cutler "put aside" his plural wives.[45] Some founding Cutlerites claimed that their discovery of plural marriage in 1849 was the principal reason for their disaffection from the Utah Mormon movement. They commented that "the first task was to eradicate any taint of plural marriage."[46] Chancy Whiting, Cutler's eventual successor, undertook this challenging task with a considerable degree of success. In spite of contradictory evidence, contemporary Cutlerites (and many of the descendants of the found-

ing group) sincerely subscribe to an interpretation of their history
that—like the emergent Reorganized Church's interpretation—held plural marriage to be an innovation of Brigham Young's. Knowledge of
plural marriage probably did influence the decisions of many of the
founders. Their knowledge—an intimate, detailed, directly experien-
tial knowledge, not ignorance—lead many Cutlerites to a growing revulsion for the practice of plural marriage, and thereby influenced decisions about continued involvement with the Young's organization.
Rejection of plural marriage was a way of justifying the Cutlerite
schism, however, not its cause.

With the formation of their schismatic movement in 1853, the Cutlerites claimed that Alpheus Cutler had been ordained at Nauvoo by
Joseph Smith through divine revelation to a special, secret quorum of
seven men entrusted with all the keys and authority of the priesthood
and Kingdom and appointed exclusively to Indian ministries. Smith's
murder, they argued, signaled God's rejection of the Mormon church but
not the priesthood or the Kingdom. Furthermore, they contended, it involved God's repudiation of the Gentiles in this dispensation, but not
the Jews or Lamanites. As the seventh member of the quorum, Cutler
had been required to wait until the six ranking members were dead (as
in the case of the first man, Joseph Smith) or in apostasy (as in the case
of the sixth man, John Smith, Joseph's uncle) before taking action.[47] Because the Gentiles had been repudiated and Cutler held exclusive authority for Lamanite ministries, he alone, the Cutlerites maintained, held
the keys to the priesthood and Kingdom. By 1853 John Smith was in
apostasy for having accepted membership in the Utah Mormon church,
the Cutlerites argued. When Cutler received a heavenly sign (two half
moons with their backs together) fulfilling Joseph Smith's prophecy to
him, he proceeded to reorganize Mormonism.

As a basic platform of faith, the Cutlerites endorsed Joseph Smith
as a prophet of God, the Bible, the Book of Mormon, and the *Doctrine and Covenants*. Reflecting their republicanism, they added the U.S.
Constitution as a sacred work. Cutlerism stressed Mormon restoration-
ism, primitivism, adventism, millennialism, communitarianism, Lamanism, and the temple theology. It reflected an entirely conventional Nauvoo Mormonism.[48]

Cutler's reorganization provided for two lines of leadership. With
the keys of the priesthood and Kingdom, he was the ultimate authority: chief counselor, God's representative on earth, and president of the
High Priesthood. He did not claim to be Joseph Smith's successor as
prophet.[49] The various priesthoods were organized by quorums with
presidents and counselors, but the Cutlerites made no provision for

apostles. The church, as opposed to the Kingdom, had a president and two counselors. A High Council was established, but by the middle 1850s it was defined as the Quorum of High Priests. The Cutlerites were theocratic; the High Council interpreted the laws of God for the people, conducted trials for those charged with law violations, and imposed judgment and sanctions. Biannual conferences of the body of the church were held to decide the more practical affairs and vote on whether to sustain official (including both lines of authority) as well as High Council actions. A republican principle thereby was combined with an otherwise theocratic notion of government.[50]

The Cutlerites founded three settlements in Iowa. In the spring of 1852, Edmund Fisher—a Cutler associate—and a committee of Silver Creek Saints explored and located the site of a new town. By 1853 about thirty-five or forty families, mostly from Silver Creek, moved to a site in Fremont County (around twenty-five miles southeast of Silver Creek), secured additional property, and constructed a village given the Book of Mormon name *Manti*. Within a few years, non-Mormons were attracted to the little frontier community, swelling its population to around three hundred.[51]

During the period 1851–54, Cutler and some of his followers pursued missionary work among the Delaware Indians on the Grasshopper River (now called the Delaware) in Kansas. The impossibility of securing title to farms and improvements created on Indian lands, troubles with the Indian agents, hardship, disease, and few converts ultimately led them to abandon the mission. Between 1853 and about 1855, additional families from the Silver Creek area and other locations in Iowa, the Indian mission, and a few dissidents from the Great Salt Lake Valley joined the Manti settlement.

By 1859 a Mormon branch at Farm Creek, another settlement they founded, had joined or affiliated with the Cutlerite church. Other former Mormons scattered over southwestern Iowa united or associated with the Cutlerite branches at Farm Creek and Manti. That the Cutlerites prospered to some extent is signified by their effort to establish a colony on the Platte River in Taylor County, Iowa, about fifty miles east of Manti.[52] By the late 1850s the Cutlerite movement had grown to more than five hundred, with three branches in southwest Iowa. The Manti Cutlerites had established a church corporation by 1860 so as to live the Order of Enoch or the "law of all things in common."[53]

The early Cutlerites were a demographically normal population. The average ages and age distribution of the group closely reflected these characteristics of the American population of the period and the early Mormons. They were about equally divided by gender, with approximately equal numbers of males and females by age. A majority of the adult population was married. The size and composition of Cutlerite families was traditional.[54]

In 1855 the Cutlerites were approached by Zenos H. Gurley, Sr., representing what became the Reorganized Church of Jesus Christ of Latter Day Saints. Cutler and his followers rejected Gurley's overture with assertions of their superior claims to Mormon succession, as well as Cutler's greater knowledge of Nauvoo Temple doctrines and ritu als. While the Cutlerites by this time shared rejection of plural marriage with the Reorganized Church, the Cutlerites—unlike Reorganization members—otherwise preserved belief in temple Mormonism. Except for plural marriage, Cutlerite beliefs and practices thereby were much closer to Young's conception of the gospel than to that of the Reorganized Church's at this time. With Joseph Smith III's acceptance of prophetic leadership of the Reorganization in 1860, most of the Farm Creek Saints and many of the Manti Cutlerites, including Alpheus Cutler's eldest son and designated successor, Thaddeus, joined with him.[55]

By 1860 Cutler's health was failing. He had little use of his legs, probably due to a stroke. His speech was blurred and ineffective, and he found this frustrating and embarrassing. He suffered from phthisic, a consumptive condition or form of pulmonary tuberculosis that became progressively worse. By 1864 he was a house-bound invalid unable to care for himself.[56] Leadership of the schismatic Mormon movement that he rather unintentionally created was passing to younger men, the Whiting brothers, Chancy, Francis Lewis and Sylvester, as well as Hiram and Lyman Murdock.[57]

When Cutler died on August 10, 1864, with a resolve and commitment reinforced by prolonged conflict and struggle with the Utah Mormons, a younger group of Cutler's most ardent supporters sustained belief in Cutlerism and successfully transmitted this resolve to subsequent generations. Reinforced by repeated conflicts and rivalry with the Reorganized Church, this was sufficient to ensure the persistence of the Cutlerite movement to the present.[58]

NOTES

In researching the Cutlerites, I am indebted to countless individuals and several organizations. I gratefully acknowledge the assistance of the Church of Jesus Christ (Cutlerite), the Reorganized Church of Jesus Christ of Latter Day Saints, and the Church of Jesus Christ of Latter-day Saints. I especially appreciate permission from the Church of Jesus Christ of Latter-day Saints to quote materials from its Archives. Myrtle Hyde and Biloine Whiting Young were also quite helpful in the preparation of this chapter.

1. Cutler was called the "Old Fox" by Orson Hyde and the Mormon High Council at Kanesville, Iowa. See Orson Hyde, George A. Smith, and Ezra T. Benson, "A Report to Presidents Brigham Young, Heber C. Kimball, Willard Richards, and the Authorities of the Church of Jesus Christ of Latter Day Saints in Zion," 1849, 12, Church of Jesus Christ of Latter-day Saints Historical Department.

2. Rupert J. and Daisy W. Fletcher, *Alpheus Cutler and the Church of Jesus Christ* (Independence: Church of Jesus Christ, 1974), chapter 1.

3. Some years before 1832, Cutler reportedly was pronounced dead by a physician but then revived. He recalled going to paradise and being told by God that he should return to earth, as a great work was before him. See Emma L. Anderson, "Others, with the Church in an Early Day," *Autumn Leaves* 2 (1889): 494–96.

4. This point is developed by Michael S. Riggs in "Nauvoo's Kingdom of God on Earth and Back to Back Half Moons in the Iowan Firmament," paper presented at the Mormon History Association Annual Meeting, Quincy, Ill., May 14, 1989, and "The Cutlerites: A Microcosm of Early Mormon Folk Magic Beliefs," paper presented at the Sunstone Theological Symposium West, San Francisco, 1990. For an outstanding discussion of the influence of magic on Joseph Smith, see D. Michael Quinn, *Early Mormonism and the Magic World View* (Salt Lake City: Signature Books, 1987).

5. This popular and frequently reported early Mormon conversion story is recounted in Inez Smith Davis, *The Story of the Church* (Independence: Herald Publishing House, 1938), 141–42. Another version is reported by Anderson, "Others, with the Church in an Early Day," 494–96.

6. Fletcher and Fletcher, *Cutler and the Church*, 18.

7. Emma Anderson, "An Incident of the Past," *Autumn Leaves,* July 7, 1895, 315–16.

8. Fletcher and Fletcher, *Cutler and the Church*, 25.

9. For details, see Sylvia Cutler Webb, "Autobiography of Sylvia Cutler Webb," *Saints Herald,* March 24, 1913, 289–93; Emma L. Anderson, "Autobiography of Emma Lacine Anderson," July 20, 1920, Reorganized Church of Jesus Christ of Latter Day Saints Library-Archives, Independence, Mo.

10. Fletcher and Fletcher, *Cutler and the Church*, 28.

11. Joseph Smith III and Heman C. Smith, *History of the Reorganized Church of Jesus Christ of Latter Day Saints* (Independence: Herald Publishing House, 1968), 2:653.

12. Margaret and Abigail Carr were born in Mecklingburg County, North Carolina. They likely became Mormon converts while living in North Carolina. Margaret was seventy-five and Abigail was sixty-six upon their marriages to Cutler. Apparently, both of the Carr sisters had been married previously, although there is no record of any children, and it seems likely that they were widowed. At the time of her marriage to Alpheus Cutler, Sally Cox was fifty-

two. She may have been a distant cousin of Joseph Smith's. She was born in Barnard, New Jersey, and probably was one of the first several hundred converts to Mormonism. She may have been married several times previously and probably was a widow, but there is no record of children by previous marriages. Daisey Caroline McCall was a native of Lincoln County, North Carolina, and forty-four at the time of her marriage to Cutler. At twenty-four, Henrietta Clarinda Miller, a native of Alfred, New York, was the youngest of Cutler's plural wives. See Clare B. Christensen, *Before and After Mt. Pisgah* (Salt Lake City: N.p., 1979), 176.

13. See Harold Schindler, *Orrin Porter Rockwell: Man of God, Son of Thunder* (Salt Lake City: University of Utah Press, 1966).

14. The subsequent Cutlerite leader Chancey Whiting's father-in-law, Isaac Morley, for example, took plural wives. His wife's sister Cordelia Morley became a plural wife of F. Walter Cox (for time only, being sealed to Joseph Smith for eternity). Cox's first wife was Whiting's sister, Emeline. Chancey Whiting was sealed to Morley in the Nauvoo Temple at this time, and it is highly probable that he witnessed some of these marriages. Chancey Whiting's eldest living brother, Edwin, took plural wives. His sister, Jane, and his widowed sister-in-law, Martha, both married the noted Mormon scout Return Jackson Redding. Most, if not all, of these ceremonies were performed in the temple before leaving Nauvoo. Calvin Beebe, a leader of the Farm Creek group and brother of Cutler's plural wife Luana, performed celestial and plural marriages in the Nauvoo Temple. One of Calvin Beebe's brothers and perhaps his father also may have taken plural wives. Silas Richards, a brother of leading Farm Creek Cutlerites and a Utah Mormon, took plural wives before leaving Nauvoo. There no doubt were other plural marriages among Cutlerite kinfolk, many of whom continued west with Brigham Young, that remain to be documented.

15. Alpheus Cutler and Reynolds Cahoon to Brigham Young and the Council of the Twelve from Upper Camp of Israel, June 12, 1846, Church of Jesus Christ of Latter-day Saints Historical Department, Salt Lake City.

16. Cutler's Park was located about two and one-half miles northwest of the subsequent site of Winter Quarters (or what is today the northern Omaha suburb of Florence). About 1988 a small memorial was erected near this site.

17. Those people who became Cutlerites commonly were members of different communities and settlements as Mormons. The Cutlers, Andersons, Murdocks, Shermans, and other eventual Cutlerite families settled in Nauvoo. Many of them knew one another, but they did not collectively comprise a distinctive faction of the Nauvoo church. A majority of the eventual nucleus of Cutler's movement lived about twenty-five miles south of Nauvoo, near what is now Lima, in and around the Morley settlement. This Mormon stake, unlike most of the outlying settlements of the Nauvoo church, was fully and intimately connected to Nauvoo Mormonism at the highest levels. The leaders of the group received instruction regarding the temple theology, including celestial marriage—from Joseph and Hyrum Smith, Brigham Young, and other apostles—as it was formulated and emerged. See Christensen, *Before and After Mt. Pisgah,* chapter 6.

18. Cutler's disaffection, it has been suggested, derived from differences with his son-in-law Heber C. Kimball because Cutler's daughters remained at the Missouri rather than accompany their husband west. Kimball's concern that he might not see these wives and his infant sons again has been seen, retrospectively, as a premonition that they would not follow him west. What Kimball thought is unclear, but conditions at Winter Quarters (poor shelter, malnutrition, disease, and death) and the perils of travel to an ambiguous western destination certainly provided reasons for anxiety. Alpheus Cutler reportedly said in 1848—with reference to their parting—that "Bro. Kimball told me that if I did not come and see him in three years, he would come and see me, so I hope to see him again" (Hyde, Smith, and Benson, "A Report to Presidents," 21).

19. Ibid., 21.

20. For a discussion of Cutler's Indian Mission, see Danny L. Jorgensen, "Building the Kingdom of God: Alpheus Cutler and the Second Mormon Mission to the Indians, 1847–1853," *Kansas History* 15, no. 3 (1992): 192–209.

21. Alpheus Cutler to Brigham Young, April 23, 1848, LDS Historical Department.

22. The eventual Cutlerites tended to convert in nuclear and even extended family groups. On this issue, see A. J. Simmonds, "John Noah and the Hulets: A Study in Charisma in the Early Church," paper presented at the Mormon History Association, Lamoni, Iowa, May 1979; and A. J. Simmonds, "'Thou and All Thy House': Three Case Studies of Clan and Charisma in the Early Church," paper presented at the Mormon History Association, Quincy, Ill. May 1989. They were related to such early Mormon leaders as Titus Billings and Isaac Morley, and they were or became related to such prominent early Mormon families as the Pratts, Pattens, Murdocks, Partridges, and Snows.

23. See Kenneth H. Winn, *Exiles in a Land of Liberty: Mormons in America, 1830–1846* (Chapel Hill: University of North Carolina Press, 1989).

24. Although critical of changing American values and concerned with their middling economic status, the founding Cutlerites did not embrace Mormonism because of socioeconomic deprivation. Nor were they rejecting American society. Rather, in Mormonism they found ways of preserving their Americanism and exemplifying its fundamental values. In all of these ways, the founding Cutlerites were like other early Mormons, including other followers of Brigham Young. There is no indication that underlying sociocultural differences between the founding Cutlerites and other Mormons contributed to the formation of their splinter movement. For an excellent recent consideration of the general Mormon alienation from American society, see Marvin S. Hill, *Quest for Refuge: The Mormon Flight from American Pluralism* (Salt Lake City: Signature Books, 1989), and Winn, *Exiles in a Land of Liberty*.

25. A significant number of the would-be Cutlerite men were members of the Quorum of Seventies, an elite missionary corps. Buckley Anderson, Wheeler Baldwin, Calvin Beebe, Luman Calkins, Thaddeus Cutler, Lewis Denna, Pliny and Edmund Fisher, Isaac Perry, William Redfield, Augustus Richards, and Almon Sherman, among other founding Cutlerites, held important positions

and performed leadership roles as members of the Mormon priesthood. Beebe, Perry, and Sherman had been members of Zion's Camp. Samuel and J. R. Badham, Amos Cox, Dexter and Clark Stillman, and Almon and Edmund Whiting served in the Mormon Battalion.

26. Orson Hyde to Brigham Young and the Council of Twelve, April 22, 1848, LDS Historical Department.

27. Hyde, Smith, and Benson, "A Report to Presidents," 11.

28. Ibid., 11–12.

29. Ibid., 15–17.

30. Ibid., 17.

31. Ibid., 18.

32. Ibid., 26.

33. Like other early Mormons, the founding Cutlerites sustained belief in Jackson County, Missouri, as the location of gathering, the temple, and Zion as prophetically revealed through Joseph Smith. Cutlerite belief that Zion would be redeemed by Alpheus Cutler, who would build a temple in Independence during their lifetimes, was not an inherently heretical idea. It was primarily at odds with the immediate practical problems concerning relocation to the Great Salt Lake Valley and establishment of permanent settlements facing the Utah Mormon leadership. See Pliny Fisher, "Book of Patriarchal Blessings," 1859, Reorganized Church Library-Archives; Danny L. Jorgensen, "The Fiery Darts of the Adversary: An Interpretation of Early Cutlerism," *John Whitmer Historical Association Journal* 10 (1990): 67–83; *Frontier Guardian* [Kanesville, Iowa], March 7, 1849.

34. Orson Hyde, ed., "Conference Minutes," *Frontier Guardian*, May 2, 1849, 1–2.

35. Hyde, ed., "Conference Minutes," 2.

36. Max Weber, *The Sociology of Religion* (Boston: Beacon Books, 1964).

37. Hyde, ed., "Conference Minutes," 1–2.

38. Brigham Young to Alpheus Cutler, October 21, 1849, LDS Historical Department.

39. Richard E. Bennett, "Lamanism, Lymanism, and Cornfields," *Journal of Mormon History* 13 (1986–87): 45–59; Richard E. Bennett, *Mormons at the Missouri, 1846–1852: "And We Should Die. . . ."* (Norman: University of Oklahoma Press, 1987).

40. The organizational stability of Young's movement was remarkable considering the dissension within Nauvoo Mormonism that partly contributed to Smith's death, the emergence of conflicting claims to movement leadership, the exodus from Nauvoo, the hardships of the Iowa trek, the scattered conditions of the membership, and the difficulties of maintaining effective lines of communication from the Mississippi River to the Rocky Mountains. The hierarchial organization of Mormonism, especially Young's capable and decisive leadership, was a source of much stability. There were, however, multiple hierarchial organizations and lines of authority. The Camp of Israel was organized on a quasi-military basis, with units of ten family heads combining into larger units of fifty and one hundred overseen by leaders with corresponding authority. As

encampments and way-stations were established, local branches were organized under the leadership of presidents and counselors. Larger gatherings, such as those at Winter Quarters and then Kanesville, elected stake authorities and high councils with municipal authority. Overlapping with these organizations was the hierarchically ordered lay priesthood headed by the First Presidency and Quorum of Twelve Apostles. Prominent Mormons, such as Orson Hyde, commonly performed multiple leadership roles without clear designation of the locus of their authority. As president of the Twelve Apostles, Hyde had an ambiguous set of responsibilities, some of which overlapped with his presidency of the Kanesville High Council; specific assignments given him by the church presidency; and authority as a member of the Melchizedek priesthood. A bitter dispute between Hyde and Almon W. Babbitt over efforts to lobby U.S. government and Iowa politicos derived in some part from a lack of clarity about Hyde's roles and corresponding authority (Hyde, Smith, and Benson, "A Report to Presidents," chapter 1). It would have been surprising had multiple and overlapping organizations and lines of authority not provoked periodic confusion and conflict.

41. Orson Hyde, ed., "Conference Minutes," *Frontier Guardian*, May 1, 1850, 1.

42. Alpheus Cutler to Brigham Young, June 13, 1850, LDS Historical Department.

43. Orson Hyde, ed., "High Council," *Frontier Guardian*, September 4, 1850, 2. With the exception of Calvin Beebe, there is no indication that any of these people continued as part of the Cutlerite movement. It therefore seems likely that they became disaffected and left Mormonism entirely. This interpretation raises interesting questions about the extent to which the Cutlerite schism had much of anything to do with belief in or commitment to Cutler's teachings.

44. Orson Hyde, ed., "Definition of Cutlerism," *Frontier Guardian*, March 21, 1851, 2.

45. What this meant, exactly, is not clear. Henrietta Clarinda Miller, as well as Cutler's daughters Clarissa and Emily (the former wives of Heber Kimball, who had remarried), subsequently died while on a mission in Kansas. Margaret and Abigail Carr, Sally Cox, and Daisey Caroline McCall disappeared from the historical record. Luana Hart Beebe continued to live among the Cutlerites, even after Alpheus Cutler's death, but she subsequently married Wheeler Baldwin and later Isaac Perry. Other Cutlerite kinfolk who were plural marriage participants continued west with Young's supporters. Hence, there is no indication that the Cutlerites practiced plural marriage after 1853.

46. Fletcher and Fletcher, *Cutler and the Church*, 44.

47. The Cutlerites have been unable to identify the other four members of the Quorum. See Fletcher and Fletcher, *Cutler and the Church*, 53–54.

48. Manti Book no. 1, record kept by Chancey Whiting, clerk of the church, commencing September 19th 1853, Church of Jesus Christ, Clitherall, Minn. (hereafter cited as Manti Book).

49. Such contemporaries as Chancey and Sylvester Whiting viewed him as

such, but Cutler never employed the titles of *prophet, seer,* or *revelator.* Cutler and his successors did not contribute prophecies to the *Doctrines and Covenants.* The contemporary Cutlerites limit their claims to exclusive authority for the priesthood and Kingdom.

50. Manti Book 1.

51. Manti was located about three miles southwest of modern-day Shenandoah in Fisher Township, Fremont County, Iowa, on Fisher's Creek just north of the hickory grove on the hill. A memorial park has been established on this site, and it includes parts of the original cemetery that was desecrated over the years.

52. A mill initially was established three miles north of contemporary Blockton on the Platte River. Because of unfavorable conditions, the settlement relocated just south of the current bridge west of Blockton. There is no record of what the Cutlerites called this settlement. It subsequently is referred to as "Mormontown."

53. The Culterites' communitarianism has been cited as a source of conflict with Young's followers. Some of Cutler's followers had been members of "The Family," a communalistic venture founded by Isaac Morley and Sidney Rigdon and practiced by their followers on the Western Reserve before their conversions to Mormonism. The "law of consecration and stewardship" formally established communitarianism as an early Mormon practice. Although it was abandoned for a tithing principle, many Mormons sustained belief in it as an ideal. Young's supporters and other Mormons periodically have experimented with communitarianism to the present day. Hence, although the Order of Enoch has received unique emphasis by the Cutlerites, there is no indication that a belief in communitarianism, as opposed to tithing, was a source of differences or conflict between them and the Utah Mormons.

54. Danny L. Jorgensen, "The Social Backgrounds and Characteristics of the Founders of the Church of Jesus Christ (Cutlerite)," paper presented at the Mormon History Association, Quincy, Ill., May 13, 1989, provides a detailed discussion of Cutlerite demographics.

55. Zenos H. Gurley, Sr., to Brother Cutler, November 29, 1855, January 3, 1856, both in the Reorganized Church of Jesus Christ of Latter Day Saints Archives; Alpheus Cutler to Zenos H. Gurley, Sr., January 29, 1856, Reorganized Church Library-Archives.

56. Mary Audentia Smith Anderson and Bertha Audentia Anderson Hulmes, eds., *Joseph Smith III and the Restoration* (Independence: Herald Publishing House, 1952), 207.

57. Within several months, Cutler's most devout followers were prepared to leave Manti. Guided by his prophecy that they would find a new home to the north between two lakes, they trekked five hundred miles north to Minnesota and founded the village of Clitherall in Otter Tail County. A year later they were joined by a second party from Manti. A few Cutlerites remained in Iowa, and several families that had gone to Minnesota returned after the first winter. Most of these former Cutlerites joined the Reorganized Church, form-

ing along with the Farm Creek Saints an important concentration of Reorganization members in southwestern Iowa.

58. With the deaths of most of the founding generation, the Cutlerite movement declined. In 1912, however, Isaac Morley Whiting assumed leadership and stimulated revitalization. During the late 1920s, a branch was established in Independence, Missouri, thereby fulfilling a Cutlerite dream of returning to Zion. Today, there are about thirty active Cutlerites with branches in Clitherall and Independence. They believe, however, in a prophecy attributed to Cutler that says that they may dwindle down to perhaps as few as three members before a new prophet emerges to lead them to Zion.

8

Stephen Post:
From Believer to Dissenter to Heretic

M. Guy Bishop

Stephen Post (1810–79) carried on a personal search for what he considered proper authority to act in the name of God from the time he converted to the Mormon faith in 1835 until his acceptance of Sidney Rigdon as the rightful successor to Joseph Smith, Jr., in 1857. From that time until his death more than twenty years later, he was an ardent defender of Rigdon's claim to be the true shepherd of Mormonism.

Post's zeal for expounding Rigdonite Mormonism knew no bounds. After embracing Sidney Rigdon as his prophet, he was almost constantly engaged in proselyting for the Church of Jesus Christ of the Children of Zion (Rigdonites). One of his most audacious efforts involved several attempts to sway Joseph Smith III, leader of the Reorganized Church of Jesus Christ of Latter Day Saints, to Rigdon's side.

Between 1865 and 1879 Post wrote several pedantic, rambling letters to Smith, urging him to "adhere to the word spoken through your father." Finally, clearly annoyed at Post's diatribes, Joseph Smith III responded in August 1879. "It is simply folly for you, and men like you, who have been conversant with the church, to construe the law [regarding succession in the church presidency] as you do," he told Post. "You have stood out and stultified your manhood," charged the Reorganization leader, "and prostituted your priesthood till you have about wasted your life in a fruitless endeavor to become learned above what is written."[1]

What brought Stephen Post to this point by 1879? Why had he chosen not to follow either of the two leading bodies of Mormonism? Post not only differed with Joseph Smith III and the Reorganization, but he also disagreed with that division of the Mormon movement that had followed Brigham Young to Utah. In 1953 Dale L. Morgan, writing about the churches of the dispersion, found Stephen Post to be "the last important champion" of Rigdonite Mormonism.[2] How and why Post arrived at that point reveals much about the state of Mormonism after the murder of Joseph Smith.

Like many others, Post based his association with Mormonism on his acceptance of the Book of Mormon. "I was convinced of the truth of [it]," he wrote, "& became determined to strive to serve my Creator until the end of my life." Responding to a 1841 request that missionaries communicate with the church's Quorum of Twelve Apostles regarding their labors, Post sent this report and autobiography to Brigham Young:

> I was just beginning for myself 6 years ago in the forests of Western Pennsylvania when I found "a marvelous work & a wonder" which arrested my attention. I found upon careful examination, with a prayerful heart; that the "law of the Lord is perfect [in] converting the soul" I therefore subscribed to the law . . . of baptism, administered by Elder Stephen Winchester. I am a blacksmith by trade, have only a small house & lot of 4 acres of land, a wife and two children (boys) . . . my wife is not a member of the church & is here surrounded by unbelieving friends.

Post informed Young in closing, "I took my license [to preach] & got it recorded April 1, 1836. I have continued to preach from time to time until present."[3] And he was still proselyting sporadically eight years later when Smith's death stunned Mormonism.

In June 1844 Joseph Smith was lynched by an anti-Mormon mob at Carthage, Illinois. His followers, doubtless including Stephen Post, were thrown into spiritual disarray. The prophet was dead! Who should now lead the church? Several claimants quickly stepped forward. Brigham Young, as senior member of the Quorum of Twelve Apostles, argued for apostolic authority in this time of crisis. Young claimed the primacy of the Twelve by virtue of Smith's having conferred upon them "all the keys and powers" related to propagating the latter-day message.[4] For a denomination as concerned with religious authority as were the mid-nineteenth-century Mormons, this position held much appeal.

Another who laid claim to the prophetic station was James J. Strang, who professed authority by appointment of Joseph Smith, Jr. At the time of the Carthage martyrdom Strang was on church assignment in Wisconsin assessing the possibilities for a Mormon relocation there. In the angelic visitation that Strang claimed at the very hour of Smith's death, the heavenly messenger advised that he was now to lead the church. Upon returning to the Mormon capital of Nauvoo, Illinois, Strang produced a letter reputedly written by Joseph Smith that named him as the successor.[5]

Finally, there was Sidney Rigdon, then an inactive member of the church's governing triumvirate, the First Presidency (the president and two counselors). Rigdon, once an important Mormon leader but by 1844 out of favor within the hierarchy, hurried to Nauvoo from his self-imposed exile in Pittsburgh to forward his position. Claiming a revelation that appointed him guardian of the church until young Joseph Smith III, then almost twelve, was ready to assume his father's mantle of leadership, Sidney Rigdon sought to wrest control from the Twelve.[6]

For Stephen Post, like many other followers of Joseph Smith, the weeks and months following his death were filled with personal decisions. Were Brigham Young and the Twelve the bearers of the true priesthood that Smith professed to have restored? Was the claim of James J. Strang, which included an angelic visitation similar to those experienced by Smith, of greater validity? Then there was Sidney Rigdon, whose offer to serve as caretaker until Joseph Smith III reached maturity may have appealed to some who saw in the boy a continuation of their beloved prophet's leadership.

In the immediate aftermath of Smith's death, Post was left largely to his own wits in deciding what to do. For whatever reason, Post almost always lived in isolation from the main body of the church. He was from the eastern United States and, despite Smith's attempt to gather the faithful at one central location, Post spent little time among other Mormons. This may have contributed to his decisions about the succession question; almost certainly it was important in his theological conceptions. He learned about doctrinal perspectives from reading and through the sermons of traveling ministers, not from senior leaders in Nauvoo.

Even so, Stephen Post lived in Nauvoo from October 1842 until April 1844, yet never seemed truly happy there. After his arrival, he attended several religious meetings, often at the home of Stephen Winchester, the elder who had baptized him seven years earlier. Twice he heard Heber C. Kimball, a member of the Quorum of Twelve Apostles, speak, and on another occasion he listened to Sidney Rigdon. Yet, for Stephen Post, something was missing. "I attended a prayer meeting at br. Winchester's," he noted on November 12, 1842. He could not help contrasting this meeting with others he had attended at Kirtland, Ohio, in 1835 and 1836. "There [in Kirtland] the majority were full of life and animation," Post recalled, "here the majority neither showed whether they were alive or dead to the cause of Zion."[7]

At Nauvoo, Post may also have heard disquieting rumors concerning plural marriage. During the early 1840s Joseph Smith began experimenting with new marriage and family patterns. These, especially plurality and the sealing of couples in eternal unions through the authority of the priesthood, highlighted the community's socio-theological development for many Mormons. Smith introduced both principles cautiously on a limited scale among the church hierarchy, but many Nauvoo residents certainly heard talk of such things.[8]

Although Post never mentioned his feelings about plural marriage during the early 1840s, within the following decade he was using his journals to oppose the practice. Later, while attending the 1850 coronation of Strang as "king in Zion," Post noted that rejection of polygamy was part of Strang's doctrine. "[A] law was proclaimed for the peace of families & for the purity of the kingdom," he wrote, "that from this time forth one man shall have but one wife." The following year Post recorded a Strangite resolution stating that "we reject the doctrines of plurality of wives, polygamy, celestial marriage and all doctrines relating there to as unfounded in the word of God and at variance with the law of the church of Jesus Christ."[9]

Post left Nauvoo before Smith's murder and, continuing through 1844, lived in Pennsylvania. He made no effort to affiliate formally with any of the Mormon factions at Nauvoo or elsewhere. He did, however, continue to preach Mormonism as he had embraced it in the 1830s. He frequently proselyted in company with his brother, Warren (1811–75), who eventually became a follower of Strang and rose to apostleship in his church.[10] By late 1845 Post was aware that Brigham Young and the Twelve were planning to move the church to the West. That November he received official word from Nauvoo about "the intention of the brethren [Brigham Young and the other apostles] to move to Oregon in the Spring."[11] Instead of going west with Young, Post eventually chose a different path—that offered by Strang. Yet in late 1845, he seemed to still recognize the authority of the Twelve, referring to them as "the brethren."

What, then, led Post to Strang and away from the influence of Brigham Young? Unfortunately, he left no solid answers about his decision, but there are many hints. Stephen Post may well serve as a paradigm for other Mormons who remained in the Midwest and East. He undoubtedly had strong family reasons to stay behind. Pennsylvania was his native state. His wife was still not a Mormon. Equally important, by the summer of 1847, his brother Warren was following Strang. A distaste for much of what he saw at Nauvoo also marked Post's vision of Mormonism. He longed for the days of Kirtland. For him, Brigham Young and the apostles represented a continuation of an emerging religious life of Nauvoo that included plural marriage, temple endowments, and a complex salvation theology.[12] Such a thought may have caused Post to pause.

By the spring of 1850, Post's two brothers, Warren and Leonard, had gone to Beaver Island in Lake Michigan to be with Strang, and in June Post joined them. He had been inclined to follow Strang since July 1846. "I have great confidence that he holds this position by revelation & the will of God," Post observed. His belief was somewhat tempered, however, when comparing Strang with Smith. "I have not as strong [of] confidence in Br. Strang as I had in his predecessor Joseph," he confided to the privacy of his journal.[13] It may well have been impossible for anyone to measure up to Smith in Post's eyes.

Stephen Post indicated something of what he sought in an 1851 letter to his brother, Warren: "Now about myself, I am looking for the consolation of Israel & long for the time to come when Zion shall arise & put on her beautiful garments & become the joy of the whole earth."[14] Post anxiously awaited the day when the earth was purified, God's people sanctified, and Christ ruled over the world. Each prophet he followed, Joseph Smith, Jr., James J. Strang, and, eventually, Sidney Rigdon, taught of an impending millennium, eternal rewards for the righteous, and a true ecclesiastical order approved by God, issues that were foremost in Post's worldview.

The choice to follow Smith was often a family matter for early Mormons, and the Posts flocked to Strang in a like manner. Strangism had many traits likely to appeal to one-time disciples of Smith. Not only did Strang claim angelic visits reminiscent of Joseph Smith's, but he also exhibited a set of reportedly ancient records bearing an uncanny similarity to Smith's golden plates whence sprang the Book of Mormon.[15]

A divine messenger had directed Strang to the Rajah Manchou plates just as Joseph Smith received direction to his ancient record from the Angel Moroni. The golden plates of the Book of Mormon had recounted a story of a civilization that colonized the Americas in about 600 B.C. In September 1845, an unnamed angel appeared to Strang and directed him to a spot near Vorhee, Wisconsin, where he unearthed similar ancient writings. In July 1850, Stephen Post had the privilege of viewing these records. "I called at br. Strang's & saw the small plates," Post wrote, "they contain hieroglyphics & appear to be of ancient workmanship of this God knows."[16]

Post left Beaver Island in July 1850, but by that time his acceptance of the prophetic nature of Strang's efforts had begun to wane. Although he returned once more in September 1853, by then, as with Joseph Smith and Nauvoo, he had become fully disenchanted with Strang. In a letter to his brother, who still lived at Beaver Island in the fall of 1853, he noted, "You need not expect me to start with my family [for

Beaver Island], I shall not put my trust in man, or make flesh my arm. & when I find by the word & spirit of God, that I am led astray from God's requirements in any particular, my determination is to retrace my steps as soon as possible."[17] Although Post's journals do not reveal what curtailed his enthusiasm for Strangism, the letter shows that he now believed Strang to be a false prophet.

Post's waining enthusiasm may well have had something to do with Strang's involvement in plural marriage, for certainly that activity prompted other followers to depart his organization. Following his 1850 coronation, Strang, perhaps hoping to recreate Joseph Smith's Nauvoo Mormondom (or more likely because he now planned to take Elvira Eliza Smith, an attractive eighteen-year-old teacher, as a plural wife), issued a revised position regarding polygamy. Reasoning that plural marriage was indeed a divine principle to be followed by God's anointed, he lived in an open relationship with Elvira Smith.[18]

Where was Stephen Post to turn now in his search for the proper priesthood authority to act in God's name? With Smith dead and Strang proven, in Post's mind, a false prophet, he had to resume his quest for the true shepherd. Post consistently adhered to a three-part test in determining a true prophet. Each step was shaped by the experience of Joseph Smith, Jr., who, for Post, remained the quintessential spokesman for God. First, Post felt that a prophet must clearly be called by divine authority. Second, there must be a lawful (scriptural) basis for such authority. Finally, any true prophet must espouse the divinity of the Book of Mormon.

These criteria were obviously drawn from historic Mormonism. God called Smith directly through a vision. He received his priesthood authority from heavenly messengers who held the power during mortality and then bestowed it upon Smith. And, as translator of the Book of Mormon, Smith was obviously its strongest proponent.

In September 1855, Post attended a conference of long-time, disgruntled Mormons in Kirtland, Ohio. Martin Harris and William Smith conducted the gathering. Harris had been an intimate of Joseph Smith's in the church's early years, and Smith was the Mormon prophet's younger brother.[19] Those in attendance hoped to bring about a new organization of the church. According to Post's information, Harris and Smith both had lately enjoyed divine directives to reorganize the church. They planned to select a new gathering place for the faithful and hoped that many of the old Saints would support their efforts.[20] Post was curious about the potential of the group and hoped that it would lead to a recovery of the kind of excitement that he had perceived in Kirtland in the mid 1830s. He was committed to the Book of Mormon, and

Harris had been one of its three witnesses. Smith also had credibility beyond what most could claim.

Post's journal shows that he paid them serious attention, even listing the actions taken at Kirtland. The conference passed resolutions accepting the Book of Mormon, Bible, and *Doctrine and Covenants*— a compilation of revelations and directions issued by Joseph Smith— as the word of God; acknowledged the restoration of the priesthood through Joseph Smith, Jr.; and stated its rejection of all doctrine not listed in the scriptures, a slightly veiled reference to endowments, sealings, and other salvation-oriented rituals from the Nauvoo era.[21]

Post might have been expected to find these positions very satisfactory. Harris and Smith purported revelations and a divine mandate, supported the Book of Mormon as the word of God, and rejected the theological innovations of Nauvoo. Yet, for Post, something intangible was still missing. In the end, disappointed, he left Kirtland and shrugged off yet another new order of Mormonism. As he had earlier assessed Nauvoo as a place without spiritual animation, Post now found a missing element here also. "I find Kirtland . . . a land barren of faith as people without a shephard," he observed. There was no one with the charisma either of Joseph Smith, Jr., or even James J. Strang leading the movement.[22]

By the time he had reached this judgment about the Kirtland group, Post was already beginning an association with Sidney Rigdon that would continue for the remainder of his life. In January 1856 Post had written to Rigdon about the state of the Mormon religion. Following his rejection in 1844 as guardian of the Mormon fold, Rigdon had returned, undaunted, to Pittsburgh, where he rallied local supporters and in April 1845 formed the Church of Christ. The subsequent death of his daughter, Eliza, seemed to affect Rigdon's mental stability. He became overly visionary, disaffecting some members of his new church. As dissension tore the Church of Christ, Rigdon decided to move church headquarters from Pittsburgh to Franklin County in south central Pennsylvania. Although a practicable alternative Mormon organization immediately after Smith's death, by 1848, due largely to Rigdon's erratic behavior, it had completely fallen apart.[23]

About the time his movement was collapsing, Rigdon moved to Friendship, New York, south of Rochester and had no involvement with Mormonism for about six years. Then, in 1856, Rigdon received a letter from Stephen Post, a communication that moved him to open communications with Post within two weeks. Claiming to have lost any interest in Mormonism during the past several years, Rigdon responded only because "common courtesy" required it. "I was called and sent forth to do a certain work before the Lord," he wrote. The summons to the ministry took place "previous to my acquaintance with J. Smith," he noted. A lengthy letter rehearsing his religious life before and after 1844 followed. "I have now indirectly answered all your interegation," observed Rigdon. He went on to express pessimism about whether the old organization (pre-Nauvoo Mormonism) could ever be rebuilt.[24]

Between January and March 1856 Rigdon must have given serious consideration to Post's letter and the deficiencies now reportedly plaguing Mormonism. In March he again wrote to Post. This time Rigdon enclosed a revelation from God, calling Post to assist Rigdon in reestablishing the work Joseph Smith had started: "Verily, verily, thus saith the Lord unto my servant Stephen Post, I have looked upon thee and seen thy works and thy desires to understand my revelations, and I have heard thy prayer. And now I the Lord say unto thee that I call [you] to a great work in assisting my servant Sidney Rigdon in preparing the way before me, and Elijah which should come." The revelation went on to assure Post that he should have the desires of his heart if he aided Rigdon and would receive an understanding of the way of the Lord. This was the type of credibility Stephen Post sought in the Lord's true shepherd, and he embraced Rigdon's prophetic role.

Further, Post was to publish a pamphlet setting forth Rigdon's claims on succession in the church. Not only was Post happy to have found the true prophet, but his allegiance was also strengthened by active involvement in the cause. He was called to help Rigdon in bringing about a mighty latter-day work. By April 1856, even as he was withdrawing from the activities of William Smith and Martin Harris, Post began preaching Rigdonism. "This evening," he wrote in his journal on April 7, "I preached . . . on the revelatons in relation to the presidency, etc." The next day he shared his revelation from Rigdon with an acquaintance, assuring him that it was "the word of the Lord to the world."[25] Perhaps his growing belief that Rigdon was the true shepherd explained why Post now found Kirtland devoid of faith.

By the fall of 1857 Post resumed preaching Mormonism, albeit a different version of the religion than he had taught previously. The Mormon gospel, as Rigdon enunciated it, taught much of the same doctrine held by the church during the Kirtland years. Polygamy was disavowed. Joseph Smith became a fallen prophet due to the theological developments springing from the Nauvoo years. Rigdon was now heralded as the divinely appointed successor to the presidency. Brigham Young and the Quorum of Twelve Apostles were vigorously condemned.[26]

In November 1857 Post was looking to Rigdon "for the redemption of Zion, the overthrow of Babylon & the bringing in of the Millennial glory."[27] These hopes were about the same as those expressed to his brother, Warren, six years before, but then he had been unable to identify a prophet who could accomplish them. In a search for truth that had seen three Mormon prophets holding his allegiance at various times, Post remained true to his vision of Zion. Was his new course one of faithful dissent or of heresy? The differences remain slight, but the distinction needs be drawn.

A dissenter disagrees with or rejects the doctrines of an established church. A heretic professes new religious beliefs opposed to the orthodox doctrines of the church. Throughout the summer of 1856 Post was a dissenter, but, as he accepted Rigdon's leadership, he moved closer to the position held by a heretic. In his quest to become (as Joseph Smith III put it in 1877) "learned above what is written," Post allowed himself to be drawn into Rigdon's realm of heresy.

In a study of dissent, the twentieth-century religious historian Edwin Scott Gaustad argues that heretics are "sinners against faith."[28] This model can be tested in the case of Stephen Post and Rigdonism by examining the doctrine propagated by Rigdon and the Church of Jesus Christ of the Children of Zion. What did they believe, and how did it differ from the teachings of mainstream Mormonism? The variety of Mormonism espoused by Brigham Young and the Utah Mormons, and that of Joseph Smith III and the Reorganization, reflected traditional dogma although they held divergent positions on similar issues. In essence, the two groups dissented from each other.

In contrast, in an undated newspaper essay, Post outlined the beliefs of the Children of Zion. Highlighting the doctrine was a belief in God and his son, Jesus Christ. An acceptance of the reality of angels and spirits who ministered the divine word to mortals and the Bible and the Book of Mormon were held up as the word of God. Credence was given to such gifts of the spirit as prophecy and speaking in tongues. Faith healing was also given credence, as was continuing revelation, an intricate part of Mormon beliefs. Of great significance to Rigdon's claim to leadership was his claim to scriptural precedent or legitimacy. As Post noted, "We believe the Gospel is an eternal order, not subject to be changed, being established upon the direct word of God."[29] Unimpeachable authority in particular was what Stephen Post considered of paramount importance. Intended for public consumption, his articles of faith for Rigdonism stated the basic beliefs of the Children of Zion and were not much beyond the basic theological conceptions of early Mormonism.

These articles of faith gave little hint of the growing Rigdonite heresy, however, for it was, in significant ways, far afield from the Mormon mainstream. While followers of Brigham Young and Joseph Smith III contended primarily over the issues of succession and Nauvoo-era theology—plural marriage and temple rites—the beliefs of each were traceable to the teachings of Joseph Smith, Jr. Several Rigdonite positions had no discernible link to Smith or premartyrdom Mormon doctrine. Three doctrines of Rigdonism boldly demonstrated its heretical tendencies: the stance that only Rigdon held the legitimate, God-given authority to succeed Joseph Smith, Jr.; that Smith had become a fallen prophet through transgressions committed at Nauvoo; and that a female priesthood should be established. Each tenet ran counter to both Utah and midwestern Mormon positions, as well as to their shared beliefs, hence constituting Mormon heresies.

Neither Brigham Young nor Joseph Smith III saw succession in the Mormon leadership in the same light, yet Rigdon's posture was an affront to both. Utah Mormonism opted for apostolic leadership after Joseph Smith, Jr.'s, murder. The Reorganization claimed lineal dissent and a father's blessing as the proper method. Rigdonites opted for an entirely different route. Casting aside the claims of both the Quorum of the Twelve and young Joseph Smith III to succeed his father, Rigdon attempted to show that only he had the right (authority) to lead the church through the most tenuous of avenues, his position as a counselor in the First Presidency.

Following Post's 1856 call to assist, Rigdon began recording revelations on every possible subject and at a rate unmatched by Joseph Smith, Jr., writings that reflected the increasingly heretical doctrines of the Children of Zion. In so doing he mimicked Smith's style as preserved in the *Doctrine and Covenants*.[30] The fourth revelation recorded by Rigdon, dated January 1864, insisted that he held a "high and lofty calling" by the will of the Lord and was to be the only spokesperson to the whole world.[31]

Rigdon also aimed his revelations at denigrating the Smith family. One charged Joseph Smith, Jr.'s, wife, Emma, with culpability for refusing to support Rigdon when he offered himself as guardian if the church in 1844 and barred her descendants from holding the priesthood. Another directed Post to warn Joseph Smith III of the dire judgments awaiting him if he did not repent. This set Post off on a crusade to convince the young man of his errors, a crusade that lasted the rest of Post's life. In the process, the Rigdonites developed a belief that Smith was evil; in an 1865 letter to Post, for example, Rigdon charged Smith with being "of the devil."[32]

While geographical distance and lack of regular contact helped spare Brigham Young and Utah Mormonism from much Rigdonite wrath, they were not overlooked entirely. In 1863, *An Appeal to the Latter-Day Saints,* a Rigdonite publication, argued for the legitimacy of Sidney Rigdon's leadership and against that of Young and the Twelve Apostles. It called the Mormons "a rebellious people ruled by twelve blasphemers." Rigdon accused leaders of Utah Mormonism of neglecting the sacred message of the *Doctrine and Covenants* and charged Young and his disciples with "attempting to prevent the order of heaven, by trying to set up the rule of twelve over the Church of the living God."[33] A December 1870 revelation blasted the people of Utah for being ignorant of the holy priesthood. Young, a "vain man," was asked whether he supposed his hypocritical and lying pretenses were acceptable to God. "Know then that your wicked corrupt and senseless career is shortly to close with the entire overthrow of you and all that you have," warned the revelation.[34]

In the meantime, Post rose quickly within the ranks of the Children of Zion. A March 1866 revelation called him to be "spokesman for my servant Sidney . . . and my servant Sidney shall be revelator." Post was promised "great wisdom" when acting for Zion.[35] He was an active and able advocate for Rigdonism, just as Rigdon had become for Mormonism in the 1830s.

As Rigdon's spokesman, Post wrote or coauthored two principal treatises. The first, *Zion's Messenger* (1864), written jointly with William Hamilton, was intended for the "benefit of the scattered Zion." It sought to show that by not following the correct law of succession most remnants of the church founded by Joseph Smith, Jr., were now lost in darkness. *Zion's Messenger* attacked the very foundations of traditional Mormonism and accused Smith of being a fallen prophet. Smith "failed to lead his people to sanctification," Post and Hamilton charged, "for they polluted their inheritance [with plural marriage]." In order to redeem Zion the Lord had called Sidney Rigdon to be "chief shepherd on the earth."[36]

Such an internal assault upon Smith as a fallen prophet was new to debates over the morality or immorality of plural marriage. Although non-Mormons as well as Mormon groups who did not accept the practice had used polygamy in attacks upon Utah Mormonism, the suggestion was unique that Joseph Smith had fallen from his prophetic stature because of it. Young's followers, of course, saw plural marriage as God's will. Although Joseph Smith III denied that his father had ever engaged in polygamy, several early leaders of the Reorganization expressed the belief that Smith had introduced the practice. By the 1880s, however, the official Reorganized Church's position was one of denial.[37]

In 1872 Post wrote another effort to bolster the Rigdonite position on true authority. In *A Treatise on the Melchisedek Priesthood and the Callings of God* he hoped to show that "no man taketh his honour [the priesthood] unto himself, but he that is called of God, as was Aaron" (Hebrews 5: 47).[38] And, in the eyes of Post and Rigdon, this usurpation of divine authority was just what Brigham Young and Joseph Smith III had done. "From very remote antiquity," Post wrote, "we have testimony reporting God calling men with his own voice." He cited Alma in the Book of Mormon, Abraham in the Old Testament, and Paul in the New Testament as examples of this direct heavenly summons. More recently, God had spoken to Joseph Smith, Jr., in a like manner and had also called Rigdon. Referring to revelations recorded in the *Doctrine and Covenants,* Post rejoiced in the knowledge that God had issued Rigdon's call.[39]

He was also supportive of Rigdonism's third heresy, the ordination of women. In an October 1864 revelation Rigdon was directed to "organize a quorum of female prophets for the benefit of Zion." An apparent rejection of traditional marital covenants and sex roles, the goal was that "the Lord might be their [women's] ruler without men or the sons of men having any claim to them by Gentile covenant."[40]

When Rigdon communicated this new doctrine to Stephen Post, now serving Rigdonism at Attica, Iowa, the location appointed as the movement's gathering place, he faithfully accepted it as God's will. Later, upon Rigdon's directive, Post began implementing a general policy of female ordination within the Attica branch early in 1869. His wife, Jane, after converting to Rigdonite Mormonism in 1865, was ordained to the office of elder in January 1868. In April she took charge of "organizing [the] branch with female officers corresponding with the Male priests, teachers, and deacons." By October 1869 at least three other Attica women were priests in a congregation of about twenty-two adults.[41]

In 1871 a revelation announced that Sidney Rigdon was not to gather to Attica so "he may escape persecution which will fall on him if he goes there at present."[42] One can only imagine the disappointment Post must have felt upon learning that his prophet would not be coming to the community he had spent the past several years trying to build. He had little time to miss Rigdon at Attica, however, for he was called on a mission to Manitoba, Canada, where he struggled to raise a Rigdonite following until his death.

In an 1875 letter to an unnamed correspondent, Post revealed why he was in Canada, "I ask myself the question why I have come to this far off Northern Country. And as I reflect upon it I have to say for my Salvation and glory in Christ's kingdom. And my love of the word of the Lord has led me to obey him, as did Abraham when he went out of Haran, Lehi from Jerusalem, Nephi separated from his brethren & the Saints [who] moved to Zion in Jackson County, Missouri leaving kindred and friends behind. We have left the United States [because of the] word of the Lord." In January 1876 the Children of Zion counted but twenty-three members in Manitoba.[43]

In July 1876 Sidney Rigdon died at Friendship, New York, and Stephen Post succeeded him as leader of the group. He died a little more than three years later, on December 18, 1879, and the Rigdonite movement quickly disintegrated. In January 1880, Canada's Children of Zion, the only survivors of Rigdonite Mormonism, met to appoint a successor to Post. There was, they felt, a "necessity of our being united in the great work of these last days." Brother Andrew J. Hinckle was then appointed president. Post's legacy, and, depending upon one's perspective, the Rigdon-Post heresy, manifested itself once more in February 1882, when Jane Post gained appointment as head of the church in Manitoba. She concluded the meeting by bearing her testimony that, if all would be faithful, "the Lord would bless them with his Holy spirit."[44]

Post based his firm support of Rigdonism during the preceding two decades on the assumption that priesthood authority and prophetic callings were closely tied to the establishment of Zion. He discussed the foundation of his faith in a 1871 letter to Sidney Rigdon: "I believe that Joseph Smith brought forth the Key of Doctrine and you [Rigdon] have brought forth the Key of Conquest, and now the Great Key of the Father will roll forth and consumate all things."[45] By now, Post's vision of Mormonism perceived Joseph Smith, Jr., as the forerunner to an even greater prophet, Sidney Rigdon, to usher in the Millennium. Post's Mormon odyssey had followed the course of stalwart disciple, then faithful dissenter, and finally ended in heresy.

NOTES

1. See Stephen Post to Joseph Smith III, February 19, 1865, June 13, 1866, and July 29, 1879; Joseph Smith III to Stephen Post, August 6, 1879, Stephen Post Collection, Church of Jesus Christ of Latter-day Saints Historical Department, Salt Lake City.

2. Dale L. Morgan, "A Bibliography of the Churches of the Dispersion," *Western Humanities Review* 7 (Summer 1953): 130.

3. Stephen Post, Journal, July 14, 1835, July 7, 1844, Stephen Post Collection; Stephen Post to Brigham Young, in Journal History of the Church of Jesus Christ of Latter-day Saints, November 10, 1841, LDS Historical Department.

4. For a solid overview of the issue of succession, see D. Michael Quinn, "The Mormon Succession Crisis of 1844," *Brigham Young University Studies*

16 (Winter 1976): 187–233; and, on the apostolic position, Ronald K. Esplin, "Joseph, Brigham, and the Twelve: A Succession of Continuity," *Brigham Young University Studies* 21 (Summer 1981): 301–41. Another perspective is found in Andrew F. Ehat, "Joseph Smith's Introduction of the Temple Ordinances and the 1844 Mormon Succession Question," M.A. thesis, Brigham Young University, 1981. Ehat contends that Smith's introduction of temple ordinances to the apostles and select others at Nauvoo passed the mantle of authority to the Twelve.

5. Roger Van Noord, *King of Beaver Island: The Life and Assassination of James Jesse Strang* (Urbana: University of Illinois Press, 1988), 1–4, 6, 7.

6. On Rigdon's claim to guardianship, see Linda King Newell and Valeen Tippetts Avery, *Mormon Enigma: Emma Hale Smith: Prophet's Wife, "Elect Lady," Polygamy's Foe* (Garden City: Doubleday, 1984), 202–4; and Leonard J. Arrington, *Brigham Young: American Moses* (New York: Alfred A. Knopf, 1985), 113–14.

7. See Post, Journal, November 2–12, 1842.

8. Regarding the introduction of plural marriage and sealing, see Lawrence Foster, *Religion and Sexuality: The Shakers, the Mormons, and the Oneida Community* (Urbana: University of Illinois Press, 1984), 123–58; Richard S. Van Wagoner, *Mormon Polygamy: A History* (Salt Lake City: Signature Books, 1985), 17–28; M. Guy Bishop, "Eternal Marriage in Early Mormon Beliefs," *The Historian* 53 (Fall 1990): 77–88; Danel Bachman, "A Study of the Mormon Practice of Plural Marriage Before the Death of Joseph Smith," M.A. thesis, Purdue University, 1975; and Ehat, "Joseph Smith's Introduction."

9. See Post, Journal, July 9, 1850, October 7, 1855. On Strang's coronation, see Van Noord, *King of Beaver Island,* 105–6, and Leonard J. Arrington and Davis Bitton, *The Mormon Experience: A History of the Latter-day Saints* (New York: Alfred A. Knopf, 1979), 89–90.

10. See, for example, Post, Journal, August 1844–June 1845.

11. Ibid., November 5, 1845.

12. On theological issues at Nauvoo, see T. Edgar Lyon, "Doctrinal Developments of the Church during the Nauvoo Sojourn, 1839–1846," *Brigham Young University Studies* 15 (Summer 1975): 400–422; and Donald Q. Cannon, "The King Follett Discourse: Joseph Smith's Greatest Sermon in Historical Perspective," *Brigham Young University Studies* 18 (Winter 1978): 179–92.

13. Post, Journal, July 12, 1846.

14. Stephen Post to Warren Post, October 3, 1851, Warren Post Correspondence, LDS Historical Department.

15. On the Post family and Strang, see Post, Journal, February 17–June 24, 1850 passim. Regarding the coming forth of the Book of Mormon, see Richard L. Bushman, *Joseph Smith and the Beginnings of Mormonism* (Urbana: University of Illinois Press, 1984), 115–19; and Jan Shipps, *Mormonism: The Story of a New Religious Tradition* (Urbana: University of Illinois Press, 1985), 11–14. For a different perspective, see Fawn M. Brodie, *No Man Knows My History: The Life of Joseph Smith* (New York: Alfred A. Knopf, 1982), 34–40.

16. Van Noord, *King of Beaver Island,* 34; Post, Journal, July 3, 1850.

17. Stephen Post to Warren Post, October 2, 1853, Warren Post Correspondence. Stephen Post's journals make no mention of this visit nor of why his feelings about Strang had changed.

18. See David Rich Lewis, "'For Life, the Resurrection, and the Life Everlasting': James J. Strang and Strangite Mormon Polygamy, 1849–1856," *Wisconsin Magazine of History* 66 (Summer 1983): 274–91; and Van Noord, *King of Beaver Island,* 100–101.

19. On William Smith's claims as a successor to Joseph Smith, see Roger D. Launius, *Joseph Smith III: Pragmatic Prophet* (Urbana: University of Illinois Press, 1988), 81–83.

20. See Post, Journal, September 23, 1855.

21. Ibid., October 7, 1855.

22. Ibid., April 11, 1856.

23. See Thomas J. Gregory, "Sidney Rigdon: Post Nauvoo," *Brigham Young University Studies* 21 (Winter 1981): 51–54; F. Mark McKiernan, *The Voice of One Crying in the Wilderness, Sidney Rigdon, Religious Reformer, 1796–1876* (Lawrence: Coronado Press, 1971).

24. Gregory, "Sidney Rigdon," 54; Sidney Rigdon to Steven Post, January 20, 1856, Stephen Post Collection.

25. Post, Journal, April 7–8, 1856.

26. See Daryl Chase, "Sidney Rigdon—Early Mormon," M.A. thesis, University of Chicago, 1931, 146; Gregory, "Sidney Rigdon," 57–60.

27. Post, Journal, November 22, 1857.

28. Edwin Scott Gaustad, *Dissent in American Religion* (Chicago: University of Chicago Press, 1973), chapter 3.

29. An undated and unidentified newspaper clipping, Miscellaneous Papers, Stephen Post Collection.

30. See "Copying Book A, Book of the revelations of Jesus Christ to The Children of Zion Through Sidney Rigdon prophet & seer & revelator," Stephen Post Collection (hereafter cited as Rigdon Revelations). The *Doctrine and Covenants,* comprised of revelations, instructions, and epistles recorded by Joseph Smith, continues to be held as sacred scripture by both the Mormon and Reorganization churches.

31. Rigdon Revelations, sec. 4.

32. Ibid., secs. 2 and 4; Rigdon to Post, N.d. [ca. July 1865], Stephen Post Collection.

33. Joseph H. Newton, William Richards, and William Stanley, *An Appeal to the Latter-Day Saints* (Philadelphia: N.p., 1863), 6, 7, 21, and 25, copy in Stephen Post Collection.

34. Rigdon Revelations, sec. 61.

35. Ibid., sec. 22.

36. Stephen Post and William Hamilton, *Zion's Messenger* (Erie: Sterrett and Gara, 1864), 2, 4–5, copy in Stephen Post Collection.

37. See Launius, *Joseph Smith III,* 199–201; Richard P. Howard, "The Changing RLDS Response to Mormon Polygamy: A Preliminary Analysis," *John Whitmer Historical Association Journal* 3 (1983): 14–29.

38. Stephen Post, *A Treatise on the Melchizedek Priesthood and the Call-ings of God* (Council Bluffs: Steam Book and Job Printers, 1872), 2, copy in Stephen Post Collection.

39. Post, *A Treatise*, 6–8, 10–11.

40. Rigdon Revelations, sec. 15. For an overview of mid-nineteenth-centu-ry American marital patterns and sex roles, see Carl N. Degler, *At Odds: Wom-en and the Family in America from the Revolution to the Present* (New York: Oxford University Press, 1970); and Christopher Lasch, *Haven in a Heartless World: The Family Besieged* (New York: Basic Books, 1977); for mid-nine-teenth-century Mormon views, see M. Guy Bishop, "Sex Roles, Marriage, and Childrearing at Mormon Nauvoo," *Western Illinois Regional Studies* 11 (Fall 1988): 30–45.

41. See Church Record Attica Branch (Iowa) of the Church of Jesus Christ of the Children of Zion, Stephen Post Collection.

42. Rigdon Revelations, sec. 63.

43. Post to a unidentified correspondent, N.d. [ca. October 1875]; Branch of Zion's church in Manitoba Canada, January 1876, included with Church Record, Attica Branch.

44. Gregory, "Sidney Rigdon," 67; Manitoba Branch Record, January 18, 1870 and February 15, 1882.

47. Post to Rigdon, March 3, 1871, Stephen Post Collection.

9

The Flight of the Doves from Utah Mormonism to California Morrisitism: The Saga of James and George Dove

Richard Neitzel Holzapfel

Religious dissent in America has a rich and varied past. The Latter-day Saint movement, popularly known as the Mormon church, among the many religious protest groups established in the United States during the nineteenth century, challenged the religious, social, economic, and political values of antebellum America.[1] Although the United States had been a seedbed of religious dissent from the earliest colonial times, founder Joseph Smith's antagonists were particularly uneasy about a man who claimed continuing revelation and introduced additional scripture. Their distaste for Smith's doctrines was mixed with their fear of his political and economic power as believers flocked to Mormonism before his death in 1844. As with other protest groups, eventually the Latter-day Saints had their own dissenters. Among them were the father and son team of James and George Dove.

The Doves followed in the footsteps of a long line of Mormon dissidents. From its beginning in 1830 many individuals sought to direct the church along lines they considered reflective of the "truth of the gospel." In many cases these dissenters established separate groups made up of fellow protesters.[2] For example, William and Wilson Law, Austin Cowles, and James Blakeslee mobilized a protest movement and eventually established a new church during the church's period in Nauvoo, Illinois (1839–46).

Following Smith's assassination on June 27, 1844, several people sought control of the church, and at least fifteen groups emerged directly from the succession struggle. The most successful of these, the Church of Jesus Christ of Latter-day Saints, removed from the Midwest to the Great Salt Lake Basin under the leadership of Brigham Young. For a short period after their arrival in Utah, the Rocky Mountain Saints found their isolated home a safe refuge from the constant persecution they had experienced earlier in New York, Ohio, Missouri, and Illinois.

Yet even in the West, the church's leadership was unable to eliminate dissent and protest from within. Among those dissenting were two generations of the Dove family. The Doves' experiences raise many unanswered questions. Why did they initially join the Mormon movement, and what eventually repelled them from it? How did the dominant institution (the Mormon church) react to their protest? Once they had developed their dissenting ideas, what were the results of their attempts to mobilize others to leave the church? What reasons best explain the rise and demise of their social and religious movement, the Church of the Firstborn?

The Dove family were among the English converts to Mormonism in the mid 1800s.[3] James and Alice Dove, the parents, were baptized by William Clayton on July 22, 1849, at Bulwell, Nottingham, England. Their commitment to the church is evident in the fact that they had their children blessed by church elders soon after their baptism.[4] Further commitment to Mormonism can be seen in James Dove's ordinations to the LDS priesthood; he was a teacher on November 16, 1850 and a priest on February 11, 1851. Like any other group, the LDS church established several types of commitment mechanisms. For the Doves, one successful commitment mechanism arose as a byproduct of the Mormon Reformation of the mid 1850s.[5]

The Mormon Reformation, an explosion of religious enthusiasm and evangelical activity in reaction to an emotional call for retrenchment, began in the Great Basin. The Mormon Reformation, however, was not limited to Utah Territory and spread to far-flung church missions, including Great Britain. Orson Pratt, the Mormon mission president in England at the time, was called by church leaders in Salt Lake City to inaugurate a similar Reformation in Britain. "There is a great reformation needed in England, Scotland and Wales," they wrote. "The Saints are dead and do not drink at the living fountain. The fire of the Almighty is not in them. And we make the same observation regarding the Elders who are sent to preach." As a measure of what Mormon leaders thought was required, the apostle Ezra T. Benson estimated that not more than half the Saints were willing to renew their covenant by being rebaptized. Accordingly, the sacrament of communion was withheld from them for several months "to afford them time and space for repentance and restitution."[6] James Dove, however, was among those who responded and was rebaptized as a sign of his recommitment.

Fueled by the spiritual fires of the Reformation, the Dove family decided to migrate to America and go to Utah. After a difficult journey, James and Alice Dove, and their children George and Sarah, immigrated to the newly established Mormon stronghold in America in

1856. The trip to Utah commenced with a voyage across the Atlantic and continued in a journey from the East Coast to the LDS staging ground near Iowa City. The Doves' trip on the Mormon trail with the Martin Handcart Company and William B. Hodgett's wagon train began in August 1856, and they arrived in Salt Lake City sometime before December 15, 1856.[7]

Once in Utah, the family was quickly incorporated into the social and religious system. James and Alice were both endowed and sealed in the Endowment House on July 16, 1857—religious ordinances reserved for the most faithful Saints. Both the endowment and sealing ceremonies were often effective commitment mechanisms, establishing loyalty to the church and to its leaders. The Reformation in England, however, did not prepare the Doves for their experiences in the Mormon Zion.

Unlike the Mormon scriptural definition of Zion, a place where the people were of "one heart, one mind, and no poor among them," Utah Territory had many Saints who were not united in heart, mind, or goods. For the Doves, this was a great disappointment. Although others disenchanted with the practice of Mormonism in Utah chose to continue their journey to California or to return East, the family's commitment to the church was strong, and they chose to try to correct the problems they perceived from inside the institution.[8]

While traveling to Utah, the Doves met other Mormon members either leaving the territory or who had already left to settle in some eastern community. For example, Elizabeth Forscutt, wife of Mark Forscutt, another British Mormon, later recalled, "Mr. and Mrs. Holt [former Utah Mormons] told us their experiences [in Salt Lake City] and urged and begged us not to go farther. Their appeals were useless. Our paths were marked to the end of our journey and we followed them cheerfully. Ah, many a time I wished I had minded them!"[9]

The Forscutts soon found much wrong with the church in Utah, however, and within six months of their arrival, "they both left the church and soon joined with the Morrisites," the small group of people led by Joseph Morris, another British convert.[10] Morris, a self-proclaimed "prophet, seer, and revelator," drew hundreds of Utah Saints into the most significant challenge to Young's authority since the Saints' arrival in Utah. Unable to wrest control of the church's central departments from Young, Morris formed a new organization, nicknamed the Morrisites, on April 6, 1861. In that same year, his followers began to gather at the foot of Weber Canyon, South Weber, in the abandoned Kingston Fort.[11]

Morris had immigrated to America with his wife and child not long after his baptism in 1847, arriving in Salt Lake City in the fall of 1853 after a two-year stay in St. Louis and Pittsburgh. By 1857 he was regarded as a religious fanatic who criticized Mormon society in general and the current Mormon leadership in particular. Trouble between Morris and local church leaders began as early as 1854, but erupted openly in 1857. Morris believed that he was called of God to continue the Mormon Reformation begun in the fall of 1856 and cut short with the death of its principal architect, the LDS church leader Jedediah M. Grant, and the Utah War in 1857.

Morris's zeal eventually brought him into conflict with Brigham Young. At first Morris intended to reform the church from within. He claimed that he was called to share the church's presidency with Young, envisioning himself as the spiritual leader and Young as the temporal president of the church. Following Morris's censure and release as a Reformation teacher in Provo, he sought comfort in prayer. The result of this prayer was his first written revelation. He received his second in 1859, and by August 1860 he had received two more revelations; in September he received thirteen. From then on, Morris received and wrote revelations regularly until his death in 1862.[12]

In addition, unlike the Mormon Reformation in England, the Utah Reformation urged many men to practice polygamy. This emphasis resulted in significant competition for wives that became so serious in many small Utah towns that several men volunteered to go on missions in an effort to find prospective brides.[13] Another result of the competition was that some older men married very young girls.[14] For many Mormon converts, unaware of polygamy when they joined the church in Europe, this was too much to bear. For the Doves, like others who became dissidents, it was a sign of the LDS church's apostasy. Within four years of their arrival, James, Alice, George, and Sarah Dove separated themselves from the church that had brought them to the Great Basin.

No contemporary account exists of the Doves' initial reactions to polygamy. That they had to deal with it is certain, because their daughter, Sarah, sixteen, was "sealed" to Thomas Higgs, a thirty-seven-year-old polygamist, and the marriage took place in Brigham Young's office on July 1, 1860.[15] A few days later, on July 18, along with her brother George, she received her endowments in the Endowment House.[16] A federal census taken a few days later, on July 23, indicated that Sarah, although married to Higgs, still lived with her parents in Salt Lake City's Twentieth Ward. Had there been any initial reservation against polygamy, the marriage precipitated a family crisis that eventually set the stage for the Doves' recruitment into a dissenting movement under Morris's charismatic leadership. James Dove later revealed his negative feelings about plural marriage:

> When the prophet [Joseph Smith] was martyred, then Brigham Young assumed control and led the people into the wilderness, found a basin in the Rocky Mountains, and called it Zion; and the hopes of the people who had been oppressed in the old countries were raised by anticipating the time when they would be in Zion enjoying a restored gospel and freedom from the evils existing in the governments of the old world; so thousands embraced the opportunity offered, and went, as they supposed, to the land of their deliverance—both temporally and spiritually— not knowing that the spirit of the Lord had departed from the priesthood, and that the one who had taken the place of the martyred prophet, had gone into idolatry and the worship of money and women.[17]

Like Morris and Forscutt, who also became a Morrisite, the Doves were disappointed with the Mormon society, especially polygamy, they discovered in Utah after they arrived from England.

The Doves' feelings of dissent did not crystallize immediately and were not publicly stated until after Dove met Morris at South Weber. In the process, both father and son began a journey that eventually took them to California, where they became leaders of a new church, the Church of the Firstborn, a remnant of the Morrisite protest movement in Utah Territory during the 1860s. But it was James Dove's son, George, who first felt a commitment to Morris. Against his father's wishes, the seventeen-year-old George moved with Morris from American Fork in Utah County to Salt Lake City in November 1859. James Dove had "several times refused permission for [me] to do this for Joseph," George wrote, "but the prophet [Morris] persisted in urging his request, and said, '[I] must do it for [him].'"[18]

Almost immediately with the rise of Joseph Morris's movement, according to George Dove, "the news spread rapidly through the Territory that a new prophet had arisen, who had not been recognized by the authorities of the Church." This alone seems to have created a curiosity and may have been a catalyst for Mormons dissatisfied with life in Utah but unable to mobilize their dissent and come forward. "Public meetings were now held in the Fort" near Ogden where Morris made his home, George Dove reported, "which were attended by people from all parts of the Territory; and in these meetings the false grounds and false assumptions of the Mormon Church were freely discussed."[19]

Morris's revelations in the early part of 1860 confirmed his initial belief that Brigham Young and other church leaders had lost the spirit and authority of the priesthood, and therefore it was now his duty to organize a new church. His move from reformer to dissident set the stage for the mobilization of a protest movement in Utah.[20] The cycle, similar to earlier situations in church history, of reform, protest, and mobilization, was complete by the spring of 1861. In this respect Joseph Morris and his disciples were not unique, because Mormonism had been fraught with division from its beginning. As many as five hundred Saints withdrew from the church and were baptized into the Morrisite movement at Weber by 1862.[21] Another five hundred became Morrisite followers in the territory, and others joined in the various other church missions. Jesse N. Smith, president of the church's Danish mission, reported, "While here the Morrisite wave swept over the mission, producing the first apostate break in the ranks of the Danish Saints."[22]

George Dove reported various motives for investigating Morris's claims in 1861: "The summary cutting off from the church, of those who had recognized his claims, cause some of the more liberal minded and thinking people of Utah to suppose that the old Church was becoming despotic." Initially, James Dove was not convinced that Morris was a proper alternative to Young. George reported that his father spoke against the "new faith in his quorum only two weeks before he himself accepted the new doctrine." In a moment of reflection years later George Dove recalled those early days nostalgically. "The demonstration of the power of God was so strong in the Fort," he recalled, "that those who came with honesty of purpose to investigate, were sure to remain; so that it became a proverb that if certain individuals went up to Weber, they must be caught."[23]

What actually happened to the skeptical James Dove when he went to South Weber to investigate Morris's claims is not known, but within a few days he returned to Salt Lake City convinced that Morris was what he claimed to be—a true prophet. Not only did Dove believe in Morris, but he also began to speak openly about his views in his home ward in Salt Lake City. Soon his local church leader sent another priesthood member, Thomas Higham, to investigate the faith of the Dove family. Higham reported to the bishop on August 1, 1861: "[I] had seen James Dove. [I] had a considerable talk with him about the way he had pursued in leaving the church and following Morris. James Dove considered he had done right. He had joined Morris on Sunday. . . . Could not say that Brigham was a prophet. Believed in Mormonism and [said] that Morris is the leader."[24]

It did not take the Latter-day Saints long to act after receiving

Higham's report. James Dove was officially excommunicated for apostasy by local ecclesiastical leaders in Salt Lake City on August 1, 1861. His rejection of Brigham Young as the spiritual leader of the church, coupled with his acceptance of the "new prophet," Joseph Morris, were the main concerns of local church leaders. The local bishop's court excommunicated Dove and his wife for "lack of following the authorities [of the LDS Church] and joining Morris."[25] It is evident that Morris was much more a prophet in Dove's eyes than Brigham Young. Before his death, Joseph Morris had recorded more than three hundred revelations—revelations that increasingly concerned the destruction of the wicked and the imminent appearance of Christ. Confident of Morris's calling, James Dove was ordained an apostle in September 1861 and took his position in the new church's hierarchy.

Dove and Morris agreed, and that might have been a fundamental attraction, that the Mormon Reformation of 1856–57 could have been the beginning of a great cleansing of the church before the dawning of the millennial day, but things had gone awry. It is certain that the Morrisites at South Weber continued to emphasize many aspects of the Reformation after its emphasis was gone in mainstream Utah Mormonism. One Reformation theme was that of cleanliness of both body and environment. John Banks reported, "The Morrisites swept the fort daily and kept it in such perfect order that not a straw was out of place. They also white washed their little huts at least once a week; and this is all because they expected Christ daily."[26]

A careful study of the Dove publications reveals several reasons why people gathered at South Weber. First, Morris claimed to be a prophet and produced scriptures like Joseph Smith. Second, Morris taught that the Second Coming was nigh, as Mormon missionaries had done during the first three decades of Mormonism. Third, Morris condemned polygamy, at least as it was then practiced by the Mormons.[27] Fourth, Morris questioned the economic disparity between the city elite and the rural poor in the Great Basin Kingdom.

As members gathered at South Weber, some Mormon neighbors became concerned about the presence of a protest movement within the boundaries of Zion. Like Joseph Smith before, Morris's detractors were particularly uneasy about a man who claimed continuing revelation and introduced additional scripture beyond the accepted canon. Their distaste for his doctrines became mixed with their fear of his political and economic power as believers flocked to him in 1861–62.[28] Eventually, the formation of this religious protest movement in Utah created intense social conflict between the Morrisites and the Mormons.

Social conflict is defined by Lewis Coser "as a struggle over values or claims to status, power, and scarce resources, in which the aims of the conflict group are not only to gain the desired values, but also to neutralize, injure, or eliminate rivals."[29] All of that would have come to nothing had not Morris been different from other dissenters in one central way: he attempted to establish a church headquarters in the very heart of Utah Mormonism. The several hundred followers who settled at Kingston Fort by 1861 found themselves increasingly at odds with civil authorities, as misunderstandings and conflicts increased between local Mormons and Morrisites.[30]

The church leaders Wilford Woodruff and John Taylor counseled local Mormons to be tolerant of the Morrisites and rebuked several members for extreme verbal attacks upon Morris, to the extent that later Morris and Dove praised Taylor's actions and words. Nevertheless, Morris reported that Woodruff provided an ominous prediction about his fate. He "stood up," Morris reported, "and prophesied that my influence should from that time go down."[31] Local Mormons, against Woodruff's and Taylor's counsel, escalated confrontation with the community as the movement gathered strength.

Legal problems between the Mormons and the Morrisites turned into an armed conflict early in 1862. It began when the Morrisite organization, like other movements, began to have its own dissenters. The first protesters among the Morrisites were severely criticized and condemned, and eventually several dissenters were retained at Kingston Fort against their will. This action set into motion the legal machinery that initiated armed conflict between the Mormons and the Morrisites. Friends and relatives of the hostages filed a complaint with the chief justice of the Third District Court at Salt Lake City. As C. LeRoy Anderson argued, "Whether justified or not, the Morrisites were clearly in violation of the law and were fast gaining the reputation of Davis County Bandits."[32]

The authorities issued warrants for the arrest of Morris and his chief lieutenant, but the men refused to surrender. For several days the Morrisites were encircled at Kingston Fort by a territorial posse, a showdown Morris perceived as a test between the "new church" and the "old church." Although a few Morrisites lost faith in Morris and his revelations (which had predicted the imminent appearance of Christ), most stood by him in the belief that the Second Coming would be accompanied by such a direct confrontation. When Morris and the others named in the writ refused to surrender in June 1862, a siege of the fort began. After several days and the deaths of individuals on both sides, the Morrisites finally succumbed. A brief skirmish, which occurred following their surrender, led to Morris's death as well as the death of his chief lieutenant, John Banks. The remaining Morrisite leaders were arrested, including James and George Dove.[33]

The Doves were arrested on June 15, 1862, and taken to Salt Lake City along with others captured at South Weber. "After this we were encamped on the South Bench," Dove later wrote, "and [were] put under a strong guard until the following morning, when we were marched to Salt Lake City. We arrived there after a march of two days; and were brought before Judge Kinney, in the Court House." The court session did not last long; each Morrisite leader was "bound over for each other, to keep the peace, on a bail of $1,500 each, for our appearance in court the following March."[34] They posted bail and were released, but both the Doves skipped bail and fled the Utah Territory before the March 1863 trial in Judge Kinney's court.

The remaining Morrisites had scattered throughout Idaho, Montana, Utah, and Nevada, so, in order to escape territorial authorities, sometime in November 1862 the Doves headed for Nevada, where they knew a sizable group had settled. James Dove reported:

> Having passed through a part of the winter in the woods, near Virginia [City], came down to Carson Valley, there finding John Livingstone talking to the people, who were anxious for us to preach; and John E. Jones, James Dove and John Livingstone met in prayer in Father Jones' house, in Jack Valley, to inquire of the Lord; and it was decided that there would be a meeting on Sunday in the Jack Valley school house, and there was a large congregation, James Dove preaching first. . . . We advanced the principles taught us in Weber. In April [1863], some were baptized.[35]

The confusion caused by Morris's unexpected death and the legal prosecution of the Morrisite church leaders resulted in factionalism from within, just as had occurred among the Mormons in Nauvoo two decades earlier. For a short period, the Doves affiliated with various Morrisite factions, yet in the end rejected all claimants. They took a long time to develop an identity that marked them as more than faithful followers and second-level leaders. But this identity change, when complete, constituted a significant attempt to reorganize and vitalize the protest movement begun at South Weber.

A reorganization of Morrisite church leadership occurred in Nevada shortly thereafter. John Livingstone, John Parson, and Richard Cook formed a church presidency; James Dove was chosen to lead the Carson Valley church. Eventually, these Nevada Morrisites felt the need for a prophet, not just a church presidency. In the winter of 1864, the six apostles (including James Dove) "met in Bro. Neils Morrison's house to ordain Bro. John Livingstone to receive communications for the guidance of the apostles."[36] Soon thereafter, another claimant, George Williams (known as the Prophet Cainan), sent letters of instruction to the Nevada Morrisites. Some confusion and eventual division occurred as a result of two men claiming a leadership role.

Eventually, James and George Dove accepted the prophetic role of George Williams and in November 1865 left Carson Valley on a mission to the eastern states on his behalf. On their way, they stopped in December 1865 in San Francisco, which would eventually be their home and the place where they organized the Church of the Firstborn, to catch a ship around Cape Horn and review local church affairs. James Dove believed that "being an apostle, [he] had the right to set in order, and he organized them."[37] They traveled from California to New Jersey with great expectations of success based on Cainan's predictions, however James Dove returned to San Francisco in January 1868, somewhat disappointed. Cainan's prophecies were working out.

When he arrived in San Francisco, James Dove, now questioning Cainan's prophetic calling, affiliated with yet another Morrisite claimant, W. W. Davies. Davies's group had been organized in San Francisco a short time before Dove's arrival, and Dove was successful in baptizing several individuals into the new group. Four years later George Dove, who had also accepted the role of Davies, arrived from a very long mission in the East. Missionary success in California was limited, although a few new converts were added yearly. James Dove, president of the local church in San Francisco, held weekly Sunday meetings. As he later wrote, "We had a very busy house for two weeks, people coming visiting and coming to the meetings, Petrie giving revelations against the high priesthood, till James had to say something about it."[38]

Ultimately dissuaded by all other claimants, the Doves began to see themselves as more than second-level leaders and followers.[39] In 1873, George Dove reported having experienced many recent spiritual communications and visions. His father, the original Morrisite apostle, announced more and more frequently to scattered believers that George was the true leader of the flock. The Doves then attempted use their publishing enterprise to mobilize support for George Dove's leadership from among the various Morrisite communities in the West. In California they published missionary tracts, pamphlets, and several books in an effort to establish their leadership and renew once again their protest against Utah Mormonism.[40]

James Dove became the strongest force in favor of his son's prophetic mission. "Bro. George continued to receive the word of the

Lord," his father wrote, "giving instructions how to proceed with the work, and giving light on many things; and principles that were given in Weber, which we did not understand before, we gained light upon." "Every time that any one has tried to lead the people on the ground of ambition," George Dove argued, "he has failed, because the love of the Father through the Son was not there. For fourteen years our food has been vanity, visions and fears. Some have been willing to take up with false shepherds, and they have gained experience thereby; while some have been unwilling to investigate anything, and have given it all up."[41]

Although George Dove was the seventh claimant, there was a difference in his call to mobilization. He did not claim to be a prophet, but to be president of the apostles "according to two revelations given in Weber about that office." His father wrote, "George S. Dove does not pretend to be a prophet, in the general acceptation of the term or to give revelations in writing. He receives communications from Jesus and Joseph, as John the revelator received communications on the Isle of Patmos."[42]

Other claimants had changed some of the objectives and goals of the movement from those set forth at South Weber by Morris, yet "we have not thrown away any of the revelations given in Weber," the Doves stated. A general epistle was sent to the scattered Morrisites:

> The times in which we live are fraught with great events; but the greatest event to the true saint of God is the establishment of a work to connect with that which was apparently broken off by the death of our beloved prophet in Weber. Let us put away all the dissensions and bickering that have occurred since that time, seek the Lord in humility, and endeavor to regain that light that was once in our possession; and with regard to the revelations given through Joseph that seem to be unfulfilled, let us not cast them away, but rather wait until the spirit of the Lord and the instructions of your brethren shall make them plain to your understanding.[43]

Through George Dove's revelations, the California Morrisites were instructed to organize themselves into a church called the Church of the Firstborn and reestablish the gathering place in Utah. The church was organized on the morning of July 2, 1876, in San Francisco, with George Dove as president. Five persons were baptized on that day, including James and George Dove, John Neilson, Joseph Taylor, and another son, Joseph A. Dove.[44] Another twenty-three individuals were baptized shortly thereafter. In Fairmount Valley, the church organized a school for children and built a church.

Once the church was organized, Dove justified its missionary activities: "Believing it to be the will of the Lord to enter upon missionary work, for the promulgation of all truth connected with the fullness of the gospel and the restoration of the faith of the Morrisite people, and in the interests of the Church of the Firstborn."[45] Initially, the Doves proselytized in Sacramento, Pleasant Grove, and Fairmont Valley and had some success in each place, but soon spread their missionary outreach to Nevada and Utah. Eventually, they visited Soda Springs, Idaho, and Beaver Valley, Montana, the two principal Morrisite enclaves. In a wider effort, such publications as *Present Knowledge and Past Revealment Combined* and *Olive Branch,* written by the Doves, were sent throughout the United States and Europe in an attempt not only to reclaim the faithful Morrisites, but also to reach out to potential new converts, both necessary resources if the social movement were to survive.[46]

James and George Dove made a significant step forward by extending their missionary efforts to Utah in August 1885. In Salt Lake City they stayed with the Holmes family in South Cottonwood. A preaching tour of Utah towns commenced soon thereafter, first in South Cottonwood and then in Sandy. On September 14, just a few weeks after their arrival, the Doves baptized ten individuals and preached to a large congregation in the Pendleton Hall. Of the Utah visit, James reported, "Visited many, and found many who were favorable, and many others who were not."[47] It was now time to test their abilities to win other Morrisites into their group.

The Doves began a trip to Montana, where a Morrisite community had been organized under the direction of George Williams. There the Doves met John R. Eardley, an influential Morrisite and former member of the Nevada Morrisite community. The first few days in Montana were hospitable and friendly. They found transportation, lodging, and accommodation to preach at every turn. A few other members of the California church were also now living in the area. Then, as the Doves pushed their leadership claims, a confrontation between James Dove and John Eardley took place.

The encounter did not stifle the attendance at the October 11, 1885, meeting in the Willow Glen schoolhouse. On that day, two meetings were held to a full house. The next settlement to be visited was Deer Lodge City, the headquarters for the Montana Morrisite faction. Several other days were spent in visiting and preaching to fellow Morrisites, including a meeting at Deer Lodge Courthouse, where more than two hundred people gathered to hear James and George Dove preach.

The Doves did convert a few new members, and on October 26 baptized several individuals. Although not as successful as they had hoped, the visit to Montana did lead to an important new mission. James Dove reported that "about this time a number of brethren began to advocate the publishing of the revelations of Joseph Morris. We told them at first that we did not think they could understand them all; we were satisfied that such would be the case; but they felt determined to have them just as they were written. Finally arrangements were made for the means to conduct that part of the work, and the brothers at Montana would have George S. Dove pledge himself that he would publish the revelations in their crude state."[48]

Their mission ended in Montana on November 18, 1885. After a brief stop in Salt Lake City, where five more individuals were baptized, George Dove returned to California with a mandate to publish the revelations of Joseph Morris and the pledged financial resources to do so.[49] His father remained in Utah in behalf of another mission—the reestablishment of a Morrisite presence in the territory.[50] Dove believed that Morris was right when he stated that South Weber was the site for the second coming of Christ. He never allowed himself to reject this notion—the Advent would be at Weber and only at Weber. This was one constant theme of his preaching and writing, and it became a means of measuring everyone's orthodoxy. For the Doves, everything that was occurring was only in preparation for that day at South Weber.

For almost a year, James Dove continued preaching in the various wards in Salt Lake City, including the First, Second, and Ninth. He held more than seventy preaching meetings during the first seven months there. The effort, however, yielded only five convert baptisms through July 1886. The mission to gather fellow Morrisites to Utah and convert Utah Saints was largely unsuccessful, but the work in California progressed. In San Francisco during the spring George Dove published a book of Morris's revelations, *The Spirit Prevails*. He finally returned to Utah in December 1886 to assist his father. Thereafter, the Doves spent most of their time preaching at public meetings except for the younger Dove's brief missionary trip to Soda Springs, Idaho, another important Morrisite community.

Eventually, South Weber drew them both back, and in May 1886 they returned and rented some land and settled to continue their religious efforts and await the Millennium. Several other Morrisites arrived not long thereafter, and a Morrisite community was born anew in South Weber more than twenty years after Morris's death. The Doves spent the next months preaching in the Ogden City courthouse. George Dove then returned to California to continue his work in the publication business, while his father remained in Utah.

Still clinging to the belief that the Second Coming would occur just as Joseph Morris had stated, James Dove remained at South Weber, attempting to gather Morrisites to the place. While there he built a home, but it was not easy, "[I] suffere[ed] considerable hardship in the winter, believing that [I] was doing the will of the Lord."[51] Heartbroken and unable to rebuild the South Weber community, he eventually returned to California. Unable to attract people back to Utah, he spent the remaining days of his life at the "temporary base" in California.

James Dove published his last pamphlet, "The Man of Sin in the Old and New Church," in 1893 in California. It was his final call to arms and attempt to garner support from possible Mormon dissidents in Utah. Following a six-year lapse, Joseph A. Dove published the last Morrisite pamphlet, "Gems of Inspiration: A Collection of Sublime Thoughts by Modern Prophets," in 1899. Instead of a plea on behalf of the California Morrisite church, it sustained the work of another Morrisite claimant, George Williams, the Prophet Cainan. The pamphlet was compiled by John R. Eardley, who had confronted the Doves several years earlier in Montana.

James Dove died sometime before the Eardley publication, and his son George no longer claimed leadership of the Morrisite church or wrote and published on its behalf.[52] By 1896, he had become a phrenologist.[53] Only Joseph Dove remained in the occupation of a printer, but it seems that publishing Eardley's work was as much a matter of income as it was of belief in the movement with which his father and brother had been associated for nearly thirty-five years.

The Morrisites were an important and significant protest movement in Utah during the early part of the 1860s. The Church of the Firstborn, on the other hand, was unable to attract the same commitment and failed to mobilize sufficient resources to continue to play a role in Utah society. Both were social movements—groups of people joining together to change conditions within the dominant culture. Like all such movements, the Morrisites also confronted the dominant culture, and this confrontation resulted in a serious predicament.

Armand L. Mauss has argued that protest movements ultimately face a dilemma if they are to survive the co-opting nature of the dominant culture and the repression that threatens such movements if they are small and lack broad appeal. "The difficulty experienced by radical movements [is] in trying both to broaden the recruitment base and to maintain intense commitment to principles," Mauss wrote.[54] Although the Morrisites attracted a significant following, still they were vulnerable. The Church of the Firstborn, even smaller, was much more precariously poised on the fringe of the dominant culture. As a result, several missions were organized in order to broaden the recruitment base.

The Doves' attempt to garner support and gather new converts became increasingly more difficult in Utah and the West as the years passed. Two major perceptions about the Morrisites thwarted mobilization. In Utah, the group was seen as criminals. Articles such as Richard W. Young's "The Morrisite War," published in Utah in 1890, emphasized this aspect of the movement.[55] The Morrisites' belief in the Law of Consecration impeded their progress outside of Utah significantly. In Utah in the 1850s it was commonly believed that this financial law, by which one gives all his or her possessions to the church, was necessary in order to establish a kingdom for Christ. For non-Mormons attuned to the laissez-faire currents of the post-Civil War era, no such background existed.

To broaden their recruitment potential the Doves made an important change in 1887, when they published a missionary tract entitled "The Articles of Faith." Dove specifically indicated that the church must live the "law of the land."[56] In his other publications during the period, George Dove emphasized that it was the Utah church that was lawless, not the Morrisites. He aligned himself with the U.S. government against the Mormons during a period known in Utah as the "Federal Raid."

For the potential convert, the financial law of the church had changed, and James Dove no longer saw consecration as a valuable commitment mechanism. "We believe that under church discipline the law of tithing is for the body of the Church," he wrote, but "those who believe in the principles and doctrines of the Church, and feel that they cannot pay tithing, or consecrate, can make a free will offering."[57] The "free will offering" was similar to the Protestant practice rather than the Mormon practice. Whatever success resulted in this attempt to broaden their appeal, it seems certain that the Doves were beginning to lose their distinctiveness and compromise their Mormon fundamentals and in certain ways were being co-opted by the dominant Protestant culture.

Another issue concerning the Doves and social conflict and collective behavior accounts for some of their grievances and how they were able to mobilize them into a social movement. Scholars have discussed the mobilization of protest groups in the pursuit of collective goals in light of a single motive such as impoverishment (economic) or disenfranchisement (political). Current mobilization theory is concerned with how people with little individual power collectively resist or challenge established groups that have a vested interest in maintaining the status quo. Although several theoretical models have been used, most sociologists have focused on what they term "substantial opposition movements" and not "with a sociology of sects, small deviant subcultures, and similar phenomena."[58]

The Morrisite movement, although falling within the sect category, is still best understood and explained by the broader theory. Several factors are necessary for the successful mobilization of a group. The first is the initiation of mobilization of conflict groups from the outside through the activities of upper-status groups in opposition to dominate culture. John Banks and Richard Cook, both prominent and wealthy members of the Mormon hierarchy, were instrumental in the rapid rise of the Morrisite movement.

Second, there usually exists a class of precipitating conditions that signal hope of success occurring at some focal point. In this case, the so-called Woodruff prophecy about the immediate demise of the movement, and the subsequent rapid growth of the Morrisites instead, could have been seen as one such focal point. Although whether Woodruff made such a statement is uncertain, a rumor that he did so spread throughout the territory and was mentioned several times by Morris at open-air meetings at Kingston Fort. The third and final condition that favors mobilization is the relationship between city and countryside. The rural-urban interchange in mobilization is not, however, completely one-sided. Here it is evident that once Morris was able to garner support, particularly economic and political support from dissatisfied city elite, the movement grew rapidly.

Paradoxically, the same factors that account for rapid mobilization also account for the centrifugal forces that lead to the dissolution of opposition movements. A central idea of the theory of mobilization is that of group recruitment and group joining as opposed to the recruitment of isolated individuals. In group recruitment, members of the group provide each other with social support. Group leaders before the movement take the initiative in mobilization, and the movement builds up rapidly through mergers of such groups. Thus a heterogeneous leadership and membership, loosely held together in pursuit of common goals, comes into being, joined by others who are attracted by the initial success of the movement. Yet the movement will have primary loyalties of the members to the component groups, leaders, and associations and not to the overarching movement itself. Ultimately, such loyalties cause factionalism when the leader dies and second-level leaders begin to vie for a major leadership role. The Morrisite movement did attract a large number of individuals dissatisfied with life in Utah. When Morris died, these loyalties to group components and ideas manifested themselves, and the result was fragmentation.

Three processes counteract these centrifugal forces: the presence of charismatic leadership (which never took place following Morris's death, John Banks, the only real alternative, was also killed at South Weber); the formation of a subculture common to all the component parts of the movement (because of the diversity of language and culture among the Morrisites this was not possible within the short period it existed); and, finally, the creation of an overarching organizational framework (this was impossible because Morris believed the Second Coming was imminent and no overarching framework was necessary, especially a succession mechanism).

When the Morrisites failed to counteract these forces, their demise was certain. The creation of a subculture common to all the members was impossible, for they were socially and economically heterogeneous. Many motives and reasons for protest and dissent in Utah were in play (a few years later, for example, the Godbeite movement challenged Young's authority).[59] Many Morrisites left the Utah church and went to South Weber, acting, once they arrived, on negative experiences they encountered in the Great Basin that concerned political, economic, social, and religious issues. This seems to be the case for Morris's secretary Mark Forscutt, who later became an important Reorganized Church leader. In some cases, such as with Morris's counselor John Banks, it was a negative experience with Brigham Young himself.[60] Still other Morrisites left Utah Mormonism because they really believed that Morris was a true prophet and Young was not. For these dissidents, the original reason for joining the Mormon church was a belief that Joseph Smith was not only a religious leader but also a prophet who received and wrote revelations.

The Doves are best understood in this context, although it is certain that other factors prepared them for their flight from Utah Mormonism to Morrisitism. James and George Dove believed Joseph Morris—he produced scripture and seemed to be more like a prophet than Brigham Young. "Notwithstanding the many objections which have been raised against the work . . . on account of the apparent failure of some of the personal promises made to Joseph Morris and others in the revelations," they wrote, "we are under the impression, and, still further, thoroughly believe, that those promises will yet be fulfilled."[61] In order to explain such failures, the Doves held a view of reincarnation—Morris could come back in the flesh to fulfill prophecy.[62] They used this same standard to judge the claims of other would-be Morrisite leaders following the death of their prophet.

In the end, the Dove family and the church they organized in San Francisco believed that only George Dove was able to claim succession rights to the important 1860s Utah Mormon protest movement. Their own movement, however, survived only until 1910. The demise of the Church of the Firstborn may be explained by examining the differential access to resources. Sociologists discuss the rise and demise of social movements based on "resource mobilization." Such resources include material resources (not limited to financial capital), numbers of potential converts, support or opposition of local government, and leadership pools.

From the very beginning, the Doves were unable to gain access to financial sources, except when they published the *Spirit Prevails* (several Morrisite factions donated money for its publication). An examination of California voter registration and federal census records indicates that the Doves continually moved residences and in later years boarded in the homes of others. It is likely that they never gained financial stability. This may explain the large spans of time between their publications, as well as the variance in size. Although the pool for potential converts in Utah may have seemed unlimited initially, it really was not. Brigham Young's death in 1877 and the succession of John Taylor to the church presidency altered the perception of the Utah church.

The insistence of James Dove on aligning himself with the U.S. government against the LDS church only antagonized the Utah Saints, who viewed themselves as being persecuted by the government. On another issue, that of continuing written revelation, whether intentional or not, John Taylor co-opted the Morrisites' argument. Unlike Brigham Young, Taylor published several revelations and wrote many others during the period. Mormons saw Taylor as a prophet. He had been with Joseph Smith at Carthage Jail when Smith was murdered; he had been a successful missionary and an influential author and defender of the faith; and his discourses were markedly different from Young's style. He was not afraid to invoke the preamble, "Thus saith the Lord" in his pronouncements. The Utah Saints did not have to go to South Weber or San Francisco to find a prophet who received revelation. They had one.[63]

James and George Doves' commitment, self-sacrifice, and untiring effort to publish and proselytize for the Morrisite faith for almost thirty-five years is impressive, especially in light of the meager success they encountered in reclaiming the dispersed and in recruiting new converts. The lack of the necessary resources to continue their protest and to mobilize their social movement resulted in the death of the Church of the Firstborn. No matter how one may explain the California Morrisites' demise, James Dove said it best: "No one came to help."[64]

NOTES

I wish to acknowledge the special assistance of C. LeRoy Anderson (University of Montana), B. Carmon Hardy (California State University, Fullerton), and Armand L. Mauss (Washington State University).

1. Originally called the Church of Christ, it later was known as the Latter Day Saint church and eventually called the Church of Jesus Christ of Latter Day Saints. Two main groups, the Church of Jesus Christ of Latter-day Saints and the Reorganized Church of Jesus Christ of Latter Day Saints, have historical roots to the church founded by Joseph Smith in 1830.

2. For a list of such groups, see Steven L. Shields, *The Latter Day Saint Churches: An Annotated Bibliography* (New York: Garland Publishing Co., 1987).

3. The principal dissenters were James Dove and his son George. James Dove was born on December 2, 1819, and George was born on May 18, 1842, both at Bulwell, Nottingham, England.

4. John Dove, born on April 1, 1849, was blessed on September 30, 1849. Selina Dove, born on January 8, 1852, was blessed on February 22, 1852. The Doves blessed their elder daughter, Sarah, on April 7, 1850. Minnie Margetts Membership Card Index, Church of Jesus Christ of Latter-day Saints Family History Library, Salt Lake City, hereafter cited as LDS Family History Library.

5. On the Mormon Reformation, see Gustive O. Larson, "The Mormon Reformation," *Utah Historical Quarterly* 26 (January 1958): 45–63; Paul H. Peterson, "The Mormon Reformation," Ph.D. diss., Brigham Young University, 1981; Gene A. Sessions, *Mormon Thunder: A Documentary History of Jedediah Grant* (Urbana: University of Illinois Press, 1982).

6. Quoted in Eugene E. Campbell, *Establishing Zion: The Mormon Church in the American West, 1847–1869* (Salt Lake City: Signature Books, 1988), 195–96.

7. William B. Hodgett, "Capt. Hodgett Company Camp Journal 1856," Archives Division, Historical Department, Church of Jesus Christ of Latter-day Saints, Salt Lake City, hereafter cited as LDS Historical Department.

8. See Leonard J. Arrington, *Brigham Young: American Moses* (New York: Alfred A. Knopf, 1985), 160–61. Surprisingly, many Saints returned to England; see Ruby C. Faunce, "Biography of Mark Hill Forscutt," *Saints' Herald*, March 13, 1934, 333.

9. Morrisite File, Newspaper Clippings, Reorganized Church of Jesus Christ of Latter Day Saints Library-Archives, Independence, Mo.

10. Ruby C. Faunce, "Biography of Mark Hill Forscutt," *Saints' Herald*, January 30, 1934, 143. The most comprehensive work on the Morrisites is C. LeRoy Anderson, *For Christ Will Come Tomorrow: The Saga of the Morrisites* (Logan: Utah State University Press, 1981).

11. The Kingston settlement was established near the mouth of Weber Canyon (known as South Weber) in 1853 by Thomas Kingston, the first Mormon bishop of Weber County. It consisted of a bowery (shade structure), church, school, and two rows of log cabins. After a wall was eventually built around

the few buildings, it was known as Kingston's Fort. The fort was abandoned during the Utah War in 1857, when all northern Utah settlements evacuated south. It remained abandoned until Joseph Morris and his followers resettled it in 1860. As converts gathered to Kingston they were forced to make temporary quarters in tents and wagon boxes. Eventually, permanent dwellings were built from walls of woven willow reed secured to corner posts. The reed walls were then filled with loose dirt for strength and insulation. Roofs were made of boughs set on supporting timber frame and covered with earth. When attack from a territorial posse seemed imminent, the Morrisites filled the gaps between the buildings with a heavy wall six feet high and eighteen inches thick, thereby enclosing the community entirely. See George A. Thompson, *Some Dreams Die: Utah's Ghost Towns and Lost Treasures* (Salt Lake City: Dream Garden Press, 1982), 50–51.

12. Morris's revelations are found in Joseph Morris, *The Spirit Prevails: Containing the Revelations, Articles and Letters writing by Joseph Morris* (San Francisco: J. A. Dove and Co., Printers, 1886). An earlier publication, *Revelations of Joseph Morris, 1857–1862* (ca. 1882), may have been an attempt by the Doves to make Morris's revelations available; nevertheless, the origins of the publication are uncertain.

13. In March 1857, one man, writing from the small community of Fillmore, reported that in that community "there were 56 single men besides all the married ones that were anxious to get more wives, and only four single women." See Campbell, *Establishing Zion,* 198.

14. To one man living at Fort Supply, Brigham Young wrote, "I don't object to your taking sisters named in your letter to wife if they are not too young and their parents and your president and all connected are satisfied, but I do not want children to be married to men before an age which their mothers can generally best determine." Ibid., 198.

15. Later Sarah Dove Higgs left Salt Lake City and joined her family in South Weber. See George S. Dove, *Roll of Membership: Names of Persons Baptized into the Fullness of the Gospel* (San Francisco: Geo. S. Dove & Co., 1886), 2.

16. Endowment House Records, Endowments Records and Sealing Records, LDS Family History Library.

17. James A. Dove, "The Man of Sin in the Old Church and the New Church" (San Francisco: Dove & Taylor Printers, 1893), 9. Copies of the Dove material were provided by the Harold B. Lee Library at Brigham Young University, the LDS Historical Department, the New York Public Library, the Reorganized Church Library-Archives, the Bancroft Library at the University of California at Berkeley, the University of California-Irvine Library, the University of California-Los Angeles Library, and the Merrill Library at Utah State University. The most complete collection of Morrisite material is located at the Merrill Library Department of Special Collections and Archives (see the register for the C. LeRoy Anderson Morrisite Collection.)

18. George S. Dove, *A Voice from the West to the Scattered People of Weber and all the Seed of Abraham* (San Francisco: Joseph A. Dove Printer, 1879), 6.

19. Dove, *Voice from the West,* 7–8.

20. The cardinal teachings of this protest movement, the Church of Jesus Christ of Saints of the Most High, were the rejection of Utah polygamy, the need for continuing written revelations, and the preparation for the imminent appearance of Jesus Christ, the Second Coming.

21. Dove, *Roll of Membership,* 8. The list contains 430 names of individuals. Dove stated, "All the names that we found in the record book are in this list. We feel assured that there were many persons baptized whose names were not recorded."

22. Jesse N. Smith, "Autobiography," LDS Historical Department.

23. Dove, *Voice from the West,* 8.

24. Salt Lake City 20th Ward, Home Teaching Minutes, LDS Historical Department.

25. Ibid.

26. John Banks, "A Documentary History of the Morrisites in Utah," 35, Special Collections, Harold B. Lee Library, Brigham Young University, Provo.

27. Forscutt explained the differences between the Reorganized Church and the Morrisite movement's attitude about the issue: "The Morrisite and Reorganized Churches were both anti-polygamic, but with this very essential difference. Polygamists were received as members in the Morrisite Church; husbands, wives, and families together. They held this as due the families who otherwise might suffer want. The gospel was designed for the people of the Orient as well as those of the occident. Polygamy was tolerated there. The Church must have a platform broad enough for all. Hence the rule adopted was this: Those who had entered into polygamous relations before entering the church ... might be received into the church fellowship, but polygamic relations must not be entered into after joining the church. If polygamists were received, they must be monogamic in life. . . . The husband was to be held strictly accountable for the maintenance and provisional comforts of all whom he had covenanted by marriage to sustain, and their offspring." Mark Forscutt, "Mark Forscutt Manuscript," LDS Historical Department.

28. This correlation did not go unnoticed among Morrisite disciples; see Karl Banks, "A Brief History of John Banks and the Morrisite Movement," 5, Special Collections Department, Marriott Library, University of Utah, Salt Lake City.

29. Lewis Coser, *Continuities in the Study of Social Conflict* (New York: Free Press, 1967), 232.

30. An interpretation of these events is found in G. M. Howard, "Men, Motives, and Misunderstandings: A New Look at the Morrisite War of 1862," *Utah Historical Quarterly* 44 (Spring 1976): 112–32.

31. Morris, *Spirit Prevails,* 672. Woodruff's diary does not mention such a statement, which is highly unusual. See Scott G. Kenney, ed., *Wilford Woodruff's Journal: 1833–1898 Typescript* (Midvale: Signature Books, 1984), 5:548–551.

32. Anderson, *For Christ Will Come Tomorrow,* 102.

33. Some Morrisites, now disappointed and despondent about their efforts

to organize a protest movement in opposition to the Utah church, found another alternative in the Reorganized Church. Among the many Morrisites who chose to join the Reorganization were Mark Forscutt and his wife. Forscutt went to England on a mission for the Reorganization and located other Morrisites, including John Eardley, in an effort to convert them, "I have hopes of bringing them into the covenant." See Faunce, "Biography of Mark Hill Forscutt," 143, 333.

34. Anderson, *For Christ Will Come Tomorrow*, 12.

35. James A. Dove, *A Few Items in the History of the Morrisites* (San Francisco: Church of the Firstborn, 1892), 1.

36. Dove, *Few Items*, 2.

37. Ibid., 2.

38. Ibid., 4.

39. James Dove listed the Morrisite claimants as George Williams, John Livingston, William Davies, Goodmund Godmundson, John Parson, Joseph Warner, and "the seventh claimant is George S. Dove." See Dove, *Voice from the West*, 14.

40. The Doves published almost twenty pamphlets and several books between 1878 and 1899 in San Francisco. See Chad Flake, *A Mormon Bibliography: 1830–1930* (Salt Lake City: University of Utah Press, 1978), 218–19, 288, 440, and Dove's advertisement printed in "Man of Sin."

41. Dove, *Voice from the West*, 5, 13.

42. James Dove indicated that the two revelations were given privately to the apostleship, one of which said: "Go and break up that quorum, and you shall not organize it again until sometime after I have delivered my people. I will send a man, and he shall preside over that quorum; until that time it shall remain disorganized." George Dove claimed the power to set in order the house of God and to give the rights to the spiritual Israel. To bolster his argument, James Dove recalled, "Mother White, at that time Mother Jones, says: 'Joseph Morris came into my house in Weber, after ordaining George S. Dove.' He said, 'We have ordained brother James Dove's son to the High Priesthood.' Then placing his hands upon his knees, as his custom was, he said: 'A noble spirit in that lad.' Repeating it several times. 'God has a great work for him to do—not such a spirit in this camp.' Mother Jones then asked him what spirit it was, and what work God had for him to do? His reply was: 'I do not know—it is in the future.' He then said: 'The old man has a good spirit, and the Lord has a work for him to do, but the lad is before his father.' I then asked him, will they do it? Joseph's reply was: 'God will make it known to them when the time comes—God will bring them to it.' From this it is plain that we can draw but one conclusion. James Dove had already been ordained an apostle by birthright; therefore, if 'the lad was before his father,' there only remained the presidency of the apostleship. This testimony of mother White's was not given until after the Church was organized, and she had been baptized on June 9th, 1877." Ibid., 14–15.

43. Ibid., 17, 22.

44. Joseph A. Dove was born in Utah in May 1861 to James and Alice

Dove. In 1899 he issued the last known Morrisite publication: "Gems of Inspiration: A Collection of Sublime Thoughts by Modern Prophets," complied by J. R. Eardley.

45. Dove, *Few Items*, 1.

46. Anderson, *For Christ Will Come Tomorrow*, 194.

47. Dove, *Few Items*, 7.

48. Ibid., 10–11.

49. George Dove reported, "The work for which we feel the most thankful to-day is the 'Spirit Prevails,' for the publication of which our friends furnished the money." See Dove, *Pearls; or, Selected paragraphs from the revelations of Jesus Christ given through Joseph Morris* (San Francisco: J. A. Dove & Co., Printers, 1891), 3. "During the conflict between the Mormon Militia and the Morrisites, Hanna Banks, wife of John Banks, took the long-hand revelations and other writings of Joseph Morris and buried them in the ground under the bowery. After three days, the widow of Joseph Morris took possession of the manuscript. At her death, her father sold it to Abraham Taylor, who retained it for over 20 years, and before his death willed it to his son, Joseph Taylor of San Francisco." See Banks, "A Brief History of John Banks and the Morrisite Movement," 9. Taylor, a member of the California Morrisite church, evidently gave it to the Doves, who were living in San Francisco at the time.

50. On this point—the appearance of Christ at South Weber—the Doves remained more faithful to Morris's revelations than any other Morrisite faction. Their arguments are present in several publications, see, for example James Dove's *Few Items*, 15–16, and *A Treatise on the Priesthood, by Spiritual Birthright; Reprobation and Election* (San Francisco: Dove and Taylor Printers, 1891), 25–28.

51. Dove, *Few Items*, 15.

52. Although a death record has not been located for either James or George Dove, an examination of census records, voting registration records, and Dove publications indicates that James lived in San Francisco in 1890 with his son George, but not in 1900. George lived there in 1900 with his brother Joseph, but not in 1910. Joseph Dove is reported living with his family (a wife and three children) in 1910. I am assuming that James died before 1900 and George before 1910.

53. California voter registration record, "Voter Record 1896," LDS Family History Library.

54. Armand L. Mauss, "On Being Strangled by the Stars and Stripes," in *The Sociology of Dissent*, ed. R. Serge Denisoff (New York: Harcourt Brace Jovanovich, 1974), 149.

55. Richard W. Young, "The Morrisite War," *The Contributor* 11 (June 1890): 281–84, 348–50, 369–72, 428–31, 466–71. Young emphasized the militaristic nature of the Morrisite camp at South Weber and the militant nature of its actions when confronted by civil authorities.

56. George S. Dove, "Articles of Faith" (San Francisco: Committee of the Church of the Firstborn, 1887), 5.

57. Dove, "Articles of Faith," 16.

58. Anthony Oberschall, *Social Conflict and Social Movements* (Englewood Cliffs: Prentice-Hall, 1973), 119.

59. Campbell, *Establishing Zion,* 321–24.

60. Banks, "Brief History of John Banks," 2–3.

61. Dove, *Pearls,* 2.

62. James A. Dove, *The Resurrection by Regeneration Compared with a Resurrection from the Grave* (San Francisco: J. A. Dove, Printer, 1891).

63. For a complete typescript of John Taylor's revelations, see Fred C. Collier, *Unpublished Revelations of the Prophets and the Presidents of the Church of Jesus Christ of Latter-day Saints* (Salt Lake City: Collier's Publishing Company, 1979).

64. Dove, "Articles of Faith," 17.

10

Henry W. Lawrence:
A Life in Dissent

John S. McCormick and John R. Sillito

Although he is little known today, Henry W. Lawrence was an important figure in Utah from pioneer days until the first two decades of the twentieth century. He was an orthodox Mormon for the first twenty years of his adult life, but by the late 1860s was increasingly critical, not so much of Mormon theology as of the Mormon church as an institution and how it conducted its affairs. His concerns found expression first in 1869 when he joined with the Godbeites, an act that led to his excommunication, and then for the next twenty years as one of the most active members of the anti-Mormon Liberal party. By the early 1890s his interests had broadened, and Lawrence moved from questioning the basic values and structures of the Mormon church to challenging those of American society as a whole. In 1893 he joined the leftist Populist party. When he joined the Socialist Party of America a few years later, his evolution from orthodoxy to radicalism in religion and politics was complete. Tracing that process is interesting in itself. More important, it illuminates larger patterns and themes in Mormon, Utah, and American history.

Lawrence was born July 18, 1835, in Pickering, near Ontario, Canada, and died in Salt Lake City on April 5, 1924. He joined the Mormon church in early childhood with his family; lived for short periods in Nauvoo and Quincy, Illinois, and in St. Louis, Missouri; worked on Mississippi River boats; and came to Salt Lake City about 1850, where he spent the rest of his life.[1] In 1859, after clerking for several businesses, he and his non-Mormon brother-in-law, John B. Kimball, founded the mercantile company of Kimball and Lawrence. The firm soon became one of the leading establishments in the territory and, along with mining and real estate activities, provided Lawrence with a substantial personal fortune, allowing him the time and resources to devote many of his efforts to political issues. At his death in 1924 he left an estate valued at more than $1 million.

Active in politics early on, Lawrence served as foreman of the territorial house of representatives in 1854, as territorial marshal from 1862 to 1863, and as a Salt Lake City councilman between 1865 and 1869. A polygamist with two wives, he was a counselor to Bishop Elijah Sheets in Salt Lake City's Eighth Ward from 1866 to 1869 and officiated in Endowment House ceremonies.[2] Clearly, during this stage of his career he had close ties to important Mormon leaders. His two elder sisters, Maria and Sarah, moreover, married Joseph Smith as plural wives in Nauvoo in the spring of 1843. Maria subsequently married Brigham Young in January 1846. Although she died soon afterward, Lawrence remained close to Young. He was also close to Heber C. Kimball, who in January 1846 married his other sister, Sarah, even though the couple was divorced in 1851 in Salt Lake City and she married Joseph Mount two years later and moved to California.[3] According to one account, reported in the *Salt Lake Tribune* on February 2, 1866, Lawrence was also a brother-in-law of Erastus Snow.

Periodically during the 1860s Lawrence accompanied Brigham Young on visits to settlements throughout the territory. While in Brigham City on one such occasion, for instance, "he bore his testimony to the truth and expressed his desire to remain faithful in it and become more useful in the work of the Lord," reported the *Tribune* on August 8, 1865. In the same publication, he recalled on November 22, 1889 that "I was taught that 'Mormonism' was the only true religion. My parents were sincere. I was sincere. . . . I was acquainted with Joseph Smith, and was taught he was a prophet of God. Was taught the same thing regarding Brigham Young."

In addition to his church activities, Lawrence helped support and build the Mormon Kingdom in a variety of other ways. A major in the territorial militia, he was active in the Echo Canyon campaign during the Utah War of 1857 as a member of the first company under Colonel Robert T. Burton that was sent into the field following word that Johnston's army was on its way to Utah. According to Orson F. Whitney, Burton's troops were ordered to "reconnoiter the country, protect the emigrant trains then on the way to the Valley, make observations respecting the numbers and equipment of the approaching army, and report the information to headquarters."[4]

In the spring of 1864 Brigham Young called Lawrence to provide food and other necessities to the poor of Washington County. The next year he donated $100 in cash to help build the St. George city hall. In 1865 Lawrence was an officer and founder of the Utah Produce Company, a cooperative marketing project of the Mormon church; in 1868 he became treasurer of the Eighth Ward Silk Producing Society; and he was one of a number of prominent Mormon entrepreneurs who were the initial investors in Zion's Cooperative Mercantile Institution (ZCMI), a church-sponsored mercantile system designed to reduce the influence of non-Mormon businessmen who, as Leonard Arrington points out, it was feared after the coming of the transcontinental railroad would "gradually assimilate the means and property of the Mormons and eventually control the Mountain Kingdom."[5] Lawrence contributed $30,000 to get it started.

In 1869 Lawrence joined a schismatic group of prominent Mormons who came to be called the Godbeites after their founder William S. Godbe. He left no account of the inner struggle he must have gone through, the doubts and fears, the conflicts and emotions he must have felt, but the decision could not have been an easy one. Lawrence was not part of the original protest group, which included Edward Tullidge, E. L. T. Harrison, Eli Kelsey, William H. Shearman, and Godbe, but he and six others soon joined them: T. B. H. Stenhouse and his wife, Fanny; Edward Tullidge's brother, John; Fred A. Perris; Joseph Salisbury; and George D. Watt.[6]

According to Ronald W. Walker, Lawrence was the group's most significant addition because of his high standing in Mormonism. The Godbeites, Walker asserts, not only disagreed with the economic and political policies of Brigham Young and called for freedom of expression within the church, but also struck at the roots of traditional Mormonism by rejecting the concept of the gathering of Zion, its social and economic blueprint. They spoke out against the kind of society Mormons sought to establish following their arrival in Utah in 1847— one in which a religious impulse so infused every activity that it was difficult to draw a line between the religious and the secular aspects of life; where members willingly submitted themselves to the direction of Mormon leaders in all matters, not only religious but also economic, political, social, and cultural; and where the emphasis was on group consciousness and activity, not on the individual. It was a society based on the concept of "disciplined and guided cooperation" that sought to exclude any outside influences antagonistic to the social ideal. To orthodox Mormons, such a society seemed perfectly reasonable, as it once did to Lawrence and his comrades, but by the late 1860s they no longer thought so.

In place of an essentially closed society, isolated both geographically and from the mainstream of American life, the Godbeites called for its transformation into one that was open, tolerant, diverse, and integrated into the larger society. To help achieve that purpose they advocated the immediate development of Utah's mining industry. They fully realized that to do so would have enormous implications. Mining would bring a new world that would alter Utah fundamentally, undermining the isolation and unity that the Mormon church sought. Before 1869 Utah was like a closely knit fabric with only a few broken threads. It was a relatively self-sufficient, egalitarian, and homogeneous society where, as Henry Wolfinger wrote, "The hand of the Church was ever-present and ever-active."[7] The development of mining would lead Utah in a different direction, helping to transform the Kingdom of God into only one among many other kingdoms of the world.

In addition to rejecting the zionic quest, the Godbeites also questioned some of Mormonism's theological tenets, including the idea of the Mormon church as the one true church with a prophet of God at its head and Mormons as chosen people with a special mission, a literal Second Advent, the physical resurrection, the Mormon concept of a personal God, the Christian Atonement, and the existence of the devil. They were also attracted to nineteenth-century American spiritualism.

The extent to which Lawrence shared these views is not entirely clear. He did to at least some degree, but they were not his main interest. He also stressed, at the outset and afterward, that he had no quarrel with Mormons themselves. "It is the system we have been opposing," he said, "not the people."[8] His primary concerns were twofold: the lack of freedom of expression and discussion within the church, and Mormonism's temporal activities. Lawrence always emphasized the primacy of individual conscience over group or party. He also stressed that the Mormon church was not only a spiritual organization, but also an economic and political one, and those aspects of the religion interested him most. "More political than religious in his orientation," Walker concludes, "he was estranged by Zion's temporal policies."[9] His concern was with what he saw as church interference in matters beyond the proper sphere of ecclesiastical activity. The Mormon church was too powerful, too controlling, too pervasive a presence. "That is simply the truth of it," Lawrence said, "there is no disguising the fact."[10] In his view, Utah needed to be integrated and controlled by secular, rather than religious, sanctions.

At first, the Godbeites' views were private and academic, but they eventually became more open. As they did so it became increasingly difficult for Mormon authorities to ignore them, and on October 25, 1869, following a piece in their *Utah Magazine* strongly critical of Brigham Young's failure to support the development of mining in Utah, the three leaders, Harrison, Godbe, and Kelsey, in what David Griffiths describes as "a medieval theo-political drama," were excommunicated in a proceeding before the Salt Lake Stake High Council.[11] The

men were not surprised. After publishing the article, Lawrence recalled
in a November 22, 1889 *Deseret News* interview, "We knew that the
conflict would come and we would have to come out of the church,
and I said to the others, 'Boys, I'll give you six weeks to stay in the
church'."

At the trial's conclusion, all those in attendance were asked to sustain the decision. Lawrence and five others refused, just as in a proceeding several weeks earlier before the School of Prophets, an ecclesiastical entity organized for study and policymaking, he had refused
to give up reading the *Utah Magazine,* which he was helping to publish through his financial contributions. As he later recollected, "Some
man jumped up near me and said: 'Henry Lawrence voted to sustain
the Utah Magazine'. Brigham Young called me to the stand, and I got
up and asserted my claim that I could not give up my manhood and
my identity, and I was in favor of the paper." [12]

Lawrence was excommunicated two months later, in December
1869, "on a charge of general apostasy" after lengthy conversations
with Brigham Young and Daniel H. Wells had failed to change his
views, he recalled in the November 1889 *Deseret News*. According to
Lawrence, "Brigham Young pleaded with me to stay with the Church."
Church leaders delayed, he suspected, hoping to keep him in the church
because "I was rather prominent in the way of business and they concluded they would hold on to me, a good paying member of the church,
. . . and my friends in the church pleaded with me to stay in the
church," whereas, he pointed out, Eli B. Kelsey, "a poor man," was
excommunicated immediately. [13]

In Lawrence's view, allegiance to one's conscience was not easy for
members of the Mormon church unless their ideas corresponded to
those of church leaders. As he saw it, Mormons "were essentially required to give up their agency," and the consequences for those who
questioned "priesthood authority" were serious. Utah was a satisfying place to live for those who shared the views of the majority and a
difficult one for those who did not. "To object to any of the counsel
of the leaders was worthy of excommunication and ostracism," he said.
"There was risk in saying anything against the church." It meant, he
added, "ostracism from your business, ostracism from society, ostracism from all family relations, . . . you were almost isolated by yourself; . . . you had to keep very quiet and go along and make no particular opposition." [14] After his own excommunication, he commented,
"My mercantile business was pretty much ruined. My former friends
and customers did not come into my store. They dared not come into
my store." Previously he was "doing a business of $15,000 to $20,000

a month," but "in a little while it was down to one third of that, and I was socially ostracized. Nobody wanted to be seen in my company," he told the *Deseret News* in November 1889.

Like other Godbeites who were polygamists, Lawrence continued his plural household after leaving the church. In October 1871 federal marshals arrested him and three others, Brigham Young, Daniel H. Wells, and George Q. Cannon, for "lewd and lascivious cohabitation." According to Orson F. Whitney, the federal government included him with the group of prominent Mormons arrested "as a show of impartiality."[15] None were ever brought to trial, however, because of irregularities in impaneling a jury, and in April 1872 the U.S. Supreme Court quashed the indictment. How long after that Lawrence remained a polygamist is not clear.

In July 1870, seven months after his excommunication, Lawrence joined with other former and non-Mormons to found the Liberal party, an opposing force to Mormon hegemony in Utah politics. The first real political party in Utah, it was established to represent the interests of non-Mormons in the territory.[16] Before this action, political parties had not existed; in elections, only one set of candidates, which Mormon leaders often nominated, appeared on the ballot, and people simply voted "yes" or "no." Under such circumstances, Liberal party organizers said, only a facade of democracy existed. In voting, people simply went through the motions. Real political power rested with Mormon leaders. Non-Mormons were effectively disenfranchised with no voice in government, and they would not have one until they formed their own political party to represent them, their interests, and their positions. Faced with this challenge, the Mormon hierarchy established its own People's party.

During the years that followed, Utah politics were lively. In an open letter to People's party officials before the February 1874 Salt Lake City municipal election, for example, Lawrence pointed out that although non-Mormons comprised between 20 and 25 percent of the city's population and provided nearly one-half of the revenue it received in property taxes and license fees, they were not represented in city government and never had been. In effect, they were subject to "taxation without representation," which "violated their sense of justice and equity as freemen," but when he and others met with Mormon officials to discuss the situation, they were "scornfully received."[17]

The next day, January 16, the church-owned *Deseret News*, in an effort to shift the emphasis from issues to personalities, described Lawrence as an example "of those who are ever ready to 'pitch into the Mormons'" and asserted that "the very stale things he said didn't amount to anything." Referring to Lawrence's remark that he had out-grown Mormonism, the paper commented, "Some people outgrow Mormonism by growing too small for it. Perhaps that is what the gentleman meant."

As Lawrence and those who joined him in the Liberal party saw it, Utah was essentially a theocracy. The Mormon church dominated political affairs to such an extent that a virtual union of church and state existed, with the state subservient to the church and the rights of Utah citizens subordinate to the wishes of a politically irresponsible priesthood. Mormon leaders dictated to their people how to vote, thereby ignoring and subverting the values and practices on which the United States was founded. As a remedy, Liberals called for separation of church and state, the right of people to vote without dictation from Mormon authorities, and the election of officials responsible to the people as a whole, not to a church or its officers. Their intention, according to Robert N. Baskin, one of the party's most important members, was to "establish republican American rule in place of the usurped rule of the priesthood of the Mormon church." They also echoed the call of the Godbeites for "the development of our extensive mineral and agricultural resources," reasoning, according to the *Tribune* on July 24, 1874, that the resulting flood of miners into the territory would overwhelm the Mormons. Non-Mormons would soon predominate and change Utah forever.

The founding of the Liberal party was part of a new era in Utah's history. During the first quarter century after Mormon settlement, Utah's most obvious feature, although the point can be overstated, was its degree of unity and cohesion. From the mid 1870s until around the turn of the century, however, the most striking characteristic, as Henry Wolfinger has pointed out, was the antagonism that existed between Mormons and the growing non-Mormon population.[18] People in Utah were essentially divided into two groups: those inside the Mormon kingdom, and those outside. That division was expressed in a number of ways, including, on occasion, separate Mormon and non-Mormon Fourth of July celebrations and, perhaps most important, in the emergence of local parties divided along religious lines, with citizens essentially aligned for or against the Mormon church.

In its early years, the Liberal party had no expectation of actually winning office. What it hoped to do was provide an organization through which Utah's non-Mormon population could focus its discontents and energies and lay a foundation for eventual full participation in the territory's political affairs. Without doubt, the opposition party was an increasingly significant force, particularly in the territory's largest cities and in mining communities. By the late 1880s it had begun to win political office. In 1889 Liberals elected mayors and a majority of city council members in Salt Lake City and Ogden—the first time non-Mormons had been elected to public office there—and in 1891 one-third of the territorial legislature.

Lawrence was one of the Liberal party's leading figures from its formation in 1870 until its dissolution in 1893. He gave substantial amounts of money to support its activities, including publication of its organ, the *Salt Lake Tribune;* he was a party officer and an important participant in party conventions and discussions; and he ran for office several times on the party ticket, twice for the equivalent of the present Salt Lake County Commission and three times for Salt Lake City mayor. During his first mayoral campaign, in 1870, he received 302 votes to 1,999 for his opponent, Daniel H. Wells of the Mormon church's People's party. During his second candidacy in 1876—when the *Deseret News* characterized his platform on August 7 as simply, "D—n the Mormons"—he received a respectable minority of votes. Finally, in 1888 Lawrence made his best showing by making light of Mormon control of the region. He described the Salt Lake City Council in the *Tribune* on February 8 as an army "where the generals are out of sight. It does just what it is told by the unseen power, for no man in the church can maintain his standing unless he implicitly obeys this power." Although he urged voters to assert their individuality and "not submit to the priests," Lawrence's campaign was unsuccessful. Reward for his political office-seeking did not come until 1891, when he and seven other Liberals were elected to the twenty-four-member lower house of the territorial legislature.

Throughout this period, the Liberal party was particularly visible during election campaigns, when it sponsored regular speeches and rallies, distributed literature, took out advertisements in local newspapers, and otherwise engaged in conventional political activity. It also carried on a range of activities throughout the years designed to both demonstrate and combat what its members believed were the pervasive influences of the Mormon church in all areas of Utah's life. Lawrence was deeply involved in those efforts. In January 1872, Robert N. Baskin, Joseph R. Walker, and Lawrence were sent to Washington, D.C., to lobby against Utah's fourth petition for statehood, arguing that as long as Mormons were in the majority, self-government would be disastrous for Utah's non-Mormon minority. Two years later, the party appointed him to a committee to "represent the interests of the minority tax-payers of this city" and inspect Salt Lake City's financial records "for the purpose of ascertaining whether the taxes paid have been equal and uniform, and also what disbursements have been made of the same after collection." After several meetings, the mayor and city council refused to allow the committee to look at the records. In the opinion of the firm of Snow and Hoge, which functioned as the city attorney, quoted in the February 25, 1874 *Deseret News,* "If the demands of the committee should be granted as a right, the same right would also belong to any and every resident of the city. This would lead to inextricable confusion and would greatly impair, if not destroy, the efficiency of the officers by preventing them from attending to their public duties."

In the fall of 1884, when the Liberal party opposed raising property taxes to build a new public school in Salt Lake City's Eighth Latter-day Saint Ward (until 1890 school districts in the city coincided with Mormon church ward boundaries), Lawrence chaired a public meeting and wrote a lengthy letter that appeared in the September 11 *Deseret News* explaining the party's reasoning. First, he said, "Utah schools are not free from sectarian biases and influences, not withstanding the statements of the Church party to the contrary." In the second place, "a large proportion of the present Territorial school fund is derived from a tax on the property of non-Mormons, who educate their children outside of the district schools. Members of the Liberal Party, and non-Mormons in general, send their children to private schools, not public ones." Finally, he noted, "When the time shall come that the school teachers are selected with more regard for their ability for teaching than for their allegiance to a certain creed, then, no doubt, the Liberals will not only send their children to the district schools, but contribute freely for their support."

Lawrence's language, and that of the Liberal party's in general, was often harsh, but it is difficult to deny the force of his arguments. He asked important questions about the role of the Mormon church in Utah's political affairs, about the nature of Utah society, and about the future direction the territory ought to take, and the assertions he made were essentially correct. Church leaders virtually dictated the political course they expected their followers to pursue, and, more broadly, the Mormon church was at odds with the fundamental values and practices of the larger society.

In addition to his activity in the Liberal party, Lawrence had a wide range of other involvements. Feeling that Utah's observance of July 24, Mormon Pioneer Day, ought not to overshadow the nation's birthday, he regularly served on Salt Lake City's Fourth of July celebration committee. Active in the Liberal Institute, which provided space for various meetings and lectures as well as for religious services for non-Mormon churches that had no buildings, he was also on the board of director's of St. Mark's Grammar School; served as president of the Deseret Agricultural and Manufacturing Society, which supervised the annual territorial fair; and in 1891 was a charter member of Salt Lake's Unitarian church and a member of its board of trustees from 1903 until 1919. (He had previously been a member of the Congregational church). In April 1887 he was a founder of the Salt Lake City Chamber of Commerce and Board of Trade, organized to promote trade, establish home industries, and attract capital and population, and, in 1890, served as its president. He was also an original member of the Alta Club. Founded in 1883, most of the club's original eighty-one members were non-Mormon mining magnates. Mormons were not admitted to the club until after the turn of the century, one more indication of the division that existed between Mormons and non-Mormons in Utah. Lawrence served on the board of directors of the Women's Industrial Christian Home, which opened in June 1889 to provide shelter for polygamist wives and their families who had left their husbands, and in 1890 was named the second receiver of Mormon church property escheated under the Edmunds-Tucker Act of 1887, succeeding Frank H. Dyer. The *Deseret News* on July 17 called his appointment "obnoxious." The *Salt Lake Tribune,* on the same day, welcomed it, however:

> There is poetic justice in the appointment. On principle Mr. Lawrence found it necessary to oppose some of the pretensions of Brigham Young. His manhood made that necessary. As a result he was excommunicated under circumstances that tried his courage to the utmost. It would have required but a word to have caused the fierce fanatics around him to rend him limb from limb. . . . Now he, as an American, is given the place of receiver to manage and dispose of the property which, under the law, has been seized from the church and is to be turned over to the school fund. No better appointment could have been made.

Beginning in the early 1890s Lawrence was also involved in efforts to improve the "moral climate" of Salt Lake City by strictly enforcing laws dealing with liquor, prostitution, and gambling. His point of view was expressed in remarks at a mass meeting at Salt Lake's First Methodist Church to discuss vice in the city and formulate a series of resolutions to be sent to elected officials. As reported in the *Tribune* on December 30, Lawrence said,

> We should guard well the good order of this city out of regard to its law and order-loving citizens. We must control our bad elements the best we can. The liquor question is a difficult

one, but we can control the saloon and it is incumbent on the city officers to control the places of wickedness in the best possible manner. The low resorts should be done away with. Rules can be adopted whereby the saloon element can be kept within bounds, and the cost of licenses can be placed so high as to shut out the lower element. There are too many saloons, and the fewer they are the better we will be.

In the 1890s Mormon leaders made a conscious decision to bring the church into the mainstream of American life. Their decision followed the federal government's passage in 1882 of the Edmunds Act, which outlawed the practice of polygamy, denied basic political rights to those people convicted of polygamy, and placed much of the government of Utah in a five-member presidential commission, and the Edmunds-Tucker Act of 1887, under which the Mormon church was disincorporated and church property was made liable to confiscation. In the face of such pressure, LDS leaders decided to undertake a process of rapprochement with their larger society.

In September 1890, church president Wilford Woodruff issued a manifesto proclaiming an end to the further performance of plural marriages; the church began a process of participation in and accommodation to the national economy; and in June 1891 Mormon leaders disbanded the People's party and sought to divide its members between the Republican and Democratic parties. Two and a half years later, after considerable debate occasioned by the fear that these measures were only temporary expedients designed to gain statehood for Utah and would be abandoned thereafter, the Liberal party dissolved.

Following the Liberal party's demise, Lawrence was briefly active in the Republican party and in 1893 was one of its candidates for the state legislature, but he quickly left the political mainstream, having lost faith in the two major parties, and in November 1893 helped found the Populist, or People's, party in Utah. By that time his concerns had begun to change. Like other Godbeites and Liberals, who, in the early 1870s, as Ronald W. Walker has pointed out, "suggested the inevitability of class conflict, questioned the supremacy of property rights, supported the fundamental aims of the Paris Commune, and predicted that organized agricultural and industrial labor would yet revolutionize American social and political conditions," Lawrence's interests had always been broad, but for twenty years his focus had been narrow.[19] He had concentrated on conditions and circumstances in Utah and the Mormon church. He continued to be concerned with those things, but now mainly directed his attention to the United States as a whole, and as he did so took an increasingly radical view, calling for a fundamental reorganization of American society, just as earlier he had called for a fundamental reorganization of the Mormon church and Utah society. In his view the United States was not a basically sound society, but one so deeply flawed that it needed to be completely restructured. Neither the Republican nor the Democratic parties were suitable vehicles through which to express that point of view and work for such changes, Lawrence thought, but the Populist party held sufficient promise to warrant support. According to David B. Griffiths, Lawrence knew in his soul that the Populists were "radical liberals committed to ending economic inequality and political injustice" whose pervasive theme was "the paradox of poverty in the midst of material abundance."[20]

The Populist party was founded on a national level at a convention in Omaha, Nebraska, in July 1892, where delegates nominated James B. Weaver of Iowa for president of the United States. He received 1,039,000 votes, the first third-party candidate ever to attract more than a million votes. Before the party's demise in 1900, the Populists had elected three governors, ten members of Congress, five senators, and about 1,500 state legislators. As Populists saw it, the country faced serious problems that the major parties were incapable of addressing, much less solving, and a new political party was necessary. The party's basic concern was the growing concentration of wealth and power in the hands of fewer and fewer individuals and corporations and the growing division of the population into two groups, rich and poor. Populists viewed the two major parties as reflecting and promoting the interests of the wealthy, acting in the interests of corporations and monopolies rather than those of the people as a whole. The names and faces of those in office changed with each election, but policies did not. Populists proposed a range of remedies: unlimited coinage of silver as an inflationary measure for the economy; government ownership of railroads, telephone, and telegraph systems; development of the initiative and referendum; elimination of the electoral college; direct election of U.S. senators by the people rather than by state legislatures; municipal ownership of streetcars, electric, gas, water, and telephone systems; exemption from taxation of most single family residences; and an eight-hour workday.

One of the great orators of the movement was Mary Ellen Lease, who has been best remembered for advising farmers to "raise less corn and more hell." In her view:

> Wall Street owns the country. It is no longer a government of
> the people, by the people, and for the people, but a government
> of Wall Street, by Wall Street, and for Wall Street.... Our laws

are the output of a system which clothes rascals in robes and honesty in rags. . . . There are thirty men in the United States whose aggregate wealth is over one and one-half billion dollars. There are half a million looking for work. . . . The people are at bay. Let the bloodhounds of money who have dogged us thus far beware.[21]

At the party's national convention in 1892, Ignatius Donnelly wrote the preamble to the platform and read it to the assemblage:

> We meet in the midst of a nation brought to the verge of moral, political and material ruin. Corruption dominates the ballot box, the legislatures, the Congress, and touches even the ermine of the bench. The people are demoralized. . . . The newspapers are subsidized or muzzled; public opinion silenced; business prostrate; our homes covered with mortgages; labor impoverished; and the land concentrated in the hands of capitalists. . . . The fruits of the toil of millions are boldly stolen to build up colossal fortunes. . . . From the same prolific womb of governmental injustice we breed two classes—paupers and millionaires.[22]

On the national level, the Populist point of view was most attractive to farmers, although most Populists saw a coalition with urban workers as a key to victory. In Utah, however, Populism appealed mainly to workers in urban areas. Before its demise in 1900 the party had some electoral success, electing a mayor in Sandy, city council members in Ogden and Vernal, a county attorney and county surveyor in Uintah County, and four state legislators. As part of an effort to build a "culture of opposition," Utah Populists published three newspapers, most importantly, Warren Foster's *Intermountain Advocate* (later renamed *Living Issues*); founded a brass band in Millville, Cache County; held "parlor meetings" with recitations, music, and speeches; established a board of labor in Salt Lake City with a free lending library and a free employment office; founded a workers' club that pressured city government to fund more municipal works projects; sponsored rallies and mass marches of the unemployed; and organized a People's Church of Salt Lake City, which all men and women interested in "rational religion, ethical culture, and social progress" were invited to join.[23] Lawrence's Mormon background and moral perspective was present in each of these activities.

In company with Warren Foster, Lawrence was the party's dominant figure and leading ideologue. His long-time friend and business associate William S. Godbe also joined the party. Lawrence provided office space for *Living Issues;* chaired the party's literary bureau, which distributed Populist literature throughout Utah; served as state party chair in 1897 and 1898; and was a delegate to the party's national convention and a presidential elector in 1896. He also ran for office several times: for governor in 1895, when he received 5 percent of the vote and led the ticket by more than five hundred votes; for Salt Lake City mayor in 1897; and for Salt Lake City treasurer in 1899. A prolific writer and speaker, Lawrence spread the Populist message however and whenever he could to both the converted and the unconverted. His remarks at Salt Lake's 1895 Fourth of July celebration, reported in the *Salt Lake Herald* on July 5, were typical:

> There is nothing grand or glorious in the nation as a nation today. When this government was founded it was based on justice and righteousness, and then it was grand and glorious, but in these days we have lost that grandeur and glory. The money power and the Shylocks rule the nation. They make laws for the benefit of the few and work injustice and oppression on the many. Money rules the Senate, money speaks in Congress, money sways our state legislatures. The money power directs each and every branch of government. Pernicious laws have fastened the millstone of debt around necks of 95% of the people of these so-called glorious United States. Sixty percent of the people present do not own their own homes. Thirty thousand people in America today own more than the balance of the 70,000,000 that form our population. The bad and pernicious legislature which has brought about this lamentable state of affairs is still going on and unless checked will end in making this a nation of white slaves. Today we are a country of millionaires by the hundreds and paupers by the millions.

At the Salt Lake County Populist convention in 1895 he advocated an eight-hour workday, arguing that "the invention of machinery and the modern appliances" should lessen manual labor and create leisure "for the improvement of the mental faculties of men and women." Instead, labor had become "degraded . . . under the social and industrial conditions forced upon the people by the old political parties."[24] At a February 1897 mass meeting of the unemployed, when Utah and the country were still in the grip of a depression that had begun in 1893, Lawrence advocated government ownership of railways, "the control by the people of machines that displace labor, and elimination of taxation on a working man's home and his tools used for earning his living," reported the *Deseret News* on February 10. In an address the next year to the party's state convention, he attacked both Democrats and Republicans for allowing the wealth of the nation to become concentrated in the hands of "less than five percent of the people"; declared that "labor and the necessities of life are controlled by monopolies and money and property—the product of man—is made to degrade and enslave humanity"; advocated that the homes of workers be exempt from taxation and foreclosure; and championed the initiative and referendum.[25]

Lawrence also expressed concern over the role of the Mormon church in perpetuating these problems in society and urged its withdrawal from politics, advocating "personal liberty and freedom and the exercise of individual judgment in all political matters."[26] The relationship of church and state in Utah was an issue in the 1896 election, when Norman Dresser, Lawrence's Populist colleague, advocated the election of Moses Thatcher to the U.S. Senate because he was "an apostle of civil and religious liberty" and his election would prove that the Mormon church has lost the power, if not the inclination, to control politics and would strengthen the spirit of independence in territorial politics. Thatcher's defeat, Dresser added in the *Intermountain Advocate* on January 1, 1897, would mean that "the church is in the saddle." In a series of articles in the fall of 1897 Warren Foster also expressed concern over the continuing role of the Mormon church in politics. Mormon leaders, he said, wanted church members

> to surrender their political consciences into their keeping; to know no will but the will of their leaders. They want to dictate how people would vote, for Democrats when it suits their purposes and for Republicans when that suits their purposes. They are to be Republicans when told to be; to be Democrats when told to be. . . . to be silent, blind serfs of the Mormon leaders all the time and under all circumstances. . . . They are to go through the farce of voting for or against this, that, or the other solely for the purpose of keeping up appearance of freedom and popular government.[27]

In subsequent issues, Foster and Lawrence charged that the Mormon church was interested in turning public schools into religious ones and that church leaders had unfairly influenced a recent school board election by telling people how to vote.

Following the demise of the Populist party after 1900, many of its members joined the Socialist Party of America. Populism and socialism had much in common, and although Populism had died, Foster said in *Living Issues* on March 9, 1900, "Its soul has gone to the better land of Socialism." Throughout the nineteenth century, socialist groups in the United States were small and had little impact on American life. At the beginning of the twentieth century, however, that began to change. In 1901 the Socialist Party of America was founded, and during the next decade a deeply rooted socialist movement emerged that had widespread support and considerable impact on American life.[28] In 1912, for example, the Socialist party had 118,000 dues-paying members and a large following in the labor union movement. Its presidential candidate, Eugene V. Debs, received nearly one million votes, several thousand socialists were elected to public office throughout the country, two socialists were serving in the U.S. Congress, and more than three hundred socialist newspapers and journals were being published across the country. After that, however, the party declined and by the early 1920s had all but ceased to exist. The reasons for this decline continue to be a source of scholarly debate.

Socialist patterns in Utah closely followed national ones.[29] The Socialist party there was a significant presence for about twenty years after its founding. It was particularly strong in mining areas, but Socialist locals existed in all but the most isolated and thinly populated of the state's twenty-nine counties. Between 1901 and 1923 the party elected nearly a hundred men and a handful of women to a variety of offices in Utah—from constable to state legislator—in more than two dozen cities and towns. In Bingham, Joseph, and Stockton, and twice in Murray and Eureka, complete socialist administrations were elected. Membership was diverse and included educators, clergy, white-collar workers, entrepreneurs, skilled and unskilled workers, and farmers and resembled the pattern of socialist support nationwide. Even members of the Mormon church were attracted to the party in considerable numbers. Forty percent of party members were Mormons, many of them active and faithful members who held important positions at the ward and stake levels. Their names often give them away: Joseph Smith Jessop, Parley Pratt Washburn, and Wilford Woodruff Freckleton. At one time, the bishop of the Eureka Ward as well as his first counselor, one of the ward clerks, and the president of the Primary Association were all active socialists.

In spite of its considerable Mormon constituency and his own antipathy for the church, Lawrence was among those former Populists who found the Socialist party a "better land" and for about a dozen years was one of its most active and visible members. He helped to organize the party in Utah, assisted in writing its state constitution, and ran for office three times. Within the party, several groupings existed.[30] Lawrence, and many Utah socialists, in particular those who were elected to public office, were part of the right, or "constructive," wing. He believed that a social and economic order based on private ownership of property, competition, and the profit motive was seriously flawed and must be replaced. For him, capitalism was not something permanent, but only a dark phase of human history and development, yet he saw no immediate prospect for a transition to pure socialism and had only a vague idea of how it might come about. He held to and nurtured a dream but had little strategy for its implementation beyond the hope and faith that the election of good men and women to office would provide the foundation and pave the way. In the meantime, he called for various measures, or what socialists called "immediate demands," that were worthwhile in themselves and might ease the way for socialism's eventual triumph: public ownership of railroad, telegraph, telephone, streetcar, and electric power systems; the initiative and referendum; compulsory education for children to the age of eighteen; an eight-hour day for workers; equal civil and political rights for men and women and "the abolition of all laws discriminating against women"; unemployment and worker's compensation; a social security system; and government regulation of hours and wages—all were specific reforms that he suggested in the *Utah Labor Journal* on April 3, 1902.

As a socialist, Lawrence continued to be troubled about the pervasive influence in Utah of the Mormon church, especially its capability to reenter politics as an advocate of socialism under ecclesiastical control. He expressed that concern in testimony before the 1906 Smoot Hearings, and in 1911 he led a successful effort to persuade the Salt Lake City School Board to allow community groups to meet in the city's public school buildings, which was necessary, he felt, to reduce Mormon church influence in public education. The first speaker under the new policy was Utah's Episcopal bishop, Franklin Spencer Spalding, a Christian socialist, who spoke under the auspices of the Socialist party on "The Development of the Social Conscience," a talk reported in the *Salt Lake Telegram* on May 25, 1911.

Utah's Socialist party was most visible during election campaigns, and Lawrence was deeply involved. During the month before the 1902 election he spoke nearly every evening, several times at the corner of Main Street and Second South in downtown Salt Lake City, as part of the party's "soap-box campaign." While running for state treasurer in 1908 he toured the state, speaking for himself and on behalf of other socialist candidates. He ran unsuccessfully once more, in 1910, for state senator, but then, in 1911, was elected to a four-year term to the Salt Lake City Commission.

In addition to conventional electoral activity, Lawrence was involved in the wide range of activities the party carried on that were meant to spread the gospel of socialism and provide mutual support for party members and sympathizers. He founded a Socialist Club in 1901 and was its first president and the next year founded the Social Science Club and was its first president. For ten years it sponsored regular lectures and programs on all phases of civic affairs and social problems. He helped arrange for such national figures as Henry Demarest Lloyd and Eugene Debs to speak in Utah; contributed to the regular "Socialist Column" that a number of Utah newspapers published; participated in discussions with Salt Lake's Unitarian minister William Thurston Brown, Socialist party leader Kate Hilliard, and the University of Utah art instructor Virginia Snow Stephen that led to the founding of the Modern School, which was based on the educational theories of the Spanish anarchist Francisco Ferrer; and in 1908 founded the Utah branch of the Political Refugee Defense League, which sought to prevent the U.S. government from returning radical political refugees to their homelands to face imprisonment and possible death.

In spite of this activity, Lawrence was expelled from the Socialist party on May 20, 1913 because he voted against a pay raise for city firefighters after the Salt Lake Federation of Labor had endorsed it. He explained that he, as a socialist, was bound to consider the good of the whole, not just the workers, and did not think the city could afford the raise. And, he said, reported the *Tribune* on May 21, 1913, "I am still a Socialist and always expect to be. While I have been read out of the party, my ideals have not been changed, and I shall pursue the same course in the future that I have in the past." At the conclusion of his term two years later, when he was eighty, he retired from public life, thanked the electorate for the opportunity to serve, and suggested in the *Tribune* of September 3, 1915 that the priority of the next mayor and city commission be the construction of a municipally owned electric power plant.

As a person of vision and courage, Henry Lawrence was a man of considerable importance in Utah, and his present relative obscurity is undeserved. He should be better known, and a full biography would be of great interest in a number of ways. Two threads run through his life. The first is a belief that ordinary people can direct their own lives, a belief in democracy as long as it remains truly responsive to the needs of the people and not to monopolies or interest groups. Lawrence's second focus was his long-term commitment to challenging undemocratic and, therefore, oppressive, values, institutions, and structures. For fifty years he was steadfast, crossing the line, confronting authority and the existing order, taking risks, putting principle above complicity and pragmatism, and standing against the current because he felt he could not remain silent without violating his principles and integrity.

He could have chosen to cling to the tranquility of accepted norms and the comforts of church membership, political orthodoxy, and received wisdom, or he might have approached things more cautiously and chosen the middle ground, saying, "There is much to be said for both sides, and the truth lies somewhere in between the two." But he did not. For him, the world was essentially divided into two groups, the party of progress and the party of order, and it was clear where he stood. Until his death in April 1924 Lawrence fought for a society of greater liberty and equality. That life-long commitment was his most impressive achievement.

NOTES

1. Many of the details of Lawrence's early life, and his subsequent years as well, remain obscure. He left no personal papers aside from a brief diary for several months of 1860, which is on deposit at the Special Collections Department, Marriott Library, University of Utah, Salt Lake City. For brief biographical sketches, see Edward W. Tullidge, *History of Salt Lake City* (Salt Lake City: Star Printing Co., 1886), biographical supplement, 50; obituaries in *Deseret News* [Salt Lake City], April 5, 1924, and *Salt Lake Tribune,* April 6, 1924; and the biographical sheet "The Lawrence Family," Special Collections, Marriott Library. Other information must be painstakingly gleaned from a variety of sources.

2. Lawrence married Jennette Sophia Kimball on December 31, 1862 in the Endowment House in Salt Lake City. Six years later he married Isabell Melvina Kimball in the Endowment House. Although both of his wives were named Kimball, they were not sisters and there is no indication that they were related. Little is known of Lawrence's second plural wife, but she was the granddaughter of Heber C. and Vilate Kimball.

3. On Maria and Sarah Lawrence, see Fawn M. Brodie, *No Man Knows My History: The Life of Joseph Smith* (New York: Alfred A. Knopf, 1945), 336–37, 339, 457–58; Linda King Newell and Valeen Tippetts Avery, *Mormon Enigma: Emma Hale Smith, Prophet's Wife, "Elect Lady," Polygamy's Foe* (Garden City: Doubleday and Co., 1984), 143–44; Margery W. Ward, ed., *A Fragment: The Autobiography of Mary Jane Mount Tanner* (Salt Lake City: University of Utah Library, 1980), 82–87.

4. Orson F. Whitney, *History of Utah* (Salt Lake City: George Q. Cannon and Sons, 1892–1904), 1:624–25.

5. Leonard J. Arrington, *Great Basin Kingdom: An Economic History of the Latter-Day Saints* (Cambridge: Harvard University Press, 1958), 298. For a fuller account of the history of this important Utah economic institution, see Martha S. Bradley, *ZCMI: America's First Department Store* (Salt Lake City: ZCMI, 1991).

6. On the Godbeites, see several works by Ronald W. Walker: "The God-beite Protest in the Making of Modern Utah," Ph.D. diss., University of Utah, 1977; "The Commencement of the Godbeite Protest: Another View," *Utah Historical Quarterly* 42 (Summer 1974): 217–45; "The Stenhouses and the Making of the Mormon Image," *Journal of Mormon History* 1 (1974): 51–72; "Edward Tullidge: Historian of the Mormon Commonwealth," *Journal of Mormon History* 3 (1976): 55–72; "The Liberal Institute: A Case Study in National Assimilation," *Dialogue: A Journal of Mormon Thought* 10 (Autumn 1977): 74–85; and "When the Spirits Did Abound: Utah's Encounter with Free Thought Radicalism," *Utah Historical Quarterly* 50 (Fall 1982): 304–24.

7. Henry J. Wolfinger, "An Irrepressible Conflict," *Dialogue: A Journal of Mormon Thought* 6 (Autumn–Winter 1971): 130.

8. *Proceedings Before the Committee on Privileges and Elections of the United States Senate in the Matter of the Protest Against the Hon. Reed Smoot, a Senator from the State of Utah, To Hold his Seat* (Washington: Government Printing Office, 1906), 4:120. Hereafter cited as *Smoot Hearings.*

9. Walker, "The Commencement of the Godbeite Protest," 235.

10. *Smoot Hearings,* 4:107.

11. David B. Griffiths, "Populism in the Far West," Ph.D. diss., University of Washington, 1969, 297.

12. *Smoot Hearings,* 4:106.

13. Ibid.

14. Ibid., 4:114.

15. Orson F. Whitney, *History of Utah* (Salt Lake City: George Q. Cannon and Sons, 1892), 2:594.

16. The standard work on the development of the Liberal party in Utah is Ronald C. Jack, "Utah Territorial Politics: 1870–76," Ph.D. diss., University of Utah, 1970.

17. *Deseret News,* January 15, 1874, see also *Salt Lake Tribune* and *Salt Lake Herald* of the same date.

18. Wolfinger, "An Irrepressible Conflict," 129–30.

19. Walker, "When the Spirits Did Abound," 319.

20. David B. Griffiths, "Far Western Populism: The Case of Utah," *Utah Historical Quarterly* 37 (Fall 1969): 397.

21. Quoted in Howard Zinn, *A People's History of the United States* (New York: Harper and Row, 1982), 282.

22. E. McPherson, ed., *A Handbook of Politics for 1892* (Washington: Government Printing Office, 1892), 269.

23. Griffiths, "Far Western Populism," 396–407.

24. *Intermountain Advocate* [Salt Lake City], October 28, 1895.

25. *Living Issues* [Salt Lake City], September 16, 1898.

26. Ibid.

27. Ibid., October 8, 1897, see also the issues of November 12, November 19, and December 10, 1897.

28. For a useful overview of socialism in the nineteenth-century United States, see Albert Fried, *Socialism in America: From the Shakers to the Third*

International (Garden City: Doubleday and Co., 1970). Much has been written about American socialism during its golden age in the early twentieth century. Among the major works are David A. Shannon, *The Socialist Party of America* (New York: Macmillan, 1955); James Weinstein, *The Decline of Socialism in America, 1912–1925* (New York: Monthly Review Press, 1967); and Richard W. Judd, *Socialist Cities: Municipal Politics and the Grass Roots of American Socialism* (Albany: SUNY Press, 1989).

29. On socialism in Utah, see John R. Sillito and John S. McCormick, "Socialist Saints: Mormons and the Socialist Party," *Dialogue: A Journal of Mormon Thought* 18 (Summer 1985): 121–31.

30. See Weinstein, *The Decline of Socialism*, 3–16.

11

Frank J. Cannon:
Declension in the Mormon Kingdom

Kenneth W. Godfrey

Early in 1905, Frank J. Cannon, a member of one of Mormonism's elite families and the son of a former member of the church's First Presidency, publicly declared that he no longer believed in the divinity of the Church of Jesus Christ of Latter-day Saints. He did so in two critical articles that appeared in the Salt Lake City newspapers. On January 22 he published "An Analysis of the Church" in the *Salt Lake Tribune,* and, on February 1, a second article, "An Address to the Earthly King of the Kingdom of God," appeared in the *Morning Examiner.*

After reading these articles, William G. Rackhon, a local church official, filed charges of unchristianlike conduct and apostasy against Cannon, and he was summoned to appear before a court presided over by Ogden Fifth Ward Bishop John Watson. Cannon refused to participate in this action, instead sending a letter stating that he did not acknowledge President Joseph F. Smith as head of the Mormon faith. He also challenged the right of the court to disfellowship him for telling the truth and for attempting to curb his free agency. Charging that the church had gone into "idolatrous bondage," he nevertheless closed the letter by affirming his love for the Mormon people, whom he hoped would soon see their errors and reform the church. Not long after this action, on March 15, 1905, Cannon was excommunicated.[1]

The church-sponsored *Deseret News* attacked Cannon after his excommunication. Bold headlines declared on April 20, "Frank J. Cannon as Contortionist. His Agility Shown in Present Attitude Than That Of Three Years Ago; How He Defended the Faith; Contribution To The Millennial Star Contained Unstilted Praise of President Joseph F. Smith." The article called Cannon a hypocrite who sold his soul in a pinch for money. It also asserted that Cannon was known for his trickery, unreliability, and for having an empty soul.

Cannon's response in the *Salt Lake Tribune,* printed under equally bold headlines, proclaimed, "Fell Under The Juggernaut! Free Speech in Utah! Hierarchy On The Throne!" The article detailed the proceed-

ings of the court that excommunicated Cannon and featured his letters to that body as well as the two editorials he had written that
prompted charges against him. A few other articles followed in some
of the state's other newspapers, questioning how a life-long Latter-day
Saint who had enjoyed both financial and political support from the
church could turn on the faith of his youth, disgrace his dead father,
George Q. Cannon, and betray his friends and admirers. Nor did the
debate end with exchanges in the newspapers. J. Golden Kimball, a
member of the church's First Council of Seventy, used the April 1905
general conference as a forum to attack Cannon publicly and to show
his moral failings while defending Joseph F. Smith.[2]

It seems a bit incongruous that Cannon would have split from the
only existence he had ever known. He had been a life-long Latter-day
Saint, and members of his family were among the church's ruling elite.
He had been born and had lived most of his life in Utah. The culture
was so much a part of him and he so much a part of it that turning
away had to have been a traumatic experience. Yet Cannon had harbored doubts about his religious heritage from very early in life. He
careened between faith affirmations and expressions of doubt and frustration. He also acted out these personal inconsistencies, engaging in
public performances that exuded conviction on the one hand and de-
bauchery on the other. He could never find a middle ground that allowed him to live a stable life. In the end, he became a caricature, performing in a grotesque vaudeville of religion as he hashed over issues
long since decided for most Americans. "Audiences listen, laugh and
sometimes applaud," the editor of the *Evening Examiner* in Ogden remarked on November 4, 1904, "but never follow him."

The long path of Frank Jenne Cannon from Latter-day Saint to heretic began almost with his birth on January 25, 1859. The year Cannon was born, his father was called into the ranks of the Quorum of
Twelve Apostles, a leading church body. From an early age Cannon
was taught the priorities of the Latter-day Saint religion, and as the
son of a leading official he was expected to adhere to them with greater
sagacity than the rank and file. Yet he had doubts, even at a young
age. Indicative of this was an incident that took place when he was
seven or eight and sought answers to his religious seeking. Thrusting
sticks lightly in the soil, Cannon prayed that "God would let them fall
over if the Prophet had not been appointed by Him to do His work."
Sometimes they fell, whereas at other times they stood, causing the boy
to view faith ambiguously.[3] Cannon was neither able to rationalize the
inconsistencies of religion that he perceived nor to rise above them.
Although he waffled back and forth, he clung to the Latter-day Saint

institution until very late in life, probably not coincidentally until after the deaths of both his father and his brother, a Mormon apostle.

At the same time, because Cannon was the son of such a high Mormon official, he endured as a child his father's frequent absence to oversee missionary efforts and ten-year stint as the territorial delegate to
Congress. These activities necessitated that he spend most of his youth
in the care of his mother, a polygamous wife. The long absences seem
to have caused Cannon to believe that his father was somehow a white
knight, a hero to be emulated yet someone whom he could never satisfy. Seeking parental approval became almost an obsession even after
Cannon reached adulthood. He perceived himself as being inadequate,
yet his career as a political figure was exceptional. He was a highly
emotional, often insecure man who seemed to never have believed that
he could live up to his father's expectations. Although he was the eldest child of an apostle who became counselor in the church's First
Presidency, Cannon also seemed always in the shadow of his apostle
brother, Abraham H. Cannon.

Cannon later admitted that he was more a social Mormon than a
converted Latter-day Saint. Like most Mormons born to Latter-day
Saint parents, he was baptized at the age of eight. Unlike most male
church members, however, his father ordained him an elder when only
thirteen years old. He never advanced further in the priesthood nor
did he ever serve a church mission. That he was never called to a high
church position or became a high priest must have disappointed his
illustrious father.

At the age of six, Cannon and the future historian-apostle Orson F.
Whitney entered the school of a German emigrant "trained in all the
strictness of rigidity of the Teutonic school." Severe, stern, and a man
showing "little mercy to the truant and idler," the pedagogue recognized Cannon's brilliance, was gentle with him, and encouraged his
extraordinary talent for learning. Cannon, Whitney remembered, was
"exceedingly sensitive . . . and when spoken to harshly . . . would quiver
like an aspen," yet he also possessed courage. However, throughout
his life he remained thin-skinned, and harsh words deeply wounded
him. His sensitivity was so acute, in fact, that it likely mirrored deep
feelings of inferiority.[4]

At the age of twelve he began his studies at the University of Deseret, and while still in his teens secured employment in the Weber
County Recorder's Office. His work set the stage for Weber County
becoming his political base during the 1890s. Until he was eighteen,
Cannon continued his service to the county recorder and then returned
to Salt Lake City to complete his education. Working as a compositor

at the *Juvenile Instructor* printing office that his father owned, he earned money to pay for his schooling. At age nineteen, in 1878, Cannon received his journalism diploma.

He also married Martha A. Brown and moved to Ogden with his bride. After a short stint as a reporter, he soon founded and edited the *Logan Journal*. In 1881, Cannon moved to San Francisco, where he worked for a short time as an editor for *The Chronicle*. Well suited for his journalistic career, Cannon was a fine writer of clear, pungent prose. He had a bright future as a writer but suffered from a lack of business sense. Virtually every newspaper he founded failed because of his inability to make good business decisions.[5]

Cannon's poor business sense was compounded, if not actually created, by his life-long struggle with alcohol. Indeed, the reason he left Utah to work in San Francisco was because of his drinking problem and the misconduct it engendered. Having abandoned his wife, Cannon had an affair with a married woman from Logan whose husband was away serving a church mission. Filled with remorse, the woman confessed her transgression, and Cannon hurriedly left town. Learning of his son's misconduct, George Q. Cannon, by then serving in the church's First Presidency, remarked that "he did not care if he never came near him again." Such a remark must have wounded Cannon severely.

Those familiar with Latter-day Saint history know that it is not unusual to charge apostates with the sin of adultery. However, Cannon's own brother recorded this incident in his diary, naming the woman with whom the adultery occurred. Moreover, the affair took place three decades before Cannon's disaffection from the church. It is highly unlikely that Abraham H. Cannon, whose diaries were remarkably honest and accurate in other respects, would have lied about his brother's sexual misconduct. Cannon also committed some other unspecified crimes, probably gambling or misusing funds, also fostered by his drinking bouts. As January 1881 dawned, therefore, Cannon hurriedly left Logan and his rowdy friends and began a new life in San Francisco, thus avoiding a church court and possibly other legal problems.[6]

When Abraham Cannon returned from his German mission in 1882, he found Frank again working in Ogden, "apparently very sorry for the course he took." But on June 29, 1882, when he met his brother and father at the Ogden railroad station, there was still much concern about Frank Cannon's life-style. They urged him to go back to Logan "and clear up, as far as possible, the disgrace which was still attached to his name." He promised to do so, and in September his brother recorded, "Frank and family are down; the former has made his affair in Logan right and now has a good recommend." We can only guess as to what he did to right his wrongs. The record is silent, too, about how Martha Cannon coped with her husband's infidelity.[7]

Cannon might have made things right in Logan, but he was still unable to control his drinking. While continuing his newspaper work, he joined with his father and brothers in forming a joint stock company. On at least one occasion when his father and brother Abraham came to Ogden to visit Cannon on business they found that he again had been drinking. Disgusted with his actions, they told him that if he ever "took a drink again, our business in Ogden would be immediately closed, as it would jeopardize our property to have it in charge of a drinker." This rebuke, disapproval, and disappointment did little to help the situation, for it further alienated Cannon, and he slipped deeper into trouble thereafter. A classic addictive pattern of binge and repentance had begun to emerge and continued throughout much of his life.[8]

Of course, as in the case of his sexual indiscretion, Cannon's drinking precipitated other indiscretions. In May 1885, for example, Kate Flint, owner and operator of several brothels, told Abraham Cannon that unless his brother's prostitution bills were paid she would sue. Wanting to avoid the publicity such a suit would cause, the Cannon family reluctantly paid the bills. Cannon went on with his binge, but on the first Sunday in June he confessed his "follies" before the evening meeting of his ward, obtained forgiveness, and applied for rebaptism.[9]

Frank Cannon's drinking and the other failures it brought forced his father to relieve him of his business duties and send his brother to Ogden to replace him. That his misconduct had forced the firing and brought another rebuke from his father only deepened Cannon's feelings of inadequacy and failure, causing still another drinking spree. Later, when he sobered up, he expressed "great sorrow at his weakness."[10]

In spite of his weaknesses, perhaps because of it and a desire to make amends with his family, Frank Cannon expressed a strong commitment to family and church during these years. He made several public gestures of support. Early in February 1886, for instance, a reward of $500 was offered for information leading to the arrest of his polygamist father. After George Q. Cannon's capture in Nevada and subsequent fall from a train that was bringing him back to Salt Lake City, Frank hurried to care for him, thus making some amends for the trouble he had caused the family. When recovered, his father posted bail and was set free pending trial. He promptly jumped bail and went on the underground.

Only a few days later U.S. Attorney William A. Dickson, while interrogating Cara Cannon, one of George Q. Cannon's wives, asked several questions that the family found "insulting and indecent." Within a week, sixteen-year-old Hugh Cannon accosted Dickson in the lobby of Ogden's Continental Hotel and struck him in the face three times. He then went to city hall and gave himself up for arrest. The next day Frank Cannon and two of his brothers were also arrested and charged with conspiracy in the assault. To relieve all others concerned, he, as the eldest, heroically pleaded guilty, was fined $150, and sent to the county jail for three months. The charges against the other brothers were then dismissed.[11]

He continued his efforts to rebuild his standing with his father from jail. While serving his term, Cannon began writing *The History of Joseph Smith the Prophet,* which was published under his father's name. Although there was only indirect evidence in the book that anyone other than George Q. Cannon wrote it, other records suggest that Frank Cannon was the author and had little collaboration. It was a very well-written work, exuding faith and filled with interesting anecdotes, probably the best biography of Smith to appear in the nineteenth century. The book also established Frank Cannon as a man who, if he did not believe Joseph Smith was God's prophet at that time, certainly had the ability to produce prose that made it appear so.[12]

Perhaps because of his model citizenship while in jail, when released Cannon was able to secure the editorship of the *Ogden Herald.* At least for awhile after he was released, his work on the paper, as well as his probably genuine efforts to reform, seem to have prompted him to shun his worst vice, alcohol. The winter of 1888 found him not drinking but rather editing his paper and making final preparations for publishing *The History of Joseph Smith the Prophet.* On February 11 he and his brother Abraham went to their father's Salt Lake farm and showed him the completed manuscript. George Cannon approved it with only a few suggested alterations and told his sons that they were "at liberty to get the manuscript into type."[13]

Cannon wanted to get the book out as quickly as possible and diligently pursued publication. It offered retribution for all that had gone before. His family, especially his father, was delighted with his work, and the book helped to resecure his father's respect and affection. The church was also pleased with Cannon's effort. It led to the appearance of a faith-promoting history, deep in reverence for Smith. With the publication of *The History of Joseph Smith the Prophet* in 1888 Frank Cannon's stock had never been higher, either with his family or the church.

The elder Cannon asked his son to go to Washington, D.C., to meet with members of Congress and open the door for the end of the crusade against polygamy. In mid 1888 he negotiated a policy that he claimed allowed the "government and the Mormons to settle outstanding difficulties over polygamy." As part of this effort, Cannon obtained the appointment of judges committed to showing leniency to Mormons on the underground who surrendered voluntarily. Cannon made a special effort to help his father, who was in hiding on the underground, securing from government officials a promise that if George Q. Cannon would voluntarily submit to trial for polygamy and plead guilty, he would receive a light sentence. "Tell Louis [George Q. Cannon] confidentially his case is fixed alone" Cannon telegraphed home on July 22, 1888.[14]

From the government's perspective, the Cannon case was a symbol to other Mormons of what they intended in their efforts against polygamy. From Frank Cannon's perspective, his successful pleading in Washington on behalf of his father helped make up for the trouble his alcoholism and moral laxity had caused his family. The effort was his first genuine foray into politics, and it felt good. The stage was set for the remainder of Frank Cannon's career.

Returning home, Cannon set about a variety of tasks, but in November 1888 he went on another drunken spree and returned to his carousing. He had been sober, at least so it seems from the available records, for more than a year. The lapse was apparently triggered by an argument with his brother over their business dealings and continued through the first half of the next year. There were long periods in May and June of 1889 in which he was not only drunk but also in the company of known prostitutes.[15] It seems that Cannon could get excited about some activity—writing *The History of Joseph Smith the Prophet* or lobbying in Washington—and have little difficulty staying sober. Without some overriding goal, however, he slid into his old habits. Difficulties with people close to him seem to have exacerbated the slide.

When he finally began to recover from his drunkenness, Frank Cannon wanted to atone once again. He worked at regaining his father's favor and apparently was successful at least in part, for in 1890 George Q. Cannon again sent him to Washington, this time to lobby against the Cullom-Strubble Bill, which would have disfranchised all Mormons. Cannon used his connections in Congress to prevent the bill's passage and in May appeared before the Senate and House committees on territories to argue against it. Cannon emphasized that the bill would only punish a "class of people who have obeyed the laws, who have avowed that they are willing to continue to obey the laws, and who swear that they will not aid or abet anybody else," in the practice of plural marriage. Polygamists, he argued, had already been disenfranchised, so why pass a bill aimed only at the innocent? Furthermore, plural marriage was dying out because young Mormons had little sympathy for it.

Cannon also persuaded Secretary of State James G. Blaine, a Republican and friend of his father's from their time together in Congress, to lobby against the proposed legislation by assuring Blaine that a compromise could be worked out concerning plural marriage, and that such a compromise might foster Utah's entering the Union as a Republican state. "President Woodruff has been praying," Cannon told Blaine, "and thinks he sees some light . . . you are authorized to say that something will be done." He also visited with members of the Senate Committee on Territories and informed its members confidentially of pending concessions by the church concerning plural marriage. Because of this activity Cannon personally took credit for having prevented the Cullom-Strubble Bill from passing.[16]

After his successful lobbying efforts, Cannon left Washington convinced that only through the Republican party would Utah ever achieve statehood. Thus, he was the first Utah editor to advocate publicly a dissolution of two political parties in Utah, organized along pro- and anti-Mormon lines, in favor of establishing a national two-party system of Republicans and Democrats in the Utah Territory. His goal was to remove the Mormon church from the political arena, a theme that would remain central during the rest of Cannon's life and one that would eventually lead to his removal from the church. To that end, Cannon, who by that time had been elected on a nonreligious ticket as a member of the Ogden City Council, and some associates organized a state Republican party in 1891, with Cannon as vice president.[17]

Cannon used the newly organized Republican institutional machinery in Utah to secure the territory's delegate position in Congress.[18] He officially launched his campaign on September 23, 1892, by speaking at a rally in Spanish Fork. His opening remarks were recollections of his mother spinning her own cloth. In this manner he introduced his thoughts regarding home industry and the protective tariff. During the next several weeks Cannon spoke throughout Utah. His opponent, Joseph L. Rawlins, a Democrat and a popular attorney, campaigned on a platform of free trade, restrictive voting laws, and against any church interference in politics. Cannon, on the other hand, advocated high tariffs, free elections, and home industry. He said nothing about the church.[19]

Late in October, the campaign became a mud-slinging contest as several newspapers published stories that cast aspersions on Cannon's moral character, commenting on his checkered past. To combat these reports, his campaign manager, Ben E. Rich, circulated a pamphlet entitled "Nuggets of Truth," complete with a picture of Joseph Smith, Jr., on the cover. The pamphlet implied that the Democrats were responsible for the persecution and suffering of the early Saints. It also included pictures of all the presidents of the church, along with short quotations from their writings to suggest that they were for protective tariff and home industry, both of which were convincing proof that they would vote Republican. The last page of the pamphlet featured a large picture of Cannon. Published anonymously but written by Ben Rich, the pamphlet was sent to all wards and stakes in the territory. The message was a not-so-implicit statement that good Mormons voted Republican. Cannon later stated that he abhorred the blatant attempt to use the prestige of the current and former church presidents to his advantage. Still, it was widely believed that he stopped circulating the pamphlet only after finding out that many church members resented its use.[20]

Cannon was willing to use the church to his advantage—if he could get away with doing so. In this instance he could not. Immediately, the Democrats cried foul and published a counter tract. They also brought into the campaign Apostle Moses Thatcher, B. H. Roberts, and Charles W. Penrose, all Mormon Democrats who actively campaigned for Rawlins. This minimized the church's influence in the election. Although Cannon denied that the church was behind or influencing his campaign, it was an unconvincing defense. The fact was that he was pleased to have support, regardless of its source, and tried to put the best public face on the affray. The publicity was sufficiently negative, however, that Cannon could not win the election, even with church support.

In 1894, Cannon was again able to secure the Republican nomination as territorial delegate, and once more his opponent was Rawlins. The outcome was different this time, however. Cannon worked hard in Washington to secure Utah's statehood. His key effort revolved around convincing Connecticut Senator Orville H. Platt to support Utah statehood, although Platt doubted that the Mormons had actually given up plural marriage. Cannon met Platt privately and told him that conditions in Utah were not exactly as described because there was still some degree of disregard of laws against polygamy. But, he continued, the outlook was positive, and the problem was dissipating as rapidly as could be expected. This, according to Platt's biographer, won the senator over and opened the way to gaining his support.[21] On January 4, 1895, Cannon sent a telegram to Mormon President Wilford Woodruff: "The land where you planted the flag is now a state of the sublime republic. May its career be magnified!"[22] It was a significant victory, one for which Cannon claimed personal credit that was not altogether deserved, but in the victory lay the seeds of turmoil that led to his eventual dissent from Mormonism.

Frank Cannon, whose political career thus far had been successful and whose time away from family and Utah had apparently helped him curb his drinking, believed that he had an excellent opportunity to become the first senator from Utah when it was admitted to the Union in 1896. Indeed, he believed that because he had done so much to make that entrance possible, the office was his right. Church officials had other plans, however. Cannon received a telegram from Wilford Woodruff, who told him that "it is the will of the Lord that your father shall be elected Senator from Utah. We want you to tell us how to bring it about."[23]

Cannon was dumbfounded. The office he desperately wanted and thought he deserved now seemed illusive. He knew, of course, that because U.S. senators were elected by state legislatures, the power of the Latter-day Saint church in Utah could ensure his father's election. But he also knew that his father, because of the wide knowledge of his polygamous marriages and his standing in the church's First Presidency, would have great difficulty in being awarded his seat by the Senate. He hoped that these issues would prompt his father to reject the position; he feared that they would not.[24]

Frank Cannon returned to Utah, immediately met with his advisors, and decided on a course of action. His strategists, Ben E. Rich and Edward Allison, an Ogden attorney, believed that the only obstacle to his election was his father's candidacy. The two men met in Ogden with Abraham Cannon and told him that Frank, because of his work for the Republican party, deserved the office. All parties agreed that the father and the son would both be denied the office if they opposed each other. The matter was not resolved for several weeks, but Abraham Cannon eventually met with Woodruff and told him that he "considered it dangerous for Father and Frank to juggle longer on this question, as the result might be that both would lose it."[25]

Woodruff learned that the elder Cannon, perhaps aware that he might face expulsion from the Senate even if elected because of his participation in plural marriage, did not favor having his name put forward. Joseph F. Smith, second counselor in the First Presidency, also felt that it would be better if the senior Cannon did not become involved in the race. A few minutes later President Woodruff said that he was impressed that his first counselor would some day be a senator, but not now, and Cannon accepted Woodruff's decision. That cleared the way for Frank Cannon's candidacy.

On January 14, 1896, George Q. Cannon publicly announced that he was not a candidate for the senatorship and declared that he could not accept that high office should it be offered to him. Frank, with his father out of the race, expected to win the Senate seat easily.[26] The territorial legislature affirmed that belief by securing the election without controversy. The *Deseret News* reported on January 22 that "it is fitting that one of the first two senators elected from the new state should be a Utah boy." Significantly, and certainly not representative of a religious dissenter, Frank Cannon met with the First Presidency just before leaving for Washington and was set apart by them in a religious ceremony as U.S. senator. On January 23, 1896, he left for Washington and entered into his official duties. He enjoyed his life there and basked in the realization that he was a full-fledged senator, not just a delegate representing a territory. He also enjoyed the status that his position gave him in the church. Cannon toured the nation speaking to groups of missionaries, where he "bore his testimony."[27]

Cannon became not only a force among the Mormons, but his Senate position also gave him stature in the national Republican party. In June 1896 he attended the Republican National Convention in St. Louis as a delegate from Utah. Once again, before going he met with the Mormon First Presidency and persuaded them to accept "silver [an inflationary position] into Republican doctrines and advocate a silver plank instead of entirely standing on a gold plank." Once in St. Louis, Cannon tried to include a plank in the party's platform favoring the free coinage of silver in addition to the gold standard. When the party refused, he and other delegates favoring bimetalism resolved to leave the convention. Cannon was selected to deliver the "speech of defiance," and he "shook the silver gauntlet at the golden towers" in spite of repeated warnings from the chair to desist. At the speech's end, the free-silver advocates, as Marriner Merrill noted, "walked majestically through the crowded hall, past the tiers on tiers of benches, filled with frowning faces and swaying forms."[28]

As a consequence, Cannon and many other westerners supported the Democratic ticket in 1896 because it had accepted the free coinage of silver. The Republicans defeated the free-silverites in 1896, and in the new order of gold standard conservatism there was little room for men like Cannon. He and other dissident Republicans organized the National Silver Republican party as a protest movement. Cannon soon became a leader of Republican dissidents and used his Senate seat to challenge the initiatives of the larger party, especially the high and

strict Dingley Tariff that had the support of the Republican administration, taking the position that agriculture was not well served by the
legislation.[29]

Cannon's opposition to the Dingley Tariff in 1897 sealed his political suicide. He not only cut all ties to the Republican party but also
alienated church leaders, who in the 1890s had begun to promote the
sugar beet industry in Utah, to which the tariff promised financial security. Mormon leadership was solidly behind the Dingley Bill and suggested that a vote against it was also a vote against both the church
and the sugar beet industry. Cannon might have survived politically
by alienating the Republican party, but he could not survive the displeasure of the Mormon church.[30]

In 1898, Republicans in Utah adopted a platform that refused to
support as senator any man who had opposed the Dingley Tariff. Cannon, in his bid for reelection, was abandoned by the party. Through
one great act of defiance he had succeeded in alienating the Mormon
leadership, the major business interests in Utah, and the Republican
party. Although he ran as an independent candidate, even his own father was allied with those interests and opposed his reelection. The elder Cannon said that his son's political stand had been "a great mistake . . . alienating the friends who have done so much for us. . . . When
a man's head is high, it is easily hit."[31]

Cannon was handily defeated in the 1898 senatorial election, and
the story of the campaign would have been of little interest but for his
expression of discontent with Mormonism that emerged from it. On
January 7, 1898, the *Daily Tribune* published two letters by Apostle
Heber J. Grant to J. Golden Kimball that suggested that the church
was meddling in the election process. The letters created a sensation.
The old charge of church interference in politics was raised anew, but
for the first time Cannon found himself echoing the charge, now knowing how it felt when the power of his church was used to support another candidate.

During this episode Cannon gave one of his most sensational speeches, renting the Salt Lake Theater and packing the house with political
malcontents. In a speech entitled "Senatorial Candidates and Phari-
sees," Cannon blasted John Henry Smith and Heber J. Grant for using the church's influence to sway the senatorial contest. Would the
Mormon church or the people of Utah, Cannon asked, dominate the
state's politics? He argued that if Utah was to progress its politics had
to be kept on a high plane, ignoring the fact that his own actions had
been suspect. Cannon implied that politics influenced by the church
could only be on a low, degrading level. With this talk he doomed

whatever slim chance he may have had for reelection. In fact, no one was elected. After 164 ballots the legislature closed, and Utah only had one senator for the next two years. Cannon deeply resented what he believed was unnecessary and inappropriate church influence in the election. The incident was an important nail in the coffin of his commitment to Mormonism. It would take years before it reached the point of burial, but the pendulum of his religion was swinging toward irrevocable doubt and despair.

Following the bitter senatorial contest, Cannon threw himself back into his business ventures, did some writing, and peppered his activities with travel. As a sop to the beleaguered Cannon, or perhaps it might have been more because of a recognition that he had numerous eastern business contacts, as the 1898 summer waned the church's new president, Lorenzo Snow, asked him to travel in the East to meet financiers who could lend or invest money in church enterprises and thereby help solve a major financial crisis.

He went East after being promised a commission and lined up several interested investors. He was again disheartened, however, to learn that in his absence the First Presidency had decided to issue half a million dollars in bonds that would be sold to local businesses and businessmen rather than on eastern markets. Cannon, having made promises to his eastern contacts, felt betrayed because he had to go back on his word. Further, he lost whatever commission he might have realized. He harbored deep resentments against Joseph F. Smith, whom he believed pressed Snow to make this decision.[32]

There was also a family reason for Cannon's resentment. Many high church officials blamed his father for Mormonism's financial difficulties. The elder Cannon had presumably made some financial arrangements for the church in the early part of the decade that had gone sour during the Panic of 1893. Brigham Young, Jr., for instance, believed that George Q. Cannon had squandered the church's money. Snow, upon becoming the church's president, created a financial committee to review past actions, and it found several deficiencies, some of which were laid at George Cannon's feet. Frank Cannon was angry at the accusations and innuendoes being hurled against his father and wanted to protect him as a matter of family honor.[33] This represented another large nail in Cannon's coffin of faith. It was one more of the many other setbacks that pushed him to dissent from the religion he had been a part of for so long.

By the next year Cannon was expressing dissatisfaction with the Latter-day Saint movement more openly. For example, he spoke to a group in Salt Lake City on "Intellectual Acceptance of the Gospel," questioned the emotional expression of faith, and derided what he called the religion's lack of rationality. Cannon's heart had no difficulty embracing Mormonism, but his mind rejected it. Those who knew him best were convinced that his faith was rooted in the shifting sands of rational intellectualism, a philosophy rooted in the scientific method and the ideas of modernity.[34]

Cannon's intellectual questioning of Mormonism took a sharp turn into full-fledged revolt during the first years of the new century, and his eventual excommunication was almost assured as a result. With the death of Lorenzo Snow in October 1901, Joseph F. Smith became the Mormon church president. At sixty-three, he was, oddly enough, the youngest, most vigorous man to lead the Mormons in more than thirty years. Both he and Cannon were men of strong opinions who had disliked each other for many years. Cannon still resented Smith because of the bond deal in 1898. Smith had championed the selling of bonds to Utahns, not to the eastern financiers whom Cannon had lined up and then had, at least from Cannon's perspective, forced him to break his word. In addition, Cannon never forgave Smith and other church leaders, including Brigham Young, Jr., for blaming his father for the church's financial difficulties in the 1890s.

Frank Cannon may never have viewed Joseph F. Smith as a prophet, but his vision of the new Mormon president was certainly dimmed because of the Reed Smoot affair in 1904, which pushed him to apostacy. Contrary to what Cannon had thought was politically expedient, Mormon leaders supported—and the Utah state legislature concurring—had elected in 1903 an apostle, Smoot, to serve in the Senate. Cannon held the view that the time had passed in which it was permissible for Mormonism to mingle church and state. He considered Smoot's election, and many non-Mormon politicos in Washington agreed, judging from the intense investigation that took place before they allowed him to take his seat, a blatant attempt to reassert the Mormon institution's influence. Promises had been made to the nation's political leaders that the church would remove its fingers from the political pie except when politics involved moral issues, and Cannon saw the election of Smoot as yet another example of church leaders failing to honor their word. It was an ill-considered idea, Cannon believed, and it was the direct result, or so he thought, of Smith's leadership.[35]

Two other issues emerged from the Smoot hearings before the Senate Committee on Privileges and Elections that pushed Frank Cannon outside the Mormon church, and both also related directly to Joseph F. Smith. The first was the admission that Mormon officials had sanctioned additional plural marriages, even after promising national government leaders that the church would end the practice. Cannon, as much as any other Mormon, had given officials assurances that, if statehood were granted, the church would indeed abandon the practice of plural marriage. Believing he was following instructions he had received from "prophets, seers, and revelators," Cannon, who had never practiced plural marriage, was astonished at the number of plural marriages that had been entered into even after statehood was secured. He was, moreover, deeply hurt that some apostles refused to testify before the Smoot hearings, fearing that their continued involvement in plural marriage might be incriminating. Fuel was added to the flames of his doubt when Smith testified that he had with forethought broken both the law of the church and the law of the land by cohabiting with his plural wives since the manifesto. Testifying further, Smith declared that he had cohabited with his wives "not openly . . . nor in a manner . . . offensive to his neighbors . . . knowing the responsibility and knowing that I was amenable to the law."[36]

The second issue concerned the prophetic office itself. Whatever conviction Cannon may have possessed at the start of the Reed Smoot hearings evaporated when newspapers announced that Smith had testified that he had never in his three years as church president received a revelation. If revelationless, the church could hardly be true, Cannon seems to have reasoned. What Smith had actually said was that he had not received "a revelation from God which had been submitted to the Apostles and sustained by a conference of the church." However, continuing his questioning, the Idaho Senator Fred Dubois asked Smith whether he had received any individual revelations since becoming church president, which would have included, by Smith's own definition, inspiration. The query was answered, "I can not say that I have." A few Mormons, Cannon among them, were concerned by Smith's testimony and publicly explicated their discomfort.[37]

With these developments Cannon's days as a loyal member of the Latter-day Saint church were numbered. His religious dissent was not of the first order. Frank Cannon was neither an Oliver Cowdery nor a William Law. In its purest form religious dissent is necessary when an individual believes that the integrity of the Gospel and the self are compromised, and Cannon never fell into that category. His dissent from Mormonism had been building over many years as an inner conflict between faith and doubt. He had gone back and forth on the issue. It was a personal debate, the kind many others have experienced both before and since. Why did he not throw off Mormonism earlier? Why did he wait until 1904 and the Reed Smoot hearings? The answers are undoubtedly complex and certainly psychological. They were probably not even fully known to Cannon himself, but they likely had to do with other influences that had previously kept him in the Latter-day Saint fold.

Two of the most important influences on Frank Cannon had passed from the scene. His younger brother, Abraham, an apostle and certainly a significant force in his life who had helped him stay sober, had tragically died of meningitis in 1896 at thirty-seven. His voice of concern and his faith in Mormonism was therefore gone from Frank Cannon's life. More important, his father, whom Cannon idolized, had died in April 1901. George Cannon had provided encouragement and reward when appropriate, and chastisement and rebuke as needed, throughout his son's life. He had probably minimized the rift between his son and the church hierarchy after the Dingley Tariff and church bond sale disagreements in 1898. He was now gone, and certainly he was missed.

That Frank Cannon was affected by his faithful family members should not be surprising. For example, when another brother, Quayle, who was editing the *Millennial Star* for the church in England, asked him to write some faith-building historical articles in 1902, he readily agreed and wrote an article about Joseph Smith, Jr., and one about Joseph F. Smith. The articles were entitled "In Honor of the Prophet" and exuded faith and extolled the virtues of both Smiths. Cannon later admitted that he had written them in that way because his brother wanted him to do so and because the Saints desired saccharine treatments.

All this changed in 1904 after the Smoot hearings and Cannon came out publicly against the church. He took up residence in Salt Lake City's Alta Club, where he formed an alliance with another former U.S. senator, Thomas L. Kearns, owner of the *Salt Lake Tribune*. Kearns made Cannon the paper's editor, and together they founded the American political party and began to attack the political and business power of the church. The American party was really a reformulation of the old Liberal Anti-Mormon party and was successful in having its candidates elected in the Salt Lake City municipal election held in November 1904. Cannon and Kearns were pleased with their success.[38]

In his *Tribune* editorials Cannon often viciously attacked the Mormon church and its financial involvements. On February 1, 1905, he published an article entitled "Are Mormons Peons?" in which he declared that the Latter-day Saints had become peons through the operation of tithing, a program actively pushed by Smith. He predicted that because of the burden Latter-day Saints carried, they were doomed to enter into an era of hopeless economic decay.[39] This led immediately to his excommunication on March 15, 1905.

His trial, excommunication, and its aftermath had so taxed Cannon that during the last week of April he went to Europe on a vacation. As he departed, there were rumors that he had quarreled with Thomas Kearns over declining circulation caused by Cannon's vicious attacks on Joseph F. Smith and the Mormon church. Regardless of the reason or reasons for the trip, Cannon and his wife did go to Europe, as rumors persisted at home that he would be replaced as the *Tribune's* editor. While on the Continent, they visited their son, who was serving a mission in Germany, reported the *Morning Examiner* on April 26.

Before returning to Utah, Cannon stopped in Philadelphia, where he conferred with Senator Dubois about how they might unseat Reed Smoot. He also met with Mrs. Frederick Schaff, president of the National League of Women, which was also opposing Smoot. In a meeting sponsored by the group he delivered an attack upon Smith and the Mormons before a large audience. Accompanied by Dubois and Schaff, Cannon traveled to New York and, again before a full house, spoke against the Mormons' secular power. Following his talk, resolutions were adopted providing for a committee of citizens to be appointed to correspond with others and pressure the Senate to expel Smoot.[40]

Back in Utah by the end of May, Cannon continued to edit the *Tribune* as well as to renew his attacks on the church. Because of his refusal to desist in his anti-Mormon articles, he finally was forced to sever his ties with the *Tribune* and move to Denver, where he secured the editorship of the *Denver Times*. Not being able to leave Mormonism alone, he willingly agreed to write articles for *Everybody's Magazine* about the menace of Mormon secular power. He also became a member of the Redpath Lyceum Bureau, which booked lecturers and entertainers into theaters around the nation, and spoke against Mormonism before more than a million American citizens in such cities as Chicago, New York, and Boston. Contacted by James S. Morten, general superintendent of the National Reform Association, Cannon also delivered talks before various Christian groups. Judge Benjamin Lindsey once remarked, "I have heard nearly all of the great orators and United States' Senators who have been on the Chautaqua and Lyceum platforms . . . and I want to say that former United States Senator Frank J. Cannon is, to my mind, the greatest of them all."[41]

At the end of the new century's first decade, Cannon, with Harvey J. O'Higgins, wrote a somewhat autobiographical book, *Under the Prophet in Utah,* that collected Cannon's many complaints about Mormonism. When the book appeared in 1911 it was favorably reviewed in the *New York Times Review of Books* on December 17: "No grimmer picture has ever been presented than that of the Mormon wife," the reviewer argued. He found it novel for a former Mormon "to prove that the Mormons [were] innocent at the time when all the country called them guilty, [and then] became guilty at the time when all the country either called them innocent or forgave them." The reviewer believed that the Utah church should speak up and answer Cannon's charges in tones more certain than they did "before the Senate Committee that investigated the charges against Reed Smoot." Cannon then helped O'Higgins write "The Other House," a tragic fictional story of a Mormon marriage, which was published in the *Delineator* in September 1911.

Two years later Cannon, together with George L. Knapp, wrote *Brigham Young and His Mormon Empire,* which detailed Young's ancestry, birth, conversion to Mormonism, and rise to the apostleship. It traced the second Mormon leader's mission to England, his rise to the church's presidency, and the trek West, as well as the carving of an empire in the Great Salt Lake Basin. Described also was the massacre at Mountain Meadows, the Mormon Reformation of the 1850s, the Godbeite movement, and the antipolygamy crusade against the Saints. The book also contained references to blood atonement and described Brigham Young's declining years. Cannon used language that mirrored his dislike of all Mormon leaders save his father. He also seemed to rely heavily on the histories of Edward W. Tullidge and T. B. H. Stenhouse for his information. *Brigham Young and His Mormon Empire* was widely read; it was even the source for an article on the Mormons that was published in an English book of political and literary essays by Evelyn Baring.[42] Throughout the rest of his life, Cannon continued to live in Colorado, writing anti-Mormon articles and enjoying the anti-Mormon lecture circuit.[43]

In time, his anger at Mormonism subsided, but he never returned to the church and always railed against its involvement in politics. As the nation prepared to celebrate Independence Day in 1933, Frank J. Cannon entered Denver Presbyterian Hospital for minor surgery. An infection attacked his body, and three weeks later he died. His body was brought to Utah, where a funeral was held on July 30, 1933, in the Ogden Elk's Lodge. The Utah state legislature sent a delegation to the service, but the Mormon church took no official part. Cannon was buried next to his wife in the Ogden Cemetery.[44]

Cannon's life was both futile and successful. He spent most of his later years in a Quixote-like fight against the church that had helped make him what he was. Earlier he had actively sought and often received its financial help and political endorsement. Then, as church leaders favored other political candidates, Cannon turned on that base of support. His attacks were too sensational, too vitriolic, and too mean for most people to sympathize with, however. Many liked to listen to him, but few believed what he had to say. At the same time, although unable to destroy the Mormon church, his dissent may have assisted in changing it. When he died in 1933, plural marriage was gone, statehood had been achieved, and the church, although still very influential, no longer dictated Utah's politics. The church had curbed its business holdings, Reed Smoot had been defeated, and no Mormon apostle has since sat in the Senate. Church leaders devoted more time to religious matters and less to secular affairs, something Cannon had always wanted. How much credit can be given to Cannon for these developments can be debated. Had he not been on the stage the same direction still would probably have been taken, although it might have been more gradual. Certainly Cannon, although only a bit player, had been on stage for most of this play.

NOTES

1. *Ogden Morning Examiner,* February 1, 1905, February 28, 1905, March 7, 1905, March 8, 1905, March 15, 1905.

2. *Ogden Standard,* April 1, 1905, April 8, 1905, April 10, 1905; *Ogden Morning Standard,* April 10, 1905.

3. Frank J. Cannon and Harvey J. O'Higgins, *Under the Prophet in Utah: The National Menace of a Political Priestcraft* (Boston: C. M. Clark Publishing Co., 1911), 326–27.

4. Orson F. Whitney, *History of Utah* (Salt Lake City: George Q. Cannon and Sons), 4:682.

5. Whitney, *History of Utah,* 4:682.

6. Abraham H. Cannon, Diary, September 18, 1880, November 26, 1880, January 11, 1881, April 6, 1881, originals in the Special Collections Library, Brigham Young University, Provo, Utah.

7. Ibid., April 6, 1881, June 29, 1882, September 1, 1882.

8. Ibid., March 2, 1885, March 3, 1885, December 22, 1884, December 23, 1884.

9. Ibid., May 9, 1885.

10. Ibid., January 10, 1886, March 3, 1886.

11. Ibid., February 26, 1886; Whitney, *History of Utah,* 3:480–491.

12. Abraham Cannon, Diary, June 29, 1888, November 7, 1887. John Q. Cannon, Frank's younger brother, revised Frank's manuscript; then, after a review by their father and Mormon apostle Joseph F. Smith, the book was published.

13. Ibid., July 19, 1887, February 22, 1888.

14. Edward Leo Lyman, *Political Deliverance: The Mormon Quest for Utah Statehood* (Urbana: University of Illinois Press, 1986), 99–100; Abraham Cannon, Diary, July 22, 1888.

15. Ibid., November 5, 1888, November 17, 1888, May 13, 1889, June 12, 1889.

16. Lyman, *Political Deliverance*, 131–32. Cannon probably took too much credit for influencing governmental officials. The church had many representatives working in Washington, including Isaac Trumbo, Brigham Young, Jr., Charles W. Penrose, Joseph F. Smith, John W. Young, and John T. Cane.

17. Ibid., 151–52.

18. *Ogden Standard*, September 16, 1892; *Deseret Evening News* [Salt Lake City], September 16, 1892; *Daily Tribune* [Salt Lake City], September 17, 1892.

19. *Ogden Standard*, September 19, 1892, September 24, 1892.

20. *Daily Tribune*, October 31, 1892; Lyman, *Political Deliverance*, 201; "Nuggets of Truth" (Salt Lake City: N.p., 1892). A copy of this pamphlet is available in the Utah State Historical Society, Salt Lake City.

21. Louis A. Coolidge, *Orville H. Platt: An Old-Fashioned Senator* (Port Washington: Kennikat Press, 1971), 1:135–36.

22. Frank J. Cannon to Wilford Woodruff, January 4, 1895, Cannon Family Papers, Latter-day Saints Historical Department, Salt Lake City. The reference is probably to the raising of the flag of the Council of Fifty on Ensign Peak by the pioneer band of which Woodruff was a member.

23. Wilford Woodruff to Frank J. Cannon, Cannon Family Papers, Latter-day Saints Historical Department, Salt Lake City.

24. That Cannon was correct in his assessment of the nation's politicians' attitude toward Mormon apostles, especially polygamous ones, is attested by the expulsion of B. H. Roberts from the House of Representatives, and the difficulty that the monogamist Reed Smoot had in securing his Senate seat only a few years later.

25. Abraham Cannon, Diary, November 17, 1895, December 5, 1895.

26. *Deseret Evening News*, January 14, 1896. Lyman states that "the earlier developments had largely favored Frank Cannon. A combination of farsightedness by his campaign managers who committed Republican state Legislative candidates to their man even before the state elections, help from a sympathetic cousin, George M. Cannon, in charge of territorial Republican machinery, and the tradition that the last territorial delegate to Congress was entitled to return to the capital in an elevated capacity all worked to his advantage over the other candidates" (*Political Deliverance*, 276).

27. "Journal History of the Church of Jesus Christ of Latter-day Saints," LDS Historical Department, January 22, 1896, 2; *Deseret Evening News*, January 25, 1896; George H. Crow, Diary, August 14, 1898, LDS Historical Department.

28. Marriner W. Merrill, Diary, 204, copy in my possession.

29. Charles L. Schmalz, "Sugar Beets in Cache Valley: An Amalgamation of Agriculture and Industry," *Utah Historical Quarterly* 57 (Fall 1989): 370–88.

30. Reuben Joseph Snow, "The American Party in Utah: A Study of a Political Party," M.A. thesis, University of Utah, 1964, 94.

31. Quoted in Richard S. Van Wagoner and Steven C. Walker, *A Book of Mormons* (Salt Lake City: Signature Books, 1982), 47.

32. Francis M. Gibbons, *Joseph F. Smith* (Salt Lake City: Deseret Book Company, 1984), 195.

33. E. Jay Bell, "The Windows of Heaven Revisited," paper presented at the Cache Valley General Authority Symposium, Logan, Utah, May 5, 1991, 5, copy in my possession; Thomas G. Alexander, *Mormonism in Transition: A History of the Latter-day Saints* (Urbana: University of Illinois Press, 1986), 6, 38, 180–81.

34. *Deseret News,* July 3, 1902; John M. Whitaker, Daily Journal, October 1, 1899, Special Collections, Marriott Library, University of Utah, Salt Lake City.

35. On the crisis in politics brought on by Reed Smoot's election, and the senatorial investigation on the subject, see Alexander, *Mormonism in Transition,* 16–29; and Milton R. Merrill, *Reed Smoot, Apostle in Politics* (Logan: Utah State University Press, 1990).

36. *Proceedings Before the Committee on Privileges and Elections of the United States Senate, in the Matter of the Protests against the Right of Hon. Reed Smoot, a Senator from the State of Utah to Hold His Seat* (Washington: Government Printing Office, 1904), 1:129. On the issue of post-Manifesto polygamy, see D. Michael Quinn, "LDS Church Authority and New Plural Marriages, 1890–1904," *Dialogue: A Journal of Mormon Thought* 18 (Spring 1985): 9–105; Richard S. Van Wagoner, *Mormon Polygamy: A History* (Salt Lake City: Signature Books, 1986), 157–94; Alexander, *Mormonism in Transition,* 60–73; and Ken Driggs, "After the Manifesto: Modern Polygamy and Fundamentalist Mormons," *Journal of Church and State* 32 (Spring 1990): 367–89.

37. *Proceedings Before the Committee,* 483.

38. B. H. Roberts, *A Comprehensive History of the Church of Jesus Christ of Latter-day Saints* (Salt Lake City: Deseret Book Co., 1976), 6:410.

39. The *Salt Lake Tribune,* January 31, February 1, and 2, 1905, contains editorials written by Cannon against the Mormon church.

40. *Deseret News,* May 2, 1905; *Morning Examiner,* May 1, 1905.

41. *Morning Examiner,* May 30, 1905, June 20, 1905; Cannon Family Papers, 6.

42. T. B. H. Stenhouse, *The Rocky Mountain Saints* (New York: D. Appleton and Co., 1873); Edward W. Tullidge, *History of Salt Lake City* (Salt Lake City: Star Printing Co., 1886); Edward W. Tullidge, *The Life of Brigham Young* (New York: Tullidge and Crandall, 1876); Evelyn Cromer Baring, *Political and Literary Essays* (London: Macmillan and Co., 1914), 342–48.

43. *The Christian Statesman,* July 1917, September 1917. There are 2,500 items in the Colorado Historical Society Library, Denver, pertaining to this period in Cannon's life. These papers were collected and processed by Susan A. Nieminem and are available for scholarly research.

44. His first wife, Martha, died on March 2, 1908, and Cannon then married her sister, who outlived him. *Deseret News,* March 2, 1908.

12

Joseph W. Musser: Dissenter or Fearless Crusader for Truth?

Martha Sonntag Bradley

Joseph White Musser's lifeline ran straight and true, marked by landmarks typical of twentieth-century Mormon men. Rites of passage for the Latter-day Saints—baptism, confirmation, priesthood ordination, temple endowment, and a lifetime of church service—defined and shaped his life. He marked time with his Mormon brothers, moving in unison for much of his adult life with the ranks of the Church of Jesus Christ of Latter-day Saints. But the last quarter of Musser's life saw a radical departure from that physical and spiritual home, for unlike most other believing Mormons he dissented from the church's decision to end the solemnizing of plural marriages. He became one of the most significant of the early twentieth century's Mormon fundamentalists.[1]

Born into a Latter-day Saint home on March 8, 1872, after his baptism at the age of eight Musser served as secretary in the presidency of his ward primary. At twelve, like most of the young men in his ward, he was ordained to the office of deacon in the Aaronic priesthood by his father, Amos Milton Musser. Musser continued to follow the predictable sequence of priesthood ordination thereafter. In two years his father once again ordained him, this time to the office of teacher, and two years later as a priest. As a young adult Joseph Musser served as the president of his ward's Young Men's Mutual Improvement Association (YMMIA), superintendent of the Sunday school, a ward missionary, a member of the stake superintendency of the YMMIA, and stake tithing clerk. He was later branch president of the Uintah branch of the Church of Jesus Christ of Latter-day Saints and as an assistant in the Uintah mission office.

On February 16, 1903, the patriarch John M. Murdock placed his hands upon Musser's head to ordain him to the office of high priest. Four years later the members of Granite Stake sustained Musser as an alternate member of their high council. President Joseph F. Smith similarly blessed him, saying, "God bless you Brother Joseph I am glad you are here and that you are in the harness. I hope they will always keep you working."[2]

Within a very few years Joseph W. Musser's lifeline—his path— veered sharply to the left and deviated from that of mainstream Mormonism to that of religious dissenter. The Granite Stake High Council excommunicated him in 1921 because of his continued belief in the doctrine of plural marriage. Therein, Musser passed from leading the faithful to assuming the position of one challenging the legitimacy of the Latter-day Saint church. In so doing, however, he did not consider himself in opposition to the "gospel," only to a hierarchy in error. Musser argued that in the hierarchy of church/priesthood/gospel the "church is subservient to the Priesthood, any action taken by it against those entering the law [plural marriage] is, null and void. A man or woman cannot properly be cut off [from] the Church for keeping a law of God, for the Church belongs to God and God cannot act a lie and remain God."[3]

According to Musser, the president of the church might or might not have been the president of the priesthood. He wrote:

> By reason of their seniority in the higher Priesthood calling, Brigham Young, John Taylor and Wilford Woodruff, each in his turn, became President of the Church, but always their Church calling was subordinate to their Priesthood positions. The greater organizes the lesser—the lesser cannot organize the greater. By authority of his Priesthood Joseph Smith organized the Church and ever after the Church was subject to his direction, because he was President of the Priesthood; a calling above that of the Church.[4]

Therefore, Musser reasoned, he was subject only to direction from those priesthood leaders who accepted the "truth" on the issue of plural marriage.

Musser further rationalized his dissenting witness with arguments about the fact that his stake president, Frank Taylor, and his counselor, John M. Cannon, both of Salt Lake City's Granite Stake, had performed plural marriages during the first decade of the twentieth century, which created a confusing, ambiguous environment for those, like Musser, who questioned the Woodruff Manifesto, the official declaration that the Latter-day Saints would no longer perform plural marriages. When Musser chose, after his excommunication, to worship God outside the parameters of the established church, he assumed a posture of dissent in the very truest sense.

Edwin Scott Gaustad describes dissent as the "distillation of the religious quest. Dissent is autonomous, inner-directed and displays all the pompous arrogance, heroic sacrifice a free spirit is capable of."[5] Musser filled the definition well after the church began to crack down on polygamists. As he wrote of his position in 1940, "It should be observed here, that while the Church Authorities have changed many of the ordinances, the Priesthood as a separate organization, has not thus gone astray and one day it will rise up and save the Church from final rejection."[6]

Musser's dissent was in part inner-directed, but it was also imitative of a seventy-year tradition of civil disobedience by the Mormon pioneers on the issue of polygamy. Despite the most obvious similarity between the historic defense of plural marriage and Musser's continued adherence to the principle after the Woodruff Manifesto, the most glaring difference was that Musser not only separated himself from mainstream America but also from the Latter-day Saint church. It is not enough, therefore, to say that he was simply continuing in the footsteps of his polygamist father, for he was making a very dramatic step to the left in choosing to worship through the "invisible" church, the "priesthood," which he believed had authority over the "visible" church as a formal organization.

Dissent, like religion, takes many forms and, as Jesus Christ told Nicodemus in describing the spirit, is as hard to define as the wind, "for you can't tell from whence it cometh or whither it goes." Dissent is uniquely individualistic. The church called modern-day polygamists "fundamentalist Mormons," those people clearly outside the official church because of excommunication proceedings against those who accepted a more literal or unique interpretation of scripture. Musser said, "The appellation 'fundamentalist' has been attached to a group of people whom the Church of Jesus Christ of Latter-day Saints, known as the Mormon Church had ostracized for adhering to its original doctrines."[7]

The road from a faithful household to one ostracized for dissenting beliefs began when Musser was a child. His father, Amos Milton Musser, was one of the assistant church historians to the Latter-day Saint movement. Musser, born in the Mormon stronghold of Salt Lake City in 1872, had a strong Latter-Day Saint background. Amos Musser and Mary Elizabeth White had left Nauvoo with the main body of Saints for the trek to Utah. They remained faithful, sacrificing members of the church throughout the difficult pioneer years and the accommodation period around the turn of the century.[8]

Musser viewed his father as living a "patriarchal life," with thirty-five children and four wives, and as being a "defender of the faith."[9]

Amos Musser received a special commission from the First Presidency to keep a record of all acts of persecution as well as the "names of the persecutors of those acts against the church of Jesus Christ of Latter-day Saints." He himself was prosecuted under the provisions of the Edmunds Act outlawing plural marriage and spent six months in the penitentiary "for acknowledging his wives and caring for the mothers of his children."[10]

Joseph Musser's religious worldview evolved in an environment that heralded the effort of those prosecuted for their righteous beliefs. "Coming from such an ancestry and being raised in a polygamous atmosphere, by parents devoted to their religious conception," he wrote, "I naturally inherited and imbibed a strong spiritual nature. From early youth I devoted my time to the church. I believed intensely in the mission of Joseph Smith, and were it possible to become fanatically religious, but not obdurate toward the religion and actions of others nor offensively dogmatic."[11]

Musser would lead much the same life as his father. At a young age, Rose Selms Borquist married him in the Logan Temple on June 29, 1892. They rented two rooms in Amos Musser's home, bought a few articles of furniture and a cookstove, and set up house on Joseph's $40 a month clerk's salary. Their first son, Joseph B., was born while his father was on a mission to the southern states.[12]

Musser would later remember that in November 1899 he and Rose received a "written invitation" from President Lorenzo Snow to go to the temple to receive "Higher Annointings." The Mussers, along with four other couples, went to the Salt Lake Temple on Thanksgiving morning, "where the most glorious blessings known to man were sealed upon us. We literally spent a few hours as in heaven 'mid the glorious calm and quiet of our holy surroundings. We were near the Lord and Oh! how happy!" Musser was twenty-seven in 1899, the husband of one and father of two. He wondered at being so favored, "for we were being sealed with the 'Holy Spirit of Promise.'"[13]

It would be Lorenzo Snow who would introduce Musser through an intermediary to the idea of entering the "principle," the way genteel Saints referred to the practice of plural marriage. "In the course of a few weeks," Musser recorded in his journal, "word came from President Snow that I had been chosen to take more wives, and help keep the law of Celestial marriage alive among the Saints. This was a distinct shock to me, as we had been given to understand that to attempt such a move would mean excommunication from the Church. The Manifesto forbade it."[14] Quite shaken by the message, Musser considered its source, the prophet of the church, and felt compelled to obey. "I did so," he would always say, "by marrying Mary Caroline Hill, a most beautiful daughter of Bishop William Hood Hill, of Mill Creek Ward." The couple would have six children: five daughters and a son, Guy, who would continue in his father's work. Musser would eventually marry and have children with a total of four women.

Musser courted his third wife, Ellis R. Shipp, while serving in the Uintah, Wasatch mission. Ellis, who had a degree in education from the University of Utah, had been called to introduce kindergarten work to the Wasatch Stake. During that same time President Joseph F. Smith issued what would later be called the "Second Manifesto." Issued in 1904, it read in part:

> Inasmuch as there are numerous reports in circulation that plural marriages have been entered into contrary to the official declaration of President Wilford Woodruff, of September 24, 1890, commonly called the Manifesto, which was issued by President Woodruff and adopted by the church at its general conference of October 6, 1890, which forbade any marriage violative of the law of the land, I Joseph F. Smith, President of the church of Jesus Christ of Latter-day Saints, do hereby affirm and declare that no such marriages have been solemnized with the sanction, consent, or knowledge of the Church of Jesus Christ of Latter-day Saints,
>
> And I hereby announce that all such marriages are prohibited, and if any officer or member of the Church shall assume to solemnize or enter into any such marriage, he will be deemed in transgression against the Church, and will be liable to be dealt with according to the rules and regulations thereof, and excommunicated therefrom.[15]

In the future, plural marriage would be punished by excommunication.

According to Musser's recollection, in 1915 an unnamed apostle conferred upon him the "sealing power of Elijah, with instructions to see that plural marriage shall not die out, President Snow had said that I must not only enter the law, but must help keep it alive. This then, was the next step in enabling me to help keep it alive. I have tried to be faithful to my trust."[16]

During the next few years Musser could feel himself growing in the "work of the Lord," even as he witnessed his brother Don pull away from Mormonism and eventually announce his apostasy. "This was a fearful blow to both Father and me," Musser would remember. He began to view himself increasingly after his excommunication as having been unjustly cast out from "its [the church's] functions and benefits." Even so, he and his wives continued to pay their tithing and fast offerings through the late 1920s despite the fact that plural marriage barred them from temple attendance, the single most significant religious experience in Mormonism. In June 1929 Ellis Musser was barred from witnessing their daughter Ellis's temple marriage, even though she was what Musser described as a "tithe payer and in good standing in her ward."[17] During the 1920s Musser emerged as a leader of a group of Mormon fundamentalists outside the church.

In spite of what he considered atrocious behavior in denying temple access to him and his wives, they all continued to wear temple garments and respect the ordinances that were performed in the temple. He told a group of fundamentalists, "The Saints must maintain the integrity of their garments. The flimsy make-shifts sold by the Jews, and at the ZCMI department store as recently advertized, are an insult to God and offer no protection as promised by the Lord. Better wear nothing by that name, than to prostitute that which is sacred. No person having lain off their garments are permitted to take them up again and Hear them without proper authority."[18] Musser also counseled his followers about theology, religion, and behavior and sought to teach them about the importance of the temple in the overall plan of Mormonism's plural marriage.

Musser developed a unique defense mechanism to explain his inability to take advantage of the temple. In 1937 he counseled a small group of fundamentalist Saints about the importance of temple work. "Don't worry about not being able to do temple work. Get your genealogies ready and the day will soon come when the temples, which are literally the houses of the Lord, will be 'set in order,' and then the work will count. Much of the work now being done will have to be done over."[19] Thus, for Musser, Mormonism would be salvaged by some reformation, which, he thought, would bring it back to the "truth."

On July 22, 1909, the president of the Quorum of Twelve Apostles, Francis M. Lyman, requested that Musser attend a meeting of his quorum at 4:30 that afternoon in the temple. At six, Lyman invited Musser into the apostles' room, where John Henry Smith, Heber J. Grant, Rudger Clawson, Orson F. Whitney, David O. McKay, George F. Richards, and Anthony W. Ivins as well as Lyman were questioning a series of suspected dissidents. For two hours the men questioned Musser's feelings on plural marriage, known violators of the 1904 prohibition on performing plural marriages, and his intentions for the future. They advised him on ways to handle delicate situations when approached about the subject of polygamy. "We want you hereafter to join with us in putting this thing down," President Ivins said, "If anybody comes to you for information or encouragement, tell them it can't be done, that it is wrong to desire and that no attentions whatever should be bestowed upon the sisters with this in view." Joseph replied, "President Lyman, I cannot do that, but I suggest if you have any instructions to give me, it should be done through my Stake President, with whom I am in harmony and I will endeavor to remain so."

Musser was sufficiently confident of his stake president's posture on the subject to decline to side with the apostles of the church. When pressured to "get in harmony," he answered in a way similar to others who had been questioned that day. "One would think these brethren had rehearsed their pieces," Lyman said. After the event, Musser moved even further from the center. Finally, on December 14, 1909, the Latter-day Saint hierarchy disfellowshipped him for his continued belief in plurality of wives.[20]

Despite the investigation— Musser called it an inquisition—Lyman called Musser to preside, after the death of his father in 1909, over the India mission, a job that could be performed through the mail. In a letter dated January 6, 1910, Lyman wrote, "Keep your hand in the good work and the Lord will bless you abundantly and so will your father and the good, good saints of India. I bless you and will continue to do so and appreciate your work as if done to me; for they seem like my own." He signed the letter, "Affectionately your brother, Francis M. Lyman."[21]

During the early 1920s Musser became increasingly conscious of the lines drawn between those who continued to practice polygamy and those who did not. He gravitated toward association with those whose ideas matched his own, particularly those who seemed to have answers to the question of priesthood authority. In 1922, after his excommunication from the Mormon church, Musser recorded several oral accounts that originated with Lorin Woolley and Daniel Bateman, who had been present in the Woolley's Centerville, Utah, home in 1886 when President John Taylor reportedly received a vision of Jesus Christ and Joseph Smith, Jr.

Such stories had been circulating for a number of years, and Musser published them for the first time in a standardized version in 1929. The document specified the date of the vision as September 26 and 27, 1886, and reported an eight-hour meeting during the day of September 27, when Taylor put the other men in attendance "under covenant" to continue the practice of plural marriage. Those present were George Q. Cannon, L. John Nuttall, John H. Woolley, Samuel Bateman, Daniel R. Bateman, Charles H. Wilkins, Charles Birrell, Samuel Seden, George Earl, Lorin C. Woolley, and two women, Julia E. Woolley and Amy Woolley. The Musser account also stated that Taylor gave five of them—Cannon, Wilkins, Samuel Bateman, and John and Lorin Woolley—authority to perform plural marriages and ordain others to do the same.[22] Perhaps because of this publication and Musser's stubborn refusal to defer to the authority of the church president, the Granite Stake High Council excommunicated him on March 23, 1921.[23]

Lorin Woolley's 1912 account of the same events, however, received limited attention. But Musser's 1929 redaction had a more profound effect on those Mormons who already questioned the church leadership's authority. He was especially able to sway those who, like Musser himself, had still failed to reconcile their feelings about plural marriage, the two manifestos, the church's increasingly severe separation from the principle of plural marriage, and the overriding issue of whether the "priesthood keys" (that is, the power) to perform plural marriages were still on the earth.

Perhaps in reaction to their unreconciled feelings about such issues, this type of sentiment, and the growing alienation between those continuing in the principle and those who were increasingly antagonistic to it, seven men met in Salt Lake City in 1929 and organized a priesthood council to fulfill the promise of the 1886 revelation. In addition to Musser, members of the first council included J. Leslie Broadbent, John Y. Barlow, Lorin C. Woolley, LeGrand Woolley, Louis Kelsch, and Charles F. Zitting. Lorin Woolley was named the senior member, and his leadership established the group as a major fundamentalist force. When he died on September 19, 1934, John Y. Barlow succeeded him as the senior member. Musser succeeded Barlow in 1949.

The seven-member council served as the precursor of the seventy-member Sanhedrin that Musser organized not long before his death in 1954. As he described it, "It was this body of men whom Moses brought before the face of the Lord. This body, when properly organized, is presided over by seven Presidents of the Great High Priest Order, the worthy Senior member being the presiding officer and the mouthpiece for the seven."[24]

Before Barlow died, he called two younger fundamentalists, LeRoy S. Johnson and J. Marion Hammon, and set them apart as apostles of Jesus Christ. He later called Guy H. Musser, Rulon Jeffs, Richard Jessop, Carl Holm, and Alma Timpson to serve as well.[25] The history of polygamy in the next half century would become, in large measure, the history of these men and their posterity, a prodigious group who, by their union, selected for themselves a peculiar destiny.

When Musser was ordained a high priest apostle and a patriarch to all the world by Barlow, himself a high priest apostle, he was instructed to see "that never a year passed that children were not born in the covenant of plural marriage." He recalled, "I was instructed to give patriarchal blessings to those applying for same and were denied access to real patriarchs in the Church."[26]

The discrepancy between Musser's belief in what he considered the "true gospel" and the reality of his relationship to the church became more complicated with each passing year during the 1930s. On his fifty-eighth birthday in 1930 he recorded in his journal, "The Church withdrew fellowship from me because of my active adherence to the principle of plural marriage, but I have a definite testimony of the truth and am seeking to live in accordance with the Gospel as the former Apostles and as the Spirit of God interprets it to me. I teach my children to pray for and sustain the authorities. I attend my meetings and am honestly trying to 'Love my neighbor as myself.'"[27] Musser then described his children as active church members and useful members of the church and the community, "yet they are my crime. How can this be? Will a corrupt fountain bring forth pure water, or a wicked tree bring forth good fruit."[28]

Musser found it increasingly difficult to find work during the early 1930s, as the official church effort at stamping out polygamy intensified. "I am out of employment and many of my erst-while friends and loved ones now Shun me. To them I seem something unclean."[29] Painfully and acutely aware of the increasing boundaries between them, he mourned the loss of friends and the support of loved ones. By 1935 Musser would find much to criticize in the state of the church that had cast him out: "Peace is taken from the earth. Men's hearts and thoughts are evil continually. Greed reigns supreme. Even the Temple of God is polluted. The Gospel, as changed, has lost much of its power and the Saints are being rapidly drawn away from the truths as revealed to Joseph Smith. Wickedness is established in the Church, and those who are sincerely trying to live the Gospel are being excommunicated and cast out."[30] This feeling of personal loss only intensified throughout the rest of Musser's life.

Similarly, LeRoy Johnson, in a sermon in 1973 before fundamentalists at Colorado City, New Mexico, spoke to the connection and sense of loss he felt toward the Mormon church. His perspective was closely related to Musser's own beliefs. "I did everything that was asked of me by the Church authorities," Johnson said. "That is where I got my training. But I did have the presence of mind enough to say 'no' when I knew people were trying to get me to do things that were not right."[31]

Musser's relationship with Mormon church president Heber J. Grant during the 1930s was particularly complicated. "I love the Gospel," he would say. "I do not endorse all that President Grant does, and many things about him I cannot admire; and yet I love and respect him as the leader of the Church, and I have it in my heart to help him in his arduous labors."[32] This respect, however, would deteriorate during the next decade as the distance between the two increased. In 1939 Musser observed that "he is prejudiced against me and that prejudice has spread throughout the council."[33]

The issue in contention among the official church leadership, and an issue of particular concern to President Grant, was the location of the power—"keys"—to perform plural marriages. Particularly after the deaths of Snow and Smith the idea was affirmed that no one was authorized to perform plural marriages anywhere on earth. The series of directives sent from the office of the First Presidency was designed to combat rumors of alternate claims to priesthood authority and undercut the credibility of those claiming to have authority to continue the practice. In 1921 President Grant "branded as plain simple liars those who undertake to say that anybody, aside from the President of the Church, had any right to give revelations to this people."[34]

The fight intensified when, in 1933, J. Reuben Clark, Grant's indefatigable counselor, drafted a definitive "Official Statement" published under the signatures of the First Presidency in the "Church News" section of the *Deseret News*. It censured the renewed interest in the "corrupt, adulterous practices of the members of this secret, oathbound organization," gave a careful accounting of the history of the controversy that had raged since the 1890 Manifesto, summarized the legal action that had been taken against the church by the federal government, cataloged doctrinal support of the principle, and described the continued practice of polygamy outside Mormonism. It stressed the contractual nature of the marriage union and the legal discontinuation of the principle, rather than the fact that it had once been evidence of a revelation.[35]

The Clark Official Statement not only solidified Mormonism's rejection of the practice of plural marriage, but it also clarified the Latter-day Saint doctrine of celestial marriage. The document carefully distinguished between celestial marriage and polygamous marriage, noting that celestial marriages were "monogamous marriages for time and eternity, solemnized in our temples in accordance with the word of the Lord and the laws of the Church."[36] This flat statement dismantled the logic for continuing any plural celestial marriages that the fundamentalists had carefully constructed. But although the statement pacified mainstream Mormons, it unified fundamentalists.

Perhaps in reaction to the flood of literature against polygamy be-

ing promulgated by the official church in June 1935, Musser began
publication of *Truth* magazine, a singleminded publication dedicated
to the defense of plural marriage. He quoted profusely from nineteenth-
century polygamous leaders—Joseph Smith, Jr., Brigham Young, and
George Q. Cannon—to justify the modern practice and always emphasized its eternal and revelatory nature. *Truth* also provided a forum
for and a means of reconciliation among the different factions of fundamentalist polygamists. Bound together solely by their belief in the
plural marriage doctrine, they had been increasingly split asunder by
alternative and competing claims to priesthood authority. Both issues
divided them from the mainstream church.

In a journal entry on March 8, 1939, Musser reflected, "I have re-
gretted more than I can tell the necessity of opposing my brethren of
the Authorities, but the doctrines they are putting out are so rank with
error I cannot refrain from publishing the truth. My desire is to establish the truth—to strike straight and fair let the blow rest where it will."
Furthermore, he spoke to the issue of his dissenting position: "But we
are said to be apostate, and yet our apostasy rests wholly on our adherence to the fullness of the Gospel as Joseph Smith established it. It
seems so strange to me—and not strange in the light of scripture—that
I should be singled out and lied about, shunned and in many ways forsaken, because I believe in the Gospel in its fullness and insist on my
right to live it."[37]

The church, in part a reaction to the growing organization of the
fundamentalists, stepped up its hunt for polygamists during the late
1930s. Furthermore, in 1938, to counteract the growing numbers of
fundamentalists, the First Presidency authorized several loyal Mormons
to conduct surveillance on persons suspected of fundamentalist sym-
pathies and worshipped in meetings in private homes in Salt Lake City
and Midvale, Utah.[38] One who conducted covert operations, Casper
Fetzer, later testified in court for the state that David O. McKay had
given him an "calling" to find offenders against the strictures of the
church and bring them to justice.[39] On June 5, 1939, Paul C. Child,
president of Salt Lake's Pioneer Stake, reportedly instructed bishops
that fundamentalists were "in very humble circumstances, being prac-
tically destitute, and if we help them we are helping to support plural
families."[40] Withholding assistance, Child believed, would help bring
a more speedy end to plural marriage.

During the same decade, the state government added to the difficulties of the polygamists. First in 1935 and then again in 1938 a number were brought to trial in Utah's courts. In his journal on September
21, 1939, Musser wrote of the *State v. Jessop* case:

The trial of these boys was a farce. It was a Church fight, the
Co. Atty [Orvin Hafen] being a counselor in the Stake Presidency there. The Dist. Atty. is a Mormon; the Sheriff who served the
papers and furnished the chief testimony. AB Prince, and the
Judge, Will L. Haft, were Mormons. The Jury of course, was comprised of Mormons. It was an effort to stamp polygamy out . . .
thereby bringing rejoicing to the heart of pres. Grant. Today the
word "JUSTICE": both in the Ecclesiastical and Civil or Criminal
Courts, in Mormon communities, is no.

The entry expresses the anger, the questioned misuse of power, and
Musser's growing sense of frustration at what he increasingly was coming to believe was the complete apostasy of the institutional leadership.

This atmosphere of subterfuge, persecution, and increased tension
between the visible and invisible church created a breach in communication between polygamists and their former church, such that it
seemed that they were no longer describing the same religion. At the
same time, the fundamentalists split further apart themselves—cluster-
ing around the personalities of Barlow, Musser, and Rulon Allred.
During the 1940s, Barlow continued to consolidate his influence in
Short Creek while Musser and Allred came to dominate fundamentalists in the Salt Lake Valley.

Nevertheless, both civil and ecclesiastical leaders identified all polygamists as representing the same problem in spite of important differences between them. The first large-scale assault on fundamentalists since the judicial crusade of the 1880s was led by U.S. attorney
John S. Boyden and Utah state attorney general Brigham E. Roberts,
a grandson of B. H. Roberts, and polygamists throughout the region
were arrested. Two heavily armed FBI agents and two Salt Lake City
police entered Musser's home at 6 A.M. on March 7, 1944. After placing Musser under arrest, they began to search his office for records.
They presented no search warrant but continued to search, despite
Musser's numerous protestations to stop. "This search continued until about 11:00 A.M. when the officers took me to the county jail," he
wrote. "Arriving there, I found a large congregation of my brothers.
Of the Priesthood Council, were John V. Barlow, myself, Charles F.
Zitting, LeGrand Woolley, Louis A. Kelsch, also Guy H. Musser and
Rulon T. Jeffs."[41] Musser was charged with federal conspiracy, state
conspiracy, and cohabitation. Thus, sixty years after his father, Joseph
White Musser joined the "honor roll" of Mormon men imprisoned for
their belief in plural marriage.

Musser was seventy-two. While in prison he was frequently ill. "The food did not agree with me, neither did the treatment nor the iron cell in which I was encased," he commented, "though I would have died there rather than renounce my faith."[42] Although this was the case at first, after six months in prison Musser and ten other polygamists applied for parole and received it on the basis of a document they signed swearing that they would not continue the practice of plural marriage. It read:

> TO WHOM IT MAY CONCERN:
> The undersigned officers and members of the so-called fundamentalist religious group do hereby declare as follows:
> That we individually and severally pledge ourselves to refrain hereafter from advocating, teaching or countenancing the practice of plural marriage or polygamy, in violation of the laws of the State of Utah and of the United States. The undersigned officers of the religious group above referred to further pledge ourselves to refrain from solemnizing plural marriages from and after this date contrary to the laws of the land; Dated September 24, 1945.

Musser's eventual release from prison on parole allowed him to continue to publish *Truth* magazine. As he wrote of the incident:

> We were told by the Parole Board we would have to live with our legal wives. We might visit the others and support our children, but we must not live with them. As Rose was my legal wife, but had not lived with me for nearly 20 years, and as my office, records, library, etc., were with Lucy, the mother of my two youngest children, Rose divorced me, thus permitting me to marry Lucy legally and maintain my residence with her. This arrangement was also endorsed by my wife Ellis. Rose made it clear she did not want a temple or a priesthood divorce; she wants our relationship to continue in eternity; and, of course, I am supporting her the best I can, as I have always done.[43]

After his release he suffered a debilitating stroke and was attended by his associate in the fundamentalist cause, Rulon Allred, who was also a physician. While under his treatment in 1949, Musser appointed Allred his successor in the senior spot in the priesthood council, passing over Barlow's choice, LeRoy Johnson. This succession crisis, pressed by others who felt they had a superior claim to seniority, divided the council, and it split into two separate bodies. Musser died five years later, on March 28, 1954.

As was true in the nineteenth century, opposition weeded out the faint-hearted, strengthened the strong, and found willing martyrs. The assumption that God required great sacrifices of the faithful provided meaning to their hardships. Guy Musser would compare his father to Jesus Christ in 1939: "he went about doing good; lifting the thoughts of men from degradation and shame; turning their eyes heavenward with a genius that marked him as a man of unfaltering courage, of vision, faith, charity, long suffering; with a heart that felt keenly the needs of his followers, . . . in many stations and in many classes of people you have been able to leave an indelibly written account of a righteous and fearless crusader for truth."[44]

Musser never deviated in his testimony of the truthfulness of the gospel. His words are a poignant reminder of both the ties that bound him to the movement and the walls that separated him:

> The Church of Jesus Christ of Latter-day Saints is the very and only Church of Jesus Christ on earth today its members who are living the fullness being members of the Church of the First Born. . . . While in many respects the Church is out of order, a condition in which the Church has always fallen through the weaknesses of men, it has not been rejected—it is still the Church of Jesus Christ, and will always remain so. . . . Meantime those attempting in perfect good faith, though weak, to live the higher law—the law of Consecration and of Celestial Marriage in its fullness, the latter of which the church rejected in the Manifesto of Wilford Woodruff, must continue on; they must endure the stigma hurled against them—of apostasy and excommunication, persecution, imprisonment, with other abuses, until the Lord sees fit to take a hand. And my faith is that when the Lord rights the wrongs of His leaders the faithful Saints will be crowned with glory and eternal lives, a consummation worth suffering for, as many are now doing."[45]

Musser's piety is the key to understanding his division from the church. As with other fundamentalist Mormons, he viewed a direct immediate private and incontrovertible experience of God as more valid than organized or authority directed religion.

Perhaps Musser's type of dissent can be understood through a comparison with another group of dissidents. In today's Israeli army there is a group of soldiers, many of whom are officers, who refuse on moral grounds to go into occupied territories taken from other nations and participate in what they call "acts of oppression." The Israeli army has a legal mandate that requires soldiers to disobey illegal orders or orders based on false interpretation of law. These soldiers, "refusniks," believe that they are only following this legal mandate. They do not want to desert from the army or separate in a substantive way, but they believe there is some higher good that goes beyond duty, that goes beyond country, and that requires of them a higher standard of morality.

Musser might have considered himself a refusnik, in fact, Francis Lyman might have affectionately called Musser a refusnik. He did not want to separate from the church; he loved it and respected its teaching as he understood them. But he would not accept the changes that were being made. He, like the refusniks, believed there was a higher good, a truer principle, a higher law than the church itself.

Joseph White Musser emerged as a dissenter from the Mormon faith from the anxiety and tension of a time when the church's effort at compromise with mainstream America was in full swing. In an effort to further separate church and state and become more palatable to American society, Mormonism gave up much of its uniqueness. The pride in the reckless, independent Mormonism of the nineteenth-century church provided Musser with a powerful incentive to resist change and retain traditional ecclesiastical forms. In the 1920s Lorin C. Woolley advised him that the fundamentalists should always avoid four faults of the visible church: (1) They should never congregate; (2) they should not proselyte; (3) they should not change; and (4) they should not compromise.

Each of these four issues seem to be reactionary, in particular a reaction to change. As the Mormon church in the early twentieth century strained to become accepted by mainstream American society, as it became a missionary church marketing not only a message but also an image, it seemed to become more like other Protestant religions than different. To maintain the pure church, the invisible church, the unadulterated church, the church of the original teachings of Joseph Smith, Jr., fundamentalists chose a road that often ran parallel to the visible church but more often moved in ever-increasing isolation, and separation—toward what they considered a straighter line to God.

NOTES

1. There are no studies of the life of Joseph W. Musser. Many discussions of polygamy in the twentieth century, however, include some information about him. See Richard S. Van Wagoner, *Mormon Polygamy: A History* (Salt Lake City: Signature Books, 1986); D. Michael Quinn, "LDS Church Authorities and New Plural Marriage, 1890–1904," *Dialogue: A Journal of Mormon Thought* 18 (Spring 1985): 9–105; Kenneth Cannon II, "Beyond the Manifesto: Polygamous Cohabitation among LDS General Authorities after 1890," *Utah Historical Quarterly* 46 (Winter 1978): 24–36; Kenneth Cannon II, "After the Manifesto: Mormon Polygamy, 1890–1906," *Sunstone* 8 (January–April

1983): 27–41; Jerold A. Hilton, "Polygamy in Utah and Surrounding Area since the Manifesto of 1890," M.A. thesis, Brigham Young University, 1965; Victor W. Jorgensen and B. Carmon Hardy, "The Taylor-Cowley Affair and the Watershed of Mormon History," *Utah Historical Quarterly* 48 (Winter 1980): 4–36; Martha S. Bradley, "Changed Faces: The Official LDS Position on Polygamy, 1890–1990," *Sunstone* 14 (February 1990): 26–33; Ken Driggs, "After the Manifesto: Modern Polygamy and Fundamentalist Mormons," *Journal of Church and State* 32 (Spring 1990): 367–89.

2. Joseph W. Musser, *Journal* (Salt Lake City: Pioneer Press, 1990), 73. This volume is a published collection of excerpts from Musser's journals over a fifty-year period.

3. Musser, *Journal,* 11.

4. Ibid., 12.

5. Edwin Scott Gaustad, *Dissent in American Religion* (Chicago: University of Chicago Press, 1973), 4.

6. Musser, *Journal,* 47.

7. Ibid., 103.

8. On the Mormon church's accommodation to the American mainstream, see Thomas G. Alexander, *Mormonism in Transition: A History of the Latter-day Saints, 1890–1930* (Urbana: University of Illinois Press, 1986).

9. Musser, *Journal,* 2.

10. Ibid., 3.

11. Ibid.

12. As an adult, the son would serve in World War II as a lieutenant, a commander, and finally a captain in the navy; he was stationed in the Pacific.

13. Musser, *Journal,* 32.

14. Ibid., 32.

15. B. H. Roberts, *A Comprehensive History of the Church of Jesus Christ of Latter-day Saints* (Salt Lake City: Deseret Book Co., 1978), 6:401–2; "Journal History of the Church of Jesus Christ of Latter-day Saints," April 6, 1904, 4, Church of Jesus Christ of Latter-day Saints Historical Department, Salt Lake City.

16. Joseph W. Musser, *Celestial or Plural Marriage* (Salt Lake City: Truth Publishing Co., 1944), 11.

17. Musser, *Journal,* 34.

18. Ibid., 44.

19. Ibid., 34.

20. *Salt Lake Tribune,* December 14, 1909, 6.

21. Musser, *Journal,* 66.

22. Van Wagoner, *Mormon Polygamy,* 190–94.

23. *Salt Lake Tribune,* March 23, 1921, 1.

24. Musser, *Journal,* 12.

25. LeRoy S. Johnson, *Sermons* (Hildale: Twin City Courier Press, 1984), 4:1606–7.

26. Musser, *Journal,* 11.

27. Joseph W. Musser, Journal, March 8, 1939, Latter-day Saints Historical Department.

28. Musser, *Journal,* 37.

29. Ibid., 43.

30. Ibid.

31. Johnson, *Sermons,* 3:5.

32. Musser, *Journal,* 38.

33. Ibid., 45.

34. James R. Clark, *Messages of the First Presidency* (Salt Lake City: Bookcraft, 1965–75), 5:194.

35. Clark, *Messages,* 5:293; D. Michael Quinn, *J. Reuben Clark: The Church Years* (Provo: Brigham Young University Press, 1983), 183–86; Van Wagoner, *Mormon Polygamy,* 195–97.

36. Clark, *Messages,* 5:293.

37. Musser, *Journal,* 46.

38. Quinn, *J. Reuben Clark,* 195.

39. Joseph W. Musser, "Who Are the Real Conspirators?" *Truth* 10 (November 1944): 141.

40. Joseph W. Musser, "True Christianity," *Truth* 5 (August 1939): 50.

41. Joseph W. Musser, "Arrest and Imprisonment," *Truth* 14 (January 1949): 330–34.

42. Musser, *Journal,* 15.

43. Ibid., 19.

44. Ibid., 46.

45. Ibid., 69.

13

Fawn McKay Brodie: Dissident Historian and Quintessential Critic of Mormondom

Newell G. Bringhurst

Every summer hundreds of faithful Mormons travel to Huntsville, Utah, a Mormon community about ten miles east of Ogden. They visit the boyhood home of David O. McKay, ninth president of the Church of Jesus Christ of Latter-day Saints and one of the most beloved figures in the twentieth-century church. However, most visitors are unaware that the old David McKay "farmhouse with [its] fourteen rooms" was also the childhood home of Fawn McKay Brodie—one of the church's most famous recent dissenters, reviled by many of the faithful with almost as much passion as her uncle is adored.[1] Such negative Mormon feelings toward Fawn M. Brodie are nurtured in large measure by her controversial book *No Man Knows My History: The Life of Joseph Smith, the Mormon Prophet,* which presented the founding Mormon prophet's motivations as primarily nonreligious or secular. In Brodie's words, "I was convinced before I ever began writing that Joseph Smith was not a true prophet."[2] Brodie, moreover, remained a quintessential critic of things Mormon following the publication of her provocative biography—a role she actively promoted for the remainder of her life.

In terms of family background, patterns of childhood behavior, and early religious beliefs, Fawn McKay Brodie seemed an unlikely dissident. Born in 1915, she came from patrician Mormon stock.[3] Her paternal grandfather, David McKay, helped found Huntsville. Her father, Thomas E. McKay, a respected church leader, served as president of the Swiss-German Mission, president of the Ogden Stake, and assistant to the Quorum of the Twelve. Politically active, he was president of the Utah state senate and later state public utilities commissioner. Brodie's uncle, David O. McKay, was a member of the Quorum of the Twelve when she was born. Her mother's father, George H. Brimhall, served as president of Brigham Young University from 1904 to 1921.

The future dissident fondly recalled her formative years in Hunts-

ville as "an idyllic childhood [insofar] as the freedom and the affection and the sense of belonging to a community was concerned." She
described the family farmhouse as "a great place to grow up" and the
larger Huntsville community as a place that she "loved madly."[4] Her
son Bruce recalled that she "always said that she had a very happy
childhood" and that he could not remember "a single negative thing
she said about it." It was "a sort of Paradise Lost," she recalled.[5]

   During her childhood, Brodie was obedient and deeply religious. She
recalled to her good friend Dale L. Morgan that she had been "supremely good and obedient."[6] On another occasion she remembered
that she had been "a model child" who had "never even indulged in a
healthy amount of mischief."[7] Brodie asserted the virtues of such obedience in her first published work, a poem entitled "Just a Minute,
Mother" that she wrote when she was ten. The poem appeared in 1925
in *The Juvenile Instructor,* a church periodical for children:

> "Just a minute, mother,"
>   Is heard in all child homes,
> From the cottage of the peasants,
>   To the castles with great domes.
>
> If mother tried to count,
>   The 'just a minutes' of each day,
> We'd find that hours and hours
>   Slip uselessly away.
>
> Let's drop our 'just a minutes,'
>   And make our mothers smile,
> And in this time we've wasted
>   Do something that's worth while.[8]

Within her Latter-day Saint religion, Brodie was active both spiritually and socially. She taught a Sunday school class and frequently spoke
or gave poetry readings as a member of the Huntsville Ward.[9] As she
approached adolescence, much of her recreation centered around the
Huntsville Capital Ward's youth group, "the Builders Club." In Huntsville ward meetings, moreover, she expressed her own religious beliefs.
Her brother Thomas recalled that in a particular fast and testimony
meeting, Brodie got up and "bore a beautiful testimony," asserting her
belief in the truthfulness of the restored gospel.[10] On another occasion,
in December 1931, she manifested her strong religious beliefs in a
Christmas story that she gave to a student devotional at Weber College, then a two-year institution run by the Mormon church, which
she attended following graduation from high school. "The Great Rush-

ing of Wings" describes the struggle and hardship of an impoverished widow whose child had been born without the use of his limbs. After suffering much misfortune, and as the result of a divinely inspired Christmas miracle, the crippled child is healed. The story concludes:

> The voice of the priest was hoarse and trembling. "A miracle, indeed, my son, a blessed miracle of faith!"
>
> "Blessed are the pure in heart," he whispered, "for they shall see God!"[11]

Brodie's religiosity appeared strong throughout her formative years. She recalled, "I was devout until I went to the University of Utah."[12] There were, however, indications of her future dissent long before her 1932 departure from Huntsville to Salt Lake City, indications stemming from certain "inner conflicts" relating to her behavior and attitudes as well as from "external conflicts" involving her family and environment.[13]

The inner conflicts arose in part from her superior intelligence and the inferiority she felt because of her physical appearance. The second of five children, she had demonstrated her exceptional intelligence as early as her third year through her ability to memorize and recite lengthy pieces of poetry, showing up her sister, Flora, who was two years her senior. By the time she was four, Brodie was able to read fourth grade-level books with ease. When she was formally enrolled in school at age six, she was given an IQ test and went "over the top score."[14] The principal promptly advanced the bright child to the third grade, and she was subsequently advanced two more grades. When she reached high school she excelled in public speaking and debate, winning two Utah oratorical contests. Brodie's precocity, however, had a price. Because she was three to four years younger than most of her classmates, she was socially "quite insecure" and reticent.[15]

Exacerbating her basic shyness was an extreme sensitivity about her physical appearance. Despite being strikingly beautiful to all who knew her, Brodie saw herself quite differently. "Almost painfully shy about her height," she reached five feet, ten inches when she was still an adolescent, making her taller than all the girls her age and most of the boys.[16] As she continued to grow, according to her elder sister, "tears would flow," for in Brodie's eyes, "tall girls were not popular." Her height combined with her intelligence and classic beauty tended to make her different from the norm as the patriarchal Mormon environment saw it. There the typical Mormon female was expected to be of average intelligence and not too tall, certainly not taller or more intelligent than the males around her. She would not stand out but would comfortably adjust to her expected status of inconspicuous subordi-

nation. "Being tall at puberty was a real hardship to Fawn's ego" recalled Flora. She was, moreover, not reassured by her father's admo-
nitions. "When she started slumping to make herself shorter," Thomas McKay would insist, "You stand up! You're beautiful."[17]

Also setting the stage for Brodie's dissent were the differing religious
views of her father and mother. In the opening section of her 1975 recollections she described both parents as "devout Mormons." Further
on, she remembered her mother as "a kind of quiet heretic which made
it much easier for me." Her mother's "heresy," Brodie recalled, "was
very quiet and took the form, mostly of encouraging me in a quiet way
to be on my own." Her father, by contrast, was "very devout" and
"always pulling me, trying to pull me back into the Mormon community." Such parental tensions "made for some family difficulties."[18]

Such difficulties, moreover, were further compounded by the troubled relationship between Brodie and her father. While she grew up,
communication between the two was limited. This was due, in part,
to McKay's varied responsibilities that took him away from Huntsville
a great deal of the time, leaving Fawn's mother primarily responsible
for raising the children. When he was at home, he worked outside with
Fawn's elder sister and younger brother while she tended to remain
inside, helping her mother. There was, moreover, a complete absence
of dialog between father and daughter. Whenever Fawn would attempt
to raise questions about her religious doubts, her father would only
say, "You've got to believe."[19] "We both found it impossible to communicate on the subject, as on most others" Brodie later recalled, attributing the lack of communication to the family's tendency to avoid
unpleasant subjects scrupulously.[20]

Thus when she arrived in Salt Lake City to attend the University of
Utah in 1932, Brodie experienced "a quiet kind of moving out . . . of
the parochialism of the Mormon community."[21] She "began doubting
the strong ties she had with the Church."[22] Facilitating the process were
the various courses and professors to which she was exposed at the
university, an institution she described as "the seat of anticlericism in
Utah." Here was found "concentrated . . . criticism of the Mormon
hierarchy."[23] She especially recalled her philosophy professor E. E.
Erickson, who through "Socratic questioning . . . gently shook the faith
of some of us who were devout." She remembered reading Milton's
Paradise Lost in one of her English classes, a tale in which Satan, despite being "wrong headed and vulnerable, had heroic qualities and
was far more likeable than the omnipotent Jehovah." The impact on
her religious faith was "subtle but indelible."[24] More important, while
at the university Brodie experienced some shock when she encountered,

for the first time, a vast body of literature that presented the Latterday Saints in a less-than-heroic light. Her discovery came as the result of her employment in the school library, where she repaired damaged books. At the conclusion of her two years at the University of Utah she had come to realize that "the center of the universe was not Salt Lake as I had been taught as a child."[25]

Despite her emerging dissent, Brodie did not discuss her growing doubts with her father or any other family member. Instead, she returned to Ogden, where she taught English at Weber College. In the meantime, she had become romantically involved with Dilworth Jensen, whom she had known for many years while growing up in Huntsville. Brodie described him as "tender, sweet, witty, [and] gallant," noting in her later recollections that she "fell passionately in love." Indeed, dating the Jensen family became a family affair for the McKay sisters; Flora dated Dilworth's elder brother, Leslie. The two couples frequently double-dated. Fawn and Dilworth's relationship was facilitated by the fact that both received graduate fellowships to attend the University of California at Berkeley beginning in the fall of 1935—an unexpected windfall, given the Great Depression.

Brodie's growing dissent, however, caused problems. Dilworth Jensen's commitment to Mormonism was much stronger than hers. He had served for two-and-a half years in the Swiss-German Mission. Thus he became "very frustrated and worried" as he observed Brodie's growing problems with church history and doctrine. Her strong attachment to Jensen notwithstanding, Brodie was concerned about their present and future religious compatibility. A potential impasse was averted when Flora McKay, over her parents' objections, eloped with Leslie Jensen. The McKays apparently feared that Fawn and Dilworth might follow suit, so she and her parents agreed that she would not go to Berkeley but would instead attend graduate school at the University of Chicago.[26]

Fawn Brodie's departure for Chicago was a major turning point in her evolution as a dissenter. Living away from Utah for the first time, "she met . . . people with tremendous intellectual curiosity and completely open minds."[27] More important, as she later recalled, "the confining aspects of the Mormon religion dropped off within a few weeks [after arriving in Chicago]. . . . It was like taking off a hot coat in the summertime. The sense of liberation I had at the University of Chicago was enormously exhilarating. I felt very quickly that I could never go back to the old life, and I never did."[28]

While at Chicago Brodie completely severed her relationship with Dilworth Jensen after meeting Bernard Brodie, a graduate student who came from a Latvian-Jewish immigrant background.[29] The couple married after a whirlwind courtship of just six weeks, on August 25, 1936, the same day she received her M.A. in English.

Shortly, thereafter, the new Mrs. Brodie began serious historical research into Mormon history—research that would ultimately result in her biography of Joseph Smith. The initial research, however, focused not on the founder of Mormonism, but rather on the church's Security Program (later known as the Welfare Program). This research led to Brodie's first but little-known publication in Mormon studies. She was encouraged by her uncle, Dean Brimhall, who was also a dissident. Brimhall had received his Ph.D. in psychology from Columbia University and had served as an administrative assistant in the Department of Labor's management of the Works Progress Administration. Even though the Church Security Program aided many destitute Mormons, Brimhall was critical of it in the wake of the program's establishment in April 1936, as church officials touted it as a Mormon version of the WPA. Brimhall felt that church officials overstated its effectiveness in taking church members off federal relief rolls, finding instead that the number of Mormons receiving public assistance remained high.

When Brodie made her own study of the Church Security Program, she arrived at essentially the same conclusions. Echoing her uncle, she felt that the church was deliberately creating the illusion that it had removed "most or all of its members from public assistance" rolls.[30] But she went one step further, suggesting that the church, in collecting tithes and other donations used in its relief efforts, was "actually making money on the whole business," adding that "if it is true . . . I think it's too good to be kept hidden." Brodie told her uncle, "I have been working up this paper which I hope will be worthwhile to someone if it ever sees the light of publication." But if it were to be published, she added, "I shall take the utmost pains to prevent anyone from home discovering who wrote it. I have too deep a regard for daddy and mother to let them know my present attitude towards the plan, and the church as a whole, especially since I am trying to make a minor move against it."[31]

Less than a year later, her article "Mormon 'Security'" appeared in the February 1938 issue of *The Nation*. As her central theme, Brodie asserted that the Church Security Program fell far short of its advertised goal of keeping its members off various New Deal relief programs, noting instead that the percentage of Utah workers on such programs was from 32 to 60 percent higher than in the nation as a whole. She claimed that "far from endangering its solid financial structure [the church] is actually the gainer from the security plan." Such gains came "in large measure" from "the voluntary labor and donations . . . from the most pious Mormons, the poorer classes, who are already heavily taxed."

These "heavy contributions" in turn had a pernicious effect in that they "materially lowered" the capacity of the average Latter-day Saint "for saving and investing, and for tiding himself over unemployment." To support her case, Brodie then asserted with more than a little irony: "The fact that in 1935 there were proportionally 25 percent more Mormons than Gentiles on relief in Salt Lake County is an indication of the serious depletion in personal resources resulting from the church's exactions from its members, for they cannot truthfully be said to be less thrifty or more industrious than are their Gentile neighbors."

Brodie then warned that "Mormon preachers . . . have reason for worry" because "federal relief is being curtailed," with "the heavy hand of economy" reaching toward the Mormon community. Concluding on a note of irony, she declared, "The Mormons have been preparing for the day of want. The day of want is upon them." Reaction within the Mormon community to Brodie and her article is difficult to gauge, because as she had indicated to her uncle, she chose to conceal her identity and wrote under the pseudonym "Martha Emery." Alluding to the ambiguous relationship with her parents and the church, yet at the same time asserting her dissent, Brodie identified "Martha Emery" in the contributors' section as "a daughter of the Mormon church."[32]

Fawn Brodie's dissent became more open between 1938 and 1945 as she focused her research energies on Joseph Smith. Some debate has emerged over exactly why she chose to undertake her controversial study of Mormonism's founder. In the immediate aftermath of the book's publication, Brodie confessed that the biography "served for me what an autobiographical novel usually does for the young novelist"— a kind of catharsis. "But there was a compulsion to self-expression too, as well as a compulsion to liberate myself wholly from Mormonism, and perhaps also certain family relationships."[33]

On another occasion, she described the writing of the biography as "a desperate effort to come to terms with my childhood."[34] Still later, Brodie indicated the influence of her Jewish husband. Attempting to answer the questions of someone "totally new to the Mormon scene [and] very fascinated by it" stimulated her "to find out the roots and sources of what Joseph Smiths's ideas were." She started out "not to write a biography of Joseph Smith but to write a short article about the sources of the Book of Mormon." But, as she pursued her research, she found there was "no good biography of Joseph Smith" and so undertook the task herself. Still another motive for researching Smith was her role as a dissenter writing for other dissenters: "It was a rather compulsive thing. I had to. It was partly that I wanted to answer a lot of questions for myself. There were many questions that no one had answered for me. I certainly did not get any of the answers in Utah. Having discovered the answers and being excited about them, I felt that I wanted to give other young doubting Mormons a chance to see the evidence. That plus the fact that I had always wanted to write, made it possible—not made it possible—made it imperative that I do a serious piece of history."[35]

One other factor encouraged Brodie in her research: the direct and indirect influence of a number of writers and scholars who also were religious dissenters and who identified with what has been termed "Mormondom's lost generation."[36] A regional literary movement with its genesis in the 1930s, it came to full flower during the 1940s. Like its earlier counterpart in the larger American literary community during the 1920s, the group tended to be alienated from its social-cultural environment. This generation of Latter-day Saints included such writers as Vardis Fisher, Paul Bailey, Maurine Whipple, Virginia Sorenson, and Samuel W. Taylor. It also included two notable non-Mormons with Utah roots, Bernard DeVoto and Wallace Stegner.[37] These writers' wide variety of work on Mormon themes was published by eastern presses and widely reviewed, thus drawing national attention to the whole field of Mormon letters. While representing "an eruption of creative vitality in response to a cultural breakdown" the group celebrated a more "heroic age" and lamented its passing.[38]

Brodie encountered the work of this generation as it appeared during the late 1930s and early 1940s. Direct influence came through her personal interaction with certain individuals who were members of the group. The first was her uncle, Dean Brimhall, whom she characterized variously as a "skeptic," "rebel," and "propagandist," which made him "beyond all question my favorite uncle."[39] As early as 1939, she acknowledged his help in the evolution of her own "naturalistic interpretation" of Joseph Smith. "I have had the most fun," she told him, "with the Book of Mormon & was able to trace almost every idea in it right down to Ontario Co. New York 1827. The lost tribe theory, the exterminated race theory, anti-Masonry, anti-Catholicism—the whole gamut of sectarian religious controversy—all of which make up the Book of Mormon." Brodie then continued: "I think your own analysis is sane & judicious, perhaps because it conforms with my own."[40]

Fawn Brodie was strongly influenced by a second Mormon dissenter, Dale L. Morgan, whom she first met in June 1943. An exact contemporary of Brodie's, Morgan was born in 1915, of Utah Mormon stock and like Brodie attended and graduated from the University of Utah. Despite his deep fascination with Mormonism's past, again like Brodie, he was not an active, practicing Latter-day Saint. Although completely deaf, by 1943 he had already established himself as a respected scholar whose numerous publications included two major books: *Utah: A Guide to the State* (1941) and *The Humboldt: Highroad of the West* (1943).[41] Almost immediately, Brodie and Morgan became fast friends, developing a long-lasting professional relationship. Morgan quickly assumed the role of chief critic "whose indefatigable scholarship in Mormon history" served as "an added spur to my own."[42]

Indeed, Morgan became a mentor to the fledgling author and critiqued a preliminary draft of Brodie's manuscript.[43] With abrupt frankness, he told her that "this draft of your book is not, properly speaking, a biography of Smith" but rather "a history" of the Mormon leader. Specifically, he viewed it as "over-simplified in its point of view." "Your own point of view, as set forth in this manuscript, is much too hard and fast, to my way of thinking," he continued, "it is too coldly logical in its conception of Joseph's mind and the development of his character. Your view of him is all hard edges, without any of those blurrings which are more difficult to cope with but which constitute a man in the round." Elaborating further, Morgan went to the heart of Brodie's thesis: "I am particularly struck with the assumption your MS makes that Joseph was a self-conscious imposter." He then declared that, despite also being a dissenter, he was "not prepared to make any final judgements about" Smith. Brodie's manuscript "was too much in the vein of 'I expose.'"

Morgan wrote that Brodie's "hard and fast" conceptualization of Joseph Smith affected her use of factual information, noting, "Your chain of reasoning looks logical, but it is attended by a string of ifs all along the line (precisely as with the orthodox Mormon reasoning), and the probability of error increases as the chain or reasoning lengthens." He urged her to "exhibit a good deal of humility with respect to the facts" and recommended that the final manuscript "be so written that Mormon, anti-Mormon, and non-Mormon alike can go to the biography and read in it with agreement—disagreeing often in detail, perhaps, but observing that you have noted the points of disagreement and that while you set forth your point of view, you do not claim that you have Absolute Truth by the tail."

Brodie acted on Morgan's recommendations, and a year later, in August 1944, gave him the entire revised manuscript. Morgan read it and returned it with a generally favorable evaluation. He proclaimed Brodie's work "downright fascinating," finding "the research . . . wide and deep without being ostentatious; the prose . . . admirably muscular," and the text "full of stimulating ideas" with a rapidly moving storyline. Most important, he felt that Brodie now had a "biography" rather than a mere "history of Joseph's life."[44]

In addition to Morgan, Brodie received important help from others identified as dissenters or part of Mormondom's lost generation. Claire Noall, also a writer and a photojournalist, provided important information and documents about Smith's practice of polygamy in Nauvoo. Noall was interested in the topic by virtue of her own research, resulting in several books that included *Intimate Disciple,* a biographical novel about her grandfather Willard Richards, who was confidant to both Joseph Smith and Brigham Young.[45] Also providing Brodie with important information on early Mormon polygamy was Stanley Ivins, the son of the one-time Mormon apostle Anthony W. Ivins. The younger Ivins's interest in polygamy "became an obsession" during the 1930s.[46]

A third individual, Vesta Crawford, also provided Brodie with important materials on early polygamy. Crawford, a Utah-based poet and writer, aided Brodie despite her own close ties to the church, as reflected in her position as editorial secretary and later associate editor of the *Relief Society Magazine.*[47] Juanita Brooks also helped Brodie; she, like Crawford, remained close to the church. Brooks, already hard at work on research that culminated in her own controversial books on the Mountain Meadows Massacre and John D. Lee, first met Brodie in 1943. The two women developed a professional and personal relationship based on mutual respect that transcended their sharply differing views about Joseph Smith and Mormon origins. Brooks readily provided Brodie relevant information from her own research, explaining to Dale Morgan, "I admire her courage, and will be glad to furnish anything I can."[48]

Even more interesting was the help that Brodie received from M. Wilford Poulson, a professor of psychology at Brigham Young University. Like Dale Morgan and Stanley Ivins, both of whom he knew well, Poulson was interested in early church history and was an avid collector of old Mormon books and diaries. Poulson was, in the words of one writer, "a closet dissenter" or "disaffected Mormon" with "an inquiring mind." His initial contact with Brodie came, most likely, through Dean Brimhall, a fellow psychologist who at one time had taught with Poulson at BYU. Poulson provided Brodie with some historical materials during the early phases of her research. More important, he apparently influenced her thinking on certain crucial aspects of Smith's career. Poulson apparently told Brodie "frankly" that "he thought Joseph Smith wrote the Book of Mormon to make money." He agreed with Brodie's conception that Thomas Dick's *The Philosophy of a Future State* "was extremely important in fixing the source of many of [Joseph Smith's] metaphysical conceptions." Poulson, like Dale Morgan, assumed the role of literary critic, reading through and critiquing a final draft of *No Man Knows My History* before its publication. After a preliminary reading of the manuscript, Poulson dropped Brodie a note expressing his belief that she "really had something."[49]

At the same time, however, Poulson manifested an ambivalence toward Brodie's work. In March 1945, just before the publication of *No Man Knows My History,* he sent Brodie "a curious little note asking that his name not be used in any form in connection with the book."[50] He then outlined his concerns about the biography: "Frankly, I had hoped your presentation would be more worthy of being characterized as DEFINITIVE. I had hoped [that] you would bring to bear the appropriate canons of historical criticism upon your sources." Then, getting to the nub of his criticism, Poulson proclaimed, "I believe that the future truly great biography of the Prophet Joseph Smith will not ungenerously trim him down to the proportions of a liar, an impostor, an adulterer and anything else mostly bad." But Poulson did concede to Brodie that "many good things" would result from her book and that it was "bound to stimulate wide and careful reading, pro and con" into the early history of the church.[51]

Indeed, *No Man Knows My History* did stimulate a variety of reactions—from applause to attack—following its publication in late 1945. Applause came mainly from writers and commentators based outside of Utah, particularly on the East Coast, where the book had been published. Most of the attacks came from Utah, primarily from individuals and publications identified with the Mormon church.[52] The most potent from within official Mormondom occurred in June 1946, when Brodie was formally excommunicated. In her official church summons, she was charged with apostasy: "You assert matters as truths which deny the divine origin of the Book of Mormon, the restoration of the Priesthood and of Christ's Church through the instrumentality of the Prophet Joseph Smith, contrary to the beliefs, doctrines, and teachings of the Church."[53]

In the eyes of Mormon officials, Fawn Brodie was no longer a mere dissenter acting from within the church but was henceforth a heretic banished beyond the Pale of Mormondom. She experienced some inner conflict in response to this drastic turn of events. According to one account, "she came to [her uncle] Dean Brimhall in tears, and . . . could hardly be comforted because she was so disrupted to be disfellow-shipped."[54] In response to the incident and reflecting her own long-standing ambivalence as a dutiful daughter, Brodie wrote to her parents, "I hope Dean didn't give you an exaggerated picture of my own attitude. It was just that I could see so clearly what it might mean for you and Daddy . . . I felt badly about it in the beginning because it seemed to symbolize how completely I had burned my bridges behind me."[55]

Despite her formal excommunication, Brodie continued to criticize Mormondom, and her views were expressed in essays that appeared in various national publications. In April 1946, shortly after the publication of *No Man Knows My History,* she produced a highly critical essay, "Polygamy Shocks the Mormons," which appeared in the *American Mercury.*[56] The essay was written in response to the arrest, conviction, and imprisonment of fifteen fundamentalist Mormons by Utah law enforcement officers in June 1944. The action, taken with the full support of Latter-day Saint authorities, represented "a strange reversal" or "curious evolution" in that Utah Mormondom was "as united against [the fundamentalists] as it was united [back in the nine-teenth century] in defending polygamy and defying the United States government."

Brodie asked the pointed question, How was it that the "overwhelm-ing majority of Mormons" could "so soon forget the savage persecu-tion of their fathers and grandfathers" and "ignore the famous mar-riage law which was so long a fundamental tenet of their theology" looking instead "with apathy or outright hostility upon the zealous handful who still cling to it"? She then proceeded to "answer" her question by attributing the current Mormon position to "a legacy of unconscious shame." Brodie noted that by the 1890s when the Mor-mons had moved to abandon polygamy, this unconventional marital practice had become "a social anachronism in Puritan America." Mor-mons, moreover, like "most other middle-class Americans . . . longed for respectability." In the current climate, Brodie continued, "Mormon historians are now not only anxious to forget the past, but actively suppress the activities of would-be researchers in Mormon archives." Thus "the magnificent immoderation with which Joseph Smith em-braced polygamy has been forgotten" along with his other "human qualities." What remains is a Joseph Smith who is "a kind of deity, a holy figure." Brodie then concluded that it was "small wonder" that the fundamentalist Mormons were "so resented" by mainstream Lat-ter-day Saints. "For by practicing and advocating polygamy they not only revive the general sense of shame and guilt which has been so successfully buried beneath a complexity of rationalizations and dimming memories, but also they cast a blight on the holy image of Joseph Smith."

A year later, in July 1947, on the centennial of Brigham Young's entry into the Great Salt Lake Valley, Brodie wrote a second essay that was published in the *New York Times Magazine* on July 20. Entitled "This Is the Place—And It Became Utah," the essay began with a brief, generally conventional historical overview of the changes that had affected both Utah and Mormonism in the hundred years since 1847. She noted, for example, that the Mormon church had "slowly and imperceptibly . . . receded from a position of complete domination over the political, economic, and moral aspects of Mormon life."

Brodie, however, was more provocative in discussing other aspects of Mormonism. She saw "the combination of idealism and solidarity which constitutes the Mormon heritage" as "responsible for [some] strange contradictions." Among the most evident was a Mormon emphasis on obedience to church authority while at the same time promoting the individual ideal of human perfectibility based on knowledge. "The church organization," she observed, "is strictly authoritarian, and the leaders, tenacious alike of their traditions and of their power, exhort their people first of all to be obedient. But if obedience to ecclesiastical authority is the primary law of the church, a belief in human perfectibility is its loftiest theological ideal." Then, clearly alluding to the origins and evolution of her own dissent, Brodie concluded, "There results, therefore, an unceasing conflict between uncompromising fundamentalism and the eager striving for perfection which is the basis of Mormon educational philosophy. For the very education of which Mormonism is so proud breeds skepticism and often outright rejection of Mormon doctrine."

Despite such expressions of dissent and criticism, Brodie spent much less time in the field of Mormon studies during the years following the completion of her Joseph Smith biography. Instead, over the course of the next forty years, she produced four major biographies of individuals completely outside of Mormonism. These included *Thaddeus Stevens: Scourge of the South* (1959), which focused on the congressional leader of Radical Republican Reconstruction. That was followed by *The Devil Drives: A Life of Sir Richard Burton*, which appeared in 1967 and concerned the life and activities of the famed British explorer and writer. In 1974 came the highly controversial *Thomas Jefferson: An Intimate History* and then her final work, *Richard Nixon: The Shaping of His Character*, in 1981.[57]

Brodie, however, continued to take an active interest in the work of others in the field of Mormon studies—an interest most vividly reflected in "New Writers and Mormonism," an essay that she wrote for *Frontier Magazine* in 1952.[58] She discussed "the phenomenon of the Mormon writer" within the context of her own dissent, elaborating on the work of other writers who also were part of Mormondom's lost generation. Such writers, she noted, are "able young men and women" who had "been raised either in the Church or alongside it" and had "found Mormonism either so fascinating or so provocative that they have been unable to resist the urge to reckon with it in print." More important, "they stand outside the official proselyters; in fact most of them are outside of the Church altogether, in spirit if not in fact." But these new writers, Brodie quickly observed, contrasted sharply with the classic anti-Mormon writers of the nineteenth and early twentieth century who "counted Mormonism a dragon to be slain." Instead, the new writers had "the ambition to be serious novelists and historians, and strive earnestly, if not always successfully for impartiality." Outlining their position as dissenters, Brodie continued, "[These] writers . . . however determined to be detached, urbane and if possible philosophic about the society which irrevocably shaped their childhood, still find themselves torn between filial loyalties and a fierce hunger for independence"—a clear allusion to her own situation.

The all-important relationship of the writers "with the [Mormon] Church," Brodie continued, "is an uneasy one." The Mormon "governing body in Salt Lake City is not publicly proud of the best Mormon novelists—Vardis Fisher, Virginia Sorenson, Maurine Whipple, and Ardyth Kennelly" and even "more suspicious . . . of its young historians" such as Dale Morgan and Juanita Brooks, "rightly counting them as a potential threat." But Mormon officials, instead of "blasting" such writers "out of the Church, as would have [been] done for the same literature a half century ago . . . contents itself with unhappy book reviews in the official *Improvement Era.*"

Brodie concluded on an optimistic note, suggesting the emergence of a more liberal climate for dissenting writers and historians. "The old terror of persecution has vanished, with the result that within the Church there is in general far greater tolerance of the dissenting voice and the genuinely creative spirit." The reason for this more tolerant attitude, Brodie suggested, was due to the relatively secure position of the Mormon church in contrast to the organization that found itself under siege from both within and without during much of the nineteenth and early twentieth centuries. The present church, she observed, "is now well entrenched, powerful and marvelously cohesive."

Despite such optimism and the fact that her major research interests carried her outside of Mormon studies, Brodie remained critical of certain Mormon attitudes and practices. She was particularly bothered by relations between Mormons and blacks and became an active critic of the now-defunct Latter-day Saint policy of excluding blacks from ordination to the Mormon priesthood. It was an issue on which she spoke out for the better part of four decades, probing the historical roots of Mormonism's black policy in three different works.[59]

In *No Man Knows My History* she was the first to acknowledge the negative nature of Mormonism's exclusionary policy toward blacks, characterizing it as "the ugliest thesis in existing Mormon theology."[60] She was also the first to probe the origins of the practice, placing it within a sociohistorical framework that stripped away the religious myth and mystery surrounding it and undermining its doctrinal legitimacy. As the church found itself under increased fire throughout the 1950s and into the 1960s for this exclusionary policy, Brodie continued to criticize it, primarily in her correspondence with various friends and associates.

In September 1970 she confronted the issue head on in a public address in Salt Lake City. "Can We Manipulate the Past?" was given in the Lafayette Ballroom of the Mormon church-owned Hotel Utah to a standing-room-only crowd of more than five hundred. Brodie asserted that the church had, for years, been "manipulating" or misreading its own past in order to justify its policy of black priesthood denial. Moreover, she questioned the use of the Book of Abraham as "scriptural precedent" for denying blacks the Mormon priesthood, characterizing it as "the least securely established" of Mormonism's canonized sacred works. Brodie concluded, "The distillation of the past . . . should not be purposefully mischievous and destructive. The past should not control the decisions we make today, especially if they are decisions reinforcing injustice."[61]

She further developed her critique concerning the origins of Mormon ideas on race and the status of blacks in a revised second edition of *No Man Knows My History* published in 1971. There, she focused mainly on the problems of authenticity surrounding the Book of Abraham.[62] Finally, in June 1978 Brodie enjoyed some satisfaction when, at long last, the church lifted its ban against ordaining blacks to the priesthood. Ironically, she was in Salt Lake City at the time and proclaimed it "a great day to be there."[63]

Such satisfaction, however, was short-lived. Two years later, in September 1980, Brodie was diagnosed with cancer, this coming on the heels of her husband's death in November 1978 from the same mala-

dy. By late 1980 her condition worsened and she required hospitaliza-
tion. In the meantime, two stories circulated concerning Brodie's past
and present relationship to the Mormon church. The first suggested
that in the immediate aftermath of the appearance of *No Man Knows
My History* she had specifically asked to be excommunicated. Thus,
in purging her name from church rolls in June 1946, church officials
were merely acquiescing to her request. This, of course, was untrue.[64]

A second story circulating in early 1981 was that Brodie had asked
to be rebaptized into the church. In fact, versions of this story had circulated since the publication of *No Man Knows My History*. The story was given impetus when Brodie's brother, Thomas B. McKay, visited her in the hospital in late December 1980. According to Brodie's
own account: "I was very glad to see [Thomas] and asked for a blessing—as my father had communicated blessings over the years as a kind
of family patriarch. This blessing he gave me, and I told him I was
grateful, saying he had said what I had wanted him to say."[65] She revealed a lingering inner conflict, however: "My delight in asking for
an opportunity for a blessing at that moment indicated simply the in-
tensity of an old hunger." But then she carefully added: "Any exag-
geration about my requests for a blessing meaning that I was asking
to be taken back into the Church at that moment I strictly repudiate
and would for all time."

A few days later, on January 10, 1981, Fawn Brodie died at age six-
ty-five. In accordance with her wishes, her body was cremated and the
ashes scattered over the Santa Monica Mountains near Pacific Palisades,
California, where she had spent the last thirty years of her life. Thus
she affirmed her position as a dissenter, albeit an ambivalent one, right
up to the end.

It is evident that Fawn Brodie's emergence as twentieth-century
Mormonism's most famous female dissenter was due to a complex set
of circumstances, particularly those of her background and upbring-
ing. Her childhood environment had been sheltered, and the extremely obedient Fawn was anxious to please her parents and others in authority. It was also a repressed environment in which the bright,
articulate youngster was inhibited from speaking out or discussing controversial issues. Thus when she left Huntsville to attend the University of Utah she found herself exposed to ideas and individuals that at
first challenged and eventually helped to undermine her Mormon faith.
These developments occurred at a time of great literary ferment manifested by Mormondom's lost generation, a group of writers and historians who profoundly influenced the course and direction of Brodie's
own literary activities during the 1930s and 1940s.

Brodie, as an emerging Mormon dissenter, "felt an intense sense of

betrayal" concerning Joseph Smith but at the same time "was working through . . . an equally intense childhood love" for the man.[66] She
came to believe that she had been "conned" and that "the whole problem of [Joseph Smith's] credibility was crying out for some explanation."[67] This strong sense of dissenting fervor, in turn, caused Brodie
to remain critical of Mormondom throughout the remainder of her life,
taking the church to task for its policy relative to blacks and its treatment of fundamentalist Mormons. Maintaining strong family ties was
of primary importance. She and her husband, despite what their son
termed "not an easy marriage," remained together for forty-two years
until Bernard's death. Brodie was, moreover, a devoted mother, acutely aware of the time necessary to properly raise her three children: Richard, who was born in 1942, Bruce in 1946, and Pamela in 1950.
She asserted on more than one occasion that being a mother gave her
much greater satisfaction than writing books. "Children are more re-
warding than books." Unlike children, "once a book is finished it is
the deadest thing in the world."[68]

Near the end of her life, Brodie became increasingly interested in
the specific issue of women and their past and present status within
Mormonism. She was no radical feminist, however. The issue of the
role of women within Mormonism came to a head in 1979 with the
excommunication of Sonia Johnson in the wake of her militant support of the Equal Rights Amendment. Johnson's stance opposed the
church's official position against the ERA, and the case received as
much publicity in the national media as Brodie's own excommunication some thirty years before. Indeed, in a short encounter Brodie reportedly told the recently excommunicated Johnson: "I think you [have]
usurped my place as the leading female Judas Iscariot" within Mormondom.[69] Sterling M. McMurrin, however, a well-known critic of
Mormon policies and practices, viewed Fawn Brodie and her impact
on Mormondom in a somewhat different light. Through her dissent,
Brodie helped usher in "A New Climate of Liberation" insofar as
Mormon letters were concerned: "Because of *No Man Knows My History*, Mormon history produced by Mormon scholars has moved toward more openness, objectivity and honesty."[70] Whatever the case, it
is clear that Fawn McKay Brodie was twentieth-century Mormonism's
most noteworthy dissenting female historian and quintessential critic.

NOTES

1. These descriptions of Huntsville and of the David McKay family home
are drawn from Fawn M. Brodie, "Biography of Fawn McKay Brodie," oral
history interview conducted by Shirley E. Stephenson, November 30, 1975,

original in Oral History Collection, Fullerton State University, Fullerton, California. Also see Fawn M. Brodie, "Inflation Idyll: A Family Farm in Huntsville," *Utah Historical Quarterly* 40 (1972): 112–21.

2. Brodie, "Biography of Fawn McKay Brodie," 10.

3. Aside from Shirley E. Stephenson's 1975 oral history interview, Brodie's sisters and brother are the most useful sources for her early life. Flora McKay Crawford has recorded her memories, "Flora on Fawn," [N.d.], typescript in my possession; and Barbara McKay Smith, "Recollections of Fawn M. Brodie," as presented at the Alice Louise Reynolds Forum, Provo, Utah [1982], typescript in my possession.

4. Brodie, "Biography of Fawn McKay Brodie," 2.

5. Bruce R. Brodie, "Monologue on Fawn M. Brodie: Biographical Data," December 8, 1983, 2, Fawn M. Brodie Papers, Special Collections, University of Utah Library.

6. Fawn M. Brodie to Dale L. Morgan, December 10, 1945, Dale L. Morgan Papers, Bancroft Library, University of California, Berkeley.

7. Brodie to Morgan, March 12, 1946.

8. Fawn McKay, "Just a Minute, Mother," *The Juvenile Instructor,* November 1925, 627.

9. Keith Jensen, oral interview conducted by Newell G. Bringhurst, August 20, 1988.

10. Thomas B. McKay, oral interview conducted by Newell G. Bringhurst, July 28, 1986.

11. "Story Given by Miss Fawn McKay," December 16, 1931, unpublished typescript in Weber State University Archives, Ogden, Utah.

12. Brodie, "Biography of Fawn McKay Brodie," 2.

13. For a discussion of the impact of these varied conflicts on the course and nature of Brodie's later writings, see Newell G. Bringhurst, "Fawn M. Brodie—Her Biographies as Autobiography," *Pacific Historical Review* 59 (May 1990): 203–25.

14. Flora McKay Crawford, oral interview conducted by Newell G. Bringhurst, September 29, 1988.

15. Pamela Brodie, oral interview conducted by Newell G. Bringhurst, January 8, 1988; Thomas B. McKay, oral interview conducted by Newell G. Bringhurst, July 24, 1987.

16. Marshall Burgess, "Fawn and Bernard Brodie: They Write, Teach, Study and Research," *Los Angeles Times Home Magazine,* February 20, 1977, reprinted as "A Talk with Fawn Brodie," *National Retired Teachers Association Journal,* July–August, 1977, 8.

17. Crawford, "Flora on Fawn," 4; Flora McKay Crawford, oral interview conducted by Newell G. Bringhurst, September 30, 1988.

18. Brodie, "Biography of Fawn McKay Brodie," 1–4.

19. Louise McKay Card, oral interview conducted by Newell G. Bringhurst, August 1, 1986.

20. Fawn M. Brodie to Dean Brimhall, November 4, 1959, Dean Brimhall Papers, Special Collections, Marriott Library, University of Utah.

21. Brodie, "Biography of Fawn McKay Brodie," 2–3.

22. Crawford, "Flora on Fawn."

23. Brodie, "Biography of Fawn McKay Brodie," 13.

24. Fawn M. Brodie, "It Happened Very Quietly," in *Remembering: The University of Utah,* ed. Elizabeth Haglung (Salt Lake City: University of Utah Press, 1981), 85–95.

25. Flora McKay Crawford, oral interview, September 30, 1988; Brodie, "Biography of Fawn McKay Brodie, 3.

26. Fawn M. Brodie to Elizabeth Jensen Shafter, October 16, 1980, copy in my possession; Pamela Brodie, oral interview conducted by Newell G. Bringhurst, January 8, 1988; Patricia Jensen, oral interview conducted by Newell G. Bringhurst, January 7, 1988; Flora McKay Crawford, oral interview, September 30, 1988.

27. Bruce R. Brodie, "Monologue on Fawn M. Brodie," 5.

28. Brodie, "Biography of Fawn McKay Brodie," 3.

29. For two good overviews of Bernard Brodie in terms of his life and activities, see Fred Kaplan, *The Wizards of Armageddon* (New York: Simon and Schuster, 1983), and Gregg Herken, *Counsels of War* (New York: Alfred A. Knopf, 1987). For a discussion of Brodie in terms of his ideas, see Barry H. Steiner, *Bernard Brodie and the Foundations of American Nuclear Strategy* (Lawrence: University of Kansas Press, 1991).

30. Fawn M. Brodie to Dean Brimhall, April 13, 1937, Brimhall Papers. On this program, see John Heinerman and Anson Shupe, *The Mormon Corporate Empire* (Boston: Beacon Press, 1985), 181–87.

31. In Brodie's letter to Dean Brimhall, April 13, 1937, Brimhall Papers, she added "of course the Church probably isn't really making money, but at any rate it is clear that the people themselves are financing every bit of the plan & and paying extra tithing besides. No Church capital is being endangered."

32. Martha Emery [pseudonym], "Mormon 'Security'," *Nation,* February 12, 1937, 182–83, 196.

33. Fawn M. Brodie to Dale L. Morgan, January 19, 1946, Morgan Papers.

34. Fawn M. Brodie to Dean Brimhall, November 4, 1959, Brimhall Papers.

35. Brodie, "Biography of Fawn McKay Brodie," 6, 10.

36. For an excellent discussion of this literary movement, see Edward A. Geary, "Mormondom's Lost Generation: The Novelists of the 1940s," *Brigham Young University Studies* 18 (Fall 1977): 89–98.

37. See Vardis Fisher, *Children of God: An American Epic* (New York: Harper, 1939); Paul Bailey, *For This My Glory* (Los Angeles: Lyman House, 1940), *Sam Brannan and the California Mormons* (Los Angeles: Lyman House, 1943), and *The Gay Saint* (Hollywood: Murray and Gee, 1944); Maurine Whipple, *The Giant Joshua* (Boston: Houghton Mifflin, 1941); Virginia Sorenson, *A Little Lower than the Angels* (New York: Reynall and Hitchcock, 1942), and *On This Star* (New York: Reynall and Hitchcock, 1946); Samuel W. Taylor, *Heaven Knows Why* (New York: A. A. Wyn, 1949), and *The Man with My Face* (New York: A. A. Wyn, 1949). See also Bernard DeVoto's early and quite critical and often sarcastic essays: "Utah," *American Mercury* 7

(March 1926) and "Centennial of Mormonism," *American Mercury* 19 (January 1930). DeVoto wrote on the Mormon experience in a somewhat more moderate and more scholarly tone in his widely acclaimed *The Year of Decision: 1846* (Boston: Little, Brown, 1943). For Wallace Stegner, see *Mormon Country* (New York: Duell, Sloan, and Pearce, 1942).

38. Geary, "Mormondom's Lost Generation," 89.

39. Fawn M. Brodie to Dale L. Morgan, January 6 and 20, 1945, Morgan Papers. Also see Brodie's general comments and analysis of these writers' works in "New Writers and Mormonism," *Frontier Magazine*, October 1952, 17–19. For a more complete discussion of the subject, see Newell G. Bringhurst, "Fawn M. Brodie, 'Mormondom's Lost Generation,' and No Man Knows My History," *Journal of Mormon History* 16 (1990): 11–23.

40. Fawn M. Brodie to Dean Brimhall, June 14, 1939, Brimhall Papers.

41. For the best account of Dale L. Morgan's life and activities, see John Phillip Walker, ed., *Dale Morgan on Early Mormonism* (Salt Lake City: Signature Books, 1986).

42. Fawn M. Brodie, *No Man Knows My History: The Life of Joseph Smith, the Mormon Prophet* (New York: Alfred A. Knopf, 1945), xi.

43. "Memo from Dale Morgan," N.d., original in Fawn M. Brodie Papers.

44. Dale L. Morgan to Fawn M. Brodie, August 28, 1944, Fawn M. Brodie Papers. Also reprinted in *Dale Morgan on Early Mormonism*, ed. Walker, 67–71.

45. Biographical material on Claire Noall is contained in her obituaries, see *Salt Lake Tribune*, September 3, 1971, *Deseret News* [Salt Lake City], September 3, 1971. Correspondence between Noall and Brodie vividly tracing their common research interests and general relationship is contained in the Claire Noall Papers, Special Collections, Marriott Library, University of Utah.

46. "Introduction," *Register to Stanley Snow Ivins' Collection*, 1–3, Utah State Historical Society, Salt Lake City.

47. For a brief description of the activities of Vesta Crawford, see Allene A. Jensen, "Utah Writers of the Twentieth Century: A Reference Tool," M.S. thesis, University of Utah, 1977, 27.

48. For an incisive overview of the life and activities of Juanita Brooks as a Mormon dissenter, see Levi S. Peterson, *Juanita Brooks: Mormon Woman Historian* (Salt Lake City: University of Utah Press, 1988), quote from 141.

49. Peterson, *Juanita Brooks*, 65, 266–67; Fawn M. Brodie to Dale L. Morgan, December 7, 1943, September 26, 1944, October 26, 1944, December 5, 1944, February 7, 1946, March 22, 1946, Morgan Papers.

50. Fawn M. Brodie to Dale L. Morgan, March 24, 1945. In describing Poulson's behavior, Brodie noted: "He gave all the reasons except the true one. Of course, I don't blame him, and in a way I am relieved, for I should hate to have been the cause of his getting into trouble with the Church. He's in a ticklish enough spot as it is. Nevertheless, his refusal is a sorry commentary on the state of academic freedom at the 'Y.'"

51. Wilford Poulson to Fawn M. Brodie, January 5, 1945, Fawn M. Brodie Papers.

52. For a discussion of the varied reactions, see Newell G. Bringhurst, "Applause, Attack, and Ambivalence—Varied Responses to Fawn M. Brodie's *No Man Knows My History*," *Utah Historical Quarterly* 57 (Winter 1989): 46–63.

53. William H. Reeder, Jr., to Fawn M. Brodie, May 23, 1946, Fawn M. Brodie Papers.

54. As related by Wallace Stegner in *Conversations with Wallace Stegner on Western History and Literature*, ed. Richard W. Etulain (Salt Lake City: University of Utah Press, 1983), 109–10.

55. Fawn M. Brodie to Thomas E. and Fawn B. McKay, June 2, 1946, Fawn M. Brodie Papers.

56. Fawn M. Brodie, "Polygamy Shocks the Mormons," *American Mercury* 62 (April 1946): 399–405.

57. For a discussion of the process of writing and influences on Brodie relative to these later works, see Bringhurst, "Fawn M. Brodie: Her Biographies as Autobiography," Bringhurst, "Fawn Brodie's Richard Nixon: The Making of a Controversial Biography," *California History* 70 (Winter 1991–92): 379–91, 424–5, and Bringhurst, "Fawn Brodie's Thomas Jefferson: The Making of a Popular—but Controversial Biography," unpublished paper given at annual meeting of the Society for the Early American Republic at Madison, Wisconsin, July 1991.

58. Fawn M. Brodie, "New Writers and Mormonism," *Frontier Magazine* 6 (December 1952): 17–19.

59. For a discussion of Brodie's role as a critic of Mormonism's racial policy, see Newell G. Bringhurst, "Fawn M. Brodie as a Critic of Mormonism's Policy toward Blacks: A Historiographical Reassessment," *John Whitmer Historical Association Journal* 11 (1991): 34–46.

60. Brodie, *No Man Knows My History*, 131–33.

61. Fawn M. Brodie, "Can We Manipulate the Past?" First Annual American West Lecture (Salt Lake City: University of Utah Press, 1970).

62. Fawn M. Brodie, *No Man Knows My History*, 2d ed. (New York: Alfred A. Knopf, 1971), 421–25.

63. Fawn M. Brodie to Jan Shipps, September 16, 1978, Fawn M. Brodie Papers.

64. Brodie's request for excommunication was reported in a January 10, 1981, Associated Press story that said that she "had asked for excommunication." See "Fawn McKay Brodie Dies: Known for Biographies of Jefferson, Mormon Leader," *Washington Post*, January 13, 1981. This was denied by Brodie's sister Barbara McKay Smith in a January 19, 1981 Associated Press story, "Relatives of Fawn Brodie Dispute Statement on Excommunication," *Los Angeles Times*, January 19, 1981. Smith stated that Brodie "had never asked to be excommunicated but had chosen not to answer a summons in June 1946 to an ecclesiastical trial called by her local church leaders in Cambridge, Mass."

65. Fawn M. Brodie, "To Whom It May Concern," December 31, 1980, Fawn M. Brodie Papers.

66. Brodie, "Monologue on Fawn M. Brodie," 12.

67. Brodie, "Biography of Fawn McKay Brodie," 7.

68. Brodie, "Monologue on Fawn M. Brodie," 9; Brodie, "Biography on Fawn McKay Brodie," 47–48.

69. Quoted in Richard S. Van Wagoner, "Fawn Brodie: The Woman and Her History," *Sunstone* 7 (July–August 1982): 37.

70. Sterling M. McMurrin, "A New Climate of Liberation: A Tribute to Fawn McKay Brodie, 1915–1981," *Dialogue: A Journal of Mormon Thought* 14 (Spring 1981): 73–76.

14

Maurine Whipple:
The Quiet Dissenter

Jessie L. Embry

Dissent has many definitions. It can involve differences of opinion "from an established church in the matter of doctrines, rites, or government." With such a broad definition, a dissenter could vary from someone such as David Whitmer, who left a church but continued to accept some of its doctrines, to people such as Sandra and Jerald Tanner, who completely left a church and then set out to disprove it. But it could also refer to someone who never formally left a church but ceased activity in it and questioned the institution's leaders and authority.

Maurine Whipple falls into the latter category. The author of *The Giant Joshua*, a novel on Mormon polygamy and the settlement of St. George, Utah, and a nonfiction tourist book, *This Is the Place: Utah*, Whipple remained very much a cultural but not an active Mormon throughout her life. She shared many characteristics of other novelists who wrote during the 1940s, referred to as "the lost generation" by Brigham Young University English professor Edward A. Geary, but unlike some others she continued to live in Utah.[1] Although not an outspoken dissenter, Whipple's life presents a useful study of how her perceptions ill-affected her ability to write, her chosen profession, as well as her religious beliefs.[2]

This discussion is based on Maurine Whipple's personal papers, which are housed in the Manuscript Division of the Harold B. Lee Library at Brigham Young University.[3] Throughout her life Whipple kept everything from Christmas cards and post cards to rough drafts of letters and manuscripts. She was a conscientious correspondent, answering every fan letter and often developing close friendships with those who admired her work. All of this information gives a clearer picture of how Whipple comprehended the world and the people around her. Although her impressions were often garbled, they influenced how she reacted to others and determined her course of action. Because so often they were only her views of the situations, where possible her opinions will be compared to others. Where it is futile to check her stories, her description of the events at least shows why she felt betrayed and became disillusioned with the Mormon church.

Maurine Whipple was born January 20, 1903, in St. George, the eldest daughter of Charles and Annie Lenzi McAllister Whipple. Her grandparents were Mormon pioneers. Brigham Young sent her maternal grandfather, John Daniel Thompson McAllister, to southern Utah, where he became a church leader, serving as president of the St. George and Manti temples. He had nine wives; Cornelia Agatha Lenzi McAllister, Whipple's grandmother, was his third. Her father, Martin Lenzi, joined the church in Philadelphia. When his wife, Elizabeth Jane Height Lenzi, was not interested in the church and would not move to Utah, he came west with the children and eventually married five more times. Elizabeth Lenzi died in 1903, and a year later Cornelia performed the temple ordinance work, having her mother endowed and sealed to her parents. Whipple's paternal grandfather, Eli Whipple, was born in New York and then moved to Utah. He eventually had three wives. After living in Pine Valley and St. George, he went to Mexico with his third wife, Mary Jane Legg. Maurine Whipple's paternal grandmother, Caroline Lytle, the second wife, stayed in Utah. The Mormon culture, especially its fundamental distinctive doctrine, polygamy, was ingrained in Maurine Whipple.

The eldest of six children, Whipple believed she had a difficult and persevering childhood.[4] From the time she was ten, she felt that she was carrying the weight of the entire family. "My parents always seemed like my children to me—in all my life it never occurred to me to go to them for help." When brother George was born, Whipple recalled, her mother was in bed for eight months, and she had to care for the new baby and do the housework. When she returned to school, the family was extremely poor, and Whipple was forced to take a part time job running a popcorn machine. Even so, she was proud of the fact that she maintained a straight A average. Throughout much of her life she continued to presume that she was the main support for her family. As she wrote in 1952, "I've had to send brothers through school, keep my brother-in-law in the hospital, help clothe their kids, help build their house, buy medicines for my mother, etc. Not that I'm complaining; . . . to me a family is important—more important than I'll ever be."[5]

Whipple remembered religion as a hotly debated topic in her home: "When I was small, I couldn't understand why, but I understood the quarrel, and resented it passionately."[6] Most of the quarrel, she realized, revolved around her father's lack of commitment to Mormonism. He "loved books and learning and travel and had no interest in orthodox religion." Her mother, on the other hand, "loved music—and religion. In fact she so loved religion that it blinded and biased her, and when the husband denied the religion of her choice, she 'punished' him by having a nervous breakdown, as women sometimes do."[7] Whipple seemed to always have resented this conflict.

Growing up in St. George, Whipple was mesmerized by happenings outside of her small world. She wanted to know about "a Somewhere remote and mysterious and utterly intoxicating." She was especially concerned about all the people out there that the Mormons called "Gentiles." She wondered:

> Did the beings who dwelt in its outer darkness know that they were doomed? . . . It worried me. . . . What was it like to be unsure of salvation? Perhaps it was like having all D's in the eighth grade and not knowing whether you would graduate. Why was it God loved some people so much more than he did others? It must be terrible to be a gentile and go through life as if you were walking on eggs, not sure of reaching even the lowest of the three heavens. At this point I usually hugged myself, because after all I was a Saint and therefore safely among the elect.[8]

But at the same time she was grateful that she was not Gentile, Whipple wanted to know all she could about them. The only non-Mormon she knew as a youth "ran the Presbyterian church" in nearby Sandtown, but that person had been there for so long that everyone called her sister, a title usually restricted to Mormons. "All in all, I was sure most of the 'gentile' had been rubbed off . . . long ago, and she, too, would be saved." Other than that, Whipple only knew Jack-Mormons such as Warren Cox, who ran the local hotel and "as an addict loves his drug, . . . loved his fellow man." Although Cox was not a real Mormon, "he didn't smoke or drink or take the Lord's name in vain, and those were the big gentile sins. In spite of public opinion I was sure the 'Mormon' was ingrained in Warren so deeply that he never could rub it off. He would still be the elect."[9]

Whipple got her chance to meet her first real "Gentile" when she went to Salt Lake City to attend the University of Utah. She rode with a Mrs. Hartog from St. George, and because the trip took two days, Whipple had "to spend the night with her." "Imagine sleeping with a gentile!" she later commented. But she quickly found out that she was also an oddity to Hartog.[10]

While Whipple was in Salt Lake City, she came in contact with numerous non-Mormons for the first time in her life and was impressed. They seemed to have "more money, and all pledged the best sororities." The boys also had better manners; unlike the Mormon boys, they didn't "expect . . . a girl to pay her own way on a date, but the boy's way too. You had to admit it: not only the gentile girls, but the boys seemed a cut above." Whipple recalled that "the high point of my college career—[was] the night of my gentile date," when "I knew a moment of pure triumph. For once I rated as highly as if I had never been a Mormon!" While sitting in a car going up Emigration Canyon, Whipple tried to explain to her uninitiated date what Mormonism meant; "tried to tell him more for my own sake than his; tried to establish in the telling some reason in a tragic history that often to my generation seemed so reasonless."[11]

After graduating from the University of Utah in 1925, Whipple wanted to work with "the magic of words." Her university professors had encouraged her to write, but she forfeited her "personal dreams" and "elected to teach school so that the brothers and sisters could have an education with some of the frills that she'd missed." Although she lost her first teaching position because she was a "sucker for lost causes" and attempted to help remove a principal accused but not convicted of killing a child, Whipple then got a job teaching in Idaho "in 50-below zero weather," where she got "appendicitis and peritonitis." While recovering, she wrote a "novelette" entitled *Beaver Dam Wash*. A friend mailed it to a publisher, and "the publisher wired her to quit teaching and go to writing. He said she had gifts."[12] She also went to a conference in Colorado and there came into contact with editors who were impressed by her style and encouraged her efforts. As a result she decided to quit teaching and concentrate on her writing. She submitted the ideas for a book on polygamy among the Mormons to Houghton-Mifflin and won a $1,000 fellowship from that company in 1938 to support her literary activities.

During the next three years she struggled to produce *The Giant Joshua*. She worked especially closely with one editor, Ferris Greenslet. Because she had no income, Whipple asked him to help her submit short stories to magazines. The first went to a number of journals, but they all turned it down. When the *Southern Review* agreed to accept it with revisions, however, Greenslet suggested that Whipple hold off making the changes until she finished the novel. To help deal with Whipple's financial dilemma, in 1939 Greenslet helped her obtain an appointment for room and board at the prestigious Yaddo writers' colony in upstate New York.[13]

The appointment was a tangible recognition of Whipple's talents as a serious writer. Although pleased, she did not find Yaddo a conducive environment for writing her Mormon novel. The colony had apparently set well with such first-cabin writers as Katherine Anne Porter and John Cheever, but Whipple found it difficult to adjust to the isolation that the colony demanded and complained about her extreme loneliness and need to relate more with other people. She complained to everyone who would listen about the inadequacies of Yaddo. Greenslet responded to her complaints with sympathy but firmness: "sorry for your loneliness, but you should judge from my experience that pain is very favorable to successful literary composition."[14] He urged her to stay at Yaddo, enjoy the discipline of the literary life, and complete her book. She did write much of *The Giant Joshua* at Yaddo but, away from the friendly confines of Mormon culture for the first time, she did not find it an enjoyable experience.

When she could no longer stand the rigors of Yaddo, Whipple returned to St. George to finish the book. Again, she had financial problems. To help her finish, Houghton-Mifflin agreed to give her an advance of $50 for each chapter. Those months of writing were apparently very lonely ones. Whipple resented the advance, commenting in a letter that it was as "if I were a tap from which they could squeeze words." Writing came slowly and usually late at night. "I was forced to work fifteen hours a day in order to make an income of fifty dollars a month and thus eventually cracked up with a preventable pneumonia and staggering doctor bill."[15]

Houghton-Mifflin invited Whipple to come to New York when *The Giant Joshua* was released in 1941 to attend autograph parties and meet people, assuring her that the book would make between $3,000 and $15,000 in advance sales.[16] However, once she got to New York she discovered that the sales amounted to only about $2,000. She was forced to lecture at Columbia University to earn enough money to pay her way back to St. George. The Advertising Department at Houghton-Mifflin believed that Whipple's novel would be a best-seller that would be promoted by the Mormon church and harvest large sales in the West. Whipple was less optimistic, however she hoped that the book would sell well, especially among the Mormons. Because none of the other books written by previous fellowship winners had covered publication expenses, Houghton-Mifflin kept most of the money from the sales and Whipple actually received very little.

If *The Giant Joshua* was not a best-seller, Whipple was pleased with its reception in the non-Mormon world. A story of Mormon pioneering in southern Utah in the latter nineteenth century, the book provides a woman's point of view of a life destroyed by polygamy. It describes one woman's battle to make her place in a unique culture that values conformity and community more than individuality and ingenuity. The struggle of a people against the land and among themselves is apparent on every page. Numerous reviewers pronounced the work excellent. The western literature critic Ray B. West, Jr., for example, concluded in the *Saturday Review of Literature* that Whipple's book caught a unique aspect of Mormon culture: "the tenderness and sympathy which existed among a people dogged by persecution and hardship, forced to battle inclement nature and struggle for each moment of happiness."[17]

While Whipple, unlike her publishers, did not expect Mormon church leaders to praise *The Giant Joshua,* she was not prepared for an exceptionally negative reaction. Although she agreed that the book had not sold well because it was released at the beginning of World War II and the whole nation was caught up in that reality, another reason, she thought, was "the violent antipathy of Mormon church leaders—who had never read the book." The only official comment from a church leader was a book review in the *Improvement Era* written by Apostle John A. Widtsoe. While he felt that the novel described the "high spiritual motives" for polygamy "with some degree of fairness," Widtsoe thought that "the example selected, a life defeated because of polygamy, leaves a bitter, angry distaste for the system," was "unfair" because "there were fewer unhappy marriages under 'Mormon' polygamy than under monogamy." Widtsoe found some positive elements, too: "One thing this novel shows is that wherever 'Mormon' history is touched, situations of epic value are uncovered. Most novels dealing with 'Mormon' life follow the trek across the plains; this book explores only a corner of subsequent settlements; yet an equally fruitful field is found."[18] But this concluding statement was not enough to counteract the review's criticism, and *The Giant Joshua* never had sufficient sales among Utah residents to satisfy either Whipple or her publisher. Even so, according to Whipple, her book was one of the most requested in the Salt Lake City public library for months.[19]

But Whipple was convinced that church leaders had done more to control her book's sales and circulation beyond writing a mixed review. She complained, "The Church exerts a despotism over Utah and its people almost as complete as Brigham Young's." Bookstores explained to her that if "they defied the Church edict" about her book "they'd be put out of business." According to Whipple, "It is a fact that the largest bookstore was forced to sell *The Giant Joshua* sub rosa—under the counter." Even in St. George, where there were "500 requests a week" in 1941 for the novel, "the Church won't let the local outlets stock it."[20]

Whipple also believed that the church's response went beyond trying to get bookstore owners not to stock the book. She complained, "Even the newspapers are owned by the Church. Fitzpatrick, publisher of the *Salt Lake Tribune,* barred any mention of my name in the paper for a whole year."[21] This is one example where Whipple's perception may have been distorted. John F. Fitzpatrick was the publisher of the *Tribune,* but the newspaper was not owned by the Mormon church. The Kearns family, who owned the paper, and Fitzpatrick were Catholics, and the newspaper had the reputation of being anti-Mormon.[22]

Whipple also complained that church leaders actively prevented her from getting employment or additional writing fellowships. She wrote, "I can't get a teaching job because of Church opposition. I was told by one official only this summer that I was an 'evil woman who has written an evil book'!" And even though she could not get a job and had little money, "I can't get on relief or even get medical attention because as one official said, 'Why don't you dig up some of that buried gold you made exploiting your people'?"[23] She complained that she did not receive a Guggenheim literary award because "one of the apostles convinced Mr. Moe that I was an infidel—which I am!"[24]

As the years passed, Whipple took pride in the fact that her book became more accepted by the Mormon community. Literary critics declared it to be the best Mormon novel. For example, Edward A. Geary explained, *"The Giant Joshua* despite its faults ... is a powerful and moving novel which is accessible to both Mormons and non-Mormons."[25] When a new edition was published in 1976 Whipple observed, *"Joshua* has forced its way back into print, a hard-back at that. And after all these years the Mormons are acclaiming it. Too bad they damned it unread in the beginning, thus cheating me of any money."[26]

Clearly, whatever seeds of discontent she may have harbored toward the Mormon hierarchy before *The Giant Joshua* was published were fertilized in the aftermath. At an intensely personal level Whipple paid the price of her individualism in Mormon society. At the same time, she was not excommunicated, as Fawn Brodie would be when her critical biography of Joseph Smith was published in 1945, and she received no official public censure.[27] Whipple would never be a fully committed Latter-day Saint again, however, in large part because she felt she had been treated unfairly.

In spite of these developments, Whipple's first attempt at writing convinced her that she wanted to continue her literary career. Rather than work directly with publishing companies anymore, she hired an agent and started thinking about where she could send articles and how she could write more books. She also lectured. One such activity involved speaking engagements for the Writers War Board early in World War II. But, she recalled, that was "mostly a thankless task since I make only expenses. But the audience reaction is satisfying and I may be able to publish some of the material in an essay."[28]

Shortly after *The Giant Joshua* was published, a regional bookstore asked Whipple to write "a book for tourists."[29] In 1943 she asked Dale Morgan, who had planned a picture book of the state as a WPA assignment, for help in obtaining pictures. Morgan, however, had his own misgivings about Whipple's latest project. He wrote to Juanita Brooks that he hoped the publisher Alfred A. Knopf had not taken the book because Whipple had promised that the Chamber of Commerce and ZCMI, a large department store in Salt Lake City, would "guarantee" to buy five thousand copies each. Morgan added, "The idea of the book is sound. That was why we wanted to do it." But he would bet "a hundred to one" it would not be a "sensational occurring on the book market. If Maurine must have easy money, she should take to safe cracking."[30]

The travel book became *This Is the Place: Utah* and was finally published in 1945. Its production was as hard on Whipple as drafting *The Giant Joshua* had been. In a letter to an agent she rehearsed the problems she had working with Bernard Smith, her editor at Alfred A. Knopf. She realized after the contract was signed that he wanted an academic book, which she would have not "dreamed of attempting having no talent nor inclination along that line." She made the attempt however because she felt obligated to do so. "I attended the funeral of the man I was marrying within the week and came home to write for Mr. Smith. I was hospitalized for a month—but I never stopped writing for Mr. Smith. . . . I don't think anyone has ever been more long suffering or struggled harder or tackled more heartbreaking obstacles for the sake of a book than I have for this one," she whined.

Whipple explained that not only did she experience these tragedies, but she also had to turn down a magazine job and two other posts, including a corresponding assignment overseas, to complete the book. She felt that Smith did not sufficiently appreciate her sacrifice. "Mr. Smith is always writing what a pain in a neck this book is to him, and yet he has a roof over his head, clothes to wear, food to eat. I don't have any of those things. I can't borrow any more money. It has even reached the stage where I can't charge any more groceries."[31]

Whipple's complaints about Smith were typical of her experiences with other editors and indicative of the perfectionism and egotism that pervaded her career. She found working with editors difficult. She wrote books or articles that were too wordy, and they complained. At first they tried to point out problems calmly, but as Whipple's anger developed, their willingness to work with her dropped. Finally, Whipple would send, either directly to the editor or to an agent, an explosive letter similar to the one in which she described her experiences with Smith. After publishing two books, she described the process as "like having a baby—easier to conceive than deliver. I feel suspiciously like the patient whose operation was a 'success' but who died."[32]

But Whipple did not hold her hard feelings for long. By the time *This Is the Place* was published, she had forgiven her editor. "Bernard Smith is one of the best and most understanding friends I have," she wrote. "We had a little difficulty doing the book, but only because, as I keep telling everyone Utah is NOT America and the same laws do not apply." She explained, for example, that someone had edited the manuscript to suggest that no one in Utah believed in Joseph Smith. "If I had let such an outright untruth go through the sale of the book would have been completely killed in Utah—every bookstore in the state would have banned it—and I would have been branded as a liar. It was on such grounds that I fought until I effected at least a compromise."[33]

As was the case with *The Giant Joshua,* Whipple was disappointed with the reception of *This Is the Place: Utah.* She explained that it was because she "let Bernard have his way often against my better judgment," and therefore "the book is not allowed on the shelves of the two main outlets in Utah." She felt that it had been "killed by the Mormon Church because the publishers insisted that I include a chapter on the Utah gentiles."[34]

The "furore" over the book not only from the Mormon church but also from state officials, Whipple said, forced her to move to Hollywood, "where I wrote for LIFE, LOOK, THE SATURDAY EVENING POST and was a member of the official COLLIERS family until the magazine died."[35] While there, she also planned to write the sequel to *The Giant Joshua.* She envisioned a trilogy that would look at the development of the "Mormon Idea" and how it had changed over time. She signed a contract with Simon and Schuster to write the sequel and started receiving advances. However, wherever she went, especially when she returned to St. George, she found it difficult to write. She was often ill, very easily depressed, and unsure of herself. Her family's reaction to the book (her father called *The Giant Joshua* trash); her community's neglect (Whipple thought she would have had more attention had she published a story in the *Relief Society Magazine* than she did for receiving the fellowship and writing the novel); and the negative response of the Mormon church leaders (Elder John A. Widtsoe's book review in the *Improvement Era*) all led to her lack of self-confidence.

After this, Whipple undertook a number of unsuccessful ventures. She aspired to study a clinic that treated alcoholics in Seattle, but her attempts to work with it and raise money for a book as well as a conference in Las Vegas fell through. She unsuccessfully applied for a grant from the Hartford Foundation. She did receive a loan from the Authors League Fund, which helped her pay for food and insurance. She wrote an Easter pageant that she wanted to produce on national forest lands in Washington County, Utah, but she had trouble funding the venture and completing it. Whipple's papers are full of letters pleading for money and support of her projects.

Not only were Whipple's writing endeavors aborted, but she also felt that people were out to get her. She theorized that the citizens of St. George hated her. She took umbrage at the residents when someone apparently shot at her dog, whom she considered her only source of protection from thieves and rapists. She facilitated a radio station from Salt Lake City in making tapes of *The Giant Joshua,* but insisted that they had been stolen by another station in Las Vegas. She was involved in a traffic accident at a poorly marked intersection and felt that the St. George police purposely sided against her. According to Whipple's account, the other driver, a woman who had a reputation for overreacting, had panicked when she saw Whipple pull out at the crossing. Rather than turn her wheel to avoid hitting Whipple, the woman took her hands off her steering wheel to shield a dog on her lap. Although she was absolved of blame in the incident, Whipple did not feel her record was completely cleared.

Whipple wrote about all of these and many other perceived injustices to anyone and everyone she could. People who wrote fan letters, editors of magazines who rejected her articles, governors of Utah and Nevada, public leaders in Utah, and friends and family members all received detailed explanations of her current difficulties. While these letters address her specific complaints, they also say a great deal about her views of the Mormon church. These and other writings express her views as a "dissenter," not just from the dictates of church leaders—whether real or merely perceived—but from any aspect of Whipple's life that did not develop along lines she thought appropriate for her.

Whipple also felt that the Mormons cheated her out of making money on her second book *This Is the Place: Utah.* She explained her initial obstacle was the state, but after the book was ready for publication, "the Church threatened to ban it unless I'd let them rewrite it for proselyting purposes! Knopf went ahead anyway and put out the most beautiful book physically in these United States. . . . But the

Church killed it for Centennial use."[36] In a letter to "dear fellow sufferers," she explained that "one or two totalitarian leaders . . . subject[ed *This Is the Place*] to every conceivable denunciation, but nobody ever once disproved a single stated fact."[37] A private investigator, A. Luke Payne from Salt Lake City, who wrote Whipple a fan letter and then corresponded with her, explained that he had a hard time obtaining a copy in Salt Lake City bookstores. He described a conversation with a clerk at ZCMI, who told him that she had no more copies of *This Is the Place* and told of the local problems stocking it. The clerk had read *The Giant Joshua* and felt "it would have had a wider sale if it had been given the backing of the church bookstores and the church itself."[38]

Although her books were not received well in Utah, Whipple theorized that they served a purpose. She perceived that a "revolution" was going on in Utah between church leaders and the Mormon people.[39] She explained the feeling in *This Is the Place*: "Persecution strengthens an ideal, a people. Today the church's conflict comes from within for the first time. There is articulate and widespread Mormon criticism of Mormondom. . . . There is a gulf between the Mormon people and their leaders."[40] In a letter to an editor at Simon and Schuster, she tried to explain the "witch-hunting" she thought she experienced in Utah but that few seemed to understand. "We speak a different language out here and people elsewhere don't have the simple mechanics of vocabulary to begin with—unless they've been in Nazi Germany." She went on to explain, "I am as apprehensive as primitive people must have been when they expected the sun to come crashing down. You had better ask Simon-Schuster if they are afraid of the Mormon Church. I can give them a book that will sell for years (I know) but it won't please the Church—the Mormon *people*, yes."[41]

Economics was one area in which Whipple especially sensed that church leaders had left the Mormon dream. To her, the Mormon pioneers believed in a "socialistic, share-and-share alike" worldview, but now Mormons were "ruthlessly materialistic."[42] She believed that the "widening gap" between the Mormon public statements and actual experiences could be demonstrated by comparing the role federal welfare played in the church.[43]

She wrote to Dale Morgan, who worked for the Utah's Writer Project with the Works Progress Administration, to ask for figures, and Morgan agreed that church welfare was not meeting the needs of all Mormons as the church publicly proclaimed. He said, for example, that 90 percent of federal relief cases in Washington County were Latter-day Saints but asked Whipple not to quote the WPA directly. "There is no desire to make it appear that WPA is attacking or belittling the church program; WPA here attends to its own business."[44]

She also approached church leaders to find WPA figures for Mormons but felt that Harold B. Lee, who worked extensively with church welfare, lost all enthusiasm for her project when she asked such questions. "He didn't approve at all because I wasn't content with generalities in the survey but kept asking for cases."[45]

Yet Whipple thought that she still had enough material to show the difference in church public relations on welfare, especially with a letter she received from a federal administrator: "I think with these suggestions you will find that the window displays of the LDS propagandists are meaningless in comparison with the actual needs as met by the State and Federal Government."[46]

Whipple felt that her writing could help sensitize the Saints to some of the inconsistencies she saw in Mormonism. She believed that *The Giant Joshua* and the never-written volumes of her projected trilogy would trace the "Idea" that supported the Mormon pioneers. In *The Giant Joshua* she had Erastus Snow explain that the church stood for the Idea. He tells Clorinda Agatha MacIntyre, the heroine, "'You may lose. . . . I may lose. Zion may lose, for the time. But the 'Idea'—he saw all those myriads, the oppressed and downtrodden, marching hand in hand straight into the dawn of a better world—'the Idea can't lose'."[47]

Whipple felt that the Mormon leaders had lost track of that Idea. In correspondence with everyone from fans to editors, she explained her concerns about the direction the Mormon church was taking. "The question seems to be: Is the idea of brotherly love so naive and impractical that it must be sacrificed if Success is to be achieved? I do not believe that such a postulation is inevitable despite events, despite Church snobbishness." Just as the "pendulum" had swung toward "success," she felt that it would swing back to the Mormon Idea of brotherhood. "I also believe (In fact, I know—as many humble people have insisted so long) that my books will help bring about their consummation; will help readjust and clarify Mormon thinking, will help reestablish this Idea."[48]

Luke Payne, for example, wrote that some Mormon people "who hold the faith and conform to all the teachings of the Church and who are as rugged and sincere as those pioneers you have written about" were interested in tolerance rather than condemning those who did not completely support present-day church leaders. He theorized that people who did not like her books "do not even have a place in their hearts for a St. Paul because he sinned before his conversion." Yet he "wonder[ed] at President [J. Reuben] Clark being so unaware of his own shortcomings in the matter of intolerance . . . to take exception to such a great work as *This is the Place* written by one of our women nurtured in our own faith."[49]

Whipple expressed her views of the Mormon church in other contexts as well. In a 1967 letter she explained, "I'm not much of a Mormon—I've seen too much hushed up."[50] One experience illustrates some of the experiences she had with the church and other writers, as well as her constant need for money. After Juanita Brooks published *The Mountain Meadows Massacre,* Warner Brothers wanted to make a movie. Brooks, however, only agreed to serve as a technical advisor to the project if she had "official Mormon consent—and obviously, the Church could never consent." Whipple complained, "Juanita is a 'fence-sitter'—she wants to have her cake and eat it, too. An impossibility, when it comes to Mormon officialdom." But she added that there was

> the material for a wonderful movie and a box-office hit. The gimmick is to go ahead, paying no attention to the church. My years of being witch-hunted and the result of two books have taught me that there is a vast schism between the Mormons and their leaders. The history of Utah politics proves that! Thus I know beyond all doubt that presented with a fait accompli, the Mormons would patronize a good movie of this incident in droves—and the church would be helpless. Juanita will never actively oppose the church which she'd have to do now, since she saw to it that the initial "Hollywood triumph" was publicized in every paper in Utah! I am under no compulsion, religious or otherwise. And I know far more of the overall picture than she, and as much of the incident in question.

Whipple wanted her suggestion to be kept quiet because she felt she would be "massacred, too, if the Church found out." She added, "Anyway, I need money so badly that any effort is worthwhile."[51]

Yet despite Whipple's misgivings about the Mormon church, she remained a very religious person and committed to some of its unique doctrines. In some notes, possibly ideas for an article, Whipple described Mormons' beliefs on the purpose of life: "LDS believe that life is a unity. We lived before birth. We'll live after death." She added, "We believe that in life, living it every second. All is life. Religion is the tissue of life itself."[52] Referring to an afterlife, she wrote, "Heaven is a condition toward which we're constantly attaining—never quite reaching. Heaven may be on earth as well as after death. Immorality is just a continuation of this life—just a struggle for greater perfection." She described the "Mormon Boy Scouts [as] the highest standard in the world," and the church's basketball program as the "largest and most efficient in the world." She commented that Mormons "believe that dancing, games, drama lead to a fuller, more worshipful life."[53] When a *Reader's Digest* editor questioned her comments about praying for rain, Whipple argued that it was "an old western custom. Lots of people think you can make rain by praying for it, and sometimes apparently do. I can remember when the town of St. George used to hold community rain-prayers that sometimes brought floods."[54]

In other letters she discussed her belief in a divine being and a pre- and post-life, "This I do know: That something lives. Something goes on. And the curtain is only gauze."[55] In a letter to a relative about a sick child she wrote: "I guess I'm the most religious one of the family. For I've seen too much not to believe in a divine force. I know that creation is no accident. . . . I know that there is some sort of immortality. I'm not convinced that any one church has the answers. But I know that faith can literally move mountains."[56]

She also expressed these religious views in *This Is the Place*: "For me, there is theology enough in the careless joy of a meadowlark's song. For me, life can hold no defeats as long as there are the assuaging solitudes, the forever resurrecting, forever prophesying wind, the peak so serene and lofty that they shed a kind of beatitude on men; no defeats as long as there is a fellow 'Jack' to cry, 'Golly, it's good to see you back.'"[57]

Increasingly as the years passed, Whipple saw herself as more a cultural Mormon than a devout member, someone who did not go along with all the beliefs and especially did not always support church leaders. But she confided that "the 'Mormon' was ingrained . . . so deeply that [she] could never rub it off."[58] Her experiences with church leaders convinced her that they did not represent the Mormon people, and she felt that they prevented her writing from being a success. Throughout all of Whipple's correspondence, the constant themes concern her lack of money, her resentment that some people were financially well-off and not able to understand her plight, her insecurities about her relationships with people and her ability as a writer, and the effects of all of these on her health. But her life was not as depressing as her letters might suggest. That may be because, as she explained in *This Is the Place*, "My generation of Mormons had learned to laugh at ourselves, and perhaps that was a great achievement, too."[59]

Despite her dislike of Mormon church leaders and of some of the people in St. George, she continued to live there. Why did she keep going back when she felt so unwelcome and when friends like Robert A.

Wilkinson, wrote, "You must get out of St. George, forget the squabbles and bigotry and create"?[60] She wrote that despite the desperate advice of Tom Wolfe's novel, "You can go home and must, . . . Going home again is a prerequisite of going anywhere else. Spiritually at least."[61] She also published her reasons for returning to Utah: "We come back because Zion is worth occasional discomfort. We come back because Zion is the most unpredictable, exciting, satisfying place in the world to live. We come back because Utah is a foreign land gone American."[62]

Although Maurine Whipple may not be the classic example of a dissenter, she is a good example of a Mormon torn between her occupation as a writer, her attempts to live well, her insecurities, and her reaction to church leaders. Her life was a cross-current of events, feelings, illusions, and complex dichotomies. As chagrined as she was, as bitter as she was toward the church from which she arose, Whipple expressed the angst and brilliance and terseness that set the stage for the creation of superior literature. Her dissent was ideological and not political; it represented some of the problems associated with the movement of the church from a position in seclusion and cohesiveness to one of accommodation and assimilation. The fact that Whipple lived in St. George until her death on Palm Sunday, April 12, 1992, indicated Mormon country's place in her view of the world. Her trilogy about the "Mormon Idea" was never completed. Even so, she was honored with a lifetime membership by the Association of Mormon Letters in January 1992, and believed during her last few months that the Mormon community was beginning to appreciate her work.

NOTES

1. Edward A. Geary, "Mormondom's Lost Generation: The Novelists of the 1940s," *Brigham Young University Studies* 18 (Fall 1977): 92.

2. There has been significant scholarly interest in Maurine Whipple's life and work in recent years. See Katherine Ashton, "Whatever Happened to Maurine Whipple?" *Sunstone* 14 (April 1990): 36–41; Maryruth Bracy and Linda Lambert, "Maurine Whipple's Story of the Giant Joshua," *Dialogue: A Journal of Mormon Thought* 6 (Autumn–Winter 1971): 55–62; Edward A. Geary, "The Poetics of Provincialism: Mormon Regional Fiction," *Dialogue: A Journal of Mormon Thought* 11 (Summer 1978): 12–20; Bruce Jorgensen, "Retrospection: *Giant Joshua*," *Sunstone* 3 (September–October 1978): 6–8; Curtis Taylor, "*The Giant Joshua* and Latter-day Fiction," *LDS Booksellers Association Newsletter*, February 1989, 6–7.

3. The Manuscript Division of the Harold B. Lee Library at Brigham Young University acquired Maurine Whipple's papers in 1977. Although the collection is not completely cataloged, some of it has been organized. The rest is

stored in boxes. Archivist Dennis Rowley allowed me to use the papers even though they are not completely cataloged. I went through the organized boxes as well as the unorganized ones. In this effort, I read several accounts of the same events. Therefore, when I give only general information that I found in the letters I do not cite a source. When I use a direct quote, I include the names and dates of the letters. Because the collection is not cataloged and all of it will be reorganized, I cannot give box and folder numbers. I will refer to the letters from this collection as the Whipple Collection.

4. Family Group Sheets, Family History Library, Church of Jesus Christ of Latter-day Saints, Salt Lake City.

5. Maurine Whipple to Bob [an editor for *Colliers*], January 28, 1952, Whipple Collection.

6. Maurine Whipple to Tom Spies, N.d., Whipple Collection.

7. Maurine Whipple to Ted Strauss, January 8, no year, Whipple Collection.

8. Maurine Whipple, *This Is the Place: Utah* (New York: Alfred A. Knopf, 1945), 18.

9. Whipple, *This Is the Place,* 18–19.

10. Ibid., 20.

11. Ibid., 21.

12. Whipple to Strauss, January 8, no year.

13. On Yaddo, see Roy Bongartz, "Yaddo at 60," *Publishers Weekly,* June 13, 1986, 32–35.

14. Ferris Greenslet to Maurine Whipple, July 25, 1939, Whipple Collection.

15. Maurine Whipple to Maximilian Becker, August 30, 1941, Whipple Collection.

16. *The Giant Joshua* was published in Boston by Houghton-Mifflin in the fall of 1941. It was reissued in 1961 by Doubleday and Co., Garden City, N.Y., and in a special edition in 1976 by Western Epics, Salt Lake City.

17. Review by Ray B. West, Jr., *Saturday Review of Literature,* January 4, 1941, 5. See also his comments on *The Giant Joshua* in Ray B. West, Jr., *Writing in the Rocky Mountains* (Lincoln: University of Nebraska Press, 1947), 34–75 passim. Other favorable reviews can be found in the *Christian Science Monitor,* February 1, 1941, 10, and the *New York Times,* January 12, 1941, 6.

18. John A. Widtsoe, "On the Book Rack," *Improvement Era* 44 (February 1941): 93.

19. Ashton, "Whatever Happened to Maurine Whipple?" 36. This may have been something akin to the heightened sales of Salmon Rushdi's, *The Satanic Verses* (New York: Viking, 1989) after the Ayatollah Khomeini called for Rushdi's execution by loyal Muslims because the book, in the Ayatollah's view, was blasphemous.

20. Maurine Whipple to Burt McBride, *Reader's Digest,* December 20, 1948, Whipple Collection.

21. Maurine Whipple to John Crowe Ransom, *Kenyon Review,* November 6, 1957, Whipple Collection.

22. O. N. Malmquist, *The First 100 Years: A History of the Salt Lake Tribune, 1871–1971* (Salt Lake City: Utah State Historical Society, 1971).

23. Whipple to Ransom, November 6, 1957.

24. Maurine Whipple to Don [Simon and Schuster], November 14, 1946, Whipple Collection.

25. Geary, "The Poetics of Provincialism," 22.

26. Maurine Whipple to Brian Stowell, March 22, 1977, Whipple Collection.

27. See Fawn M. Brodie, *No Man Knows My History: The Life of Joseph Smith* (New York: Alfred A. Knopf, 1945); Newell G. Bringhurst, "Fawn M. Brodie, 'Mormondom's Lost Generation,' and *No Man Knows My History,"* *Journal of Mormon History* 16 (1990): 11–23.

28. Maurine Whipple to Dale L. Morgan, May 29, 1943, Dale Morgan Collection, Special Collections, Marriott Library, University of Utah, Salt Lake City. The originals of the Morgan Collection are at the Bancroft Library, University of California–Berkeley. The University of Utah has a microfilm copy.

29. Maurine Whipple to Burt McBride, editor for the *Reader's Digest,* December 20, 1948, Whipple Collection.

30. Dale L. Morgan to Juanita Brooks, July 31, 1943, Juanita Brooks Collection, Utah State Historical Society, Salt Lake City.

31. Maurine Whipple to Harold Ober, N.d., Whipple Collection.

32. Sketch, Whipple Collection.

33. Whipple to Don, November 14, 1946.

34. Maurine Whipple to Mrs. Claire M. Smith, Harold Ober Associates, August 9, 1974, Whipple Collection.

35. Whipple to Smith, August 9, 1974.

36. Whipple to McBride, December 20, 1948.

37. Maurine Whipple to "dear fellow sufferers," April 8, 1952, Whipple Collection.

38. A. Luke Payne to Maurine Whipple, August 7, 1948, Whipple Collection.

39. Whipple to Don, November 20, 1948.

40. Whipple, *This Is the Place,* 166.

41. Whipple to Don, November 14, 1946.

42. Notes, Whipple Collection.

43. Dale L. Morgan to Juanita Brooks, November 9, 1941, Brooks Collection.

44. Dale L. Morgan to Maurine Whipple, November 25, 1941, Whipple Collection.

45. Maurine Whipple to Dale Morgan, December 6, 1941, Morgan Collection.

46. Dean R. Brimhall to Maurine Whipple, November 18, 1941, Whipple Collection.

47. Whipple, *Giant Joshua,* 621.

48. Whipple to Ransom, November 6, 1957.

49. A. Luke Payne to Maurine Whipple, February 2, 1947, Whipple Collection.

50. Maurine Whipple to Ernest Linford, August 18, 1967, Whipple Collection.

51. Whipple to Strauss, January 8, no year, Whipple Collection.

52. Notes, Whipple Collection.

53. Ibid.

54. Whipple to McBride, February 3, 1949.

55. Whipple to Linford, August 18, 1967.

56. Maurine Whipple to Carol, December 6, 1969, Whipple Collection.

57. Whipple, *This Is the Place*, 184.

58. Ibid., 18–19.

59. Ibid., 50.

60. Robert A. Wilkinson, New York, to Maurine Whipple, March 23, 1967, Whipple Collection.

61. Notes, Whipple Collection.

62. Whipple, *This Is the Place*, 176.

15

Richard Price:
Leading Publicist of the Reorganized
Church's Schismatics

William D. Russell

Since the late 1950s, the Reorganized Church has been moving from
its traditional position as a sect that considered itself the one true
church of Jesus Christ to a denomination that considers itself merely
one of many Christian churches, each with its own strengths and weaknesses. In the 1950s the Reorganization's leadership and membership
were predominantly sectarian. By the time women were first ordained
to the Reorganization's priesthood in November 1985, however, the
leadership and a considerable number of members had embraced the
denominational perspective.[1] This transition prompted a backlash in
the Reorganized Church that threatened to rip the institution apart.
The new synthesis, embraced by the organization's leadership and many
of its members, found opposition from a sizable minority of more traditional members who viewed it as an apostasy. The leading strategist
and publicist of Reorganization fundamentalism, as the dissenting
movement is called, has been Richard Price, a long-time loyal member
of the priesthood.

The seeds of the dissent of Richard Price and other fundamentalists
date from the late 1950s. The beginning of W. Wallace Smith's reign
as Reorganized Church president in October 1958 can be seen as the
beginning of a significant drive by the Reorganized Church's leadership toward a more liberal or ecumenical interpretation of the gospel.[2]
When President Israel A. Smith died and his brother W. Wallace Smith
became president, Maurice L. Draper was added to the First Presidency, Clifford A. Cole and Charles D. Neff were ordained to the Quorum of Twelve Apostles, and Roy A. Cheville became presiding patriarch. All were identified early in their careers as progressive leaders
with fairly liberal interpretations of scriptures, theology, and history.
In the years that followed, these four men played significant roles in
the direction of the church.[3]

At about the same time, Graceland College in Lamoni, Iowa, the church's primary institution of higher education, hired four new professors in theology and philosophy—Lloyd R. Young (1958), Leland Negaard (1959), Paul M. Edwards (1960), and Robert Speaks (1960)—who also were considered more open and less doctrinaire toward religious knowledge. Speaks and Negaard had graduate degrees from two of the leading Protestant theological seminaries in the country, the University of Chicago and Union Theological Seminary in New York, respectively. And a few years before their arrival, two historians, Robert Bruce Flanders and Alma R. Blair, began to examine Latter Day Saint history critically with the tools of their discipline.[4] These faculty members were often criticized during the 1960s for undermining the faith of students.

Meanwhile, at the church's publishing house, a twenty-eight-year-old moderate, Roger Yarrington, replaced the very conservative Chris B. Hartshorn as managing editor when Hartshorn retired in 1960.[5] Previously, the managing editor had scrutinized materials submitted for possible publication to see whether they contained statements "not in harmony" with traditional Reorganization teachings. Unlike Hartshorn, Yarrington did not see his editorial role as that of a protector of the traditional faith. The result was a liberalizing of the church's print media.[6]

Meanwhile, in the early years of W. Wallace Smith's presidency, the staff of the Department of Religious Education at the Reorganized Church's headquarters in Independence, Missouri, headed by Clifford Buck, began taking courses at a Methodist seminary in Kansas City—Saint Paul School of Theology—when it opened its doors in 1959. Buck and his associate, Richard Lancaster, became the first Reorganized Church graduates of the seminary in 1965. Other staff members in the department had graduate degrees from Protestant theological institutions.

All of these men were part of a de facto "Young Turk" uprising within the Reorganized Church, a group that questioned traditional systems of belief and raised challenging perspectives on fundamental issues. By the early 1960s, fundamentalists such as Richard Price had become concerned about the three primary sources of liberal thought in the church at the time: the theology of the liberal professors at Graceland, the new editors at Herald House, and the staff of the church's Department of Religious Education. The fundamentalists thought that the threat to orthodoxy came from the well-educated staffs of church departments and institutions but did not think that the new ideas were accepted by top church leaders themselves.[7] At first Price and those who shared his views seemed to see it as their mission to inform the leaders about the dangerous things that their underlings were teaching.

By the late 1960s, however, Richard Price and other fundamentalists had become concerned that the highest leaders of the church were infected with what he referred to as the "liberal heresy." Two events particularly awakened Price to the idea that ecumenism was being accepted by the top leadership—within the First Presidency and the Quorum of Twelve Apostles particularly. The first event was his and other fundamentalists' discovery in 1969 of certain facts relating to a new curriculum that the Religious Education Department was developing.[8] Certain theological papers—"Position Papers"—had been written by members of a curriculum committee as a means of building a base for revising Sunday school materials. The set of discussion papers was liberal; for example, the author of the essay on the Book of Mormon suggested that it might be fiction and that Joseph Smith, Jr., might have been its author.[9] Although the papers were written by young staff members, the fact that one member of the First Presidency (Duane E. Couey) and three apostles (Clifford A. Cole, Earl T. Higdon, and Alan D. Tyree) were on the departmental committee for whom the papers were written was seen as a sign that the hierarchy was secretly leading the church in a liberal direction, using the curriculum as an instrument of that goal. The papers were leaked to the church public by conservatives. Other fundamentalist Saints who read them were shocked at their liberal contents, which seemed to deny traditional Restoration teachings.

The second event came in the late 1960s, when fundamentalists learned about some private theological seminars that had been arranged for the eighteen members of the church's Joint Council of the First Presidency, Quorum of Twelve Apostles, and Presiding Bishopric.[10] At these seminars, which began in 1967, faculty members at Saint Paul School of Theology, such as the theologian Paul Jones and Carl Bangs, a religious historian, tutored the church's top leaders on issues in theology and history.[11] The seminars focused on the concept of incarnation, stressing that the church is "true" only to the extent that it reflects the spirit and personality of Jesus Christ.[12] Having no formal theological education, the Reorganization leaders were in some cases being exposed for the first time to scholarship that undercut some cherished Restoration concepts. When fundamentalists later heard about the seminars, they were appalled. As one delegate told the 1970 World Conference, "These other schools have nothing to teach us," referring to Protestant seminaries such as Saint Paul.[13] Price and others were afraid that the church would abandon its Restoration distinctives in favor of ecumenical Protestantism.

Many fundamentalists began to wonder whether the prophet himself approved of the liberal theology that was being produced by staff members at the church headquarters. Many held out hope that W.

Wallace Smith was simply not well informed about the heresies of his subordinates, and that when he became informed he would bring the liberal movement to a screeching halt. After all, why would leaders of the true church find any need to be taught by theologians from Protestant churches or to accept any of their conceptions? Joseph Smith, Jr., had been told to "join none of them" because they were "abominations" before God.[14] For fundamentalists such as Price, Protestant churches possessed a lesser share of the gospel than the Restoration.

For a brief period in the early 1970s a newspaper called *Zion's Warning* sounded the alarm to fundamentalist Saints about apparent departures from the Restoration tradition. "The Old Jerusalem Gospel Being Ousted by Top R.L.D.S. Officials" announced its banner headline in its first issue, dated February 1970.[15] But by 1973 *Zion's Warning* was no longer in existence, and before long, its publisher, Barney Fuller, had left the Reorganized Church and become a charismatic Protestant preacher. Fuller's departure left Richard Price, the most significant fundamentalist spokesman, to fill the void left by the loss of *Zion's Warning*.

Born on February 28, 1924 in Boise, Idaho, Price was raised in a traditional Reorganization environment. His maternal grandmother, Alice Mary Dennis Parks, was the first member of the family to join the church. She had been baptized by Apostle Frederick A. Smith (Joseph Smith's grandson) in 1890. After his father, Chauncy Price, died when Richard was two, his mother, Arlie Abercrombie Price, married a Mormon elder, Earl Player. But Alice raised her children in the Reorganized Church and saw Earl Player join the Reorganization when Richard was eleven years old.[16] After fourteen years of marriage, they divorced when Price was seventeen. Alice then married another Mormon elder, Walter Prince. Thus Price was able to see firsthand the diverse aspects of Mormonism, especially its midwestern and Rocky Mountain variations.

A turning point for Price came at a Reorganized Church Sunday school when he was sixteen and had a profound, born again-type of spiritual experience that made him a devout believer in the Reorganization gospel. He attended Graceland College, then a two-year school, from 1943 to 1945. He then transferred to Central Missouri State College in Warrensburg, and graduated in 1948 with majors in education and history. In the same year he married Pamela Kirksey, a Reorganized Church member from Fisher, Arkansas. After teaching high school English for two years in Idaho and Washington, the Prices "gathered to Zion" in 1950, moving to Independence, Missouri.

Richard Price had accepted a call to the office of priest in 1947 in

Idaho. In Independence he and his wife attended the Enoch Hill Congregation, where he was called to the office of elder in 1953. The Price family remained in the Enoch Hill Congregation until 1984, except for a two-year period from 1958 to 1960, when he served as pastor of the Chillicothe, Missouri, Mission. An example of the Prices' dedication to the work of the Reorganized Church can be seen in their two years at Chillicothe. Although he worked at the Bendix Corporation in Kansas City six days a week, on Sundays he drove his family from Independence to Chillicothe, approximately ninety miles each way, where they spent a long day attending services and doing church work.

Even as a young man in the 1940s and 1950s, Price was troubled by what he regarded as a lack of thorough commitment to traditional Restoration principles and an overemphasis on careerism by the church's appointee ministers. His concern increased during the 1960s and reached a point of serious action when, in December 1969, a friend, Thomas Willis, handed Price a bootlegged copy of the Position Papers. Price was alarmed when he read them. Although the papers were written by staff members, he felt that the papers reflected the opinions of church leaders. He thus began to write a pamphlet as a rebuttal. Some fundamentalist high priests told him that they could circulate his reply. What was originally intended to be a pamphlet, however, soon grew into a 260-page book, *The Saints at the Crossroads*, finally published in 1974.[17] The book, the first thorough critique of the apparent liberal direction of the Reorganized Church's leadership, is still one of the most significant to appear.

When the manuscript of *The Saints at the Crossroads* was completed, Price took it to Charles Hield, the retired former president of the Quorum of Twelve Apostles, and to Leon Look, who held the priesthood office of Seventy, a calling to do missionary work. They read it with approval and encouraged him to have it published in time for the 1974 World Conference. Clark Printing in North Kansas City was willing to start production as soon as it had received $1,800 of the estimated $6,500 cost of printing ten thousand copies, and Price said, "I'll have it next Saturday." With only seven days to raise the money, he called upon his fundamentalist friends for assistance. They loaned him $2,000, and Price was prepared to mortgage his house to cover any other loans needed to finance the publication of the book.

On Monday before the World Conference of April 1974, two thousand copies of *The Saints at the Crossroads* were delivered to the Price home in Independence. The family stacked boxes all over the living room, dining room, and kitchen. That night Price called twenty people and asked them to help distribute the book. A thousand copies went out that same night. He planned to sell the book for $1.50 as a means of recovering the printing costs, but many were given away. For instance, all World Conference delegates were given a free copy. "One millionaire delegate came and insisted that he be given his free copy," he recalled, "so we gave it to him." Price and his friends also mailed free copies of the book to the presiding elder of every Reorganized Church in Missouri, Iowa, Kansas, and Nebraska.[18]

The Saints at the Crossroads sounds the warning more effectively than any previous attempt to tell the Saints about what fundamentalists regard as the rejection of the true gospel. More than 11,500 copies of the book had been sold or given away through 1992. In the book Price documents the liberal direction in which he feels the hierarchy is moving the Reorganized Church. A true conservative, he assumes that the gospel is a fixed body of doctrine that is both unchanging and unchangeable. If church leaders take positions contrary to that set of beliefs, he argues, then they have left the church, and those remaining loyal to the Reorganization's original teachings are "the church."

Price asserted that the Reorganization's hierarchy was trying to have the organization admitted into the National Council of Churches and the World Council of Churches, and that the leadership was trying to make admission more possible by shedding distinctive Restoration beliefs, thereby making the church's theology consistent with the liberal Protestant theology held by many prominent persons in leading ecumenical churches. On the first page of the book, he asks, "Do you know that the Book of Mormon, the Doctrine and Covenants, and the Inspired Version of the Bible are being discarded, and that the Church is being changed into a Protestant denomination? Do you know that the New Curriculum actually teaches vulgar, profane, and Communistic material to our children? Have you noticed that Joseph Smith is no longer really upheld as a true prophet?"[19]

Price suggests that future church historians would regard the 1970s as the "era of the liberalist heresy" when it came to light that "the leaders had been a decade in the process of secretly abandoning the Three Standard Books and other distinctives of the Church's heritage—and taking the Church into the ecumenical movement."[20] He also speculates that a split in the church would probably occur: "God may have to raise up another people to do His work."[21]

The heart of Price's book consists of a detailed critique of the controversial Position Papers written by the staff of the Department of Religious Education, principally Donald D. Landon, head of the department, and Geoffrey F. Spencer, Wayne Ham, and Verne Sparkes.[22] Price viewed these papers as deliberate attempts by ecumenically oriented church employees to make the Reorganization into a Protestant denomination, a desire he thought abominable.

Price argues in *The Saints at the Crossroads* that the gospel contains two fundamental elements: "(1) the good news that Jesus Christ atoned for sins, and (2) the set of rules whereby individuals may obtain the benefits of that atonement."[23] He argues that the Position Papers erred by asserting that the first element was all that was important in the gospel, and that the second element had to be discarded so that the leaders could take the church into the ecumenical movement. Position Paper Number 6, he continues, "goes to great lengths to eradicate from the minds of the saints any thought that the gospel is a set of beliefs."[24] Price says that the Position Papers held that Joseph Smith's New Translation of the Bible (called the "Inspired Version" by the Reorganization) was not a restoration of the original biblical text, and that in some instances the accuracy of the text is weakened by the changes introduced by Smith. The changes were apparently introduced to make the biblical passages in question support ideas already held by Smith and the Saints.[25] In a similar vein, Price shows that the Position Papers regarded the Book of Mormon as a product of Smith's nineteenth-century American environment.[26]

Price was puzzled, however, by the fact that the Position Papers scarcely mentioned the *Doctrine and Covenants*. But, "since they have expressed the belief that both [the Inspired Version and the Book of Mormon] are products of Joseph's own creation, it follows that they would consider the Doctrine and Covenants the same."[27] Perhaps Price should not have been so surprised that the *Doctrine and Covenants* was not subjected to the same critical analysis as the Book of Mormon and the Inspired Version of the Bible. He is right that it would follow that liberals should regard the revelations of the *Doctrine and Covenants* as products of Smith's environment, but the power to bring revelations to the church gives the Reorganization prophet a tremendous weapon for settling matters of church policy. Since the 1950s, the Reorganization president has brought forth several revelations settling policy debates about such diverse issues as whether missionaries called to the priesthood office of "Seventy" should be self-sustaining, whether all elders should be delegates to World Conference, whether polygamous persons in the third world should be baptized, and whether women should be ordained.[28]

Price argues that the departure from past Restoration distinctives left the church in an identity crisis. He quotes a statement in Position Paper Number 7, "The Nature of the Church," that said that "the ecumenical revolution around us, the erosion of distinctives which we felt we possessed, and an awareness of our historical rootedness in 19th century enthusiastic religion have all combined to create an identity crisis for us."[29] Price indicates that the Position Papers claim that the church was merely a fellowship of believers but deny that it had a particular structure—doctrines, officers, and ordinances; the authors viewed the Reorganized Church as only a fragment of Protestantism. Position Paper Number 7 held, according to Price, that God saves people equally in all denominations and all churches are capable of saving people.[30]

Price contends that for these liberal writers, "the entire concept of the New Testament Church, apostasy, and Restoration vanishes." He adds, "Paper #10 claims that Joseph Smith did not restore the New Testament Church's organization, since there was no Church to restore." He concludes, "This approach makes Joseph Smith a false prophet, and leaves the Restored Church entirely without foundation." For the liberals, Restoration concepts were simply answers to religious questions in Joseph Smith's day.[31]

Price holds that in the paper on Zion, liberals had interpreted "Zion" to mean ecumenism.[32] The Position Papers tried to prove that Zion was a nineteenth-century idea adopted by Joseph Smith from other community builders of his time; that Smith's Zion does not fit into present cultural conditions; that now Zion should be seen as an attitude of service and a "moving target" rather than one holy city; and that the Saints had to give up old ideas of Zion and accept new ones.[33]

"The New Positionists," wrote Price, "have discarded the idea of Zion as a holy city in one geographical place, and have construed the word to mean a 'witness and process' by which Zion can be anywhere."[34] For the liberals, he argues, the Zionic ideal has "to do with the task of making every city more compassionate, more humane, more responsive to man's need and more receptive to God's grace."[35] He adds, "The new concept of Zion is interpreted as being the social gospel."[36]

Price concludes that the current period in the Reorganized Church will be regarded by historians as

> the time when the most outspoken leaders of the Church forsook the Lord's true gospel and followed after the age-old worldly religion called liberalism. This big change has caused a problem which is greater than the one created by Brigham Young. He set aside the Three Standard Books and led the Saints into the heresies of polygamy, the Adam-God theory, and blood atonement, causing a split in the Church from which it is still suffering. Today's problem is greater because the leaders are not just setting the Three Books aside, but they are discarding them.[37]

In all, Price's book is a remarkable critique of the policies of the Reorganization's hierarchies and sounded the call to conflict between the more conservative members and the liberal hierarchy. He has written a great deal since *The Saints at the Crossroads,* but his position on the theological heresy remains much the same.

The experience of writing *The Saints at the Crossroads,* and its reception by those in the church who questioned what they saw happening in the presiding quorums, led Price to expand his activities. In 1975 the Prices and Paul and Diana Ludy of Bates City, Missouri, decided to form a publishing company, Cumorah Books, to present the fundamentalist case against increasing Reorganization liberalism. Their first publication dealt with the ordination of women. W. Wallace Smith had been interviewed by two talk-show hosts who asked about the issue. Price was convinced that the interview revealed that Smith favored ordaining women, and Cumorah Books published it to expose what Price thought was a heretical idea.[38]

The same year, Cumorah Books published a forty-five-page pamphlet, "Decision Time," essentially an abbreviated version of *The Saints at the Crossroads* with some updating based on the events that had transpired in the year since the book's appearance. Since its publication in 1975, "Decision Time" has been printed three times, and twenty-five thousand copies have been distributed. After a 1984 revelation to permit women's ordination, Price revised it to reflect these new circumstances.[39]

In response to the publication of "Decision Time," the First Presidency sent a letter to 1,500 church administrators, saying that the booklet "contains many allegations against a number of the general officers of the church as well as others" and suggested that "the author of the pamphlet writes with questionable integrity when he quotes from persons not identified with the leadership of the church and suggested that, because such persons write articles published in the *Saints' Herald* occasionally, they represent the views of the First Presidency and of other general officers."[40] The First Presidency also said that Price was "guilty of teaching false doctrine when he states that the very basis of the Reorganized Church of Jesus Christ of Latter Day Saints is founded in the Three Standard Books." The sentences that followed did not make the basis of the church's beliefs clear but, as Price saw it, W. Wallace Smith and his two counselors were claiming that their interpretations of revelations determined the church's position. For Price, such a position was a replay of the "Brighamite heresy."

"Decision Time" produced the first threat of legal action by the Reorganized Church against Richard Price. After "Decision Time" was published, he received a letter from Thomas Bennett, the church's legal counsel, which charged him with misuse of the church's name by displaying it prominently on Cumorah Books' stationery and in the pamphlet. The objection rested on the possibility that it was unclear that "Decision Time" was a private and not a church-sponsored publication. Pamela Price believes that her husband was inspired to call Don Carlos Smith of Independence, a descendant of Joseph Smith, Jr.'s, to discuss this matter. Smith referred the Prices to an attorney named George Hare, who arranged a meeting between Bennett, Price, and Paul Ludy. The result was that Price and Ludy agreed to add the word *individuals* to their Cumorah Books letterhead.[41] From then on, Cumorah products read, "Cumorah Books, Incorporated, is composed of individuals who publish religious literature for members and friends of the Reorganized Church of Jesus Christ of Latter Day Saints. The purpose of the company is to publish materials which defend and proclaim the original doctrines of the Church."[42]

Late in 1975, Cumorah Books published the original *Position Papers*. Price was nervous about whether Cumorah Books would be sued by the Reorganized Church on a claim of copyright violation after the *Position Papers* appeared, but there was no legal action.[43] By 1978 the board of Cumorah Books was comprised of Richard and Pamela Price, Paul and Diana Ludy, Pamela Price's brother Nathan Kirksey, and Merva Bird.[44] The board decided that year that the best means of informing the church membership about the liberal direction of the church, as well as of providing a clearinghouse of information for other fundamentalists, was to publish a magazine. *Restoration Voice* was patterned somewhat after the Reorganization's official magazine, the *Saints' Herald*. *Restoration Voice* has been published six times a year since its first issue, which was dated September-October 1978. Ten thousand free copies of the first issue of the thirty-two-page, slick-format magazine were distributed. The publication, which is supported entirely by donations, continues to be mailed to interested persons free of charge. [45]

Near the same time in 1978 that Price was launching *Restoration Voice*, Gregory I. Donovan, a lay elder in the Reorganization from Detroit, wrote to ask his assistance in scheduling a retreat at Graceland College. The event, which Donovan called a "Restoration Festival," was to be a weekend filled with sermons, lectures, prayers, testimonies, and hymn singing in the traditional restoration mode. Donovan did not know many leading fundamentalists and so asked Price's help in arranging for speakers. Price suggested the former apostle Charles R. Hield, the popular Book of Mormon investigators Thelona D. Stevens and Roy E. Weldon, and several others. He also helped publicize the Restoration Festival by sending an announcement to the approximately one thousand names on his list of persons known to have purchased *The Saints at the Crossroads*. An estimated 1,500–2,000 persons attended the festival at Graceland on September 22–24, 1978.[46]

The First Presidency chose not to oppose the holding of the Restoration Festival, although Graceland President Franklin S. Hough was criticized for renting college facilities to Donovan for the event. When a second festival was held in Kansas City, Missouri, in the fall of 1980, the First Presidency opposed it and took the position that those in the priesthood who participated in meetings, which competed with regular Sunday church services in Reorganization congregations, jeopardized their priesthood standing. Donovan and other leaders of the Restoration Festival were "silenced"—the official term for removal of priesthood status in the Reorganized Church—in the fall of 1980 for ignoring the hierarchy's dictums.[47]

After the second festival, Donovan became ill, and Price took over the leadership of Restoration Festival, Inc. Price and his associates began to hold quarterly Restoration Festival gatherings in the Independence area, with Price making most of the arrangements. He even published a newsletter announcing the Restoration Festivals. The event was short-lived, however. Board members began to quarrel over such doctrinal issues as whether the revelations as published in the 1833 *Book of Commandments* should be preferred over the revisions of those revelations later published in the *Doctrine and Covenants*. The problems went unresolved, and at the 1982 summer reunion—a week-long camp meeting—sponsored by the Restoration Festival, board members quarreled still more, and the organization soon broke up.[48]

At a business meeting for the Restoration Festival in January 1983, one faction was voted off the board. According to Price, the members ousted were those who had done the most work. The Restoration Festival soon ceased to be a functioning organization, although it remained legally organized. Richard Price had already resigned from the board and was beginning to move toward the development of his independent branch concept, which would be the primary strategy of the fundamentalists in dealing with the church hierarchy during the late 1980s.[49]

The next major publication of Price's was triggered by what became known as the "Presidential Papers." The First Presidency called all appointees and executive officers and their wives to Independence in January 1979 for a series of lectures. In these lectures the First Presidency set forth a theological basis for the church in the 1980s. The papers were not intended for public dissemination, but an appointee's wife allowed a relative to have a copy. Soon bootleg copies were circulating in the fundamentalist underground. To counter this leak, the First Presidency made the papers public and reproduced copies for anyone who wanted them. Many did want them and some, such as the retired Presiding Bishop G. Leslie DeLapp and his former counselor Henry Livingston, wrote discussions of what was wrong with the papers.

David Sheehy, an Independence businessman and uncle of Howard S. Sheehy of the First Presidency, gave Richard Price a copy of the papers. Price thought them a continuation of the Position Papers of a decade earlier and further evidence of the liberal heresy in the church. He spent three months writing comments on the Presidential Papers. Then Pamela Price worked with him for another month to complete the response. The result was the publication of the *Presidential Papers,* which consisted of the papers themselves along with Price's comments.[50]

Price felt that the *Presidential Papers* revealed that the First Presidency was heading the church toward such further heresies as ordaining women, conducting open communion, and espousing the idea of a universal church in which the Reorganized Church would be seen as no better than any other church. The *Presidential Papers,* written by members of the First Presidency, confirmed for fundamentalists that the Position Papers, written by staff members a decade earlier, clearly signaled the direction in which the leadership was taking the church.[51] Price would later come to the theological conclusion that, on that day in January 1979, "Wallace Smith lost his authority to be the president and prophet of the church and since that day the higher quorums of the church have been spiritually vacant and there are no apostles and there are no prophets in the church today on the higher church level." He concluded, "It is true that there is no authority left."[52] David Sheehy provided the money to print the *Presidential Papers.* Some of those involved feared being sued for copyright infringement and so rented a post office box in Raytown, Missouri, to handle orders for the book. There were no legal repercussions, however, and more than five thousand copies have been distributed.

Price had also been concerned about the proposed Reorganization temple in Independence ever since it was been called for in the revelation approved at the 1968 World Conference.[53] He believed at the time that the temple would not be built in the right spot. He also came to believe that it would be built for the wrong reasons and with the wrong design. Accordingly, the Prices wrote *The Temple of the Lord,* in which they noted that Joseph Smith, Jr., had designated that the temple in Independence should be built on the highest spot on the temple lot, which was one-half mile west of the city's square.[54] This would place the temple on land owned by the Church of Christ (Temple Lot). But the Reorganized Church built across River Street, according to Price a block east of the spot on which the temple had been intended. Construction of the temple was completed in 1993.

Price believed that the real reason behind the First Presidency's push to build was to gain the support of the Reorganization's membership and create a tourist attraction.[55] The temple has also been promoted as an "ensign for peace," but the Prices believe it to be a departure from the original intent of the temple. As Jeremiah said, in the last days they will cry, "peace, peace, when there is no peace," indicating that the Reorganized Church's hierarchy have been fulfilling the prophecy.[56] Instead, the Prices wrote that the temple's real purpose was to prepare a place for God to appear to the pure in heart. It should also be a house of prayer, a place of thanksgiving, a place for priesthood instruction, the place for Christ and God to dwell while in Zion, the place to bestow the endowment, and the place from which Christ shall govern Zion.[57]

The next major controversy in which Price involved himself concerned church history. In September 1983 the Reorganized Church historian Richard P. Howard published a carefully worded article on polygamy in the independent *John Whitmer Historical Association Journal.* Howard avoided answering the question of whether Smith was a polygamist, but noted that important early Reorganization leaders believed him to be. Because opposition to polygamy was a central issue on which the Reorganized Church was built, fundamentalists were upset at Howard's conclusions, even if they were stated rather vaguely.[58] Price again wrote a rebuttal to the latest publication that revealed how far afield liberals were taking the church. In less than a month the rebuttal was published as a full-page advertisement in the October 22, 1983, issue of the *Independence Examiner.* According to Pamela Price, the $812 fee for the advertisement was paid entirely by contributions from employees at the Reorganized Church headquarters in Independence.[59] Later Price published a booklet about what he termed the polygamy conspiracies. He concluded that "the fourth group which is trying to prove Joseph Smith, Jr., to be a polygamist is the present day liberal element in the RLDS Church. Why are these people pushing the polygamy issue now? The reason is because they are determined to take the RLDS Church into the National and World Council of Churches so it can be a part of the New Age Movement. In order to do this, they must discard the entire Restoration Movement, including the Prophet Joseph Smith."[60] Price viewed Howard's historical research as another example of the church leaders' conspiracy to reject all that was important in the Restoration.

Price's worst fears over the direction of the church were realized when, at the April 1984 World Conference, delegates approved a revelation allowing the ordination of women. Section 156 of the *Doctrine and Covenants* "will go down in history as the false document that finally split the Church," Price commented the following year.[61] It was the last straw for many fundamentalists, forcing them to answer the question of whether they could continue to participate in the Reorganized Church as it was constituted. For Price and many others, it was time for action.[62] Yet when Rudy Leutzinger and Patrick McKay, Sr., approached him shortly after the April 1984 World Conference to suggest that they form an independent branch, he was not yet ready.[63] He suggested in June 1984, two months after the church's decision to ordain women, that "many stalwart fundamental saints are determined to attend regular services in their congregations as long as possible in order to testify of the Restoration." He continued, "They have determined to stay in the RLDS Church, holding fast to the precious Restored gospel, without supporting the apostate leadership. This may require a special kind of courage as they face the possibility of silencing or even expulsion. But they know that God's work cannot be frustrated and that God will yet build Zion through the RLDS Church, after this 'liberal apostasy' has passed into history."[64]

The First Presidency established the date of November 17, 1985, as the first day in which women would be ordained. That was a day that "shall certainly live in infamy," Price later wrote, borrowing from Franklin Delano Roosevelt.[65] For a year and a half before that date, he had labored at writing a book about women's ordination and wanted to publish it before November 17. In late summer, the Prices went to Nauvoo, Illinois, for a week to work uninterrupted on the book manuscript. They finished the 224-page book but fell short of their publication goal. *Action Time* was released a day or two after the first ordinations were performed.

Price reported that while writing in Nauvoo, he was inspired by an idea of how best the Reorganized Church was to survive. He recalled how what became the Reorganization had survived as individual branches after the martyrdom of Joseph Smith, Jr., in 1844. Pamela Price reported that the idea had occurred to her, too, before her husband mentioned it. Thus both felt that they were independently led by the Holy Spirit to the same idea. What began as a book about women's ordination became a book about how the "true church" could survive in the face of what Price called the "liberal heresy." More than six thousand copies of *Action Time* had been distributed by 1990.[66] While the strategy of the Restoration Festival had been to hold occasion weekend gatherings while the fundamentalists remained active in their regular congregations, Price's strategy now was to quit attending the regular congregations and organize separate branches.

Price's actions had bothered the Reorganization hierarchy for years, but leaders had been unwilling to take action until 1985. That year, after the Center Stake president decided to remove Price's priesthood license, he received official notice of the silencing in a March 22, 1985, letter from O. C. Henson, Jr., president of Center Stake in Independence. Henson cited the reason as the fact that he published attacks "on the church leadership." Henson stated that these publications conflicted with conference resolutions that gave the First Presidency the power to preside over the church and discouraged publication of prophecies other than those accepted by the institutional church.[67] By the time of Price's silencing, the priesthood status of many other fundamentalists had also been removed. Price and his associates refused to recognize these silencings, believing that the fundamentalists were the true Reorganized Church and that the liberal leaders were in apostasy.

In an April 1986 address in Independence, "The Restoration Branches Movement," Price set forth his strategy for the survival of the church. He asked, "How shall the church be preserved when those in high places have complete control" and "are completely eradicating the restoration movement?"[68] He noted that some groups had left the Reorganized Church completely, saying that a new church had to be started. Some ten or fifteen men had declared themselves the "One Mighty and Strong" prophesied by Isaiah. They were premature, he believed; Saints should not leave the church, but should remain the "loyal remnant" within the organization. In time, he asserted, God would redeem the church.

Price believed that fundamentalists needed to agree to a set of restoration principles and worship in independent branches, according to pure Restoration principles, until God acted to set the church aright. He proposed commitment to fifteen principles.

1. The Inspired Version of the Bible, the 1908 Reorganized Church's edition of the Book of Mormon, and sections 1–144 of the Reorganization's *Doctrine and Covenants* are divinely sanctioned scriptures that contain the law of the church. By stopping at section 144, he rejected all of the revelations of W. Wallace Smith and his son, President Wallace B. Smith. According to Price, the church had been "without true leadership since W. Wallace Smith came into office in 1958."[69]

2. The first four volumes of the official Reorganized Church

history are "a correct rendition of the history of the church."

3. The Epitome of Faith—a Reorganization revision of the 1842 Wentworth Letter—is a correct and official statement of belief.

4. That there are two separate persons in the Godhead, and those who teach that there is one person are teaching false doctrine.

5. Joseph Smith, Jr., was a true prophet, and his experiences such as the "First Vision" in the grove and the obtaining of the Book of Mormon plates were actual facts of history.

6. The church that Smith established in 1830 was the true church restored, and the Reorganized Church is the lawful continuation of it.

7. Joseph Smith III, Frederick M. Smith, and Israel A. Smith were true prophets, and their interpretations of the doctrine and history were correct to be used in guiding the present-day church.

8. God has always been and continues to be unchangeable and so are the doctrines and structures of the church. They have been the same in every age.[70]

9. The present leaders of the Reorganized Church were in apostasy because they espoused liberalism, humanism, and ecumenism, which are false doctrines. They also rejected the Restoration movement and the idea that the "Three Standard Books" are true.

10. The present leaders of the church and all those who follow them have lost all of their authority.

11. Those who still proclaim the original Restoration beliefs still have their authority, and the church continues to exist through them. "Joseph Smith III said," according to Price, "that whenever a church is founded and its principles of faith are formulated, those declarations and principles become the constitution of its corporate and legal existence. When change is introduced, that portion that remains in adherence to the original faith is the church. Nor does it make any difference in law how few in numbers they be, the church is that part of the members that remain true to the original tenets."[71]

12. In his own due time, God will remove the liberal faction and recover the church, and will use it to fulfill his promises concerning Zion.

13. The church can be preserved through restorationists who determine to stay within the church and to save it from within. Voluntarily surrendering membership is a mistake; there may come a time when restorationists will be able to sue for possession of church buildings.

14. Priesthood who proclaim the original doctrines have full authority, even if they have been silenced or expelled by the hierarchy.

15. Saints must cease to support the liberal faction, financially or otherwise.[72]

Price argued that independent branches should preserve the gospel, with a set of common beliefs, as had been done in the earliest years of the Reorganized Church. "The word independent means that they are totally free of the hierarchy," he noted, "the term Restoration means that they are true to the original doctrines of the Reorganized Church. The word Branch is used to signify that they consider themselves a definite part of the Reorganized Church of Jesus Christ of Latter Day Saints, and that they are determined to remain loyal to its original beliefs."[73]

According to Price, the branches should each have a president and two counselors and keep records of business meetings and ordinances performed. They should not be dominated by one leader, but should operate by common consent. They should seek to become stable, and then can send delegates to conferences to elect men to be temporary officers until God sends a new prophet. The historical precedent of the rise of the Reorganization in the 1850s was a source of inspiration for Richard Price. He believed that the new prophet would be a descendent of Joseph Smith's male line. His name, of course, would have to be Smith. He also believed that the new prophet would not have to announce himself.

The strategy that Price set forth has been a prudent course for those who believe that the gospel is unchanging and that the hierarchy is leading the church into apostasy. The independent Restoration branches can probably survive for some time by offering the kind of worship and congregational life that appeals to fundamentalist Saints. Eventually, however, they will have to agree upon a prophet or the movement will fragment into many different groups that may dwindle away. But the efforts of people such as Richard Price, who publicize and promote the independent Restoration branches' strategy, seem to offer hope for the fundamentalist cause.

By 1987 the Reorganized Church's hierarchy had decided to take formal action to expel Price from the church. O. C. Henson wrote to him on January 9, 1987, saying that "serious consideration is being given to charging you in a Bishop's Court with unchristian conduct which could affect your church membership." The charges were based upon Price's alleged disregard for truth. Cited as examples were the two books, *The Saints at the Crossroads* and *Action Time;* the pamphlet "Decision Time"; and two articles published as advertisements in the *Independence Examiner,* the October 22, 1983, rebuttal to Richard Howard on polygamy and a December 20, 1986, article on the apparent move of the Reorganization hierarchy toward involvement in the World and National Councils of Churches.[74]

Price responded to the charges by offering to apologize if the leaders could show any untrue statements in his writings. Because he was being charged for criticisms he had made publicly against church leaders and not for a personal moral offense, Price saw no reason for the trial to be private, as was normal church procedure. He insisted on allowing the public to attend or, at a minimum, to allow a court reporter to transcribe the proceeding or to tape record the trial. David Simons, bishop of Center Stake and the presiding officer of the trial, insisted on following church policy of holding confidential trials and denied Price's demands. After much pretrial maneuvering, the trial was finally held in Independence on July 25, 1987. Price refused to participate in a private proceeding, so Karen McDonald, an attorney who was a church employee, was appointed to represent him. The trial proceeded, and he was expelled. He appealed to the Standing High Council of the church for review of his case, but the expulsion was upheld.

The expulsion process was widely publicized, and many regarded it as bad publicity for the Reorganized Church. One Reorganization member reported to his Sunday school class that an employee at Bendix Corporation, where Price had worked for thirty-four years, asked, "Why is your church persecuting a nice man like Richard Price?" Whether or not the church regarded it as bad publicity, the trial was an expensive process, both financially and otherwise. Perhaps for that reason the weapon of expulsion has not been used against fundamentalists since.

The question that remains, How long can fundamentalists remain united behind the strategy articulated by Richard Price? Although some fundamentalists march to the beat of a different drummer than Price, the majority of fundamentalist groups have operated in general consistency with his strategy. The main division within the fundamentalist movement is between those who, like Price, claim to be Reorganized Church members and are waiting for a prophet to set the church in order, and those who are organizing new churches and do not feel that there is any chance of saving the Reorganized Church.

Some fundamentalist groups began organizing almost immediately at the general church level. The Church of Christ, Restored, which has its base in Michigan, organized in 1987 and ordained eight apostles. The man selected to be senior apostle died a few months later. Another group, led by fundamentalists from the Quorum of Seventies, called a general assembly that in April 1991 effected a reorganization of the church, adopting the name "Restoration Church of Jesus Christ of Latter Day Saints." They also ordained eight apostles. Unity among this faction was short-lived, and the group split in early 1992.

Price asserts that such efforts have been premature. There have also been several self-proclaimed prophets, none of whom have impressed Richard Price. The most famous and notorious is Jeffrey Don Lundgren, now on death row in Ohio, convicted of murdering a family of five in 1989. Lesser known are the prophets Bob Baker, Ron Livingston, Eugene Walton, Robert Murdock, and John Cato.

Concerned about the division within fundamentalist ranks, in the summer of 1989 Price began publishing *Vision,* a thirty-two-page, slick-format magazine. He urged each local independent branch to be self-governing, to be free to make its own decisions but wanted consensus on the essentials of doctrine. So the purpose of *Vision* was "to keep the movement united while it is not united"—united in theology but free in self-government.[75] Price wanted to find a way to work together and yet not give too much power to a few.

Richard Price continues to enunciate his beliefs and to serve as the chief spokesperson for the fundamentalist cause. However, other leaders are growing impatient with Price's caution and are pushing for more serious organizing beyond the local level. It remains to be seen what Price's strategies will bear; he has been a tremendously influential dissenting voice in the late twentieth-century Reorganized Church and has given direction to an amorphous dissident element in the Reorganization during a chaotic period. Without his efforts, the fundamentalist movement would have probably been even more fragmented. Whether or not one agrees with him, Price formulated a cautious, prudent strategy in a situation where feelings run high on both sides and compromise between the hierarchy and the fundamentalists appear unlikely.

NOTES

1. This process was described as early as 1964 in Maurice L. Draper, "Sect-Denomination-Church Transition and Leadership in the Reorganized Church of Jesus Christ of Latter Day Saints," M.A. thesis, Kansas University, 1964. See also, Howard J. Booth, "Shifts in Restoration Thought," *Dialogue: A Journal of Mormon Thought* 13 (Fall 1980): 79–92; Larry W. Conrad and Paul Shupe, "An RLDS Reformation? Construing the Task of RLDS Theology," *Dialogue: A Journal of Mormon Thought* 18 (Summer 1985): 92–103; William D. Russell, "Beyond Literalism," *Dialogue: A Journal of Mormon Thought,* 19 (Spring 1986): 57–68.

2. See Richard Price, *Action Time: The Problem of Fundamentalism versus Liberalism in the Reorganized Church of Jesus Christ of Latter Day Saints, and Suggestions for Coping with that Problem* (Independence: Price Publishing Co., 1985), 118, 146.

3. Although these men were moderate in most of their conceptions, they were far to the left of many of the church's rank and file. They expressed their more open ideas in numerous publications and followed their beliefs in forming and executing church policy. Many of their ideas were presented in such published works as Maurice L. Draper, *Credo: I Believe* (Independence: Herald Publishing House, 1983); Clifford A. Cole, *Faith for New Frontiers* (Independence: Herald Publishing House, 1959); Peter A. Judd and Clifford A. Cole, *Distinctives: Yesterday and Today* (Independence: Herald Publishing House, 1983); Roy A. Cheville, *Spirituality in the Space Age* (Independence: Herald Publishing House, 1962).

4. Robert Flanders, especially, excited the ire of more traditional Saints by suggesting that among other, less attractive features of his persona, Joseph Smith, Jr., had instituted the Mormon practice of polygamy. See Robert Bruce Flanders, *Nauvoo: Kingdom on the Mississippi* (Urbana: University of Illinois Press, 1965).

5. Indicative of Yarrington's standards were his observations on ethics. See Roger Yarrington, *Restoration Ethics Today* (Independence: Herald Publishing House, 1963).

6. Two excellent examples of the more liberal approach are James E. Lancaster, "By the Gift and Power of God," *Saints' Herald,* November 15, 1962, 798–802, 806, 817, reprinted with minor revisions in the *John Whitmer Historical Association Journal* 3 (1983): 51–61, and in *The Word of God: Essays on Mormon Scripture,* ed. Dan Vogel (Salt Lake City: Signature Books, 1990), 97–113; and Lloyd R. Young, "Concerning the Virgin Birth: Comments on the Doctrine," *Saints' Herald,* February 1, 1964, 77–78, 94. The first questions the traditional conception of how the Book of Mormon had been translated and raises the specter of seer stones and magic. The second challenges the probability of the virgin birth of Christ. Both raised a furor within the church.

7. Personal interview with Richard Price, December 7, 1990, Independence, Mo.

8. William J. Knapp, "Professionalizing Religious Education in the Church: The New Curriculum Controversy," *John Whitmer Historical Association Journal* 2 (1982): 47–59.

9. Price Publishing Company in Independence, Missouri, published *The Position Papers;* the paper on the Book of Mormon was also published. See Wayne Ham, "Problems in Interpreting the Book of Mormon as History," *Courage: A Journal of History, Thought, and Action* 1 (September 1970): 15–22.

10. Donald D. Landon, *A History of Donald D. Landon while under General Conference Appointment, 1951–1970: An Oral History Memoir* (Independence: Department of History, Reorganized Church of Jesus Christ of Latter Day Saints, 1970), 94.

11. Knapp, "Professionalizing Religious Education," 49.

12. Ibid., 49; Donald D. Landon to William D. Russell, January 28, 1987.

13. William D. Russell, "Reorganized Mormons Beset by Controversy," *Christian Century,* June 17, 1970, 770.

14. This was from Joseph Smith's 1842 account of his "First Vision." It has been kept continually in print as *Joseph Smith Tells His Own Story* (Independence: Herald Publishing House, N.d.), a tract issued by the church, until recently. For an analysis of Reorganized Church perspectives on the First Vision, see Richard P. Howard, "An Analysis of Six Contemporary Accounts Touching Joseph Smith's First Vision," in *Restoration Studies I,* ed. Maurice L. Draper and Clare D. Vlahos (Independence: Herald Publishing House, 1980), 95–117.

15. *Zion's Warning* [Independence, Mo.], February 1970, 1.

16. Personal interview with Richard Price, December 7, 1990, Independence, Mo.

17. Ibid.; Richard Price, *The Saints at the Crossroads* (Independence: Cumorah Books, 1974).

18. Personal interview with Richard Price, July 25, 1990, Independence, Mo.

19. Price, *Saints at the Crossroads,* iv.

20. Ibid., 21.

21. Ibid., 94. As a means of supporting this assertion Price cited Joseph Smith, Jr., writing from Kirtland, January 11, 1833. See Joseph Smith III and Heman C. Smith, *History of the Reorganized Church of Jesus Christ of Latter Day Saints* (Independence: Herald Publishing House, 1967), 1:267–68.

22. Spencer and Ham graduated from Saint Paul School of Theology, and Landon also studied there. Sparkes was a graduate of Union Theological Seminary in New York. Landon and Sparkes soon left church employment, but Spencer and Ham rose to prominent positions in the church hierarchy. Spencer became president of the Quorum of Twelve Apostles, and Ham was placed in charge of temple ministries in Independence.

23. Price, *Saints at the Crossroads,* 92.

24. Ibid., 93.

25. Ibid., 101.

26. Ibid., 102–12.

27. Ibid., 112.

28. *Book of Doctrine and Covenants* (Independence: Herald Publishing House, 1970), secs. 143:3 (1954), 147:6 (1964), 150:10–11 (1972), 156 (1984).

29. Price, *Saints at the Crossroads,* 114; *Position Papers* (Independence: Cumorah Books, 1975), 46.

30. *Position Papers,* 49–50; Price, *Saints at the Crossroads,* 118.

31. Price, *Saints at the Crossroads,* 131; *Presidential Papers* (Independence: Cumorah Books, 1979), 98.

32. Price, *Saints at the Crossroads,* 136.

33. Ibid., 136–39; *Position Papers,* 117–26.

34. Price, *Saints at the Crossroads,* 139.

35. Ibid., 138; *Position Papers,* 122.

36. Price, *Saints at the Crossroads,* 139.

37. Ibid., 223–24.

38. "President Smith's [March 31, 1975] Television Interview" (Independence: Cumorah Books, N.d.).

39. Richard Price, "Decision Time" (Independence: Cumorah Books, 1975); personal interview with Richard Price, July 25, 1990, Independence, Mo..

40. First Presidency to Administrative Officers and Appointees, December 29, 1975, copy in my possession.

41. Personal interview with Richard Price, July 25, 1990, Independence, Mo.

42. This statement, or one similar in wording and identical in intention, has appeared on most of the publications issued by Cumorah Books and its successor, Price Publishing Co., between 1976 and the present.

43. Personal interview with Richard Price, July 25, 1990, Independence, Mo.

44. Merva Bird later wrote the widely circulated pamphlet, "Women's Ordination? No!" published by Cumorah Books in 1980.

45. *Restoration Voice* has served as the primary source for communicating the traditional Reorganization message. While it contains testimonies, fiction, history, and theology written by present-day fundamentalists, much of the material is composed of articles that originally appeared in the *Saints' Herald,* especially during the 1940s and 1950s, the period that the fundamentalists view as the last era before the rise of liberal heresy.

46. The program and papers of this event were published. See *Restoration Festival, September 22–24, 1978* (Independence: N.p., 1978); personal interview with Richard Price, July 25, 1990, Independence, Mo.

47. To forestall the attraction of the Restoration Festival, the institutional church tried in 1979 to organize its own weekend to appeal to the same traditions within the church. An attempt to co-opt the opposition and make room for the expression of fundamentalist concepts, the retreat was only moderately successful. See *Faith of Our Fathers: The Call to Establish the Cause of Zion, Sermon and Presentation Transcripts, November 23–25, 1979* (Independence: Creative Ministries Inc., 1979).

48. Personal interview with Richard Price, March 22, 1989, Independence, Mo.

49. Personal interview with Richard Price, July 25, 1990, Independence, Mo.

50. Ibid.; *Presidential Papers.*

51. Personal interview with Richard Price, July 25, 1990, Independence, Mo. See also "Presidency Confirms Presidential Papers," a four-page introduction to the *Presidential Papers* (1984 ed.).

52. Richard Price, "The Restoration Branches Movement," unpublished address, April 27, 1986, Independence, Mo.

53. *Book of Doctrine and Covenants,* sec. 149:6.

54. Richard Price and Pamela Price, *The Temple of the Lord* (Independence: Price Publishing Co., 1982, 1985).

55. Personal interview with Richard Price, December 7, 1990, Independence, Mo.

56. Ibid.; Jeremiah 8:14; *Book of Doctrine and Covenants*, sec. 156:3, 5a.

57. Price and Price, *Temple of the Lord*, 117.

58. Richard P. Howard, "The Changing RLDS Response to Mormon Polygamy: A Preliminary Analysis," *John Whitmer Historical Association Journal* 3 (1983): 14–29. In this essay Howard offered a detailed analysis of the origins of the doctrine, suggesting that it was a historical accident that grew near and immediately after the death of Joseph Smith, Jr. This conservative discussion of polygamy's origins is opposed to such countervailing arguments as Lawrence Foster, *Religion and Sexuality: Three American Communal Experiments of the Nineteenth Century* (New York: Oxford University Press, 1981); Danel W. Bachman, "A Study of the Mormon Practice of Plural Marriage before the Death of Joseph Smith," M.A. thesis, Purdue University, 1975; Richard S. Van Wagoner, *Mormon Polygamy: A History* (Salt Lake City: Signature Books, 1985); Danel W. Bachman, "New Light on an Old Hypothesis: The Ohio Origins of the Revelation on Eternal Marriage," *Journal of Mormon History* 5 (1978): 19–31.

59. Richard Price, "Polygamy: How the Latter Day Saints Were Betrayed by Men Nearest the Prophet," *Independence Examiner*, October 22, 1983; Lisa Wade, "The Dividing Line," *Independence Examiner*, October 22, 1983; personal interviews with Richard and Pamela Price, July 25, 1990, Independence, Mo.

60. Richard Price, *The Polygamy Conspiracies* (Independence: Cumorah Books, 1984), quote from 31.

61. Price, *Action Time*, 34.

62. Personal interview with Richard Price, July 25, 1990, Independence, Mo.; Dale Ratliff, "Deception," *Restoration Foundation*, Winter 1984, 1–2; Bird, "Women's Ordination?"; "Women's Ordination Questionnaire" (Independence: Cumorah Books, 1983), with a letter-writing campaign to oppose the practice.

63. Personal interview with Richard Price, March 22, 1989, Independence, Mo.

64. Price, "Decision Time," 48 (3d printing June 1984).

65. Price, *Action Time*, 44.

66. Personal interview with Richard Price, July 25, 1990, Independence, Mo.

67. O. C. Henson, Jr., to Richard Price, March 22, 1985, copy in my possession; *Rules and Resolutions* (Independence: Herald Publishing House, 1980), General Conference Resolutions 386 and 709; "Silencing of Richard Price," audio cassette of interview of Price and O. C. Henson at time of silencing, March 12, 1985.

68. Price, "The Restoration Branches Movement"; Richard Price and Larry Harlacher, "Restoration Branches Movement: Pamphlet No. 1: Forming of Restoration Branches" (Independence: Price Publishing Co., 1986). Some of Price's publications were aimed at helping other fundamentalists develop strat-

egies for opposing the hierarchy. See *Blue Valley Packet* (Independence: Price Publishing Co., N.d.), and *Buckner Packet* (Independence: Price Publishing Co., N.d.).

69. Price, *Action Time,* 59.

70. Ibid., 2.

71. *Independence Examiner,* April 9, 1988; Price, *Action Time,* 112–13.

72. The fifteen points are contained in the Price, "The Restoration Branches Movement."

73. Price, "Restoration Branches Movement."

74. Price published four "Expulsion Packets" containing correspondence and other documents relative to his trial. Unless otherwise noted, information on Price's expulsion is taken from these sources.

75. Personal interview with Richard Price, July 25, 1990, Independence, Mo.

16

Apostate Believers:
Jerald and Sandra Tanner's Encounter
with Mormon History

Lawrence Foster

For more than three decades, Jerald and Sandra Tanner have devoted their lives to exposing and trying to destroy Mormonism. They have succeeded in upsetting Mormons of various persuasions, largely because of their abrasive writing style, which is most nearly reminiscent of FBI undercover agents reporting back to J. Edgar Hoover on the terrible continuing threat of the worldwide communist (read: Mormon) conspiracy. Yet the Tanners have been more than simply gadflies; in curious and often indirect ways, their work has also been a factor helping to stimulate serious Mormon historical writing. In addition to publishing many hard-to-find Mormon historical documents, their criticisms have highlighted issues that professional Mormon historians, operating from a very different perspective, have also sought to address. Above all, the Tanners reflect both the strengths and weaknesses of the very Mormonism which, rather paradoxically, they are trying to destroy. Their life and work can tell us much about the dynamics of dissent in exclusivistic religious movements.[1]

The distinctiveness and depth of the Tanners' sense of mission can best be understood by looking initially at the nature of their activities since they first began producing literature critical of Mormonism in 1959. The most widely known apostates in Mormonism or in other religious movements usually make one dramatic break, produce one great exposé, or go on one major speaking tour before gradually sinking from sight or moving on to engage in other activities. Whether the break be basically idealistic in motivation, as in the case of a William Law or a T. B. H. Stenhouse, or primarily opportunistic, as in the case of a John C. Bennett or an Ann Eliza Webb, apostates seldom sustain a broad-ranging and historically valuable career of exposure over many years. Similarly limited is the historical contribution of missionaries from other religious traditions who devote their lives to trying to con-

vert Mormons to another faith. Such missionary anti-Mormons tend
to be obviously self-serving, with little regard for history except as a
polemical device to try to turn Mormons into Baptists, Methodists,
Catholics, or followers of some other tradition.

Jerald and Sandra Tanner's career is more complex than either the
typical apostate or anti-Mormon patterns. Not only have they been
unusually persistent and dedicated, producing a continuing stream of
documents and polemical pieces, but the caliber of their writing has
also in recent years been higher than that typically found in this literature. The sheer volume of their writing is impressive. Scott Faulring's
bibliography of their publications from 1959 through 1982 lists more
than two hundred items.[2] These range from Jerald Tanner's first one-
page broadside "Does the Book of Mormon Teach Racial Prejudice?"
to their massive, closely argued, six-hundred-page study *Mormonism—
Shadow or Reality?* Reprints of Mormon historical and religious writings, important manuscripts, and anti-Mormon exposés comprise forty-four of their publications. And forty-nine of their items are polemical
pieces of twenty pages or more that debate virtually every significant
topic that has surfaced since the 1960s in Mormonism. The Tanners
were productive during the restrictive 1960s when primary Mormon
historical publications were often difficult to secure; they remained
active during the halcyon days of the more liberal 1970s, which saw
the great flowering of Mormon historical writing; and they continued
to be in the news during the 1980s, at a time when serious Mormon
scholarship was forced increasingly on the defensive.

The roots of this extraordinary career lay in Jerald Tanner's early
disillusionment with Mormonism. He had been reared as a Mormon
who "believed that Joseph Smith was a prophet of God and that I belonged to the only true church."[3] During his teens, however, he began
to feel personally at loose ends and to question the inconsistencies in
the historical record of Mormonism. His initial questioning in 1958
did not cause him to reject Mormonism entirely. Rather, he joined
Pauline Hancock's group, headquartered in Missouri, which believed
in the Book of Mormon but renounced nearly all other beliefs that dis-
tinguish Mormonism from fundamentalist Protestantism. Tanner began holding evening religious meetings in Salt Lake City, while learning to be a machinist during the day.

Sandra McGee entered the picture in 1959 when she attended one
of the meetings that the nineteen-year-old Jerald was holding. She had
grown up as a fairly conventional Mormon in the Los Angeles area,
although she had been independent-minded, questioning what she had
been taught. When Sandra met Jerald in Salt Lake City, she was ini-

tially more interested in him than in his religion. "It seemed that the only way I was going to get him, though, was through his religion."[4] Two months after their first meeting, they were married.

From that point, their joint career gradually developed. Four months after their marriage, Sandra converted to evangelical Protestantism. The couple began putting out fliers, then pamphlets, books, and historical documents, explaining their position and trying to work through their own understanding of Mormonism and where it had gone wrong. From the very beginning, the Tanners' concerns were not simply doctrinal, but also social. Jerald's fierce opposition to Mormon racism, for example, has been a recurrent motif throughout his career and has contributed to many of his most important researches into Mormon religious documents such as the Book of Abraham.[5] The Tanners' publication in 1961 of the complete edition of *A Book of Commandments* (1833), the earliest book of Joseph Smith's revelations, marked their first venture into making vital and hard-to-find Mormon historical and religious documents available to a larger audience. Much of the motivation behind such publication appears to have been the polemical concern to embarrass present-day Mormons by showing the inconsistencies and changes in Mormonism since its earliest years. The larger impact of such publication efforts, however, has been to help some Mormons become more aware of their rich heritage and to encourage scholarly attention to the fascinating early days of the Mormon movement.

Another important transition in the Tanners' career came in 1964, when Jerald quit his machinist job to devote all his time to their anti-Mormon publishing. That work has always been conducted on a shoestring and threatened with closing because of Jerald's ill health and the recurrent shortages of funds. The Tanners carry on their publication activities from their large and somewhat ramshackle old house at 1350 South West Temple in Salt Lake City, across from the Derks Field Stadium, where they also maintain their bookstore. At first, they named their organization the Modern Microfilm Company because of their short-lived use of microfilm, but they soon switched to the more convenient photo-offset process, which they continue to use. Also in 1964, the Tanners put out the first of more than seventy issues of their flier, the *Salt Lake City Messenger*, an occasional publication that for more than twenty-five years has provided a fascinating, albeit polemical, perspective on the latest Mormon controversies, new discoveries in Mormon history, and the state of various anti-Mormon research and activities.

Finally, 1964 also saw the first publication of the Tanners' major work, *Mormonism—Shadow or Reality?* It had appeared previously in briefer form under another title and would later be enlarged in 1972, 1982, and 1987, for a final total of more than six hundred pages. *Mormonism—Shadow or Reality?* has sold more than fifty thousand copies in its various editions and its 1980 abridgment and incorporates the Tanners' most important research, discoveries, and allegations that have appeared in their other publications.[6] The 1980 abridgment of the book, *The Changing World of Mormonism*, published by the Moody Press in Chicago, reflected the Tanners' move toward more mainstream evangelical anti-Mormon work. Also suggesting a partial shift in direction was the Tanners' decision, which went into effect in 1983, to become a nonprofit corporation and change the name of their organization from the somewhat anachronistic Modern Microfilm Company to the Utah Lighthouse Ministry, Inc.

Why was the Tanners' disillusionment with Mormonism so deep and their hostility toward it so sustained? A key factor was Jerald Tanner's reaction to his initial naive and unrealistic understanding of Mormonism. As a youth, he appears to have believed that Joseph Smith was perfect and that the Latter-day Saint church had all the answers and could do no wrong. When his research increasingly showed him that Smith had flaws, that the eternally true (and some assert, changeless) church had in fact changed, and that Mormon leaders had sometimes made mistakes, even very serious ones, he was furious. He felt that he had been cheated—sold a bill of goods—that the church had willfully lied to him about matters of the highest importance. The anger, even fury, that emerges from much of the Tanners' writing, with its frequent obtrusive underlining, LARGE CAPITALS, and <u>LARGE CAPITALS WITH UNDERLINING</u>, along with sharp attacks on the personal motives of Joseph Smith and other church leaders, seems to be crying out for the Mormon church either to prove that it is perfect or else cease making its exclusivistic claims to truth. Sandra Tanner summarized this aspect of their feelings toward Mormonism when she observed:

> I see the Mormon Church leadership failing to come to grips with the problems in their own history. They won't even admit there are problems. . . . Certainly there are problems in the history of any group of people you get together to do anything, . . . but the difference is, Mormonism is claiming they are *The* Church that God's directing, as opposed to all the other ones just doing it on manmade ability. So when you make that kind of a distinction, one expects a better performance record. . . . They are not just saying that they are a nice church down the street that's doing a

little better job than the Baptists, they're claiming to be the only true one and that the very sincere Baptist minister is totally wrong. . . . When they make those kinds of specific claims, I expect their history to conform with the kinds of claims they make for it.[7]

Yet there was surely more to Jerald Tanner's hostility than a purely intellectual disillusionment with his childhood understanding of Mormon truth claims. Many people who have become intellectually disillusioned with Mormonism have nevertheless continued to express appreciation for the Mormon life-style and the culture the church has helped to create. Although the Tanners do make perfunctory acknowledgment of Mormon social strengths, their overall tone is far more bitter than that of the average former Mormon. Perhaps this is because Jerald's social as well as intellectual contacts with Mormonism appear to have been disappointing. As described in the Faulring interviews with Sandra Tanner, Jerald's family life seems to have been filled with stress. Both he and his family appear to have been isolated from many positive aspects of Mormon culture. His father developed a drinking problem, and Jerald himself, during his teenage years, began to drink so heavily that for a time he feared that he might become an alcoholic.[8] Some of Jerald's Mormon friends also were outsiders who drank and did not conform to the ideal pattern the church has sought to develop. Quite possibly Jerald's failure to find satisfying social contacts in the Mormon church contributed to the deep bitterness he eventually developed toward it. By comparison, Sandra Tanner, whose social experiences with Mormonism while growing up were positive, expresses a more balanced understanding of the personal appeal of Mormon culture, even when she criticizes specific Mormon truth claims.

Whatever the roots of Jerald's disillusionment and bitterness may have been, the factors that have sustained the Tanners' anti-Mormon activities over more than three decades also call for explanation. Of prime importance was the cooperative relationship that developed between Jerald and Sandra Tanner. Neither individual alone could have been so effective; together they have compensated for each other's weaknesses and have developed a remarkably strong partnership. Jerald, an intense and almost painfully shy man, is primarily responsible for the research and writing. His own drive, more than any other factor, sustains their operation. Whether Sandra would even have become an active anti-Mormon had she been by herself is open to question. On the other hand, Jerald would hardly have been effective by himself, either. Sandra, whose personality is warmer and more outgoing, takes major responsibility for dealing with the public. Whereas Jerald is often socially inept and strident in his writing, Sandra conveys a real warmth and caring that only close associates have the opportunity of experiencing with Jerald. Together the Tanners have reared a family and have developed an unusual career for themselves, a career with far more intellectual challenge than the machinist work that Jerald initially intended to pursue.

Accidents of history also furthered the development of the Tanners' career of exposure. Jerald had the good fortune to begin his anti-Mormon writing and publication at a time when Mormon intellectuals were already independently becoming increasingly self-conscious about their past and seeking to understand it better. In the early 1960s, most nineteenth-century Mormon publications could be found in a few major libraries, but only dedicated and assiduous scholars were able to locate and work with them. When the Tanners began publishing complete and scrupulously accurate reproductions of classic early Mormon documents that were in the public domain, that publication opened up the possibility of serious home study. A small but significant market began to develop among Mormons who wanted to be able to explore their own past, even though they might resent the Tanners' other, purely polemical tracts. Yet support was often tenuous. On at least one occasion, in 1966, the Tanners considered giving up their publication work and instead going to Africa as missionaries.[9] They nevertheless remained, largely because their own career and polemicism increasingly tied them to Mormonism, albeit as critics and not believers.

To understand the Tanners' career, one must compare their approach to that of four other types of people who have sometimes sustained an unconventional relationship with Mormonism. One group with whom the Tanners have often been erroneously linked is the professional historians, whose chief goals have been to reconstruct the Mormon past and help modern Mormons better to appreciate their distinctive heritage. Second are the "closet doubters," individuals who have quietly bracketed their points of uncertainty or disagreement with Mormonism while continuing to be active and creative participants in the church, primarily for social reasons. Third are the embittered former Mormons who have given up not only Mormonism but also all other religious belief, convinced that if Mormonism is not "true," then no religion is. Fourth are the former Mormons who have converted to an alternative religious faith and are actively trying to convert Mormons to that faith as well. These four types of individuals differ widely in background and motivation, yet sometimes they all have been assumed to fit into one mold.[10]

Despite some similarities with each of these groups, the Tanners have close affinity with only one of them. Unlike the Mormon historians who try to understand the Mormon past so that the church can more effectively deal with the present, the Tanners seek to use every bit of historical evidence they can find (even if it would seem objectively favorable to Mormonism) to attack the church. The Tanners also have little in common with the closet doubter because they now feel that they already "know" that the Mormon church is "false" and hence are only collecting evidence to support that predetermined position. Likewise, the Tanners differ from those disillusioned former Mormons who have rejected not only Mormonism but all religious truth. Although the Tanners do retain from Mormonism a belief that a religion is either "true" or "false," they are convinced that they have located ultimate truth in their new faith—which happens to be a form of Protestant fundamentalism.

The institutional embodiment of the Tanners' faith is an evangelical Protestant denomination of more than two hundred thousand members in the United States and some two million adherents worldwide: the Christian and Missionary Alliance. The Tanners and their three children have been active in that church in Salt Lake City since the 1970s. Jerald serves as an elder and is involved with various social outreach activities. When the Tanners write about their own religious convictions, as in *A Look at Christianity*, they avoid discussing their specific institutional affiliation and instead focus, in typical Protestant fundamentalist fashion, on the importance of conversion, being "born again."[11] By contrast to the often-harsh rhetoric of their attacks on Mormonism, in person they can be kind, even gentle individuals. Disciplined, hard-working, and committed, they might seem to be almost an ideal model for Mormon missionaries—except that they have devoted their lives to trying to destroy the Mormon church.

What have the reactions of Mormon scholars been toward the Tanners, and what significance has their work had for the development of Mormon historical studies? To say that Mormon intellectuals have been ambivalent about the Tanners would be an extreme understatement. Although many Mormon scholars are disturbed by some of the same Latter-day Saint weaknesses that the Tanners also criticize, the scholars' dissatisfactions derive from an almost wholly different perspective from that of the Tanners. Many Mormon historians, for example, dislike the way in which the conservative element of Mormon leadership has frequently made access to the church's own records difficult for even its finest and most loyal scholars and has in subtle and far-from-subtle ways controlled, rewritten, or even suppressed candid scholarly studies of the faith. If Mormonism is, as it claims, the true religion, then its history, if properly understood, should support that status. Many of the finest Mormon historians thus believe that the full truth, if fairly and honestly portrayed, would best serve the long-term interests of the church.

By contrast, the Tanners are critical of what they term the Mormon "suppression" of documents and evidence for a very different reason: they believe that the full record of Mormonism, if it could be made available, would utterly refute the church's claims to truth and lead to the destruction of the faith. At every point, the Tanners see fraud, conspiracy, and cover-ups. They always assume the worst possible motives in assessing the actions of Mormon leaders, even when those leaders faced extremely complex problems that had no simple solutions. And the Tanners judge the validity of Mormon beliefs not so much within the context of the church's own framework as by contrast with a normative Christianity that early Mormonism emphatically rejected and claimed to supersede.

Such radically different approaches lead to radically different uses of identical evidence by historians and by the Tanners. In general, the primary goal of the historians has been to understand and appreciate the remarkably complex and multifaceted movement that constitutes Mormonism. Toward that end, Mormon historians, like historians in all fields, seek to sift through all pertinent evidence in order to reconstruct the fullest possible picture of the past and its significance for the present. Both positive and negative factors are candidly considered in trying to come to a realistic understanding of Mormon development.

By contrast, the Tanners sound like high school debaters. Every bit of evidence, even if it could be most plausibly presently in a positive way, is represented as yet another nail in the coffin being prepared for the Mormon church. There is no spectrum of colors, only blacks and whites, good guys and villains, in the Tanners' published writings. Even when they backhandedly praise objective Mormon historical scholarship, they do so primarily as a means of twisting that scholarship for use as yet another debater's ploy to attack the remaining—and in their eyes insurmountable—Mormon deficiencies.

All too often, the Tanners' work simply provides a mirror image of the very Mormonism that it is attacking. The Tanners have repeatedly assumed a holier-than-thou stance, refusing to be fair in applying the same debater standards of absolute rectitude that they demand of Mormonism to their own actions, writings, and beliefs. Whereas the Mormon church, for example, has frequently argued that the end (supporting Mormonism) justifies the means (withholding or suppressing evidence), the Tanners have, in effect, simply reversed the argument while continuing to use the same true-false framework. They argue that the end (destroying Mormonism) justifies the means (publishing anything they believe could prove damaging to Mormonism).

This ends-justifies-means approach extends not only to reprinting older published Mormon or anti-Mormon works that are now in the public domain or to reproducing archival material without authorization. It also includes publishing contemporary scholarly work of living individuals without their permission. As my own interview with Jerald and Sandra Tanner in May 1982 indicates, they genuinely appear not to see themselves in violation of U.S. copyright law or Christian ethics when they published and sold a scholarly paper without any attempt to secure the permission of its author.[12] Such behavior has caused even some Mormon scholars who are critical of Mormon church restriction of access to documents and writings to become frustrated and angry about the Tanners' methods.

The Tanners' own writing style also is essentially a mirror image of that of unsophisticated Mormon writers. The stereotypical Mormon thesis in history or religious studies, for example, begins with a ringing affirmation of faith in the Mormon church, is followed by a long and poorly digested presentation with obtrusive block quotations and little analysis, and ends (no matter what has been said previously) with yet another ringing affirmation of faith in Mormonism. The Tanners' basic format, by contrast, begins with a sharp attack on Mormon perfidy, is followed by numerous long quotations interspersed with purple prose, and ends (no matter what has been presented) with a ringing denunciation of the vile delusion of Mormonism. One cannot help but be reminded of James Thurber's parable of "The Bear Who Left It Alone," the moral of which was "You might as well fall flat on your face as lean over too far backward."[13]

Yet if the Tanners' own work falls short as history, it nevertheless has helped stimulate historical studies. Jerald is a brilliant analyst of detail, with an almost uncanny ability to spot textual inconsistencies that demand explanation. His analysis showing that a pamphlet denunciation of Mormonism attributed to Oliver Cowdery was, in fact, a clever forgery, is only one example of research and analysis that would do credit to any professional historian.[14] More recently and significantly, Jerald stood almost alone among those studying Mormon history in publicly raising doubts about the authenticity of the "Salamander letter," purportedly describing Joseph Smith's early experiences that led to the production of the Book of Mormon. The vast majority of Mormon scholars had accepted as genuine this and other documents that subsequently have been shown to be forged by Mark

W. Hofmann. Jerald, despite his desire to find evidence discrediting the conventional Mormon story, felt that something did not ring true about the letter, and he was prepared to voice his doubts publicly. The letter seemed to him almost *too* close to expectation to be correct.[15]

The impact of the Tanners' publication of primary Mormon printed documents also must not be underestimated. Those who began their scholarly work on Mormonism during the more open period of the 1970s may find difficulty realizing the problems earlier scholars encountered in gaining ready access to basic Mormon publications. Even essential early journals such as the *Evening and Morning Star, Messenger and Advocate, Elders' Journal, Times and Seasons,* and *Millennial Star* were all but unavailable to the general public until the Tanners began their republication. That republication and the controversy associated with it in turn stimulated further efforts by other publishers and even the Mormon church itself to reprint its own writings. Yet without the goad provided by independent critics of the church, such activity might well have proceeded more slowly, if at all.

A third and much more problematic impact of the Tanners on Mormon scholarship has come through their unauthorized publication of Mormon archival materials. Although such publication has been relatively infrequent, it has generated some of the most sensational cases and has produced the greatest distress among both Mormon scholars and the hierarchy alike. Usually the Tanners have published brief extracts or short documents such as letters. In themselves, these documents are interesting but usually not particularly sensational—until the Tanners' unauthorized publication generates controversy. The precise channels through which the Tanners have secured copies of some of the documents have understandably remained secret. In cases in which their general methods are known, however, the techniques by which their materials have been acquired appear to leave much to be desired, ethically speaking.

The most problematic recent case involved publication of extracts from the Nauvoo diary of William Clayton, Joseph Smith's private secretary. Typed extracts from the diary, which had been made legitimately by the Mormon historian Andrew Ehat, were photocopied and distributed without his knowledge or permission by a third party. When the Tanners secured the items, they proceeded to publish them despite Ehat's strenuous objection. Although the Tanners initially were judged guilty of theft of personal property, the state appeals court eventually overturned the conviction, largely on the grounds of the weakness of Ehat's own claims to have special rights to use the primary manuscript sources with which he had worked.[16]

Despite the Tanners' extensive publication record and the hostility they have aroused, few public analyses of their work have appeared. When the Tanners' arguments have been attacked in Mormon publications, as has occurred on many occasions, their names and the titles of their writings have almost never been cited. Indeed, until recently even such independent Mormon scholarly journals as *Dialogue: A Journal of Mormon Thought* and *Sunstone,* which discuss all manner of controversial issues, have largely avoided mentioning the Tanners by name, much less analyzing their work explicitly.

What accounts for this reluctance to discuss the Tanners? The Tanners' answer is simple: The Mormon church is afraid of them. In their view, it has been engaged in a "conspiracy of silence" because it cannot answer their objections. The Tanners argue that if the church were to try systematically to answer their objections, it would realize the error of its ways and collapse. By failing to deal with them directly, the church, in the Tanners' opinion, is providing yet another proof of its underlying fraudulence and repressive mind control.

This interpretation fails to deal with many complex factors that have contributed to Mormon reticence about discussing the Tanners in print. The most obvious point is that neither conservative nor liberal Mormons think that the Tanners are really serious about wanting a truly open discussion or considering approaches that differ from their own chip-on-shoulder, anti-Mormon mindset. On the one hand, the Tanners have repeatedly demanded that Mormonism live up to standards of rectitude impossible for any human organization to achieve or else give up its truth claims. On the other hand, the Tanners simultaneously tell the Mormon church that even if it were somehow able to live up to its impossibly high standards, it still would be false because it is not normative Christianity as they understand it.

In short, probably nothing that the Mormon church could realistically do in the foreseeable future would satisfy the Tanners. They have set up a logically closed system within which they can refute Mormonism to their satisfaction either if it is true to its original distinctive mission or if, as now appears to be happening, it increasingly seeks to moderate its historic uniqueness and adopt a position closer to the form of Protestant fundamentalism the Tanners themselves espouse. The Tanners seem to be playing a skillful shell game in which the premises for judgment are conveniently shifted so that the conclusion is always the same—negative. For example, the Tanners could attack the Mormon church for its racist policy of excluding blacks from full participation before 1978; but after that date, when the policy was courageously eliminated, they turned around and attacked the church on the grounds that it is supposedly all-knowing and changeless on matters of principle.[17] Similarly, the Tanners have strongly criticized the Mormon temple ceremony, yet instead of praising the changes in that ceremony in April 1990 that made it more acceptable to ecumenical and women's concerns, they instead argued that the changes simply discredited it further.[18]

Faced with such resolute unwillingness to consider anything Mormonism does in a positive light or to engage in a constructive dialog about differing approaches, the Mormon church as an organization has understandably chosen to ignore the Tanners as much as possible. By the Tanners' own admission, their following is a small, albeit loyal, one.[19] The church sees no advantage in engaging in vitriolic polemic with virtual unknowns and thereby giving them publicity.[20] A much more effective approach is to try to stand above the battle. Furthermore, as the knowledge somehow percolates through the church that there are still nasty apostates somewhere attacking the true faith, average Mormons are thereby encouraged to further support the church.

The reluctance of Mormon intellectuals to discuss the Tanners in writing has more complex roots. Initially, serious historians were just getting into the relevant primary material and trying to make sense of it themselves. Although these scholars had a better understanding of some of the difficult issues that the Tanners highlighted, their understanding was at first very tentative and certainly not sufficiently developed to go into print. The historians also had problems of their own as their research began leading them into a slow but major reconstruction of Mormon history (and most recently, theology), which itself posed a substantial challenge to the conventional wisdom of present-day Mormonism.

Many Latter-day Saint historians have been as profoundly frustrated as are the Tanners by the historical naiveté of some church leaders. The Tanners have made a career of attacking such naiveté as though it constituted the essence of Mormonism. In effect, some of the less well-informed church leaders are providing the very rope by which the Tanners are trying to hang them. Such leaders have confused the truth of Mormonism with their limited understanding of the truth of Mormonism. Many historians are frustrated that their church, which could have such a strong case to present to the world, has instead often deliberately chosen to make its case in weaker and less defensible ways.

Latter-day Saint historians, in their role as constructive rather than destructive critics of the church, have had great difficulty handling a two-front controversy with church conservatives, on the one hand, and the Tanners, on the other. In order to be effective in refuting the "straw

man" view of Mormonism that the Tanners have conveniently chosen
to attack, the historians must gently point out to Mormon conservatives that their own understanding of the faith also is incomplete. Conservatives, in turn, have often argued that the historians and the Tanners are bedfellows, when this in fact is not the case at all. The result,
in the opinion of some Mormon historians, is that the Tanners' long-
term impact has been to retard rather than advance serious Mormon
historical scholarship, providing Mormon conservatives with an excuse
to restrict access to Mormon historical records again in the 1980s.

What has the larger significance of the Tanners been for the development of Mormonism and for understanding the strengths and weaknesses of the Latter-day Saint movement as a whole? Religious dissidents often highlight aspects of a religious movement that might
otherwise be overlooked. They bring to light problems in a faith that
need to be resolved and understood before a realistic assessment of a
group's strengths and weaknesses can be made. Although it is easy to
dismiss religious dissidents simply as troublemakers or disturbed individuals, they can also play a highly creative role in prodding a faith to
clean up its own house and be true to the best in its testimony.

"Career apostates," as I have termed those who devote their whole
lives to trying to destroy a faith in which they once deeply believed,
provide a particularly illuminating angle from which to view religious
movements.[21] Such individuals can be seen as occupying a curious mid-
point in the continuum of religious involvement that ranges from (1)
believers of all varieties, through (2) seceders from a religion, (3) career apostates, (4) converts to an alternative religious faith, and (5)
founders of new religious movements. Caught betwixt and between the
end points of the spectrum, career apostates remain in a sort of lim-
bo, unable either to be satisfied believers in their original faith or to
break cleanly with it and develop a positive alternative synthesis of their
own. Like the unfortunate divorcees who continue to squabble over
the financial settlement and custody of the children rather than moving on to make a new and more happy life for themselves, career apostates tend to define themselves more in terms of what they are against
than what they are for. Yet their personal ambivalence also may reflect an ambivalence at the heart of the movement with which they
maintain such an intense love-hate relationship.

Circumstances play an important role in determining the way in
which religious dissidence, including career apostasy, develops. Using
the case of Roman Catholicism, for example, one can see a spectrum
of responses by the institutional church that helped define the nature
of the religious dissidence it faced. At one point, those with an intense

sense of religious vocation could be constructively channeled into monastic orders. At another time, similar individuals could be branded as heretics and burned at the stake. And at still other times, individuals such as Martin Luther could break free entirely from the parent body and successfully form a new religious synthesis of their own. Much depended, in each case, on how the parent organization responded to the challenge. Either an extreme authoritarian approach or an extreme laissez-faire style could be equally conducive to stimulating dissidence.[22]

Protestantism has been particularly prone to religious dissidence of all kinds. By replacing loyalty to an all-inclusive church organization with an emphasis on individual interpretation of the Bible as the ultimate basis for religious authority, the Protestant movement encouraged fissure, as different individuals found very different messages in the same biblical record. In the United States alone, where the splintering has been most pronounced, there are by latest count nearly 1,600 distinct religious organizations, more than nine hundred of which claim to base themselves on the same biblical record.[23]

Mormonism, reacting against the cacophony of religious claims in nineteenth-century America, sought to return to an authoritative church structure with similarities to that of Roman Catholicism.[24] A major goal of Mormonism was to create a New Israel, a total culture stressing salvation by works rather than the more conventional Protestant emphasis on the Pauline concept of salvation by faith. At the same time, however, Mormonism retained the Protestant emphasis on individual Bible interpretation and, in fact, went still further by developing the concept that continuing revelation, including new scripture, was possible in different dispensations. The result, rather paradoxically, has been that the authoritarian Mormon movement has produced more splintering and diversity than that found in any comparable Protestant group, with the exception of the Baptists. By a recent count, more than 150 identifiable Mormon factions emerged during the first 150 years of the movement.[25]

The diversity within the Mormon movement is by no means necessarily a sign of weakness. Many students of religion have argued, in fact, that a key to the success of a religious movement is its ability to hold seemingly contradictory elements in tension within itself. This is true because reality is always more complex than our verbal understanding of it can be. The word *water,* for example, cannot convey the full characteristics of the substance that we know as water. Similarly, talking about religious experience or formulating creedal statements of belief is not the same as having a religious experience oneself. As in the case of the blind men and the elephant, the full complexity of reality invariably eludes our limited understanding.

Both Christianity and its Mormon offshoot provide classic examples of religious movements whose success has been based, in part, on their ability to hold apparent opposites in creative tension. Christianity, to use only one possible illustration from the movement, maintains that Jesus Christ was simultaneously "wholly God" and "wholly man." Although this is a paradox and a logical impossibility, it has proved a remarkably durable and effective belief—so long as both sides of the paradox are maintained. Similarly, one of the greatest non-Mormon scholars of Mormonism, Thomas F. O'Dea, argues that the great strength of the movement lies in its ability to maintain a creative tension between seeming opposites—hierarchical structure and congregationalism, rationality and charisma, consent and coercion, conservative family ideals and equality for women, political conservatism and social idealism, and patriotism and particularism.[26]

Thus, much of what the Tanners view as inconsistency and weakness in Mormonism may actually be a necessary feature of the movement if it is to be fully successful. If Mormonism were as onesided as the Tanners' analysis (and that of some of the more naive church leaders whose perspectives the Tanners criticize), then the faith might well have had far less appeal. Like the leaders of many Mormon splinter groups, including the Mormon fundamentalists who practice polygamy, the Tanners have emphasized only one side of the paradox of Mormonism. They have assumed that Mormonism must be eternally true and unchanging when one of the most distinctive affirmations of the movement is its claim to receive "continuing revelation"—its ongoing effort to find new ways whereby principles believed to be eternally valid can better be understood and creatively expressed in the face of ever-changing temporal circumstances.

The Tanners assume that Mormonism is false because it deviates from Pauline Christianity. By the same reasoning, however, Christianity could be said to be false because it deviates from orthodox Judaism. If such a standard of religious truth were universally and consistently applied, it would negate the possibility of religious development and creative change. As Jesus observed, "new wine must be put into new wineskins" (Matt. 9:17). Mormonism under Joseph Smith claimed to be a new revelation that included yet also superseded all previous human truth in a new synthesis for the "dispensation of the fullness of time."[27] Whatever one may think of this assertion, it must be taken seriously in any balanced analysis of the Mormon movement.

Yet if the Tanners' understanding of the dynamics of Mormon development is incomplete, their criticisms do highlight disagreements within the movement that must be handled constructively if Mormonism is to remain healthy. Since World War II, Mormonism has experienced a phenomenal sevenfold increase in membership. Many converts have come from the Baptist churches and from other Protestant fundamentalist groups whose underlying beliefs are sharply opposed to those of earlier Mormonism, including Mormon notions of the Godhead and continuing revelation. Faced by the onslaught of such new members and the Mormon desire to convert Protestant fundamentalists, the church has begun backing away from, or even denying, some of its earlier testimonies. A certain ossification and rigidity of belief have started to develop as present-day Mormon leaders try to limit the free-wheeling speculation of earlier years. Mormons increasingly are talking about and suffering expulsion for "heresy," a concept that was largely absent from early Mormonism.[28] It is supremely ironic that a present-day Mormon leader could include among his list of the "seven deadly heresies" of Mormonism at least one belief that was firmly held by major nineteenth-century Mormon leaders such as Brigham Young.[29]

In the face of such misunderstanding or misrepresentation of the record of Mormonism by some Latter-day Saints, the Tanners have sometimes played a positive role. Every organization, especially if it is highly authoritarian, is dependent for its ongoing health and vitality on its critics, both internal and external. Such individuals, whatever their motives may be, can provide essential information that might otherwise be overlooked, blow the whistle on errors and excesses, and in general help force the organization, whether it be religious or secular, to live up to its ideals and to keep honest, fit, and trim. The Tanners have challenged the Mormon church, if it really believes in its own ideals, to live up to those ideals. They have challenged the Mormon church, if it really believes in its own history, to find out what that history was. They have challenged the Mormon church, if it purports to be a universal church, to correct its sectarian provincialisms such as its former policy of excluding blacks from full church membership. Although such challenges obviously have not been popular and the Tanners have generally failed to give the church due credit when it *has* met them, nevertheless through such challenges the Tanners have prodded the church, however haltingly and imperfectly, to begin to develop a more realistic sense of itself.

The complex love-hate relationship that the Tanners have sustained so long with the Mormon church must not be forgotten. By devoting more than thirty years of their life to attacking Mormonism, the Tanners have borne the most eloquent possible witness to the importance that they ascribe to the Mormon faith, even though they view it as mistaken. In discussing their motives, the Tanners quote a powerful letter from Duane Stanfield that explains why some "apostate Mormon and anti-Mormon critics" of the Latter-day Saint church devote so much time and energy to their cause: "I would say its because they feel the truth is important; in fact nothing really matters in life but the truth. They feel that they had found the truth, and they gave it their heart, mind, and strength; and then found themselves to be, as they felt, in error. And when you have been deceived on such a scale, you want others to know about it, just as one so dedicated and committed wants others to know about the [Mormon] Gospel."[30]

Mormonism appears to have disappointed the Tanners because they found it unable to provide them with a sense of total religious security, a faith that had all the answers. Instead, the Tanners have turned to Protestant fundamentalism for such security. Yet the painful irony is that had the Tanners put the same effort into analyzing Protestant fundamentalism that they have into analyzing Mormonism, they would have realized that Protestant fundamentalism also is a historically limited movement that ultimately cannot provide them with the total religious security they are seeking. It developed out of a nineteenth-century counterreaction to new currents of thought, including the higher biblical criticism and new scientific and anthropological knowledge. Such knowledge appeared to undercut a monistic interpretation of truth. In response, Protestant fundamentalists increasingly demanded rigid adherence to certain specific beliefs such as the "inerrancy" of the Bible and the doctrine of the Virgin Birth. They also rejected or radically reinterpreted scientific knowledge such as that pertaining to evolutionary biology in order to shore up their literalistic interpretation of biblical stories such as the six-day creation account in Genesis.[31] The result, in the view of many Christians, was that the Protestant fundamentalist movement tended to lose sight of the forest for the trees. Christianity had traditionally adopted a more flexible approach to truth than the Pharasaic-type literalism put forward by nineteenth- and twentieth-century fundamentalists.[32]

The Tanners, like many of the Mormon conservatives whose views they criticize, have not yet developed a faith that is sufficiently inclusive to encompass the full depth and richness of a mature Christianity. Yet if the Tanners' perspective remains limited, their efforts nevertheless call attention to real challenges the Mormon movement must meet if it is to remain healthy and vital. There are great dangers in being either too rigid or too open-minded. Too-great rigidity limits our ability to seek truth wherever it may lead us. Too-great open-mindedness risks leaving us with no vital beliefs or standards by which to judge our complex experiences. If Mormonism is to remain strong, it must continue to achieve a balance between its paradoxical polarities, especially between faith and works. Only time can tell whether Mormonism will be able to live up to its full potential, creatively combining seemingly opposed elements into a compelling new synthesis reflecting that higher truth that is always beyond full human comprehension.

NOTES

1. This chapter draws heavily upon Lawrence Foster, "Career Apostates: Reflections on the Works of Jerald and Sandra Tanner," *Dialogue: A Journal of Mormon Thought* 17 (Summer 1984): 35–60. Copyright 1984 by Lawrence Foster. Valuable critiques of the Tanners include Ian Barber, *What Mormonism Isn't* (Auckland, New Zealand: Pioneer Books, 1981), and the analysis by the anonymous "Latter-day Saint Historian" entitled *Jerald and Sandra Tanner's Distorted View of Mormonism: A Response to* Mormonism—Shadow or Reality (Privately printed, 1977; repr. Sandy, Utah: Mormon Miscellaneous, 1983). Jerald and Sandra Tanner's rejoinder to that latter pamphlet appeared in both original and enlarged editions in 1978 as *Answering Dr. Clandestine: A Response to the Anonymous LDS Historian* (Salt Lake City: Modern Microfilm Company). That controversy is analyzed in Foster, "Career Apostates," 50–53.

2. Scott Harry Faulring, "Bibliography of Modern Microfilm Company, 1959–1982," included in his 487-page "An Oral History of the Modern Microfilm Company, 1959–1982," Oral History Project, Department of History, Brigham Young University, 1983, is a key source for any serious work on the Tanners. In quotations from it here, punctuation has been standardized. More recent sources are included in H. Michael Marquardt, "A Tanner Bibliography, 1959–1983," *Restoration Research* 3 (July 1984): 3–28, and "Tanner Bibliography: Update," *Restoration Research* 6 (April 1987): 22–23. A nearly complete collection of the Tanners' writings, as well as Faulring's "Oral History," is available in the Special Collections Department, Marriott Library, University of Utah, Salt Lake City. For more complete bibliographic citations than can be presented here, see the notes in Foster, "Career Apostates."

3. Jerald and Sandra Tanner, *Mormonism—Shadow or Reality?* (Salt Lake City: Modern Microfilm Company, 1982), 568.

4. As quoted by Jack Houston, "The Jerald Tanners vs. Mormonism," *Power for Living*, June 15, 1970, 3.

5. For an example of the Tanner's continuing concern with this issue, see "Excommunication: Mormon Leader Expelled After Charging Church with Racism," *Salt Lake Messenger*, No. 73 (October 1989): 1–4.

6. Tanner and Tanner, *Mormonism—Shadow or Reality?* Preface.

7. Faulring, "Oral History," 158–59. This was stated in an interview of September 17, 1981.

8. Ibid., 9–11. For Jerald Tanner's discussion of his teenage drinking problems, see his *Is There a Personal God?* (Salt Lake City: Modern Microfilm, n.d.), 19–20.

9. Faulring, "Oral History," 83.

10. For treatments of many of these approaches, see the numerous articles in *Dialogue: A Journal of Mormon Thought, Journal of Mormon History,* and *Sunstone.* On Mormon historians, see Leonard J. Arrington, "The Search for Truth and Meaning in Mormon History," *Dialogue: A Journal of Mormon Thought* 3 (Summer 1968): 56–65, and "Reflections on the Founding and Purpose of the Mormon History Association, 1965–1983," *Journal of Mormon History* 10 (1983): 91–103; Davis Bitton, "Ten Years in Camelot: A Personal Memoir," *Dialogue: A Journal of Mormon Thought* 16 (Autumn 1983): 9–20; Martin E. Marty, "Two Integrities: An Address to the Crisis of Mormon Historiography," *Journal of Mormon History* 10 (1983): 3–19; Lawrence Foster, "New Perspectives on the Mormon Past: Reflections of a Non-Mormon Historian," *Sunstone* 7 (January–February 1982): 41–45; and David E. Bohn, "Our Own Agenda," *Sunstone* 14 (June 1990): 45–49. A major resource on the philosophical attitudes of Mormon historians is found in Louis Midgley and David J. Whittaker, "Mapping Contemporary Mormon Historiography: An Annotated Bibliography" (unpublished draft, August 6, 1990). For closet doubters, see D. Jeff Burton, "The Phenomenon of the Closet Doubter," *Sunstone* 7 (September–October 1982): 34–38.

11. For a powerful example of this perspective, see L. Jackson Newell, "An Echo from the Foothills: To Marshall the Forces of Reason," *Dialogue: A Journal of Mormon Thought* 19 (Spring 1986): 26–34.

12. The paper in question was D. Michael Quinn's "On Being a Mormon Historian." It was originally presented in 1981 before the student history association at Brigham Young University as an eloquent response to the attacks on Mormon historians that had been made by Apostles Ezra Taft Benson and Boyd K. Packer. Although Quinn decided not to publish the paper immediately, he did circulate some copies to interested individuals. One copy eventually came into the hands of Jerald and Sandra Tanner. They published it without any attempt to secure Quinn's permission and have continued to sell it despite the severe criticisms historians have made of their ethics in the matter. It was published in a revised form in *Faithful History: Essay on Writing Mormon History,* ed. George D. Smith (Salt Lake City: Signature, 1992), 69–111.

13. James Thurber, *The Thurber Carnival* (New York: Delta, 1964), 253. Original italics removed.

14. Jerald and Sandra Tanner, *A Critical Look—A Study of the Overstreet "Confession" and the Cowdery "Defense"* (Salt Lake City: Modern Microfilm, 1967).

15. For Jerald Tanner's fullest account of his role in questioning the authenticity of the document, see his *Tracking the White Salamander: The Story of Mark Hofmann, Murder and Forged Mormon Documents* (Salt Lake City: Utah Lighthouse Ministry, 1987), which contains his *Confessions of a White Salamander.* The Tanners' role in unravelling this case, which shook the Mormon

church and the Mormon historical fraternity, also is discussed in Linda Sillitoe and Allen D. Roberts, *Salamander: The Story of the Mormon Forgery Murders* (Salt Lake City: Signature Books, 1988); Robert Lindsey, *A Gathering of Saints: A True Story of Money, Murder and Deceit* (New York: Simon and Schuster, 1988); Steven Naifeh and Gregory White Smith, *The Mormon Murders: A True Story of Greed, Forgery, Deceit, and Death* (New York: Weidenfeld & Nicolson, 1988); and Richard E. Turley, Jr., *Victims: The LDS Church and the Mark Hofmann Case* (Urbana: University of Illinois Press, 1992).

16. For their own account of this affair, see Jerald and Sandra Tanner, *The Tanners on Trial: Concerning Stolen Documents, the Mormon Underground, and the Question of Copyright Violations* (Salt Lake City: Utah Lighthouse Ministry, 1984)..

17. Tanner and Tanner, *Mormonism—Shadow or Reality?* 262–93. The Tanners express pleasure that the policy itself was changed (a social interpretation), but they argue that such change serves to further undercut Mormon claims to possess true religious authority (a doctrinal interpretation).

18. "Temple Ritual Altered: Mormon Leaders Delete Some of the 'Most Sacred' Parts of Ceremony," *Salt Lake Messenger*, No. 75 (July 1990): 1–16.

19. Interview of Sandra Tanner by James V. D'Arc, September 19, 1972, in Faulring, "Oral History," 377.

20. The Tanners have reacted to serious scholarly efforts to analyze their work in much the same way that they criticize the Mormon church for reacting to them—by trying to ignore criticisms that they cannot answer effectively. For instance, in 1982 the Tanners did not respond at all to my request for an interview with them as background for a scholarly paper I was writing on them. After more than a month of waiting—and sending a second, follow-up letter—I learned through a mutual acquaintance that the Tanners were uneasy about meeting with me and had not decided whether they would agree to an interview. I then drafted a press release to go out to every radio and television station in the Salt Lake City area, noting that the anti-Mormon writers Jerald and Sandra Tanner, who have repeatedly criticized the Mormon church for not responding to their inquiries, had themselves not been willing to meet with a prominent non-Mormon scholar attempting to make an objective study of their life and work. Only after I passed word of this proposed press release to a mutual contact did the Tanners promptly agree to an interview.

Subsequent to the publication of my article "Career Apostates," the Tanners have never directly alluded to it in print, nor have they ever written to me to express approval or disapproval of any aspect of it. Just as the Mormon church's interests are not served by telling its more insular members about the Tanner's criticisms of Mormon weaknesses, so too the Tanners' interests are not served by alerting their own somewhat insular readers to scholarship critical of the serious weaknesses inherent in the Tanners' approach.

21. For my discussion of the concept of the "career apostate" as applied to the persistent anti-Shaker writer Mary Dyer, see Lawrence Foster, *Religion and Sexuality: The Shakers, the Mormons, and the Oneida Community* (Urbana: University of Illinois Press, 1984), 51–54.

22. There are very few "career apostates" because historical circumstances usually make sustaining such a position very difficult. On the broader implications of never passing beyond what has been described as a chronic state of "liminality," see J. Gordon Melton and Robert L. Moore, *The Cult Experience: Responding to the New Religious Pluralism* (New York: Pilgrim Press, 1982), 59–60.

23. J. Gordon Melton, *The Encyclopedia of American Religions,* 3d ed. (Detroit: Gale Research, 1989).

24. For some of the divergent perspectives on this early period, see Mario S. De Pillis, "The Quest for Religious Authority and the Rise of Mormonism," *Dialogue: A Journal of Mormon Thought* 1 (March 1966): 68–88; Marvin S. Hill, "The Shaping of the Mormon Mind in New England and New York," *Brigham Young University Studies* 9 (Spring 1969): 251–72; and Jan Shipps, *Mormonism: The Story of a New Religious Tradition* (Urbana: University of Illinois Press, 1985). It may not be accidental that two of the most perceptive non-Mormon students of Mormon history, Thomas F. O'Dea and Mario S. De Pillis, both came out of the Roman Catholic tradition, which also places a strong emphasis on church authority.

25. Groups that have emerged from the Latter Day Saint movement are discussed in Steven L. Shields, *Divergent Paths of the Restoration: A History of the Latter Day Saint Movement* (Bountiful, Utah: Restoration Research, 1982). The most detailed listing of such groups is Albert J. Van Nest, *A Directory to the 'Restored Gospel' Churches: A Survey of Churches and Groups that Have Based Their Beliefs and Teaching on the 'Restored Gospel' as Brought Forth by Joseph Smith* (Evanston: Institute for the Study of American Religions, 1983). Van Nest identifies 167 past and present groups. It is worthy of note that despite such fissure, more than 99 percent of the followers of Joseph Smith belong to one of the two main groups: the Church of Jesus Christ of Latter-day Saints, headquartered in Salt Lake City, Utah, and the Reorganized Church of Jesus Christ of Latter Day Saints, headquartered in Independence, Missouri.

26. Thomas F. O'Dea, *The Mormons* (Chicago: University of Chicago Press, 1957), 222–57.

27. Joseph Smith did make certain public relations gestures to try to downplay his divergences from traditional Christianity, yet the core of his message consisted of the assertion that he was helping to introduce a new dispensation that would include yet supersede all previously valid human truth. Because he and his followers radically reinterpreted the meaning of many common Christian terms, many Mormons today are unaware of how great Smith's departures from normative Christianity really are. On these points, see Sterling M. McMurrin, *The Theological Foundations of the Mormon Religion* (Salt Lake City: University of Utah Press, 1965); Shipps, *Mormonism;* and Sandra Tanner, *The Bible and Mormon Doctrine* (Salt Lake City: Modern Microfilm, 1971).

28. Changing conceptions of heresy, both in mainstream Christianity and in Mormonism, are discussed in Michael Hicks, "Do You Preach the Ortho-

dox Religion: Thoughts on the Idea of Heresy in the Church," *Sunstone* 6 (September–October 1981): 29–34; and David Christie-Murray, *A History of Heresy* (New York: Oxford University Press, 1989).

29. In his speech of June 1, 1980, at Brigham Young University, Bruce R. McConkie identified "Heresy No. 6" of the "seven deadly heresies" of Mormonism as the belief in the Adam-God doctrine. This doctrine was, however, advocated publicly by Brigham Young as an important belief of the Mormon church. See Gary James Bergera, "The Orson Pratt–Brigham Young Controversies: Conflict within the Quorums, 1853–1868," *Dialogue: A Journal of Mormon Thought* 13 (Summer 1980): 7–49, for details of Brigham Young's belief in the Adam-God doctrine. For extracts from the McConkie speech, see Tanner and Tanner, *Mormonism—Shadow or Reality?* 178c. If one were to follow McConkie's line of reasoning to its logical conclusion, one would have to conclude that Brigham Young, while head of the Mormon church, had been guilty of "deadly heresy." It is difficult to imagine that any apostate or anti-Mormon statements could possibly be more damaging to the faith of sincere Latter-day Saints than the ill-informed and intemperate assertions made recently by some Mormon leaders.

30. From a letter to *Dialogue,* Winter 1968, 10–11, as quoted in Tanner and Tanner, *Mormonism—Shadow or Reality?* 573.

31. For the best historical treatment of the development of Protestant fundamentalism in America, see George M. Marsden, *Fundamentalism and American Culture: The Shaping of Twentieth Century Evangelicalism, 1870–1925* (New York: Oxford University Press, 1980).

32. The significance of Jesus' parables, to use only one example, never depends on whether the stories are literally true, but rather on the underlying moral message. A lengthy analysis could be written on the limitations of Protestant fundamentalism when it is viewed as the sole valid approach to Christianity. For a lively parable suggesting a starting point for moving toward an understanding of mature Christianity, see Nels F. S. Ferre, *The Sun and the Umbrella* (New York: Harper, 1953). For examples of how mature biblical criticism can move beyond a preoccupation with the literal historicity of primary Christian documents, see Raymond E. Brown, *The Birth of the Messiah: A Commentary on the Infancy Narratives in Matthew and Luke* (Garden City: Doubleday, 1979), and Norman Perrin, *The Resurrection According to Matthew, Mark, and Luke* (Philadelphia: Fortress Press, 1977).

In their rebuttal to the anonymous Latter-day Saint historian, the Tanners concede that they do not dare to apply the same scholarly standards of evidence to their analysis of the Bible that they do to Mormon writings because to do so, in their opinion, would be to destroy the credibility of the Bible ("Dr. Clandestine," 16–20). This conclusion is true only if one accepts the Tanners' limited view of what constitutes religious truth. For an account of apparent inconsistencies in accounts of the Resurrection narratives that the Tanners have thus far refused to address—even as they call attention to similar apparent historical inconsistencies in early Mormon records—see Reginald H. Fuller, *The Formation of the Resurrection Narratives* (Philadelphia: Fortress Press, 1980).

Until the Tanners are prepared to use consistent standards of judgment for their own faith as well as that of others, their stance cannot be taken seriously by scholars or by the general public.

17

Sonia Johnson:
Mormonism's Feminist Heretic

Alice Allred Pottmyer

Sonia Johnson, previously unknown other than to her family and close friends, garnered major media attention in mid November 1979 and continued in the headlines for several weeks after receiving a summons to an ecclesiastical court in the Church of Jesus Christ of Latter-day Saints. She was officially excommunicated from the Mormon church on December 5, 1979. In the process, she became a symbol of opposition to Mormon political conservatism and inflexibility in dealing with members who are vocal in holding opposing positions on political issues.[1]

It was common knowledge to all those watching the Latter-day Saint church's proceedings against Johnson—and most informed Americans were watching it in one form or another because it became a media cause célèbre—that the controversy swirled around her efforts to publicize the church's heavy-handed efforts to defeat the passage of the Equal Rights Amendment (ERA). The Mormon leadership publicly opposed the proposed Twenty-seventh Amendment to the U.S. Constitution, arguing that it would lead to an erosion of family values and promote gender conflict. They quietly used the church's bureaucracy and institutional structure to mobilize opposition, thrusting the church into a political sphere usually reserved for secular organizations in modern American society. Because of this effort, Sonia Johnson helped to found in 1978—along with friends Hazel Rigby, Maida Withers, and Teddie Wood—the small Mormons for ERA organization. Johnson's efforts to protest the church's activities against the ERA, therefore, placed her in a direct adversarial position to her church. The lines of apposition and the strength of commitment of the two groups ensured that the disagreements could not be resolved amicably.[2]

In spite of this, Johnson's public activities in 1979 to expose the church's anti-ERA politics and organizational attempts to defeat the measures were not mentioned in the letter of excommunication. Instead, she was asked:

1. Have your actions influenced members and non-members to oppose church programs, i.e., the missionary program?

2. Have your actions and statements advocated diminished support of church leaders?

3. Have you presented false doctrine which would damage others spiritually?

The judgment on these questions also avoided discussion of the ERA issue. "You testified that you believe and have taught that missionaries should not be invited into people's homes," the court found. In an especially indicting conclusion, the tribunal also asserted that Johnson had "testified that you believe and have publicly stated that our society, specifically including church leaders, has a savage misogyny; when, in fact, it is church doctrine that exaltation can be gained only through the love that results in the eternal bonding of man and woman."[3] This conclusion about celestial marriage sealed her fate before the court.[4]

Notwithstanding her excommunication from the Mormon church in December 1979, Sonia Johnson was one of the most unlikely of dissenters. Born Sonia Harris in February 1936 in Malad, Idaho, the middle of five children, she had been brought up in a fairly traditional Mormon family. She described her early history in her autobiography.

> Mom and Dad had driven the nearly snow-blocked roads to the small town hospital in Malad, Idaho. At that time, they were living in Washakie, a Shoshone Indian reservation just over the state line in Utah. They were school teachers there grateful to the Lord to be working for the government during the depression, teaching and feeding the "Lamanites," as Indians are called by Mormons. Dad was collecting Shoshone Indian legends for his master's thesis, while Mom did most of the teaching as well as preparing the daily lunch the school was required by law to give the Indian youngsters. Two children had already preceded me into the family: Joyce, aged nine, and Paul, four.[5]

Soon after her birth, the family moved to Ferron, Utah, but three years after, they moved to Preston, Idaho, where her father taught seminary for the Mormon church. In seminary, Mormon high school students study LDS history and the scriptures. In the summer of 1948, when she was twelve, the family moved to Logan, Utah. Soon thereafter, she became organist for the junior Sunday school in the Logan First Ward, a large congregation, and kept that position for years.[6]

When Sonia Johnson burst into the headlines in 1979, only a few people in Logan were not surprised. Even so, there were hints in her life that she would not willingly accede to the status quo. When she was fifteen, for instance, she rose in a Logan First Ward fast and testimony meeting to criticize what she considered an error on the part of a temple worker who had spoken at the "chastity night" meeting for teenage girls held earlier in the week. During that presentation to about twenty girls and their mothers, the speaker discussed the evils of necking, petting, and physical intimacy between males and females. As she spoke, the lecturer tore off white rose petals in a bud vase situated in front of her. At the conclusion of her speech she picked up the petals and attempted to fit them back onto the stem. "You are just like this rose. If you sully your body by allowing boys to touch it in forbidden ways, you can never be whole or beautiful or pure again, just as the petals of this rose can never be pure and white again. No good man will ever want to marry you." Johnson went on, "So I rose and told the congregation that day that a temple worker had come and preached false doctrine to us young women. I described her performance and attacked her conclusion on the basis that Christ had taught repentance as a method of becoming totally whole and pure and beautiful again: 'though your sins be scarlet, they shall be white as snow.'"[7]

Johnson's remarks were considered improper for several reasons. First, Mormonism has traditionally valued obedience to ecclesiastical authority above all else except perseverance. Second, as a girl Johnson was expected to defer to her elders. Third, the place in which she chose to express her minority opinion, the fast and testimony meeting of her entire congregation, ensured that the Mormon hierarchy would learn of it and raise questions about the entire group. Finally, she had challenged some of the sexual mores of the Latter-day Saint movement. The response from leaders was prompt. The president of the young women's organization castigated Johnson from the pulpit for her insensitivity to the temple worker's speech. Friends also chastised her, and her father scolded her and worried what others would think. Her mother, however, comforted her.

Johnson reflected on this and other similar incidents in her autobiography, indicating that they were the first instances in which she became aware of a persistent male chauvinism of Mormonism. She repeatedly found this theme in her church thereafter. From the all-male priesthood to the conservative social values espoused by the institutional leadership, she concluded that sexism was a perpetual part of the Latter-day Saint experience.[8] "Looking back," Sonia Johnson recalled, "I recognize that what most outraged me about the temple worker's rose drama and about polygamy was the sexism, the blatant sexism; it was a non-concept. But I know that its manifestations invariably outraged me. And confused me, because I could not, as the phrase goes today, get a handle on it."[9]

Johnson did not dwell on these concerns, however, and her life took a common course into adulthood. She completed high school in Logan and attended Utah State University during the late 1950s. Away from home and attending an institution that prided itself on its secular perspective, Johnson confronted for the first time the issues of modernity that had destroyed the traditional Protestant worldview that had held sway in the nineteenth century.[10] While in school at Utah State University in 1958, she began dating a classmate, Richard Johnson, a stormy looking "Easterner" from Wisconsin. A nonmember, Rick, as he was known, challenged Johnson's perspectives and prompted her to study and to defend her beliefs. Although she was enamored with him, she refused to consider him as a future husband, telling a summer school roommate who raised the possibility, "Don't be ridiculous, he's not even a member of the church." She soon helped to change that, and in November 1958 Richard Johnson was baptized.[11]

The couple married on August 21, 1959. Soon afterward Rick Johnson finished his master's degree at Utah State University and in February 1960 he, Sonia, and her fifteen-year-old brother, Mark, went to western Samoa. The Johnsons both taught there in the church's educational system, but not on religious subjects. In 1961 they moved to Minneapolis, where Rick began working on a Ph.D. in educational psychology at the University of Minnesota. Sonia supported the couple by working in the neurology department of the university's hospital. Rick, however, persuaded her to quit her job and to enroll in the M.A. program in English at the university. These were busy years. In 1963 Rick finished his Ph.D. and accepted a teaching position at Rutgers University in New Brunswick, New Jersey. Their first child, Eric, was also born in July 1963. At Rutgers, Sonia continued her education. She completed her master's degree and Ed.D. dissertation before giving birth to their daughter, Kari, in 1965. The Johnsons left Rutgers in the mid 1960s and moved westward to Palo Alto, California, where Rick accepted a position at Stanford University. Their third child, Marc, was born in Palo Alto in 1967. By that time Sonia was teaching night school.[12]

The Johnson family did not remain long in Palo Alto, however, for in the late 1960s they relocated first to Korea and then to Malaysia, where another son, Noel, was born. They returned to Stanford in 1974, and almost immediately began having marital difficulties. Sonia Johnson recalled that Rick was "finding other women attractive, he told me, and this worried him." He decided that the best way to preserve their marriage was to find a job they could do together. They took a position with the U.S. Office of Education, teaching educators how to evaluate their federally funded projects. "We bought a motor home, put all the kids in it, and set off for the next year," Sonia recalled. "Twenty-one bicentennial states, hundreds of hours of teaching our own children and of feelings of severe strain on our marriage later, we came to Virginia. On Kari's eleventh birthday, June 25, 1976, we bought the house in which the seeds of feminism, planted long ago in Logan and watered and cultivated along the way by various repressive church programs and edicts, finally sprouted. 'Hello Virginia, Sterling Park Ward, ERA, feminism, and the new world!'"[13]

Soon after arriving in Virginia, she telephoned Hazel and Ron Rigby, friends from their University of Minnesota graduate school days who now lived in the Washington, D.C., area. Although they had kept in touch for fifteen years, they had not seen each other during that time. After her conversation with Hazel Rigby, Sonia Johnson expressed surprise at how Rigby had changed. At age forty-two, Sonia Johnson had just spoken to her first feminist. Both her Mormon background and the fact the Johnsons had spent several years outside the country kept her from hearing about current trends in the women's movement. Hazel Rigby informed her that the women's movement was for everyone, even women like Sonia who were content with their lives. She introduced Johnson to a few Mormon feminist friends, and one recommended that she read *I'm Running Away from Home, but I'm Not Allowed to Cross the Street* by Gabrielle Burton. An avid reader, Johnson also read Germaine Greer's *Female Eunuch* and Kate Millett's *Sexual Politics.*[14]

Sonia Johnson also caught up on the political issues swirling around the women's rights movement. While she had been out of the country, she had heard little about the intense political battles that women had been waging in the United States. She also knew little about the proposed Equal Rights Amendment. Johnson was especially ignorant of the concerted efforts of the LDS church to prevent its passage. She did not know, for example, that Utah members of the conservative John Birch Society had fought the amendment as early as 1973. She had not read the *Church News* editorial of January 11, 1975, opposing the amendment. She also had not read the January 14, 1975, article in the *Salt Lake Tribune* quoting M. Byron Fisher, a member of the Utah legislature, as saying, "It is my Church, and as a bishop, I'm not going to vote against its wishes."[15]

A month before the Johnsons moved to Sterling, Virginia, the *Washington Evening Star* printed a front-page interview with Barbara Smith, president of the General Relief Society, a Mormon organization for women, under the title "A Mormon Tells Why She Opposes ERA." The reporter, Randy Sue Coburn, asked whether Smith's reasons for opposing the ERA lay in the church's traditional emphasis on the value of family life. Smith replied:

> Yes, this is the reason we took this position in the first place, because we feel unless a man is given the responsibility of providing for his family, and not putting the woman and the man in the same position that they both must provide equally, it will destroy the family. Now, I really don't think that's going to happen immediately. I think as far as you and I are concerned, you could teach your family and I could teach mine. It's future generations I'm concerned about, if legally it is written that both men and women would have the same responsibilities. I think it will destroy our nation and our country. I believe it was Napoleon who said France has need of good mothers, for that you'll have good sons.

Smith was also asked of the ERA, "What do you see as the harmful aspects?" She replied, "Well, we see that it's so vague and so broad and so all-encompassing that instead of defining any rights we have, it's just a hope that the things that we want to take place will take place."

The article caused the small group of pro-ERA Mormons in northern Virginia to laugh and complain, but they did nothing. The small group of Mormon ERA supporters, which did not yet include Sonia Johnson, was pleased when on May 27, 1976, a letter to the editor from Phoebe Phaehler of Rockville, Maryland, appeared in the *Evening Star*. In support of the ERA, Phaehler said that Barbara Smith did not speak for everyone in the church. She admitted that she was a "Mormon convert who is enthusiastically for ERA" and said, "I am also a member of NOW, and we have gone over the anti-ERA arguments for years. Women will not be forced to provide half of the financial support and responsibilities of a family if ERA is passed, nor will they be drafted. ERA will simply offer women a fair choice in their lives."

In the fall of 1976, a few months after the Johnsons moved to Virginia, a small band of Mormons for ERA marched in their first parade. In Alexandria, Virginia, Rick and Sonia Johnson and their four children joined the parade to commemorate early women's suffrage.[16] Seemingly in response, the Mormon First Presidency issued a formal statement against ratification of the ERA on the ground that it "could indeed bring them far more restraints and repressions. We fear it will even stifle many God-given feminine instincts."[17]

In 1977, Mormon church activity against the ERA began to heat up. On January 8, Apostle Boyd K. Packer, a Mormon general authority, spoke at a rally in Pocatello, Idaho.[18] He specifically asked that the amendment, originally passed by the Idaho legislature with a two-thirds majority, be rescinded. On the platform with Packer was Allen Larsen, speaker of the Idaho House of Representatives, who was also a Mormon stake president. A week later, Barbara Smith gave an anti-ERA speech in Coeur D'Alene, Idaho, and strongly urged that the ERA in Idaho be rescinded. Perhaps it was coincidence, perhaps not, but the Idaho legislature rescinded the ERA a few days later by a simple majority. A series of orchestrated actions on the part of anti-ERA Mormons also took place during the next few months.[19] On February 1, Utah Senator Jake Garn, another faithful Mormon, inserted an anti-ERA speech by Apostle Boyd Packer into the *Congressional Record*.[20] In March and April, Florida Mormons lobbied heavily in Tallahassee against the ERA. On June 4, Barbara Smith gave another anti-ERA speech in Newport Beach, California. Phyllis Schlafly, whom Smith praised, also spoke at the meeting. Schlafly believed, among other things, that twentieth-century American politics has been the product of a conspiracy by a concerted effort of "a small group of secret kingmakers" who "manipulated the Republican National Convention to nominate candidates who would sidestep or suppress the key issues" and thereby allow Democrats to win the White House and sell the country down the river.[21]

Later, in 1977, the anti-ERA campaign hit closer to Johnson's heart. Mormon ERA protestors showed up at several International Women's Year (IWY) activities. For example, on June 24, approximately fourteen thousand Mormon women and men crowded the IWY conference at Salt Lake City. They voted down all the proposals brought forward in the meeting, including those in favor of world peace.[22] On July 9, the IWY conference in Hawaii was also taken over by anti-ERA Mormons, who elected an anti-ERA slate of candidates to attend a national IWY meeting in Houston. Apparently, the anti-ERA forces had targeted Hawaii because it was the first state to ratify ERA and had a state equal rights law.[23] Near the same time, anti-ERA Mormons tried to take over IWY meetings in Ellensburg, Washington. Mormon men with walkie-talkies instructed the women on which meetings to attend and how to vote. Even closer, in her Sterling Park, Virginia, congregation on April 24, Johnson's stake president, Clifford Cummings, gave an anti-ERA speech. In the fall, Brigham Young University professor Stan Taylor gave another anti-ERA speech at Johnson's stake center.[24]

By August 1977 an ever-increasing body of evidence indicated that the Mormon hierarchy was making a concerted effort to fight the Equal Rights Amendment. Sonia Johnson would become the center of a network of more reform-minded Latter-day Saints who were ERA activists within the church. The internal aspects of this pro-ERA effort soon caught the attention of the national media. When Johnson exploded into the headlines in the latter part of the year, other pro-ERA Mormons began calling her and writing from all over the country. Some, with their husbands and children, formed a small group and marched down Pennsylvania Avenue in the Women's Equality Day parade of August 1977 with ten thousand other marchers. After the parade, the pro-ERA advocate Maida Rust Withers, formerly of Salem, Utah, was well received at a White House convocation. The rest of the small group of Mormon pro-ERA marchers, however, met a different response in Lafayette Park at a post-parade rally. Two recently returned male Mormon missionaries challenged the marchers and the sign they carried that read, "Mormons for the ERA." "They were horrified by our views," recalled Withers, "and we were horrified at their emotional reactions."[25]

In January 1978, the small and loose group of Mormons for ERA decided to actually form an organization, and Sonia Johnson was chosen president. This was partly the case because she had a part-time teaching job but was basically a homemaker; most of the other leaders worked full-time and raised children. Because of his political position as senator from Utah, membership on the Senate Judiciary Committee, and his proximity to Johnson's organization in the Washington area, the conservative Republican Orrin Hatch played an important role in the evolution of the Mormons for ERA movement.

On May 26, 1978, Hatch inserted the official Mormon position against the ERA into the *Congressional Record:*

> The Church of Jesus Christ of Latter-day Saints (Mormon) has a profound veneration for the Constitution of the United States of America. We believe it was divinely inspired and we take a serious interest in any proposed amendments to that basic document and the process itself by which the Constitution is amended. Furthermore, the Church has a very deep and everlasting commitment to the preservation and strengthening of the family, including its individual members. As a people who have in our history known the loss of our constitutional rights, we have long been concerned with the rights and interests of both men and women.

Hatch also inserted into the record an October 22, 1976, statement from the LDS First Presidency, which opposed ratification of the Equal Rights Amendment:

> From its beginnings, The Church of Jesus Christ of Latter-day Saints has affirmed the exalted role of woman in our society. . . .
>
> There have been injustices to women before the law and in society generally. These we deplore.
>
> There are additional rights to which women are entitled.
>
> However, we firmly believe that the Equal Rights Amendment is not the answer.
>
> While the motives of its supporters may be praiseworthy, ERA as a blanket attempt to help women could indeed bring them far more restraints and repressions. We fear it will even stifle many God-given feminine instincts.
>
> It would strike at the family, humankind's basic institution. ERA would bring ambiguity and possibly invite extensive litigation.
>
> Passage of ERA, some legal authorities contend, could nullify many accumulated benefits to women in present statutes.
>
> We recognize men and women as equally important before the Lord, but with differences biologically, emotionally, and in other ways.
>
> ERA, we believe, does not recognize these differences. There are better means for giving women and men the rights they deserve.[26]

The small group of Mormons for ERA had enjoyed sitting around at their potluck suppers and talking on the telephone, complaining about the church's 1976 anti-ERA statement, but before this action had done little outside of internal support and a few marches for the proposed amendment. The group was not aware for some time that Hatch had inserted the statement into the *Congressional Record*. All this now would change. The church quickly followed with other serious actions aimed at defeating the amendment. In June 1978, for instance, the LDS Washington, D.C., area public communications director Dale Ensign concluded a regional meeting by giving out the names of the members of Congress who were on the fence about the ERA extension. He encouraged everyone in the room to contact those members of Congress and lobby against the amendment.[27]

When I, as the Arlington Ward public communications director, mentioned this act to Johnson, she and other Mormons for ERA decided that it was time to act. They sent their first letter to Congress, although at that point they did not even have letterhead. Twenty names went onto the letter, including those of supporters from all over the country. The small group also marched in the pro-ERA parade in July 1978. Sonia Johnson recalled the event:

> In July of 1978, the year I was converted heart and soul to the Equal Rights Amendment, we marched, one hundred thousand of us, for an extension of time to ratify it, seven years having proved too little time for such a revolutionary concept as legal equality to be properly understood by the country. Knowing that time limits imposed by Congress upon amendments are arbitrarily chosen and not constitutionally mandated, we felt confident that an extension would not violate our basic American document. On the hottest day of that summer, about twenty of us marched under the Mormons for ERA banner—and no one who ever saw that banner ever forgot it.[28]

The ERA extension measure passed the House of Representatives and was soon placed in the hands of Senator Birch Bayh (D-Indiana), chair of the Senate Subcommittee on Constitutional Rights, who was charged with managing deliberations on it. Among other hearings scheduled for the ERA, Bayh asked his staff to assemble religious leaders for a series of hearings that he would hold on the matter in August 1978. One of the senator's staffers remembered seeing the Mormon pro-ERA banner in the parade and decided that it would be good to have a representative from that group in the discussions. It took some time to track down Sonia Johnson, but a week beforehand the subcommittee invited her to participate in the hearing. Because the family had planned to leave the next day for a trip to visit relatives in Utah, they decided that Rick and the children would go without her.[29]

Sonia Johnson understood that this was the opportunity that the Mormons for ERA had been working for since its organization. It was the ideal vehicle to demonstrate that not all Mormons opposed the amendment. She spent the days before her testimony praying and preparing for what was supposed to be a five-minute testimony. On the panel with her were Joan Martin, a black Presbyterian minister from New York who represented the National Council of Churches and the Religious Committee for the ERA; Judith Hertz, representing the National Federation of Jewish Temple Sisterhoods; and Father William Callahan, a Catholic priest. Because she had only recently become political, Johnson was unaware that Hatch, a former Mormon bishop, was also a member of the subcommittee and would question her at the hearing. Being alerted to the agenda, Hatch and his staff had notified other Mormons who opposed the proposed amendment, and many were present in the hearing room.

When the day came, the proceedings were relatively mundane until after Sonia Johnson gave her testimony. Reporters woke up when Hatch began questioning her. "He began innocuously enough," she recalled. "You couldn't have foreseen that he was about to found Mormons for ERA on a national scale." Johnson wrote in her journal about Hatch's inquiries, "'It is implied by your testimony that you're more intelligent than other Mormon women, and that if they were all as intelligent as you, they would all support the Equal Rights Amendment.' And then he banged his fist on the table in angry emphasis and shouted, 'Now that's an insult to my wife'!"[30]

United Press International reporter Cheryl Arvidson reported in articles that appeared nationally on August 5, 1978, including in the *Washington Post* and *Salt Lake Tribune,* that

> Sen. Orrin Hatch, R-Utah, a member of the Church of Jesus Christ of Latter-day Saints, clashed Friday with a woman of that faith who claimed a substantial number of female members are opposing the church's mandated opposition to the Equal Rights Amendment.
>
> She questioned how Mormon leaders, in their official statement opposing the ERA, can talk about the "exalted role of woman in our society" and yet follow policies in the church that push women into secondary positions.
>
> "Where equality does not even pertain, the word 'exalted' is a mockery," she said. "One wonders if the leaders of the church would gladly exchange their sex and become so exalted."[31]

Bayh also asked Johnson "whether she expected difficulty within the Mormon church because of her strong statements on behalf of the ERA." "I hope there won't be," she replied. "So do I," he said.

Immediately after her appearance, Mormons for ERA stalwart Teddie Wood sent Johnson's testimony, along with an affidavit from Hazel Rigby, to all the general authorities of the church. "In her statement, Hazel recounted how the Mormon anti-ERA women who besieged me afterward felt I should not have made it a Mormon issue, and how I replied that the church had made it a Mormon issue by choosing to publish their opposition widely, in the *Congressional Record,* for example."[32] These actions sparked outward evidence of support for the ERA among many Mormons. For example, on August 19, 1978, the *Salt Lake Tribune,* once an anti-Mormon newspaper but by this time a more dispassionate voice in the Great Salt Lake Basin, published a letter from ten Mormon women to Orrin Hatch. They said that he was "wrong in assuming that only 1/10th of 1 percent of Mormon women support ERA. The names listed below belong to a segment of Mormon women that are not afraid to sign their names in the support of the Equal Rights Amendment. We urge other LDS women who share our views to step forward and do the same."

The ERA issue heated up around the country late in August 1978. Sonia Johnson learned that Utah's other senator, Jake Garn, another conservative Republican and a Mormon, was threatening to filibuster against the ERA extension bill to prevent it from coming to a vote during the current session of Congress. From her parents' home in Logan, where the family was vacationing, she sent Senators Garn and Hatch a telegram (with copies to the news media) on August 18: "Since you have announced your intention to filibuster when the ERA extension bills comes before the Senate, I am announcing my intention to begin fasting on the Capitol steps in Washington as soon as the filibuster begins—a genuine Mormon fast, without food or liquid—and to continue until you stop talking or I die."[33]

Upon returning to Virginia, Johnson planned to make good on her threat and applied for a permit to stand on the front steps of the Capitol Building. At the same time, the Mormons for ERA began planning a family home evening program to be held on the Capitol steps. "To my immense relief, however, Garn decided not to filibuster," Johnson wrote. "I don't know why, and he would deny it violently, but I rather think that neither the church nor the Utah senators were willing to chance the sensational headlines: 'Mormon Woman Dies of Mormon Senator's Prolixity.'"[34] The extension bill passed the Senate.

After the Bayh hearing and the unexpected publicity, Johnson began to receive mail from other pro-ERA Mormons, and her small group started to expand. "Mormons all over the country who had been suffering under the conviction that they were the only members of the church who support the ERA (which says volumes about how little one dares communicate with others in the church on this issue) had read one of the wire stories about Hatch and me, had thought, with boundless relief, 'Now there are two of us'!" She soon became the center of protest against the Mormon official position.[35]

During the fall of 1978, the church stepped up its political activities against the proposed amendment. It organized officially against it in Virginia in November. Gordon B. Hinckley, a member of the Council of Twelve Apostles and the head of the Special Affairs Committee, a political action arm of the church, according to Johnson, "instructed two regional representatives in the Washington, D.C., area, Julian Lowe and Don Ladd, to organize the Mormon women there into an anti-ERA lobbying coalition."[36] During the initial organization meeting held on November 8, a meeting to which all women in the Oakton Stake were invited, Johnson commented, "Dapper little Bob Beers, Mormon political action coordinator in Virginia for Schlafly's Stop ERA, contributed this gem: 'If you go to your state senator and say that he should be against the Equal Rights Amendment because the prophet is against it, you are going to get nowhere. That may be why we are against it, but when you are trying to convince a legislator to do something, you better talk his language, not yours.'"[37]

After the organizational meeting, Johnson, Hazel Rigby, and Maida Withers met with Regional Representative Julian Lowe. "We urged him to be above board about the whole thing, to send out a press release right away announcing the formation of the coalition and informing the public that it was a church-sponsored, church-organized, church-financed, and church-directed political action committee." They informed him, "President Lowe, if you don't tell, we will." It proved to be a prophetic statement.[38]

In November 1978, the LDS Citizens Coalition was organized, and the male leaders selected Beverly Campbell, a professional public relations person, as chair. The coalition printed brochures—"concerns sheets"—held meetings, had petitions signed, and lobbied in Richmond, activities of typical lobbying organizations. However, when the deadline arrived for lobbying groups to report to the secretary of the Commonwealth of Virginia their lobbying expenses over $100 for the recently concluded session of the Virginia General Assembly, the LDS Citizens Coalition decided not to file a report. This led to scandal.

Washington Star staff writer Marcia Ruth Fram broke the story on March 6, 1979, commenting that "the Virginia LDS (Latter-day Saints) Citizens Coalition failed to register as a lobbying group but engaged in substantial lobbying efforts." She added that the coalition had spent $3,500 in its efforts to defeat the ERA in Virginia but had claimed that only $88.60 went for "material presented directly to legislators." Because of the backlash from this revelation, on March 15 Fram reported that the group had agreed to register with the state as lobbyists. "According to Campbell, the coalition was financed by contributions from individual citizens sent to an organization called Families Are Concerned Today (FACT), based in Potomac, Maryland," a posh Washington suburb. They had used this approach because otherwise "it would look like it was a church thing—which it is not. It is church people," she said, "But it's not the church." Johnson had let Fram know of this discrepancy in the manner in which the church had been trying to get across its anti-ERA position, and the news created bad publicity for the LDS church.[39]

At the same time, Johnson tried to meet with LDS president Spencer W. Kimball. She asked for letters from all over the church for presentation to him, with the impression that if he could just hear the alternative positions on the ERA within the church he would reverse the official LDS opposition. "After I had accumulated a hundred or so pro-ERA Mormon letters heavy with pain and need," she recalled, "I wrote to him again, offering to bring them to him personally because I knew he needed to read them." She also wanted to confront him about "whether he knew what was in the hearts of the women of the church. I wanted to ask him outright whether he had a revelation from God on this subject, and if so, to plead with him to make his revelation or lack thereof public." She never got the chance. Kimball's executive secretary, Francis W. Gibbons, always blocked any contact with him. In one letter Gibbons told Johnson that "President Kimball regrets that he will be unable to meet with you as suggested. He also asked me to say that he is conscious of the needs of the sisters of the church, and with the aid of the priesthood, and the Relief Society, and under the direction of the Lord, is endeavoring to fill these needs."[40] Johnson decided to get the pro-ERA message to the church leadership in the best way she could. Her group hired a tow plane to fly over the April 1979 LDS General Conference on Temple Square in Salt Lake City. The plane displayed a banner that read, "Mormons for ERA are everywhere!"[41]

Johnson was becoming a media star and a popularly acclaimed expert on Mormon activities. Accordingly, in the early summer of 1979 she received a call from the president of the small Kalispell, Montana, chapter of the National Organization of Women (NOW), who asked for her help in combating LDS anti-ERA efforts. The LDS had been instrumental in an almost successful effort to reverse the ERA decision that had been passed in the previous session of the Montana legislature. Johnson could help by visiting Kalispell and telling them "what to do about their Mormons." She recalled that "I delivered the most innocuous speech of my career, especially considering that the subject was Mormons in politics. Fortuitously (and you can say it's a coincidence if you wish) NOW had that speech videotaped, giving me permanent proof that one of the newspaper quotes contributing to my excommunication was in error." The next day she picked up a newspaper in the hotel lobby and "read what I was supposed to have said in my speech the day before: 'Don't let Mormon missionaries into your home.'"[42]

A few days after she returned to Virginia, Johnson and Hazel Rigby drove to New York City, where she delivered a speech entitled "Patriarchal Panic: Sexual Politics in the Mormon Church." She was part of a panel entitled "Some Reflections on Women, Religion, and Mental Health" at the American Psychological Association's annual meeting. The context of the speech was "as you sow, so shall you reap."[43]

During this same period, the church began holding area conferences all over the country. In September 1979 Spencer W. Kimball was scheduled to attend the Washington, D.C., conference at the Capital Centre in Largo, Maryland. In another attempt to see him, Johnson wrote to Kimball and asked for an appointment. Regional Representative Donald Ladd telephoned her with the news that President Kimball would not be able to see her.[44] Perhaps it was coincidence, but a few days before the conference, Kimball was hospitalized and was unable even to attend the conference. Even so, the church public communications representatives made extensive efforts to bring the media to the conference, and Johnson took advantage of the opportunity.

Mormons for ERA again arranged for a tow plane, and as they departed the conference people were greeted by sixty picketers spread over all the exit roads and carrying signs such as "men of quality are not threatened by women for equality." The media loved it, and once again Johnson and her group were in the political spotlight. The *Washington Post* on September 14, 1979, even devoted the entire top of a page to a photograph of the banner flown by the tow plane: "Mother in Heaven Loves Mormons for ERA," the only mention of the conference in the newspaper.

Rick Johnson had returned from an extended trip to Liberia just in time to assist with the September 1979 Capitol Centre picketing, but the situation was not a happy one in the Johnson household. Stresses from years of marital difficulties, coupled with the new situation, created a rift. "But by the winter of 1979, when Rick began talking about going off to Africa, I had become a feminist and was finding that I could not accommodate to his escapist tactics anymore. He was after all an adult. He had helped bring these children into the world. Now he could stick around, put his personal preferences aside for a while, and work up the courage to tackle the problems parents have to tackle."[45] Instead, he moved to a room over the garage and asked Sonia for a divorce. He also admitted that he had fallen in love with another woman.

In the meantime, Sonia Johnson continued her political activism. She spoke in October on another panel, this time at the University of Utah. Her speech, "Off Our Pedestals, or Chronicles of the Uppity Sisters," combined portions of letters from Mormon women across the United States. It was, she recalled, a "low-key, humorous, moving, and less strident" speech than many she had given. One phrase, however, stuck out among the others—"savage misogyny"—and that would be used against her during her excommunication trial.[46] It was used in this context:

> This made me think of one of my favorite rejected slogans for our airplane banner tow: PEDESTALS ARE THE PITS. It's true, of course, pedestals are the pits. I wish there were time to talk at length about why the pedestal, as a symbol of women's immobilization and isolation in our male-centered society, more than any other symbol—the gilded cage, the doll's house—reveals our savage misogyny. Briefly, it is physically, intellectually, and spiritually cramped. It is precarious and a fall is dangerous, if not fatal. It maroons women and keeps us emotionally stranded from one another. And placing us in the position customarily occupied by statues, reveals society's attempt to render us as conveniently non-human, mindless and will-less as the [statues].[47]

Linda Thielke, a part-time reporter for United Press International, commented on the speech in her story, which appeared in the *Deseret News* on October 27, that "hatred of women" had been applied to the church: "'Pedestals are the pits,' said Ms. Johnson. It shows most vividly the savage misogeny in the Mormon Church."

This news clipping soon joined those from Montana and other places on her bishop's desk in Virginia. In early November 1979, the bishop of the Sterling Park, Virginia, Ward, Jeffrey Willis, called Johnson into his office and told her that "he was in the process of deciding whether or not to call me to trial."[48] She did not have to wait long to learn of his decision. As Johnson was reading her five-year-old son his bedtime story at 9 P.M. on November 14, someone knocked at her door. The two counselors in the Sterling Park Ward bishopric handed her a summons to a church court scheduled for Saturday, November 17. She had no idea how these courts operated, and, because the summons mentioned no charges, she was at a loss over how to prepare. "When she received the original court summons, the news had been leaked to Salt Lake media (UPI and AP) through a series of phone calls initiated by Sheldon Rampton, a Princeton student who visits the Johnson home and was on hand when the summons was delivered."[49]

With three days to prepare her defense against unspecified accusations, Johnson went to work on how best to respond. She met with Willis the following evening and asked for written charges. He refused but agreed to consider postponing the trial until December 1, 1979, allowing Johnson to round up witnesses who had heard her speak in various parts of the country. The next evening, Friday, November 16, Willis visited Johnson again to tell her that he had reconsidered and had set the court date for 6:30 P.M. on November 27. However, on the instructions of the Stake President Earl Roueche, Willis returned to her home later that evening to ask Johnson for her temple recommend and tell her that the stake president was taking charge of her case. The trial had been rescheduled for 11 the next morning.[50]

For five hours that Saturday, she was behind closed doors with the Bishopric. She temporarily fought off efforts to excommunicate her. The central questions in the trial revolved around Johnson's stand on the ERA in relationship to the involvement of the LDS hierarchy in the political situation. As the *Washington Post* summarized the controversy on November 28:

> Is she influencing people in the church to distrust the leadership. "Am I just being purely political or am I attacking the church?" she paraphrased.
>
> Is her ERA stand undermining the teachings of the president of the church, who Mormons believe receives his revelations directly from God?
>
> Is she "knowingly teaching false doctrine?"

When the court was over, no final decision had been made, but the Bishopric determined to bring Johnson before a stake court to answer charges of apostasy. She was informed on November 28 that the court would take place on December 1, three days hence, in the Oakton, Virginia, Stake Center. The summons stated that the court, scheduled to meet at 8:30 P.M., would "be strictly held to one hour and thirty minutes."[51]

More than two hundred people, including approximately forty Mormon supporters of the Equal Rights Amendment, braved 20-degree weather on December 1 to stand in the parking lot of the Oakton Stake Center with the media while Johnson was "informed that she was charged not only with hampering the church's worldwide missionary effort, but with damaging other church programs, including temple work, the welfare program, family home evening, genealogy, and family preparedness (food storage)." The magnitude of the charges were hard to imagine; some thought that the hierarchy had lain every negative aspect in the church at Johnson's feet. The charge of teaching false doctrines remained but was not detailed. Witnesses were almost superfluous in such a setting and after the "trial," Johnson told the crowd waiting in the cold that the entire episode had been "unsatisfactory." Then her bishop, Jeffrey Willis, appeared and read a prepared statement, complete with press copies, which affirmed that Johnson's ERA activism had not been considered by the court nor had any issue of immorality been raised or pondered. She had been tried solely on ec-clesiastical grounds. He also said that no decision had yet been reached; it would be deliberated and then announced. The reaction of the crowd was predictable. When Willis denied that the trial had not been con-nected with ERA, boos of disbelief drowned out his remarks. Because a decision had not been made Saturday night, Johnson was in the Ster-ling Park Ward on Sunday morning, participating in full view of the congregation as the ward organist.

She learned from reporters that she would receive a registered let-ter on December 5, announcing the Stake Court's decision. It arrived by way of two Mormon officials, and its contents came as no real sur-prise. The judgment was excommunication. The charges had been changed and were carefully worded: "You testified that you believe and have publicly stated that our society, specifically including church lead-ers, has a savage misogyny; when, in fact, it is church doctrine that exaltation can be gained only through the love that results in the eter-nal bonding of man and woman."[52] Johnson appealed to the next lev-el of jurisdiction for review of the decision, that of Stake President Earl Roueche, but the appeal was denied. She next appealed to the LDS First Presidency, but in June 1980 that appeal was also denied.[53]

Stake President Roueche read her the First Presidency's verdict, but she was not allowed to see or keep a copy of the document. However, because of the Gregg shorthand that she learned in high school, she made accurate notes. "What do I have to do to get back into this church," she asked Roueche after he read her the verdict. He told her that the church's stand on the ERA was inspired revelation from God and that, to show her repentance, she would have to oppose the ERA publicly. "Why don't you say that to the press?" she countered. "You'd like that, wouldn't you?" he answered angrily. "Yes," she said. "I'd like it if you'd tell the truth."[54] After the excommunication, she made public her divorce. A few months later, Rick requested that his name also be removed from the rolls of the Mormon church, and he was excommunicated at his request.

Thereafter, Johnson began to support herself by speaking and writ-ing on the cause closest to her heart: the feminist goal of equality for women. "The children," she said, "are very proud of me. I think the period of mourning about the divorce, the period of mourning over my misery [over being ousted from the Mormon church] is largely over," she told a *Washington Post* reporter, Majorie Hyer, in an inter-view published on December 29, 1980. Doubleday published her au-tobiography *From Housewife to Heretic* in 1981, and she continued to work for passage of the ERA. In 1982 she even fasted in Illinois for thirty-seven days with a group of women while the legislation was under consideration. Later that year, she ran unsuccessfully for the presidency of the National Organization for Women. In 1984, she accepted the nomination of the Citizens party to run for the presidency of the United States.

In 1987, the Crossing Press published *Going Out of Our Minds: The Metaphysics of Liberation*. In her chapter, "High Treason," Johnson admitted that three years after her divorce and excommunication she had become attracted to another woman, Susan. "The struggle against the taboo of loving someone of the same sex had taken place unconsciously. I hadn't been aware of it at all. Who knows how long it raged in there or how fiercely. The important fact is that I was victorious over immense forces, and that I consciously chose to act on that victory. Having made the choice, I broke through the terrifying, albeit ultimately absurd, patriarchal barrier as if it were rice paper, as if it were no big deal."[55]

Sonia Johnson sold the Sterling Park home and moved to Arlington, Virginia, where she shared a townhouse for several years with her children and Susan, also her business manager. She then bought several acres near Estancia, New Mexico, in the Albuquerque area, where she established a small women's community and continues to write and lecture. Her Wildfire Books Company published *Wildfire: Igniting the She/Volution* in 1989 and *The Ship That Sailed into the Living Room: Sex and Intimacy Reconsidered* in 1991. Both were autobiographical.

In *The Ship That Sailed into the Living Room*, Johnson discussed the break-up of her lesbian relationship. "It was during our fifth year together, that I began to be aware that I was suffering on some deeper, less visible level than I'd noticed before, that I was in a subtler, more constant sort of pain than my usual 'having relationship problems' discomfort."[56] She commented that "during neither of my marriages—to Rick and then to Susan—had I needed to ask myself whether I felt sexually excited, because I thought I was sure that I was—or that if I wasn't, I could become so in plenty of time to join in honestly."[57] She had believed that she should want to, as least some of the time, but in *The Ship That Sailed* she posits a form of relationship that goes beyond sex.

I live now with several women in the mountains of New Mexico. We have only recently come together and are still in the first stages of learning. At our home in Freedom, though we are not going to live together in the same space, we plan eventually to build a common bathhouse—with hot tub, sweat house, cold plunge, showers, and, perhaps, swimming pool. Seeing one another naked every day, being together without clothing, massaging, stroking, holding one another when we haven't the false barrier of cloth between us, we will get lots of practice in non-sexual, non-stimulus-response, touching. In my vision of us, we will find out how to go beyond sex, where no touch is sexual or can be interpreted as sexual because we are in the moment, in our power, not using touching as a means to some other end. Like our wild archaic sisters, we will have no inclination to do "it" because there will be no "it" to do. Sex as a concept will become extinct among those of us who choose this way.[62]

The journey from a Mormon belief system, and its acceptance of conservative gender roles and patriarchy, to feminist political activist was never one on which Johnson consciously set out. It came in fits and starts, with a growing awareness of the inequities of the institutions that were so much a part of her life. Once begun, however, the Latter-day Saint organization pushed and probed in ways that forced Johnson to react further away from the church. Although outside the Mormon church, Johnson continues as a martyr to LDS hierarchical power and a symbol of women's struggles inside the institution for greater equality. In 1990 she described her life, in a letter to me, as "going just dandy." Her fifth book is a novel based on personal experiences, and she engages in a variety of activities, especially with "the multitudes of women visitors who come through and she enjoys endless hours of rich conversation. But most of all she is enjoying herself, coming to know herself and take great pleasure in that knowledge."[63]

NOTES

1. Studies of Sonia Johnson can be found in Linda Sillitoe and Paul Swenson, "A Moral Issue," *Utah Holiday*, January 1980, 18–20, 22–34; Linda Sillitoe, "Church Politics and Sonia Johnson: The Central Conundrum," *Sunstone* 5 (January–February 1980): 35–42; Teresa Carpenter, "Courage and Pain: Women Who Love God and Defy Their Churches," *Redbook*, April 1980, 155–56; Christine Rigby Arrington, "One Woman against the Patriarchal Church," *Savvy*, October 1980, 28–33; Mary L. Bradford, "The Odyssey of Sonia Johnson" and "All on Fire: An Interview with Sonia Johnson," *Dialogue: A Journal of Mormon Thought* 14 (Summer 1981): 14–26, 27–47; Jan Shipps, "Sonia Johnson, Mormonism and the Media," *Christian Century*, January 2, 1980, 5–6; "A Savage Misogyny," *Time*, December 17, 1979, 80; Lisa Cronin Wohl, "Feminist Latter-Day Saint: Why Sonia Johnson Won't Give up on the ERA or the Mormon Church," *People*, March 1980, 39–40, 42; K. Lanlois,

"Interview with Sonia Johnson," *Feminist Studies* 8 (Spring 1982): 7–18; Linda Sillitoe, "Off the Record: Telling the Rest of the Truth," *Sunstone* 14 (December 1990): 17–19. Scholarly studies of Mormon excommunication include Lester E. Bush, Jr., "Excommunication: Church Courts in Mormon History," *Sunstone,* July–August 1983, 24–30; Mark P. Leone, *Roots of Modern Mormonism* (Cambridge: Harvard University Press, 1979), 111–47; Edwin Brown Firmage and Richard Collin Mangrum, *Zion in the Courts: A Legal History of the Church of Jesus Christ of Latter-day Saints, 1830–1900* (Urbana: University of Illinois Press, 1988).

2. Numerous studies have documented the orchestrated Mormon effort to defeat the ERA. See O. Kendall White, Jr., "Overt and Covert Politics: The Mormon Church's Anti-ERA Campaign in Virginia," *Virginia Social Science Journal* 19 (Winter 1984): 14–16; O. Kendall White, Jr., "Mormonism and the Equal Rights Amendment," *Journal of Church and State* 31 (Spring 1989): 249–67; Anson D. Shupe and John Heinerman, "Mormonism and the New Christian Right: An Emerging Coalition?" *Review of Religious Research,* 27 (December 1985): 146–57; John Heinerman and Anson D. Shupe, *The Mormon Corporate Empire* (Boston: Beacon Press, 1985), 144–52; James T. Richardson, "The 'Old Right' in Action: Mormon and Catholic Involvement in an Equal Rights Amendment Referendum," in *New Christian Politics,* ed. David Bromley and Anson D. Shupe (Macon: Mercer University Press, 1984), 210–33. Broader studies of the politics of the ERA can be found in Jane J. Mansbridge, *Why We Lost the ERA* (Chicago: University of Chicago Press, 1986); and Mary Frances Berry, *Why ERA Failed: Politics, Women's Rights, and the Amending Process of the Constitution* (Bloomington: Indiana University Press, 1986).

3. Sillitoe and Swenson, "A Moral Issue," 30; Carl Beauchamp, "The Sonia Johnson Trial," *Women's Political Times* 4 (December 1979): 1, 8; Ben A. Franklin, "Mormon Church Excommunicates a Supporter of Rights Amendment," *New York Times,* December 6, 1979, A26; Ben A. Franklin, "Mormon Feminist Awaiting Verdict of Her Church Trial," *New York Times,* December 3, 1979, A18; Elisabeth Bumiller, "Sonia Johnson's Sea of Troubles," *Washington Post,* February 23, 1980, B1, B5; O. Kendall White, Jr., "A Feminist Challenge: 'Mormons for ERA' as an Internal Social Movement," *Journal of Ethnic Studies* 13 (Spring 1985): 29–50.

4. The concept of celestial marriage has been discussed in Bruce R. McConkie, *Mormon Doctrine* (Salt Lake City: Bookcraft, 1966), 117–18; David John Buerger, "The Development of the Mormon Temple Endowment Ceremony," *Dialogue: A Journal of Mormon Thought* 20 (Winter 1987): 33–76; Carol Cornwall Madsen, "Mormon Women and the Temple: Toward a New Interpretation," in *Sisters in Spirit: Mormon Women in Historical and Cultural Perspective,* ed. Maureen Ursenbach Beecher and Lavinia Fielding Anderson (Urbana: University of Illinois Press, 1987), 80–110; and in several essays in Gary James Bergera, *Line upon Line: Essays on Mormon Doctrine* (Salt Lake City: Signature Books, 1989).

5. Sonia Johnson, *From Housewife to Heretic* (Garden City: Doubleday and Co., 1981), 66.

6. Johnson, *From Housewife to Heretic*, 71.

7. Ibid., 74–75.

8. The Mormon hierarchy has been especially important in defining this structure. Even when trying to demonstrate equality, they failed. The LDS apostle Franklin D. Richards made a convoluted attempt to show that men and women were equal before the Mormon God in 1888 when he said, "I ask any and everybody present who have received their endowments, whether he be a brother Apostle, Bishop, High Priest, Elder, or whatever office he may hold in the Church, What blessings did you receive, what ordinance, what power, intelligence, sanctification or grace did you receive that your wife did not partake of with you? . . . I hold that a faithful wife has certain gifts and blessings and promises with her husband, which she cannot be deprived of except by transgression of the holy order of God" (*Woman's Exponent*, September 1, 1888, 54).

The important aspect of this is the necessary linkage of women to men. A faithful wife had gifts and promises and blessing with her husband, not in her own right, and this helped ensure her subservience. Although most Mormon women were quite pleased with this position—after all, it placed them in a much higher position than non-Mormons—there is little question that the sexes were not equal. Melodie Moench Charles concluded that Mormon theology allowed women "no authority nor power; she gets no acknowledgment for her distinctive contributions, whatever they are. She has no self apart from her husband." See "The Need for a New Mormon Heaven," *Dialogue: A Journal of Mormon Thought* 21 (Fall 1988): 73–87, quote from 84–85.

9. Johnson, *Housewife to Heretic*, 77.

10. This is dealt with in Martin E. Marty, *Modern American Religion*: Vol. 1, *The Irony of It All, 1893–1919* (Chicago: University of Chicago Press, 1986), and O. Kendall White, Jr., *Mormon Neo-Orthodoxy: A Crisis Theology* (Salt Lake City: Signature Books, 1987).

11. Johnson, *Housewife to Heretic*, 2, 28.

12. Ibid., 37–38, 40–41.

13. Ibid., 88.

14. Gabrielle Burton, *I'm Running Away from Home, but I'm Not Allowed to Cross the Street* (Pittsburgh: Know, Inc., 1972); Germaine Greer *The Female Eunuch* (London: MacGibbon and Kee, 1970); Kate Millet, *Sexual Politics* (Garden City: Doubleday and Co., 1970).

15. "Equal Rights Amendment," *Church News*, January 11, 1975, 16; "ERA Effort Fails to Take Hold," *Salt Lake Tribune*, January 22, 1975, A4; Robert Gottlieb and Peter Wiley, *America's Saints: The Rise of Mormon Power* (New York: G. P. Putnam's Sons, 1984), 204–5; "Chronology—The Mormon Anti-ERA Campaign," *Mormons for ERA Newsletter* 5 (February 1983): 5.

16. Collection of Utah Women's Issues, 1970s–80s, Western Americana, Marriott Library, University of Utah, Salt Lake City; Paul Swenson and Alice A. Pottmyer, "The Church, the Press and the ERA," *Utah Holiday*, September 1978, 14.

17. Spencer W. Kimball, N. Eldon Tanner, and Marion G. Romney statement, *Deseret News,* October 22, 1976, A1.

18. *Salt Lake Tribune,* January 9, 1977, B4. Boyd K. Packer has enjoyed a long career as a voice of conservatism in Mormonism. He has, for instance, publicly denounced Mormon historians for being too secular in interpretation, Brigham Young University professors for teaching Darwinian evolution, and defined the arts as faith-promoting illustrations of gospel principles. See Boyd K. Packer, "The Mantle Is Far, Far Greater than the Intellect," *Brigham Young University Studies* 21 (Summer 1981); 259–78; Boyd K. Packer, "Come, All Ye Sons of God," *Ensign* 13 (August 1983): 68–69.

19. *Salt Lake Tribune,* January 9, 1977, B4; "Chronology—The Mormon Anti-ERA Campaign," 5.

20. *Congressional Record,* February 1, 1977, Senate 1980–88.

21. Phyllis Schlafly, *A Choice Not an Echo* (Alton: N.p., 1964), 25–26.

22. Patricia Brim, "The IWY Conference in Utah," 4, Box 4, Folder 35, Collection of Utah Women's Issues, University of Utah; Linda Sillitoe, "Women Scorned: Inside the IWY Conference," *Utah Holiday,* August 1977, 26–28, 63–69; Sheri L. Dew, *Ezra Taft Benson: A Biography* (Salt Lake City: Deseret Book Co., 1987), 453–54; "10,000 Jam Hall, Foyer at Women's Sessions," *Deseret News,* June 24, 1977, A1; "Mormon Turnout Overwhelms Women's Conference in Utah," *New York Times,* July 25, 1977, 26; Lisa Bolin Hawkins, "Report on the Utah International Women's Year Meeting," typescript, Box 2, Folder 5, Collection of Utah Women's Issues, University of Utah; "Papers of the International Women's Year Conference, Utah," Western Americana, Marriott Library, University of Utah; Dixie Snow Huefner, "Church and Politics at the Utah IWY Conference," *Dialogue: A Journal of Mormon Thought* 11 (Spring 1978): 58–75.

23. Conservative Women Opposed to the Equal Rights Amendment Collection, MSS SC 1827, Archives, Harold B. Lee Library, Brigham Young University, Provo; "Bitter Battle Expected at Women's Meeting," *Honolulu Star-Bulletin,* July 8, 1977; "Conservative Bloc Exceeds Liberals," *Honolulu Star-Bulletin,* July 9, 1977, 2.

24. "Chronology—The Mormon Anti-ERA Campaign," 5.

25. Swenson and Pottmyer, "The Church, the Press and the ERA," 14.

26. *Congressional Record,* May 26, 1978, Senate S8442.

27. "Chronology—The Mormon Anti-ERA Campaign," 5; White, "Mormonism and the Equal Rights Amendment," 254–55. See also "The Church and the Era," *Vienna Vision* [Vienna, Va., ward newsletter], August 1978; "Prophet Called for Positive Action Against ERA," *Oakton, Virginia Stake Newsletter,* November 1978, both in Box 3, Folder 10, Collection of Utah Women's Issues, University of Utah; Sheldon M. Rampton, "To All Families in the Oakton Virginia Stake," September 8, 1978, Box 7, Folder 27, Sonia Johnson Papers, Marriott Library, University of Utah; Ken Driggs letter to the editor, *Dialogue: A Journal of Mormon Thought* 11 (Autumn 1978): 6.

28. Johnson, *From Housewife to Heretic,* 121.

29. Ibid., 124.

30. Ibid., 135.

31. United Press International story, August 5, 1978, Johnson Papers, University of Utah.

32. Johnson, *From Housewife to Heretic,* 137.

33. Ibid., 147.

34. Ibid., 148.

35. Ibid., 151.

36. Ibid., 164.

37. Ibid., 166.

38. Ibid., 174.

39. *Washington Star,* March 6, 1979; White, "A Feminist Challenge," 29–50.

40. Johnson, *From Housewife to Heretic,* 154.

41. Ibid., 156.

42. Ibid., 191–92.

43. Ibid., 193.

44. Personal notes of author, November 1979.

45. Johnson, *From Housewife to Heretic,* 210.

46. "A Savage Misogyny," 80.

47. Sillitoe and Swenson, "A Moral Issue," 23, 24.

48. Johnson, *From Housewife to Heretic,* 227.

49. Sillitoe and Swenson, "A Moral Issue," 31.

50. Ibid., 24; Marjorie Hyer, *Washington Post,* November 18, 1979.

51. Sillitoe and Swenson, "A Moral Issue," 26.

52. Ibid., 30.

53. Arrington, "One Woman against the Patriarchal Church," 33.

54. Ibid., 33.

55. Sonia Johnson, *Going Out of Our Minds: The Metaphysics of Liberation* (Freedom, Calif.: The Crossing Press, 1987), 108.

56. Sonia Johnson, *The Ship That Sailed into the Living Room: Sex and Intimacy Reconsidered* (Estancia, NM: Wildfire Books, 1991), p. 9.

57. Johnson, *The Ship That Sailed,* 37.

58. Ibid., 313–14.

59. Sonia Johnson to Alice Allred Pottmyer, February 26, 1990; Jean Tait (for Sonia Johnson) to Alice Allred Pottmyer, February 1, 1993, both in possession of the author.

Contributors

LEONARD J. ARRINGTON is professor emeritus at Brigham Young University. He served as Latter-day Saint church historian between 1972 and 1980 and as director of the Joseph Fielding Smith Institute for Church History at Brigham Young University before his retirement. He is the author of numerous books and articles on Mormon history, including *Great Basin Kingdom: An Economic History of the Latter-day Saints, 1830–1900* (Harvard University Press, 1958) and *Brigham Young: American Moses* (Alfred A. Knopf, 1985).

M. GUY BISHOP received his Ph.D. in 1981 from Southern Illinois University, Carbondale. He contributed a chapter to *Religion and Society in the American West,* edited by Carl Guareri and David Alvarez (University Press of America, 1987). His biography of Henry W. Bigler will be published by the University of Utah Press.

MARTHA SONNTAG BRADLEY, whose Ph.D. is from the University of Utah, is a faculty member at Brigham Young University and coeditor of *Dialogue: A Journal of Mormon Thought.* She is completing a book on post-manifesto polygamy among the Mormons.

NEWELL G. BRINGHURST is a member of the history faculty of the College of the Sequoias, Visalia, California. His many publications include *Saints, Slaves and Blacks: The Changing Place of Black People within Mormonism* (Greenwood Press, 1981) and, for the Library of American Biography series, *Brigham Young and the Expanding Western Frontier* (Little, Brown, 1986). He is at work on a biography of Fawn M. Brodie.

PAUL M. EDWARDS is president of the Temple School of the Reorganized Church of Jesus Christ of Latter Day Saints in Independence, Missouri. His Ph.D. is from St. Andrews University, Scotland, and he is the author of *Our Legacy of Faith: A Brief History of the Reorganized Church of Jesus Christ of Latter Day Saints* (Herald Publishing House,

1991); *The Chief: An Administrative Biography of Fred M. Smith* (Herald Publishing House, 1988); *Ethics: The Possibility of Moral Choice* (Herald Publishing House, 1987); and *Preface to Faith: A Philosophical Inquiry into RLDS Beliefs* (Signature Books, 1986). He was also coeditor of *The Restoration Movement: Essays in Mormon History* (Coronado Press, 1973), with F. Mark McKiernan and Alma R. Blair.

JESSIE L. EMBRY is director of the Oral History Program at the Charles Redd Center for Western Studies at Brigham Young University. She is the author of *Mormon Polygamous Families: Life in the Principle* (University of Utah Press, 1987) and has completed a manuscript on black Americans and the Mormon experience.

LAWRENCE FOSTER is professor of history at the Georgia Institute of Technology, Atlanta. He is the author of *Religion and Sexuality: Three American Communal Experiments of the Nineteenth Century* (Oxford University Press, 1981), and *Women, Family, and Utopia: Communal Experiments of the Shakers, the Oneida Community, and the Mormons* (Syracuse University Press, 1991).

KENNETH W. GODFREY is area director of the Latter-day Saints Institutes of Religion, Logan, Utah. He is the author of numerous articles and coauthor of *Women's Voices* (Deseret Book Co., 1978).

RICHARD NEITZEL HOLZAPFEL is member of the Department of Church History and Doctrine, Brigham Young University. He is the author, with T. Jeffery Cottle, of *Old Mormon Nauvoo, 1839–1846: Historic Photographs and Guide* (Grandin Book Co., 1990) and *Old Mormon Kirtland and Missouri: Historic Photographs and Guide* (Fieldbrook Publications, 1991), and *Every Stone a Sermon* (Deseret Book Co., 1992), a history of the Salt Lake Temple.

RICHARD P. HOWARD has been the church historian of the Reorganized Church of Jesus Christ of Latter Day Saints in Independence, Missouri, since 1965. He is the author of *Restoration Scriptures: A Study of Their Textual Development* (Herald Publishing House, 1969), and *The Church Through the Years* (Herald Publishing House, 1992–93), a two-volume history of the Reorganized Church.

DANNY L. JORGENSEN is professor of religion at the Center for Interdisciplinary Studies in Culture and Society at the University of South Florida, St. Petersburg. He has written several articles relating to sociological research and a book, *Participant Observation: A Methodology for Human Studies* (Sage Publications, 1989).

ROGER D. LAUNIUS is chief historian for the National Aeronautics and Space Administration in Washington, D.C. He has written *Joseph Smith III: Pragmatic Prophet* (University of Illinois Press, 1988), *Invisible Saints: A History of Black Americans in the Reorganized Church* (Herald Publishing House, 1988), and *Zion's Camp: Expedition to Missouri* (Herald Publishing House, 1984).

JOHN S. McCORMICK is on the faculty of the Salt Lake Community College in Utah. He had published widely on the Socialist party in the West in the *Utah Historical Quarterly* and several other professional journals.

ALICE ALLRED POTTMYER is a freelance writer and has worked for several Washington, D.C., trade associations. She participated with Sonia Johnson in the Mormons for ERA organization and has written several essays for such magazines as *Utah Holiday* on their efforts.

RONALD E. ROMIG is church archivist for the Reorganized Church of Jesus Christ of Latter Day Saints in Independence, Missouri. He is the author of several articles relating to early Mormonism, many of which have investigated the historical geography and demographics of the church in Jackson County, Missouri.

WILLIAM D. RUSSELL is a professor with the Division of Social Sciences at Graceland College, Lamoni, Iowa. A past president of the Mormon History Association, he has written several articles about the development of Mormonism, notably "History and the Mormon Scriptures," his MHA presidential address, which appeared in the *Journal of Mormon History* in 1983. He is at work on a history of the liberal-conservative split in the Reorganized Church.

RICHARD L. SAUNDERS is on the staff of the Special Collection Division, University of Montana. A junior scholar in Mormon studies, he is working on a biography of Francis Gladden Bishop.

JOHN S. SILLITO is an archivist with Weber State University in Ogden, Utah. His articles on the Socialist party's role in the development of the American West have appeared in the *Utah Historical Quarterly* and *Dialogue: A Journal of Mormon Thought*.

LINDA THATCHER is coordinator of collections at the Utah State Historical Society, Salt Lake City. A librarian by training, she has served as president of the Conference of Inter-mountain Archivists and the Utah Women's History Association. In addition, her historical work has appeared in such journals as *Dialogue: A Journal of Mormon Thought, Utah Historical Quarterly,* and *Sunstone Review.*

KENNETH H. WINN is the state archivist for Missouri, Jefferson City. His *Exiles in a Land of Liberty: Mormons in America, 1830–1846* (University of North Carolina Press, 1989) analyzed Mormonism from the standpoint of the ideology of "Republicanism" present in American culture during the early nineteenth century.

DAN VOGEL, an independent scholar in Columbus, Ohio, has written *Indian Origins and the Book of Mormon: Religious Solutions from Columbus to Joseph Smith* (Signature Books, 1986) and *Religious Seekers and the Advent of Mormonism* (Signature Books, 1988). He is also editor of *The Word of God: Essays on Mormon Scripture* (Signature Books, 1990).

Index

Adam-God doctrine, 364n29
Adams, George J.: Joseph Smith III and, 147
Aldrich, Hazen, 130
Allred, Rulon, 274
Alta Club (Salt Lake City): Henry W. Lawrence and, 229
American pluralism, 25
American political party, 256
Anderson, C. LeRoy: on Morrisites, 203
"Articles of Faith" (Doves' publication), 210
Atchison, David, 54
Avard, Sampson, 9, 62

Banks, John: death of, 204, 212; Morrisite movement and, 211
Barlow, John Y.: ordains Joseph White Musser, 269–70; LeRoy Johnson and, 274
Baskin, Robert N., 227
Bates, Irene M.: on William Smith, 147
Beebe, Luana Hart: Orrin Porter Rockwell and, 162; Alpheus Cutler and, 162
Bennett, John C.: William E. McLellin and, 87–88
Bishop, Francis Gladden: biography of, 102; joins Mormon church, 103–4; visions of, 103, 105, 109–10; called as missionary, 106–7; receives endowments, 107; Gibson Smith's complaints about, 107; suspended from church, 107; charges against, 108–9; excommunication of, 109; James J. Strang and, 111; marriage of, 112; writings of, 112; followers of Charles B. Thompson and, 113; letters to Brigham Young, 113; in Salt Lake City, 114; death of, 114

Blair, Alma R., 320
A Book of Commandments (1833), 345
Book of Esdras: predictions of, 122–23, 128–30; publication of, 122, 125; denounciation of, 125
Book of Mormon: David Whitmer's perceptions of, 24–25; release of, 26; John Corrill's feeling about, 47; Reorganized Church and, 321
Borquist, Rose Selms: Joseph White Musser and, 265
Brewster, James Colin: biography of, 120; in Kirtland, Ohio, 120; vision of, 121–22; writings of, 122; reorganizes church, 123; editorial by John Taylor and, 125; excommunication of, 125; "To the Mormon Money Diggers," 125; exodus from Nauvoo and, 128; Esdras publication and, 128; letter to James J. Strang, 130; as counselor Church of Christ, 130; as editor of Olive Branch, 131; Kinderhook plates and, 131; in Colonia, N.M., 132; dissolves group, 133; returns to United States, 133; joins Sidney Rigdon's church, 134
Brewster, Zephaniah: money digging and, 126–27; priesthood and, 127
Briggs, Jason W., 150–51
Brigham Young and His Mormon Empire (Frank J. Cannon), 258
Brimhall, Dean, 284, 286
Brodie, Bernard, 284
Brodie, Fawn McKay: biography of, 279–81; mother and, 282; at University of Utah, 282–83; at Weber College, 283; Dilworth Jensen and, 283; at University of Chicago, 283; Bernard Brodie and, 283, 284; LDS Church Security

Program and, 284–85; as "Martha Emery," 285; researches Joseph Smith, 285–89; Dale L. Morgan and, 286–88; Claire Noall and, 288; Juanita Brooks and, 288; Vesta Crawford and, 288; Stanley Ivins and, 288; Wilford M. Poulson and, 288–89; excommunication of, 289–90, 294, 299n64; on 1944 polygamy arrests, 290–91; publications of, 291–92; on racial relations, 293; illness of, 293; death of, 294; as a feminist, 295

Brooks, Juanita, 288

Brown, Martha A.: Frank J. Cannon and, 244

Campbell, Beverly, 378

Cannon, Abraham, 256; death of, 256

Cannon, Frank J.: as dissenter, 13; excommunication of, 241–42, 256; biography of, 242–44; adultery charges and, 244–45; alcohol and, 244–45, 247; jailed, 246; in Washington, D.C., 247, 248; two-party system proposal and, 248; campaign for territorial delegate, 248, 249; career in U.S. Senate, 250–53; silver question and, 251; National Silver Republican party and, 251; Dingley Tariff and, 252; Lorenzo Snow and, 253; Brigham Young, Jr., and, 253–54; Joseph F. Smith and, 253–54; Reed Smoot and, 254–57; American political party and, 256; Thomas Kearns and, 256; Abraham Cannon and, 256; Senator Dubois and, 257; publications of, 246, 256–58; death of, 258; marriage of, 261n44

Cannon, George Q., 244–45; U.S. Senate and, 250–51; LDS Church business interests of, 253; death of, 256

Cannon, John M., 263

Carr, Abigail: Alpheus Cutler and, 162; biography of, 173–74n12

Carr, Margaret: Alpheus Cutler and, 162; biographical information, 173–74n12

The Changing World of Mormonism (Jerald and Sandra Tanner), 346

Cheville, Roy A., 152

Church of Christ (Aldrich): organizion

of, 130; move to California and, 131–33

Church of Christ (McLellin), 89

Church of Christ (Rigdon), 83; "Preamble and Resolutions," 83–84; 1845 conference, 84–85; formation of, 186, 188; beliefs of, 188–89; Stephen Post and, 190; disintegration of, 192

Church of the Firstborn (Dove), 205, 207; failure of, 209, 210, 213

Church of Jesus Christ (Cutlerite), 158

Church of Jesus Christ of Latter-day Saints: beginnings of, 3; David Whitmer's perceptions of, 24–25; reorganization of, 148; Church Security Program of, 284–85; New Israel and, 356; diversity and, 356

Citizens Coalition, 378

Clark, J. Reuben: on polygamy, 271

Clay County (Mo.), 57

Clayton, William: on William Smith, 146; publication of journal of, 352

Cole, Joseph M., 84

Comunitarianism: revelation, 63–64; John Corrill and, 64

Cook, Richard: Morrisite movement and, 204, 211

Corrill, John: biography of, 45–46; as primitist, 48; joins church, 48; as missionary, 49; role in Missouri, 49; on Law of Consecration, 51; as negotiator, 52; patriarchal blessing and, 55; receives endowments, 55; Joseph Smith and, 50, 55–56, 64–65; Kirtland Temple and, 56; tries to find Mormons new home, 57; as "Keeper of the Lord's Storehouse," 58; republicanism and, 59; quote on branches, 59–60; reason for dissent, 62; elected to Missouri legislature, 63; on Danites, 63; on comunitarianism, 64; sent to Daviess County, 66; negotiates for peace, 67; excommunication of, 69; death of, 69; family and, 70n6; Lyman Wight and, 72n34; personal property of, 75n87

Council of Fifty (Nauvoo, Ill.): Alpheus Cutler and, 161–62

Cowdery, Oliver: as Book of Mormon witness, 7; introduces David Whitmer

Restoration, 23; letter to Joseph Smith, 27; on separation of church and state, 34; transgression of, 35; break with church, 35–36

Cowdery, Warren, 9

Cowles, Austin, 131

Cox, Sally: Alpheus Cutler and, 162

Crawford, Vesta: Fawn Brodie and, 288

Cumorah Books, 327–28

Cutler, Alpheus: biography of, 159; move to Nauvoo, 160; joins Mormon church, 160; Kirtland Temple and, 160; *Doctrine and Covenants* and, 160; at School of the Prophets, 160; Nauvoo Temple and, 161; Council of Fifty and, 161–62; plural marriages of, 162, 169; Joseph Smith and, 163; Lamanite mission and, 164; Orson Hyde and, 165–68; excommunication of, 169; Joseph Smith III and, 172; Heber C. Kimball and, 175n18

Cutler, Clarissa: Heber C. Kimball and, 162–63

Cutler, Emily: Heber C. Kimball and, 163

Cutlerites: formation and beliefs of, 170–71; polygamy and, 174n14, 177n45; Jackson County, Mo., and 176n33; comunitarianism and, 178n53; decline of, 179n58

Cutler, Lois H.: Almon W. Sherman and, 160

Cutler, Louisa Elizabeth: Tunis Rappleye and, 160

Cutler Peak (Neb.), 174n16

Danites: purpose of, 9; creation of, 62; John Corrill on, 63

"Decision Time," 327–28

Delaware Indians: Alpheus Cutler and, 169, 171

Deseret Agricultural and Manufacturing Society: Henry W. Lawrence, and, 229

Doctrine and Covenants: Joseph Smith, Jr., and, 6; Church of Christ (Rigdon) and, 84; William E. McLellin and, 84; Alpheus Cutler and, 160; Sidney Rigdon and, 190; Richard Price and, 325, 329

Doniphan, Alexander, 54

Donovan, Gregory I., 328–29

Dove, George: on Morrisites, 201; excommunication of, 202; arrest of, 204; mission to eastern states, 205; as phrenologist, 209; succession, 212–13; death of, 218n52

Dove, James: baptism, 197; migrates to America, 197–98; plural marriage and, 200; arrest of, 204; as leader of Carson Valley (Nev.) Morrisites, 204; mission to eastern states, 205; in Montana, 207; missionary efforts in Salt Lake City, 207–8; publications of, 207, 209, 213; return to South Weber, 208–9; U.S. government and, 213; revelations of, 217n42; death of, 209, 218n52

Dove, Joseph A., 206; birth of, 217–18n44

Dove, Sarah, 199

Dresser, Norman, 234

Dubois, Fred Thomas: Frank J. Cannon and, 257

Eardley, John R., 207

Ehat, Andrew, 352

Eighth Ward Silk Producing Society: Henry W. Lawrence and, 221

The Ensign, 81

Equal Rights Amendment (ERA): Church of Jesus Christ of Latter-day Saints and, 366; Sonia Johnson and, 366; anti-ERA lobbying coalition organized, 377–78

Far West (Mo.), 37; settlement of, 57; arrival of Joseph Smith, 60

Fetzer, Casper, 272

Flanders, Robert Bruce, 320

Forscutt, Mark, 212

Foster, Warren, 232

From Housewife to Heretic (Sonia Johnson), 383

Gallatin (Daviess County) Mo.: riot in, 65–66

Garn, Jake, 377

Geary, Edward A.: on *The Giant Joshua*, 307

The Giant Joshua (Maurine Whipple), 304–6, 307, 309

Gladdenites: in Utah, 113

Godbeites: Henry W. Lawrence and, 222;
    beliefs of, 222–23
Godbe, William S.: excommunication of,
    223–24; Populist party and, 232
Grieg, J. M., 91–92

Harris, Mark, 369
Harris, Martin: Book of Mormon
    witness, 7, Church of Christ (McLellin)
    and, 89
Harrison, E. T.: excommunication of,
    223–24
Hatch, Orrin: Sonia Johnson and, 376–
    77
Haun's Mill (Mo.): massacre at, 66
Hedrick, Grandville: William E. McLellin
    and, 95–96
Higham, Thomas: on George Dove, 201
Hill, Mary Caroline: Joseph White
    Musser and, 266
Hinkle, George M.: William E. McLellin
    and, 80–81
The History of Joseph Smith the Prophet
    (Frank J. Cannon), 246
Hubble, (Mrs.): end of revelations, 7;
    challenge to Joseph Smith, 16–17
Huntsville, Utah: Fawn McKay Brodie
    and, 279–80
Hyde, Orson: Alpheus Cutler and, 165–
    69

Independence (Mo.), 51–53
India Mission, 268
International Women's Year conference
    (Salt Lake City), 372
Ivins, Stanley: Fawn Brodie and, 288

Jackson County (Mo.), 29, 30; violence
    against church members, 31; Mormon
    expulsion from, 32, 53; Culterites and,
    176n33
Jensen, Dilworth: Fawn Brodie and, 283
Johnson, LeRoy, 270, 274
Johnson, Richard: Sonia Harris and, 369;
    excommunication of, 383
Johnson, Sonia Harris: excommunication
    of, 366–67; 381–83; biography of,
    367–69; early experiences in Mormon
    church, 368–69; early married life,
    369–70; feminist issues and, 370–72;

Senate Subcommittee testimony of,
    375–76; Orrin Hatch and, 376–77;
    Jake Garn and, 377; Spencer W.
    Kimball and, 379–80; marriage and
    divorce of, 380, 383; From Housewife
    to Heretic, 383; fast of, 383–84;
    publications of, 384; National
    Organization of Women and, 384; later
    life, 384–85

Kearns, Thomas, 256
Kelsey, Eli: excommunication of, 223–24
Kimball and Lawrence, 220, 224–25
Kimball, Heber C.: Clarissa Cutler and,
    162–63; Emily Cutler and, 163;
    polygamous wives and, 175n18
Kimball, John B., 220
Kimball, Spencer W.: Sonia Johnson and,
    379–80
Kinderhook plates, 131
Kingston settlement (Weber County,
    Utah), 214–15n11
Kirtland Bank, 58
Kirtland (Ohio), 29
Kirtland Temple: dedication of, 34, 56–
    57; John Corrill and, 56; Alpheus
    Cutler and, 160

Lamanites, 164–66
Law of Consecration: David Whitmer on,
    30; growing discontent over, 31;
    Morrisite beliefs on, 210
Law of lineage: William Smith and, 150
Law, William: as counselor to Joseph
    Smith, Jr., 9–10; withdraws from
    church, 17; William E. McLellin and,
    82
Lawrence, Henry W.: biography of, 220;
    political career of, 220–21; Utah War
    and, 221; as polygamist, 221, 225;
    joins Godbeites, 222; Utah Magazine
    and, 224; excommunication of, 224;
    Liberal party and, 225–27; runs for
    political office, 227; taxes and, 227–
    28; civic duties and, 228–30; politics
    and, 227, 230, 231–34, 235–37;
    testifies at Smoot hearings, 236;
    marriage of, 238n2; death of, 328
Lawrence, Maria: Joseph Smith and
    Brigham Young and, 221

Lawrence, Sarah: Joseph Smith and Heber C. Kimball and, 221
Liberal party, 225; in Utah, 226–27
Living Issues, 233
Livingstone, John, 204–5
Logan Journal, 244

Manifestos, 230, 266
Manti (Iowa), 178n51; Cutlerite followers leave, 178–79n57
Marsh, T. B., 85
McCall, Daisey Caroline: Alpheus Cutler and, 162
McKay, David O., 272
McKay, Thomas E., 279
McLellin, Emeline Miller, 98n11
McLellin, William E.: as dissenter, 13; David Whitmer and, 38, 88–89, 92–93, 97; joins church, 76; Joseph Smith and, 77, 80, 89–90; attempt to write a revelation, 77; Quorum of Twelve Apostles and, 78, 82–83; Missouri High Council and, 78; called to repent, 78; disfellowshipped, 79; move to Hampton, Ill., 80; excommunication of, 80; George M. Hinkle faction and, 80–81; letter to Sidney Rigdon, 82, 86; William Law's group and, 82; Church of Christ and, 83–84, 88, 99n27; father and, 85; revelation by T. B. Marsh, 85 and; James J. Strang and, 86–88; John C. Bennett and, 87–88; missionary work of, 78, 91; James J. Strang on contact with Whitmer, 92; J. M. Grieg on, 91–92; Joseph Smith III and, 94–95; Grandville Hedrick and, 95–96; death of, 97; *Doctrine and Covenants* and, 98n6; marriage of, 98n11
Melchizedek and Aaronic Herald, 149
Miller, Henrietta Clarinda: Alpheus Cutler and, 162
Missouri High Council: David Whitmer ordained as president of, 32; John Whitmer and W. W. Phelps and, 60; William E. McLellin and, 78
Modern Microfilm Company, 345
Morgan, Dale L.: Fawn Brodie and, 286, 287, 288
Mormon Reformation of 1856–57: in Great Britain, 197; in Utah, 199; George Dove and Joseph Morris on, 202
Mormonism—Shadow or Reality (Jerald and Sandra Tanner), 344, 346
Mormons for ERA, 366, 374–75, 377
Morris, Joseph: biography of, 198–99; revelations and beliefs of, 202; warrant for arrest, 203; death of, 203–4; publication of revelations, 208
Morrisites, 198; Mormons baptized into, 201; George Dove on, 201; information about, 203; conflict with, 203; Wilford Woodruff and John Taylor on, 203; in California (Dove), 206; differences from Reorganized Church, 216n27
Musser, Amos Milton, 264–65
Musser, Joseph White: as polygamist, 14; biography of, 262–63; excommunication of, 263; marriage to Rose Selms Borquist, 265, 274; Lorenzo Snow and, 265; plural marriage and, 265, 266, 274; Mary Caroline Hill and, 266; Ellis R. Shipp and, 266; temple relationship of, 267; Quorum of Twelve Apostles and, 267–68; India mission and, 268; disfellowshipped, 268; excommunication of, 268; Lorin Woolley and, 268–69; ordained by John Y. Barlow, 269–70; Heber J. Grant and, 270–71; *Truth* magazine and, 272; on *State v. Jessop,* 272–73; arrested, 273–74; Rulon Allred and, 274; death of, 274

National Silver Republican party, 251
Nauvoo Expositor, 10
Nauvoo High Council: Alpheus Cutler and, 161
Nauvoo (Ill.): James Brewster and, 128
Nauvoo Temple, 161
Neilson, John, 206
New Church, 113
Noall, Claire: Fawn Brodie and, 288
No Man Knows My History (Fawn M. Brodie), 289, 293

Ogden Herald, 246
Olive Branch, 130, 131

"On Being a Mormon Historian" (D. Michael Quinn), 361n12

Ordination of women: Sidney Rigdon and, 191; Reorganized Church and, 332

Page, Hiram: end of revelations, 6; letter in *Olive Branch,* 100n52

Pagels, Elaine, 16

Parson, John, 204

Partridge, Edward: excommunication of, 8; clashes with Joseph Smith and Sidney Rigdon and, 50

Patten, David W.: on William E. McLellin, 79; Alpheus Cutler and, 160

Pettegrew, David: on Rigdon conference (1845), 84–85

Phelps, W. W.: trial of, 60–61; William Smith as patriarch and, 144

Plural marriage: Culterites and, 174n14, 177n45; Stephen Post and, 182–83; James J. Strang and, 185; Reorganized Church and, 190; Mormon Reformation on, 199; after manifesto, 254–55; Joseph White Musser and, 263, 265–66, 274; 1944 arrests for, 273, Brodie on, 290–91

Poorman, John, 42n25

Populist party: founding and beliefs, 231–32; Henry W. Lawrence and, 231, 233–34; demise of, 234

Position Papers (Reorganized Church), 324–28.

Post, Stephen: baptizes James Brewster, 134; Joseph Smith III and, 180; joins Mormon church, 181; Stephen Winchester and, 182; plural marriage and, 182–83; James J. Strang and, 183–85; Martin Harris and, 185–86; William Smith and, 185–86; Sidney Rigdon and, 186–89, 192; Church of Christ (Rigdon) and, 190

Poulson, M. Wilford: Fawn Brodie and, 288–89

Pratt, Parley P.: on William Smith, 146

"Presidential Papers," 329–30

Price, Richard, 16; biography of, 322–23; beliefs of, 324; on Position Papers, 324–27; *Doctrine and Covenants* and, 325; begins Cumorah Books, 327–28;

publications of, 328, 337; Restoration Festival and, 329; "Presidential Papers" and, 330; polygamy and, 331; ordination of women and, 332; silencing of, 333; Restoration principles of, 333–35; Reorganized Church and, 335–36

Primitivists, 47

Quorum of the Twelve Apostles: selection of, 33; William E. McLellin and, 78, 82–83; role of patriarch in, 145; Joseph White Musser and, 267–68

Rajah Manchou plates, 184

Rappleye, Tunis, 160

Redfield, Harvey, 31

Reorganized Church of Jesus Christ of Latter Day Saints: William E. McLellin and, 94–96; leadership of, 150, 319; William Smith and, 150–51; leadership of, 152–53; plural marriage and, 190; differences from Morrisites, 216n27; Methodist church and, 320; Book of Mormon and, 321; theology and, 321; ordination of women and, 332; organization plan by Richard Price and, 335

Restoration Festival, 329, 333

Restoration principles, 333–35

Restoration Voice, 328

Rigby, Hazel: Sonia Johnson and, 370

Rigdon, Sidney: David Whitmer on, 29; as first counselor, 29; John Corrill and, 46; "Salt Sermon," 61; letter from William E. McLellin, 82; Church of Christ and, 83–84; succession of Joseph Smith and, 181; Stephen Post and, 186–89, 192; revelations of, 189; *Doctrine and Covenants* and, 190; ordination of women and, 191

Rockwell, Orrin Porter, 32; Luana Hart Beebe and, 162

Ryland, Judge, 54

The Saints at the Crossroads (Richard Price), 323–27

"Salamander letter:" Jerald Tanner and, 351–52

Salt Lake City Chamber of Commerce and Board of Trade, 229

Salt Lake City Messenger, 345

Salt Lake Tribune, 227, 256–57

School of the Prophets (Kirtland Temple): Alpheus Cutler and, 160

Separation of church and state: David Whitmer on, 34; Liberal party and, 226

Sheen, Isaac, 149

Sherman, Almon W., 160–61

Shipp, Ellis R.: Joseph White Musser and, 266

Shumway, Sally, 112

Smith, Alexander H., 152

Smith, Barbara, 371, 372

Smith, Bernard: Maurine Whipple and, 308–9

Smith, Elbert A., 152

Smith, Gibson, 107

Smith, Hyrum: death of, 10; revelation by Joseph Smith on, 143

Smith, Jesse N.: on Morrisites, 201

Smith, John, 148

Smith, Joseph F.: Frank J. Cannon and, 253–54; revelations of, 255; Joseph White Musser and, 263; issues Second Manifesto, 266

Smith, Joseph, Jr.: dissent from established authority, 3–4; Kirtland Temple and, 9, 10; David Whitmer on, 24; pluralism and, 25; revelation on David Whitmer, 25, 27; scope of church and, 26; charisma of, 28; John Corrill and, 48, 50, 55–56, 64–65; abandons Zion's Camp, 54; arrival in Far West, Mo., 60; sends troops to Daviess County, Mo., 66; William E. McLellin and, 77–78, 89–90; leaves Kirtland, 122; Esdras manuscript and, 124; treasure seeking and, 126; succession and, 130; William Smith and, 142; revelation on Hyrum Smith, 143; Alpheus Cutler and, 163; burial of, 163; succession of, 181–82; plural wives Maria and Sarah Lawrence and, 221; Fawn Brodie on, 285–89; Jerald Tanner on, 346

Smith, Joseph, Sr.: on money digging, 126; ordination of, 143

Smith, Joseph III: William E. McLellin and, 94–96; leadership of Reorganized Church and, 150, 152; Stephen Post and, 180; Rigdonites and, 180

Smith, W. Wallace, 319–22

Smith, William: in Nauvoo, 16; biography of, 141–42; as patriarch, 144–45; Brigham Young and, 145; as apostle and patriarch, 146; excommunication of, 146–47; Strangites and, 148; Baptist church and, 148; revelations of, 148–49; Isaac Sheen and, 149; Reorganized Church and, 150–51

Smoot, Reed, 254, 255

Snow, Lorenzo: Frank J. Cannon and, 253; Joseph White Musser and, 265

Social Science Club (Salt Lake City), 237

Socialist Club (Salt Lake City), 237

Socialist party, 234–37

State v. Jessop: Joseph White Musser on, 272–73

Strang, James J.: William E. McLellin and, 86–88, 91–92; Francis G. Bishop and, 111–12; William Smith and, 148; succession to Joseph Smith, 181–82; Stephen Post and, 183–85; plural marriage and, 185

Tanner, Jerald, and Sandra McGee Tanner: publications of, 344–48; Protestant fundamentalism and, 349, 359; on Mormonism and Mormon history, 344, 346, 348; life in LDS church, 347; Mormon scholars and, 349–50; copyright and, 351; as historians, 351; "Salamander letter" and, 351–52; publishing controversies and, 352; Mormon church and historians on, 354–55; as "career apostates," 355; criticism and, 362n20

Taylor, Frank, 263

Taylor, John: editorial on Brewster, 125; William Smith and, 145; on Morrisites, 203

Taylor, Joseph, 206

Temple ceremonies: washing and anointing, 34

The Temple of the Lord (Richard Price), 330

Temple (Reorganized): Richard Price and, 330–31

Thatcher, Moses, 234

This Is the Place: Utah (Maurine Whipple), 308, 310–11

Thompson, Charles B., 113
Truth magazine, 272

Under the Prophet in Utah (Frank J.
    Cannon), 257, 258
Unitarian Church: Henry W. Lawrence
    and, 229
Utah Magazine: Henry W. Lawrence and,
    224
Utah Produce Company, 221
Utah statehood, 227; Frank J. Cannon
    and, 249
Utah War: Henry W. Lawrence and, 221

Visions: Francis G. Bishop and, 103,
    105, 109–10; James Brewster and,
    121–22

Walker, Joseph R., 227
Whipple, Maurine: biography of, 302;
    religion and, 302–3; as teacher, 304; at
    University of Utah, 303–4; at Yaddo
    writers' colony, 304–5; *The Giant
    Joshua* and, 304–6, 309; employment
    of, 307; as writer and lecturer, 307–8;
    Bernard Smith and, 308–9; *This Is the
    Place: Utah* and, 308, 310–11; moves
    to Hollywood, 309; complaints of,
    309–11; on Mormon "revolution,"
    311; on LDS church, 311–13; on
    Juanita Brooks, 313; on Mormon
    beliefs, 313–14; as cultural Mormon,
    314; death of, 315
Whitmer, Christian, 24
Whitmer, David: as Book of Mormon
    witness, 7, 25; biography of, 23;
    Joseph Smith and, 23–25, 32–33, 38–
    39; questions church's direction, 30; on
    separation of church and state, 34;
    transgression of, 35; church and, 36,

37; William E. McLellin and, 38, 92–
    93, 97
Whitmer, John: trial of, 60–61; 1849
    meeting with William E. McLellin, 92–
    93
Whitmer, Mary Musselman, 23
Whitmer, Peter, Sr., 23, 26
Widtsoe, John A.: on *The Giant Joshua,*
    306
Wight, Lyman: John Corrill and, 72n34
Williams, George (Prophet Cainan), 205
Winchester, Benjamin, 9
Winchester, Stephen, 182
Winter Quarters: Alpheus Cutler and,
    163, 164
Women's Industrial Christian Home:
    Henry W. Lawrence and, 229
Woodruff, Wilford: on Morrisites, 203
Woolley, Lorin: Joseph White Musser
    and, 268–69

Yaddo writers' colony: Maurine Whipple
    and, 304–5
Young, Brigham: rise to leadership of,
    11; Nauvoo experience of, 16; Francis
    G. Bishop and, 113; William Smith
    and, 143–45; William Smith and, 146–
    47; reorganizes church, 148; Alpheus
    Cutler and, 166, 168; leadership of,
    176–77n40; Maria Lawrence and, 221;
    mining and, 223
Young, Brigham, Jr.: Frank J. Cannon
    and, 253, 254, 258
Young, Richard W., 210

Zion's Camp: disaster at, 8; relief project,
    32; purpose of, 54
Zions Cooperative Mercantile Institution,
    222
Zion's Warning, 322